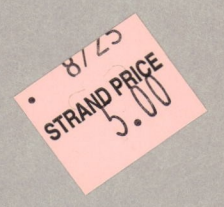

Cyclopedia of World Authors
REVISED EDITION

Ode-Z

CYCLOPEDIA
of
WORLD AUTHORS

REVISED EDITION

VOLUME THREE—ODE-Z

Edited by
Frank N. Magill

Associate Editors
DAYTON KOHLER
TENCH FRANCIS TILGHMAN

Salem Press, Incorporated
Englewood Cliffs, New Jersey

Copyright © 1958, 1974 by FRANK N. MAGILL
All rights in this book are reserved. No part of this work may be used or reproduced in any manner whatsoever or transmitted in any form or by any means, electronic or mechanical, including photocopy, recording, or any information storage and retrieval system, without written permission from the copyright owner except in the case of brief quotations embodied in critical articles and reviews. For information address the publisher, Salem Press, Inc., Englewood Cliffs, New Jersey 07632.

An earlier edition of this work
appears under the title of
MASTERPLOTS CYCLOPEDIA OF WORLD AUTHORS

PRINTED IN THE UNITED STATES OF AMERICA

Cyclopedia of World Authors
REVISED EDITION

———

Ode-Z

CLIFFORD ODETS

Born: Philadelphia, Pennsylvania
Date: July 18, 1906

Died: Los Angeles, California
Date: August 14, 1963

Principal Works

PLAYS: *Waiting for Lefty*, 1935; *Awake and Sing*, 1935; *Till the Day I Die*, 1935; *Paradise Lost*, 1935; *Golden Boy*, 1937; *Rocket to the Moon*, 1938; *Night Music*, 1940; *Clash by Night*, 1941; *The Big Knife*, 1949; *The Country Girl*, 1950.

Clifford Odets, born in Philadelphia, Pennsylvania, on July 18, 1906, was reared in middle-class surroundings but grew up to write some of the most controversial proletarian dramas of our time. Educated in the Bronx, New York City, he left high school after his second year to seek a career in the entertainment field. From 1925 to 1927 he directed a drama group on the radio, and read poetry there and in vaudeville. Other jobs included announcing, script writing, creating sound effects arranging, and acting with a stock company on a summer theater circuit. These activities led him to work with the Theatre Guild in 1928 and to membership in the Group Theatre at the beginning of the depression in 1930. It was while acting with this latter organization that he wrote and had produced by it three plays in 1935, *Awake and Sing!*, *Waiting for Lefty*, and *Till the Day I Die*. In tune with the prevailing mood of pessimism, the plays were not only financially successful: they won Odets the Yale Drama Prize for that year and an invitation from Hollywood to write motion picture scripts. Though failing to produce a memorable film, he wrote *Golden Boy* in 1937, his best play and perhaps the only one (with the possible exception of *The Country Girl*) likely to survive on the basis of good theater.

All of Odets's plays of the 1930's were basically social criticism or propaganda for proletarian collectivism. All the characters are Americans dispossessed not only of economic opportunity but also of their very dignity. The Berger family in *Awake and Sing!* could find suicide of the old to collect insurance the only method of survival for the young. During World War II Odets frankly espoused the Russian way of life with his adaptation of *The Russian People*. He was not incuriously silent after the war, in the light of the revelations of Russian manners. The beginning of the 1950's saw him turning toward the world of American entertainment, out of which came *The Big Knife* and *The Country Girl*, the latter made into a prize-winning motion picture in 1954.

BIBLIOGRAPHICAL REFERENCES: A useful volume is *Six Plays of Clifford Odets*, Modern Library, 1939. The only full-length studies are R. Baird Shuman, *Clifford Odets*, 1962; and Edward Murray, *Clifford Odets: The Thirties and After*, 1968. See also Burns Mantle, *Contemporary American Playwrights*, 1938; and Joseph Wood Krutch, *The American Drama Since 1918: An Informal History*, 1939. An interesting profile is John McCarten's "Revolution's Number One Boy," *New Yorker*, Jan. 22, 1938, 21–27. See also E. J. Isaacs, "Clifford Odets," *Theatre Arts Monthly*, XXIII (1939), 257–264; John Gassner, "The Long Journey of Talent," *ibid.*, XXXIII (1949), 25–30; and R. S. Warshow, "Poet of the Jewish Middle Class," *Commentary*, I (1946), 17–22.

SEÁN O'FAOLÁIN

Born: Cork, Ireland
Date: February 22, 1900

Principal Works

NOVELS: *A Nest of Simple Folk*, 1933; *Birds Alone*, 1936; *Come Back to Erin*, 1940.
SHORT STORIES: *Midsummer Night Madness and Other Stories*, 1932; *There's a Birdie in the Cage*, 1935; *A Purse of Coppers*, 1937; *Teresa*, 1946; *The Man Who Invented Sin*, 1948; *The Finest Stories of Seán O'Faoláin*, 1957; *I Remember! I Remember*, 1962; *The Heat of the Sun*, 1966; *The Talking Trees and Other Stories*, 1970.
BIOGRAPHY: *The Life Story of Eamon De Valera*, 1933; *Constance Markievicz*, 1934; *King of the Beggars: A Life of Daniel O'Connell*, 1938; *The Great O'Neill*, 1942; *Newman's Way: The Odyssey of John Henry Newman*, 1952.
PLAY: *She Had to Do Something*, 1938.
TRAVEL AND MISCELLANEOUS: *The Silver Branch*, 1938; *An Irish Journey*, 1940; *The Irish*, 1948 (rev. ed. 1969); *Summer in Italy*, 1950; *South to Sicily*, 1953.
CRITICISM: *Vanishing Hero: Studies in Novelists of the Twenties*, 1956.
AUTOBIOGRAPHY: *Vive Moi*, 1964.

Seán O'Faoláin was born in Cork, Ireland, February 22, 1900, the son of Denis Whelan and his wife Bridget Whelan. An Irish nationalist, he adopted the Gaelic variant of his name as part of a personal campaign to reassert the values of the Irish past.

O'Faoláin's education began at the Presentation Brothers' School in Cork and continued with advanced study at the National University of Ireland, which awarded him an M.A., and as a Comonwealth Fellow at Harvard University from 1926–1928, where he received a second master's degree. He fought in the Irish Revolution (1918–1921) and then, when the Sinn Fein party split into a right and left wing because of differing policies concerning the treaty with England, O'Faoláin took the Republican side during the civil war and became director of publicity for the Republican Army.

O'Faoláin spent the academic year 1928–1929 at Harvard as a John Harvard Fellow. During the following year he taught Gaelic at Harvard and Anglo-Irish literature at Boston College. During the next three years he was lecturer in English at St. Mary's Training College, Strawberry Hill. He did not enjoy teaching and consequently welcomed the freedom which soon came through his fiction and biographies.

His first volume of short stories, *Midsummer Night Madness and Other Stories*, was published in 1932 and immediately brought him to the attention of those who were looking for the distinctive Irish combination of compassion for the "simple folk" of Ireland and a sense of the close relationship between heroism and a spirit of independence. The stories are concerned with Irish life from the period of the Easter Rebellion of 1916, a consequence of the Sinn Fein movement for complete independence of Ireland, through the days following the establishment in 1921 of the Irish Free State. The book was nominated for the Femina Prize and brought an invitation to him to become a charter member of the Irish Academy of Letters. With his first novel, *A Nest of Simple Folk,* he achieved the kind of critical and popular response which made financial independence as a writer possible. He returned to Ireland where he continued his writing, becoming more and more interested as time went on in the writing of biographies and travel books.

Since World War II he has traveled in Europe and the United States, spending some time as a lecturer in 1954 at the Graduate School of Princeton University. Perhaps his most controversial and widely read piece in the United States has been his article, "Love Among the Irish" which appeared in *Life Magazine* on March 16, 1953. In that article he developed many of his familiar themes: the restrictive effects of Irish family traditions, the dangers of church censorship, the marriage problem for the Irish young people whose lives are conditioned and inhibited by provincial traditions of church, state, and family. His attitude has made him a controversial writer, a critic as well as a realist; but in his work there is a stubborn devotion to Ireland which belies his advice to the young to get out of Ireland.

His reputation as a biographer and travel writer has gradually supplanted his earlier fame as a short story writer and novelist. Although there has been a change of literary medium O'Faoláin continues to be concerned with realistic portrayals of the people and the country of Ireland, and consequently there is a continuity to his work.

BIBLIOGRAPHICAL REFERENCES: A recent study is M. Harmon, *Seán O'Faoláin,* 1967. For criticism and comment see further Seán O'Faoláin, Introduction to *The Finest Stories of Seán O'Faoláin,* 1957; Malcolm Cowley, "Yeats and O'Faoláin," *New Republic,* XCVIII (February 15, 1939), 49–50; and J. V. Kelleher, "Seán O'Faoláin," *Atlantic Monthly,* CXCIX (May, 1957), 67–69.

LIAM O'FLAHERTY

Born: Aran Islands, Ireland
Date: 1896

Principal Works

NOVELS: *Thy Neighbor's Wife*, 1923; *The Black Soul*, 1924; *The Informer*, 1925; *Mr. Gilhooley*, 1926; *The Assassin*, 1928; *The House of Gold*, 1929; *The Puritan*, 1931; *Skerrett*, 1932; *The Martyr*, 1933; *Famine*, 1937; *Land*, 1946; *Insurrection*, 1950.

SHORT STORIES: *Spring Sowing*, 1926; *The Tent and Other Stories*, 1926; *The Fairy-Goose and Two Other Stories*, 1927; *The Mountain Tavern and Other Stories*, 1929; *The Wild Swan and Other Stories*, 1932; *Two Lovely Beasts and Other Stories*, 1948; *The Stories of Liam O'Flaherty*, 1956; *Short Stories*, 1961.

AUTOBIOGRAPHY: *Two Years*, 1930; *Shame the Devil*, 1934.

BIOGRAPHY: *The Life of Tim Healy*, 1927.

Liam O'Flaherty is an Irish novelist who has always had a direct knowledge of the land and a genuine compassion for the people of Ireland. He has concerned himself in his work almost exclusively with the poor and the laboring, and his efforts as a writer have been to communicate a sense of their dignity and their worth. Born in the Aran Islands in 1896, O'Flaherty began life in a struggling community where primitive conditions were imposed by a barren land. As Robert Flaherty's motion picture, *Man of Aran*, shows, no setting would be more likely to give a youth the full appreciation of the problems of bare survival and of the courage it takes to resolve those problems. O'Flaherty's novels express his acute awareness of the stubborn courage and perseverance demanded of those who would live in the Aran Islands and in other barren parts of Ireland.

He was educated by Catholic priests as a postulant for the priesthood, and then at Rockwell College, Blackrock College, and University College in Dublin. He left the college to join the Irish Guards and served on the Western Front, in France, for six months during the First World War. He was wounded in 1917 and discharged with a disability pension.

As O'Flaherty relates in his autobiographical *Two Years*, the two years after his discharge from the army were a period of extensive travel and experience in various temporary jobs. His travels ranged from Ireland to South America, through the United States and Canada, and to Turkey. During the course of his travels he undertook menial employment of various kinds. According to his report—not always trustworthy, say the critics—he was a lumberjack in Canada, a brewer's fireman, a night porter in a hotel, a miner, a printer's devil in Boston, a worker in a canned milk factory, a waiter, a dish washer, a bank clerk, a stoker, and a deckhand. While working in a tire factory in Hartford, Connecticut, he began writing short stories.

Whatever the actual facts of his wanderings—facts which may never be determined because of what one reviewer called O'Flaherty's "magnificent lies"—there is no question but that he did travel extensively, probably over four continents, and that he was usually associated with the poor and the laboring class wherever he happened to be.

After working at a number of jobs on the eastern coast of the United States, he returned to Ireland and promptly achieved notoriety and expulsion from Ireland for joining unemployed workers in seizing a public building in Dublin. This was but one instance of his active left-wing political activity, motivated apparently not by intellectual idealism but by a spontaneous and intimate sympathy for the underprivileged.

After being forced to leave Ireland, he traveled to England and established residence there. In 1923 his first novel, *Thy Neighbor's Wife*, appeared, followed the next year by *The Black Soul*. With his third novel, *The Informer*, O'Flaherty won a mass audience. His vivid treatment of the psychological and political aspects of common Irish life in a time of civil war made this novel a particularly effective work of naturalistic realism. The force of the novel was retained in translations and O'Flaherty achieved world recognition. He was married to Margaret Barrington in 1926. His travels have resulted in *A Tourist's Guide to Ireland* (1929) and *I Went to Russia* (1931).

O'Flaherty's earlier novels tended to focus upon some one troubled individual, while his later works, such as *Famine* and *Land* are novels of nineteenth century Ireland, depicting the general character of Irish life and conveying its distinctive mood. With *Insurrection* in 1950 O'Flaherty once again won the wholehearted endorsement of most critics, many of whom acknowledged the book as equal to or better than *The Informer*. The action takes place during the 1916 Easter uprising in Ireland and concerns a young Irishman who is killed helping the cowardly son of a woman he meets in a pub. The book has been praised for its poetry and its pathos; it was regarded as "taut, humorous, tragic," and the *Saturday Review of Literature* critic declared that it may be the best O'Flaherty has done. Although some reviewers thought that the novel needed greater scope and that O'Flaherty should have given his characters more individuality, the consensus seemed to be that O'Flaherty's skill as a writer and his knowledge of common life in Ireland keep him very much in the forefront of contemporary Irish writers.

BIBLIOGRAPHICAL REFERENCES: For biographical material see O'Flaherty's two autobiographical studies, *Two Years*, 1930, and *Shame the Devil*, 1934. For criticism see J. N. Zneimer, *The Literary Vision of Liam O'Flaherty*, 1970. For brief criticism see also William Troy, "The Position of Liam O'Flaherty," *Bookman*, LXIX (1929), 7–11; C. H. Warren, "Liam O'Flaherty," *Bookman* (London), LXXVII (1930), 235–236; Vivian Mercier, "Man Against Nature: The Novels of Liam O'Flaherty," *Wascana Review*, I, ii (1966), 37–46; and Michael H. Murray, "Liam O'Flaherty and the Speaking Voice," *Studies in Short Fiction*, 5 (1968), 154–162. O'Flaherty is also discussed in J. von Sternemann, "Irische Geschichten," *Die Neue Rundschau*, XLII (1931), 521–539.

JOHN O'HARA

Born: Pottsville, Pennsylvania
Date: January 31, 1905

Died: Princeton, New Jersey
Date: April 11, 1970

Principal Works

NOVELS: *Appointment in Samarra,* 1934; *Butterfield 8,* 1935; *Hope of Heaven,* 1938; *A Rage to Live,* 1949; *The Farmer's Hotel,* 1951; *Ten North Frederick,* 1955; *From the Terrace,* 1958; *The Big Laugh,* 1962; *Elizabeth Appleton,* 1963; *The Lockwood Concern,* 1965; *The Instrument,* 1967; *The Ewings,* 1968; *Lovely Child: A Philadelphian's Story,* 1969.

SHORT STORIES: *The Doctor's Son,* 1935; *Files on Parade,* 1939; *Pal Joey,* 1940; *Pipe Night,* 1945; *Hell Box,* 1947; *A Family Party,* 1956; *The Hat on the Bed,* 1963; *The Horse Knows the Way,* 1964; *Waiting for Winter,* 1966; *And Other Stories,* 1968; *The O'Hara Generation,* 1969.

PLAYS: *Five Plays* (*The Farmer's Hotel, The Searching Sun, The Champagne Pool, Veronique, The Way It Was*), 1961.

John O'Hara, novelist and short story writer, was one of the chief practitioners in the so-called hard-boiled school of American fiction. His writing is marked by a callous tone and a blunt attitude toward sexual matters; his characters typically belong to the moneyed Ivy League country club set or are members of the demimonde of Broadway and Hollywood. O'Hara gilds his realism, however, with an encyclopedic knowledge of group customs and manners combined with an accurate reproduction of characteristic speech. In a way, he is a special sort of social historian, a tough Horace Walpole. There is, nonetheless, a peculiar ambivalence in O'Hara's attitude toward his material: although he detests the snobbery of his rich characters, the author himself is somehow fascinated by their way of life. Readers who strongly object to O'Hara's brutality perhaps fail to realize that his presentation of frustration and cruelty is in fact an indictment of lives that have abandoned their potentiality for understanding and generosity.

Born on January 31, 1905, in Pottsville, Pennsylvania—which is probably the Gibbsville of his fiction—O'Hara attended preparatory schools but not college. After serving an apprenticeship at an assortment of jobs, he succeeded at screen writing and journalism. In 1934 *Appointment in Samarra* launched him as a promising literary figure. This work, which may be his best, is set in Gibbsville during the prohibition era and describes the circumstances leading to the suicide of a member of the young married set. *Butterfield 8* deals with the death of a party-girl, and is probably based on the Starr Faithful case. *Hope of Heaven* treats the unsuccessful love affair of a screen-writer. *A Rage to Live* is a large work dealing with a married woman who is unable to stay her amatory urges. *The Farmer's Hotel,* a novelette, describes a violent crime among a group of snow-bound travelers. *Ten North Frederick,* also set in Gibbsville, is a strongly-written story of the dissolution of a successful lawyer who secretly longs to be president. This novel received the National Book Award.

O'Hara was also a prolific worker in the short story field. He was especially expert at what has become known as the *New Yorker* type of story, a tight sketch in which a character exposes some lack in his nature or in which a dramatic situation is undramatically stated. His stories have been collected in *The Doctor's Son, Files on Parade, Pipe Night,* and *Hell Box. Pal Joey,* a series of loosely connected letters by a shallow night-club entertainer, was used by O'Hara for the book of a Rodgers and Hart musical in 1940. One of the first well-plotted musical dramas, it had a highly successful revival in 1952. *A Family Party* is a short story issued as a book. *Sweet and Sour* (1954) is a collection of newspaper columns.

Although it is likely that John O'Hara learned some lessons from Hemingway and Fitzgerald, his work is sufficiently individualized to place him as one of the most distinctive American writers of his generation. The novels and stories of his last decade had the same critical reception as his earlier work: some critics complained of the monotonous preoccupation with sex; others praised his realistic technique, and, especially, his ear for genuine American speech.

BIBLIOGRAPHICAL REFERENCES: There are two full-length studies: Edward R. Carson, *The Fiction of John O'Hara, Critical Essays in English and American Literature,* No. 7, 1961; and S. N. Grebstein, *John O'Hara,* 1966. For shorter critical articles see John Portz, "John O'Hara Up to Now," *College English,* XVI (1955), 493–499, 516; Louis Auchincloss, *Reflections of a Jacobite,* 1961, 139–155; and Jessie Bier, "O'Hara's *Appointment in Samarra*: His First and Only Real Novel," *College English,* XXV (1963), 131–141. See also *Book Review Digest,* 1934 ff.; and Finis Farr, *John O'Hara: A Biography,* 1973.

ZOÉ OLDENBOURG

Born: Leningrad, Russia
Date: March 31, 1916

Principal Works

NOVELS: *Argile et cendres,* 1946 (*The World Is Not Enough*); *La Pierre angulaire,* 1953 (*The Cornerstone*); *Réveillés de la vie,* 1956 (*The Awakened*); *Les Irreductibles,* 1958 (*The Chains of Love*); *Les Brûles,* 1960 (*Destiny of Fire*); *Les Cités charnelles,* 1961 (*Cities of the Flesh*); *La Joie des pauvres,* 1970 (*The Heirs of the Kingdom*).

HISTORY AND BIOGRAPHY: *Le Bûcher de Montségur,* 1958 (*Massacre at Montségur*); *Les croisades,* 1956 (*The Crusades*); *Cathèrine de Russie,* 1965 (*Catherine the Great*).

Zoé Oldenbourg-Idalovici, who writes under her maiden name Zoé Oldenbourg, was born in what was then the city of Petrograd on March 31, 1916. Her paternal grandfather was Perpetual Secretary of the Academy of Science there; her father, Sergius Oldenbourg, was a journalist and historian; her mother was a mathematician. The parents emigrated to Paris in 1925, taking their four children with them: Mlle. Oldenbourg, her sister, and her two brothers. She displayed an interest in writing as a child, was encouraged by her father, and wrote steadily after she was twelve; although she does not consider the works produced during those early years important in themselves, she feels they were invaluable as exercises and as practice. She was also interested in art, and at one time intended to make painting her career. She received her *baccalauréat* from the Lycée Molière, Paris, in 1934, and attended the Sorbonne; she then studied painting at the Académie Ranson. In 1938 she studied theology in England. During the war years she decorated articles produced by a small Paris workshop. She was married in 1948 to Heinric Idalovici, Parisian art-gallery owner.

Publication of her first novel, *The World Is Not Enough* (1946), and its very favorable reception, determined her vocation. A historical novel of life in the twelfth and thirteenth centuries, it was praised for the vividness with which it re-created a medieval family and their world. A sequel, *The Cornerstone,* appeared in 1953 and was awarded the Prix Femina. These works were widely hailed as the best historical novels to appear in many years.

She has written two contemporary novels, *The Awakened* (1956) and its sequel, *The Chains of Love* (1958). These are stories of young *èmigrès* in Paris during the 1930's; *The Awakened* contains some of her own vivid memories of a childhood spent in exile. Critical reactions to the two novels were sharply divided, perhaps because of the author's viewpoint. The people of whom she writes have customarily been placed in a romantic light by the literary and artistic world of this century. She sees them instead as the truly displaced persons of our age—homeless, weary, corroded by loneliness and divided loyalties, more tragic than colorful.

The next two novels, *Destiny of Fire* (1960) and *Cities of the Flesh*

(1961), are both concerned with the Albigensian Crusade of the thirteenth century and its violent suppression by the Church. In addition to these novels, a history entitled *Massacre at Montségur* and dealing with the same subject appeared in 1958. Criticism was again somewhat mixed, with some reviewers feeling there had been an overemphasis on the horrors of the period.

The Crusades, a history of the first three crusades and of the kingdom of Jerusalem up to the time of its conquest by Saladin, appeared in 1956. It was followed by a biography, *Catherine the Great,* in 1965. Both have been well received.

Mme. Oldenbourg continues to paint as an avocation, and has been a member of the Prix Femina Jury since 1961.

BIBLIOGRAPHICAL REFERENCES: There is a brief discussion of Miss Oldenbourg in the *Wilson Library Bulletin,* XXXIV (March, 1960), 523.
For a review of various works see Frank N. Magill, *Survey of Contemporary Literature,* 1971. For a review of *The Heirs of the Kingdom* see *ibid., Masterplots 1972 Annual,* 1972, 163–167.

EUGENE O'NEILL

Born: New York, N. Y.
Date: October 16, 1888

Died: Boston, Massachusetts
Date: November 27, 1953

Principal Works

PLAYS: *Thirst and Other One-Act Plays*, 1914; *Bound East for Cardiff*, 1916; *Before Breakfast*, 1916; *The Moon of the Caribbees and Six Other Plays of the Sea*, 1919; *Beyond the Horizon*, 1920; *Gold*, 1920; *The Emperor Jones, Diff'rent*, and *The Straw*, 1921; *The Hairy Ape, Anna Christie*, and *The First Man*, 1922; *The Dreamy Kid*, 1922; *All God's Chillun Got Wings*, 1924; *Welded*, 1924; *Desire Under the Elms*, 1925; *The Great God Brown, The Fountain*, and *The Moon of the Caribbees*, 1926; *Marco Millions*, 1927; *Lazarus Laughed*, 1927; *Strange Interlude*, 1928; *Dynamo*, 1929; *Mourning Becomes Electra*, 1931 (*Homecoming, The Hunted*, and *The Haunted*); *Ah! Wilderness*, 1933; *Days Without End*, 1934; *The Iceman Cometh*, 1946; *A Moon for the Misbegotten*, 1952; *Long Day's Journey into Night*, 1956; *A Touch of the Poet*, 1957.

Eugene (Gladstone) O'Neill, American playwright, is often regarded as the most important writer for the theater this country has produced. He was born in New York City, October 16, 1888, the son of the popular melodramatic actor James O'Neill and of the latter's wife, Ella Quinlan. In O'Neill's posthumous and frankly autobiographical play *Long Day's Journey into Night* (completed by 1941 but neither published nor produced until 1956) the father appears as an improvident bohemian, lavish in speculation and with boon companions but parsimonious and unsatisfactory as the head of a family; the mother as a loving, somewhat conventional woman wrecked by the habit of drug-taking contracted during an illness and encouraged by the disorderliness of the domestic establishment. The future playwright attended various private schools, sometimes accompanied his father on tour, and grew into an unhappy, rebellious young man. He was dismissed at the end of his first year at Princeton University and spent five years as a drifter, going as a common sailor on voyages to South America and Europe, later working briefly as a reporter on the New London (Conn.) *Telegraph*.

Some months spent during 1912 in a tuberculosis sanitarium marked the turning point of his life. In the hospital he read widely in the modern drama and, profoundly impressed by Ibsen, even more by August Strindberg, he determined to become a playwright. He spent some time as a student in Professor George Pierce Baker's course at Harvard and saw the first production of one of his plays in 1916, when an amateur group calling itself The Provincetown Players acted his short romantic melodrama, *Bound East for Cardiff*, first at Provincetown, Massachusetts, then at its tiny theater in New York's Greenwich Village. Other one-act melodramas, based like the first on his experience as a sailor, followed, and in 1920 his first full-length, professionally produced play, *Beyond the Horizon*, won the Pulitzer Prize. Passionately committed to his task and extremely prolific, he was soon turning out a rapid succession of plays, all somber in tone but otherwise exhibiting a great variety of themes and styles. Some were commercially produced, others by amateur and semi-amateur groups; but all helped make him before long the most discussed American playwright.

Among the more notable plays of this period were *The Emperor Jones, The Hairy Ape,* and *The Great God Brown,* together with his earlier, first great popular success, *Anna Christie,* which differed from these other plays in being realistic rather than "experimental" and "expressionistic" in method. The success of *Desire Under the Elms* in 1924 led to his association with the Theater Guild, the leading "art theater," which produced his two most widely discussed plays, the enormously long *Strange Interlude* in 1928 and the trilogy, *Mourning Becomes Electra,* a modernization of the Greek legend as told by Aeschylus, in 1931. Less notable plays appeared between these outstanding successes, which were not again approached until *The Iceman Cometh* was produced in 1946. In 1936 he became the first American playwright to receive the Nobel Prize, but ill health resulting from Parkinson's disease made composition increasingly difficult for him during the next decade. Two late plays failed to achieve Broadway production during his lifetime, and O'Neill was physically almost incapacitated for several years before his death in Boston on November 27, 1953. He was survived by his third wife, the actress Carlotta Monterey, who became his literary executor.

O'Neill was the author of one comedy, *Ah! Wilderness,* but this play is by no means a completely merry work. The most persistent characteristic of his total writing is its tragic view of life, presented in various ways and seeming to range from prosaic, pessimistic naturalism, through the classic version of man redeemed and ennobled by suffering, to the mystical exultation of *Lazarus Laughed.*

In all of O'Neill's plays, in one way or another, the phrase used by his master Strindberg, "Men are pitiable creatures," is always implicit. The great and even bewildering variety of styles and subject matter is, like the presence of different sociological and psychological theories, less the result of changes in thought than simply of repeated attempts, none found quite satisfactory, to objectify and express his tragic sense of life. Men are seen as pitiable creatures for many reasons, but most significantly they want something which the universe does not seem to provide. O'Neill explicitly stated that it was this seeming "maladjustment" to the universe rather than any political or social maladjustment which interested him most. What does seem to change from play to play is the conclusion to be drawn from man's situation in an alien universe. Sometimes, as in *The Iceman Cometh* (the most nihilistically pessimistic of the plays), O'Neill seems to say that only the deluded are either happy or wise; in other plays he seems to be saying, instead, either that man's aspiration toward the unattainable is his justification and his glory or even, as in *Lazarus Laughed* and perhaps also in *Days Without End,* that the universe does hide a saving secret which an occasional individual can penetrate.

O'Neill's greatness has not been universally recognized, and during the decade before his death some insisted that he had been greatly over-estimated. The surprise occasioned by *Long Day's Journey into Night*—one of the most impressive of his plays—stimulated a debate which seems likely to swing definitely in his favor. His unfriendly critics have brought many charges, accusing him especially of over-ambition in his attempt to rival the great tragic writers of the past, of relying too heavily upon Freudian psychology, and of a lack of either precision or beauty in the writing of dialogue. To the first of these charges it is sometimes replied that high ambition was precisely what the modern drama, too content with small subjects and small themes, most conspicuously lacked and that the Freudianism evident enough in some of his best-known work is not a doctrine being preached but simply a proper use of what is, after all, one of the most important ways in which modern man is accustomed to look at himself and his problems. The third charge was more serious. O'Neill wrote rapidly, sometimes clumsily and repetitiously. There is little wit and in the words little of that poetry upon which Tragedy is sometimes said to depend. Yet the effectiveness of his plays was demonstrated at the time when they were new and continues to be demonstrated today by both the posthumous plays and several revivals. Whatever absolute value may ultimately be put upon O'Neill's work, it seems likely that he will continue to be regarded as the most impressive playwright so far to appear in the United States.

BIBLIOGRAPHICAL REFERENCES: *O'Neill and His Plays,* edited by Oscar Cargill, N. Bryllion Fagin, and William J. Fisher, 1961, contains criticism and a bibliography. For further study see Croswell Bowen, *The Curse of the Misbegotten,* 1959; and Arthur and Barbara Gelb, *O'Neill,* 1962. A collected edition is *The Plays of Eugene O'Neill,* 12 vols., 1934–1935. See further Barrett H. Clark, *Eugene O'Neill: The Man and His Plays,* 1947 (rev. ed.). Other studies include S. K. Winther, *Eugene O'Neill: A Critical Study,* 1934; R. D. Skinner, *Eugene O'Neill: A Poet's Quest,* 1935; and Edwin A. Engel, *The Haunted Heroes of Eugene O'Neill,* 1953.

See also "The Playwright Unbound: Eugene O'Neill," in T. H. Dickinson, *Playwrights of The New American Theater,* 1925; "Eugene O'Neill, Poet and Mystic," in Arthur H. Quinn, *A History of the American Drama from the Civil War to the Present Day,* Vol. II, 1936 (rev. ed.); "Tragedy: Eugene O'Neill," in Joseph Wood Krutch, *The American Drama Since 1918,* 1939 (rev. ed.); *idem,* Introduction to *Nine Plays,* 1941; Barrett H. Clark, "Aeschylus and O'Neill," *English Journal,* XXI (1932), 699–710; Homer E. Woodbridge, "Eugene O'Neill," *South Atlantic Quarterly,* XXXVII (1938), 22–35; Clara Blackburn, "Continental Influences on Eugene O'Neill's Expressionistic Drama," *American Literature,* XIII (1941), 109–133; F. I. Carpenter, "The Romantic Tragedy of Eugene O'Neill," *College English,* VI (1945), 250–258; and George Jean Nathan, "O'Neill: A Critical Summation," *American Mercury,* LXIII (1946), 713–719.

JOSÉ ORTEGA Y GASSET

Born: Madrid, Spain
Date: May 9, 1883

Died: Madrid
Date: October 18, 1955

PRINCIPAL WORKS

ESSAYS AND STUDIES: *España invertebrada*, 1922 (*Invertebrate Spain*); *El tema de nuestro tiempo*, 1923 (*The Modern Theme*); *La deshumanización del arte*, 1925 (*The Dehumanization of Art*); *La rebelión de las masas*, 1930 (*The Revolt of the Masses*); *Misión de la universidad*, 1930 (*The Mission of the University*); *Del Imperio romano*, 1941 (*Concord and Liberty*); *Historica como sistema*, 1941 (*Towards a Philosophy of History*).

One of the most eminent Spanish philosophers of modern times, a figure whose influence was felt beyond his native country, José Ortega y Gasset, was born in Madrid on May 9, 1883. He was educated at a Jesuit school at Málaga and at the University of Madrid, where he later held the professorship of metaphysics. From 1906 to 1910 he studied in Germany. Returning to Spain, he obtained his professorship in 1911. He published widely in newspapers and reviews, and in 1923 founded the *Revista de Occidente*, which became an important and influential periodical. His announced mission at the time was to "Europeanize Spain" and to combat its traditional cultural isolation.

Ortega y Gasset, long a foe of the monarchy, naturally favored the revolution that overthrew Alfonso XIII in 1931. Indeed, he has been called one of the "Fathers of the Republic," and was elected a deputy from León. But the victory of Franco drove him from Spain, and he spent many years in exile in France, Portugal, and South America. For a time he held a professorship at the University of San Marcos in Peru. In 1945 he returned to Spain.

The first of his books to be translated into English, and the work on which his reputation in the English-speaking world chiefly rests, is *The Revolt of the Masses,* which attained considerable popularity in this country during the 1930's. The title is, to some degree, deceptive, for the author was not dealing with proletarian revolution, as the word "masses" might suggest. Rather, he was concerned with what he regarded as the significant phenomenon of the twentieth century: the emergence of the "mass man" into a position of power. The author recognizes, among human beings, two types: the superior man, intellectually disciplined, cultivated, always demanding more of himself and striving to raise himself still higher; and the "common" man, self-satisfied, lacking in standards, making no demands upon himself, content to be like everyone else. These two classes, the author takes pains to emphasize, have nothing to do with the traditional social divisions; indeed, Ortega y Gasset rather scorns the old European nobility. It is a question of a moral and intellectual elite, the members of which may come from any social milieu.

The fantastic increase in the population of Europe—according to the author, it never rose above 180 millions from the sixth century to 1800, but by 1914 it had reached 460 millions—has produced a continent swarming with people; and the "mass man," thrust upward by sheer force of numbers, has taken over all the functions previously exercised by the superior minority. Through him, all traditional values of European civilization are threatened: "the vulgar proclaims and imposes the right of vulgarity, or vulgarity as a right." Since the masses "neither should nor can direct their own personal existence, and still less rule society in general," Europe is in danger of being destroyed by a kind of internal barbarian invasion.

Ortega y Gasset was not, as his words might seem to imply, an admirer of the dictatorships emerging into European politics at that time; on the contrary, he detested them. He was merely re-emphasizing the traditional European reliance on a small group of genuinely superior men to direct its affairs. This attitude, so different from the American enthusiasm for the "age of the common man," may account for much of the popularity of the book in this country. Ortega y Gasset died in Madrid on October 18, 1955.

BIBLIOGRAPHICAL REFERENCES: Ortega y Gasset's principal works are available in translation. For biography and criticism see Joaquín Iriarte, *Ortega y Gasset*, 1942; José Ferrater Mora, *Ortega y Gasset*, 1957; R. Alonso, *En torno de pensamiento de Ortega y Gasset*, 1946; Julian Marias, *Ortega y Gasset y la idea de la razón vital*, 1948, and *Ortega y tres antípodes*, 1950; E. R. Curtius, "*Spanische Perspektiven*," in *Die Neue Rundschau*, XXXV (1924); L. Araquistain, "Ortega y Gasset: profeto del fracas de las masas," in *Leviatán*, VII (1934) and VIII (1935); and D. White, "One of the Twelve: The Life and Thought of Ortega y Gasset," *Religion in Life*, XXV (1956), 247–258. A more specialized study is José Sanchez Villaseñor, *Ortega y Gasset: Existentialist*, 1949, an examination of Ortega y Gasset's philosophical attitudes in the light of modern existentialist doctrine. Three recent books are José Ferrater Mora, *Ortega y Gasset, An Outline of His Philosophy*, 1963; Julián Marías Aquilera, *José Ortega y Gasset, Circumstance and Vocation*, 1970; and Robert McClintock, *Man and His Circumstances: Ortega as Educator*, 1971.

GEORGE ORWELL
Eric Hugh Blair

Born: Motihari, India
Date: 1903

Died: London, England
Date: January 23, 1950

Principal Works

novels: *Burmese Days,* 1934; *A Clergyman's Daughter,* 1935; *Keep the Aspidistra Flying,* 1936; *Coming Up for Air,* 1939; *Nineteen Eighty-Four,* 1949.
satire: *Animal Farm: A Fairy Story,* 1945.
essays: *Inside the Whale,* 1940; *Critical Essays,* 1946; *Shooting an Elephant,* 1950.
autobiography: *Down and Out in Paris and London,* 1933; *Such, Such Were the Joys,* 1953.
miscellaneous: *The Road to Wigan Pier,* 1937; *Homage to Catalonia,* 1938.

Eric Hugh Blair was born in 1903 at Motihari in Bengal, India, the son of a Customs and Excise official of Scottish descent. Although his father soon retired on a small pension, the modest family resources were strained to send the boy in 1911 to a fashionable English preparatory school. Accepted at a reduced rate because of the likelihood of his winning a scholarship, he crammed successfully and won one to Eton in 1917. Lonely, imaginative, and insecure among the children of the well-to-do, he studied at Eton until 1921, reading Shaw, Wells, and other advanced writers and doing some writing of his own. Deciding not to try for a scholarship to Cambridge, he took a job in the Indian Imperial Police, intending to choose his own way of life when he would be pensioned off at forty. The five years between 1922 and 1927 which he spent in this service in Burma were unhappy ones. He was torn between opposed feelings: shame, guilt, and outrage at the often brutal workings of colonialism, and inability to feel more than contemptuous sympathy for its native victims.

Returning home on leave in 1927, he quit the service, took his terminal leave pay, and went to Paris to live on it for a year and a half while he wrote short stories and novels which no one published. With his money spent and the depression on, he plummeted down into the depths of poverty, at times seeming to make his plunge an act of expiation for feelings of guilt attaching to his Burma days. By a combination of public charity, a dishwashing job (in Paris), and a few loans, he managed to survive, tasting the bitterness of extreme penury in both Paris and London. The years between 1929 and 1935 saw him supporting himself as a private tutor, a teacher in cheap private schools, and (for a year and a half between 1932 and 1934) a part-time assistant in a Hampstead Heath bookshop. By this time, however, he had been published, as George Orwell, in various magazines such as *The Adelphi,* and in January, 1933, his first book, the autobiographical *Down and Out in Paris and London,* had appeared to receive high praise from the critics. His portraits of the people of this nether world and his etchings of the miseries of their surroundings were lit up by the flame of his social consciousness.

In his first novel, *Burmese Days,* he presented a decaying empire, his writing—not illusioned like Kipling's or sympathetic like Forster's—serving him as a purgative for some of his feelings of guilt at having been part of a system he loathed. In *A Clergyman's Daughter*, Orwell drew upon his experience as a schoolteacher, hop-picker, and down-and-outer. This novel, with its amnesic protagonist, shows the inadequacy of the Church and its philosophy in an acquisitive society. There was now a slight income from his writing (an average of $15 a week from 1930 to 1940) to permit him to escape to Essex, where he kept a pub, a village store, and a flock of hens. In 1936 he married Eileen O'Shaughnessy. In the same year *Keep the Aspidistra Flying* was published. A novel about a young man who escapes from, but finally capitulates to, the advertising industry in order to permit rather unromantic matrimony, it presents a gray, shabby middle-class life dominated by money. Increasingly active as a Socialist by this time, Orwell recorded the experiences of his stay in a depressed area of Britain in *The Road to Wigan Pier*. A choice of the Left Book Club, this documentary study displayed Orwell's strong sympathy for the laboring classes.

By Christmas of 1936 Orwell had decided to go to Spain to do a series of newspaper articles about the Spanish Civil War. When he arrived there, he felt compelled instead to join the military force of the anarchist-affiliated P.O.U.M. organization, fighting on the side of the Loyalists. A bullet through the throat put an end to his service in May, and when the Communists crushed the P.O.U.M. in Barcelona, Orwell barely escaped the country. All this was recorded graphically in clear, vivid prose in *Homage to Catalonia*.

Despite the tuberculosis aggravated by his hardships in Spain, Orwell continued to work, publishing in 1939 *Coming Up for Air*. This novel of a man returning to find the old home town destroyed by gray suburban developments was dominated by the conviction of impending war. When the war came, Orwell served as a sergeant in the Home Guard and as a member of the Indian Service of the B.B.C. In the last year of the war, as his own health further declined, his wife died suddenly from the combined effects of a minor operation and poor nutrition.

Animal Farm, published in 1945, was his most successful single work, a classically-written Swiftian animal story which was on one level a satiric allegory of Stalinism and on another of **totalitarianism in general**. Now a prominent, successful author and journalist, the ill, tired man went in 1947 to live with his sister and adopted son on the island of Jura, off the west coast of Scotland. He had hoped there to complete a new novel about the totalitarian future he saw, but in 1949 he found it necessary to enter a sanatorium in Gloucestershire. *Nineteen Eighty-Four*, completed in University College Hospital, London, was a horrifying vision of a world in which all the old values were systematically eradicated, language was deliberately made rudimentary to prevent unorthodox thought, and three superstates dominated an enslaved planet. The author's avowed faith in the proletarians was but a feeble flicker against the overpowering gloom of this fictional relation of personal and national horror. By late 1949, when he had married Sonia Brownwell, George Orwell had envisioned another novel. Planned as a new departure into a study of human relationships, it died with him when he succumbed after a tuberculous hemorrhage on January 23, 1950.

BIBLIOGRAPHICAL REFERENCES: The *Collected Essays, Journalism, and Letters* were edited by Sonia and Ian Angus, 4 vols., 1968. There are four interesting and significant biographical and critical studies of Orwell by Laurence Brander, 1954, John Atkins, 1954, Christopher Hollis, 1956; and George Woodcock, *The Crystal Spirit*, 1966. See also Tom Hopkinson, *George Orwell*, 1955 (pamphlet); Kenneth M. Hamilton, "G. K. Chesterton and George Orwell: A Contrast in Prophecy," *Dalhousie Review*, XXXI (1951), 198–205; Charles I. Glicksberg, "The Literary Contribution of George Orwell," *Arizona Quarterly*, X (1954), 234–245; Philip Rieff, "George Orwell and the Post-Liberal Imagination," *Kenyon Review*, XVI (1954), 49–70; Richard J. Vorhees, "George Orwell: Rebellion and Responsibility," *South Atlantic Quarterly*, LIII (1954), 556–565; R. H. Rovere, "George Orwell," *New Republic*, CXXXV (1956), 11–15; Robert F. Gleckner, "1984 or 1948?" *College English*, XVIII (1956), 95–99; and Richard J. Vorhees, *"Nineteen Eighty-Four:* No Failure of Nerve," *ibid.*, 101–102.

JOHN OSBORNE

Born: London, England
Date: December 12, 1929

Principal Works

PLAYS: *Look Back in Anger,* 1957; *The Entertainer,* 1957; *Epitaph for George Dillon,* 1958; *The World of Paul Slickey,* 1959; *Luther,* 1960; *Inadmissable Evidence,* 1964; *A Patriot for Me,* 1965; *A Bond Honoured,* 1966; *The Hotel in Amsterdam,* 1968; *Time Present,* 1968.

English actor, dramatist, and screenwriter, John Osborne erupted into fame and fortune with the production of *Look Back in Anger* at the Royal Court Theatre, London, in 1956. He had written several plays before that time; his first had been produced as early as 1949, but until the appearance of *Look Back in Anger* his career in the theater was undistinguished. This play's successful run in London, its brilliant performance in Paris, New York, and Berlin, its long and happy career with touring companies on the road, and its superb film version, in which Richard Burton and Mary Ure, Osborne's second wife, starred in the leading roles, made it unquestionably the best serious English play, commercially as well as artistically, in the post-World War II period. When Sir Lawrence Olivier played the lead role in *The Entertainer,* written earlier than *Look Back in Anger* but not produced until 1957, Osborne's place as a playwright in the contemporary English theater was secure beyond doubt.

But *Look Back in Anger* is more than a great play; it is also the manifesto of a generation, and much of its success surely resulted from its being the source for the title and the attitudes of the Angry Young Men, Britain's youthful postwar critics of the Establishment. In it, as in all his plays, Osborne has focused upon the tension between children and parents as a vehicle for probing into the grim battle for survival between the past and present. Writing from an existentialist bias that, unlike the abstract rationalistic one of the French, is concretely social and personal, he has repeatedly insisted that life is *now* and that it is worth whatever risk it entails in attacking the intellectual and social *status quo*. His art is rebellious, but only in order to free and affirm the person or integrity of his suffering and creative self, not to replace one dehumanized order with another. "We've only ourselves," as Jean, the daughter of the protagonist in *The Entertainer,* puts it; so the Angry Young Man—for instance, Jimmy Porter in *Look Back in Anger*—attacks vigorously whatever gets in the way of authentic living or of loving in "good faith." So did Luther, one of history's Angry Young Men, who would not compromise his religious or intellectual perceptions to satisfy the Church's demand that its security and his, as well as all Europe's, not be tampered with. Luther disrupts Europe, to his own dismay over the chaos and cruelty he releases, but at the same time he abandons the Church, taking a nun as wife and begetting a son.

The prevalence of the will to be

1344

and the affirmation of life in Osborne's work can perhaps be traced back to his origins in a London tenement district, where he was born of working-class parents on December 12, 1929. They may also be reflected in his leaving school at sixteen and getting his education in the world as a writer for trade journals and an actor rather than in the ivy halls of the English public schools and universities. Certainly he has remained faithful in his allegiance to working-class values and to its tough sense of life as a struggle against powers that would hold one down. Regardless of their source, the will and affirmation are vividly present in his work from the beginning and survive intact in his successful "Tom Jones," a film he adapted from Henry Fielding's eighteenth century novel. His continuing interest in the movies is reflected in his association with Woodfall Films, a company he formed with Tony Richardson, the director of "Tom Jones."

BIBLIOGRAPHICAL REFERENCES: Three important studies of Osborne's life and work are R. Hayman, *John Osborne,* 1968; Simon Trussler, *The Plays of John Osborne: An Assessment,* 1968; and Martin Banham, *Osborne,* 1969. His work is also discussed in most books on contemporary drama. See John Russell Taylor, *Anger and After,* 1962, revised edition, 1969; K. Allsop, *The Angry Decade,* 1958; W. A. Armstrong, ed., *Experimental Drama,* 1963; K. M. Baxter, *Speak What We Feel: A Christian Looks at the Contemporary Theatre,* 1964; Raymond Williams, *Drama from Ibsen to Brecht,* 1968; and John Kershaw, *The Present Stage,* 1966.

THOMAS OTWAY

Born: Trotton, Sussex, England
Date: March 3, 1652

Died: Tower Hill (?), London, England
Date: April 14 (?), 1685

Principal Works

PLAYS: *Alcibiades,* 1675; *Don Carlos,* 1676; *The Cheats of Scapin,* 1677 (adapted from Molière); *Friendship in Fashion,* 1678; *The Orphan,* 1680; *The Soldier's Fortune,* 1681; *Venice Preserved, or a Plot Discovered,* 1682; *The Atheist,* 1684 (the second part of *The Soldier's Fortune*).

Although the son of a poor Anglican curate, Thomas Otway, born at Trotton, March 3, 1652, was educated at Winchester School and Oxford University. He left the university in 1672, however, before receiving a degree. Just what he did between leaving the university and the production of his first play, the bombastic *Alcibiades,* is unknown. The following year a second play, a tragedy in heroic couplets entitled *Don Carlos,* was produced, an adaptation of St. Real's French tragedy with the same title. *Don Carlos* proved successful on the stage and made Otway's reputation as a leading playwright of the time. His success gave Otway acquaintance and friendship with the famous people of the stage and court. Otway wrote mainly for the famous actor Betterton, including a number of tragedies and comedies adapted from the French drama of Molière and Racine.

Rejected by a self-seeking actress, Mrs. Barry, for whom he bore a lifelong love, Otway joined the English army in 1678 and received a commission as ensign within a short time. He returned to London the next year and began writing again, turning to blank verse in his domestic tragedy, *The Orphan, or The Unhappy Marriage.* *The Soldier's Fortune* was a successful original comedy which utilized Otway's military experience. His greatest play, *Venice Preserved,* followed in 1682. One more play, *The Atheist,* a continuation of *The Soldier's Fortune,* was produced in 1684. Although successful on the stage and in print, Otway's works were insufficient to produce an income for him, and his life was full of financial difficulty. He was an impetuous man and reputedly fought several duels successfully. He died in questionable circumstances. Several accounts, none verified, have been offered as to the manner of his death in his thirty-fourth year, but the most common is that he died in a shop near the sponging house in which he was then living. In his plays Otway illustrated the tendency of the drama of the Restoration period to move away from heroic bombast to sentimentality and pathos.

BIBLIOGRAPHICAL REFERENCES: The outstanding edition of Otway is J. C. Ghosh's, *Works,* 2 vols., 1932, reprinted 1968. The sole biography is R. G. Ham, *Otway and Lee,* 1931. Aline M. Taylor, *Next to Shakespeare: Otway's "Venice Preserv'd" and "The Orphan," and Their History on the London Stage,* 1950, is the most recent full study devoted to Otway; it includes a bibliography. Still valuable for a survey of the subject is Bonamy Dobrée, *Restoration Tragedy,* 1929. See also Aline Mackenzie, "*Venice Preserv'd* Reconsidered," *Tulane Studies in English,* I (1949), 81–118.

OUIDA
Marie Louise de la Ramée

Born: Bury St. Edmunds, England
Date: January 7, 1839

Died: Viareggio, Italy
Date: January 25, 1908

Principal Works

NOVELS: *Held in Bondage,* 1863; *Strathmore,* 1865; *Chandos,* 1866; *Idalia,* 1867; *Under Two Flags,* 1867; *Tricotrin,* 1868; *A Dog of Flanders,* 1872; *Pascarel,* 1873; *Signa,* 1875; *Ariadne,* 1877; *Moths,* 1880; *A Village Commune,* 1881; *In Maremma,* 1882; *Othmar,* 1885; *The Tower of Taddeo,* 1890; *The Massarenes,* 1897; *La Stregha,* 1899; *The Waters of Edera,* 1900.

ESSAYS: *Critical Studies,* 1900.

Ouida, born at Bury St. Edmunds, England, January 7, 1839, was the pseudonym of Marie Louise Ramé, daughter of a French language teacher and an Englishwoman. As a young woman Ouida changed her surname to what seemed to her the more romantic and dignified "de la Ramée." The family background and childhood of Ouida are vague. Her father disappeared while she was still a child, and she and her mother, then in France, returned to England to take up residence in London. In 1860, just in her twenties, Ouida began to contribute fiction to *Bentley's Miscellany.* Her stories were about glamorous, unreal, and romantic life, but they found an enthusiastic, even fascinated, body of readers, so that for a time Ouida was a very popular author. Sir Arthur Quiller-Couch was among the critics who praised her. Her first novel was *Held in Bondage,* her first real success *Strathmore,* and her best-known, and probably best, *Under Two Flags.*

Even as a child, Ouida, as she preferred to be called even in private life, was egocentric. She displayed an unusual propensity for falling in love, a trait which caused her unhappiness, for her love was often unrequited, and probably led to the misanthropy which she made so obvious in later life. Once a success, Ouida tried to make herself into a great lady. She moved to Florence, Italy, and purchased a large house. She became an irritating, even despicable, personality, insulting her friends, her acquaintances, and her publishers. In 1894 she removed to Lucca, Italy, to live on a more lavish scale than ever, with no attention to the expense of her way of life. But declining popularity as an author cost her the large income she once had, and the last decade of her life she spent almost in poverty. Her only real income in that time was a small pension from the British government. In old age she suffered from blindness in one eye and painful illness. She died in Viareggio, Italy, on January 25, 1908, and was buried in that country. Although adults have almost forgotten her work, children still find such stories as *Two Little Wooden Shoes* and *A Dog of Flanders* interesting.

BIBLIOGRAPHICAL REFERENCES: The New York edition of Ouida's *Complete Works* was published in 12 volumes. Elizabeth Lee, *Ouida: A Memoir,* 1914, is a good biography, but it is inferior to Eileen Bigland, *Ouida, the Passionate Victorian,* 1950, probably the best single work on Ouida's life and art. The only full-length critical work is Yvonne ffrench's *Ouida: A Study in Ostentation,* 1938, containing a good bibliography. The most recent biography is Monica Stirling, *The Fine and the Wicked: The Life and Times of Ouida,* 1958. Critical essays in books include G. S. Street, "An Appreciation of Ouida," in *Quales Ego,* 1896; Max Beerbohm, *More,* 1899; Carl Van Vechten, *Excavations,* 1926; and Malcolm Elwin, *Victorian Wallflowers,* 1934. A brief magazine article is Rose Macaulay, "Eccentric Englishwomen, IV: Ouida," *Spectator,* CLVIII (1937), 855–856.

OVID
Publius Ovidius Naso

Born: Sulmo, Italy
Date: March 20, 43 B.C.

Died: Tomi (Now Constanta, Rumania)
Date: A.D. 18

Principal Works

POEMS: *Amores; Heroides* (Letters from Heroines); *Ars amatoria* (Art of Love); *Remedium amoris* (Love's Remedy); *Medicina faniei* (Face Lotions); *Metamorphoses*, all written before A.D. 8; *Tristia* (Sorrows); *Ex Ponto* (Letters from Pontus), A.D. 8–18.

Publius Ovidius Naso (Ovid) was born in the Italian Apennines, northeast of Rome, at Sulmo on March 20 of the last year of the Republic. He was brought up under the absolute rule of Augustus. His works depict the life of rich and fashionable Romans during the second half of Augustus' reign, and with his death the Golden Age of Roman literature came to an end.

Ovid's father, of an equestrian family whose estates were never confiscated, sent the boy and his brother from Abruzzi to Rome, where they were educated by two famous rhetoricians, Arellius Fuscus and the Spanish-born friend of Seneca, Marcus Porcius Latro, who formed Ovid's literary style. Horace read his poems to Ovid, and Aemilius Macer, who traveled with him to Athens, Troy, and Sicily, made him acquainted with the writings of Vergil.

On their return to Rome, Ovid was offered a political career in the Senate, but he chose literature. He married three times. Personal experience undoubtedly inspired the creation of his imaginary Corinna whom he celebrated in forty-four short poems and the five-volume *Amores* which he later prudently reduced to three. His fourth marriage, to a girl of the Fabian family, brought him favor with the Empress Livia. Women were influential in Roman life, and women figure largely in Ovid's poetry, with a balance between romance and realism and a tongue-in-cheek humor. His *Letters from Heroines* were imaginary epistles from the old heroines of antiquity to their absent husbands and lovers.

His *Art of Love* caused the greatest furor. This guide book for lovemaking, with two volumes for men and one for women, has been called the most immoral book ever written by a man of genius. Because it ran counter to Augustus' attempts at moral reforms, Ovid tried to repair the damage by writing *Love's Remedies*, telling how to end love affairs, but he was banished in 8 A.D. to the half-barbaric town of Tomi at the mouth of the Danube, more probably for what he knew of scandals at court than for what he had disclosed.

Though he wrote scores of letters to influential Romans and five volumes of *Sorrows* to describe the wretchedness of his exile and to present pleas for forgiveness, even Tiberius upon his succession to the throne refused to pardon him, thus suggesting that the reason for Ovid's banishment was something more than licentious writing or even meddling in the love intrigues of Augustus' granddaughter Julia. He remained in Tomi until his death in A.D. 18.

Ovid's greatest work was the fifteen

books of *Metamorphoses*, written in hexameters to recount miraculous transformations that range through classical mythology from the change of chaos to cosmos in the world down to the tale of Julius Caesar's metamorphosis into a star. The Alexandrian poets as well as old legends provided material for this cyclic work. At the time of his banishment, he burned his own manuscript, but other copies had been made and so the work has survived.

BIBLIOGRAPHICAL REFERENCES: There are a number of modern translations: Robinson Ellis, *The Amores of Ovid*, 1912; F. A. Wright, *Ovid's The Lover's Handbook*, 1923; F. J. Miller, *Metamorphoses*, 2 vols., 1916; A. L. Wheeler, *Tristia and Ex Ponto*, 1924; J. H. Mozley, *The Art of Love and Other Poems*, 1929; and Rolphe Humphries, *Ovid: The Art of Love*, 1957. See also Edward K. Rand, *Ovid and His Influence*, 1925; Herman Frankel, *Ovid, a Poet Between Two Worlds*, 1945; Gilbert Highet, *Poets in a Landscape*, 1957; and Brooks Otis, *Ovid as an Epic Poet*, 2nd ed., 1971.

WILFRED OWEN

Born: Oswestry, England
Date: March 18, 1893

Died: Sanbre Canal, France
Date: November 4, 1918

Principal Works

POEMS: *Poems* (edited by Siegfried Sassoon, 1920); enlarged edition, with a memoir by Edmund Blunden, 1931.

Wilfred Owen was born and raised in the Shropshire countryside made famous by another poet, A. E. Housman. Born in Oswestry, Owen moved to Shrewsbury for a year, and then to Birkenhead where, in 1900, he entered school. In 1911, he matriculated at London University. According to his friend Edmund Blunden, whose *Memoir* (1931) is an affectionate and detailed account of the poet's short life, Owen was a quiet, imaginative boy, not given to sports, whose greatest pleasure was to be read to by his mother. Owen was writing verse by the time he reached London University, and was deep in his earliest love—Keats. He was awarded the Military Cross on October 1, 1918, and killed in action on November 4. His life and his poems reveal a young man highly sensitive, idealistic, and given to aestheticism who was transformed by the horrors of trench warfare into a quietly courageous leader of men, a biting social critic, and a poet of hard, tough truthfulness and humanity. He is generally regarded as the greatest English war-poet.

As a boy, Owen read widely, not only Keats, but Dickens, Scott, George Eliot, and Ruskin, for whose work he had great respect, except "that Prophet . . . warned us so feebly against the war." He played the piano, studied botany and archaeology, and in August of 1913 became a tutor in English at the Berlitz School, Bordeaux. After some private tutoring he returned to England in 1915 and joined the Artist's Rifles. His friendship, in Bordeaux, with M. Laurent Tailhade was his first contact with a genuine man of letters, for, despite Owen's love of poetry, he had never been part of a literary circle. At the time he contemplated music as a profession, and painting, but was aware that poetry was his first love.

Owen went to war after Christmas in 1916, with the Lancashire Fusiliers. That spring he fell into a shellhole and suffered a concussion, the effect of which was to affect his nerves so that, on June 26, 1917, he was sent back to Craiglockhart Hospital, Edinburgh, where he met and became close to Siegfried Sassoon, a poet and a sharp critic of the public illusions regarding the war. It was in the long talks with Sassoon that Owen completed his maturity as a poet. Henceforth his poems, for example, "Dulce et Decorum Est," toughened to the task of expressing with both bitterness and deep humanity the conditions, the waste, stupidity, and terror, of war. He once observed that "Tennyson, it seems, was always a great child." The world had changed radically since the war began, and Owen's poetry, like that of Sassoon, Blunden, Rosenburg, and others, had turned sharply away from Victorian and aesthetic models. No one in France, except one captain, knew that

Owen was a poet. His letters to his mother are, perhaps, the most vivid record written of the actual conditions of life, or better, of death during the Great War. In them he describes the fetid mud, "three, four, five feet deep," the lonely terror of outpost and reconnaisance duty in No-Man's Land, the sensation of being drenched with the warm blood of a man killed by his side. But with all the horrors and realism of his poems and letters, with all the scornful and bitter criticism of those at home who still regarded the war as a sort of pilgrimage or holy crusade, Owen maintained the selfless pity and love for his fellows that make his poems—and his life—memorable.

BIBLIOGRAPHICAL REFERENCES: A good introduction to Owen's poetry is Edmund Blunden's memoir in *The Poems of Wilfred Owen*, 1931. Harold Owen's *Journey from Obscurity: Wilfred Owen, 1893–1918*, 3 vols., 1963–1965, is an indispensible biographical study. A fine recent edition of Owen's work is *The Collected Poems*, edited by C. Day Lewis, 1963.

See also Dennis S. R. Welland, *Wilfred Owen, A Critical Study*, 1960; Gertrude M. White, *Wilfred Owen*, 1969; I. M. Parsons, "The Poems of Wilfred Owen," *New Criterion*, X (1931), 658–699; Bernard Bergonzi, *Heroes' Twilight: A Study of the Literature of the Great War*, 1965; John H. Johnston, *English Poetry of the First World War*, 1964; and C. M. Bowra, *Poetry and Politics, 1900–1960*, 1966.

For additional material see William White, *Wilfred Owen, 1893–1918: A Bibliography*, 1966.

THOMAS NELSON PAGE

Born: Hanover County, Virginia
Date: April 23, 1853

Died: Hanover County
Date: November 1, 1922

PRINCIPAL WORKS

NOVELS: *On Newfound River*, 1891; *Red Rock*, 1898; *Gordon Keith*, 1903; *John Marvel, Assistant*, 1909; *The Red Riders*, 1924.

SHORT STORIES: *Marse Chan*, 1884; *In Ole Virginia*, 1887; *The Burial of the Guns*, 1894.

JUVENILES: *Two Little Confederates*, 1888; *The Old Gentleman of the Black Stock*, 1897.

ESSAYS AND STUDIES: *The Old South*, 1892; *Social Life in Old Virginia*, 1897.

BIOGRAPHY: *Robert E. Lee, Man and Soldier*, 1911.

Thomas Nelson Page was a product of the ante-bellum South, and the romance of the pre-Civil War period influenced all his thinking and his writing, as did the Civil War itself. He was born on a plantation in Hanover County, Virginia, on April 23, 1853, and lived there until he entered college. He attended Washington College (later Washington and Lee University) from 1869 to 1872, but was forced to leave before graduation by lack of sufficient money for his expenses. An important influence upon him during those undergraduate years was Robert E. Lee, president of the institution, who took a personal interest in young Page. After leaving college, Thomas Nelson Page found employment as a tutor and studied law with his father. In 1873 he entered the University of Virginia and received the LL.B. degree in 1874. During the following decade he practiced law, married, and continued the writing he had begun while at Washington College.

Page's first fame came with the publication of a story in Negro dialect, "Marse Chan," in the *Century Magazine*. In 1893 he left the practice of law altogether and moved to Washington, D.C., for by that time he had acquired sufficient reputation as a man of letters and a lecturer to assure himself of an income. In the next twenty years he lectured and wrote, his stories, novels, and social studies being almost completely about the South before, during, and immediately after the Civil War. His works reflected his own romantic and idealized notions about the South. He believed that the ante-bellum South had been a happy place for both slaves and masters, and he attempted in his writings to present such a sympathetic picture that the North would change its views and the breach between the two sections be healed.

From being a man of letters, Page became a diplomat in 1913, when President Wilson appointed him ambassador to Italy, a post Page held until 1919. He was sympathetic toward the Italians and tried to support Italy's position in the peace negotiations at Paris after World War I. Failing to be helpful that way, he wrote a highly sympathetic volume, *Italy and the World War* (1920). Ill health prevented any further serious writing during the remainder of his life, and his last novel, *The Red Riders*, was left unfinished when he died at his Hanover County home on November 1, 1922.

BIBLIOGRAPHICAL REFERENCES: The collected edition is *The Novels, Stories, Sketches and Poems of Thomas Nelson Page,* 18 vols., 1906–1918. The official biography by Rosewell Page is not altogether satisfactory, *Thomas Nelson Page: A Memoir of a Virginia Gentleman,* 1923. The only recent work is Theodore L. Gross, *Thomas Nelson Page,* 1967. Of importance is the major study of Southern literature, Jay B. Hubbell, *The South in American Literature, 1607–1900,* 1954. See also Edwin Mims, "Thomas Nelson Page," *Atlantic Monthly,* C (1907), 109–115; and Charles W. Kent, "Thomas Nelson Page," *South Atlantic Quarterly,* VI (1907), 263–271.

THOMAS PAINE

Born: Thetford, England
Date: January 29, 1737

Died: New Rochelle, New York
Date: June 8, 1809

Principal Works

POLITICAL PAMPHLETS AND ESSAYS: *The Case of the Officers of the Excise,* 1772; *Common Sense,* 1776; *The Crisis,* 1776–1783; *Public Good,* 1780; *Dissertations on Government,* . . . *Bank and Paper-Money,* 1786; *The Rights of Man,* 1791–1792; *Opinion de Thomas Paine* . . . *concernant le judgement de Louis XVI,* 1792; *Letter to George Washington,* 1796.

DEISTIC PHILOSOPHHY: *The Age of Reason,* 1795–1797.

Thomas Paine was born at Thetford, England, on January 29, 1737, the son of Frances Cocke and Joseph Paine. After grammar school he was apprenticed at thirteen in his Quaker father's trade as a corsetmaker until he left home at nineteen. Briefly a privateer, a schoolmaster, a grocer, and a tobacconist, he was twice discharged as an exciseman. His second discharge resulted from lobbying at Parliament for higher salaries for excisemen. He met Benjamin Franklin at Westminster and received letters of introduction from him when Paine left for America in 1774.

After his arrival at Philadelphia, Paine edited *The Pennsylvania Magazine,* contributed articles to the *Pennsylvania Journal* on recent inventions, in which he was widely read, and wrote miscellaneous papers. Publication of *Common Sense* in 1776 established his fame and probably sold 500,000 copies at a loss. He urged America's moral obligation to the world to seek independence for its own sake and to free the almost-uncontaminated continent from monarchy by establishing a strong federal republic. Enlisting in the Continental army in the same year, he began *The Crisis* essays with the phrase "These are the times that try men's souls." The influence of the sixteen *Crisis* pamphlets did much to preserve morale during the winter at Valley Forge.

Secretary of the Continental Congress, 1777–1779, Paine became needlessly embroiled in disputes concerning the administration of secret French aid and was dismissed from his post at French request. Clerk of the Pennsylvania Assembly, 1779–1781, he resigned to undertake a brief mission to France. After the Revolutionary War, New York gave him a farm at New Rochelle and Pennsylvania gave him £500 for his services.

While living at New Rochelle and at Bordentown, New Jersey, 1782–1787, he continued his writings for efficient taxation, against paper money, and for federal supervision of western lands occupied by Virginia. He also experimented in iron bridge construction, which led him to England in 1787. His bridge was successful in all ways except financially. Paine was welcomed in England by Charles James Fox and Edmund Burke and in France by Condorcet. In reply to Burke's condemnation of revolutionary France, Paine published in 1791–1792 his *Rights of Man,* in which he urged an English revolution to establish a republic as the only way to guarantee equal, individual rights of liberty, porperty, security, and resistance to oppression. This book sold about 200,000 copies and caused Paine's banishment from Great Britain.

Although ignorant of French, Paine took advantage of honorary French citizenship to gain election to the French Convention. Associated with the Girondists, he played a minor role, except for speaking against the execution of Louis XVI. Arrested and deprived of citizenship, 1793–1794, he was freed upon James Monroe's instance. Living at Paris until 1802 with the Bonneville family, he published there the epitome of deism, *The Age of Reason* in which he discounted the Trinity, claims for Biblical consistency, and the paternity of Christ, while stoutly asserting the existence of a God. He also wrote the unjust *Letter to Washington,* accusing the president of conniving at his arrest in France.

These two last publications made Paine anathema to the Federalists and an embarrassment to the Republicans, whose states-rights cause he embraced upon his return to America in 1802. His last years were spent as an ill, bohemian resident of New York and New Rochelle with inconsequent literary production. Cared for by Madame de Bonneville, he died at New Rochelle on June 8, 1809, and was buried on his farm because consecrated ground was denied him. In 1819, William Cobbett transferred his remains to England. He was twice married without issue: first, to Mary Lambert, who died within a year of their marriage in 1759, and lastly to Elizabeth Ollive in 1771, from whom he was legally separated in 1774.

Paine's talents as a revolutionary propagandist were not excelled in the last quarter of the eighteenth century. Although subsequently damned as an atheist, his religious views were not exceptionable in his own day; however, they still cloud his name.

BIBLIOGRAPHICAL REFERENCES: The critical edition of Paine's works is *The Writings of Thomas Paine,* edited by Moncure D. Conway, 4 vols., 1894–1896. W. M. Van der Weyde's *The Life and Works of Thomas Paine,* 10 vols., 1925, does not add substantially to the Conway edition. The standard biography is Moncure D. Conway, *The Life of Thomas Paine,* 2 vols., 1892, a study which exaggerates the importance of its subject but is generous in citation of sources. Also authoritative is W. E. Woodward, *Tom Paine: America's Godfather,* 1945. Howard Fast, *Citizen Tom Paine,* 1943, exaggerates his leftist proclivities. The best brief sketch is Crane Brinton, "Thomas Paine," *Dictionary of American Biography,* XIV, 159–166. See also Alfred O. Aldridge, *Man of Reason: The Life of Thomas Paine,* 1959. A convenient one-volume edition is *Thomas Paine: Representative Selections,* edited, with an introduction, by H. H. Clark, American Writers series, 1944.

FRANCIS PARKMAN

Born: Boston, Massachusetts
Date: September 16, 1823

Died: Jamaica Plain, Massachusetts
Date: November 8, 1893

Principal Works

TRAVEL SKETCHES AND IMPRESSIONS: *The California and Oregon Trail,* 1849.
HISTORY: *History of the Conspiracy of Pontiac,* 1851; *Pioneers of France in the New World,* 1865; *The Jesuits in North America in the Seventeenth Century,* 1867; *The Discovery of the Great West,* 1869 (*La Salle and the Discovery of the Great West,* 1879); *The Old Regime in Canada,* 1874; *Count Frontenac and New France Under Louis XIV,* 1877; *Montcalm and Wolfe,* 1884; *A Half Century of Conflict,* 1892.
NOVEL: *Vassall Morton,* 1856.

Francis Parkman's background was a fortunate one for a person who was to become a writer. He was born, September 16, 1823, into a wealthy and cultured Boston family; his father was a clergyman, and his mother came from a socially prominent New England family. Even when Parkman later became an invalid, he always had enough of his grandfather's fortune on which to live comfortably. Few men have so carefully and sensibly prepared themselves for their life's work. Although he showed moderate aptitude in his studies and some skill at writing, his most pleasurable hours were spent tramping through wooded country. In 1840 he entered Harvard, where he joined several clubs and was popular with his fellow students. He always did well in courses he liked—he was quite fond of poetry—and he was elected to the Phi Beta Kappa fraternity. Even then he was intensely interested in Indians and frontier life. Here, too, he often went on extended expeditions into wild country on foot or by canoe. He was a sportsman and a good shot.

In 1843, while still a student at Harvard, Parkman went to Europe and toured the Continent. On his return he was graduated and entered the law school. His first publication, in 1845, was a series of five sketches on his rambles during vacations, published in *The Knickerbocker, or New York Magazine.* His most important trip took him west as far as Wyoming, and from there he returned by way of the Southwest. On this trip he gathered much material about Indians and the Oregon Trail, about which he was to write so knowingly.

On his return Parkman was struck by the extreme nervous disorder that was to plague him for the rest of his life. In 1846 he retired to Boston to regain his health. There he had a major breakdown and went to Brattleboro, Vermont, to cure himself. He then started to write *The California and Oregon Trail,* published in 1849. In 1848 he started his *History of the Conspiracy of Pontiac,* the first of a series of volumes on his main historical topic, the struggle between France and England for the possession of the North American continent. He wrote this, and his other histories, under severe strain from his ailment, the sufferings of which are hinted in his one novel, *Vassall Morton.*

The book that definitely established his reputation as a great American historian was *Pioneers of France in the New World.* In this work, as well as in all his others, Parkman was scrupulous in using primary sources to document his statements. His last two books, *Montcalm and Wolfe* and *A Half Century of Conflict*, completed his historical survey of the titanic conflict of the two great European powers for control of North America.

Beset by ill health and its depressing mental effects, Parkman was never morbid; and although he could have lived comfortably without working, he always felt that he must have an occupation. His careful preparation for this occupation and his diligence in trying to capture the spirit of a past time, along with a rich and colorful narrative style, have made him, in the opinion of many readers, the greatest of American historians. His interests were varied, and he was professor of horticulture in the Harvard agricultural school, 1871–1872. He died at Jamaica Plain, near Boston, on November 8, 1893.

BIBLIOGRAPHICAL REFERENCES: Parkman's *Works* are collected in the New Library Edition, 12 vols., 1902. An important *Representative Selections* was edited by W. L. Schramm, 1938, with critical introduction, notes, and bibliography. The *Letters* were edited by Wilbur R. Jacobs, 1960. There are four authoritative biographies: Henry Dwight Sedgwick, *Francis Parkman*, American Men of Letters Series, 1904; C. H. Farnham, *A Life of Francis Parkman*, 1910; Mason Wade, *Francis Parkman, Heroic Historian*, 1942; and Howard Doughty, *Francis Parkman*, 1962. Critical works include Otis A. Pease, *Parkman's History: The Historian As Literary Artist*, 1953; John Fiske's essay on Parkman in *A Century of Science and Other Essays*, 1900; and E. F. Wyatt, "Francis Parkman: 1823–1893," *North American Review*, CCXVIII (1923), 484–496.

VERNON LOUIS PARRINGTON

Born: Aurora, Illinois
Date: August 3, 1871

Died: Seattle, Washington
Date: June 17, 1929

PRINCIPAL WORKS

CRITICISM: *Sinclair Lewis: Our Own Diogenes,* 1927.
LITERARY HISTORY: *Main Currents in American Thought,* 1927–1930.

V. L. Parrington, after whom Parrington Hall is named at the University of Washington, took his B.A. degree at Harvard in 1893. A midwesterner by birth, he returned to his native region, taking an M.A. at the College of Emporia, in Emporia, Kansas, in 1895. While there he taught English and French; he also tried for election, on the Populist ticket, to the local schoolboard. From 1897 to 1908 he was a member of the faculty of the University of Oklahoma, becoming Professor of English in 1898. During 1903–1904 he spent a year of academic leave in Europe, occupying himself with research at the British Museum in London and the Bibliothèque Nationale in Paris. In 1908 he joined the staff of the English department at the University of Washington, where he taught until his death in 1929. He was married in 1901 and had two daughters and a son. His son, Vernon Louis Parrington, Jr., is himself the author of a highly reputed study of the Utopian novel in American literature.

Vernon Louis Parrington singlehandedly wrote a great history of American literature; probably he will be the last single scholar ever to accomplish such a task. Moreover, his approach to the study of literature influenced a whole generation of scholar-professors in American literature, leading them to study it as a part of our cultural history, to see that our authors and their works are an integral part of the American scene from the earliest days of exploration and settlement to the twentieth century. Although later scholars have noted that Parrington was too strictly guided by a Jeffersonian view of American history and, occasionally, too greatly influenced by his personal enthusiasm for a particular writer (as in the case of James Branch Cabell), there is no doubt that *Main Currents in American Thought* is one of the great and influential works of American scholarship. It was only fitting that the second volume, "The Romantic Revolution in America, 1820–1860," won for Parrington the Pulitzer Prize in history in 1928.

Although he spent most of his available time working on *Main Currents in American Thought,* Parrington also contributed to scholarly journals and to such standard reference works as the *Cambridge History of American Literature,* the *Dictionary of American Biography,* and the *Encyclopedia of Social Science.*

BIBLIOGRAPHICAL REFERENCES: For commentary on Parrington's work and his place in American intellectual history see *Books that Changed Our Minds,* edited by Malcolm Cowley and Bernard Smith, 1939; Lionel Trilling, *The Liberal Imagination,* 1950; Louis Filler, "Parrington and Carlyle: Cross Currents in History and

Belles-Lettres," *Antioch Review,* XII (Summer, 1952), 203–216; M. D. Peterson, "Parrington and American Liberalism," *Virginia Quarterly Review,* XXX (Winter, 1954), 35–49; J. L. Colwell, "The Populist Image of Vernon Louis Parrington," *Mississippi Valley Historical Review,* XLIX (June, 1962), 52–66; R. A. Skotheim and Kermit Vanderbilt, "Vernon Louis Parrington: The Mind and Art of a Historian of Ideas," *Pacific Northwest Quarterly,* LIII (July, 1962), 100–113; David W. Noble, *Historians Against History,* 1965; Richard Hofstadter, *The Progressive Historians,* 1968; and R. H. Gabriel, "Vernon Louis Parrington," *Pastmasters,* edited by Marcus Cunliffe and Robin Winks, 1969. Hofstadter's book includes an extensive bibliography.

BLAISE PASCAL

Born: Clermont-Ferrand, France
Date: June 19, 1623

Died: Port Royal, France
Date: August 19, 1662

Principal Works

essays: *Provinciales*, 1656–1657; *Pensées*, 1670.

Blaise Pascal, born on June 19, 1623, was a precocious child tutored at home in Clermont-Ferrand and, later, in Paris by his father. During Pascal's boyhood his father displeased Cardinal Richelieu by objecting to the Cardinal's handling of some financial matters and went into temporary exile. The Cardinal later relented and appointed Pascal's father intendant of Rouen in 1639, a post he held for nine years. During the years in Rouen, Pascal became acquainted with Corneille, the famous dramatist. In 1646 the Pascal family became interested in Jansenism, although Blaise Pascal himself seems to have been at the time more interested in science than in religion. He had written a geometric treatise at the age of seventeen, and his first complete demonstration of the barometer in 1647 was only one of his many achievements in mathematics and physics.

In 1650 the Pascal family returned to Paris, where Pascal's father died in the following year. Jacqueline Pascal, a sister, joined a convent at Port Royal. During this period, in which Pascal seems to have written his essays on the passions of love, the author is supposed to have led a dissolute life. In 1654 he underwent a mystic experience at the convent at Port Royal and a few months later retired from the world. During 1656 he came out of retirement briefly to defend Antoine Arnauld from an attack by the Jesuits, publishing a series of letters entitled *Provinciales*.

Pascal continued to live a quiet, religious life within the walls of Port Royal until his death on August 19, 1662. Eight years later a committee of Jansenists, headed by the Duc de Roannez, Pascal's friend, edited and published the *Pensées*, fragments salvaged from a projected but unfinished work to be called *Apologie de la religion catholique*. Because of religious biases, however, this and other early editions failed to do justice to Pascal. Only nineteenth century and later editions, made from the original manuscripts, are trustworthy. It is rather as a pioneer in science and mathematics than as an author that Pascal is an important person in world history.

bibliographical references: The Pascal bibliography is extensive. Among recent studies in English are Morris Bishop, *Pascal: The Life of a Genius*, 1936; H. F. Stewart, *Pascal's Apology for Religion*, 1942; F. T. H. Fletcher, *Pascal and the Mystical Tradition*, 1954; Ernest Mortimer, *Blaise Pascal: The Life and Works of a Realist*, 1959; and Albert N. Wells, *Pascal's Recovery of Man's Wholeness*, 1965. See also Jacques Chevalier, *Pascal*, 1922; Ehrhard Bucholz, *Blaise Pascal*, 1942; Henri Lefebre, *Pascal*, 1949; Jean Mesnard, *Pascal, l'homme et l'œuvre*, 1951 (tr. 1952); and Jean Steinmann, *Pascal*, 1954. An interesting comparative study is D. G. M. Patrick, *Pascal and Kierkegaard*, 1948. See also R. H. Soltau, *Pascal: The Man and the Message*, 1927.

BORIS LEONIDOVICH PASTERNAK

Born: Moscow, Russia
Date: February 10, 1890

Died: Moscow
Date: May 30, 1960

Principal Works

NOVEL: *Dr. Zhivago,* 1957 (English translation, 1958).
SHORT STORIES: *Aerial Ways,* 1924.
POEMS: *Sestra moya zhizn',* 1922 (*My Sister, Life*); *Temy i variatsii,* 1923 (*Themes and Variations*); *God 1905,* 1926 (*The Year 1905*); *Vtoroye rozhdenie,* 1932; *Poetry of Boris Pasternak,* translated by George Reavey, 1959.
TRANSLATIONS INTO RUSSIAN: *Hamlet, Antony and Cleopatra, Othello, Romeo and Juliet.*

Boris Pasternak was the son of Leonid and Rosa (Kaufman) Pasternak. The father was a famous Russian painter, and the mother a recognized concert pianist. Thus the boy who was to become the most renowned modern Russian writer grew up where art was a way of life. One of the close family friends was the composer Scriabin, who influenced Pasternak's youthful ambitions in music. Finishing his early schooling at a *gymnasium* in Moscow, young Pasternak undertook the serious study of music, hoping to become a composer. In 1910 he turned to the study of law at Moscow University. Two years later came another change: he went to Germany to study philosophy at the University of Marburg. After a year there under Professor Hermann Cohen, he traveled in Italy and then returned to Moscow during 1913–1914. He had broken a leg in childhood and, because of that old injury, did not serve in the tsarist forces during World War I; he worked instead in a factory in the Ural Mountains. Shortly after the revolution he was back in Moscow, working in the library of the Soviet Commissariat of Education. By this time he had been writing poetry seriously for several years, with his first volume, *Twin in the Clouds,* being published in 1914. He was influenced by his close friend, Vladimir Mayakovsky, and became himself a leader in the then-current symbolist movement. What was probably his most important volume of poetry, *My Sister, Life,* was published in 1922. In the following decade Pasternak was active as a writer of both poetry and prose. Among his prose works was *Aerial Ways,* a collection of short stories which included "The Childhood of Lyuvers," the beautiful, sensitive tale of a young girl's emergence into womanhood. The first collected edition of his work, in Russian, came in 1933.

Early in the 1930's Pasternak's refusal to condone the execution of Soviet generals in one of the Stalinist purges caused him to fear for his life, but though he came into some disfavor he was not even imprisoned. But he left off creative writing almost entirely, turning to translation. He translated poetry into Russian, poetry from other language groups of the U.S.S.R., as well as from the works of Goethe, Kleist, Paul Verlaine, Ben Jonson, and Percy Bysshe Shelley. Particularly popular in Russia, and highly regarded by critics, were his translations of Shakespearean plays. All these translations were official in the sense that they were published by the government publishing house. During the early 1940's he wrote a quantity of poetry inspired by his country's successful withstanding of the Nazi onslaught.

For many years Pasternak worked on *Dr. Zhivago,* his novel about a poet-doctor in the Russian revolution who sees that revolution failing to conform to his vision of what it might be. The novel was accepted and then rejected by the State Publishing House. In the meantime foreign rights had been sold to Feltrinelli, a publisher in Milan, who issued the novel in an Italian translation in 1957. Other translations followed, with American publication in 1958. That same year the Royal Swedish Academy announced that Pasternak had been awarded the Nobel Prize for literature. Though he immediately announced his pleasure at the honor, he found that he was expelled from the Soviet Writers Union that same month, and was labeled a traitor by writers in Soviet publications. Pasternak refused to accept the Nobel Prize, which was held in trust for him, and wrote a letter to Nikita Khrushchev acknowledging political weakness and begging to be spared exile from his native land. In the last months of his life he continued to live at the writers' colony at Peredelkino, not far from Moscow, where, it is reported, he spent his time gardening and talking with his colleagues and friends about philosophy and literature, his long-time interests in life. He died at the age of seventy, in 1960, apparently from disorders caused by his age.

BIBLIOGRAPHICAL REFERENCES: D. L. Clark, *Pasternak's Lyrics,* 1966; Mary F. and Paul Rowland, *Pasternak's Doctor Zhivago,* 1967; D. A. Davie and A. Livingston, *Pasternak,* 1969; Marc Slonim, "Boris Pasternak: The Voice of the Other Russia," *Soviet Russian Literature,* 1964, 218–230; and F. D. Reeve, "Doctor Zhivago," *The Russian Novel,* 1966, 360–378.

WALTER PATER

Born: London, England
Date: August 4, 1839

Died: Oxford, England
Date: July 30, 1894

Principal Works

ESSAYS AND STUDIES: *Studies in the History of the Renaissance,* 1873; *Appreciations, with an Essay on Style,* 1889; *Plato and Platonism,* 1893; *Miscellaneous Studies,* 1895.

NOVELS: *Marius the Epicurean,* 1885; *The Child in the House,* 1894.

TALES AND SKETCHES: *Imaginary Portraits,* 1887.

Walter (Horatio) Pater was born in London on August 4, 1839. Having attended King's School in Canterbury and graduated B.A. from Queen's College, Oxford, he was made Fellow of Brasenose College, Oxford, from which he received his M.A. degree in 1865. With this college he was connected in some capacity during most of the rest of his life. During vacations, however, he often traveled on the Continent. He died at Oxford after a brief illness, on July 30, 1894.

Much of Pater's literary output consisted of critical essays on aesthetic subjects, most of which were collected in such works as *Studies in the History of the Renaissance* and *Appreciations, with an Essay on Style.* Critics have spoken of his sensual approach to art, and some are bothered by a certain subjective impressionism in his criticism. Pater also wrote a few romances, the most famous of which is *Marius the Epicurean.* There is a relation between these romances and his critical works because in the romances he seems to advocate that life itself be approached as an art. Through elaborate sentences with delicate shadings he worked continually for perfection of expression in his prose style. Although Pater spent most of his life in academic seclusion, he had a profound influence on a group of perceptive younger artists and critics.

BIBLIOGRAPHICAL REFERENCES: Pater's works are collected in the New Library Edition of the *Works of Walter Pater,* 10 vols., 1910. The *Letters* were edited by Lawrence Evans, 1971. The standard bibliography is C. A. and H. W. Stonehill, *Bibliographies of Modern Authors,* Series 2, 1925. The best biographies are Thomas Wright, *The Life of Walter Pater,* 2 vols., 1907; and A. C. Benson's *Walter Pater,* English Men of Letters Series, 1906, which includes a critical bibliography. Other critical works include Helen H. Young, *The Writings of Walter Pater: A Reflection of British Philosophical Opinion From 1860 to 1890;* 1933; R. C. Child, *The Aesthetic of Walter Pater,* 1940; R. V. Johnson, *Walter Pater: A Study of His Critical Outlook,* 1961; and Gordon McKenzie, *The Literary Character of Walter Pater,* 1967. Short critical articles are T. S. Eliot, "Arnold and Pater," in *Selected Essays,* 1932; G. G. Hough, "Walter Pater" in *The Last Romantics,* 1949; Geoffrey Tillotson, "Arnold and Pater: Critics Historical, Aesthetic, and Otherwise," in *Criticism and the Nineteenth Century,* 1951; R. V. Johnson, "Pater and the Victorian Anti-Romantics," *Essays in Criticism,* IV (1954), 42–57; and Lord David Cecil's published lecture, *Walter Pater: The Scholar-Artist,* 1955.

ALAN PATON

Born: Natal, South Africa
Date: January 11, 1903

Principal Works

NOVELS: *Cry, the Beloved Country,* 1948; *Too Late the Phalarope,* 1953.
SHORT STORIES: *Debbie Go Home,* 1961; *Tales from a Troubled Land,* 1961.
SOCIAL STUDIES: *The Land and People of South Africa,* 1955; *South Africa in Transition,* 1956 (with Dan Weiner); *Hope for South Africa,* 1958.
PLAY: *Sponono,* 1965 (with Krishna Shah).
MEDITATIONS: *Instrument of Thy Peace,* 1968; *For You Departed,* 1969.

Perhaps more a great humanitarian than a novelist, sensitive Alan Paton has nevertheless written two very fine novels about racial problems in Africa. Born in Pietermaritzburg, Natal, on January 11, 1903, he writes out of lifelong familiarity with the land and its people, white and black.

Though always interested in literature, Paton first chose a career in science and became a science teacher in the school at the African village of Ixopo, which was later to figure in *Cry, the Beloved Country.* Later he was for a number of years the principal of a reformatory for African boys. There he brought many badly needed improvements to the institution. Today he is considered one of South Africa's leading experts on prison reform.

In 1928 he married Doris Olive Francis; their work is among tuberculosis patients in Natal. They have two children, David and Jonathan. By religion, Paton is an Anglican.

After abandoning two novels, Paton began *Cry, the Beloved Country* in 1946 while on a tour studying prison systems. The book, published in 1948, enjoyed an overnight success. *Too Late the Phalarope,* probably because of its heavy style, has not been as well received. Both novels have been dramatized.

In addition to his hospital work, Paton is also active in a Non-European Boys' Club movement, and in the Liberal Association of South Africa, which, challenging white supremacy in Africa, favors all and any civilized men.

BIBLIOGRAPHICAL REFERENCES: There is only one full-length study: Edward Callan, *Alan Paton,* 1968. Sheridan Barker, "Paton's Beloved Country and the Morality of Geography," *College English,* XIX (1957), 56–61, presents an interesting explication of *Cry, the Beloved Country.* See further Edmund Fuller, "Alan Paton: Tragedy and Beyond," *Books with Men behind Them,* 1962, 83–101; and Fred H. Marcus, "*Cry the Beloved Country* and *Strange Fruit:* Exploring Man's Inhumanity to Man," *English Journal,* LI (1962), 609–616. See also F. Charles Rooney, "The 'Message' of Alan Paton," *Catholic World,* CXCIV (1961), 92–98.

OCTAVIO PAZ

Born: Mixcoac, Mexico
Date: March 31, 1914

Principal Works

POEMS: *Bajo tu Clara Sombra* (*1935–1938*), 1941; *Entre la Piedra y la Flor*, 1941; *A la Orilla del Mundo*, 1942; *¿Aguila o Sol?* (*Eagle or Sun?*), 1951; *Semillas para un Himno*, 1954; *Piedra de Sol*, 1957; *La Estación Violenta*, 1958; *Libertad bajo Palabra: Obra Poética, 1935–1957*, 1960; *Salamandra, 1958–1961*, 1962; *Blanco*, 1967; *Topoemas*, 1968; *Ladera Este, 1962–1968*, 1969.

ESSAYS: *El Laberinto de la Soledad* (*The Labyrinth of Solitude*), 1950; *El Arco y la Lira*, 1956; *Las Peras del Olmo*, 1957; *Corriente Alterna*, 1967; *Conjunciones y Disyunciones*, 1967; *Posdata*, 1970.

Considered the most personal Mexican poet of the period and one of the best poetic voices in Spanish, Octavio Paz has devoted his life to both letters and diplomacy. Born in Mixcoac, on the outskirts of Mexico City, he studied at the National University of Mexico and later, having been granted a Guggenheim Fellowship, went to the United States to study Spanish-American poetry. He visited Spain during the period of the Civil War and adhered to the Republican cause; from these circumstances was born one of his earliest works, *¡No pasarán!* (*They Will Not Trespass!*). After his return to Mexico, he collaborated in *Taller*, 1938–1941, and *El Hijo Pródigo*, 1943–1946, literary periodicals of considerable prestige, especially the second, in Mexican literature of this century. Paz entered the Foreign Service of his country, and since 1943 he has held posts in France, Japan, Switzerland, India, and other countries. He resigned his position as ambassador to India as a protest against the shooting of Mexican students in 1968 during the regime of President Díaz Ordaz. His prestige has been greatly increased by the translations made of his works and by the bestowing of one of the most renowned literary awards in the world, the *Grand Prix International de Poésie*, in the sixth contest of the International Congress of Poetry at Knokke-le Zoute, Belgium, in 1963.

Paz has been a writer in many fields. Not only poetry but the essay, literary and political criticism, drama, and translations are expressions of his activity as a man of letters. The present article attempts only to touch on his most recurrent poetic themes and includes a brief presentation of his best essays.

Libertad bajo Palabra (*Freedom and the Word*), published in two editions, is a book that constitutes Paz's first important personal anthology, from 1935 to 1948 in the first edition; from 1935 to 1957 in the second. In this work, the poet travels a spiritual road departing from solitude in search of communication. This communication is made through liberty and words, namely, through poetry. The poetic style of Paz, commonly drawing upon surrealism, fills his work with symbolism of generally hermetic message. Under these symbols appear the yearning for participation, the wish of eternization, the perception of poetry as a dream, desperation, solitude, silence. The poet finishes by thinking that life is a mirror reflecting his own image, the solitude of his conscience and the conscience of his solitude. But he has to struggle against this situation and transcend his tragedy by going to others, the only way of realizing his own existence. Going to others is love; love is the unique means of liberty that sends man to the very center of his sources, far beyond end and beginning.

Piedra de Sol (*Sun Stone*), 1957, represents a transitional step in Paz's poetry. Though the theme of time had already appeared in some of his earlier productions, it is in this poem that he goes deep into temporality, in this particular instance set against the ancient Mesoamerican mythologies. The title of the poem evokes at once the Aztec calendar. Written in 584 hendecasyllabic lines—the same number of days that it takes the planet Venus to complete its synodic period—the poem presents the contradictory elements of life and myths, in a recurrent, cyclical way. This is the poem of the eternal return of matter, life, and time. In Paz's constant search for unity and reconciliation, *Piedra de Sol* constitutes an attempt to integrate love and death, time and eternity, reality and irreality, word and the world.

Paz's next personal anthology, *Salamandra, 1958–1961,* contains some of his most cryptic poems. This book presents one of the basic tenets of surrealism—the struggle of language in quest of originality and authenticity. These poems are not, however, pure verbalism. The author wants to unite his conscience with the world through words, the main way to go to others, to "the other shore" of communication.

Another trip to India in 1962 gave Paz a new perspective of man. He had already glimpsed the cultural differences between the western and the eastern mentalities—the West is disjunctive, dual, manichean; the East is based on unity conjunction, and conciliation. In *Ladera Este,* 1969, he goes beyond the inclusion of toponyms, mythologies, and customs of India. He transcends them and assumes a more integral attitude toward man and history. This universality comes as a result of the acceptance and unification of opposite concepts of life, time, and the world. Thus, Paz reaffirms his theory of poetry as the union of contrary elements.

In the field of the essay, Paz has explored several topics. Perhaps the best known books in this genre are *El Arco y la Lira* (2nd. ed. 1967), and *El Laberinto de la Soledad* (*The Labyrinth of Solitude*), 1950. The first work is one of the deepest treatments on the essence of poetic creation ever written in the Spanish world. It should be mentioned that the second edition of this book differs somewhat from the first because of Paz's adoption of the structuralistic theories of the French philosopher and anthropologist Claude Lévi-Strauss, who has influenced Paz's latest production. One sentence from the book might summarize its whole idea: "The poem is a series of symbols looking for a meaning." *El Laberinto de la Soledad* comprises several essays on the Mexican character, its historic roots and its solitude. With exceptional insight, Paz delves into the ingredients that have shaped, according to him, the Mexican soul—atavism, burden of racial origins, love of death. The last chapter ends with an analysis of the solitude inherent in every human being. By doing this,

Paz equates the Mexican people with the rest of the world. Man, by definition, is a solitary being. Going to others in love is his only means of self-realization.

BIBLIOGRAPHICAL REFERENCES: Arturo Rivas Sáinz, "La Poesía de O.P.," *Letras de México*, I, 6 (June 15, 1943), 1–2; 5, 8; Rodolfo Usigli, "Poeta en Libertad," *Cuadernos Americanos*, (January–February, 1950), 293–300; Ramón Xirau, "La Poesía de O.P.," *Cuadernos Americanos*, LVIII, 4 (July–August, 1951) 288–298; Fernando Charry Lara, "Tres Poetas Mexicanos, III: Octavio Paz," *Universidad de México*, XI, 5 (January, 1957), 14–17; Manuel Durán, "Octavio Paz en su libertad," *México en la Cultura*, no. 408 (January 14, 1957), 2; and "Liberty and Eroticism in the Poetry of Octavio Paz," *Books Abroad*, XXXVII (1963), 373–377; John M. Fein, "El Espejo como imagen y tema en la poesía de Octavio Paz," *Universidad de México*, XII, 3 (November, 1957), 8–13; Luis Leal, "Octavio Paz: El Laberinto de la Soledad," *Revista Iberoamericana*, 49 (January–July 1960), 154–186; Lloyd King, "Surrealism and the Sacred in the Aesthetic Credo of Octavio Paz," *Hispanic Review*, XXXVII, 3, (July, 1969), 383–393; Julio Ortega, "Notas sobre Octavio Paz," *Cuadernos Hispanoamericanos*, 231 (March, 1969), 1–14; Emir Rodríguez-Monegal, "Octavio Paz: crítica y poesía," *Mundo Nuevo*, 21, (March, 1968), 55–62; Raymond D. Souza, "The World, Symbol and Synthesis in Octavio Paz," *Hispania*, XLVII, 1 (March, 1964), 60–65; Ramón Xirau, *Octavio Paz: el Sentido de la Palabra* (México, 1970); Saúl Yurkievich, "La Topoética de Octavio Paz," *Caravelle*, 12 (1969), 183–189.

Revista Iberoamericana devoted its No. 74 (January–March, 1971) to Octavio Paz. It contains a very valuable collection of articles, plus a bibliography.

THOMAS LOVE PEACOCK

Born: Weymouth, England
Date: October 18, 1785

Died: Lower Halliford, England
Date: January 23, 1866

Principal Works

NOVELS: *Headlong Hall,* 1816; *Melincourt,* 1817; *Nightmare Abbey,* 1818; *Maid Marian,* 1822; *The Misfortunes of Elphin,* 1829; *Crotchet Castle,* 1831; *Gryll Grange,* 1860.

POEMS: *The Monks of St. Mark,* 1804; *Palmyra and Other Poems,* 1806; *The Genius of the Thames,* 1810; *The Philosophy of Melancholy,* 1812; *Sir Proteus: a Satirical Ballad,* 1814; *Rhododaphne,* 1818.

Thomas Love Peacock, born at Weymouth, Dorsetshire, England, on October 18, 1785, was a literary barnacle, following the ship of English Romanticism for the ride though not a part of it. Until his early thirties he wrote poetry that was intended to inspire readers as that of the Romantics did. However, it was only the shell of poetry; it contained rhyme and meter and exotic material, but the meat—emotion—was absent. This passage from *Rhododaphne* is typical:

All other fires are of the earth,
And transient: but of heavenly birth
Is Love's first flame, which howsoever
Fraud, power, woe, chance, or fate may sever
From its congenial source, must burn
Unquenched, but in the funeral urn. (Canto VII)

Actually Peacock was in spirit and temperament a classicist. He was precocious as a child and although he did not attend college, he was well-read in Latin and Greek (having taught himself the two languages for pleasure's sake). Among his favorite classical authors were Sallust, Tacitus, and Lucian. Of an even disposition, he walked along country roads and stopped by graveyards and mountain streams as was the prevailing practice of the Lake poets. But he collected ideas, not emotional experiences. (One idea was that a Welsh girl whom he had met on a walking tour through Wales would be a good wife to marry; when he had advanced in the East India Company to a salary sufficient to support a family ten years later he wrote to her to be his bride. She remembered and accepted.) However, he was not ignorant of the Romantic movement; many of the poets, like Shelley, were his good friends. And it was the combination of his practical brain, his enjoyment of literature, and his sense of humor that produced his real contribution to literature, a series of seven novels satirizing the whole intellectual and artistic movement of the day.

In reality a conservative, successful businessman, Peacock was unsympathetic to the new ideas of the time primarily because they went beyond reason, which is to say they were to him unreasonably romantic. Using the method of irony, he satirized radicalism, medievalism, and transcendentalism as well as individual romanticists like Wordsworth, Coleridge, Byron, and Shelley. Five of the seven novels —all but *Maid Marian* and *The Misfortunes of Elphin*—follow the same plan: a group of eccentric guests at a house party reveal the folly of their romantic persuasions in witty talk and inane action. Each guest, of course, is a caricature of a contemporary figure. The other two novels are burlesques of legends, the first of Robin Hood and the second of the Welsh (supra). The critic Saintsbury felt that this last novel was the best, although *Crotchet Castle* has remained the most popular. The main purpose of all the works was "to make a joke of things." Peacock died at Lower Halliford, Chertsey, on January 23, 1866.

BIBLIOGRAPHICAL REFERENCES: The standard edition of Peacock's works is the Halliford Edition, edited by H. F. B. Brett-Smith and C. E. Jones, 10 vols., 1923–1924; it includes a biographical introduction and full bibliographical and textual notes. J. B. Priestly, *Thomas Love Peacock* in the English Men of Letters Series, 1927 (revised edition 1966), is the most adequate biography, although Carl Van Doren, *The Life of Thomas Love Peacock,* 1911, is still important. Critical works include A. Martin Freeman, *Thomas Love Peacock, a Critical Study,* 1911; A. B. Young, *The Life and Novels of Thomas Love Peacock,* 1904; H. R. Fedden, "Peacock," in *The English Novelists,* edited by D. Vershoyle, 1936; and Olwen W. Campbell, *Peacock,* in the English Novelists Series, 1953. Recent works are Carl Dawson, *Thomas Love Peacock,* 1968; and Howard Milk, *Peacock: His Circle and His Age,* 1969. An important article is O. Burdett, "Thomas Love Peacock," *London Mercury,* VIII (1923), 21–32.

DONALD CULROSS PEATTIE

Born: Chicago, Illinois
Date: June 21, 1898

Died: Santa Barbara, California
Date: November 16, 1964

Principal Works

NATURE AND NATURAL HISTORY: *Cargoes and Harvests*, 1926; *Bounty of Earth*, 1926 (in collaboration with his wife); *Vence: The Story of the Provençal Town Through 2000 Years*, 1930; *Flora of the Sand Dunes and the Calumet District of Indiana*, 1930; *Trees of North America*, 1934; *An Almanac for Moderns*, 1935; *The Happy Kingdom*, 1935 (in collaboration with his wife); *Old Fashioned Garden Flowers*, 1936; *A Book of Hours*, 1937; *A Child's Story of the World*, 1937; *A Prairie Grove*, 1938; *This Is Living*, 1938 (in collaboration with Gordon Aymar); *A Gathering of Birds*, 1939 (editor); *Flowering Earth*, 1939; *Forward the Nation*, 1942; *Journey into America*, 1943; *Immortal Village*, 1945; *American Heartwood*, 1949; *A Cup of Sky*, 1950 (in collaboration with his son Noel); *A Natural History of Trees of Eastern and Central America*, 1950; *Sportsman's Country*, 1952; *A Natural History of Western Trees*, 1953; *The Rainbow Book of Nature*, 1957.

BIOGRAPHY: *Singing in the Wilderness: A Salute to John James Audubon*, 1935; *Green Laurels: The Lives and Achievements of the Great Naturalists*, 1936; *Lives of Destiny*, 1954.

AUTOBIOGRAPHY: *The Road of a Naturalist*, 1941.

REFERENCE WORKS: *Flora of the Tryon Region of North and South Carolina* (six volumes), 1928–1932.

NOVELS: *Up Country*, 1928 (in collaboration with his wife); *Port of Call*, 1932; *Sons of the Martian*, 1932; *The Bright Lexicon*, 1934.

MISCELLANEOUS: *Parade with Banners*, 1957.

Donald Culross Peattie, son of Robert Burns Peattie and Elia Wilkinson Peattie, was born in Chicago June 21, 1898. His father was a journalist, his mother a novelist. Young Peattie graduated from Chicago University High School in 1916; he entered the University of Chicago with a scholarship in English literature which he had won in a competitive examination. After two years at that institution, he moved to New York. He later entered Harvard where he specialized in the natural sciences—not with the intention of becoming a scientist but because he considered them essential background for his chosen career of nature writer. He graduated *cum laude* in 1922; in the same year he received the Witter Bynner Poetry Prize. He worked as a botanist in the Department of Agriculture from 1922 until his first book, *Cargoes and Harvest*, appeared in 1926. He had married novelist Louise Redfield in 1923; she collaborated with him on several of his early works.

Although he produced several works of fiction, Peattie is best known for his many nature books, which have always been deservedly popular. *An Almanac for Moderns* (1935), the day-to-day observations and reflections of a sensitive naturalist, was awarded the Gold Medal of the Limited Editions Club. He was granted a Guggenheim Fellowship for creative writing in 1936 and 1937. His *Flowering Earth* (1939) was named the best horticultural book of the year and in 1940 received a silver medal from the Commonwealth Club of California. *The Road of a Naturalist,* an autobiographical work, was awarded a prize by Houghton Mifflin in 1941. In addition to writing his numerous books, Peattie conducted nature columns in the Washington *Evening Star* and the Chicago *Daily News;* he was also a roving editor for *Reader's Digest.*

Donald Culross Peattie has been called America's most lyrical naturalist. He was essentially a poet; in his writing he combined science and the spirit of poetry. His work reveals a strong appreciation for beauty and a sense of the unity of nature, considerable philosophic insight, and a concern for good prose. Although he has been criticized in some instances for an oversentimentalized approach to his material, he has nonetheless produced enduring works of high literary quality. He was a popularizer in the highest sense of the term.

BIBLIOGRAPHICAL REFERENCES: Peattie has received little attention from the critics, especially in recent years. For brief comment see Mark Van Doren, "A New Naturalist," *North American Review,* CCXLIV (August, 1937), 162–171; Mangum Weeks, "Artist and Backwoodsman," *Virginia Quarterly Review,* XIII, (January, 1937), 140-143; and K. Hendrick, "Peattie's Talk About Writing," *Christian Science Monitor Magazine,* September 23, 1950, 14.

For a review of *An Almanac for Moderns* see Frank N. Magill, *Masterplots:* Comprehensive Library Edition, 1968, 115–117.

GEORGE PEELE

Born: London, England
Date: 1558

Died: London (?)
Date: 1596

Principal Works

PLAYS: *The Arraignment of Paris*, 1584; *Edward the First*, 1593; *David and Bethsabe*, 1594; *The Old Wives' Tale*, 1595.
POEMS: *Polyhymnia*, 1590; *The Honour of the Garter*, 1593; *Anglorum Feriae*, 1595.

George Peele was born in London in 1558 and died in 1596. He studied at Oxford and after leaving the university wrote for the stage and produced various patriotic occasional poems, of which the best known are *Polyhymnia*, *The Honour of the Garter*, and *Anglorum Feriae*. These poems suggest that he moved in court circles, and such is certainly the impression left by his first play, *The Arraignment of Paris*, which was performed before Elizabeth by the Children of the Chapel Royal. The Peele canon offers many difficulties, and only the publication dates of his plays are known. In addition to *The Arraignment of Paris*, these comprise *Edward the First*, *David and Bethsabe*, *The Old Wives' Tale*. The two last named are pirated and corrupt texts.

Very little is known about Peele's life, except that his latter days were spent in poverty and sickness. He was evidently very much a public figure in his own day. Many tales and pranks were attributed to him, and his reputation as a jester survived long after his death. The character George Pieboard (i.e. a peel or baker's shovel) in the pseudo-Shakespearian comedy, *The Puritan Widow* (1607), doubtless presents him as his contemporaries saw him.

Peele does not rank high as a dramatist, but it is not unreasonable to regard him as a lyric poet who, for pecuniary advantage, turned to a medium for which he was not naturally suited. Of his lyrical gifts there can be no doubt and the songs in his plays have a verbal felicity that is almost Tennysonian. *The Arraignment of Paris* and *The Old Wives' Tale* are successful within their limits precisely because they exist at a gentle and unconstrained pastoral level which allows full scope for lyricism. *David and Bethsabe*, which draws freely on *Samuel* and *The Song of Solomon*, is a notable attempt to present Hebrew pastoral but the general effect is marred by Peele's attempts to bring off the more heroic parts of his material in the grand Marlovian manner. There is probably a measure of topical satire in *The Old Wives' Tale*, but the merit of the play lies in its deft and impalpable presentation of a tale of magic and spells. It has affinities with *Comus* (1634), and it is likely that Peele's work influenced Milton far more than is generally recognized.

BIBLIOGRAPHICAL REFERENCES: The only complete edition of the plays is *The Works of George Peele*, edited by A. H. Bullen, 2 vols., 1888. See also F. B. Gummere in *Representative English Comedies*, edited by C. R. Gayley, 1903; E. K.

Chambers, *The Elizabethan Stage*, Vol. III, 1923; *Dictionary of National Biography*, Vol. XV; and P. H. Cheffaud, *George Peele*, 1913. For bibliography see Thorleif Larsen, "A Bibliography of the Writings of George Peele," *Modern Philology*, XXXII (1934).

CHARLES-PIERRE PÉGUY

Born: Orléans, France
Date: January 7, 1873

Died: Villeroy, France
Date: September 5, 1914

Principal Works

PLAYS: *Jeanne d'Arc*, 1897; *Le Mystère de la charité de Jeanne d'Arc*, 1910.

PERIODICAL: *Cahiers de la quinzaine*, 229 vols., 1900–1914 (Fortnightly Notebooks).

POEMS: *La Tapisserie de Ste.-Geneviève et de Jeanne d'Arc*, 1912; *La Tapisserie de Notre-Dame*, 1912; *Eve*, 1913; *Œuvres poétiques complètes*, 1941.

Charles-Pierre Péguy was born and grew up in that part of France where Joan of Arc had lived four centuries earlier. His life and his work was strongly influenced by the history of Joan, who became the subject of a considerable portion of his writings. Péguy was reared by his mother and grandmother, for his father died when the child was less than a year old. A bright boy, he earned a scholarship to the *lycée* at Orléans. He spent a year in the French military service and then attended Lycée Louis-le-Grand and the Collège de Sainte-Barbe. In 1894 he entered L'École Normale Superieure, where he came under the influence of Henri Bergson and Romain Rolland, although he did not finish his studies. Instead, he married Charlotte Baudouin. Shortly after his marriage his *Jeanne d'Arc* was published, in 1897. The following year he used some of his wife's money to open a Socialist publishing house and bookstore in Paris. He was an ardent defender of Dreyfus, and his store soon became a meeting place for political activities. While still a young man he began the publication of the *Cahiers de la quinzaine*, which for fourteen years carried his own writings, as well as those of such famous French authors as Romain Rolland, Anatole France, and Jean Jaurès.

As a poet, Péguy taught his readers that patriotism is real, that earthly history is but a part of divine history, and that classicism is the true temper of a life of liberty among men. As a political man, Péguy thought of himself as a socialist, but he declined to be a part of the Socialist Party. As a religious man, he was an atheist during his student days, but he found his faith restored later and considered himself a Catholic, even though his civil marriage prevented his being received by his Church. A symbol of his own love for his country, he died during the fighting on the first day of the Battle of the Marne, during World War I.

BIBLIOGRAPHICAL REFERENCES: The *Œuvres Complètes* were published in 20 volumes, 1916–1955. The *Œuvres Poétique Complètes* with an introduction by Francois Porché and notes by Marcel and Pierre Péguy was published in 1941 and in a revised edition in 1957. Other recent editions include *Œuvres en vers* and *Œuvres en prose*, edited by Marcel Péguy, 1958, 1963. M. Péguy also edited Péguy's *Lettres et Entretiens*, revised edition, 1954.

Translations include *Basic Verities, Prose and Poetry*, translated by Anne and Julian Green, 1943; *God Speaks: Religious Poetry*, translated by Julian Green, 1945;

Men and Saints: Prose and Poetry, translated by Anne and Julian Green, 1944; *The Mystery of the Charity of Joan of Arc,* translated by Julian Green, 1950; and *The Mystery of the Holy Innocents and Other Poems,* translated by Pansy Pakenham, 1956.

For critical comment see André Rousseaux, *Le Prophète Péguy,* 3 vols., 1942–45; Louis Perche, *Essai sur Charles Péguy,* 1957, which includes a good bibliography; Jean Roussel, *Charles Péguy,* 1953; Bernard Guyon, *Péguy,* 1960; D. Halevy, *Péguy et les Cahiers de la Quinzaine,* 1947; M. Villiers, *Charles Péguy: A Study in Integrity,* 1965; and H. Schmitt, *Péguy: The Decline of an Idealist,* 1967.

SAMUEL PEPYS

Born: London (?), England
Date: February 23, 1633

Died: Clapham, England
Date: May 26, 1703

Principal Works

MEMOIRS: *Diary, 1660-1669,* 1825; first complete publication, 1848-1849. *Memoirs Relating to the State of the Royal Navy of England,* 1690.

Samuel Pepys, born on February 23, 1633, probably in London, was a man of wide interests and varied affairs: an inveterate playgoer and a minor patron of the arts, a conscientious husband and householder, a responsible public official, and a friend (sometimes a self-acknowledged flatterer) of the great and the powerful. All this we know from his *Diary,* his own candid and unaffected portrayal of himself. Yet it must be remembered that the *Diary,* as detailed and as thorough as it is for its own specified time, deals with only nine years in a life that lasted a full seventy.

Although not much of importance had happened to Samuel Pepys before he began his famous project in 1660, his many affairs continued long after poor eyesight forced him to give up his record in 1669; and twice, in the period between the ending of the *Diary* and the quiet ending of his life in 1703, his fortunes fell and rose again. Although the full publication of the *Diary* in 1849 transformed him suddenly into a literary figure, it should also be remembered that he was not, neither to himself nor to his contemporaries, primarily a man of letters. He was what would be called in modern terminology a "career" admiralty official. He served twenty-eight years in the Admiralty Department, was twice Secretary of the Admiralty, and was acknowledged, after the "Bloodless Revolution" ended his career in 1688, as the foremost authority on naval matters in all England.

His admiralty career began significantly enough with the restoration of the Stuarts in 1660. His life up to that time had been a genteel struggle with poverty, for his family, though well connected, was, by his own admission, "never very considerable." He had gone through Magdelene College, Cambridge, as a scholarship student (receiving a B.A. in 1653 and an M.A. in 1660), had married in 1655 the fifteen-year-old daughter of a penniless French expatriate, and had lived for some time under the patronage of a wealthy cousin, Sir Edward Montagu. This nobleman, later the first Earl of Sandwich, was a stanch supporter of Charles II and played no small part in the triumph of the royal cause. As his good fortune swelled with the resurgence of the Stuarts, so the good fortune of Samuel Pepys increased as well. Pepys' first official appointment was to a minor position in the Exchequer, but on July 13, 1660, he moved to the Navy Office, becoming, later that same year, Clerk of the Privy Seal and a Justice of the Peace.

This triumphal year is covered by the *Diary.* During the remaining eight years of that chronicled account, the triumphs continue. Pepys' finances improve. Able to afford books, he begins the collection of his famous library (now preserved at Cambridge); he can dress his wife in cautious finery;

and he can, when his basically puritan conscience allows, indulge in his favorite delights, the theater and wine. His prestige increases, too; he is known to the king. The Duke of York becomes his friend and his pupil in naval matters. By 1689 the lowly government clerk has become a prominent official; the unknown Cambridge scholar has become a respected practical authority; the former Roundhead sympathizer has become a friend of royalty.

But, as Pepys well learned, one who attaches himself to the politically great and who enjoys their triumphs must also endure their defeats. Once the national relief at the removal of the Puritans had died away, the reaction against the policies of the two royal brothers—a reaction accelerated greatly by popular disapproval of their personal conduct and, particularly, of James's avowed Catholicism—set in. The reaction had immediate repercussions; since there was much disapproval over the temporary Dutch naval supremacy, and the Duke of York was closely associated with the Navy, the Admiralty received much of the reactionary force. The first of a number of setbacks came even before the end of the *Diary,* but the honor of the Admiralty was saved by Pepys himself. In 1688, in an eloquent speech before the House of Commons, he defended his colleagues of the Navy Department against a charge of financial mismanagement and temporarily, at least, kept the anti-Stuart forces at bay.

The reaction being too strong to be held back indefinitely, Pepys was to be injured by it personally before it was finally ended. Following an excursion to France and Holland in 1669, he returned to England to stand for Parliament. He was supported in this venture by the Duke of York, but he lost the election when his interests were turned from politics to bereavement over his wife's death. He stood again, after having been appointed Secretary of the Admiralty for the first time, in 1673; and here his connections with the future James II worked against him. He won the election but was not, for some months, allowed to take his seat because of a trumped up charge that he, like his royal friend and patron, was a Roman Catholic.

This was not the only time that he was to be the victim of conspiracy and guilt by association. On May 22, 1679, he was imprisoned in the Tower of London on a charge of collaborating with the French, an accusation as spurious as the earlier one. When his accusers could not muster enough evidence to have him brought to trial, he was eventually released. Although no action was taken against him, he was forced to remain in the Tower from May to the following February, even though it was widely admitted that he was guiltless.

In June of 1684, after a visit to Tangier, he was reappointed to his Admiralty Secretaryship and was once again elected to Parliament. He continued in office during the brief reign of the fourth Stuart and retired, peacefully enough, when William of Orange arrived to become the constitutional co-monarch of England. Even in retirement Pepys was harassed for his long friendship with the now-deposed king. Once again (June, 1689) he was imprisoned. Once more he went untried. Finally, in deference to his age and his ill health, he was released, uncharged, and was allowed to live out his remaining four years in the quiet retreat of Clapham.

From this last retirement came the only written work published under his name during his lifetime, his *Memoirs of the Royal Navy*. These papers were accepted as his final vindication. He died on May 26, 1703, with full honors restored, secure in his reputation as a naval authority, as a valuable man of public office, and as a respected former President of the Royal Society. Thus his reputation remained, fading slowly in the pages of Restoration history, until the first deciphering of his *Diary* over a century later.

BIBLIOGRAPHICAL REFERENCES: The standard edition of the *Diary* is that edited by Henry B. Wheatley, 10 vols., 1893–1899; but eventually this work will be superseded by the unabridged trancription in preparation edited by Robert Latham and William Matthews: 10 vols. projected, Vol. I–V, 1970–1971. Another edition of the *Diary*, edited from Mynors Bright and with an introduction by John Warrington, 1953, is available in the Everyman Library. Other published writings by Pepys include *Memoirs Relating to the State of the Royal Navy*, edited by Joseph R. Tanner, 1906; *Private Correspondence and Miscellaneous Papers*, edited by Joseph R. Tanner, 2 vols., 1926; *Further Correspondence*, edited by Joseph R. Tanner, 1929; *Letters and Second Diary*, edited by R. G. Howarth, 1932; *Shorthand Letters*, edited by Edwin Chappell, 1933; *The Tangier Papers*, edited by Edwin Chappell, 1935; and *The Letters of Samuel Pepys and His Family Circle*, edited by Helen Truesdell Heath, 1955.

The standard biography is Sir Arthur Bryant, *Samuel Pepys*, 3 vols., 1933–1938. See also Henry B. Wheatley, *Samuel Pepys and the World He Lived In*, 1880 (2nd ed.); Joseph R. Tanner, *Samuel Pepys and the Royal Navy*, 1920, and *Mr. Pepys: An Introduction to the Diary*, 1925; Lord Arthur Ponsonby, *Samuel Pepys*, 1928; John Drinkwater, *Pepys: His Life and Character*, 1930; and Clara Marburg, *Mr. Pepys and Mr. Evelyn*, 1935. For briefer studies see, further, *Occasional Papers Read at Meetings of the Samuel Pepys Club*, 2 vols., 1917–1925.

JOSÉ MARÍA DE PEREDA

Born: Polanco, Spain
Date: February 6, 1833

Died: Polanco
Date: March 1, 1906

PRINCIPAL WORKS

NOVELS: *El buey suelto*, 1877 (*Footloose*); *Pedro Sánchez*, 1883; *Sotileza*, 1884; *Nubes de estío*, 1891 (*Summer Clouds*); *Peñas arriba*, 1895 (*Ascent to the Heights*).

Spanish literature is full of regional novelists who describe in their fiction the people and customs of the corner of Spain in which they live. Of them all, the greatest was José María de Pereda, the youngest of twenty-two children of a wealthy family of Polanco, near Santander, Spain, where José was born February 6, 1833. Having grown up full of the conservative ideas of his social class, he journeyed, at the age of nineteen, to Madrid, to enter artillery school. There his dislike of mathematics and his disgust with mob rule as he saw it during the revolution of 1854 turned him against the capital. Although he returned later to serve in Congress, political corruption made even more attractive the quiet of his country home in the north, and he spent the rest of his life in Santander.

For something to do, Pereda founded a newspaper, *La abeja montañesa* (*The Mountain Bee*), and for it he wrote a series of descriptive sketches. Later he collected eighteen of them into his first volume, *Escenas montañesas* (*Mountain Scenes*), published in 1864. This book revealed Pereda as the Spanish writer with the truest feeling for nature. Mountains and sea play as important a part in his stories as people do. Civilization, he believed, destroys men's souls.

The traditions of his mountainous homeland, never overrun by the Moors who conquered most of the rest of Spain, are more truly Spanish than those of southern Spain, occupied by foreigners through the fifteenth century. For his portrayal of the patriarchal life of his region, the conservative Pereda was accepted during his lifetime as more truly Spanish than any of his contemporaries. Some of his books can still serve as guidebooks for tourists to the city and countryside of Santander. Also, it is hard to imagine that this novelist who believed that liberal thinkers are the incarnation of all that is evil could have had as his greatest friend the liberal Benito Pérez Galdós, with whom he took a walking trip through Galicia and Portugal and who sponsored his election to the Spanish Academy in 1897.

Pereda was against anything new. His fervent Catholicism turned him against the naturalism of Zola which colored the work of other writers of Spain. But in spite of the idealization of some of his characters, Pereda was not a true romanticist. Menéndez y Pelayo classifies Pereda's style as "idealized realism." Especially realistic is his reproduction of the speech of the common people. Though he was an aristocrat, his sympathetic short story, "La leva" ("The Draft"), telling of the conscription of lowly Santander fishermen, is one of the greatest ever written in Spain.

Uncertain at first of his capabilities as a writer, Pereda was very sensitive to critical opinion. Following the publication of *De tal palo, tal astilla* (*Chip of the Old Block*) in 1879—his uncompromising answer to Pérez Galdós' anti-clerical novels—critics declared that his painting of love was cold. In 1882 he replied with *El sabor de la tierruca* (*Redolent of the Soil*), an idyl describing village life and the charms of the Santander region. When this work provoked the comment that his novels had a limited horizon, he changed his scene to Madrid in the unsettled times he had known there as a student, and wrote Spain's best modern picaresque novel, *Pedro Sánchez*, the story of a political adventurer.

His most popular novel, *Sotileza*, one of the two best sea tales in Spanish literature, was written to portray the noble virtues and incorruptible faith of Santander fishermen, as well as their miserable living conditions. Ten years later, when the critics declared he was "written out," Pereda replied with *Ascent to the Heights*, considered by many his best novel. This work describes the healing effects of nature on a Madrid idler who takes over his uncle's mountain estate. With its sale of 5,000 copies during the first week equaled in its time only by Pérez Galdós, the book brought about Pereda's election to the Spanish Academy in 1897.

Pereda's flaws lie in the weakness of his plots and his inability to portray women, especially those of the upper class, who appear in his pages chiefly as snobs or caricatures. Only the lower class women get sympathetic treatment in his pages, as in his handling of the orphan heroine of *Sotileza*.

Pereda showed little understanding of modernism. For this reason, during his lifetime, some critics were blinded to his talents by their dislike for his social and religious beliefs. A later revaluation of his writing, however, won for him a high place among Spanish novelists for his vivid style, his delicacy of observation, his forceful and enormous vocabulary, and his realistic creation of living people. He died in Polanco on March 1, 1906.

BIBLIOGRAPHICAL REFERENCES: For biographical and critical material see Boris de Tennenberg, *L'Espagne littéraire*, 1903; J. Montera, *Pereda: Biografía crítica*, 1919; E. Gómez de Baquero, *El renacimiento de la novela española en el siglo XIX*, 1924; J. Camp, *José María de Pereda, sa vie, son œuvre, et son temps*, 1937; R. Gullon, *Vida de Pereda*, 1944; José A. Balseiro, *Novelistas españoles contemporáneos*, 1947; and Sherman H. Eoff, "A Fatherly Word According to Design," *The Modern Spanish Novel*, 1961, 21–50.

BENITO PÉREZ GALDÓS

Born: Las Palmas, Canary Islands
Date: May 10, 1843

Died: Madrid, Spain
Date: January 4, 1920

Principal Works

NOVELS: *Saragossa*, 1874; *Doña Perfecta*, 1876; *Gloria*, 1876–1877; *Marianela*, 1878; *Fortunata y Jacinta*, 1886–1887; *Angel Guerra*, 1890–1891; *Episodios nacionales*, 1872–1912 (*National Episodes*).

PLAYS: *La loca de la casa*, 1893 (*The Madwoman in the House*); *La de San Quintín*, 1894; *Electra*, 1900; *Mariucha*, 1903; *El abuelo*, 1904 (*The Grandfather*).

Regionalism in the Spanish novel developed because of Spain's circumscribed provinces and the difficulty of traveling from one to another. So each novelist wrote best about his "patria chica" or restricted region. Benito Pérez Galdós, born at Las Palmas, the Canary Islands, May 10, 1843, had an eye for the whole of the nation. His English school environment in the Canary Islands may also explain why he differed on so many social questions from the views of most Spaniards.

At the age of twenty Pérez Galdós was sent to Madrid to study law, but books bored him. He liked people. When he found that his pen could earn him a living, he tried his hand at plays and short novels. His first long book, begun in 1867, was finally published in 1870. Between then and 1918, he wrote seventy-seven novels and twenty-one plays. His greatest success lay in the novel. Because he believed that fictional people should behave and talk like real people, he became the father of the modern Spanish novel and its greatest practitioner, with only his friend Pereda to contest that claim. But he was realistic only as one who cannot forget that beauty is also essential.

A trip to Paris, where he became acquainted with the novels of Balzac, determined Pérez Galdós to re-create in fiction the history of nineteenth century Spain. In 1873, the first volume of *National Episodes* appeared, called *Trafálgar*, dealing with the naval battle of 1805. In two years he completed the first series of ten volumes, ending with the battle of Arapilis in 1812 and including in Volume VI an account of the heroic defense by the citizens of Saragossa against the French. The next series of ten volumes, covering events through 1834, was started at once and completed in four years. Then Pérez Galdós abandoned the project for twenty years. He started again in 1898 and wrote feverishly until his blindness in 1912 prevented the careful research on which he based his historical novels. By this time he had completed forty-six of the series, covering seventy years of Spain's history and weaving in a vast panorama of 1,243 people, according to a dictionary compiled by Professor Glenn Barr.

Of his other novels, those called by the author "novels of the first epoch," three are among his best. He deals with the clerical problem in *Doña Perfecta* and with religious bigotry in *Gloria*, a theme also handled in his *La Familia de León Roch* (*The Family of Leon Roch*) in 1879. To this period also belongs *Marianela*, considered Spain's best sentimental novel, the tragedy of an ugly orphan after the blind boy who has idealized her regains his sight.

The rest of Pérez Galdós' fictional output, his "contemporary novels" about social and ethical themes, includes the great but lengthy *Fortunata y Jacinta*, which presents the idea that the hope of Spain is in its lower class; *Angel Guerra*, which deals with the mysticism of a political idealist, and *Misericordia* (1897), another novel about the lower class, its central figure a Christlike priest.

While turning out novels, Pérez Galdós realized that more money could be earned by successful plays than by books, and so he dramatized some of his novels and wrote original plays. His aim was to correct the exaggerated situations and unnatural dialogue then in vogue. Because he lacked a basic sense of the dramatic as well as a feeling for the stage, however, only a few of his plays were successful. *The Grandfather* is probably the best.

In 1897 he accepted an invitation to become a member of the Royal Spanish Academy, an honor he had previously refused. He also took up politics and entered Congress as a reform delegate against a corrupt monarchy and its supporters. As president of the Coalition, he wrote and campaigned until blindness ended his political activities. For a time he kept on writing, dictating a few plays and a novel, but by that time other writers had captured the public fancy. Political enmities, financial troubles, and the fact that he had never married, brought him loneliness at the end of his life. He died in Madrid, January 4, 1920.

In his many novels, even those produced because of financial necessity, Pérez Galdós reveals a vigorous creative power and a knowledge of people, especially of Madrid, through whose streets he roamed all his life. He is the interpreter of the national spirit; and while his preaching sometimes flaws his writing, he was the outstanding novelist of Spain in the nineteenth century.

BIBLIOGRAPHICAL REFERENCES: For studies of Pérez Galdós in English see Isaac Goldberg, *The Drama of Transition*, 1922; Salvador de Madariaga, *The Genius of Spain*, 1923; L. B. Walton, *Pérez Galdós and the Spanish Novel of the Nineteenth Century*, 1927; H. C. Berkowitz, *Pérez Galdós: Spanish Liberal Crusader*, 1948; W. T. Pattison, *Benito Galdós and the Creative Process*, 1954; and Alfredo Rodríguez, *An Introduction to the* Episodios nacionales, 1967. In Spanish, Clarín, *Galdós*, 1912; Salvadaor de Madariaga, "Benito Pérez Galdós," in *Semblanzas literarias contemporáneos*, 1924; J. Casalduero, *Vida y obra de Galdós*, 1943 (Buenos Aires); José A. Balseiro, *Novelistas españoles contemporáneos*, 1947; and A. del Río, *Estudios galdósianos*, 1953.

ST.-JOHN PERSE

Born: An island near Guadeloupe
Date: May 31, 1887

Principal Works

POEMS: *Éloges,* 1910; *Anabase,* 1924 (*Anabasis*); *Amitié du Prince,* 1924 (*The Friendship of the Prince*); *Exil,* 1942; *Vents,* 1953; *Éloges and Other Poems,* 1956; *Seamarks,* 1958; *Chronique,* 1961.

Alexis St.-Léger Léger, the French poet who writes under the pseudonym of St.-John Perse, was born May 31, 1887, on a small, family-owned island, the Island of St. Léger les Feuilles, off Guadaloupe. His early education explains in part the symbolic and esoteric nature of his poetry; his first intellectual influences came from a Roman Catholic bishop and from a nurse who was a Hindu priestess of Shiva. His formal education, begun in France when he was eleven years old, was liberal in the fullest sense of the word. The studies of medicine, letters, and law all combined to fashion the background that was to make him not only a poet but also a distinguished statesman.

It was as a diplomat that he became known to his countrymen, and it was in the French diplomatic corps that he made his public career. He entered the foreign service in 1914, served in Peiping from 1917 to 1921, and acted as consultant on Asiatic affairs during the Washington conference on disarmament in 1922. He served in the foreign office under Aristide Briand and on Briand's death became Permanent Secretary of Foreign Affairs, holding that position until the Nazi invasion of France. Refusing to become a collaborationist, he fled to England, traveled from there to Canada, and finally, at the behest of Archibald MacLeish, came to the United States to act as Consultant of French Poetry to the Library of Congress.

Léger's career as a poet ran concurrently with his career as a diplomat, but he had managed, at least as far as reputation was concerned, to keep the two separated. He published little, and always under the pseudonym St.-John Perse, concealing his artistic identity so well that few, if any, of his colleagues in the diplomatic service knew of his literary career. Among fellow poets, however, he became known, despite the infrequency of his publications, as a writer of great accomplishment and considerable scope.

His first collection of poems, *Éloges,* came out in 1910, and though a few individual lyrics had been pirated earlier, this was his first acknowledged appearance in print. Fourteen years later *Anabasis,* the work now considered his masterpiece, was published. This work established him as a worthy successor to Arthur Rimbaud in the school of French Symbolism; the poem was compared favorably with Rimbaud's *A Season in Hell,* and its author praised for his ability to portray the "subconscious mastered by reason." *Anabasis* also brought him to the attention of poets in this country and in England, and T. S. Eliot published an English translation in 1930. Whatever work Léger produced between 1924 and 1940 will never be seen, much less praised. His manuscripts were left behind when he fled the

Nazis. Since the war Léger has published two additional volumes, both equal in merit to those done earlier in France, *Exil* in 1942 and *Vents* in 1953. In 1960, he was awarded the Nobel Prize in Literature.

BIBLIOGRAPHICAL REFERENCES: The Bollingen edition of *Chronique*, 1961, contains an extensive bibliography. For brief studies of Saint-John Perse in English see T. S. Eliot, Preface to *Anabasis*, 1930, reissued with additional notes by Hugo von Hofmannsthal, Valery Larbaud, and Giuseppe Ungaretti, 1949; Archibald MacLeish, "A Note on Alexis Saint-Léger Léger," *Poetry*, LIX (1942), 330–337, and "The Personality of Saint-John Perse," in *Exile and Other Poems*, 1949; John Gould Fletcher, "Like a Sky Above Orchards," *New Republic*, CXI (1944), 282; Roger Caillois, "The Art of Saint-John Perse," translated by H. M. Chevalier, *Sewanee Review*, LIII (1945), 198–206; Wallace Fowlie, "Saint-John Perse," *Poetry*, LXXIX (1951), 31–35; and K. G. Chapin, "Saint-John Perse: Notes on Some Poetic Contrasts," *Sewanee Review*, LX (1951), 65–81.

For more extended biographical and critical studies see also Maurice Saillet, *Saint-John Perse*, 1952; Alain Bosquet, *Saint-John Perse*, 1953; Roger Caillois, *Poétique de Saint-John Perse*, 1954; Pierre Guerre, *Saint-John Perse et l'homme*, 1954; and Arthur Knodel, *Saint-John Perse: A Study of His Poetry*, 1966.

FRANCESCO PETRARCH

Born: Arezzo, Italy
Date: July 20, 1304

Died: Arquà, Italy
Date: July 19, 1374

Principal Works

POEMS: *Epistles,* 1326–1374; *Le Rime,* after 1327; *Africa,* 1338–1342; *I Trionfi,* c. 1352–1374 (*The Triumphs*).
BIOGRAPHY: *De viribus illustribus,* c. 1338 (*Concerning Famous Men*).
PHILOSOPHICAL AND RELIGIOUS TREATISES: *Secretum,* 1343 (*Inmost Thoughts*); *De vita solitaria,* 1346–1356 (*On Solitary Life*); *De otio religiosorum,* 1347–1356 (*On Religious Freedom from Care*); *De remediis utriusque fortunae,* c. 1350–1374 (*On the Remedies for Good and Bad Fortune*).

Francesco Petrarch (Petracco), the most famous literary man of Italy next to Dante, was born in Arezzo on July 20, 1304, while his father, the notary Ser Petracco, was a political exile under the edict of 1302. His mother took him to the Tuscan town of Incisa, but when he was nine they joined his father in Avignon. At fifteen Petrarch was studying law, first in Montpellier from 1316 to 1320 and later, until 1323, at Bologna in Italy. The death of his father removed the pressure that he become a lawyer, but it also deprived him and his brother of their inheritance. Under the encouragement of Giacomo (or Jacopo) Colonna, he took minor church orders and turned to the classics. Late in 1326 or early in the next year he returned to Avignon, home of the Pope.

That was a fateful move. There, on April 6, 1327, he saw a lovely lady in the church of Santa Clara. He never revealed her identity, but always referred to her as Laura, and to her he wrote a total of 366 poems making up a collection of odes, sonnets, and lyrics that ranks as one of the world's greatest volumes of love poems. Others have identified her as a French lady, Laura de Noves, who had married a rich burgher two years earlier and who had eleven children by him before her death, during the plague, on April 6, 1348. (Petrarch's patron, Bishop Colonna, died about the same time.) In the traditions of chivalry, Laura welcomed the tribute of the poet, but held him at a distance for twenty years.

Petrarch's poems to Laura run the gamut from passion to anger at love unrequited, and even express struggles with his conscience over his religious obligations. But his feelings for her did not prevent his having affairs with other women, by whom he had children, a son Giovanni in 1337, and a daughter Francesca in 1343. They were later legitimatized by a papal decree.

In 1335, Colonna secured for Petrarch a canonry at Lombez, in the region of the Pyrenees. Two years later Petrarch bought himself a small house at Vaucluse, near Avignon, with the intention of becoming a recluse and devoting himself to writing. An eager student of history, he produced a series of biographies, *Concerning Famous Men,* and began an epic in classical Latin about Scipio Africanus and the Punic Wars. He called it *Africa.*

Always eager for acclaim, Petrarch arranged for a public ovation for himself at the court of King Robert of Naples early in 1341, and another one, in Rome, in April of the same year, when he was crowned poet laureate. He tried to return to his writings, but, well-known by this time, he had many calls for his services. Although he had boasted of his republican theories, rulers and even Pope Clemente VI sent him on diplomatic missions. Rarely had he leisure to write more sonnets of delicacy and technical excellence that later set the form for the Elizabethan sonnet of England, through translations by Henry Howard, Earl of Surrey, and Sir Thomas Wyatt.

In 1350, Petrarch, on his way to Rome, stopped in Florence to see his great friend Boccaccio (1313–1375). For a time, beginning in 1362, he lived in Padua, where he was a canon of the Church, and then in Venice, where he and Boccaccio met for the last time. In 1369 he moved to a villa in nearby Arquà, where he died quietly five years later, on July 19, 1374.

Petrarch has been called the "First Modern Man of Letters." With his interest in ancient cultures, his collection of books, coins, and medals of antiquity, he was a forerunner of Humanism. Through him, the medieval period made its transition to the Italian Renaissance.

BIBLIOGRAPHICAL REFERENCES: Petrarch's sonnets are available in several translations, the latest being that by Joseph Auslander, 1931. For biography and commentary see J. H. Robinson, *Petrarch, the First Modern Scholar*, 1898; H. Holloway-Calthorp, *Petrarch: His Life and Times*, 1907; Henry Reeve, *Biography of Petrarch*, 1912; E. H. R. Tatham, *Petrarca, the First Modern Man of Letters: His Life and Correspondence*, 1925–1926; J. H. Whitfield, *Petrarch and the Renascence*, 1943; Ernest H. Wilkins, *Life of Petrarch*, 1961; and Morris Bishop, *Petrarch and His World*, 1963; also Umberto Bosco, *Francesco Petrarca*, 1946; and Rosario Verde, *Studio sulla Rima del Petrarca*, 1950. Central to all modern Petrarchan scholarship is *Studi petrarcheschi*, edited by C. Calcaterra, 3 vols., 1948–1950. Briefer studies in English include Murray Potter, *Four Essays*, 1917; and E. H. Wilkins, *Studies in the Life and Works of Petrarch*, 1955.

PETRONIUS
Gaius Petronius Arbiter

Born: Unknown
Date: Unknown

Died: Cumae, Italy
Date: c. 66

Principal Work

picaresque satire: *Satyrica*, c. 60 (*Satyricon*).

A certain Gaius Petronius did exist. Plutarch, probably by a slip, referred to him as Titus Petronius, but Tacitus, in his annals for A.D. 66, tells of the death of Gaius Petronius, a brilliant, cynical man of pleasure who was as famous for his idleness as most men are for their industry. This Petronius was a man of culture, noted for his frankness. Tacitus also cites his political experiences, first as a proconsul of Bithynia, and later as a consul and administrator. When Petronius abandoned diplomacy and returned to the licentiousness of Nero's court, he became the emperor's *Arbiter Elegantiae,* the arbiter of elegance and master of the court revels.

Envy brought about his death. The emperor's previous favorite, Tigellinus, forced a slave to testify to Petronius' plots with the traitor Scaevinus and soldiers were sent to place Petronius under house arrest at Cumae. Disgraced and politically suspect, Petronius knew how to die elegantly. He cut his veins in such a way that his death would seem natural, and during his last hours he bandied conversation and songs with his companions. In his will, instead of lauding the emperor, as was customary, he attacked Nero's unnatural vices, describing them so accurately that the emperor searched among his courtiers for an informer. His suspicions finally fell on a companion of his revels, Silia, the wife of a senator, and she was executed.

There is no positive proof that Petronius wrote the *Satyricon*, usually attributed to him. However, the medley of ribaldry, anecdotes, and cynical philosophy and moralizing is just what Nero's favorite might have written, a supposition strengthened by the fact that a first century grammarian referred to the author as "arbiter."

Whether he or some other Roman of the same name wrote all that has been lost and the 146 chapters of Books 15 and 16 that are still preserved, the author of the *Satyricon* was forced to invent the narrative formula for adventures involving his mouthpiece Encolpius and two friends. It was necessary to forget courtly speech and put into the mouths of his characters the plebian Latin of the market place, with its wealth of slang, puns, and obscenities difficult for the ordinary student of Latin. The result is such a remarkable picture of the ordinary Roman citizen that one regrets the lost portion of the work but is grateful that its popularity among ancient anthology compilers preserved as many episodes as we still have of a work which offers entertainment on every level, from the outrageously scabrous in human conduct to delicate and refined judgment in literature and art.

bibliographical references: The *Satyricon* is available in a number of translations of varying quality and completeness. See in particular those by J. M. Mitchell,

1922, and M. Heseltine, Loeb Classical Library, 1913. *Trimalchio's Dinner* was translated by H. T. Peck, 1898. See also E. H. Haight, *Essays on Ancient Fiction,* 1936; and H. W. Hawley, "Quaestiones petronianae," in *Harvard Studies in Classical Philology,* II (1891), 1–40. The standard background study is J. W. Duff, *Roman Satire,* 1936. See also Kenneth Rexroth, "Petronius: *The Satyricon,*" *Classics Revisited,* 1968, 99–103; and Patrick G. Walsh, *The Roman Novel: The Satyricon of Petronius and the Metamorphoses of Apuleius,* 1970.

BORIS PILNYAK
Boris Andreyevich Vogau

Born: Mozhaysk, Russia
Date: September 29, 1894

Died: ?
Date: 1937 (?)

Principal Works

NOVELS: *Goly god,* 1922 (*The Naked Year*); *Ivan da Marya,* 1923 (*Ivan and Maria*); *Tretya stolitsa,* 1923 (*The Third Capital*); *Mashiny i volki,* 1925 (*Machines and Wolves*); *Mat' syra zemlya,* 1926 (*Mother Damp Earth*); *Mahogany,* 1929; *Volga vpadayet v Kaspiyskoye more,* 1930 (*The Volga Falls to the Caspian Sea*); *Rozhdeniye cheloveka,* 1935 (*The Birth of a Man*); *Sozrevaniye plodov,* 1936 (*The Ripening Fruit*).

SHORT STORIES: *Bylyo,* 1920; *Tales of the Wilderness,* 1925.

Perhaps Boris Pilnyak, famous for *The Naked Year,* a portrait of Russia in chaos, can be regarded as a symbol of the distinctive confusion and tragedy that is characteristic of the U.S.S.R. under Communist domination. As a revolutionary intellectual, he tended to accept the Communist revolution as a genuine people's revolt; as a student of nature and a sympathizer with the common man, he tended to discover and to report the degenerating effects of communism on the people of Russia. Because of the adverse criticism implicit in his writings, he was criticized by government leaders, although in other times he has been honored by them. The result is that since 1938 there has been no news of Pilnyak from the U.S.S.R., and there is a rumor that he has been executed.

The son of educated, middle class parents of German, Slavic, and Tartar extraction, he was born Boris Andreyevich Vogau in a small town near Moscow on September 29, 1894. Graduated from the Nizhni-Novgorod school in 1913, he also attended the University of Kolomna and the Moscow Institute of Commerce, where he studied business finance and administration. As one exempt from military service because of poor eyesight, he was able to devote a considerable amount of time to writing, much of it unpublished; his pseudonym is derived from the title of an unpublished novel. He achieved fame with *The Naked Year,* published seven years after Pilnyak had begun to sell some of his work. The book is an electrifying portrait of the revolution, reflecting in a realistic and fresh way its enthusiasm, its horror, and its human spirit.

Pilnyak's concern for the people of Russia and the elementary forces at work within the great land led him to be critical in his later works of the brutalized Bolsheviks and of the careless waste of human lives, as set forth in his account of the building of the dam at Kolomna in *The Volga Falls to the Caspian Sea.* His short novel *Mahogany,* published in Berlin in 1927, was denounced as anti-revolutionary and banned in the U.S.S.R. Pilnyak traveled extensively in Russia, Germany, England, the Near East, and the Far East. In 1931 he toured the United States and wrote a bitter commentary on his experiences in *O.K.* (1933).

Pilnyak's fate remains a mystery. He was last heard of in 1937, and it is believed that he was liquidated in the Stalinist purge of that year.

BIBLIOGRAPHICAL REFERENCES: For a brief study of Pilnyak in English see Gleb Struve, *Twenty-five Years of Soviet Russian Literature*, 1944. See also A. Voronsky, "Boris Pilnyak," in *Literaturnye tipy*, 1927; A. Paley, *Literaturnye portrety*, 1928; and B. P. Kozmin, "Boris Pilnyak," in *Pisateli sovremyonnoi epokhi*, Vol. II, 1937. See further Lev Trotsky, "The Literary 'fellow-travelers' of the Revolution," *Literature and Revolution*, 1960, 56–115; Vera Alexandrova, "Boris Pilnyak," *A History of Soviet Literature*, translated by Mirra Ginsburg, 1963, 135–149; and Marc L. Slonim, "Boris Pilnyak: the Untimely Symbolist," *Soviet Russian Literature*, 1964, 59–66.

PINDAR

Born: Cynoscephalae, Greece
Date: c. 522 B.C.

Died: Argos, Greece
Date: c. 443 B.C.

Principal Works

POEMS: *Epinicia,* 502–452 B.C.

Pindar was born at Cynoscephalae, near Thebes, about 522 B.C. Through his parents, Daiphantus and Cleodice, of a family claiming descent from Cadmus, founder of Thebes, Pindar could regard ancient Greek gods and heroes as part of his family. As training for his poetic career, Pindar began to study the flute, first in Thebes under his uncle Scopelinus, later in Athens. He began writing odes at the age of twenty, losing in his first competition to a poetess named Corinna, because he neglected to use mythology. His lesson learned, for the next fifty years he was highly regarded for his paeans to Apollo and Zeus and his hymns to Persephone and others.

The home of this Boeotian was chiefly Thebes, but he frequently visited Athens, then coming into literary supremacy, and spent several years at the court of Hieron of Syracuse. There he wrote what was to be called the Pindaric Ode, the epinician, a poem to welcome home the victors in the national games—the Pythian, the Isthmian, the Nêmean, and the Olympic. Pindar's formula was to select a myth and then in some way relate it to the victor and provide words for the chorus to use in the parade. From internal evidence, many of the forty-five odes that survive intact can be dated by the games whose victors he celebrates.

High moral tone, patriotism, and religious fervor characterize the works of this outstanding Greek lyric poet. Though he wrote them to order, and was paid for them, the odes show no signs of cheapening art for cash. Not until they were imitated in England in the seventeenth and eighteenth centuries did the form become debased. Only fragments of Pindar's other poems survive. He died in Argos about 443.

BIBLIOGRAPHICAL REFERENCES: The fullest translation of Pindar in English is L. F. Farnell, *The Works of Pindar*, 3 vols., 1930–1932, a work valuable for critical commentary. Earlier translations are those in prose by Ernest Myers, 1874, and in verse by T. C. Baring, 1875. An excellent recent translation is Richard Lattimore, *The Odes of Pindar*, 1947. For critical comment see also D. M. Robinson, *Pindar, Poet of Eternal Ideas*, 1936; Gilbert Norwood, *Pindar*, 1945; J. H. Finley, *Pindar and Aeschlyus*, 1955; Robert B. Downs, "Theban Eagle: Pindar," *Famous Books, Ancient and Medieval*, 1964, 48–51; and Moses I. Finley, "Silver Tongue," *Aspects of Antiquity*, 1968, 38–43.

SIR ARTHUR WING PINERO

Born: London, England
Date: May 24, 1855

Died: London
Date: November 23, 1934

Principal Works

PLAYS: *Mayfair*, 1885; *The Profligate*, 1889; *Lady Bountiful*, 1890; *The Hobby Horse*, 1892; *The Second Mrs. Tanqueray*, 1893; *The Weaker Sex*, 1894; *The Notorious Mrs. Ebbsmith*, 1895; *Trelawney of the Wells*, 1898; *The Gay Lord Quex*, 1899; *Iris*, 1901; *His House in Order*, 1905; *The Thunderbolt*, 1909; *Mid-Channel*, 1909; *The Big Drum*, 1915; *The Enchanted Cottage*, 1922.

Arthur Wing Pinero had a career and a theater deeply interesting to the historian of the English drama; in his work one sees the partial impact of Continental themes and ideas, from Sardou, the master of the well-made play, to Ibsen, the creator of the theater of ideas. In Pinero, for two decades, the English found their leading practicer of these imported skills.

Pinero, born on May 24, 1855, was the son of a Jewish solicitor in London. With a private school education as a foundation, he read for the law in his father's office, but with no serious intentions of becoming a solicitor. At the age of nineteen he joined the Theatre Royal in Edinburgh, soon supplementing his bit-role acting by writing short dramatic pieces as supplements to longer plays. After the success of *The Money Spinner* (1880) he was able to forego the pretense of being an actor and to devote his time to playwriting. Between 1885 and 1887 he wrote three successful farces for the Court Theatre in London. In these he presented "possible people doing improbable things"; that is, he shifted the emphasis from farcical situations to character. This was a foreshadowing of his greater successes during the 1890's, beginning with *The Second Mrs. Tanqueray* in 1893. In this play, and those that followed, he added to his technically deft work the themes and social insights which his public regarded as daring and thought-provoking. For two decades the English press and public regarded each new Pinero play as a likely source of controversy, for his plays usually amounted to a criticism of the current sexual patterns based, Pinero would have his audiences believe, on appearances rather than on sincere attraction and devotion. As a matter of fact, Pinero's homegrown versions of the Continental "problem plays" always contained incidents quite as shocking to current taste as the slamming of the door at the end of Ibsen's *A Doll's House;* for example, in *The Notorious Mrs. Ebbsmith* the rebellious heroine momentarily throws the Holy Scriptures into the fire. Dramatic strokes like these won Pinero his temporary reputation as an iconoclast.

It was a reputation that waned. During the last twenty years of his life Pinero had the bitterness of seeing his fame and public dwindle. To audiences that began to respond to Eugene O'Neill and Sean O'Casey, Pinero's representations of upper-class infidelity came to seem mannered and unreal. Of his more than fifty pieces, many found neither a producer nor a publisher; it was no comfort for him to recall that he had been knighted in 1909. His last successful play, *The Enchanted*

Cottage, is a strange blend of the delicate sentimentalism of J. M. Barrie and cynical realism. Although his is no longer a great name in the theater, it cannot be denied that he measured shrewdly the taste of a generation. Pinero died in London on November 23, 1934.

BIBLIOGRAPHICAL REFERENCES: There is no collected edition, but Clayton Hamilton edited *The Social Plays of Arthur Wing Pinero,* 1917–1919, with a general introduction and critical prefaces to each play. For biography and criticism see Wilbur D. Dunkel, *Sir Arthur Wing Pinero: A Critical Biography with Letters,* 1941, reprinted 1967; also H. H. Fyfe, *Sir Arthur Wing Pinero's Plays and Players,* 1930; Edward Everett Hale, *Dramatists of Today,* 1911; and Cecil W. Davies, "The Drama of Reputation," *English,* XIV (1962), 13-17. A good foreign estimate is Wilibald Stöcker, *Pineros Dramen: Studien über Motive, Charaktere und Technik,* 1911.

HAROLD PINTER

Born: London, England
Date: October 10, 1930

Principal Works

PLAYS: *The Room*, 1957; *The Birthday Party and Other Plays*, 1958; *The Caretaker*, 1960; *A Slight Ache and Other Plays*, 1961; *The Collection* and *The Lover*, 1963; *The Homecoming*, 1965; *Tea Party and Other Plays*, 1967; *Landscape* and *Silence*, 1968.
POEMS: *Poems*, 1968.
MEMOIRS: *Mac*, 1968.

Harold Pinter is a British playwright who has recently become one of the leading practitioners in the dramatic mode known generally as the Theatre of the Absurd. Born in 1930, the son of a Jewish tailor in Hackney, a part of East London, Pinter began his literary career in his teens by writing poetry for the little magazines. At the same time, however, he was studying acting at the Royal Academy of Dramatic Art and the Central School of Speech and Drama. This led to a career in acting. Under the stage name of David Baron, he performed in many parts of Ireland with a Shakespearean company and also did a considerable amount of repertory work in the provinces. Before turning to plays, he started a novel entitled *The Dwarfs*, which he failed to complete. But in 1957, he was actually commissioned to write his first play. He spoke of an idea for a play to a friend of his in the drama department of Bristol University, and the friend was so attracted by the idea that he requested Pinter to write the play. Pinter composed it in four days.

The result of this nimble, almost impulsive feat of composition was a one-act drama called *The Room*, first performed at Bristol University in May of 1957. It was followed shortly by a second one-act play, *The Dumb Waiter*, also written in 1957 but not performed until January 21, 1960, when it was presented at the Hampstead Theatre Club in London. After this came Pinter's first full-length play, *The Birthday Party*, which opened at the Arts Theatre in Cambridge on April 28, 1958. Unsuccessful at first, the play was soon transferred to the Lyric Theatre in Hammersmith, and Pinter himself directed it the following year in Birmingham. After an enthusiastically received performance by the Tavistock Players at the Tower Theatre in Canonbury, London, it was broadcast on television to millions of Britons in the spring of 1960. It crossed the Atlantic in July of the same year, when it was presented by the Actors Workshop in San Francisco.

Besides *The Caretaker*, his second full-length play (and first great public success), Pinter's work for the stage includes a number of other scripts—among them *The Lover* and *The Collection*, two one-act plays performed in Boston during the spring of 1965. In addition, he has written extensively for the screen, radio, and television. On the B.B.C.'s Third Programme, Britons have heard his radio plays *A Slight Ache*, first broadcast on July 29, 1959; *A Night Out*, first presented in March, 1960; and *The Dwarfs*, based on his unfinished novel, first performed on December 2, 1960. On television, they have seen a viewer's version of *A Night Out* (April, 1960), as well as *Night School,* a television play first broadcast in July of 1960. Pinter is the author of the script for *The Pumpkin Eater,* a film released in 1964 with a cast that includes James Mason, Anne Bancroft, and Peter Finch. In 1963 he was awarded an Italian prize for his television scripts, and in 1966 he was made a Commander of the Order of the British Empire.

BIBLIOGRAPHICAL REFERENCES: Important studies of Pinter include Martin Esslin, *The Peopled Wound: The Work of Harold Pinter,* 1970; Katherine H. Burkman, *The Dramatic World of Harold Pinter: Its Basis in Ritual,* 1971; Ronald Hayman, *Harold Pinter,* 1968; Walter Kerr, *Harold Pinter,* 1967; Arlene Sykes, *Harold Pinter,* 1970; L. Gordon, *Strategems to Uncover Nakedness: The Dramas of Harold Pinter,* 1969; Arnold P. Hinchliffe, *Harold Pinter,* 1967; John R. Taylor, *Harold Pinter,* 1969; James R. Hollis, *Harold Pinter: The Poetics of Silence,* 1970; and Herman T. Schroll, *Harold Pinter: A Study of His Reputation, 1958–1969,* 1971.

See also Martin Esslin, *The Theatre of the Absurd,* revised edition, 1969; John Russell Brown, editor, *Modern British Dramatists,* 1968; Louis MacNeice, *Varieties of Parable,* 1965; John Kershaw, *The Present Stage,* 1966; and Allardyce Nicoll, *English Drama: A Modern Viewpoint,* 1968.

LUIGI PIRANDELLO

Born: Girgenti, Sicily
Date: June 28, 1867

Died: Rome, Italy
Date: December 10, 1936

PRINCIPAL WORKS

PLAYS: *Così è—se vi pare*, 1917 (*Right You Are—If You Think So*); *Il Piacere dell' onesta*, 1917 (*The Pleasure of Honesty*); *L'uomo, la bestia e virtù*, 1918 (*Man, Beast, and Virtue*); *Sei Personaggi in cerca d'autore*, 1921 (*Six Characters in Search of an Author*); *Vestire gli ignudi*, 1922 (*Naked*); *Enrico IV*, 1922 (*Henry IV*); *Ciascuno a suo modo*, 1924 (*Each in His Own Way*); *Lazzaro*, 1929; *Come tu mi vuoi*, 1930 (*As You Desire Me*); *Questa sera si recita a soggetto*, 1930 (*Tonight We Improvise*).

NOVELS: *L'esclusa*, 1901 (*The Outcast*); *Il fu Mattia Pascal*, 1904 (*The Late Mattia Pascal*); *Si gira*, 1916 (*Shoot*); *I Vecchi e i giovani*, 1913 (*The Old and the Young*).

SHORT STORIES: *Amori senza amore*, 1894; *Beffe della morte e della vita*, 1902; *Bianche e nere*, 1904; *Erma bifronte*, 1906; *Il Carneval dei morti*, 1921.

ESSAYS AND STUDIES: *Umorismo*, 1908; *Arte e scienza*, 1935.

Luigi Pirandello, winner of the Nobel Prize for literature in 1934, became a force in twentieth century drama by calling attention to the limitations of the school of the "well-made" play, the poetic drama, and the naturalistic drama of the nineteenth century. He offered in their place a "theater" that the Italians called "grottesco" and that elsewhere has been called expressionistic. However named, Pirandello's theater directs our attention to the psychological reality that lies beneath social appearances and overt social action. He found inadequate the "well-made" plays of Scribe and Sardou which, like later Hollywood products, are cleverly contrived to excite and divert. He rejected the overwrought and often insincere language of the poetic drama of Gabriele D'Annunzio and Sem Benelli, for he aimed at language closer to that of normal impassioned speech. Finally, he rejected not so much the subject matter of the naturalistic theater of Brieux as its assumptions: that drama is a branch of sociology. Drama, if a branch of anything, was to Pirandello a branch of psychology; and it is superior to psychology in that the dramatist who investigates mental states is not bound by a theory or dogma as are Freud and Jung. The dramatist's only obligation is to be faithful to his insights into the particular situation he treats. (With Pirandello, it is usually an abnormal situation upon which the dramatist broods imaginatively.)

But it was not only opposition to literary fashions in the Italian world that was productive in Pirandello. The conditions of his own life made contributions to his literary production; these conditions created problems that, in his many plays and almost countless stories, he tried to study and resolve.

Pirandello was born on June 28, 1867, of a well-to-do family in Girgenti, Sicily, which at that time was a backward and violent section of Italy, a region in which each man had to protect his own rights and live in expectation of violence. Pirandello was also early impressed by the special civil and religious privileges accorded the upper classes to which he as a boy belonged. In short, he did not need wider experience to reveal to him the elements of hypocrisy and cruelty implicit in human life.

Later experiences helped to underline this lesson. When he attended the University of Rome, he encountered academic pedantry and was saved from total disgust only by a kindly professor. After further training in Germany, Pirandello returned to Sicily and discovered that he and his fiancée of long standing had lost interest in each other. Instead, in 1894, he married a girl of his father's choosing, Antonietta Portulano. For some years the young couple lived easily in Rome, but Signora Pirandello's allowance from her father ceased; the Sicilian sulphur mines of the father had been ruined by floods. When Signora Pirandello became insane, Pirandello did not confine her to an asylum but, until her death in 1918, lived with her and watched over her. During these years his life and the lives of his three children were distorted by the jealous frenzies of Signora Pirandello, who unceasingly accused her husband of infidelity. The family was also poor; Pirandello taught in a teachers' college. During these years he also continued to write and publish; he tried to give expression to the insights that his life, early and late, had stimulated in him. Until after World War I, Pirandello was ignored in his own country. It was the international popularity of *Six Characters in Search of an Author* that finally won him recognition, a recognition that was still grudging on the part of the Italian Fascist government, which regarded Pirandello as decadent.

Decadent or not, Pirandello's themes are now generally regarded as important. As early as 1904, in his novel, *The Late Mattia Pascal*, Pirandello had called attention to the gap between what a man is and what he must seem to be if he is to live in conformity with his social role. *Six Characters in Search of an Author* makes a similar contrast between the conventional bonds that hold persons together and the real bonds of passion and injury that connect one person with another. *As You Desire Me* presents an amnesia victim whose sense of identity depends not on her self-knowledge but on whether a man—possibly her former husband—believes that she is the person she claims to be. *Henry IV* poses another difficult problem, typical of Pirandello and, we now know, closely related to his personal tragedy: what does the word "sanity" mean? And is "sanity" the possession of the "normal" majority or of the persons endowed with a peculiar and distorting insight?

As this inspection suggests, Pirandello was an asker of questions. He questioned the wisdom of taking sense impressions, surface appearances, and sanity for granted. In this respect he resembles many other twentieth century writers. Pirandello's influence has been considerable, especially in his own country, where more recent Italian writers like Ugo Betti and Diego Fabbri have imitated his technique and have continued his merciless and exhaustive scrutiny of human motives and actions. He died at Rome on December 10, 1936.

BIBLIOGRAPHICAL REFERENCES: For criticism of Pirandello in English see Domenico Vittorini, *The Drama of Luigi Pirandello*, 1935; Lander MacClintock,*The Age of Pirandello*, 1951; Alba Fazia, *Luigi Pirandello and Jean Anouilh*, 1954; Oscar Büdel, *Pirandello: Studies in Modern European Thought and Literature*, 1966; Glauco

Cambon, ed., *Pirandello: A Collection of Critical Essays*, 1967; and Olga Ragusa, *Luigi Pirandello*, 1968. See also J. L. Palmer, *Studies of the Contemporary Theatre*, 1927; William A. Drake, *Contemporary European Writers*, 1928; and Eric Bentley, Introduction to *Naked Masks: Five Plays by Luigi Pirandello*, 1952.

PLATO

Born: Athens, Greece
Date: 427 B.C.

Died: Athens
Date: 347 B.C.

Principal Works

PHILOSOPHIC DIALOGUES: The order of the *Dialogues* is not known, but the following sequence has been suggested by Campbell and Lutoslawski: *Apology, Euthyphro, Crito, Charmides, Laches, Protagoras, Meno, Euthydemus, Gorgias, Lysis, Cratylus, Symposium, Phaedo, Republic, Phaedrus, Theaetetus, Parmenides, Sophist, Politicus, Philebus, Timaeus, Critias, Laws.*

Born at Athens in 427 B.C. and named at birth Aristocles, Plato, the most famous and probably the most important of the Greek philosophers, was the son of Ariston and Perictione, Athenian aristocrats. The family of Ariston traced its descent to Codrus, presumably the last king of Athens, and Perictione was a descendant of Solon, the Athenian lawgiver. Plato probably enjoyed a comfortable boyhood as the youngest member of a wealthy family. He had two brothers, Glaucon and Adeimantus, and a sister, Potone.

When Plato was still a child his father died, and his mother then married Pyrilampes, an active supporter of the policies of Pericles. His uncle, Charmides, and another relation, Critias, were also involved in the political life of the time and were prominent in the oligarchy that came into power at the end of the Pelopennesian War in 404 B.C. Under these circumstances it was natural for Plato to regard political life as one of the duties of the conscientious citizen, and the philosophy of politics as one of the scholar's noblest pursuits.

From his boyhood Plato was acquainted with Socrates, and his friendship with the elderly philosopher convinced him that the search for truth, philosophy, was essential to any effective political life. Plato's early ambition to be a statesman was encouraged by Charmides and his friends, but when Plato observed that the thirty rulers of Athens, among them his relatives and associates, were even more vicious in their governmental practices than their predecessors, and, furthermore, that they were attempting to involve Socrates in the illegal arrest of a fellow citizen, he began to have qualms as to a career in politics. His misgivings were confirmed when the leaders of the democracy that followed the oligarchy charged Socrates with impiety and with corrupting the youth of Athens; Socrates was brought to trial, condemned, and executed. Plato decided that until philosophers became kings, or kings became philosophers, there was no practical value to be gained if an honest man entered political life.

In all probability, Plato was more than once engaged in active military service. He possibly entered service when he was eighteen and may have served for five years with the cavalry during the last years of the Peloponnesian War. He may also have been involved in 395, when Athens was once more at war.

After the death of Socrates in 399 Plato went to Megara with some other friends of Socrates and visited Euclides, a distinguished philosopher who had been present at the death of Socrates. He may have traveled, but he soon returned to Athens and began his own writing.

When Plato was about forty years old, he made a trip to Italy and Sicily, where he was dismayed by the luxurious, sensual life customary among the wealthy. On the positive side, he made friends with Archytas, the virtual ruler of Tarentum, in Italy. Archytas was not only a strong and respected leader, but also an eminent mathematician, and he and Plato discussed many of the interesting features of Pythagoreanism, with which Plato had first become fascinated in Athens. In Sicily, Plato visited Syracuse, where he became acquainted with Dionysius, the tyrant of the city, and with Dion, the brother-in-law of Dionysius. Dion, then about twenty years old, was inspired by Plato's ideas about the proper kind of state and resolved to become the kind of noble political leader that Plato sketched out for him. While inspiring Dion, however, Plato was irritating Dionysius, who had little interest in philosophy. According to some sources, Plato was seized by a Spartan envoy who shipped him off to Aegina, where he was offered for sale as a slave but was saved by Anniceris, a friend from Cyrene, who ransomed him.

When he returned to Athens about 387 Plato founded a school in which scientific and political studies would be undertaken by young men actually engaged in the task of acquiring knowledge. The school was located outside the city gates where Plato owned a house and garden. Since the place was known as the "Academy," the school acquired that name, and for forty years Plato devoted most of his time to the school. The *Dialogues* for which he is famous were composed, in great part, at the Academy and in connection with its activities. Among the young men who became his pupils were Dion, who followed Plato to Athens; Aristotle, who joined the school when he was eighteen, and others who were either princes or destined to become important political figures.

In 367, Dionysius of Syracuse died and his power, which by that time extended over Hellenic Sicily and Italy, passed to his son, Dionysius II. Through the influence of Dion, who was the new ruler's uncle, Plato was invited to Syracuse to teach philosophy to the young Dionysius; and he reluctantly accepted. Instruction was practically impossible because of suspicion and intrigue at court, and four months after Plato's arrival Dion was banished on the ground that he was plotting against the ruler. When the war with Carthage broke out, Plato left Sicily, promising to return when peace was established if Dion should be allowed to return to Syracuse.

In 361, Plato returned to Sicily at the urging of Dion, still under banishment. When Dionysius continued to refuse to allow Dion's return and made matters worse by confiscating his property, Plato protested. He was made a virtual prisoner and was in danger from Dionysius' bodyguards, but finally he was released through the intervention of his friend Archytas of Tarentum. He returned to Athens in the summer of 360.

For the next thirteen years Plato taught and wrote at the Academy, composing the later dialogues, among them the *Laws*. He died in 347 and was buried on the grounds of the Academy.

Plato is famous for the intellectually

lively portrait of Socrates which he presented in his earlier dialogues, and for his theory of Ideas, eternal, changeless forms of things by reference to which knowledge is possible. In his *Republic* he set forth his ideas of the ideal state, one founded on conceptions of law and justice.

BIBLIOGRAPHICAL REFERENCES: The standard translation is Benjamin Jowett, *The Dialogues of Plato*, 5 vols., 1892, reprinted in various modern editions. An excellent book of selections is John Burnet's translation of *Euthyphro, Apology, Crito, and Phaedo*, 1924. Perhaps the best introduction to the man and the writings is A. E. Taylor, *Plato: The Man and His Work*, 1927. For analysis and criticism see also J. A. Stewart, *The Myths of Plato*, 1905, and *Plato's Doctrine of Ideas*, 1909; A. E. Taylor, *Platonism*, 1924; John Burnet, *Platonism*, 1928; Paul Shorey, *What Plato Said*, 1933, and *Platonism, Ancient and Modern*, 1938; G. M. A. Grube, *Plato's Thought*, 1935; A. D. Winspear, *The Genesis of Plato's Thought*, 1938; Raymond Sinneterre, *Introduction à l'étude de Platon*, 1948; Guy C. Field, *The Philosophy of Plato*, 1949; Victor Goldschmidt, *La religion de Platon*, 1949; David Grene, *Man in His Pride: A Study in the Political Philosophy of Thucydides and Plato*, 1950; Catherine Rau, *Art and Society: A Reinterpretation of Plato*, 1951; William D. Ross, *Plato's Theory of Ideas*, 1951; R. B. Levinson, *In Defense of Plato*, 1953; R. Allen, *Studies in Plato's Metaphysics*, 1965; Raphal Demos, *The Philosophy of Plato*, 1966; Constantin Ritter, *The Essence of Plato's Philosophy*, 1968; and John Randall, *Plato: Dramatist of the Life of Reason*, 1970. An excellent background study is G. C. Field, *Plato and His Contemporaries*, 1930.

PLAUTUS
Titus Maccius Plautus

Born: Sarsina, Italy
Date: c. 255 B.C.

Died: Rome (?), Italy
Date: 184 B.C.

Principal Works

PLAYS: *Miles Gloriosus*, c. 206 B.C. (*The Braggart Soldier*); *Stichus*, 200; *Aulularia*, c. 195 (*The Pot of Gold*); *Pseudolus*, 191 (*The Trickster*); *Bacchides*, c. 189; undated: *Amphitruo*; *Asinaria* (*The Ass Comedy*); *Captivi* (*The Captives*); *Casina*; *Cistellaria* (*The Casket*); *Curculio*; *Menaechmi*; *Mercator* (*The Merchant*); *Mostellaria* (*The Haunted House*); *Rudens* (*The Slipknot*); *Trinummus*; *Vidularia* (*The Chest*).

Titus, son of Titus, was born about 255 B.C. in Sarsina, the capital of the Umbrian people of central Italy, only a dozen years after they came under the sway of Rome. Being a freeman, the ambitious Titus could leave home and go south along the Flaminian Way to Rome, which was still a city of thatch and timber. Because some of the Roman generals had become lovers of the theater in Syracuse, where they saw adaptations by a Greek slave, Andronicus, a Greek tragedy and a comedy had featured the Ludi Romani of 240 B.C. Temporary wooden platforms made the theater, and the audience brought their own chairs. (Rome's first permanent theater was built by Pompey, in 55 B.C.) This rude drama attracted young Titus. History records he worked "in operis artificium scenicorum," which might mean he was a stage carpenter, a minor actor, or even a flute player who entertained the spectators between the acts. It has been said that he was nicknamed Maccus after a dissolute character of the farces and that he himself, with characteristic humor, assumed the name Plautus (Flatfoot).

Somehow he made money, and quickly lost it. Scholars speculate that he hired a ship to carry merchandise for sale in Greece; this circumstance would explain his knowledge of Greek and the poverty that drove him to grinding corn for a baker. About 206 B.C. he wrote two plays based on Greek originals. One, *The Braggart Soldier*, was especially successful. With actors clamoring for more of his productions, Titus soon became an established playwright.

At this time, besides Greek plays in translation, Roman audiences had three kinds of dramatic entertainment: satirical medleys of songs and stories, dialogues attacking political and military leaders, and broad farces, performed by masked actors, imitating the coarsest sort of Greek pantomime. Plautus, who knew the "New Comedy" of Athens that had replaced the genre of Aristophanes after the loss of Athenian independence made it dangerous to lampoon citizens, borrowed some light social drama of Menander and his imitators, incorporated some of the technique of the farces, and, while retaining the Greek setting, added Roman local color and topics to give them greater appeal, often so timely that it is possible to date the year of composition.

Apparently the audience did not find it incongruous to have supposedly Greek characters mentioning Roman praetors and aediles, or using the verb *pergraecari* (to act like a Greek) when they meant "lead a dissolute life."

When his popularity with comedies about deceitful servants and parasitical followers earned Roman citizenship for the Umbrian, he changed his nickname Maccus, with its connotation of "clown," into the patrician name Maccius, and became Titus Maccius Plautus. In his day he had detractors; Quintilian criticized him, and Horace commented that if Plautus got his cash he never cared whether his comedies stumbled or stood. Modern critics attack his immorality and the use he made of comedy's early privilege, because of its religious connections, to gloss over its licentiousness. It is true that he was not an originator; the plays whose plots he invented show him at his worst. But when he stays close to his Greek sources, embellishing his work with the salty flavor of common Latin speech, he merits his reputation as the master of Roman comedy.

Originally 130 plays were attributed to him. Later Varro (116–27 B.C.) reduced to twenty and a fragment the number definitely accredited, with nineteen more possibly his work. As he himself borrowed from Greek predecessors, so later playwrights made use of his work. The *Menaechmi* inspired Shakespeare's *Comedy of Errors*. His *Aulularia* was rewritten by Ben Jonson, Molière, Thomas Shadwell, and Hooft, and it probably influenced Fielding in the composition of *The Miser*. Dryden, too, adapted his work. Plautus' humor, combined with pictures of the homely life of the common people and lively satire of the wealthy, makes him one of the greatest of Roman dramatists. He died, probably in Rome, in 184 B.C.

BIBLIOGRAPHICAL REFERENCES: For translations of the extant plays of Plautus, see G. E. Duckworth, *The Complete Roman Drama*, 2 vols., 1942; and Paul Nixon, *Plautus with English Translation*, 5 vols., 1916–1938. For critical and background studies see also A. Y. Sellar, *The Roman Poets of the Republic*, 1889; W. W. Blancké, *The Dramatic Values in Plautus*, 1918; J. T. Allen, *Stage Antiquities of the Greeks and Romans*, 1927; Gilbert Norwood, *Plautus and Terence*, 1932; F. A. Wright, *Three Roman Poets*, 1932; William Beare, *The Roman Stage*, 1950; and Erich W. Segal, *Roman Laughter; The Comedy of Plautus*, 1968.

PLINY THE YOUNGER

Born: Comum, Italy
Date: 61

Died: Unknown
Date: Before 114

Principal Works

LETTERS: Books I–IX, 97–109; Book X, c. 111.
ORATION: *Panegyricus*, 100.

Pliny the Younger, or Gaius Plinius Caecilius Secundus, was born in Comum, Italy, in A.D. 61. His was an aristocratic family of much importance in the Comum area where several inscriptions relating to the family have survived. His father was Gaius Caecilius and his mother was Plinia, the sister of Gaius Plinius, or, as he is more commonly known, Pliny the Elder, the soldier, lawyer, scholar, and author of the famous *Natural History*. In 71 the younger Pliny's father died, leaving his son to the guardianship of his brother-in-law, the elder Pliny. In 79 the elder Pliny adopted the younger by will, and the young man combined his adopted father's name with his own. From both his father's and his mother's side of the family, Pliny the Younger inherited considerable wealth and, more important, influence.

Pliny's early education was overseen by his mother, his uncle, and his tutor, one Virginius Rufus. We know that from his early years Pliny was devoted to writing; in one of his letters he tells us that he wrote a tragedy in Greek when he was fourteen. A lesson assignment given him by his uncle on the day in 79 when Vesuvius erupted and buried Pompeii kept Pliny from accompanying his scientifically curious uncle to the site of that cataclysm, and thus spared him from the disaster that killed his uncle. Pliny's later education was at least in part guided by the greatest of Roman teachers, Quintilian.

At the age of eighteen Pliny began to practice law in Rome. Most of his legal career was spent pleading before the court of the Centumviri, and thus he dealt primarily with cases having to do with wills and inheritances. He also dealt with other kinds of cases, however, and achieved a wide reputation as a lawyer. He is known to have pleaded before the Senate.

Thanks to the influence of his family and to his own talents, Pliny from his earliest years served in a succession of important public offices. While a young man he was a military tribune in Syria, where he heard the Stoic philosophers Eurphrates and Artemidorus. Afterwards, he was a quaestor, a praetor (around 93), and in 100 he achieved the consulship. In honor of his appointment to that position he wrote his *Panegyricus*, a rather stilted oration in praise of the Emperor Trajan, who had given him the post. The *Panegyricus* is the only surviving oration of the many that Pliny published. Other offices Pliny held from time to time were the prefecture of the military treasury, the prefecture of the state treasury, the custodianship of the banks and channel of the Tiber, the propraetorship of Pontica, and, about 111, the governorship of Bithynia—a position to which he was appointed, it is thought, because of his skill in fiscal matters. The finances of Bithynia were in some disorder. It is to his tenure as governor of Bithynia that we owe

Pliny's most important single letter (10.96), his inquiry to the Emperor Trajan as to how he should treat members of the young, growing, and troublesome Christian sect.

His body and health, it appears, were never robust; nevertheless, throughout his life he was a model of the active Roman gentleman. We see this reflected in great detail in the 338 surviving texts in the ten books of his letters. (Books I–IX are letters to various friends. Book X, which was probably published by someone other than Pliny, contains letters from Pliny to Trajan concerning his governorship of Bithynia. Book X also includes many of the Trajan's replies to Pliny.) Pliny was a patron of the arts (Martial was one of the poets he helped at one time or another), a sponsor of public works, a good landlord, a good master to his slaves, a helpful, and generous friend, a public spirited civil servant, an astute lawyer, an amateur scholar (one of his close associates was the great historian, Tacitus), a careful overseer of his wealth and estates, a connoiseur of the good life, and an observer of the bounties and beauties of nature. He married twice, both marriages were without issue. His second wife was Calpurnia, grand-daughter of Calpurnius Fabatus. She was much younger than her husband and is said to have been an accomplished woman. Pliny praises her for her kind attentions to him. Nothing is known of the place and exact date of Pliny's death, or of his activities in his last years.

BIBLIOGRAPHICAL REFERENCES: The standard text is the *Epistles*, edited by R. A. B. Mynors, 1963. The *Panegyricus* was edited by M. Durry, 1938. Translations include *The Letters of the Younger Pliny*, translated by Betty Radice, 1963, for Penguin Books; and the Loeb Classical Library edition with a translation by William Melmoth, revised by W. M. L. Hutchinson, 2 vols., 1961–1963. Betty Radice's translation also appears in a new Loeb Library edition, 2 vols., 1969.

Indispensible for studies of Pliny is A. N. Sherwin-White's *The Letters of Pliny: A Social and Historical Commentary*, 1966. Sherwin-White also edited *Fifty Letters of Pliny*, 1967. See also A.-M. Guillemin, *Pline et la vie littéraire de son temps*, 1929; Moses Hadas, *A History of Latin Literature*, 1952; and Frank O. Copley, *Latin Literature*, 1969. Scholarly articles are listed annually in the *Annél Philologique* under the heading Plinius Minor.

PLUTARCH

Born: Chaeronea, Boeotia, Greece
Date: c. 45

Died: Chaeronea
Date: c. 125

Principal Works

BIOGRAPHY: *Parallel Lives*, 105–115.
ESSAYS AND TREATISES: *Opera moralia* (*Moral Works*).

Plutarch the biographer was born about A.D. 45 at Chaeronea, in Boeotia, a district that had always had the unlucky reputation of producing stupid men. Plutarch himself shared the belief, though he could have professed that in his own person he belied it. He came of a wealthy magisterial family. In youth he studied philosophy under Ammonius of Delphi, who is thought to have been of the Academic school, or possibly of the Stoic. Plutarch's works show traces of Stoic teaching, especially as regards steadfastness under pain, but they reject the Stoic idea of rewards and punishments for the dead. They embrace the Pythagorean doctrine of metempsychosis. Plutarch is said to have visited Egypt; in view of the knowledge of Egyptian mythology and religion exhibited in his *On Isis and Osiris*, the probability is high. He is known to have been initiated into the Dionysiac mysteries. He journeyed to Rome, and there, it is assumed, wrote his moral treatises. There, certainly, he became renowned as a teacher of philosophy, and he is declared by some authorities to have been appointed Trajan's tutor. He gained the friendship of the consul Sosius Senecio, and was himself elevated by Trajan to the consular rank. On his retirement, he returned to Greece, where he held the procuratorship under Hadrian. He passed his later years at Chaeronea, where he died about A.D. 125, as archon and as priest of Apollo. Although his Roman literary contemporaries are silent concerning him, he was revered by Eusebius and Aulus Gellius.

In medieval and modern times, Plutarch has been one of the most widely read Greek authors, chief attention being accorded to his *Parallel Lives*. The collection, first printed at Florence in 1517, enjoyed the particular distinction of providing Shakespeare, through Sir Thomas North's English translation (1579) of the Amyot French version, with the plots of *Julius Caesar, Antony and Cleopatra, Coriolanus*, and (in part) *Timon of Athens*. The plan of the *Lives*, which seem to belong to Plutarch's later period, was to set beside each other, in pairs, illustrious Greek and Roman commanders or statesmen and then, in a separate esssay, to compare their traits of character for the purpose of moral instruction. Thus, with Theseus he compared Romulus; with Alcibiades, Coriolanus; with Aristides, Cato; with Demosthenes, Cicero. In all, forty-six lives are extant; to these are appended four others unconnected with one another. Furthermore several of the comparative essays have been lost. The greatest virtue of the *Lives* consists in Plutarch's richness of anecdotal detail, for his circumstantial disclosures of homely incident are often illuminating as well as startling. The *Lives* are deeply learned and must have required an enormous amount of research. Their greatest flaw results from Plutarch's tendency to distort facts when dealing with personages concerning whom, for moral reasons, he was biased.

His other works, far more voluminous, have a good deal of philosophic and antiquarian interest. They fall into various classifications in accordance with their emphasis upon political, scientific, historical, moral, or religious matters. Among them should be mentioned *The Malignity of Herodotus*, reflecting Plutarch's dislike for that historian's preference of Athens to Sparta; the essay *On the Face Appearing on the Disk of the Moon;* the treatise *Whether an Old Man Ought to Engage in Politics;* and the disquisition *On Isis and Osiris,* a source of much material to early students of Egyptian culture. In the esssay *On the Cessation of Oracles* occurs the memorable story of the voice that cried, from the island of Paxi, "Great Pan is dead!"—a tale often stimulating, in later times, to the romantic fancy. Plutarch wrote a *Consolation to Apollonius,* much imitated in the Renaissance, and a *Consolation to His Wife,* by which he hoped to mitigate her grief over the death of their little daughter Timoxena.

BIBLIOGRAPHICAL REFERENCES: The *Lives,* translated by Bernadotte Perrin, 11 vols., 1914–1926, are in the Loeb Classical Library. Another edition, translated by John Dryden, 1683, and revised by Arthur Hugh Clough, 1864, has been reprinted as a Modern Library Giant. The basic translation of the *Moralia* is that by Philemon Holland, 1603. The translation by F. C. Babbitt and others, 14 vols., is also in the Loeb Classical Library. T. G. Tucker and A. O. Prickard have also translated selections from the *Moralia,* 2 vols., 1913–1918. For commentary see R. C. Trench, *A Popular Introduction to Plutarch,* 1873; John Oakesmith, *The Religion of Plutarch,* 1903; K. M. Westaway, *Educational Theory of Plutarch,* 1931; Moses Hadas, *A History of Greek Literature,* 1950; J. R. Hamilton, *Plutarch: Alexander; A Commentary,* 1969; and C. P. Jones, *Plutarch and Rome,* 1971.

EDGAR ALLAN POE

Born: Boston, Massachusetts
Date: January 19, 1809

Died: Baltimore, Maryland
Date: October 7, 1849

Principal Works

POEMS: *Tamerlane and Other Poems,* 1827; *Al Aaraaf, Tamerlane and Minor Poems,* 1829; *Poems,* 1831; *The Raven and Other Poems,* 1845; *Eureka: A Prose Poem,* 1848.
SHORT STORIES: *Tales of the Grotesque and Arabesque,* 1840 (2 vols.); *Tales,* 1845.
NOVELLA: *The Narrative of Arthur Gordon Pym,* 1838.
CRITICISM: *The Literati,* 1850.

The parents of Edgar Allan Poe were David Poe and Elizabeth Arnold Poe. They had three children: William Henry Leonard, Edgar, and Rosalie. Edgar was born on January 19, 1809, in Boston. His mother died in Richmond, Virginia, on December 8, 1811, and the circumstances of David Poe's death are unknown. It is believed that he died not long before or after the death of his wife. The pretty little boy, Edgar, though not legally adopted, became a member of the childless family of John Allan, a Scottish tobacco merchant of the Richmond firm of Ellis and Allan. He was given the name of Edgar Allan and treated as the son of the family. When Mr. Allan sailed for England to establish a branch of the firm, Edgar went with him and his wife. He was kept in an English school most of the time until the Allans returned home in 1820. After further school days in Richmond, Poe was taken to Charlottesville where on February 14, 1826, he was entered as a student in the University of Virginia. He continued as a student for the more than ten months' session until it closed in December. He excelled in his classes, but he accumulated some debts over which he and Mr. Allan quarreled; and as a result Poe left Richmond a penniless youth.

Why Poe chose to go to Boston is unknown but he arranged there for the publication of a little volume of poems, *Tamerlane and Other Poems,* and on May 26, 1827, he enlisted under the name of Edgar A. Perry in the United States Army. In 1829 he secured a discharge from the army and entered West Point in 1830 as a cadet. After the death of his first wife, John Allan married again. Soon afterward there was a final break with Poe and Poe himself was dismissed from the Academy. He had published *Al Aaraaf, Tamerlane and Minor Poems* in 1829 and upon leaving West Point he published *Poems, Second Edition,* 1831. There followed an obscure period in Baltimore before he went to Richmond in 1835 to work on the *Southern Literary Messenger* until the end of 1836. He had married his cousin, Virginia Clemm, in 1836, and he now took her and his aunt, Mrs. Clemm, to New York, but soon he removed to Philadelphia where he became first an associate editor of *Burton's Gentleman's Magazine* and later editor of its successor, *Graham's Magazine.* In April, 1844, he returned to New York and in 1846 rented the little cottage in Fordham, just out of the city, where Virginia died on January 30, 1847, and where Poe and Mrs. Clemm continued to live until Poe's death. He had published stories and articles in various magazines and had worked on the New York *Mirror* and edited the *Broadway Journal.*

Of his books, *The Narrative of Arthur Gordon Pym* was published in 1838, *Tales of the Grotesque and Arabesque,* in two volumes, in 1840, *Tales* and *The Raven and Other Poems* in 1845, and *Eureka* in 1848. The publication of his prize-winning story, "The Gold Bug" in the Philadelphia *Dollar Newspaper* in 1843 brought him some recognition, but he became famous in 1845 with the printing of "The Raven" in the *Evening Mirror* and the *Whig Review*. In 1849, the year in which appeared "Annabel Lee," "The Bells," and others of his best-known poems, Poe visited Norfolk and Richmond on a lecture tour. He had broken his engagement to marry the poetess, Mrs. Helen Whitman, and in Richmond he had become engaged to his former sweetheart, Sarah Elmira Royster, now the widow Shelton. From the time of his leaving Richmond his movements are unknown until he was found in an unconscious condition in Baltimore. He died in a hospital on October 7, 1849. In the churchyard of the Westminster Presbyterian Church he was interred the next day. His wife, Virginia, was later removed from the vault of the Valentines, owners of the Fordham cottage, to a place beside his grave.

Edgar Allan Poe is as important for his influence upon the literature of the world as he is for the works in themselves. He is known as poet, critic, short story writer, and mystic theorist. The quality of about twenty of his poems is unique. He was an innovator in the field of pure poetry and of symbolism. Of lesser importance was his mastery of certain technical devices, such as assonance, rhythm and rhyme, as evidenced in his "The Raven," "The Bells," and "Ulalume." His influence was especially great in France through Baudelaire, Mallarmé, and the Symbolists. Certainly, "To Helen," "Annabel Lee," "The Haunted Palace," "The Raven," "Israfel," "The City in the Sea," and "Ulalume" are among the most universally admired short poems in the language.

Poe, at the time of his death, was best known in America as a critic. He defined the short story and developed the theory of what has come to be known as "pure poetry."

His prose tales were unique for his day. He invented the detective story, as illustrated by such tales as "The Murders in the Rue Morgue" and "The Purloined Letter." His most characteristic tales were stories of impressionistic effect, often containing a psychological theme or built on a study of conscience, as seen in "Ligeia" or "William Wilson"; or tales of terror, such as "The Black Cat," "The Telltale Heart," or "The Cask of Amontillado."

The magic of Poe, his power to arouse our terror, and to make us partake of the sensations that he evokes by his stories as though we had lived them, are the effects of his conscious art. His poems are remarkable for their beauty and melody, his tales for the intensity with which the artist brings us under his spell. He is associated especially with his dark and terror-filled stories with which all readers are familiar and he is, perhaps, the world's master of the macabre. He was the product of the Gothic influence infused with the curiosity as to all things psychological that came from Germany. When all the stories that he wrote, however, are considered, he is seen to have a wider range as a prose writer than is generally recognized.

BIBLIOGRAPHICAL REFERENCES: The standard editions are *The Complete Works of Edgar Allan Poe*, edited by James A. Harrison, 17 vols., 1902, now out of print, and the less complete but reliable *Works of Edgar Allan Poe*, edited by George E. Woodberry and Edmund C. Stedman, 10 vols., 1894–1895 (reprinted 1914); but a new edition is needed to incorporate the letters and other findings of recent scholarship. One such contribution is John W. Ostrom, *The Letters of Edgar Allan Poe*, 2 vols., 1948. The best editions of the short stories are James Southall Wilson, *Tales of Edgar Allan Poe*, 1927; and Killis Campbell, *Poe's Short Stories*, 1927. The latter also edited *The Poems of Edgar Allan Poe*, 1917. An edition in 3 vols. of the *Collected Works*, edited by Thomas Oliver Mabbott, is in progress, Vol. I, *Poems*, 1970.

The standard biography is Arthur H. Quinn, *Edgar Allan Poe: A Critical Biography*, 1941. See also J. H. Ingram, *Edgar Allan Poe: His Life, Letters, and Opinions*, 2 vols., 1880; George E. Woodberry, *The Life of Edgar Allan Poe, Personal and Literary*, 2 vols., 1885 (rev. ed., 1909); Hervey Allen, *Israfel: The Life and Times of Edgar Allan Poe*, 2 vols., 1926; N. B. Fagin, *The Histrionic Mr. Poe*, 1949; and Edward Wagenknecht, *Poe: The Man behind the Legend*, 1963.

See also Margaret Alterton, *Origins of Poe's Critical Theory*, 1925; Norman Foerster, *American Criticism*, 1928; S. F. Damon, *Thomas Holley Chivers, Friend of Poe*, 1930; Killis Campbell, *The Mind of Poe and Other Studies*, 1933; Gay Wilson Allen, *American Prosody*, 1935; Van Wyck Brooks, *The World of Washington Irving*, 1944; and "Edgar Allan Poe," in *The Literary History of the United States*, Vol. II, edited by Robert E. Spiller, Willard Thorp, Thomas H. Johnston, and Henry S. Canby, 1948.

For briefer criticism and special studies consult the extensive bibliography in *The Literary History of the United States*, Vol. III, 689–696.

POLITIAN
Angelo Ambrogini

Born: Montepulciano, Italy
Date: July 14, 1454

Died: Florence, Italy
Date: September 24, 1494

PRINCIPAL WORKS

PLAY: *Orfeo*, 1480 (*Orpheus*).
POEMS: *Sylvae*, 1512; *Le Stanze*, 1518.
ESSAYS: *Miscellanea*, 1489.

Angelo Ambrogini, who called himself Poliziano and Politian, from his birthplace, was a humanist who studied the philosophy of Plato under Marsilio Ficino and Aristotle under Argyropulos. A true man of the Renaissance, he displayed a modern spirit in his ability to express his classical learning in understandable, popular forms.

At the age of nineteen he attracted the attention of Lorenzo de' Medici (1449–1492) by his Latin version of a part of the *Iliad*, and he was asked to tutor Lorenzo's son Piero. Besides being canon of the cathedral of Florence, he developed the scientific method of textual criticism in his lectures on Greek and Roman literature at the University of Florence, where he had among his students Johann Reuchlin and William Grocyn. His pastoral play, *Orpheus*, was produced in Mantua in 1480, during a brief period of estrangement from the Medicis. After his death his original verses in Latin, including *Manto, Rusticus, Nutricia,* and *Ambra*, were published in twelve books in Paris in 1512. He also wrote poems in Italian, of which the most famous is *Le Stanze*, written to celebrate the skill and courage of Giuliano de' Medici in a tournament. His translations from the Greek include works by Plato, Epictetus, and Plutarch.

As one of the earliest poets of the Italian Renaissance, he revealed the lyrical qualities of the Italian language in *Le Stanze*. His idyllic *Orpheus* is one of the first plays in that language, and since it was also set to music, it can be classified as an early Italian opera. Born in Montepulciano, Italy, on July 14, 1454, he died at Florence, September 24, 1494.

BIBLIOGRAPHICAL REFERENCES: There is a translation of *Orpheus* by Louis E. Lord, 1931. For biographical studies see W. P. Gresswell, *Memoirs of Angelus Politianus*, 1805; Pietro Serrasi, *Vita de Angelo Poliziano*, 1808; and M. A. Boccalaro, *Angelo Poliziano: it poeta del bel canto*, 1951. For background and related materials see also William Roscoe, *Life of Lorenzo de' Medici*, 1803 (10th ed., 1889); H. O. Taylor, *Thought and Expression in the Fifteenth Century*, 1920; John Addington Symonds, *The Renaissance in Italy*, 1875–1886, Modern Library, 1935; Warman Welliver, *Botticelli's Court of Venus, Poliziano's Stanze, and Lorenzo*, 1960; and A. Bartlett Giamatti, *The Earthly Paradise and the Renaissance Epic*, 1966.

MARCO POLO

Born: Venice (?), Italy
Date: c. 1254

Died: Venice
Date: January 9, 1324

Principal Work

description and travel: *The Travels of Marco Polo,* c. 1299.

Much of Marco Polo's early life is still in question, including the place and date of his birth. Marco's father was one of three Venetian brothers who had formed a business partnership as merchants. Nicolo Polo, Marco's father, and Maffeo Polo are known to have been at the court of Kublai Khan in the 1260's. The Khan apparently became interested enough in religion to send the two men back to Italy to request that the Pope send Christian missionaries to his land. When the Polos arrived home in 1269, they found that Pope Clement IV had died the year before. They waited for the election of a new Pope before setting off once again for China, taking with them young Marco Polo and letters explaining the cause for their delay. They were followed some months later by two Dominican monks, but these missionaries never reached their destination.

According to Marco Polo's own account, his father and uncle hoped to journey to China by sea, taking ship on the Persian Gulf. Finding that plan impossible to follow, they traveled overland to the court of Kublai Khan, passing on their way through lands explored by no other white man until the nineteenth century and arriving at their destination in 1275, when Marco Polo was about twenty or twenty-one years old. Kublai Khan, pleased to see the Venetians, made them welcome at his court. Young Marco studied the languages of Kublai Khan's dominions and entered the service of that great ruler.

Traveling for the Khan took Marco Polo over much of Asia: into the Chinese provinces of Shansi, Shensi, Szechuen, and Yunnan, and into the areas now known as Burma and Tibet. Marco Polo, finding that the Khan took great interest in all phases of life, took many notes on his travels and reported in great detail to Kublai Khan, who seems to have listened personally to the young Venetian. Apparently Kublai Khan esteemed Marco Polo, for the latter even served for a time as the governor of the province of Yangchow. Apparently the two elder Polos served Kublai Khan in the capacity of military advisers.

So important and rich did the three Europeans become that they grew fearful of what jealous courtiers or a new ruler might do to them in the event of Kublai Khan's death. Fearing the worst, they petitioned the Khan to permit them to return to their homeland; their wish was not at first granted, however. An opportunity presented itself finally in 1286. The Khan of Persia, a relative of Kublai Khan, sent a delegation to request a Mongol bride for their ruler, and the envoys who presented the request asked that the three Venetians might accompany them back to Persia. In 1292 the party set out by sea for Persia. Two years later they arrived at the court of Arghan Khan and were given permission to continue on to Venice. They arrived in their home city in 1295, twenty-four years—almost a quarter of a century—after their departure. Having left Venice a stripling, Marco Polo returned a mature and experienced man of about forty.

During 1298 a war broke out between Venice and Genoa. The Genoese assembled a fleet to attack Venice, and the latter city prepared to defend itself. A Venetian naval force under Andrea Dandolo set out to meet and destroy the attacking Genoese vessels; aboard one of the Venetian galleys, as its commander, was Marco Polo. The Venetians were defeated, and among those who found themselves prisoners of war was Marco Polo, who remained a captive in Genoa for almost a year, not being freed until the summer of 1299. During his imprisonment at Genoa, Marco Polo wrote his famous narrative of travels and adventures, or rather he dictated them to a fellow prisoner, one Rusticiano of Pisa, who acted as amanuensis, taking down the *Travels* in French.

Little is known of Marco Polo's life after his release from Genoese imprisonment. By his will, made on January 9, 1324, the day he died in Venice, it is known that he left a wife and three daughters, but other information is scanty. Indeed, aside from his own account, little is known of any of Marco Polo's life. Scholars have searched diligently in the Venetian archives, but they have found little information of consequence. And yet Marco Polo was influential for more than two centuries, through the detailed account of his adventures that he left behind. Many of the maps of the fourteenth and fifteenth centuries were based on his information; even Christopher Columbus owned a Latin translation of the *Travels*, into which he wrote notes.

The Travels of Marco Polo is in two parts. The first part is the actual narrative, while the second part consists of passages describing various places and parts of Asia, particularly portions of the empire of Kublai Khan. The earliest manuscript, perhaps the original, is believed to be one in the National Library at Paris. Altogether there are some eighty manuscripts in existence, and as is usually the case the various manuscripts differ considerably. While the *Travels* have importance as a historical document, the book is of negligible literary value. It is a plainly written account of experiences fascinating in themselves.

BIBLIOGRAPHICAL REFERENCES: Convenient editions of *The Travels of Marco Polo, the Venetian* are the Everyman's Library, 1921, and the Modern Library, 1931. The most generally useful volume on Polo is Henry H. Hart, *Venetian Adventurer*, 1947, with a full bibliography. Other studies are R. Alluli, *Marco Polo*, 1923; and Luigi F. Benedetto, *Marco Polo*, translated 1931. The stories of several great travelers are included in Merriam Sherwood and Elmer Mantz, *The Road to Cathay*, 1928. A valuable general study is J. N. L. Baker, *The History of Geographical Discovery and Exploration*, 1931. See also Henry H. Hart, *Marco Polo, Venetian Adventurer*, 1967; and Sir Edward D. Ross, "Marco Polo and His Book," *Proceedings of the British Academy*, XX (1934), 181–205. For fictionalized accounts of Marco Polo's adventure see Donn Byrne, *Messer Marco Polo*, 1921; and Eugene O'Neill, *Marco Millions*, 1928.

HENRIK PONTOPPIDAN

Born: Fredericia, Denmark
Date: July 24, 1857

Died: Ordrup, Denmark
Date: August 21, 1943

PRINCIPAL WORKS

NOVELS: *Det forjættede Land*, 1891–1895 (*The Promised Land*); *Lykke-Per*, 1898–1904 (*Lucky Peter*); *Dødes Rige*, 1912–1916 (*The Kingdom of the Dead*); *Mands Himmerig*, 1927 (*Man's Heaven*).
SHORT STORIES: *Stækkede Vinger*, 1881; *Landsbybilleder*, 1883; *Krøniker*, 1890.
PLAY: *De vilde Fugle*, 1902.

Much of the major writing done in Scandinavia for the last seventy-five years has been in some degree pessimistic, for writers there have been very much aware of the intellectual currents flowing through Europe, chiefly of scientific materialism which conflicted with the traditional values of a Christian society. Most of the intellectuals accepted the methods of scientific inquiry and were disillusioned with democracy because of the people's reluctance to accept social change that would bring the social organization into harmony with scientific principles. Ibsen, Strindberg, and Hamsun are all, to some extent, tragic artists. Henrik Pontoppidan also protested against the complacency of his society because it refused to be honest in facing the new knowledge.

Born in Fredericia, Denmark, on July 24, 1857, Henrik Pontoppidan, son of a provincial clergyman, went to Copenhagen to study engineering. At the age of twenty, while engaged in scientific studies, he suddenly realized that he wished only to be a writer. He left college and supported himself by teaching high school. He hated the facile religious sentimentality prevalent in the school, and he disliked the easy-going way of life of the Danish people because it lacked the emotional and intellectual intensity that he respected.

Pontoppidan's early work, of which *The Promised Land* is representative, protests against the injustices of peasant life; his hopes for reform rest with liberal politics, though he is aware that the hardness of human hearts cannot easily be overcome. A little later, in the eight volumes of *Lucky Peter,* he used autobiographical material to portray the life of a representative Dane in modern Denmark. In *The Kingdom of the Dead,* Pontoppidan reached the nadir of his pessimism: in five volumes he shows his disappointment with the results of liberalism and despairs of social progress. He never fully emerged from this pessimism. Though he had entered politics and had served a short time in the Danish legislature, he withdrew from public life entirely during his last years. He wrote little after his retirement; his last important novel, *Man's Heaven,* is a bitter attack upon those who failed Denmark during World War I: the politicians, the journalists, the isolationists, and the war profiteers.

Pontoppidan, under the influence of Georg Brandes, took up the techniques of realism and wrote with great accuracy of various social groups. His style is smooth and apparently effortless. He represents the most modern elements in Danish thought; it was for this that he was awarded the Nobel Prize for literature in 1917. He died at his home at Ordrup, Charlottenlund, Denmark, on August 21, 1943.

BIBLIOGRAPHICAL REFERENCES: A good introduction to Pontoppidan in English is Hanna Astrup Larsen, "Pontoppidan of Denmark," *American-Scandinavian Review*, XXXI (1943), 231–239. The most carefully documented study of his life and work is C. M. Woel, *Henrik Pontoppidan*, 2 vols., 1945. A brief sketch also appears in Annie Russell Marble, *The Nobel Prize Winners in Literature, 1901–1931*, 1932. See further Ernst Ekman, "Henrik Pontoppidan as a Critic of Modern Danish Society," *Scandinavian Studies*, XXIX (1957), 170–183; and W. Glyn Jones, "Henrik Pontoppidan, The Church and Christianity after 1900," *Scandinavian Studies*, XXX (1958), 191–197.

ALEXANDER POPE

Born: London, England
Date: May 21, 1688

Died: Twickenham, England
Date: May 30, 1744

Principal Works

PASTORAL POEMS: *Pastorals*, 1709; *Windsor Forest*, 1713.
DIDACTIC POEMS: *Essay on Criticism*, 1711; *Moral Essays*, 1731–1735; *Essay on Man*, 1733–1734.
SATIRES: *The Rape of the Lock*, 1712–1714; *The Dunciad*, 1728–1743; *Imitations of Horace*, 1733–1737; *The Epistle to Dr. Arbuthnot*, 1735.
TRANSLATIONS: Homer's *Iliad*, 1715–1718; the *Odyssey*, 1725–1726.

Alexander Pope, English poet, was born in London, May 21, 1688, son of a prosperous linen merchant and his second wife. The fact that Pope's parents were Roman Catholics had a bearing on the amount of education he received and his economic and social status. Schools and universities were closed to him; he could not buy or inherit land; he paid double taxes, and he could not legally live within ten miles of London. He was educated at irregular times by private tutors, mostly priests, but for the most part he, on his own, "dipped into a great number of English, French, Italian, Latin and Greek poets." This was no meager education in itself, for poets of the early 1700's copied many forms and ideas from the classical writers of ancient Rome and the period was called the Augustan Age. Pope himself became known as the "prose and reason" poet.

At the age of twelve a serious illness left him a hunch-backed cripple, four feet, six inches tall. Yet before he was seventeen he was admitted into the society of London wits, and men of fashion encouraged this young prodigy. By the time he was thirty he was acclaimed the chief poet of his times.

Pope's first important publication was his *Pastorals* in 1709. Two years later at the age of twenty-three his more famous *Essay on Criticism* was published. As very polite conversation, it is typical of the eighteenth century "salon"-type verse. Here Pope gives some of his popular sayings: "A little learning is a dangerous thing"; "To err is human, to forgive divine," and "Fools rush in where angels fear to tread." In the first section of the poem he tells of the chaotic state of criticism of his time; in the second he expounds his main rule of following nature, and in the final part he explains that the rules to be observed in writing must be studied in the works of great classical writers—Horace and Vergil, for example. They should not be slavishly imitated but should serve as guides. Pope himself was greatly influenced by Milton and Dryden. *The Rape of the Lock*, printed as a short poem in 1712 and in an elaborate form in 1714, is one of the finest early eighteenth century products. In a satirical way it catches, sums up, and presents in artistic form the spirit of the age. His use of myth makes it unusual for the period.

In his translation of *Homer*, his chief employment for twelve years, Pope consciously dressed Homer in the language of his century. In so doing he accustomed the English ear to the regular rhythms and beats of Homer. He also undertook a translation of the *Odyssey*, done partly by directing collaborators. The two translations were so successful in sales that Pope is reportedly the first English poet to make a fortune by his writing.

"Eloisa to Abelard," which appeared in a volume of poems in 1717, has medieval color and a melancholy tone. Pope left this romantic type, however, and returned to neo-classical forms.

In 1718 he moved to Twickenham on the Thames, where he lived with the widowed mother to whom he was devoted. Pope never married. His love for Lady Mary Wortley Montagu came to a bitter end. Later he fell in love with Martha Blount, and during the last ten years of his life he spent some part of every day with her.

Toward the end of his life Pope's fame as a moralist and satirist increased. Most of the distinguished men of his day were among his friends or enemies. The latter he ridiculed in the mock-heroic *Dunciad,* published in 1728 and republished in 1729.

The *Essay on Man* was also connected with controversies of the time. Designed as one of a series of philosophic poems, it gives proof that by training and temperament Pope was not a philosophical poet, at the same time presenting excellent examples of Pope's technique in building from abstract observation or a general idea to particular illustrations. Also noteworthy of his later years was his *Epistle to Dr. Arbuthnot,* which shows artistic progress in his ability to handle the couplet. Here he gives it ease and a conversational quality in contrast to the stiff and more formal use in *Essay on Criticism.*

The "school of Pope," with its great attention to matters of style and its concern for poems technically "perfect," was considered dull and lifeless and was detested by nineteenth century artists. Pope and his contemporaries are more kindly received today. In them we see elegant, correct, useful, and reasonable literature, although this writing is not necessarily profound.

Pope died at his Twickenham, Middlesex, villa on May 30, 1744.

BIBLIOGRAPHICAL REFERENCES: Earlier standard editions of Alexander Pope are being superseded by the continuing volumes of the Twickenham Edition, edited by Geoffrey Tillotson and others, 1938 ff. The best one-volume edition is Aubrey Williams, ed., *Poetry and Prose,* 1969. The best general biography is W. J. Courthope, *Life of Pope,* in Vol. V of Pope's *Works,* edited by Whitwell Elwin and W. J. Courthope, 10 vols., 1871–1889. See also Samuel Johnson, *Lives of the Poets,* 1781; Edith Sitwell, *Alexander Pope,* 1930; George Sherburn, *The Early Career of Alexander Pope,* 1934; R. K. Root, *The Poetical Career of Alexander Pope,* 1938; and Peter Quennell, *Pope: The Education of Genius,* 1969.

For criticism see also Geoffrey Tillotson, *On the Poetry of Pope,* 1938; J. E. Tobin, *Alexander Pope, 1744–1944,* 1945; Austin Warren, "The Mask of Pope," in *Rage for Order,* 1948; Cleanth Brooks, "The Case of Miss Arabella Fermor," in *The Well-Wrought Urn,* 1949; W. K. Wimsatt, "Rhetoric and Poems: The Example of Pope," in *English Institute Essays,* 1949; and Maynard Mack, " 'Wit and Poetry and Pope': Some Observations on His Imagery," in *Pope and His Contemporaries: Essays Presented to George Sherburn,* edited by James L. Clifford and Louis A. Landa, 1949. See further Maynard Mack, ed., *Essential Articles for the Study of Alexander Pope* (essays by various hands), 1964.

JANE PORTER

Born: Durham, England
Date: 1776

Died: Bristol, England
Date: May 24, 1850

Principal Works

NOVELS: *Thaddeus of Warsaw,* 1803; *The Scottish Chiefs,* 1810.

Born in Durham, England, in 1776, Jane Porter was the daughter of an army officer who died when she was three years old. Soon afterward the widowed mother took the family to Edinburgh to live, but shortly before 1803 the entire family moved to London, where Jane Porter began to write. Her first book was the story of a Polish exile entitled *Thaddeus of Warsaw.* The book had an amazing success with critics and the public; among the people who sent a congratulatory message to the author was Kosciusko, world-renowned Polish patriot. With the publication of her novel, Jane Porter became as well known as her brother, Sir Robert Ker Porter, a painter, and her sister, Anna Maria Porter, also a popular novelist of the period.

The best novel to come from her pen was *The Scottish Chiefs,* a historical romance of the kind later made famous by Sir Walter Scott, who was a childhood friend of Jane Porter. Indeed, *The Scottish Chiefs* is one of the few historical novels prior to Scott's Waverley series which still commands a body of readers. After her initial success as a novelist, Jane Porter turned to the writing of plays. Her first effort was never staged, and her second was a failure so complete that it ended her career as a dramatist. A number of later novels were written and published, but none caught the public or critical fancy as did her first two. Jane Porter, who never married, spent much of her life in literary and artistic society and lived a happy and serene life, although somewhat financially embarrassed in her later years. She died in Bristol on May 24, 1850.

BIBLIOGRAPHICAL REFERENCES: For a study of Jane Porter and her times see Mona Wilson, *These Were Muses,* 1924.

KATHERINE ANNE PORTER

Born: Indian Creek, Texas
Date: May 15, 1894

Principal Works

NOVELETTES AND SHORT STORIES: *Flowering Judas,* 1930 (enlarged 1935); *Hacienda,* 1934; *Noon Wine,* 1937; *Pale Horse, Pale Rider,* 1939; *The Leaning Tower and Other Stories,* 1944; *Collected Stories,* 1965; new edition with preface by the author and 3 additional stories, 1967.
NOVEL: *Ship of Fools,* 1962.
ESSAYS: *The Days Before,* 1952; *Collected Essays and Occasional Writings,* 1970.
TRANSLATIONS: *Katherine Anne Porter's French Song-Book,* 1933; *The Itching Parrot,* by José Joaquín Fernández de Lizárdi, 1942.

The critical reputation of Katherine Anne Porter is in inverse ratio to the volume of her published work. Never one to rush into print, she has eyed her writing with such sharp scrutiny that only a comparatively small amount of it has appeared in book form, yet on the basis of one novel, five novelettes and three collections of short stories she has been acclaimed as one of the outstanding literary figures of her generation, an important influence on younger writers, and a stylist comparable to Hawthorne and Flaubert.

A descendant of Franklin Boone, Miss Porter was born on May 15, 1894, in a small community near San Antonio, Texas. She spent her girlhood in Texas and Louisiana and received most of her formal education in small convent schools in the South. More important to her development was the fact that she spent her childhood in a home in which there existed both incentive and opportunity to read. By the time she was fifteen she had absorbed a wide variety of literature; she once said that it would be possible for her to write an autobiography based on her reading alone. She spent her youth writing and destroying manuscripts "quite literally by the trunkful," and she was thirty before her first story was published. In the meantime she had eked out a living by doing book reviews, political articles, editing, rewriting, and what she terms "hack writing of every sort." Twice married and divorced and the recipient of a number of literary honors and awards, she has lived in New Orleans, Chicago, Bermuda, Mexico, New York, Berlin, Paris, and Hollywood.

If the surface aspects of her life appear unfixed and variable, they are in sharp contrast to her inner self, which has remained constant in her efforts to resolve life's complexities in art. In her own words, "This has been the basic and absorbing occupation, the intact line of my life which directs my actions, determines my point of view, and profoundly affects my character and personality, my social beliefs and economic status and the kinds of friendships I form." The first fruits of her apprenticeship appeared in 1930 with the publication of *Flowering Judas,* which was reissued in 1935 with four stories added. *Pale Horse, Pale Rider,* containing three novelettes, followed in 1939. Although Miss Porter liked the title story best, most readers have preferred *Noon Wine,* a psychological tale involving events of unexpected violence on a small farm in Texas. Her most recent book of fiction is *The Leaning Tower and Other Stories*. In 1952 she published *The Days Before*, a collection of her critical writings and essays. For some time now she has committed herself to two long-term projects, a biography of Cotton Mather and a full-length novel. The latter, at which her publishers have darted hopeful glances from year to year, has thus far inspired two titles, *No Safe Harbor* having been discarded in favor of *The Ship of Fools*.

Perhaps the most obvious reason for Miss Porter's importance, in spite of so small an output, is that she is an incomparable stylist. Precise, subtle, poetic, strong yet delicate, her prose has above all a rare quality of stylistic verisimilitude. Unlike many modern authors, whose language always sounds characteristically like themselves, she has a genius for adapting her prose to the specific situation and character under discussion, and for reflecting the personality, background, and quality of thought and vocabulary of each of the widely varied characters she depicts. Rhythm, tone, imagery, and choice of words contribute to the organic unification of her prose and its subject matter. Only the purity, sharpness, and concentration of the writing provide the clues that the thoughts and words of the poor dairy farmer in *Noon Wine* and of the harassed, bullying movie producer in *Hacienda* are creations of the same mind. Writing always in the third person, Miss Porter is nonetheless extraordinarily successful in making what she writes seem to flow from within the brain of the character she is portraying.

Closely related to style is the skill with which she handles her subject matter. Modern Americans of all sorts, their relationships, and the extreme difficulty of self-fulfillment and self-understanding in the world of today are her concern. Two of the "Miranda" novelettes, *Old Mortality* and *Pale Horse, Pale Rider,* deal respectively with the rather conventional themes of self-understanding and the will-to-death. But the last words of the first story indicate the precarious and temporary nature of Miranda's climactic realization of herself, while the ending of the second portrays the quiet awfulness of being doomed to live. Avoiding the extremes of romantic optimism and nihilistic pessimism, the author presents her quiet negativism, her recognition of the wasteland that is modern life, with a subtlety that stops just short of inconclusiveness. With quiet but dramatic irony as her chief tool, whether it is the irony of reflection in the "Miranda" stories or the horrifying irony of action in *Noon Wine*, Miss Porter brilliantly portrays the difficulties involved in ordinary, decent everyday living in our time. Carefully treading the narrow way between objective realism and aesthetic sensibility, she presents a vision of the world which is completely her own, familiar to our view and yet capable of suggesting the deeper realities of symbol and myth.

Miss Porter's position in contemporary fiction was further heightened by the publication of her one novel, *Ship of Fools,* in 1962. Parts of the book had been appearing in magazines since 1945; it had become a kind of publishing legend. The densely-woven story of a cosmopolitan group of travelers sailing from Mexico to Nazi Germany and of their complicated and endlessly shifting relationships won the highest critical praise as being one of the finest contemporary novels.

BIBLIOGRAPHICAL REFERENCES: For full-length critical studies see Harry John Mooney, Jr., *The Fiction and Criticism of Katherine Anne Porter,* 1957; George Hendrick, *Katherine Anne Porter,* 1965; and M. M. Liberman, *Katherine Anne Porter's Fiction,* 1971. Of particular importance in an understanding of Miss Porter's background of subject matter and method of composition is her essay, " 'Noon Wine': The Sources," in *The Yale Review,* XLVI (1956), 23–39. For additional critical studies see also Ray B. West, Jr., "Katherine Anne Porter: Symbol and Theme in 'Flowering Judas,' " in *The Art of Modern Fiction,* by R. B. West, Jr., and R. W. Stallman, 1949; and "Katherine Anne Porter and 'Historic Memory,' " in *Southern Renascence,* edited by Louis D. Rubin, Jr., and Robert D. Jacobs, 1953; Edmund Wilson, *Classics and Commercials,* 1950; Lodwick Hartley, "Katherine Anne Porter," *Sewanee Review,* XLVIII (1940), 206–216, and "The Lady of the Temple: The Critical Theories of Katherine Anne Porter," *College English,* XIV (1953), 386–391; Margaret Marshall, "Writers in the Wilderness: Katherine Anne Porter," *Nation,* CL (1940), 473–475; Robert Penn Warren, "Katherine Anne Porter: Irony with a Center," *Kenyon Review,* IV (1942), 29–42; Vernon A. Young, "The Art of Katherine Anne Porter," *New Mexico Quarterly,* XV (1945), 326–341; Robert B. Heilman, "The Southern Temper," *Hopkins Review,* VI (1952), 5–15; and Charles A. Allen, "Katherine Anne Porter: Psychology as Art," *Southwest Review,* XLI (1956), 223–230. For bibliography see Edward Schwartz, "Katherine Anne Porter: A Critical Bibliography," with an introduction by Robert Penn Warren, *Bulletin of the New York Public Library,* LVII (1953), 211–247. Some articles on *Ship of Fools* are Theodore Solotaroff, "*Ship of Fools* and the Critics," *Commentary,* XXXIV (1962), 277-286; Lodwick Hartley, "Dark Voyage: A Study of Katherine Anne Porter's *Ship of Fools,*" *University Review,* XXX (1963), 83–94; Sister M. Joselyn, "On the Making of *Ship of Fools,*" *South Dakota Review,* I, ii (1964), 46–52; Paul W. Miller, "Katherine Anne Porter's *Ship of Fools,* a Masterpiece Manqué," *University Review,* XXXII (1965), 151–157; and M. M. Liberman, "The Responsibility of the Novelist: The Critical Reception of *Ship of Fools,*" *Criticism,* VII (1966), 377-388.

EZRA POUND

Born: Hailey, Idaho
Date: October 30, 1885

Died: Venice, Italy
Date: November 1, 1972

Principal Works

POEMS: *A Lume Spento*, 1908; *A Quinzaine for This Yule*, 1908; *Personae*, 1909; *Exultations*, 1909; *Provença*, 1910; *Canzoni*, 1911; *Ripostes*, 1912; *Lustra*, 1916; *Quia Pauper Amavi*, 1919; *Hugh Selwyn Mauberley*, 1920; *Umbra*, 1920; *Poems, 1918–1921*, 1921; *A Draft of XVI Cantos*, 1925; *Personae: The Collected Poems of Ezra Pound*, 1926; *A Draft of Cantos 17–27*, 1928; *A Draft of XXX Cantos*, 1930; *Eleven New Cantos, XXXI-XLI*, 1934; *Homage to Sextus Propertius*, 1934; *The Fifth Decad of Cantos*, 1937; *Cantos LII-LXXI*, 1940; *The Pisan Cantos, LXXI-LXXXV*, 1948; *The Cantos of Ezra Pound*, 1948; *Section: Rock-Drill, 85–95 de los cantares*, 1956; *Thrones: 96–109 de los cantares*, 1959; *Selected Cantos*, 1970.

ESSAYS AND STUDIES: *Pavannes and Divisions*, 1918; *ABC of Economics*, 1933; *Jefferson and/or Mussolini*, 1935; *Social Credit: An Impact*, 1935; *Polite Essays*, 1937; *Culture*, 1938 [*Guide to Kulchur*]; *What Is Money For?*, 1939.

LITERARY CRITICISM: *The Spirit of Romance*, 1910; *Instigations*, 1920; *How to Read*, 1931; *The ABC of Reading*, 1934; *Make It New*, 1934.

BIOGRAPHY AND AUTOBIOGRAPHY: *Gaudier-Brzeska*, 1916; *Indiscretions, or Une revue de deux mondes*, 1923.

TRANSLATIONS: *The Sonnets and Ballate of Guido Cavalcanti*, 1912; *Cathay*, 1915 (Translated for the most part from the Chinese of Rihaku, from the notes of Ernest Fenollosa); *Certain Noble Plays of Japan, from the Manuscripts of Ernest Fenollosa*, 1916; *Dialogues of Fontenelle*, 1917; *The Natural Philosophy of Love*, by Remy de Gourmont, 1922; *Confucius: The Great Digest and The Unwobbling Pivot*, 1947; *The Classic Anthology Defined by Confucius*, 1954; Sophocles' *Women of Trachis*, 1957.

LETTERS: *The Letters of Ezra Pound, 1907–1941*, 1950.

Ezra Pound's is a special case in the literary history of our time. One of the most controversial figures in a confused and stormy period, an imitator on the one hand and a brilliant innovator on the other, he has been highly praised and savagely attacked. Certainly no one can doubt his influence on the technique of contemporary verse; there are few poets who have written since the 1920's who have done so without knowledge of the *Cantos*, Pound's tremendous but obscure work in progress. Time alone can tell whether he will survive as a major poet in his own right or as an influential poetry propagandist. However, since his poetry as well as his promotion of literature is discussed widely and freely at the present time, both the man and his work demand, and receive, considerable critical attention.

Ezra (Loomis) Pound was born in Hailey, Idaho, on October 30, 1885, but when he was two he was taken to Pennsylvania by his parents. His mother was a distant relative of Henry Wadsworth Longfellow. A precocious youth, he attended the University of Pennsylvania when he was fifteen but later transferred to Hamilton College, where he received the degree of Ph.B. in 1905. For the next two years he taught Romance languages at the University of Pennsylvania. However, the disciplines of teaching bored him, and after a short time at Wabash College in Indiana he went to Europe in 1908. There he remained, proclaiming that American civilization in general was unbearable, shifting his residence whenever the possibility of a new poetry group appeared, inspiring or attacking other writers while creating on his own. *A Lume Spento*, his first book of poems, was printed in Venice in 1908. *Personae*, his first characteristic book of poems, was published in London in 1909.

Pound was in and out of London until 1920, positively helping such varied writers as T. S. Eliot (who once called him "il miglior fabbro"), William Butler Yeats, and Wyndham Lewis to shape their styles, and for two years serving as London editor of the *Little Review* (1917–1919). During this time successive volumes of his own poetry appeared, all employing Imagist or experimental techniques. Between 1920 and 1924 he lived in Paris, one of the leaders of the expatriate "lost generation" group of writers who congregated there after World War I. In 1924 he went to Italy to live, his long residence at Rapallo broken only by a visit to the United States in 1939. Refusing to leave Italy at the beginning of World War II, he became a radio propagandist for the fascist Italian government. After the war he was imprisoned to stand trial for treason; however, when he was declared insane, he was committed to St. Elizabeth's Hospital in Washington, D. C.

Early in his career Pound demonstrated the intensity and extrasensory foresight of a prophet. He anticipated the fad for things Oriental with his publication of *Cathay*, a free translation into English of verse by the Chinese poet Rihaku. In addition, continuing his scholarly research, begun years before, into medieval literature, especially the Italian and the Provençal, he made free translations of such buried writers as Cavalcanti in *The Sonnets and Ballate of Guido Cavalcanti*, Arnaut Daniel, Sextus Propertius, and others. R. P. Blackmur in his *Language As Gesture* states that Pound is a better poet as a translator than as an originator, for "lacking sufficient substance of his own to maintain an intellectual discipline, he is always better where the discipline of craftsmanship is enough." Certainly this is true of Pound's major opus, a series of original cantos with sources grounded in medieval and modern history, Greek mythology, Chinese culture, and minor classics, which will number about one hundred when finished. In the ninety-five cantos now published there is a juxtaposition of past worlds and the present that reminds one of Eliot's *The Waste Land* (1922). However, here the parallel ends, for the allusions to the past are all to the special past Pound found in his special readings, rather than to a heritage in great works familiar to readers. In addition, in the *Cantos* Pound uses language ideographically, as if the English words could serve the same function as Chinese characters. The result is often unintelligible, but at the same time there are individual lines of great beauty. It was for this work that Pound received the Bollingen Prize in Poetry in 1949, an award which provoked one of the most heated critical battles of the decade.

Pound was probably the best teacher of language of his generation. His encouragement of the early works of others who later became rightfully famous was always just, and what he has written of writing generally, as in his *The ABC of Reading,* is clear and true. (Curiously, outside the field of literature his judgments were twisted to the point of monomania.) It is as a teacher and propagandist that he best served: an odd, wild, gifted man.

In 1958, thanks to the efforts of several poets, among them Eliot, Frost and MacLeish, the charges of treason were dropped, and Pound was allowed to return to Italy, where he and his wife lived at Merano in the Italian Alps.

BIBLIOGRAPHICAL REFERENCES: There is no collected edition of Pound's poetry or prose. All the verse he wishes to preserve, exclusive of the *Cantos,* was printed in *Personae,* 1926; reissued with additional poems, 1949. His major critical writings have been collected in *Literary Essays of Pound,* edited and with an introduction by T. S. Eliot, 1952.

There is as yet no definitive biographical study. The most detailed critical study of his poetry is Hugh Kenner, *The Poetry of Ezra Pound,* 1951. Earlier estimates of his work include T. S. Eliot, *Ezra Pound: His Metric and Poetry,* 1917 (unsigned), and the introduction to *Selected Poems,* 1928; Carl Sandburg, "The Work of Ezra Pound," *Poetry,* VII (1916), 249–257; Conrad Aiken, *Scepticisms,* 1919; and Louis Untermeyer, *American Poetry Since 1900,* 1923. The basic essay for all recent Pound studies is Richard P. Blackmur, "The Masks of Ezra Pound," in *The Double Agent,* 1935. See also F. R. Leavis, *New Bearings in English Poetry,* 1932; Edith Sitwell, *Aspects of Modern Poetry,* 1934; Allen Tate, *Reactionary Essays on Poetry and Ideas,* 1936; Alice S. Admur, *The Poetry of Ezra Pound,* 1936; Babette Deutsch, *Poetry in Our Time,* 1952 (rev. ed., 1956); and H. H. Watts, *Ezra Pound and the Cantos,* 1952. *Examination of Ezra Pound,* edited by Peter Russell, 1950, contains a collection of essays by various hands.

The controversy over the Bollingen Prize in Poetry is aired in two volumes of specialized critical studies: *The Case of Ezra Pound,* edited by Charles Norman, 1948, and *The Case Against the Saturday Review,* edited by the editors of *Poetry,* 1949. The Pound bibliography is constantly proliferating. For recent biography and criticism see Charles Norman, *Ezra Pound,* 1960; William Van O'Connor, *Ezra Pound,* 1963; Donald Davie, *Ezra Pound: Poet as Sculptor,* 1964; Harry Meacham, *The Caged Panther,* 1967 (an account of Pound at St. Elizabeth's); and Noel Stock, *The Life of Ezra Pound,* 1970.

ANTHONY POWELL

Born: London, England
Date: December 21, 1905

Principal Works

NOVELS: *Afternoon Men,* 1931; *Venusberg,* 1932; *From a View to a Death,* 1933; *What's Become of Waring,* 1939.

NOVEL SEQUENCE: *The Music of Time,* including *A Question of Upbringing,* 1951; *A Buyer's Market,* 1952; *The Acceptance World,* 1955; *At Lady Molly's,* 1957; *Casanova's Chinese Restaurant,* 1960; *The Kindly Ones,* 1962; *The Valley of Bones,* 1964; *The Soldier's Art,* 1966; *The Military Philosophers,* 1968; *Books Do Furnish a Room,* 1971.

BIOGRAPHY: *John Aubrey and His Friends,* 1948.

Anthony (Dymoke) Powell is the son of Lieutenant Colonel P. L. W. Powell, of Britain's Welch Regiment. As the child of an army officer, he spent his boyhood in the many places his father was stationed, including Finland. His schooling came at a day school in London, a boarding school in Kent, and Eton, which he entered in 1919. After Eton he went up to Balliol College, Oxford, taking his A.B. in 1926, after which he returned to London and went to work for Duckworth, a publishing company. His first novel, *Afternoon Men,* was published by his employer in 1931. Other novels followed regularly. In 1934 Powell married Lady Violet Georgiana Pakenham, daughter of the 5th Earl of Longford. He left publishing for journalism in 1936, taking employment with the London *Daily Telegraph.* Among other assignments, he had a signed review column in the newspaper. He also became a scenario writer for the motion pictures, working with Warner Brothers in Great Britain. Attracted by the movie industry, he traveled to the United States to work in Hollywood. Being disappointed in his efforts to find suitable employment there, he returned after a brief stay to England.

As a reserve officer, Powell was called to active duty in the British army in 1939, shortly after World War II began. After a year and a half of service with troops as a lieutenant of infantry he was transferred to the Intelligence Corps, serving at the War Office as a liaison officer with the Polish, Belgian, Czechoslovakian, Luxembourg, and French forces. During the war he rose to the rank of major. His war honors include the Order of the White Lion from Czechoslovakia, the Order of Leopold II from Belgium, and the Oaken Crown and Croix de Guerre from Luxembourg. In 1956 he was also honored by his own government with the Commander, Order of the British Empire.

After being released from military service in 1945, at the end of World War II, Powell returned to research on John Aubrey, the celebrated seventeenth century writer, on whose life and work he had been engaged before the war began. His biographical volume, *John Aubrey and His Friends,* appeared in 1948, with an edition of selections from Aubrey's writings appearing the following year. Since 1950 Powell has been working on a sequence of novels he calls *The Music of Time*, with volumes appearing frequently since the first, *A Question of Upbringing*, in 1951. Originally he had contemplated a series of at least six novels; ten have been published, the most recent being *Books Do Furnish a Room* (1971). As a novelist Powell is essentially a realist, portraying the world in which he lives in the twentieth century. His work has enjoyed a healthy popularity among readers in both America and Europe. His *At Lady Molly's* (1957) won the James Tait Black Memorial Prize.

In 1962 Powell accepted the responsibility of being a trustee of Britain's National Portrait Gallery. In 1963 his first novel, *Afternoon Men*, was adapted for the stage by Riccardo Aragno. Although Powell had lived most of his adult life in London, in the early 1950's he acquired a Regency period house called The Chantry, near Frome, Somersetshire, in western England, where he now lives.

BIBLIOGRAPHICAL REFERENCES: Full-length studies include Robert K. Morris, *The Novels of Anthony Powell*, 1968, and John David Russell, *Anthony Powell, A Quintet, Sextet, and War*, 1970. See also Bernard Bergonzi's pamphlet, *Anthony Powell*, 1962, revised 1971; J. Hall, *The Tragic Comedians*, 1963; V. S. Pritchett, *The Working Novelist*, 1965; Arthur Mizener, *The Sense of Life in the Modern Novel*, 1965; Paul West, *The Modern Novel*, 2 vols., 1965; Charles Shapiro, editor, *Contemporary British Novelists*, 1965; and Raymond G. McCall, "Anthony Powell's Gallery," *College English* XXVII (1965), 227–232.

JOHN COWPER POWYS

Born: Shirley, Derbyshire, England
Date: October 8, 1872

Died: Wales
Date: June 17, 1963

Principal Works

NOVELS: *Wood and Stone*, 1915; *Rodmoor*, 1916; *Ducdame*, 1925; *Wolf Solent*, 1929; *A Glastonbury Romance*, 1932; *Weymouth Sands*, 1934; *Jobber Skald*, 1935; *Maiden Castle*, 1936; *Morwyn*, 1937; *Owen Glendower*, 1940; *Porius*, 1951; *The Inmates*, 1952.

SHORT STORIES: *The Owl, the Duck, and—Miss Rowe! Miss Rowe!* 1930.

POEMS: *Odes and Other Poems*, 1896; *Poems*, 1899; *Wolf's-bane*, 1916; *Mandragora*, 1917; *Samphire*, 1922.

ESSAYS AND STUDIES: *Visions and Revisions*, 1915; *Confessions of Two Brothers*, 1916 (with Llewelyn Powys); *Suspended Judgments*, 1916; *The Complex Vision*, 1920; *Psychoanalysis and Morality*, 1923; *The Religion of a Sceptic*, 1925; *The Meaning of Culture*, 1929; *In Defence of Sensuality*, 1930; *Dorothy M. Richardson*, 1931; *A Philosophy of Solitude*, 1933; *The Pleasures of Literature* [*The Enjoyment of Literature*], 1938; *The Art of Growing Old*, 1944; *Dostoievsky*, 1947; *Rabelais*, 1948; *In Spite Of: A Philosophy for Everyman*, 1953; *Atlantis*, 1954.

AUTOBIOGRAPHY: *John Cowper Powys: Autobiography*, 1934.

John Cowper Powys, born in Derbyshire, England, on October 8, 1872, is a member of an extraordinarily artistic family. His father was a minister of the Church of England, his mother was a descendant of the poets William Cowper and John Donne. Although John Cowper Powys is an exceptionally prolific writer, his two brothers, Llewelyn and Theodore Francis, turned out before they died a volume of work almost equal to his own. Of the other eight Powys children, one sister became a novelist and poet, another sister a painter, another brother an architect. All of them shared an inheritance of Celtic imagination.

Powys, graduated from Corpus Christi College, Cambridge, began his career as a lecturer in the United States and Britain. His approach to figures like Carlyle, Ruskin, and Tennyson was peculiarly romantic; he would try to intuit the essential nature of the man about whom he was speaking and would often identify himself with that person. As a result, his literary criticism is emotionally based and his comments frequently reveal more about Powys than they do about the subject of the lecture. Despite this subjective quality, or perhaps because of it, he was a very successful lecturer.

His father having granted him an annuity of sixty pounds, Powys began the risky career of writing. He had been influenced by the pantheism of Wordsworth and the Celtic romanticism of the early Yeats. Soon after his graduation from Cambridge he met Thomas Hardy, who advised him to study the bizarre techniques of Edgar Allan Poe. Consequently, Powys' novels frequently deal with subject matter from the Welsh past that lends itself to a presentation of grotesque and fantastic scenes. *Porius*, for example, exploits fifth century Wales for its Arthurian romance and for the exotic religious rituals of the Druids. His historical novels allow his imagination free rein; as a result they are frequently overloaded and lacking in artistic control. His novels of the present are likely (as in *The Inmates,* the story of a love affair in an insane asylum) to deal with bizarre subjects and characters.

After 1910 a case of ulcers caused Powys frequently to spend his winters in America. In 1928 he settled in the United States, living mostly in New York and Hollywood until he returned to England in 1934.

He lived out his life in Wales, the land in which his imagination almost continually dwelt.

BIBLIOGRAPHICAL REFERENCES: There is only one full-length biographical or critical study devoted to John Cowper Powys alone: H. P. Collins, *John Cowper Powys: Old Earth-man,* 1966. The best source for information about his life and work is his *Autobiography,* supplemented by *Confessions of Two Brothers,* written with Llewelyn Powys, 1916. For studies of his family background and related material see also Richard H. Ward, *The Powys Brothers,* 1935; Louis N. Wilkinson, *Welsh Ambassadors,* 1936, and *The Brothers Powys,* 1947; R. C. Churchill, *The Powys Brothers,* 1962; Kenneth Hopkins, *The Powys Brothers: A Biographical Appreciation,* 1967; John Cowper Powys, "Four Brothers," *Century,* CX (1925), 553–560; and Gilbert E. Govan, "The Powys Family," *Sewanee Review,* XLVI (1938), 74–90.

LLEWELYN POWYS

Born: Dorchester, England
Date: August 13, 1884

Died: Davos Platz, Switzerland
Date: December 2, 1939

Principal Works

ESSAYS AND STUDIES: *Ebony and Ivory*, 1923; *Thirteen Worthies*, 1923; *Black Laughter*, 1924; *The Cradle of God*, 1929; *The Pathetic Fallacy: A Study of Christianity*, 1930; *Impassioned Clay*, 1931; *Now That the Gods Are Dead*, 1932; *Earth Memories*, 1934; *Glory of Life*, 1934; *Damnable Opinions*, 1935; *Dorset Essays*, 1935; *The Twelve Months*, 1936; *Somerset Essays*, 1937; *Rats in the Sacristy*, 1937; *A Baker's Dozen*, 1939; *Swiss Essays*, 1947.

NOVELS: *Apples Be Ripe*, 1930; *Love and Death*, 1939.

TRAVEL SKETCHES AND IMPRESSIONS: *A Pagan's Pilgrimage*, 1931.

AUTOBIOGRAPHY: *Confessions of Two Brothers*, 1916 (with John Cowper Powys); *Skin for Skin*, 1925; *The Verdict of Bridlegoose*, 1926.

BIOGRAPHY: *Henry Hudson*, 1927.

Llewelyn Powys, born in Dorchester, England, August 13, 1884, was the eighth of eleven children of Charles Francis Powys, an Anglican clergyman. Two of his elder brothers, John Cowper and Theodore Francis, became well-known writers.

In spite of his close relationship with his oldest brother, John Cowper, Llewelyn went through Sherborne School and Cambridge, and began to teach school with little thought of becoming a writer. In 1909 he contracted tuberculosis and spent several years in Switzerland. After he had recovered to some extent, he went to Africa to become a stock farmer in Kenya. During his five-year stay in Africa (1914–1919) he began to write. He published two series of essays and sketches about his life in Africa as *Ebony and Ivory* and *Black Laughter*. In 1920 he came to New York, writing stories, articles, and personal essays for various periodicals. While in America, he married Alyse Gregory, managing editor of *The Dial*. His autobiographical observations of America, sparked with a sharp wit, appeared in *The Verdict of Bridlegoose*. Powys' essays covered a great range, any subject from a sensory description of a street to herbalism in the sixteenth century. Despite his wide range of concern, knowledge, and literary allusion, his work has been criticized as too much concerned with trivia about well-known people, too journalistic, or too gossipy.

In 1928 Powys traveled to Palestine; his work thereafter demonstrated considerably more substance. The account of the trip to Palestine, *A Pagan's Pilgrimage*, shows an interest in an appreciation of theology and biblical tradition from the point of view of a non-believer. Powys followed this book with *Impassioned Clay*, which attempts to survey man's history and constant search for comfort in the supernatural. Powys, calling upon youth to be strong and free from the need for spiritual comfort and religious systems, referred to this book as the "Devil's handbook."

In his last years, Powys' tuberculosis forced him to live in Switzerland. He kept writing, ever more seriously calling for independence from religion and opposition to Nazism. His most comprehensive work, published posthumously as *Love and Death*, is an "imaginary autobiography" in which he attempted to get at the meaning of all his experience. After a long illness he died at Davos Platz, Switzerland, on December 2, 1939.

Powys' work found a devoted audience, especially in America. For many readers, his elaborate and allusive style enriched the value of his observations. For others, his style seemed too elaborate, pretentious, and falsely poetic. Between these extremes, however, it is generally agreed that he always maintained a great range of observations and a genuinely independent sense of judgment.

BIBLIOGRAPHICAL REFERENCES: The fullest biographical study is Malcolm Elwin, *Life of Llewelyn Powys*, 1946. Other books and articles dealing with the Powys' family are listed in the bibliography of John Cowper Powys. See also R. L. Blackmore, ed., *Advice to a Young Poet: The Correspondence between Llewelyn Powys and Kenneth Hopkins*, 1969.

T. F. POWYS

Born: Shirley, Derbyshire, England
Date: December 20, 1875

Died: Sturminster Newton, England
Date: November 27, 1953

Principal Works

NOVELS: *Black Bryony,* 1923; *Mark Only,* 1924; *Mr. Tasker's Gods,* 1925; *Mockery Gap,* 1925; *Innocent Birds,* 1926; *Mr. Weston's Good Wine,* 1927; *Kindness in a Corner,* 1930; *Unclay,* 1931; *Make Thyself Many,* 1935; *Goat Green,* 1937.

SHORT STORIES: *The Left Leg,* 1923; *Feed My Swine,* 1926; *A Strong Girl,* 1926; *A Stubborn Tree,* 1926; *What Lack I Yet?,* 1927; *The Rival Pastors,* 1927; *The Dewpond,* 1928; *The House with the Echo,* 1928; *Fables,* 1929 (reissued as *No Painted Plumage*); *Christ in the Cupboard,* 1930; *The Key of the Field,* 1930; *Uriah on the Hill,* 1930; *The White Paternoster,* 1930; *The Only Penitant,* 1931; *Uncle Dottery,* 1931; *When Thou Wast Naked,* 1931; *The Two Thieves,* 1932; *The Tithe Barn,* 1932; *Captain Patch,* 1935; *Bottle's Path and Other Stories,* 1946; *God's Eyes A-Twinkle,* 1947.

ESSAYS AND STUDIES: *An Interpretation of Genesis,* 1908; *The Soliloquy of a Hermit,* 1916.

Of the three Powys brothers distinguished in literature—John Cowper, Theodore Francis, and Llewelyn—the second, though not the most famous, was without doubt the one with the most original genius. T. F. Powys, whether owing to some occult Cymric strain or to some chance of breeding, may be numbered among those writers to whose narrative talent is added a mystical insight. Born in Derbyshire on December 20, 1875, and educated at private schools, he had reached the age of forty-seven before his first volume of fiction appeared; but he had practiced his craft in silence for many years. In general he may be grouped with such writers as Violet Paget, Lord Dunsany, Algernon Blackwood, Kenneth Grahame, and Arthur Machen, all of whom drew inspiration from the hypothesis that nature is tenanted by animistic forces. The Edwardian decade and after was a great period of haunted literature, as much an age of tales about fauns, banshees, and goblins as it was of social-protest novels and comic-opera romances. This was the period when Powys began to write.

Unlike those of his contemporaries who, in the tradition of Celtic folklore, contrasted the normal human world with a realm of supernatural creatures, Powys depicted an inward haunting, the presence of the cosmic powers of good and evil in man himself. His human characters are almost incarnations, and hence they often have an allegorical quality: in *Unclay* the central figure, John Death, is Death; in *Mr. Weston's Good Wine* Mr. Weston is God. But Powys always emphasized human traits; his personages seem as homely and local as the rustic Dorset villages through which they move.

Powys' technique arose from his acute perception of nature's unseen powers. It would be misleading to speak of "possession," or of "immanent spirits," or to regard him as an ordinary pantheist. Such terms imply a dualism in which the material and the spiritual, however intermingled, remain distinguishable. Powys conceived rather a complete, monistic identification of all nature, human and external, with the passionate intelligence of a Creator responsible alike for beauty and for pain. Powys' insistence on the truth of matter explains the occasional elements of horror, and even of foulness, in his stories.

His philosophical essays, *An Interpretation of Genesis* and *The Soliloquy of a Hermit*, set forth the ideas that later became visible in his fiction. Powys, after his marriage in 1905, went to reside in the small Dorset community of Sturminster Newton, staying in comparative seclusion there until his death on November 27, 1953.

BIBLIOGRAPHICAL REFERENCES: The only full-length study is H. Coombes, *T. F. Powys*, 1960. The best critical article on T. F. Powys is Donald MacCampbell, "The Art of T. F. Powys," *Sewanee Review*, XLII (1934), 460–473. For background studies of the Powys family and related materials see the bibliography of John Cowper Powys.

WILLIAM HICKLING PRESCOTT

Born: Salem, Massachusetts
Date: May 4, 1796

Died: Salem
Date: January 28, 1859

Principal Works

HISTORY: *History of Ferdinand and Isabella*, 1837; *History of the Conquest of Mexico*, 1843; *History of the Conquest of Peru*, 1847.

When Washington Irving decided to write the history of Columbus and the Spaniards in the New World, he found the field already occupied by William Hickling Prescott, son of an eminent lawyer and a graduate of Harvard University, class of 1814. After considerable travel in Europe, Prescott had abandoned the idea of following in his father's footsteps and decided to become a writer specializing in historical narratives.

Despite an accident of his college days that had blinded him in one eye and left him only limited vision in the other, he devoted himself assiduously to research in preparation for his chosen career. Foreign works were read to him and he wrote on a frame for the blind, producing in 1837, after ten years of toil, his monumental *History of Ferdinand and Isabella*. At regular intervals thereafter he issued multiple-volume works that described in colorful and dramatic detail, reminiscent of Sir Walter Scott, the Spanish struggle for the dominance of Latin America. He considered his greatest accomplishment to be *History of the Conquest of Mexico*. Its companion work is *History of the Conquest of Peru*. To Prescott, history was primarily the vivid account of heroic figures, such as Cortez and Montezuma; in spite of his scholarly mastery of his sources he was not a writer of philosophic depth or scientific thoroughness. In 1858, while at work on the third volume of his *History of Philip II*, he suffered an apoplectic stroke. He died in Salem on January 28, 1859, the town in which he had been born on May 4, 1796.

BIBLIOGRAPHICAL REFERENCES: The standard edition is the Montezuma Edition of *The Works of William H. Prescott*, edited by Wilfred H. Munro, 22 vols., 1904. Prescott's great-grandson, Roger Wolcott, edited *The Correspondence of William Hickling Prescott, 1833–1847*, 1925—a work supplemented by Clara L. Penny, ed., *Prescott: Unpublished Letters to Gayangos in the Library of the Hispanic Society of America*, 1927. Useful one-volume editions are the *Conquest of Mexico* and the *Conquest of Peru*, issued together in the Modern Library, 1936, and *William Hickling Prescott: Representative Selections*, edited by William Charvat and Michael Kraus, American Writers Series, 1943.

The standard biography is George Ticknor, *Life of William Hickling Prescott*, 1864. See also H. F. Cline, C. H. Gardiner, and Charles Gibson, *William Hickling Prescott: A Memorial*, 1959. The best brief biographical sketch is that by Roger B. Merriman in the *Dictionary of American Biography*; the best critical sketch is the introduction to Charvat and Kraus, *Prescott: Representative Selections*, 1943. See also Rollo Ogden, *William Hickling Prescott*, American Men of Letters Series, 1904; Harry T. Peck, *William Hickling Prescott*, English Men of Letters Series, 1905; and Van Wyck Brooks, *The Flowering of New England*, 1936.

THE ABBÉ PRÉVOST

Born: Hesdin, Artois, Flanders
Date: April 1, 1697

Died: Chantilly, France
Date: November 23, 1763

Principal Works

NOVELS: *Mémoires et aventures d'un homme de qualité*, 1728–1731 (*Memoirs and Adventures of a Man of Quality*); *L'Histoire du Chevalier des Grieux et de Manon Lescaut*, 1731 (*The History of the Chevalier des Grieux and Manon Lescaut*); *Le Philosophe anglais, ou Histoire de Monsieur Cleveland, fils naturel de Cromwell*, 1731–1739 (*The English Philosopher, or the History of Mr. Cleveland, Natural Son of Cromwell*); *Le Doyen de Killerine*, 1735–1740 (*The Dean of Coleraine*); *Histoire d'une Grecque moderne*, 1740 (*The History of a Modern Greek Lady*).

MISCELLANEOUS: *Histoire de Marguerite d'Anjou, Reine d'Angleterre*, 1740; *Histoire de Guillaume le Conquérant*, 1742; *Histoire générale des voyages*, 1745–1770; *Lettres de Mentor à un jeune seigneur*, 1764 (*Letters of Mentor to a Young Nobleman*).

Antoine François Prévost, who called himself "Prévost d'Exiles," and who is generally referred to as the Abbé Prévost, was born on April 1, 1697, at the village of Hesdin, in Artois, Flanders. Influenced by his masters at the Jesuit school there, he entered upon a novitiate in Paris in 1713, at the age of sixteen. After two years he proceeded to the Collège de La Flèche, but for reasons now unknown he stayed only one year. Enlisting as a soldier, he completed a term of service, following which he applied, without success, for readmission to his novitiate. It is said that he was tricked by the military into re-enlisting, and that he deserted and escaped to Holland. At length he made his way home. Conjecturally, he soon thereafter met the girl who was to become the heroine of his most famous prose romance, *The History of the Chevalier des Grieux and Manon Lescaut*, but the factual basis of the tale is obscure. Whatever may have occurred, the issue was tragic, and in 1720 Prévost revived his earlier intention of becoming a churchman. He first went to the monastic community of St. Maur at the Abbey of Jumièges, and, being taken into the priesthood six years later at St. Germer de Flaix, he continued with the Benedictines until 1728. In that year, while at the abbey of St.-Germain-des-Prés, he abandoned the order, very much as he had abandoned the army, and took ship for London.

He remained in England some months, working on *Memoirs and Adventures of a Man of Quality*, of which *Manon Lescaut* was the seventh volume, and on *Cleveland*, another long, episodic romance full of swashbuckling. He spent the years between 1729 and 1733 in Holland, where he wrote a few translations. Various improbable legends became attached to his name in these years. After another sojourn in London, he obtained forgiveness of the Benedictines and was reinstated. Having no great fondness for the conventual life, he secured office outside the monasteries and devoted much time to literature and gallantry. In 1754 he received preferment as Abbé of St. Georges de Gesnes. He died near Chantilly on November 23, 1763.

Prévost was on friendly terms with both Voltaire and Rousseau. He translated John Dryden's *All for Love*, Frances Sheridan's *Memoirs of Miss Sidney Bidulph*, and Samuel Richardson's novels (though doubt has been raised as to his responsibility for the version of *Pamela*) and converted them into shallow narratives of rapid action. His fame rests on his contribution to French romantic prose.

BIBLIOGRAPHICAL REFERENCES: The standard biography is V. Schroeder, *L'Abbé Prévost, sa vie, ses romans*, 1898. See also Henry Harrisse, *L'Abbé Prévost, histoire de sa vie et de ses œuvres*, 1896; and Henri Roddier, *L'Abbé Prévost, l'homme et l'œuvre*, 1955. A more specialized study is Paul Hazard, *Études critiques sur Manon Lescaut*, 1929. See also Berenice Cooper, *The Abbé Prévost and the Modern Reader*, Transactions of the Wisconsin Academy of Sciences, Arts and Letters, XLII, 1953, and *The Abbé Prévost and the Jesuits, ibid.*, XLIII, 1954; R. L. Frautschi, "Manon Lescaut: The Exemplary Attitude," *French Review*, XXXVII (1964), 288–295; and Stephen G. Nichols, "The Double Register of Time and Character in *"Manon Lescaut,"* Romance Notes, VII (1966), 149–154.

REYNOLDS PRICE

Born: Macon, North Carolina
Date: February 1, 1933

Principal Works

NOVELS: *A Long and Happy Life*, 1962; *A Generous Man*, 1966; *Love and Work*, 1968; *Permanent Errors*, 1970.
SHORT STORIES: *The Names and Faces of Heroes*, 1963.

Edward Reynolds Price was born and reared in North Carolina, a place that has provided a setting for much of his fiction. After graduating *summa cum laude* from Duke University in 1955, he attended Merton College, Oxford, as a Rhodes Scholar. In 1958 he returned to Duke University where he teaches English. Price's first novel, *A Long and Happy Life*, was widely praised, winning the William Faulkner and Sir Walter Raleigh awards. His remarkable ear for dialect, and his ability to describe familiar Southern settings with freshness and conviction, make memorable the sensitive innocence of Rosacoke Mustian, whose search for love is rendered without descending to the sentimentality such a story risks.

Price's short stories, collected in *The Names and Faces of Heroes*, are also concerned with the search for love, especially as it is embodied in the relationships between fathers and sons. His dense, almost poetic style is itself a source of narrative power.

More recently, Price has extended his range somewhat; *Love and Work*, for example, is a brief but absorbing exploration of young Thomas Eborn's attempts to reconcile his life as a college teacher, his rural Southern past, and his tendency to use writing as an escape from human contact.

BIBLIOGRAPHICAL REFERENCES: There are as yet no long studies devoted to Price. See John W. Stevenson, "The Faces of Reynolds Price's Short Fiction," *Studies in Short Fiction*, III (1966), 300–306; Daniel R. Barnes, "The Names and Faces of Reynolds Price," *Kentucky Review*, II, no. 2 (1968), 76–91; Clayton L. Eichelberger, "Reynolds Price, 'A Banner in Defeat,'" *Journal of Popular Culture*, I (1968), 410–417; and Frederick J. Hoffman, *The Art of Southern Fiction*, 1967. Reviews of the novels also contain valuable discussion.

J. B. PRIESTLEY

Born: Bradford, Yorkshire, England
Date: 1894

Principal Works

NOVELS AND TALES: *Adam in Moonshine*, 1927; *The Good Companions*, 1929; *Farthing Hall* 1929 (with Hugh Walpole); *Angel Pavement*, 1930; *Faraway*, 1932; *Wonder Hero*, 1933; *The Doomsday Men*, 1938; *Blackout in Gretley*, 1942; *Bright Day*, 1946; *Jenny Villiers*, 1947; *Festival at Farbridge*, 1951 [*Festival*]; *The Thirty-first of June*, 1961; *The Shape of Sleep*, 1962; *Sir Michael and Sir George*, 1964; *It's an Old Country*, 1967.

PLAYS: *Dangerous Corner*, 1932; *The Roundabout*, 1933; *Eden End*, 1934; *Laburnum Grove*, 1934; *Time and the Conways*, 1937; *Music at Night*, 1938; *The Plays of J. B. Priestley*, Vols. I-III, 1948-1950.

ESSAYS AND STUDIES: *George Meredith*, 1926; *Thomas Love Peacock*, 1927; *Apes and Angels*, 1928; *English Humour*, 1929; *English Journey*, 1934; *Midnight on the Desert*, 1937; *Rain Upon Gadshill*, 1939; *Thoughts in the Wilderness*, 1957; *Literature and Western Man*, 1960; *Charles Dickens: A Pictorial Biography*, 1961; *Margin Released: A Writer's Reminiscences and Reflections*, 1962; *The Prince of Pleasure and His Regency*, 1969; *The Edwardians*, 1970; *Anton Chekhov*, 1970; *Victorian Heyday*, 1972.

J(ohn) B(oynton) Priestley was born in Bradford, England, in 1894. After secondary schooling at Bradford, he enlisted in the army at the beginning of World War I, served with the army in France, and was invalided out as an officer. Convalescing, he entered journalism by writing for the *Yorkshire Observer*. He entered Cambridge in 1919, and established a reputation for himself as essayist and critic before receiving his degree from Cambridge. His literary criticisms and reviews had made Priestley a well-known figure before he started his career as a novelist with *Adam in Moonshine* in 1927.

Priestley's first major success in fiction was *The Good Companions*, which appeared in 1929. It enjoyed a very large success in both Britain and America. During 1929 he collaborated with his friend Hugh Walpole to write a humorous romance, *Farthing Hall*, which was published in the same year. Similar in appeal to *The Good Companions*, *Angel Pavement*, a long romantic novel, English in tradition, appeared in 1930. Other representative novels include *Wonder Hero*; *The Doomsday Men*, an adventure; *Blackout in Gretley*, a story of and for wartime; *Bright Day*, another war novel; *Jenny Villiers*, a story of the theater; and *Festival at Farbridge*, published in America as *Festival*.

Mr. Priestley has been three times married: to Miss Patricia Tempest, who died in 1925, to Miss Mary Wyndham Lewis, and to Miss Jacquetta Hawkes, with whom he has collaborated on the travel sketches appearing in *Journey Down a Rainbow* (1955).

BIBLIOGRAPHICAL REFERENCES: For biography and criticism see David Hughes, *J. B. Priestley*, 1958; Gareth Lloyd Evans, *J. B. Priestley, the Dramatist*, 1964; and Susan Cooper, *J. B. Priestley: Portrait of an Artist*, 1970. See also Edward Shanks, "Mr. Priestley's Novels," *London Mercury*, XXVI (1932), 240–247; T. Frederick,

"J. B. Priestley," *English Journal,* XXVII (1938), 371–380; and R. W. Whidden, "Priestley and His Novels," *Queen's Quarterly,* XLVIII (1941), 57–62.

MATTHEW PRIOR

Born: Wimborne Minster, England
Date: July 21, 1664

Died: Wimpole, England
Date: September 18, 1721

Principal Works

POEMS: *The Hind and Panther Transvers'd to the Story of the Country Mouse and the City Mouse,* 1687; *An English Ballad,* 1695; *Carmen Saeculare,* 1700; *Poems on Several Occasions,* 1709; *Lyric Poems,* 1741.
PROSE: *Miscellaneous Works,* 1740.

Matthew Prior, poet and diplomat, was born at Wimborne Minster, England, on July 21, 1664. He distinguished himself while still a child as a remarkable classical student, and was sent first to Westminster School and then to Cambridge. His poetry and his character attracted the notice of patrons, particularly Lord Dorset. Prior's satires pleased his friends, and his achievements as a diplomat pleased the Court. He became employed in a variety of important situations: secretary to the embassy at The Hague; secretary to the negotiations of the peace of Ryswick (1697); secretary to the embassy in France (1698); undersecretary of state (1699); member of Parliament (1701).

Prior's literary work reflected not only the classical interest of the early eighteenth century, but the very specific interest of that age in the art of satire. He won the admiration and friendship of Jonathan Swift for his keen satires on poets and politicians. He shared Swift's Tory sympathies, and while that party was in power had a good deal to do with government affairs in England. After 1714, however, the year the Tory Party was replaced by the Whigs, Prior was removed from political office. He was, according to the ferocious political practices of his time, impeached and jailed. While in custody he wrote his most important long poem, "Alma; or, the Progress of the Mind," a discussion of humanity and its motivations. The tenor is fundamentally skeptical, a tone perhaps to be expected from a man writing while in prison. After 1717, when he was released, he was able to devote himself until his death to those things that mattered greatly to the eighteenth century: reading, writing, and good living. He was particularly fond of the last, and was known as a *bon vivant* of formidable capacities.

During his lifetime Prior was widely praised for his satire and for his pastoral poems. He himself stated that poetry was not his principal vocation; he preferred to think of himself as a man of affairs. Poetry was, he noted, the product of his leisure hours. Modern critics believe that Prior was too modest, and they are ready to grant him qualities that he and his contemporaries seem to have ignored: a high degree of intellectual power and the skill to adapt classical themes and genres to the poetry of his own age. Perhaps the most significant of Prior's poetic achievements was his reinstatement of the colloquial mode in verse; few other poets were able to take such resolutely commonplace words and make them the substance of art. He experimented in couplets and quatrains, in parodies and pastorals, and proved that, far from being wholly imitative, the early eighteenth century had its own share of literary experimentalists.

BIBLIOGRAPHICAL REFERENCES: The best edition of Prior's literary works is that by H. Bunker Wright and Monroe K. Spears, *The Literary Works of Matthew Prior,* 1959. A study of the life is C. K. Eves, *Matthew Prior, Poet and Diplomatist,* 1939. One of the best general studies is R. W. Ketton-Cremer, *Matthew Prior,* 1957. See also W. P. Barrett, "Matthew Prior's Alma," *Modern Language Review,* XXVII (1932); Monroe Spears, "Some Ethical Aspects of Prior's Poetry," *Studies in Philology,* XLV (1948), 606–630.

FREDERIC PROKOSCH

Born: Madison, Wisconsin
Date: May 17, 1909

Principal Works

NOVELS: *The Asiatics,* 1935; *The Seven Who Fled,* 1937; *Night of the Poor,* 1939; *The Skies of Europe,* 1941; *The Conspirators,* 1943; *Age of Thunder,* 1945; *The Idols of the Cave,* 1946; *Storm and Echo,* 1948; *Nine Days to Mukalla,* 1953; *A Tale for Midnight,* 1955; *Ballad of Love,* 1960; *The Seven Sisters,* 1962; *The Dark Dancer,* 1964; *The Wreck of the Cassandra,* 1966; *The Missolonghi Manuscript,* 1968.

POEMS: *The Assassins,* 1936; *The Carnival,* 1938; *Death at Sea,* 1940; *Chosen Poems,* 1944.

Frederic Prokosch was born at Madison, Wisconsin, May 17, 1909. His father, Edouard P. Prokosch, was a distinguished philologist and Sterling Professor of Linguistics at Yale. His mother, Mathilde Dapprich Prokosch, was a concert pianist. Both parents were Austrian. Since the family traveled considerably, the boy was educated at schools in Wisconsin, Pennsylvania, New York, Texas, Connecticut, England, Austria, France, and Germany. He attended Haverford College and was graduated at the top of his class in 1926. He received his M.A. degree from Haverford in 1928.

Prokosch began his graduate work for the Ph.D. in English Literature at the University of Pennsylvania and was awarded the degree in 1932 after further work at Yale University. His thesis subject, based upon a study of pseudo-Chaucerian manuscripts, was entitled "Chaucerian Apocrypha." From 1931–33 he taught at Yale, and continued there as a research fellow for two more years.

In 1935 Prokosch's first novel, *The Asiatics,* met an encouraging critical reception. His extensive academic background, together with experience in travel and a poetic and philosophic temperament, yielded a rare kind of book for a writer of that period, a book which differed from realistic novels with American settings in concerning itself with Asiatic scenes and philosophic attitudes. This peculiar and effective combination became characteristic of most of his work. His book of poems, *The Assassins,* published the following year, showed that he was a capable writer in more than one dimension.

During the academic year 1936–37 Prokosch taught at New York University and then, as a Guggenheim Fellow, he continued his work at Cambridge University. His best-known book, *The Seven Who Fled,* appeared in 1937 as the winner of the Harper Novel Award. The story of seven European refugees traveling from Central Asia to Shanghai and critically surveying their lives on the way provided the author with ample apportunity to express his pessimistic, anti-materialistic point of view. Once again he followed a prose work with a volume of poetry, *The Carnival,* in 1938. A third volume of poems, *Death at Sea,* appeared two years later, and the following year, 1941, he received the Harriet Monroe Lyric Prize from *Poetry* magazine.

During World War II Prokosch worked abroad for the Office of War Information, spending two years (1943-1944) as an attaché in the American Legation in Stockholm. After the war he went to Rome on a Fulbright Scholarship.

During his college days and afterward Prokosch developed championship skill in tennis and squash; he was squash champion of Connecticut in 1933, and he won the squash rackets championship of France in 1939, the championship of Sweden in 1944.

Although some critics have charged Prokosch with being decadently romantic, arguing that by his preoccupation with Oriental and African settings he has neglected the realities of life in favor of travel fantasies, others have found in his novels and poems a careful craftmanship and a poetic sense which give them literary stature. In addition, his poetry and fiction represent an attempt to portray and probe into the intellectual and spiritual malaise characteristic of this century. His poems particularly reflect a sincere preoccupation with the dark state of the world. Most of his novels follow the experiences of a small group of perplexed Westerners traveling through new countries and thereby acquiring new perspectives and insights. An underlying serious intent saves his novels from the merely exotic class. Of his more recent novels, *The Missolonghi Manuscript* received, perhaps, the best critical reception. The "inner story" of the book purports to be a journal kept by Lord Byron and discovered by an American professor who is a specialist in the Romantic era. The book was praised for its sensitive probing of the "Byron personality" and for its historical accuracy. The other novels written during the 'sixties did not fare so well at the hands of the critics.

Prokosch now makes his home in Paris.

BIBLIOGRAPHICAL REFERENCES: There is no full-length study available. For brief critical studies see Dayton Kohler, "Frederic Prokosch," *English Journal*, XXXII (1943), 413–419; and Richard C. Carpenter, "The Novels of Frederic Prokosch," *College English*, XVIII (1957), 261–267.

SEXTUS PROPERTIUS

Born: Assisi, Italy
Date: 50–48 B.C.(?)

Died: Unknown
Date: 16 B.C.–A.D. 2(?)

Principal Works

POEMS: *Elegies*, I, 26 B.C.(?); II, 24–23 B.C.(?); III, 22–21 B.C.(?); IV not earlier than 16 B.C.

Sextus Propertius was born in the province of Umbria, probably in the town of Assisi. Both his birth and death dates are conjectural. Judging from a few bits of evidence in his poetry and in the few contemporary remarks made about him, however, we can with some confidence assume he was born between 48 and 50 B.C. As for his death, we can only say he died after 16 B.C. (some of the poems in his last book of elegies mention events that occurred that year) and before A.D. 2, when Ovid speaks of him in language appropriate only to one already dead. The maximum length of his life, then, could have been fifty-two years, though it was probably shorter.

Propertius was born into a family of equestrian rank. While still a young child he lost his father, and his patrimony was considerably diminished when some of his family's land was confiscated in the great distribution of land to the veterans of Octavian and Antony in 41 and 40 B.C. As a youth he was destined by his mother to study law, but very quickly he turned to poetry. Soon after he had put on the toga of manhood, he fell in love with one Lycinna. But two years later, when he was about twenty, he met and fell in love with Cynthia.

Cynthia's real name was Hostia. She was a high-class prostitute or courtesan who had her own elaborate private establishment—she had eight personal slaves. She lived by pleasing wealthy men. Cynthia was the great passion of Propertius' life, and was the most important subject of his poetry. Their affair, as we see it in the poetry, was tempestuous, marked by mutual infidelities and recrimination, and lasted about five years, at the end of which time Propertius finally broke with her (probably before 21 B.C.). Cynthia died before 16 B.C., and Propertius' fourth and last book of elegies mentions her death. As for the poet's life after his rupture with Cynthia, we know nothing. He may have married and had children, however, since Pliny the Younger (A.D. 62–113) says that Passennus Paullus, a poet, claimed Propertius as an ancestor. Paullus was a resident of Assisi, where an inscription containing his name has been found.

Propertius left four books of elegies. The first, probably published about 26 B.C. is almost wholly concerned with Cynthia. It was a great success and opened the way for the poet to enter the circle of Maecenas, the great Roman patron of letters, and Augustus' unofficial propaganda minister. As a member of Maecenas' group, Propertius became acquainted with Horace, who did not like him. The younger poet Ovid, however, knew and respected Propertius. Book II of the elegies was published about 24 or 23 B.C., and book III about 22 or 21 B.C. Book IV, we know for reasons mentioned above, was published not earlier than 16 B.C.

BIBLIOGRAPHICAL REFERENCES: There are two excellent annotated modern editions: *The Elegies of Propertius,* edited by H. E. Butler and E. A. Barber, 1933, and *Propertius: Elegies,* edited by W. A. Camps, 4 vols., 1961–1967. There are verse translations by Constance Carrier, 1963, and A. E. Watts, 1966. Of special interest are Ezra Pound's versions of several of the elegies in *Homage to Sextus Propertius,* 1934.

Critical discussions may be found in D. R. Shackleton Bailey, *Propertiana,* 1956; E. H. W. Meyerstein, *The Elegies of Propertius,* 1935; J. P. Boucher, *Études sur Properce,* 1965; J. P. Sullivan, *Ezra Pound and Sextus Propertius, A Study in Creative Translation,* 1964; Clarence W. Mendell, *Latin Poetry: The New Poets and The Augustans,* 1965; W. Y. Sellar, *The Roman Poets of the Augustan Age,* 2 vols., 1892; K. P. Harrington, *The Roman Elegiac Poets,* 1914; Moses Hadas, *A History of Latin Literature,* 1952; Frank O. Copley, *Latin Literature,* 1969; and Archibald W. Allen, "Sunt Qui Propertium Malint," *Critical Essays on Roman Literature, Elegy and Lyric,* edited by John P. Sullivan, 1962.

MARCEL PROUST

Born: Paris, France
Date: July 10, 1871

Died: Paris
Date: November 18, 1922

Principal Works

novels: *A la recherche du temps perdu*, 1913–1927 (*Remembrance of Things Past*), in seven parts: *Du Côté de chez Swann*, 1913 (*Swann's Way*); *A l'ombre des jeunes filles en fleurs*, 1918 (*Within a Budding Grove*); *Le Côté de Guermantes*, 1921 (*The Guermantes Way*); *Sodome et Gomorrhe*, 1921 (*Cities of the Plain*); *La Prisonnière*, 1923 (*The Captive*); *Albertine disparu*, 1925 (*The Sweet Cheat Gone*); *Le Temps retrouvé*, 1927 (*The Past Recaptured*); *Jean Santeuil*, 1951.

essays and studies: *Les Plaisirs et les jours*, 1896 (*Pleasures and Days*); *Pastiches et mélanges*, 1919; *Contre Sainte-Beuve*, 1954 (*Against Sainte-Beuve*).

Marcel Proust was born in Paris on July 10, 1871. His father was a successful physician, wealthy enough to provide abundantly for his family. He married a Jewess who was a devoted mother to her sons, but since the younger Robert was robust and quite normal, she gave special attention to the weaker Marcel. Until the age of nine, Marcel lived a normal if sheltered life. Then a violent attack of asthma increased his dependence on his mother. A very strong attachment between them grew up and colored the rest of Marcel's life.

In spite of his physical weakness Marcel went to school fairly regularly, and in the Lycée Condorcet excelled in philosophy and composition. His schoolmates recognized his ability. The chief contributor to a precocious periodical put out by the most intellectual members of his class, he made enduring friendships among them. At the age of seventeen his formal schooling ended, but even before this time Proust had been visiting the literary salons. He was handsome and witty and became a favorite of the famous. Among the men of letters he met were the younger Dumas, Renan, Halévy, and Anatole France. He wrote short pieces which won him a kind of reputation as a precious dilettante, and his gift for mimicry assured him a place in the most brilliant salons. This phase of his life was interrupted in 1889 when he was called up for military service. He ranked seventy-third in a company of seventy-four. At the end of his year of service he returned to Paris, quite content to live on a generous allowance from his parents. To please his father, he made some attempt to prepare for a profession, even reading law for a while. Then by means of an examination, he was appointed honorary attaché at the Mazarine library. He served several years, but his work was only nominal; he frequently took long leaves on the plea that he was engaged in urgent writing. His first book, a slender volume of diverse pieces called *Pleasures and Days* appeared in 1896.

Toward the end of the 1890's the Dreyfus affair, with its sinister overtones of anti-Semitism, rocked France. To his credit, Proust took an active role in the agitation to clear Captain Dreyfus, to some extent because he himself was part Jewish. In 1903 his father died, and the family was further disrupted by Robert's marriage. Proust's health became worse; his bouts with asthma were appallingly severe, and he went out only infrequently. By 1905 he had recovered sufficiently to accompany his mother on a trip to Evian, but their holiday was cut short by Mme. Proust's illness. He brought her home to die.

From 1905 until his own death in 1922 Proust lived as an invalid, leaving his bed only at intervals, morbidly conscious of his wasted youth, unable to surmount the melancholy of the loss of his mother. True, he had written one book, translated several of Ruskin's works into French, contributed to periodicals, and worked secretly on a novel, but he felt himself capable of more serious work. And indeed he was. Between 1906 and 1913 he finished the plan of what has been called the greatest novel of the century, *Remembrance of Things Past*, and completed the first part, *Swann's Way*, published in 1913; the succeeding six parts (three published posthumously) were written between debilitating asthmatic spells and bronchial attacks.

In view of Proust's personality and health, his achievement is remarkable. Most of his productive years after 1905 were spent propped up in bed, the air thick with vapors to ease his breathing, the windows closed and shuttered. He always had his linen warmed before putting it on, and he habitually wore numerous woolen waistcoats. He left the house only after sundown on the occasions when he was well enough to get up, muffled in a heavy overcoat even in summer, and carrying an umbrella. From time to time he invited in a few friends who dined sumptuously around his bed on chicken and beer. On rarer occasions he dined alone late at night at the Ritz, swathed in fur coat and scarf, his hands covered with dirty white gloves, surrounded by obsequious waiters whom he tipped extravagantly.

Although he retained the friendship of many women, and although he several times made attempts at love affairs, he felt himself incapable of love for women; the theme of homosexuality clouded his life and found expression in parts of his novel. Balancing this inversion is the fact that all sorts of people were attracted to him, and he was lavishly generous to anyone in distress.

The publication of *Swann's Way* was little noticed; in fact, Proust had to bring it out at his own expense. Even so perceptive a critic as Gide could see little merit in it. The second volume, delayed by the war, was almost equally unnoticed for a time by the public, but a number of critics saw the great merit of the work. Léon Daudet especially was convinced of its greatness, and thanks largely to his efforts, Proust was awarded the Prix Goncourt at the age of forty-seven.

At last Proust was famous. He enjoyed briefly the letters that poured in and the homage of friends and admirers, but he kept on working. Proofs were revised and rewritten until the margins were covered and the edges tattered. Before his death in Paris on November 18, 1922, he completed the vast work, a monument to his genius.

Remembrance of Things Past is a search for lost days, an evocation of mood and emotion. It is also a resigned acknowledgement that time is a destroyer, that the past is dead. In form the novel is an innovation—it is built on recurring themes of people, loves, ambitions, frustrations. It is in large part autobiographical, and Proust's circle furnished models for many of the characters. In spite of unconventional sentences and long sections without paragraph breaks, Proust was a meticulous craftsman, detailed and realistic in his descriptions. In addition to its intensely personal dissection, the work is a canvas of social history.

As artist and innovator, Proust is unique. As a person he was weak, abnormal, handicapped. In comparison his novel becomes a more astonishing feat. Since it continues increasingly to attract critical attention, its place in world literature seems assured.

Shortly after World War II Bernard de Fallois, French scholar, discovered among Proust's notebooks and unclassified manuscripts two previously unknown early works, the apprentice and unfinished novel, *Jean Santeuil*, and an important critical study, *Contre Sainte-Beuve*. These works throw considerable new light on Proust's literary activities and his development as a writer.

BIBLIOGRAPHICAL REFERENCES: The definitive biography is George D. Painter, *Proust*, Vol. I, 1959, Vol. II, 1965, which contains an extensive bibliography. A useful general study in André Maurois, *À la recherche de Marcel Proust*, 1949 (English translation, *Proust: Portrait of a Genius*). For biographical and critical studies in French see Robert de Billy, *Marcel Proust: Lettres et conversations*, 1930; Ramon Fernandez, *Proust*, 1930; Jacques Bret, *Marcel Proust: Étude critique*, 1946; Edmond Kinds, *Marcel Proust*, 1947; François Mauriac, *Du côté de chez Proust*, 1947 (Proust's Way); in English, Clive Bell, *Proust*, 1929; Derrick Leon, *Introduction to Marcel Proust*, 1940; Harold March, *The Two Worlds of Marcel Proust*, 1948; F. C. Green, *The Mind of Proust*, 1949; and Walter A. Strauss, *Proust and Literature: The Novelist as Critic*, 1957.

See also Joseph Wood Krutch, *Five Masters*, 1931; Edmund Wilson, *Axel's Castle*, 1931; Wallace Fowlie, *Clowns and Angels*, 1943; Martin Turnell, *The Novel in France*, 1950; Janko Lavrin, "Dostoievsky and Proust," *Slavonic Review*, V (1927), 609–627; and A. J. Roche, "Proust as a Translator of Ruskin," *Publications of the Modern Language Association*, XLV (1930), 1214–1218.

JAMES PURDY

Born: Ohio
Date: 1923

Principal Works

NOVELS: *Malcolm,* 1959; *The Nephew,* 1960; *Cabot Wright Begins,* 1964; *Eustace Chisholm and the Works,* 1967; *Jeremy's Version,* 1970.
SHORT STORIES AND NOVELLAS: *Don't Call Me by My Right Name,* 1956; *63: Dream Palace,* 1956; *Color of Darkness,* 1957; *Children Is All,* 1962
PLAYS: *Children Is All* and *Cracks* (printed in *Children Is All*), 1962.

James Purdy was thirty-two years old when he resolved to make his way by writing, and he was no doubt aware that for Hemingway, Faulkner, or Fitzgerald this was a ripe age. He nevertheless resigned his teaching position at Lawrence College in Wisconsin, arranged the necessary financing for a limited edition of *63: Dream Palace,* and sent copies to well-known literary figures in England. The ebullient praise that he received in the *Times Literary Supplement* of London caught the attention of the American publishers who had previously rejected his manuscripts, and his collection of stories was published here in 1957 under the title *Color of Darkness.* Dame Edith Sitwell repeated her enthusiastic response in an introduction, and James Purdy was established.

Nor were the critics wrong to urge him on, for Purdy sometimes writes clear, smooth, simple prose, and often seeks to increase his reader's awareness of human capability. One feels, for the most part, that he is honest, that he selects his stones before he scales them across the pond.

But *Malcolm,* his first novel, published in 1959, does not move smoothly. In picaresque fashion it allows its young hero to gallop headlong into disconnected adventures. He becomes an involved onlooker in the lives of casual acquaintances, and has no story of his own. The reader is confronted with a midget who denies his limited stature, a pre-marital ritual in a tattoo parlor, and an exchange of spouses, among other details. Perhaps the satire fails because it is difficult to recognize the subject being satirized, but one can detect unmistakable echoings from *Color of Darkness.*

In his second novel, *The Nephew,* Purdy has achieved, perhaps, his greatest success to date. Here he abandons the fashionable bizarre and the confusing fantastic to tell the simple story of Alma Mason's fears and doubts and ignorance about her young nephew who was killed in Korea. The small town, probably like the one in Ohio in which Purdy was born, comes alive for us through all the subterranean intrigues of its basically uncomplicated inhabitants. At the conclusion of the novel the reader knows more about the people involved than any individual character whose life makes up part of the whole. When Alma is shown how beautiful is the wisteria growing near her own house, we are reminded that none of us ever sees the distant attractiveness of his life unless, like Alma, we are invited to use a neighbor's window. Purdy's novel is successful because he draws the reader gently to his casement and shows him the lives of a part of his own family.

The Nephew was published in 1960. It was followed by a second collection of stories called *Children Is All* which came out in 1962. A number of these seem little more than exacerbating exercises in dialogue built around a central situation; dramatic movement is lacking. The two one-act plays, one of which gives the book its title, appear contrived, like a children's impromptu game. One has the feeling that these stories are part of Purdy's earliest work, and that they were published after, but possibly written before, the stories in *Color of Darkness*. In *Cabot Wright Begins,* he returned to the grimly fantastic to make a satiric examination of American values. This time the subject was a graceful and generous rapist of 300 women. The novel rambles between Chicago, where Purdy attended the University, and Brooklyn Heights, his home, but never really decides which story to tell, with the result that much of the novel reads like notes from underground in a world where an unbridgeable gulf separates the individual and society, the fantastic and the real.

The influence of Sherwood Anderson—of *Winesburg, Ohio,* in particular—has always been light but pervasive in Purdy's fiction. This is especially true of the trilogy, *Sleepers in Moon-Crowned Valleys,* on which he is now at work, a story of life in a Midwestern town more than a generation ago. Once more he is shaping violence and sex into an apocalyptic metaphor of the contemporary human condition. *Jeremy's Version,* the first novel of the series, was published in 1970.

BIBLIOGRAPHICAL REFERENCES: For comment on Purdy's work see Warren French, "The Quaking World of James Purdy," *Essays in Modern Literature,* 1963; Paul Herr, "The Small Sad World of James Purdy," *Recent American Fiction: Some Critical Views,* edited by J. J. Waldmeir, 1963; Regina Pomeranz, "The Hell of Not Loving: Purdy's Modern Tragedy," *Renascence,* XVI (1964), 149–153; and Gerald Weales, "No Face and No Exit: The Fiction of James Purdy and J. P. Donleavy," *Contemporary American Novelist,* CLXXXVII (Spring, 1964), 143–154. For additional articles see the *Bulletin of Bibliography,* XXVIII, no. 1 (1971), 5–6.

P'U SUNG-LING

Born: Tzu-ch'uan, Shantung, China
Date: June 5, 1640

Died: Shantung, China
Date: February 5, 1715

Principal Works

NOVELS AND TALES: *Liao-chai chih-i*, 1766 (*Strange Stories from a Chinese Studio*); *Hsing-shih yin-yuan chuan*, 1870 (*Marriage as Retribution*); *Liao-chai Ch'üan-chi*, 1936 (*Collected Works*, excluding the two above).

P'u Sung-ling's ancestors were probably of Turkic origin and came to China with the Mongol armies around the middle of the thirteenth century. Two of them were governors of Shantung in the last two or three decades of the Yuan dynasty (1279–1368), but nothing was heard of the family again until 1592, when a granduncle of the author became a *chin-shih* and later served a term as magistrate. P'an, the author's father, also studied for the examinations, but after failing several times to pass the first hurdle, he turned to trade. He was apparently the most distinguished member of the clan in his day, for it was recorded that in 1647 he led a successful defense of his village against a band of marauders who had sacked several neighboring cities.

P'u Sung-ling was the third of four sons. He passed his *hsiu-ts'ai* examinations with highest honors in 1658. In 1685 he became a salaried licentiate, and in 1710 a senior licentiate; but the *chü-jen* degree, the next in order, eluded him, though he attended the examinations regularly until he was past sixty. As a result he was thwarted in his ambition, shared by all literocrats of traditional China, of entering government service, and he was forced to content himself with serving as secretary to more fortunate friends (from 1670 to around 1692) and in teaching in the family schools of the local gentry (until 1710).

The major portion of *Strange Stories from a Chinese Studio* must have been completed by 1679, the date of the preface, but internal evidence suggests many subsequent additions, one as late as 1707. The book was circulated in manuscript during the author's lifetime and was much esteemed by some of his more prominent contemporaries. Upon its publication in 1766, it was an immediate success and became *the* collection of strange tales for literate readers. For the traditional literocrat, his stories are masterpieces of the polished, allusive, classical style; for the modern reader, they represent a radical advance over all previous examples of the same genre because of the richness of invention displayed by the author and the touch of humanity which he gives to all his ghosts, fox fairies, and flower spirits, and which make them seem real, if not probable.

Until 1932, the *Chih-i* was about the only work by which P'u Sung-ling was known. But in that year Hu Shih published his study of the *Hsing-shih Yin-yuan chuan* (*Marriage as Retribution*) and proved conclusively that this epic novel of a hen-pecked husband, which had appeared anonymously in 1870, was also written by P'u. Because of the interest aroused by this discovery and the recognition of this hitherto neglected novel as one of the two or three greatest works of Chinese fiction (the other two being the *Chin P'ing Mei* and the *Hung Lou Meng*), the unpublished works of the author were sought out and published in 1936 under the title of *Liao-chai Ch'üan-chi* (*Collected Works*). The two books of prose and three of verse in the literocratic tradition included in the collection occasioned no surprise, but the rest of the material would have seemed incredible if Hu Shih's study had not prepared us for it, for this comprises seven short satires and eleven longish romances in the *ku-tz'u* or *t'an-tzu* forms (somewhat like the *chante-fable* of medieval French) of the popular tradition. Some of these last, elaborations of stories of wicked mothers-in-law, jealous wives, and hen-pecked husbands, had appeared in briefer forms in the *Chih-i*. In thus dealing with the same set of themes in three different mediums—first in the short tale form, then as romances in prose and verse, and finally in a long epic novel—P'u Sung-ling is unique in the history of Chinese literature.

BIBLIOGRAPHICAL REFERENCES: The best and most comprehensive biographical study of P'u Sung-ling in English is the article by Fang Chao-ying in *Eminent Chinese of the Ch'ing Period*, edited by A. W. Hummel, 1944. Full-length biographies are unknown to traditional Chinese literature; the official biographies as found in histories, in family archives, or on tomb inscriptions are always sketchy and unrevealing. The most detailed biographical information is cast in the form of a chronological record (*nien-p'u*), in which the known facts of the subject's life, in so far as it is possible to determine through his own and other people's writings, are set down in the words of the sources, generally without comment. There is such a record of P'u Sung-ling appended to the *Liao-chai ch'üan-chi;* it was compiled by Lu Ta-huang, editor of the collected works. For a discussion of the circumstances surrounding the *Strange Stories from a Chinese Studio* see Jaroslav Průšek, *Studia Serica*, 1959, 128–146.

ALEXANDER PUSHKIN

Born: Moscow, Russia
Date: June 6, 1799

Died: St. Petersburg, Russia
Date: February 10, 1837

Principal Works

poems: *Ruslan and Ludmila,* 1821; *Kavkarski plennik,* 1820–1821 (*The Prisoner of the Caucasus*); *Eugeny Onegin,* 1823–1831 (*Eugene Onegin*); *Graf Nulin,* 1825 (*Count Nulin*); *Poltava,* 1828; *Medny vsadnik,* 1832 (*The Bronze Horseman*).
novels: *Arap Petra Velikogo,* 1828 (*The Negro of Peter the Great;* unfinished); *Dubrovsky,* 1832–1833; *Kapitanskaya dochka,* 1836 (*The Captain's Daughter*).
short stories: *Pikovaya dama,* 1834 (*The Queen of Spades*); *Povesti Belkina,* 1834 (*The Tales of Belkin*).
plays: *Boris Godunov,* 1826; *Rusalka,* 1836.
folk tales: *Skazki,* 1831–1834 (*Fairy Tales*).

Alexander (Sergeyevich) Pushkin, Russia's first important and still greatest poet, was descended on his father's side from a family of impoverished nobility and on his mother's from an Abyssinian officer in the service of Peter the Great. Pushkin was proud of both heritages, and the distinctive character of his verse, a combination of classical form and romantic feeling, may have been influenced by them.

Born in Moscow on June 6, 1799, he studied at home and at the Lyceum (1811–1817), where he absorbed Latin and eighteenth century French literature and began publishing verses: spirited anacreontics, political epigrams, and in 1820 a long narrative poem, *Ruslan and Ludmila.* This work, like much of his later work, was based on folk material. At the age of twenty he was already acknowledged the new leader of Russian poetry. To the tsarist government he was also (and continued to be throughout his life) politically suspect. He was as precocious in love as he was in verse and in St. Petersburg (1818–1820) threw himself with his characteristic love of life into a round of sensual adventures.

In 1820, as the result of his patriotic "Ode to Liberty," he was sent to the Caucasus as a nominal state official but in reality an exile. There, during the next four years, he wrote his first mature poems, *The Prisoner of the Caucasus, The Fountain of Bakhchisaray* (1822), *The Robber Brothers* (1822), and *The Gypsies* (1823–1824), all showing in their exotic settings and romantic characterizations the influence of Byron. He also began in 1823 his masterpiece, *Eugene Onegin,* a novel in verse modeled on Byron's *Don Juan* and not completed until 1831. But Pushkin's poem resembles Byron's only superficially (and less as the work proceeds) in its buoyant tone and theme of love. It has greater unity of form, mellower wisdom, and more profound characterization; the story of Eugene, the callow amorist, simply rejected by the romantic, noble Tatyana who continues to love him even after she is married to another, merits the claim of having launched the great Russian novel.

Dismissed from the service in 1824, for the next two years Pushkin was confined by the government to his mother's estate near Pskov. Here, seeking a less subjective theme, he wrote his play, *Boris Godunov,* an imitation of Shakespearean tragedy rather stilted in tone and lacking in cumulative effect. Although Pushkin's theme is individual rather than political freedom, the play was censored as anti-monarchial. Its reputation today rests chiefly on the Moussorgsky opera based on Pushkin's text.

After 1826 Pushkin was kept under closer government surveillance in Moscow and St. Petersburg. Several notable short verse plays dealing with kinds of evil (*The Covetous Knight, Mozart and Salieri, The Stone Guest*) were written in 1830 just before his marriage to Natalia Goncharova, a beautiful empty-headed girl much younger than he, who, if we can trust one of his letters to a friend, was his one hundred thirteenth conquest. After this date he wrote mostly history, criticism, and fiction. His most important stories, written in terse, bare narrative style, are *The Queen of Spades,* a tale of supernatural evil, and *The Captain's Daughter,* a romantic novel of love and heroism played out against a background of provincial life and the Pugachev Rebellion of 1773.

Forced into a dull round of court affairs by his wife and subject to continuous government censorship and restraint in spite of his patriotic poems, *Poltava* and *The Bronze Horseman,* Pushkin found married life onerous. Involved in domestic intrigue and scandal, he challenged a guardsman named d'Anthès and was fatally wounded in a duel fought to defend his wife's honor. He died two days later on February 10, 1837, at St. Petersburg.

Pushkin's reputation, at its height in the 1820's, fell during the last years of his life but revived rapidly after 1880, when Dostoevski delivered the famous commemorative address in which he stressed Pushkin's role in the formation of a Russian national consciousness. It is still too low in the West because of the special difficulties in translating his work, particularly his large body of lyric poetry beloved by Russian-speaking peoples.

BIBLIOGRAPHICAL REFERENCES: Pushkin's most important works are available in translation. The *Letters* were translated and edited by Thomas J. Shaw, 1967. For biographical and critical studies in English see D. S. Mirsky, *Pushkin,* 1926; E. J. Simmons, *Pushkin,* 1937; Janko Lavrin, *Pushkin and Russian Literature,* 1947 and *Russian Writers,* 1954; Walter N. Vickery, *Pushkin: Death of a Poet,* 1968; and John Bayley, *Pushkin: A Comparative Commentary,* 1971; in French, Henri Troyat, *À Pouchkine; biographie,* 2 vols., 1953 (translated 1971). For bibliography see also Avrahm Yarmolinsky, *Pushkin in English,* 1937.

FRANÇOIS RABELAIS

Born: Chinon, France
Date: c. 1495

Died: Paris (?), France
Date: 1553

PRINCIPAL WORK

SATIRE: *Gargantua and Pantagruel*, 1532–1564.

Concrete facts about the life of François Rabelais are few and far between. The dates and places of his birth and death are at best only guesswork—the best guesses being 1495 at Chinon, France, for his birth and 1553 at Paris for his death—and the gaps in his career are many. As is so often true of men with colorful personalities but uncertain biographies, his life is obscured by a mist of legend and anecdote. There is, for instance, the story that Rabelais, finding himself without money in Lyons, obtained free transportation to Paris by pretending that he was involved in a plot to poison the king. Probably equally apocryphal are the well-known words attributed to him on his deathbed: "Down with the curtain; the farce is done! I am going to seek a great perhaps." Our understanding of Rabelais the man is further confused by his relationship to the bitter religious and political controversies that raged in Europe during his lifetime. As an exponent of rationality and common sense, and enemy of narrow-minded dogmatism of any sort, it was almost inevitable that Rabelais should become the victim of bigotry and cant, and that he and his writing should be denounced by extremists on both sides of moderation. He was characterized by Calvin as a debauched libertine, and by the Catholics as an infamous drunkard; and both epithets, whether justified or not, have stuck.

About all we know for certain about Rabelais is that he was, at various times, a monk, a doctor of medicine, an editor, and, for all time, a writer. The first specific record that we have of him is his signature on the certificate of a purchase made by the Franciscan monastery at Fontenay-le-Comte in 1519, evidence that suggests, because of his apparent importance in the abbey, that he had taken orders several years earlier. We next hear of Rabelais corresponding with Guillaume Budé, secretary to King François I and one of the foremost scholars in Europe. At the same time he was familiar with the group of scholars gathered around André Tiraqueau, one of the most learned judges in France. Moved, it would seem, by a growing interest in intellectual matters, Rabelais received permission from the Pope in 1524 to transfer from the Franciscans at Fontenay to a Benedictine monastery at Maillezais, a change which gave him the advantage of both the protection of his friend, Geoffroi d'Estissac, Bishop of Maillezais, and the relative sophistication and scholarship of the Benedictines. By 1530 he had left the order and taken on secular garb, and in November of that year he was graduated as bachelor of medicine from the University of Montpellier.

In 1532 Rabelais was in Lyons, the intellectual center of France, where he edited and published some medical and scholarly works, was physician at the Hôtel-Dieu, and produced his first original work in *Pantagruel,* or Book II of what was later to become *Gargantua and Pantagruel*. The following year his work was censured by the

Faculty of Theology of the University of Paris. In 1534 Rabelais went to Rome in the train of his friend and patron, Cardinal Jean du Bellay, apparently in hopes of regularizing his somewhat anomalous relationship with the Church. His wishes were realized, and in reply to his petition excusing his leaving the order, a papal bull was issued permitting him to rejoin the Benedictines, to assume ecclesiastical office, and to practice medicine. Rabelais, who in the meantime had published *Gargantua,* or Book I of his masterpiece, took advantage of this dispensation almost immediately, becoming canon of St. Maur the next year and, in 1537, taking the degrees of licentiate and doctor of medicine at Montpellier. In 1540 he seems to have been in Italy, and by 1546 he was in Metz, while the recently published *Tiers Livre,* Book III of *Gargantua and Pantagruel,* was being condemned by the Sorbonne. Two years later part of Book IV was published in Lyons—for which a rare copyright was granted by Henry II—and in 1552 the completed Book IV appeared in Paris, to be immediately proscribed by Parliament. In 1553 Rabelais resigned two curacies which he had received several years before from the du Bellay family, and some time before the end of the year he was dead. Nine years later, in 1562, sixteen chapters of what is now Book V appeared under the title, *Ringing Island by Master François Rabelais,* and in 1564 the complete Book V was published in Paris. Its authenticity has often been questioned, and it is probable that some parts of it were edited from unfinished notes left by the author. In 1567 all five books were published together for the first time.

Apart from such inferences as can be gleaned from these meager biographical data, all our knowledge of the philosophy or personality of the man called Rabelais is based on his one extant work and masterpiece, *Gargantua and Pantagruel.* This rollicking and uninhibited tale of the birth, education, and adventures of the "huge giant Gargantua" (Book I) and of his son Pantagruel (Books II–V) leaves the reader with the impression that its author was a man of keen satiric wit, of comprehensive, if not profound, learning, but above all, of a tremendous and all-inclusive enthusiasm for life. Rabelais ends his prefatory address "To My Reader" with the admonition, "Live Happy," and this *joie de vivre* colors every word he wrote. Himself a monk, he was the inveterate enemy of scholasticism, pedantry, superstition, the unnatural rigors of monasticism, and all that was narrow or crabbed or fanatic. An admirer of what was best and noblest in Renaissance humanism, Rabelais had a profound respect for enlightened education and learning (he would make Pantagruel "an abyss of knowledge"). At the same time, reason, for Rabelais, is very close to instinct, and to "follow nature" (where nature is civilized and well-bred) is the true road to the happy life. The one rule of the saturnalian Abbey of Thélème (Book I) is, "Do as thou wilt"; nature is good, and everything that limits and restricts the freedom to "be yourself" is rotten. But Rabelais was not simply a pagan hedonist; instinct for him seems to include faith in God and a future life. "Laughter is the essence of mankind," and joy is the highest form of worship. Consistent with these principles, Rabelais has added immeasurably to the joy of mankind.

BIBLIOGRAPHICAL REFERENCES: The basic and best-known translation in English is *The Works of the Famous Mr. Francis Rabelais,* translated by Sir Thomas Urquhart and Peter Le Motteux, 1653–1694. Recent translations include those by Samuel P. Putnam, 1929; and Jacques Le Clercq, 1936. An abridgement of the Putnam translation was published as *The Portable Rabelais* in 1946. Among the recent biographical and critical studies in English are A. F. Chappell, *The Enigma of Rabelais,* 1924; Samuel P. Putnam, *Rabelais, Man of the Renaissance,* 1929; John Cowper Powys, *Rabelais: His Life,* 1948; D. B. Wyndham Lewis, *Doctor Rabelais,* 1957; and Marcel Tetel, *Rabelais,* 1967; in French, J. Plallard, *La Vie et l'œuvre de Rabelais,* 1939; and J. Charpentier, *Rabelais et la génie de la Renaissance,* 1941.

JEAN BAPTISTE RACINE

Born: La Ferté-Milon, France
Date: December, 1639

Died: Paris, France
Date: April 26, 1699

Principal Works

PLAYS: *Andromache*, 1667; *Les Plaideurs*, 1668; *Britannicus*, 1669; *Bérénice*, 1670; *Bajazet*, 1672; *Mithridate*, 1673; *Iphigénie*, 1674; *Phèdre*, 1677; *Esther*, 1689; *Athalie*, 1691.

Jean Baptiste Racine is remembered, along with Pierre Corneille, as a leader of the classical revival in the drama of seventeenth century France. His father was a solicitor and local official in the town of La Ferté-Milon, but both parents died soon after Jean's birth in December, 1639, and the boy was brought up by his Jansenist grandparents. He attended school, first at Beauvais, and later at the famous Jansenist monastery of Port-Royal, where he wrote quite passable odes in both Latin and French while still in his teens. By the time he had left the Collège d'Harcourt he had composed an ode in honor of the marriage of Louis XIV which had earned him 600 livres from the monarch, written two unsuccessful dramas, formed a friendship with La Fontaine and liaisons with several of the leading actresses of the day. A few years later he also became a friend of the famous critic and arbiter of French taste, Boileau, who remained his mentor and friendly censor for much of his life.

The years between 1664 and 1673 were marked by the highly favorable reception of two plays, *La Thébaïde* (1664) and *Alexandre Le Grand* (1665), the second of which raised Racine to the rank of Corneille in public opinion, and by an extremely unpleasant exchange of pamphlets with the Jansenists at Port-Royal, who hated the theater and his involvement in it. It was in *Andromache* that Racine displayed the heights of his particular genius, the ability to combine the strict requirements of the highly formalized Senecan drama which dominated the French stage with a revived interest in human motivation and characterization. Like his other great tragedy, *Phèdre*, *Andromache* not only employs a classical Greek theme, but also follows the classical rules and unities of Aristotle as they had come to be interpreted on the seventeenth century French stage by the master of the classical renaissance, Corneille. At the same time Racine devotes all his skill to the creation of warm, human characters, and in such figures as Hermione and Phèdre draws a highly sympathetic (some say sentimentalized) picture of the victims of grand and fatal passions. Like Corneille, he regards human passion as a destructive force but, unlike his rival, he feels a genuine sympathy for its victims. This outlook, combined with almost uniformly brilliant versification, has made Racine almost as popular in our century as he was in his own.

Andromache was followed in fairly close succession by a long series of successful plays on classical, biblical, or Oriental themes: *Les Plaideurs* (his charming and only comedy), *Britannicus*, *Bérénice*, *Bajazet*, *Mithridate*, and *Iphigénie*. In 1677 the series was climaxed by *Phèdre*, the story of the Grecian woman whose uncontrollable love for her stepson brings on a series of disasters and her own destruction. Perhaps the greatest of Racine's tragedies, it was also, however, the unluckiest. Influential enemies had commissioned another *Phèdre* to be written for presentation at the same time as his, and Racine's play was nearly driven from the stage in consequence. After this blow the playwright retired almost completely from dramatic writing, abandoned his lifelong libertine habits in favor of a reconciliation with the puritans of Port-Royal, married, and settled down to a comfortable life as a courtier and royal historiographer. He also raised seven children, two sons and five daughters.

Racine wrote only two more plays during the remaining twenty years of his life, both composed especially for the young girls who attended the school at St. Cyr established by Louis XIV's last mistress, Madame de Maintenon, for the education of poor girls from noble families. *Esther* and *Athalie*, while lacking the intense passions of the earlier tragedies, possess a delicacy and perfection of construction, characterization, and versification all their own. The choruses, set to the music of Moreau, the court composer, are particularly lovely.

Except for a short history of Port-Royal and several minor pieces, Racine was silent after 1691. His declining years were marked by a loss of friends and of literary and royal favor. He died in Paris on April 26, 1699. He was buried at Port-Royal.

BIBLIOGRAPHICAL REFERENCES: The standard edition of Racine is that edited by Paul Mesnard in the *Collection des grands écrivains de la France*, 1865–1874. There is also an English edition, *The Dramatic Works of Jean Racine*, translated by R. B. Boswell, 1889–1890. For recent studies of the playwright see Alexander F. B. Clark, *Jean Racine*, 1939; Jean Giraudoux, *Racine*, 1950; Geoffrey Brereton, *Jean Racine: A Critical Biography*, 1951; Bernard Weinburg, *The Art of Jean Racine*, 1963; and Odette de Mourges, *Racine: Or the Triumph of Relevance*, 1967.

MRS. ANN RADCLIFFE

Born: London, England
Date: July 9, 1764

Died: London
Date: February 7, 1823

Principal Works

NOVELS: *A Sicilian Romance,* 1790; *The Romance of the Forest,* 1791; *The Mysteries of Udolpho,* 1794; *The Italian, or, The Confessional of the Black Penitents,* 1797; *Gaston de Blondeville,* 1826.

Mrs. Ann (Ward) Radcliffe, although little known today, was considered the greatest romanticist of her age, both for her imaginative plotting and for her poetic prose. Her novels have become a minor landmark in English literary history because their author formulated a Gothic school of writing that owed more to her invention than to the influence of her contemporaries in the same genre, and her tales of terror are unblurred by the awkward supernaturalism of Walpole, the sentimentality of Clara Reeves, or the turgid horrors of Matthew Gregory Lewis.

Born in London on July 9, 1764, Ann Ward included among her ancestors the celebrated classical scholar, Dr. S. Jebb. Stimulated by her wide reading, she delighted as a child in daydreams of things supernatural; however, a shy, asthmatic girl isolated in a society of her elders, she was not encouraged to exercise her abilities or to express herself. At twenty-three, pretty and demure, she married William Radcliffe, the future editor of the *English Chronicle.* Living in London, intimate with literary people, and childless, she began to write. Her first book, *The Castles of Athlin and Dunbayne* (1789), went almost unnoticed, but her second, *A Sicilian Romance,* established her reputation as a master of suspense and description. With *The Romance of the Forest,* published in 1791, she attracted the attention of a wide reading public. For her fourth novel, *The Mysteries of Udolpho,* she received £500 before it was published.

This novel typifies the two strongest elements in Mrs. Radcliffe's fiction: the suggestion of imminent evil and the atmosphere of refinement and beauty. Juxtaposed, each element intensifies the other. Mrs. Radcliffe carries the reader into a beautiful Eden, and by contrasting excellent description with vague references to impending doom an effect of mystery and terror results. That some terrible mystery suggested by a low groan from a distant tomb or an uncertain light on a castle stairs turns out to be wind or moonlight does not alter the effect of the story. Mrs. Radcliffe discriminated carefully between terror and horror, and her ability to evoke the former while avoiding the latter points to her skillful handling of atmosphere and dramatic situation.

Mrs. Radcliffe's novels are built on the same plot: a chaste, helpless young woman achieves a good marriage after a series of attempts on her life by sinister villains in an exotic setting. Although the plots are improbable and the characters are two-dimensional to the modern reader, the novels had great influence on other writers of the time, notably Scott and Byron; early in Scott's career he was hailed as Mrs. Radcliffe's successor, and certainly Schedoni, the villain of *The Italian,* is the forerunner of the Byronic hero.

Although she was in literature a mistress of the strange and picturesque, her own biography is commonplace because of the regularity of her life, and modern scholarship now discounts the contemporary belief that madness, induced by the terrors she created, accounts for the long interval of time between the publication of *The Italian* and her posthumous *Gaston de Blondeville*. A figure deserving more attention in literary history than she has received, Mrs. Radcliffe died in London on February 7, 1823.

BIBLIOGRAPHICAL REFERENCES: The edition of 1824 was reprinted in 1971. A modern edition of *The Italian* was issued as *The Confessional of the Black Penitents* by the Folio Society of London in 1956. For biography and criticism see Clara F. McIntyre, *Ann Radcliffe in Relation to Her Time*, Yale Studies in English, LXII, 1920; and A. A. S. Wieten, *Mrs. Radcliffe: Her Relation to Romanticism*, 1926. For more general studies of the Gothic Revival and its writers see also Dorothy Scarborough, *The Supernatural in Modern English Fiction*, 1917; Edith Birkhead, *The Tale of Terror*, 1921; Eino Railo, *The Haunted Castle*, 1927; the Rev. Montague Summers, *The Gothic Quest*, 1938, and *A Gothic Bibliography*, 1941. See further Donald Thomas, "The First Poetess of Romantic Fiction: Ann Radcliffe," *English*, XV (1964), 91–95; and Harrison Ross Steeves, "The Gothic Romance," *Before Jane Austen*, 1965, 243–271.

SIR WALTER RALEIGH

Born: Devonshire, England
Date: c. 1552

Died: London, England
Date: October 29, 1618

Principal Works

POEMS: Poems, c. 1580–1618, published in various sixteenth century anthologies.
HISTORY: *A Report of the Fight About the Iles of Açores*, 1591; *The Discoverie of . . . Guiana*, 1596; *History of the World*, 1614.

Sir Walter Raleigh, or Ralegh, epitomizes the merchant adventurers who lent glamour to the court of Elizabeth I and spread her fame throughout the Old World and the New. Born into the landed gentry, which was just beginning to realize its potential power, Raleigh had to make his way through his own ability, ambition, and charm, like so many other outstanding men of his generation.

Raleigh was born about 1552 in Devonshire. He attended Oriel College, Oxford, in 1568, but within a year he left the University to fight for the Huguenot cause in France. Although he returned to study at the Inns of Court in 1575, the North American expedition being planned by his half-brother, Sir Humphrey Gilbert, interested him far more than his law books. He is reported to have commanded one of the ships on this illfated venture in 1579; the fleet was broken up by the Spaniards and returned to England soon after its departure.

Raleigh had been introduced at court in 1577, and, through the efforts of Gilbert and other friends, he was appointed captain of a troop of foot soldiers in the Irish campaign of 1580. Returning to court with dispatches the following year, he won the favor of Queen Elizabeth and his career flourished; he was knighted, given a number of lucrative monopolies, made a member of Parliament, and, in 1587, named Captain of the Yeomen of the Guard. During these years he planned and invested heavily in colonies in North America, but none of his settlements survived.

The rise of the Earl of Essex in the queen's favor made Raleigh's position precarious, and he incurred the royal wrath by his hasty marriage with Elizabeth Throckmorton, or Throgmorton, one of Elizabeth's Maids of Honor. The Raleighs were briefly imprisoned in the Tower of London, then exiled from the court. Sir Walter again turned his attention westward. He commanded an expedition to Guiana in 1595, believing firmly that untold riches lay just ahead of him, but he returned empty-handed to England. The most successful result of this voyage was his book, *The Discovery of the Empire of Guiana* (1596).

Partially reconciled with the queen, Raleigh served as Rear Admiral in the fleet which destroyed the Spanish navy at Cadiz in 1596. Friction with Essex and misplaced trust in Robert Cecil, who had succeeded his father, Lord Burghley, as chief minister of state, marked Raleigh's next few years, but he lived comfortably until Elizabeth's death. Cecil, who desired undisputed control of the government without the interference of the domineering Raleigh, had laid careful plans and cleverly turned the peace-loving

James I against Sir Walter, who tactlessly greeted the new king with plans for military campaigns.

In 1603, Raleigh was arrested and tried for treason for his alleged involvement in a plot to put Lady Arabella Stuart on the throne. Sir Edward Coke, one of England's ablest legal minds, attacked Raleigh viciously, and in spite of his impassioned plea of innocence, Sir Walter was convicted and sent to the Tower, where he remained until 1616, four years after Cecil's death. He passed a part of his imprisonment writing a *History of the World*, with which he hoped to gain royal clemency.

Raleigh was freed to undertake another voyage to Guiana to find gold for the ever-empty treasury of the king, but this expedition, too, failed, and Raleigh's eldest son lost his life in a battle with Spanish colonists. Spanish influence was high at the English court at this time, and at the insistence of the King of Spain, James ordered Raleigh's execution on October 29, 1618.

Although Raleigh's arrogance and his opportunism had made enemies among both the nobility and the commoners, he became a great popular hero during his imprisonment, and he was widely mourned. His terse, understated poems and his fine prose works are highly valued by modern students of sixteenth and seventeenth century literature, but it is as a colorful personality rather than as a writer that history best remembers him.

BIBLIOGRAPHICAL REFERENCES: The only complete edition is the *Works*, edited by Oldys and T. Birch, 8 vols., 1829. The standard edition of the poetry is that edited by Agnes Latham, revised edition, 1951. Miss Latham also edited *Sir Walter Raleigh: Selected Prose and Poetry*, 1965.

There are a number of good biographical and critical studies, including D. B. Quinn, *Ralegh and the British Empire*, 1947; E. Thompson, *Sir Walter Ralegh: The Last of the Elizabethans*, 1935; Eleanor G. Clark, *Ralegh and Marlowe*, 1941; P. Edwards, *Sir Walter Ralegh*, 1953; W. Oakeshott, *The Queen and the Poet*, 1960; A. L. Rowse, *Sir Walter Ralegh: His Family and Private Life*, 1962; and N. L. Williams, *Sir Walter Ralegh*, 1962.

Important commentary on Raleigh's place in intellectual history is found in E. Strathmann, *Sir Walter Ralegh: A Study in Elizabethan Skepticism*, 1951; M. C. Bradbrook, *The School of Night*, 1936; Christopher Hill, *Intellectual Origins of the English Revolution*, 1965; and Pierre Lefranc, *Sir Walter Ralegh, Ecrivain, L'oeuvre et les idées*, 1968.

CHARLES-FERDINAND RAMUZ

Born: Cully, Switzerland *Died:* Cully
Date: November 24, 1878 *Date:* May 23, 1947

Principal Works

NOVELS: *Le Règne de l'esprit malin,* 1917 (*The Reign of the Evil One*); *Présence de la mort,* 1922 (*The End of All Men*); *La Grande Peur dans la montagne,* 1926; (*Great Fear in the Mountain*); *La Beauté sur la terre,* 1927 (*Beauty on Earth*); *Derborence,* 1935 (*When the Mountain Fell*).

Charles-Ferdinand Ramuz was born on November 24, 1878, in Cully, a small town on Lake Geneva in the canton of Vaud. He studied at the University of Lausanne and in 1902 moved to Paris where he intended to develop his capacities as a writer and to achieve independence of style and originality in content. During the next twelve years he wrote diligently, producing several novels and numerous poems and short stories. Becoming increasingly dissatisfied with life in Paris and with his work, he began to believe that isolation in France neither liberated him nor provided him with the kind of material he was best equipped to handle. Consequently, he resolved to return to his birthplace and to write in the midst of the life he remembered and valued. In 1914 he settled down once more in Cully and began a flow of work about the Swiss people he understood so well, writing of fishermen and simple farmers, of craftsmen and peasants.

His decision was soon shown to be wise. A series of novels concerned with Swiss life came from Cully, bringing success and recognition to their author. Writing in a sympathetic way about the people he knew, he won a wide audience; and although there were critics who claimed that he was allowing his metaphysical and mystical interests to cloud his clear vision of the people of Switzerland, there was enough of the beauty and virtue of the land in his books to make them widely acceptable. Ramuz explained in a critical discussion of his work that he intended to communicate the basic emotions of actual life not by philosophic analysis and not by contrived situations, but by selecting those features of actual life which would best exemplify the very qualities he was concerned to share.

He was considered for the Nobel Prize in 1945, a tribute to the enduring quality of his work and to his productivity. Two years later, on May 23, 1947, he died at Cully as the result of an operation.

BIBLIOGRAPHICAL REFERENCES: There is no helpful criticism of Ramuz in English. See Emmanuel Buenzod, *C.-F. Ramuz,* 1928; P. Kohler, *L'Art de C.-F. Ramuz,* 1929; C. Guyot, *Comment lire C.-F. Ramuz,* 1946; André Tissot, *C.-F. Ramuz, ou, Le drame de la poésie,* 1947, and *L'Expérience poétique de C.-F. Ramuz,* 1947; Bernard Voyenne, *C.-F. Ramuz et la sainteté de la terre,* 1948; Lucien Girardet, *Notre Ramuz,* 1952; and Hélène Cingria, *Ramuz, notre parrain,* 1956.

JOHN CROWE RANSOM

Born: Pulaski, Tennessee
Date: April 30, 1888

Principal Works

POEMS: *Poems About God,* 1919; *Chills and Fever,* 1924; *Grace After Meat,* 1924; *Two Gentlemen in Bonds,* 1927; *Selected Poems,* 1945, revised and enlarged 1963, 1969.
CRITICISM: *The World's Body,* 1938; *The New Criticism,* 1941.
ESSAYS AND STUDIES: *I'll Take My Stand: The South and the Agrarian Tradition,* by Twelve Southerners, 1930; *God Without Thunder: An Unorthodox Defense of Orthodoxy,* 1930.

John Crowe Ransom, besides being a fine, though hardly prolific poet in his own right, is perhaps the most influential critic in America of the past quarter century. His influence has stemmed from three sources: the examples he has set in his own poetry; the pronouncements he has made as the leader of two related but distinct literary movements, Southern Agrarianism and the New Criticism; and the power of selection he has exerted in the past twenty years as the editor of the *Kenyon Review.* His influence has been strongly felt, not in literary circles alone, but in the academic world as well (though it must be admitted that today, as far as poetry is concerned, it is difficult to distinguish between the two sectors, so greatly do they overlap). A college teacher himself since 1914 and a professor, first at Vanderbilt and then at Kenyon, since 1924, Ransom's application of the principles of the New Criticism to the teaching of literature has challenged the older historical approach and has been adopted, in part at least, by many of his adherents throughout the country.

Ransom was born in Pulaski, Tennessee, on April 30, 1888, and he began his academic training at Vanderbilt, the original seat of the Southern Agrarians. He was graduated from Vanderbilt in 1909, and then, after studying for four years as a Rhodes Scholar at Oxford, he returned to Vanderbilt as an instructor in English in 1914. There he remained, except for two years spent as a Field Artillery Officer in France during World War I, until he moved to Kenyon in 1937.

His literary activity, which can be divided into two distinct parts (the poetic corresponding to the period at Vanderbilt, the critical to the one at Kenyon), began in 1919 with the publication of *Poems about God.* In 1922 he became one of the founders of the Agrarian magazine, *The Fugitive,* which he edited until its demise in 1925. The previous year had marked the publication of *Chills and Fever,* his second, and, aside from his *Selected Poems,* best volume of verse. In it he realized most fully his own critical conditions for a modern poetry of metaphysical wit, of clarity and restraint, and of a "perfect anonymity"; and at least two of the pieces—the title poem and "Bells for John Whiteside's Daughter"—can readily be cited among the best that have been written in the century. In 1925 he was also one of the "Twelve Southerners" who contributed to the Agrarian manifesto, *I'll Take My Stand.*

Two other slim volumes of verse appeared before his departure from Vanderbilt, but the publication of *Chills and Fever* was the high point of his work as a poet, though the appearance of his *Selected Poems* in 1945 reestablished his reputation, and his receiving of the Bollingen Prize in Poetry and the Russell Loines Memorial Award from the American Institute of Arts and Letters in 1951 has kept it deservedly alive.

BIBLIOGRAPHICAL REFERENCES: A comprehensive survey is *Homage to John Ransom: Essays on His Work as Poet and Critic*, a symposium by various of his contemporaries, *Sewanne Review*, LVI (1948), 367–476. Recently have appeared Karl F. Knight, *The Poetry of John Crowe Ransom*, 1964; Robert Buffington, *The Equilibrist*, 1967; and Thomas D. Young, ed., *John Crowe Ransom: Critical Essays and a Bibliography*, 1968. See also Vivienne Koch, "The Poetry of John Crowe Ransom," in *Modern American Poetry*, edited by B. Rajan, 1952; Isabel Gamble, "Ceremonies of Bravery: John Crowe Ransom," in *Southern Renascence: The Literature of the Modern South*, edited by Louis D. Rubin, Jr., and Robert D. Jacobs, 1953; and John M. Bradbury, "Ransom as Poet," *Accent*, XI (1951), 45–57.

RUDOLPH ERICH RASPE

Born: Hanover, Germany
Date: 1737

Died: Muckross, Donegal, Ireland
Date: 1794

Principal Work

MOCK-HEROIC CHRONICLE: *Baron Münchausen's Narrative of His Marvellous Travels and Campaigns in Russia,* 1786.

While most people have heard of the mendacious Baron Münchausen, whose *Narrative* competes in foreign translation with classics like *Robinson Crusoe, Gulliver's Travels,* and *Pilgrim's Progress,* the author of the book is practically a forgotten man. Perhaps this is just as well, since Rudolph Erich Raspe, born at Hanover, Germany, in 1737, had little admirable about him except a misused ability to absorb. Little is known about his lower-class family, though they provided him with funds for his study at the universities of Göttingen and Leipzig between 1756 and 1760. After graduation, he spent a year tutoring the son of a noble. Later he became a librarian, first at Hanover, then at Göttingen. Here he translated from the French a philosophic work by Leibniz, published by the university in 1765, wrote verses in Latin, studied Percy's *Reliques of Ancient English Poetry,* and composed a long allegorical poem on a medieval theme. With Jakob Mauvillon (1743-1794), he founded *The Cassel Spectator,* for which he wrote articles about his many interests and hobbies.

For his study of mammoths during the Ice Age, the Royal Society of England made him an Honorary Fellow, and after the appearance of a volume on ancient gems and medals, the landgrave sent him to Italy to collect specimens. When he was detected stealing and selling the best of them, he was arrested but escaped and fled to England. The warrant for his arrest provides a description of him, as "a long-faced man with small eyes, crooked nose, red hair under his stumpy periwig, and a jerky gait."

In England Horace Walpole and other admirers helped pay his debts until details of his rascality arrived from the Continent; he was then expelled from the Royal Society. Because of his smattering of geology, he became an assayist with a mining company at Dolcoath, in Cornwall. Here he did the only writing that has survived him. In Germany he had known an eccentric old soldier, Hieronymus von Münchausen (1720-1797), who amused his guests and burlesqued his exaggerating gamekeeper by telling highly imaginative yarns as solemn truth. Sure that a book published in England would never reach the eyes of the original Münchausen, Raspe set down some of the yarns he remembered, invented others, and issued the book locally. A great success, the work was republished at Oxford in 1786. Neither brought Raspe much cash, but when a London bookseller bought the rights and sandwiched the original tales between a prefatory chapter and fifteen additional sketches at the end, the volume began a literary trend that still prevails in tall-story fiction. The first German edition of the tales appeared in 1786.

Raspe, having concocted a scheme for amalgamating silver and gold, collected money for his experiments and then fled to a remote section of Ireland, where he died of scarlet fever in 1794.

BIBLIOGRAPHICAL REFERENCES: There are many editions of the tales of Baron Münchausen. A recent biography is John Carswell, *Romantic Rogue, Being the Life and Times of Rudolf Erich Raspe,* 1950. See also Thomas Seccombe, Introduction to *The Surprising Adventures of Baron Münchausen,* 1895. A more specialized study is Carl Muller-Frauruth, *Die deutschen Lügendichtungen auf Münchausen,* 1881.

MARJORIE KINNAN RAWLINGS

Born: Washington, D.C.
Date: August 8, 1896

Died: St. Augustine, Florida
Date: December 14, 1953

Principal Works

NOVELS: *South Moon Under,* 1933; *Golden Apples,* 1935; *The Yearling,* 1938; *The Sojourner,* 1953.
SHORT STORIES: *When the Whippoorwill,* 1940.
SKETCHES: *Cross Creek,* 1942.

Marjorie Kinnan Rawlings was born in Washington, D.C., on August 8, 1896. She attended the University of Wisconsin, where she was graduated in 1918. Later she worked with the Young Women's Christian Association at national headquarters as publicity writer and magazine assistant. There followed a period of writing feature articles for various newspapers until her retirement to Florida in 1928 to raise oranges in her grove at Cross Creek and to devote more time to creative writing of her own. Most of her published work has its setting in central Florida in the section around Cross Creek, where she made her home and was accepted by the natives.

Her first novel, *South Moon Under,* appeared in 1933 and was selected as the choice of one of the national book clubs. Its period is about 1900, its theme the difficulties of a hunter's life in the Florida scrub country. In 1935 came *Golden Apples,* which tells the struggles of a young boy and his sister who take over an abandoned estate, raise oranges, and find satisfactions in their progress; it is set in the 1890's.

Marjorie Kinnan Rawlings' best novel, *The Yearling,* appeared in 1938. It is the story of twelve-year-old Jody Baxter as he grows from boyhood to an early maturity. Jody makes a pet of a fawn, Flag, which grows to maturity, ruins the crops, and has to be killed. Jody's story, set in 1870, is one of the great regional works in Ameircan writing, and it has had tributes comparing it with *Huckleberry Finn. The Yearling* won the Pulitzer Prize as the outstanding novel of 1938.

Mrs. Rawlings has written short stories in *When the Whippoorwill* (1940), an autobiographical account of the author's life in Florida in *Cross Creek* (1942), and a delightful discussion of food and its preparation in *Cross Creek Cookery* (1942). Her last book, *The Sojourner,* was her first novel with a northern setting. Mrs. Rawlings' death from a cerebral hemorrhage occurred in St. Augustine, Florida, on December 14, 1953.

BIBLIOGRAPHICAL REFERENCES: Very little has been written about Marjorie Kinnan Rawlings. There is only Gordon E. Bigelow, *Frontier Eden: The Literary Career of Marjorie Kinnan Rawlings,* 1966. See also Harry R. Warfel, *American Novelists of Today,* 1951; also *Book-of-the-Month Club News,* March, 1938.

CHARLES READE

Born: Oxfordshire, England
Date: June 8, 1814

Died: London, England
Date: April 11, 1884

Principal Works

NOVELS: *Peg Woffington*, 1853; *Christie Johnstone*, 1853; *It Is Never Too Late to Mend*, 1856; *The Cloister and the Hearth*, 1861; *Hard Cash*, 1863; *Griffith Gaunt*, 1866; *Foul Play*, 1868; *Put Yourself in His Place*, 1870; *A Terrible Temptation*, 1871; *A Woman Hater*, 1877.

PLAYS: *The Ladies' Battle*, 1851; *Angelo*, 1851; *A Village Tale*, 1852; *Masks and Faces*, 1852 (with Tom Taylor); *The Lost Husband*, 1852; *Gold*, 1853; *The Courier of Lyons*, 1854 (*The Lyons Mail*); *Peregrine Pickle*, 1854; *Drink*, 1879.

Charles Reade, born at Ipsden House, June 8, 1814, was the youngest in a family of eleven children born to a wealthy family of the landed gentry in Oxfordshire. Unlike his brothers, who were given the usual "public school" education, Charles Reade was educated at home by tutors. As a result of the private education he was faced with difficulties, personal and academic, when he entered Oxford. He had not learned to get along with people, nor had he acquired the academic knowledge he should have had. During his four years at Oxford, from 1832 to 1835, he received honors, apparently more by luck than ability and, in the case of a Vinerian Scholarship, by absolute chicanery. After leaving Oxford he went to London, studied law, and in 1843 was admitted to the bar, although he never actively practiced law. From 1837 to 1848 Reade, who was independently wealthy, spent his time in relative idleness. He traveled a great deal in Europe, adding to his collection of Cremona violins. Returning to London in 1849, he began to write plays. His first successful production was a comedy, *The Ladies' Battle*. Within two years five other plays were produced, and Reade made many friends among theatrical people, among them Laura Seymour, the famous actress, who was his friend and adviser until her death in 1879.

It was at the suggestion of Mrs. Seymour that Reade first turned to fiction. She suggested that he turn a play into a novel, and so *Masks and Faces* became the novel *Peg Woffington*. In 1856 Reade's first long novel was published, *It Is Never Too Late to Mend*. Following the publication of this novel, Reade turned his efforts almost exclusively to writing fiction rather than drama. His *White Lies* appeared in serial form in the *London Journal*, in 1856–57. Serial publication was common at the time. His greatest novel, *The Cloister and the Hearth*, appeared in 1861. Part of that novel had been published earlier under the title "A Good Fight" in a periodical, *Once a Week*. The story had proved so popular that Reade decided to expand it into its eventual four-volume length.

Probably under the influence of Charles Dickens, who was Reade's friend, the author turned from writing historical romances to writing problem novels. Just how much influence Dickens had on this change is impossible to assess, but as the editor of *All the Year Round*, in which much of Reade's fiction appeared, the influence was probably great. After his change to problem novels, Reade wrote such volumes as *Hard Cash, Griffith Gaunt,* and *Foul Play.* During his career as a writer, Reade wrote more than twenty novels, and he wrote, too, almost as many plays. Of all his works, only *The Cloister and the Hearth* draws any wide group of readers today. His problem novels deal with problems that have long since been solved or alleviated, and so are uninteresting to modern-day readers. The plays are deemed by most scholars to be too stagy and melodramatic. None has found any acceptance on the stage for years, although Reade himself thought that his dramatic work was more important than his fiction, even to requesting that the title of dramatist be put first upon his tombstone. He never lost interest in the novel, however, and when he died in London, April 11, 1884, he left a completed novel, *A Perilous Secret* (1884), ready for publication.

BIBLIOGRAPHICAL REFERENCES: The authorized biography is C. L. and Compton Reade, *Charles Reade, A Memoir,* 2 vols., 1887. A more recent study is Malcolm Elwin, *Charles Reade, A Biography,* 1934. See also A. C. Swinburne, *Miscellanies,* 1886; Walter C. Philips, *Dickens, Reade and Collins, Sensation Novelists,* 1919; A. M. Turner, *The Making of the Cloister and the Hearth,* 1938; and Wayne Burns, *Charles Reade: A Study in Victorian Authorship,* 1961.

FORREST REID

Born: Belfast, Ireland
Date: June 24, 1876

Died: Warrenpoint, Ireland
Date: January 4, 1947

PRINCIPAL WORKS

NOVELS: *The Kingdom of Twilight,* 1904; *The Garden God,* 1906; *The Bracknels,* 1911; *Following Darkness,* 1912 (reissued as *Peter Waring,* 1937); *The Gentle Lover,* 1913; *At the Door of the Gate,* 1915; *The Spring Song,* 1916; *Pirates of the Spring,* 1920; *Pender among the Residents,* 1922; *Uncle Stephen,* 1931; *Brian Westby,* 1934; *The Retreat,* 1936; *Young Tom,* 1944.

SHORT STORIES: *Retrospective Adventures,* 1941.

ESSAYS AND STUDIES: *W. B. Yeats: A Critical Study,* 1915; *Illustrators of the Sixties,* 1928; *Walter de la Mare: A Critical Study,* 1929; *Milk of Paradise, Some Thoughts on Poetry,* 1946.

AUTOBIOGRAPHY: *Apostate,* 1926; *Private Road,* 1940.

Forrest Reid, Irish author of childhood and the supernatural, was born on June 24, 1876, in Belfast, Ireland, the son of Robert Reid and his wife Frances Matilda Parr Reid. He was the youngest of twelve children. Perhaps when Forrest Reid became a novelist he never demanded commercial success because he had grown accustomed in his childhood to having enough, but never more than enough, of the necessities of life. His father met with business misadventures and lost considerable money investing in ships which tried unsuccessfully to run a Civil War blockade to the United States. As a boy, Reid enjoyed a close family life, but spent a large amount of time by himself, roaming the fields of Ulster and developing his imaginative powers to the point where dream and reality became almost, but not quite, indistinguishable. He became interested in memory, in time, in the spiritual demands of animals, and in a kind of youthful pantheism. He was tutored at home until he was eleven; he hardly ever attended church, perhaps because he found his needs met during his wanderings over the countryside.

He was educated at the Royal Academical Institution in Belfast and then at Christ's Church, Cambridge, where he received his B.A. He was not impressed by Cambridge, nor by intellectual company of the sort he found there, and he was happy to return to Belfast. He lived in a small suburban house, doing most of his own housekeeping and leading a simple life. He took a job as a clerk in a Belfast tea warehouse and enjoyed working there, performing simple duties, receiving an adequate income, and using his mind imaginatively in the creation of ideas and stories.

His first novel was *The Kingdom of Twilight,* a book he later wished he could disown; but the story was good enough to interest Henry James, who wrote to Reid and encouraged him. Reid responded by dedicating his second book, *The Garden God,* to James. In 1911 he made the acquaintance of E. M. Forster, to whom he dedicated *Following Darkness.* This book was later rewritten and appeared as *Peter Waring* in 1937.

Reid continued to write novels and critical studies, building a small but enthusiastic group of readers. He amused himself by playing croquet, at which he was so expert that he became a champion and made periodic trips to England to engage in tournaments. He loved dogs, as his readers know, and made them his close companions. He had a loyal group of literate and appreciative friends. He enjoyed bridge, book hunting, print collecting, dog shows, and stamp collecting. These interests were satisfied by the small income he received from his books, and he was content to be free to write as he pleased.

His trilogy, *Tom Barber* (published in one volume in 1955), will probably endure as his masterpiece, for as the culmination of his work in the novel it has all the virtues of Reid at his best: the radiance of happy childhood, the peculiar aura of supernatural elements, a continuous beauty of setting and character, and a charming and restrained humor. The trilogy is composed of novels written in reverse order to the chronology of the story: *Uncle Stephen*, the last of the series, appeared first in 1931; *The Retreat*, in 1936; and *Young Tom*, with which the trilogy begins, in 1944. Probably no better expression of the spirit of Reid's own childhood can be found than in this evocation of the experiences of Tom Barber.

In his work he sought what in his autobiography, *Apostate*, he called "a sort of moral fragrance." But since his novels present that atmosphere of good and evil as it made itself felt to him in his childhood, his novels are not burdened but enlightened by the depth of his moral involvement. His biographer, Russell Burlingham, characterized his work as "a world full of sunlight and earth's loveliness, yet ever haunted by mystery and fringed with dream."

Reid was a member of the Irish Academy of Letters, and a recipient of an Honorary D.Litt. from Queen's University in Belfast in 1933. Unmarried, he lived most of his life at 13 Ormiston Crescent in Belfast. He died on January 4, 1947, at Warrenpoint, Ireland.

BIBLIOGRAPHICAL REFERENCES: The fullest account of Reid's life is given in his two autobiographical accounts; in addition, *Private Road*, 1940, contains an interesting analysis of his novels in the light of his personal vision of experience. For biography and criticism see also Russell Burlingham, *Forrest Reid: A Portrait and a Study*, 1953, with an introduction by Walter de la Mare; also E. M. Forster, *Abinger Harvest*, 1936.

ERICH MARIA REMARQUE
Erich Paul Remark

Born: Osnabrück, Germany
Date: June 22, 1897

Died: Locarno, Switzerland
Date: September 25, 1970

Principal Works

NOVELS: *Im Westen nichts Neues*, 1929 (*All Quiet on the Western Front*); *Der Weg zurück*, 1931 (*The Road Back*); *Drei Kameraden*, 1937 (*Three Comrades*); *Flotsam*, 1941; *Arc de Triomphe*, 1946 (*Arch of Triumph*); *Der Funke Leben*, 1952 (*Spark of Life*); *Zeit zu Leben und Zeit zu Sterben*, 1954 (*A Time to Live and a Time to Die*); *Der schwarze Obelisk*, 1956 (*The Black Obelisk*); *Der Himmel kennt keine Günstlinge*, 1961 (*Heaven Has No Favorites*); *Die Nacht von Lissabon*, 1963 (*The Night in Lisbon*); *Shadows in Paradise*, translated 1972.

Erich Maria Remarque, author of *All Quiet on the Western Front*, perhaps the outstanding novel of modern war, was from a Roman Catholic family of French descent. His father was a bookbinder and the family name was Remark.

Educated in Osnabrück, where he was born on June 22, 1897, he was drafted into the German Army during World War I when he was eighteen. He was wounded several times. After his discharge he received a government-sponsored education for teaching, but a year's experience convinced him that he was not suited to the academic life. He tried his hand at various occupations: drama critic, a salesman for a tombstone company, test driver for a Berlin tire company, advertising copywriter for an automobile company, part-time organist in an insane asylum, and assistant editor of *Sportbild*, an illustrated sports magazine. Some of his bizarre experiences were later incorporated in his satirical novel, *The Black Obelisk*.

In his spare time and between jobs he worked on a war novel, *All Quiet on the Western Front*, which was an immediate success when it was published in 1929, selling over a million copies during the first year of its sales in Germany and enjoying a similar success in translation. There have been three motion picture versions of the book, and it is likely that the simplicity and directness of the style will enable the book to stand beyond its own time as a memorable portrait of men at war.

In 1932, after a divorce which ended a nine-year marriage, he married for a second time. In order to find the freedom to write and to regain his health, Remarque and his wife built a house at Porto Ronco on Lake Maggiore in Switzerland, where Remarque had been living intermittently since 1929.

His second novel, *The Road Back*, represented an attempt to convey a sense of the overwhelming challenge facing soldiers returning to a defeated country. His third book, *Three Comrades*, continued his narrative exposition of the effects of war on Germany, the subject matter that has most concerned Remarque. His continued protests against uncivilized force made him one of the targets of Nazi vilification, and early in their rise to power the Nazis included his books among those that were publicly burned.

The Switzerland stay ended in 1939, when Remarque moved to the United States. In 1947 he became a naturalized citizen. After that time he lived in Los

Angeles and New York and made return visits to his home at Lake Maggiore.

One of his later novels, *The Black Obelisk,* although new in method, since it can be characterized as a tragic farce, seemed particularly suited to Remarque, for it allowed him to be humane while desperate, satirical while moral, compassionate while censorious, and sane while commenting on lunacy. The novel aroused considerable attention and intensified an interest in Remarque's play, *The Last Station,* which had an enthusiastic reception in Berlin and Vienna.

BIBLIOGRAPHICAL REFERENCES: There is no full-length biographical or critical study. See W. K. Pfeiler, *War and the German Mind,* 1941; James Gray, *On Second Thought,* 1946; and Robert Van Gelder, *Writers and Writing,* 1946.

MARY RENAULT
Mary Challans

Born: London, England
Date: September 4, 1905

Principal Works

NOVELS: *Purposes of Love,* 1939; *Kind Are Her Answers,* 1940; *The Friendly Young Ladies,* 1944; *Return to Night,* 1946; *The Charioteer,* 1953; *The Last of the Wine,* 1956; *The King Must Die,* 1958; *The Bull from the Sea,* 1962; *The Mask of Apollo,* 1966; *Fire from Heaven,* 1970.

JUVENILE LITERATURE: *The Lion in the Gateway,* 1964; *The Persian Boy,* 1972.

Mary Renault, a pseudonym used by Mary Challans, was born in London and educated at Oxford. After her formal studies, she entered nurse's training and spent the war years as a military nurse. In 1948 she moved to South Africa, where she currently lives.

Miss Renault began publishing while still a nurse. Although well received, none of her early works gained wide popularity. A vacation trip to Greece in the late 1940's led to a fascination with the culture of ancient Greece, and Miss Renault has achieved major success by fictionalizing ancient history and myth.

Her first major triumph was *The Last of the Wine* (1956), a fictional retelling of the Peloponnesian War's final years. Mary Renault's success continued with *The King Must Die* (1958), which recounted the adventures of Theseus in Knossos and his battle with the Minotaur. The same myth provided the basis for her next novel, *The Bull from the Sea* (1962), the story of Theseus' wife Phaedra and her incestuous passion for her stepson, Hippolytus.

The Mask of Apollo (1966) described Plato's attempts to influence the tyrants of Syracuse. *Fire from Heaven* is a fictional biography of the young Alexander of Macedon, following his life from childhood until he succeeded his father, Philip II.

All Miss Renault's novels are carefully researched, and are filled with realistic detail of everyday ancient life. Her works are usually written in the first person; the viewpoint is most often that of a minor historical figure or of a wholly fictional one. Only in *Fire from Heaven* has she employed the third person narrative.

Although she is occasionally criticised for too much historical detail, which is said to intrude upon the narrative, and although her prose has been termed stilted, Mary Renault's novels have, for a vast audience, made ancient Greece alive and exciting.

BIBLIOGRAPHICAL REFERENCES: The first full-length study is Peter Wolfe, *Mary Renault,* 1969. See also M. L. Holton, "Mary Renault," *Wilson Library Bulletin,* XXXVIII (1963), 353, and Landon C. Burns, Jr., "Men Are Only Men: The Novels of Mary Renault," *Critique,* VI, no. iii (1963), 102–121.

For reviews of various works see Frank N. Magill, *Survey of Contemporary Literature,* 1971.

ALFONSO REYES

Born: Monterrey, Mexico
Date: May 17, 1889

Died: Mexico City, Mexico
Date: December 27, 1959

PRINCIPAL WORKS

ESSAYS AND STUDIES: *Cuestiones estéticas*, 1911 (*Esthetic Questions*); *Visión de Anáhuac*, 1917; *Retratos reales e imaginarios*, 1920 (*Portraits, Real and Imaginary*); *Simpatías y Diferencias*, 1921–1926 (*Sympathies and Differences*); *Cuestiones Gongorinas*, 1927 (*Questions Relating to Góngora*); *Capítulos de Literatura Española*, 1939 (*Chapters concerning Spanish Literature*); *La Crítica en la Edad Ateniense*, 1941 (*Criticism in the Athenian Age*); *La Experiencia literaria*, 1942 (*Literary Experience*); *Ultima Thule*, 1942; *El Deslinde: Prolegómenos a la Teoría literaria*, 1952 (*The Boundary Line: Prolegomenon to Literary Theory*).

SHORT STORIES AND TALES: *El Plano Oblicuo*, 1920 (*The Oblique Plane*); *Quince Presencias*, 1955.

POEMS: *Obra poética*, 1952 (*Poetic Works*).

"The art of expression," wrote Alfonso Reyes, "did not appear to me as a rhetorical function, independent of conduct, but a means of realizing human feeling." Thus this Mexican writer defined and justified his literary vocation, so faithfully and completely fulfilled during the fifty years of his writing that he has justly been called by one of his critics, "the most accomplished example of the man of letters in México."

Born in Monterrey, capital of the State of Nuevo León in Mexico, on May 17, 1889, he was the son of General Bernardo Reyes, at that time governor of the state and a prominent politician in the regime of President Porfirio Díaz.

Having begun his schooling in his native city, Alfonso Reyes moved later to Mexico City where, in 1913, he received the professional title of lawyer. Here in Mexico City, in 1909, there appeared a generation of writers who engaged in a vigorous intellectual revolution which had enormous repercussions in Mexican culture. These writers were united in a movement called "El Ateneo de la Juventud" (The Athenaeum of Youth). Reyes was the youngest member of this group and was side by side with other writers who, afterwards, were also primary figures in the intellectual life of modern Mexico: José Vasconcelos, Antonio Caso, Martín Luis Guzmán, Enrique González Martínez. The basic aims of this group were the study and understanding of Mexican culture, the assimilation of current philosophies, literary criticism, and, above all, interest in and knowledge of universal ideas.

Immersed in these intellectual currents, Reyes left for Europe in the service of Mexican diplomacy. France, Spain, Argentina and Brazil gave testimony to his great culture and to his diplomatic skill. In Madrid he collaborated with the Center of Historical Studies as a member of the Department of Philosophy under the direction of D. Ramón Menéndez Pidal, and was also invited to contribute to the pages of *El Sol* (*The Sun*), headed by José Ortega y Gasset. In 1939, after twenty-five years—except for a few intermissions—of diplomatic service, he returned to Mexico and pursued his literary activities with the greatest enthusiasm. The universities of California, Tulane, Harvard, Havana, Princeton, and Mexico conferred honorary degrees on him, and in 1957, in recognition of his faithful and constant dedication to letters, he was named president of the Mexican Academy of Language, of which he had been a corresponding member since 1918.

The Alfonso Reyes bibliography is very extensive. During his fifty years as a writer—in 1906, at the age of seventeen, he wrote his first sonnet, "Mercenario"—his indefatigable pen has produced no less than three hundred titles, among them books of poems, criticism, essays, memoirs, plays, novels and short stories, prefaces, newspaper articles, non-literary works and translations. As a constant element of his work one finds, as much in his prose as in his verse, the lyricism that gives to his books a tone that is agreeable and gracious, ingenious and subtle. In his poetry are evident the influences of Góngora and Mallarmé combined with a personal taste for the picturesque and colloquial. In his preferred medium, the essay, he treats of a great variety of subjects. His best literary criticism is to be found in the essays of *Literary Experience,* in which he pours forth his own experiences in the profession of a writer, and in "Sobre la estética de Góngora," with which he opens the doors to the modern study and understanding of that baroque Spanish poet. Important among his strictly literary works is *Visión de Anáhuac,* a poetic study of Mexican history; among the humanistic studies, *Discurso por Virgilio, (Address in Behalf of Virgil,* 1931) containing both profound classical and American flavor; among the works with fantastic and dreamlike themes so much to Reyes' taste are included those in *Arbol de pólvora.*

In 1952, with a profound understanding of the function of a writer, Reyes produced a volume, the greatest of his critical works, on the literary phenomenon: *The Boundary Line: Prolegomenon to Literary Theory.* Here he analyzes the limitations of the artistic work of expression, style, aesthetic problems, semantics, philology, and the philosophy of language.

"American, European, universal," thus Federico de Onís has described Reyes. These epithets are well spoken if one considers that this Mexican writer, through his native sensibility, his classic form, and the universality of his subjects, is, as the same critic avers, "the most successful example of a citizen of the international world of letters, both ancient and modern."

BIBLIOGRAPHICAL REFERENCES: A work that is indispensable to all Reyes studies is the two-volume *Páginas sobre Alfonso Reyes* (I: *1911–1945,* II: *1946–1957*), a critcial anthology with an extensive bibliography compiled at and published by the University of Nuevo León, Monterrey, Mexico, 1955–1957. See, in particular, Jean Cassou, "Alfonso Reyes"; Azorín, "Azorín habla de la personalidad literaria de Alfonso Reyes"; Gabriela Mistral, "Un hombre de México"; Juan Ramón Jiménez, "Alfonso Reyes"; Karl Vossler, "El Monterrey de Alfonso Reyes"; Waldo Frank, "Note on Alfonso Reyes"; José María González de Mendoza, "Los temas mexicanos en la obra de Alfonso Reyes"; Federico de Onís, "Alfonso Reyes"; J. B. Trend, "Alfonso Reyes"; Luis Leal, "La Generación del Centenario"; Raimundo Lida, "Alfonso Reyes y sus Literaturas"; and José Luis Martínez, "La Obra de Alfonso Reyes." Supplementing this monumental work is the *Catálogo de índices de los libros de Alfonso Reyes,* with a foreword by Alfonso Rangel Guerra, a bulletin of the University of Nuevo León University Library, 1955.

Carlos González Peña, *History of American Literature*, translated 1943 (rev. ed.), contains a section on Reyes. See also Luis Garrido, *Alfonso Reyes*, 1954 (Mexico); Raimundo Lazo, *La personalidad, la creación y el mensaje de Alfonso Reyes*, 1955 (Havana); Manuel Olguín, *Alfonso Reyes, ensayista: vida y pensamiento*, 1956 (Mexico); José Luis Martínez, "La prosa de Alfonso Reyes," in *Literatura mexicana siglo XX, 1910–1949*, I, 1949 (Mexico); José María González de Mendoza, Introduction to *Verdad y Mentira*, 1950; and Manuel Alcalá, "Alfonso Reyes, el mexicano universal," *Filosofía y Letras*, XXVII (1955), Nos. 53–54, 149–164. "Our Alfonso Reyes," essays by Albert Guerard, Muna Lee, Ramón Sender, Antonio Castro Leal, and others, appeared in *Books Abroad*, XXIX (Spring, 1955).

LADISLAS REYMONT

Born: Kobiele Wielkie, Poland
Date: May 7, 1867

Died: Warsaw, Poland
Date: December 5, 1925

Principal Works

NOVELS: *Komedjantka*, 1896 (*The Comedienne*); *Fermenty*, 1897; *Ziemia obiecana*, 1899 (*The Promised Land*); *Sprawiedliwie*, 1899 (*Justice*); *Chłopi*, 1902–1909 (*The Peasants*); *Marzyciel*, 1910 (*The Dreamer*); *Wampir*, 1911 (*The Vampire*); *Rok 1794*, 1914–1919 (*The Year 1794*).

SHORT STORIES: *Przed switem*, 1902; *Burza*, 1908; *Przysięga*, 1917; *Za frontem*, 1919 (*Behind the Lines*); *Bunt*, 1924; *Krosnowa i swiat*, 1928.

Ladislas Reymont, Polish novelist and short story writer and 1924 winner of the Nobel Prize in Literature was born Wladyslaw Stanislaw Rejment, on May 7, 1867, at Kobiele Wielkie, the son of a comparatively poor country church organist. His childhood was unhappy and far from promising; he was not only poor in his studies, but so erratic in his efforts that he never completed school. He was several times apprenticed to various shops and trades but failed to hold any position long. His father, himself concerned about earning enough as organist and farmer to keep his family going, was particularly unsympathetic and stern with the boy; and the mother's piety merely made his failures seem worse. His one saving grace was his enthusiastic interest in the books which his brother brought to him, and in solitude the family's black sheep began to build the interest in literature which was ultimately to make him one of Poland's notable novelists. He was particularly interested in the book *Lilla Weneda*, (1840) a romantic historical novel by Słowacki. Later on he found the historical novels of Sienkiewicz, and he read them eagerly, vowing to pattern his work after Sienkiewicz.

His first adventures away from home were with a traveling theatrical company with which the penniless boy traveled for a year. His experiences were later reflected in *The Comedienne*.

When he returned from his theatrical venture, his father found employment for him on the Warsaw-Vienna railroad, where he managed to hold a job long enough to get a considerable amount of reading done. When he was about twenty-six years old, even though he had no funds, he decided to take a chance on establishing himself in Warsaw. He lived there in poverty and consoled himself by writing short stories. The stories finally were accepted by the Cracow *Myśl* (*Thought*) and the Warsaw *Prawda* (*Truth*). Having come to the attention of editors, although not yet famous, Reymont managed to win an assignment to write a report on Jasna Góra, a Polish shrine at Częstochowa, with which he was well acquainted, having spent some months there and having at one time considered becoming a lay brother at the shrine. The result was *Pielgrzymka do Jasnej Góry* (1895), *A Pilgrimage to Jasna Góra*).

The following year saw the publication of the novel about his theatrical wanderings, *The Comedienne*, and that moderately successful work was followed by *Fermenty* in 1897. Reymont was beginning to establish himself as a realistic writer who had considerable sympathy for the workers of Poland but very little faith in an industrialized society. His lack of enthusiasm for the then prevalent positivistic faith in science and industry was even more marked in the novel *The Promised Land,* a severe criticism of industry and its leaders, so colorful and bitter in its content that certain passages were deleted by the censor. The novel, like most of his work, reflected his own experience, this time the experience of working in a factory in Łódź, a job he held in 1897.

The positive side of his criticism of industrialized society was given in what turned out to be his most famous novel, *The Peasants,* a long, somewhat disorganized portrait of the severe life of the peasants, written over a seven year period and published from 1902 to 1909. Despite Reymont's pessimistic and fatalistic predilections, he managed to make the point that, at least from his point of view, the hard life of the peasants contributed more to the dignity of man than the city could. Reymont had been injured and had to spend a year and a half in bed; it was while convalescing that he began work on *The Peasants.*

After *The Peasants,* Reymont's work failed to satisfy the expectations which his previous novels had aroused. Becoming interested in spiritualism through Madame Blavatsky in England, he decided to write stories in which he would emphasize the psychological aspects of life. Unfortunately he was not adept at such a level, and he confused the psychological with the phenomena of spiritualism. The result was *The Dreamer* and *The Vampire,* two mediocre novels.

He regained some critical respect with his novel *The Year 1794,* a story of eighteenth century Polish political and social life, but the book was not as effective as the earlier emotional, turbulent books of factory and peasant life.

Reymont visited the United States in 1920 and traveled to various large cities to raise money for Polish relief. He was awarded the Nobel Prize in Literature in 1924 and was honored the following year by a folk congress in which his novels and his social action were reviewed and praised. Four months later he died in Warsaw, on December 5, 1925.

BIBLIOGRAPHICAL REFERENCES: Reymont's best fiction is available in translation. For biographical and critical studies see Ignacy Matuszewski, *Twórczośći Twórcy,* 1904; Jan Lorentowicz, *Ladislas Reymont, Essai sur son œuvre,* 1925; Frank L. Schoell, *Les Paysans de Ladislas Reymont,* 1925; Z. Falkowski, *Władysław Reymont, Człowiek i tworca,* 1929; and J. Krzyżanowski, *Władysław Stanisław Reymont, Tworca i dzieło,* 1937. Brief studies of Reymont in English include Ernest Boyd, "Wladyslaw Reymont, *Saturday Review of Literature,* I (November 29, 1924), 317–318; A. Stender-Peterson, "Reymont, Winner of the Nobel Prize," *Living Age,* CCCXXIV (1925), 165–169; and E. M. Almedinger, "Ladislas Reymont, Peasant and Writer," *English Review,* XLII (1926), 119–122.

ELMER RICE

Born: New York, N. Y.
Date: September 28, 1892

Died: London, England
Date: May 8, 1967

Principal Works

PLAYS: *On Trial*, 1914; *The Adding Machine*, 1923; *Close Harmony*, 1924 (with Dorothy Parker); *Wake Up, Jonathan*, 1928 (with Hatcher Hughes); *Cock Robin*, 1929 (with Philip Barry); *Street Scene*, 1929; *See Naples and Die*, 1930; *Counsellor-at-Law*, 1931; *We, the People*, 1933; *Between Two Worlds*, 1935; *American Landscape*, 1939; *Flight to the West*, 1941; *Dream Girl*, 1945; *The Grand Tour*, 1951; *The Winner*, 1954; *Cue for Passion*, 1959; *The Iron Cross*, 1965.

NOVELS: *A Voyage to Purilia*, 1930; *Imperial City*, 1937; *The Show Must Go On*, 1949.

AUTOBIOGRAPHY: *Minority Report*, 1963.

Elmer (L.) Rice, born Elmer Reizenstein in New York City on September 28, 1892, was considered during the 1920's to be as expert as O'Neill in the use of symbolism in drama. However, unlike O'Neill, only one successful play, *Dream Girl*, has come from his hands in the past quarter of a century. Though Rice did not complete high school, he managed to work his way through the New York University Law School and was graduated *cum laude* in 1912; he passed the bar examinations the same year. However, dissatisfied with the lack of quick success the legal profession presented, he wrote *On Trial* evenings, and when it was successfully produced in 1914 he gave up the law for literature. He collaborated with Hatcher Hughes, Dorothy Parker, and Philip Barry on plays and wrote movie scenarios also.

Two of his best-known plays are *The Adding Machine* and *Street Scene*; each stresses a main thesis of the playwright, that metropolitan life corrodes character and causes unnecessary alienation among people. The first is the most symbolic of any of his plays in technique, with scenery and action distorted in an expressionistic manner as seen through the eyes of the main character, Mr. Zero, a man who has as much emotional life as the adding machine he punches all day. The second play is an example of selective realism at its best, with a slice of a city tenement area as the protagonist. The effect is one of deep pity and terror. Rice had difficulty in finding a producer for *Street Scene*, and the producer who finally presented it was at first considered unwise. However, it won the Pulitzer Prize for drama and later was made into a highly successful movie. After its success Rice produced successfully the next two of his own plays. He was a regional director of the Federal Theatre in 1935 and directed dramatic shows in a housing settlement. After World War II he joined Maxwell Anderson, S. N. Behrman, Sidney Howard, and Robert Sherwood to form the Playwrights' Producing Company, an organization for the financing and producing of plays by the playwrights themselves.

BIBLIOGRAPHICAL REFERENCES: A convenient volume is *Seven Plays*, 1950. The only full-length study is Robert Hogan, *The Independence of Elmer Rice*, 1965. Brief critical estimates may be found in three works: A. H. Quinn, *A History of the*

American Drama from the Civil War to the Present Day, 1936; Burns Mantle, *Contemporary American Playwrights,* 1938; and Joseph Wood Krutch, *The American Drama Since 1918: An Informal History,* 1939. Of basic importance is R. L. Collins, "The Playwright and the Press: Elmer Rice and His Critics," *Theatre Annual,* VII (1948–49), 35–58. See also Meyer Levin, "Elmer Rice," *Theatre Arts Monthly,* XVI (1932), 54–62.

I. A. RICHARDS

Born: Chesire, England
Date: February 26, 1893

Principal Works

CRITICISM: *Foundations of Aesthetics* (with C. K. Ogden and J. Wood), 1921; *The Meaning of Meaning* (with C. K. Ogden), 1923; *Principles of Literary Criticism,* 1924; *Science and Poetry,* 1925; *Practical Criticism,* 1929; *Mencius on the Mind,* 1931; *Coleridge on Imagination,* 1934; *Interpretation in Teaching,* 1938; *How to Read a Page,* 1942; *Basic English and Its Uses,* 1943; *Speculative Instruments,* 1955; *So Much Nearer: Essays Toward a World English,* 1968; *Design for Escape: World Education Through Modern Media,* 1968.

POEMS: *Goodbye Earth and Other poems,* 1958; *The Screens and Other poems,* 1960; *Tomorrow Morning, Faustus,* 1962; *Internal Colloquies,* 1971.

Ivor Armstrong Richards, University Professor Emeritus of Harvard University, is one of the most influential figures in twentieth century scholarship. His primary impact comes from the series of volumes written in the 1920's which remain primary texts in fields as diverse as literary criticism and communicology.

Richards is perhaps most famed for his critical trilogy: *Principles of Literary Criticism, Science and Poetry,* and *Practical Criticism.* In the first of these volumes, he stated his basic theory of poetry and of criticism. *Science and Poetry* examined the role of poetry in life and forecast its future, while the final book was an application of the precepts explicated in the first two.

The critical system outlined and applied in the three volumes has often been misunderstood; Richards has been accused of dismissing the imaginative aspect of poetic creation. His interest in the neurological aspects of aesthetic appreciation has been interpreted to mean that the enjoyment of poetry rests solely upon minor interactions of brain waves.

Richards' critical precepts are, in fact, quite different from the coldly scientific position often ascribed to them. He attempted to place the poetic act on a scientifically sound basis. It is important to recall that his work appeared in reaction to Romantic critics, who emphasized the reader's ineffable emotional feelings. Richards denied the validity of such an approach to criticism. Rather, he said, the poem as an art object was a completed whole which communicated experience directly to the reader. A poet was a creator whose organization of experience was more efficient and more meaningful than that of ordinary men.

Richards' influence upon the field of communicology is due to his work with C. K. Ogden in semantics; their book, *The Meaning of Meaning,* was the first serious attempt to explore semantics and its relationship to effective communication.

BIBLIOGRAPHICAL REFERENCES: Important studies of Richards' work are W. H. N. Hotopf, *Language, Thought and Comprehension: A Case Study of the Writings of I. A. Richards,* 1965, and J. P. Schiller, *I. A. Richards' Theory of Literature,* 1969. His contributions to literary criticism are considered in many studies, among them are John Crowe Ransom, *The New Criticism,* 1941; S. E. Hyman, *The Armed*

Vision, 1948; D. G. James, *Critiques and Essays in Criticism,* edited by R. W. Stallman, 1950; George Watson, *The Literary Critics: A Study of English Descriptive Criticism,* 1962; Cleanth Brooks and William K. Wimsatt, *Literary Criticism: A Short History,* 1957; Rene Welleck, *Concepts of Criticism,* 1963; Lee T. Lemon, *The Partial Critics,* 1966; and Gerald E. Graff, "The Later Richards and the New Criticism," *Criticism,* IX (1967), 229–242.

DOROTHY M. RICHARDSON

Born: Berkshire, England
Date: 1873

Died: Beckenham, England
Date: June 17, 1957

Principal Works

NOVELS: *Pilgrimage: Pointed Roofs*, 1915; *Backwater*, 1916; *Honeycomb*, 1917; *The Tunnel*, 1919; *Interim*, 1919; *Deadlock*, 1921; *Revolving Lights*, 1923; *The Trap*, 1925; *Oberland*, 1927; *Dawn's Left Hand*, 1931; *Clear Horizon*, 1935; *Dimple Hill*, 1938.

MISCELLANEOUS: *The Quakers Past and Present*, 1914; *John Austen and the Inseparables*, 1930.

Like James Joyce, Marcel Proust, Virginia Woolf, and Katherine Mansfield, Dorothy M. Richardson, who was born in Berkshire in 1873, began early in her career to use what were then still experimental techniques in order to portray with fullness and intimacy her own sensitive reactions to experience. Unlike them, however, she has seen her works less and less read with the passage of time, although both critics and fellow novelists have noted and praised her part in enlarging the scope of the novel.

A secluded early childhood was followed by the traumatic experience of the breakup of her home when she was seventeen. Although she continued her work—writing poems, short stories, and essays—her first book was not published until fifteen years later, when *The Quakers Past and Present* appeared in 1914. The twelve-volume autobiographical novel, *Pilgrimage*, began in 1916 with *Pointed Roofs*, the first book in the series. The most recent one, *Dimple Hill* came out in 1938, the same year as the omnibus edition of *Pilgrimage*. The central figure, Miriam Henderson, has been likened to Joyce's Stephen Dedalus. Everything in the novels is filtered through the consciousness of the protagonist and presented by means of the stream-of-consciousness technique. Although the subtlety and sensitivity of the artist's perceptions have been praised, the absence of important action and the lack of sufficient selectivity and condensation have been criticized. The wife of artist Alan Odle, Miss Richardson died at Beckenham, England, on June 17, 1957.

BIBLIOGRAPHICAL REFERENCES: Criticism of Dorothy Richardson's fiction is not extensive. See John Cowper Powys, *Dorothy M. Richardson*, 1931; May Sinclair, Introduction to *Pointed Roofs*, 1919; Caesar R. Blake, *Dorothy Richardson*, 1960; Lawrence Hyde. "The Work of Dorothy Richardson," *Adelphi*, II (1924), 508–517; and Harvey Eagleson, "Pedestal for a Statue," *Sewanee Review*, XLII (1934), 42–53. Edward Wagenknecht discusses her work in the chapter titled "Stream-of-Consciousness," *Cavalcade of the English Novel*, 1943 (rev. ed., 1954).

HENRY HANDEL RICHARDSON
Ethel Florence Richardson Robertson

Born: Melbourne, Australia
Date: January 3, 1870

Died: Hastings, England
Date: March 20, 1946

Principal Works

NOVELS: *Maurice Guest,* 1908; *The Getting of Wisdom,* 1910; *The Fortunes of Richard Mahony,* 1930 (a trilogy comprising *Australia Felix,* 1917; *The Way Home,* 1925; *Ultima Thule,* 1929); *The End of a Childhood,* 1934; *The Young Cosima,* 1939.

AUTOBIOGRAPHY: *Myself When Young,* 1948.

When Sinclair Lewis said in 1941 that *The Fortunes of Richard Mahony* was "a truly major work of fiction of the twentieth century," he was giving belated recognition to one of the most neglected novelists of modern times. "Henry Handel Richardson" was the pseudonym of Ethel Florence Lindesay Richardson (also known as Henrietta Richardson), born in Melbourne, Australia, on January 3, 1870. After her education in Melbourne she went to Germany about 1890 and studied to become a concert pianist. In 1895 she married J. G. Robertson, who in 1903 became professor of German literature at the University of London. Turning from music to literature, she published at widely separated intervals the novels which have caused her to be hailed since her death as the most distinguished among Australian novelists.

An uncompromising realist, she made the facts of her family the facts of her fiction. Her first novel, *Maurice Guest,* is the story of a musician who suffers ostracism for living like a genius when he was not one; this is probably the most imaginative of her books. *The Getting of Wisdom* partly reflects the writer's schooldays and the experiences that may cause a sensitive young girl to become a writer. Then came the novels that make up *The Fortunes of Richard Mahony: Australia Felix, The Way Home,* and *Ultima Thule.* The trilogy traces the career of a man who went to Australia to find success, failed, and returned home to renew his former position. Rejected in his earlier associations and surroundings, he disintegrated spiritually and died. The work is based on the life of the writer's father. Critical recognition and some measure of popular success came with the last novel of the series. In 1934 Miss Richardson published *The End of a Childhood,* a sequel to her second novel. Her final work of fiction was *The Young Cosima,* a biographical novel dealing with twelve years in the life of the daughter of Franz Liszt. Miss Richardson died at her home in Sussex on March 20, 1946. Her unfinished autobiography, *Myself When Young,* appeared posthumously.

BIBLIOGRAPHICAL REFERENCES: The most comprehensive literary studies are Nettie Palmer, *Henry Handel Richardson,* 1950 (Sidney); and Vincent Buckley, *Henry Handel Richardson,* 1962 (Melbourne). See also Norman Bartlett, "Pioneers of a New World Literature," *South Atlantic Quarterly,* LXIX (1950), 30–41.

SAMUEL RICHARDSON

Born: Derbyshire, England　　　Died: London, England
Date: 1689　　　　　　　　　　　Date: July 4, 1761

Principal Works

NOVELS: *Pamela, or Virtue Rewarded,* 1740; *Clarissa, or The History of a Young Lady,* 1747–1748; *Sir Charles Grandison,* 1753–1754.
LETTERS: *The Correspondence of Samuel Richardson,* 1804.

About Samuel Richardson's life and personality there seems to be a great deal of information, most of it uninteresting. He was born in 1689, the son of a Derbyshire joiner and a pious but nowise unusual mother. As a boy, his thoughtful and serious nature would have recommended him for the Church, but his parents could not afford the requisite education. Instead, after moderate schooling, he was apprenticed to a London printer, John Wilde. He proved a conscientious worker for a demanding master, and in due time reaped his reward by marrying his employer's daughter and succeeding to the business. By dint of hard work and honesty his became one of the most prosperous and sought-after publishing concerns in London.

There is no evidence that Richardson had any youthful ambitions to be a writer; he was over fifty, and a successful businessman, when he stumbled, quite by accident, into his role as "father" of the English novel. From youth to old age, Richardson was unusually fond of what he characteristically called "epistolary correspondence." As a boy in Derbyshire he had been commissioned by various young ladies to compose or embellish their love letters, and in the process he had gained considerable insight into feminine emotional life and had developed an imagination that took pleasure in creating in detail fantasies concerned with the distresses of love. Later, as an apprentice, he carried on a long correspondence, often on moral subjects, with a man he describes as being a "master of the epistolary style." With this background in letter-writing, it was not unusual that two bookseller friends should suggest that he turn his talents to account by publishing a volume of model letters of various sorts. Richardson took up the idea, but characteristically amended it by proposing that the letters should teach not only how to write but also "how to think and act justly and prudently in the common concerns of human life."

The book, entitled *Familiar Letters,* appeared in 1741, but in the meantime Richardson, while writing a connected group of letters "to instruct handsome young girls, who were obliged to go out to service, . . . how to avoid the snares that might be laid against their virtue," remembered an appropriate story told him some twenty-five years before, and *Pamela,* published in 1740, was born. Perhaps the best concise description of this milestone in the development of the novel is given by Richardson himself on the title page: *Pamela: or Virtue Rewarded. In a Series of Familiar Letters from a beautiful Young Damsel, to her Parents. Now first published in order to cultivate the Principles of Virtue and Religion in the Minds of the Youth of both Sexes. A Narrative which has its Foundation in Truth and Nature; and at the same time that it agreeably entertains, by a Variety of curious and affecting Incidents, is entirely divested of all those Images, which, in too many Pieces calculated for Amusement only, tend to inflame the Minds they should instruct.* The book was not only an immediate and unparalleled success—with the average reader for its detailed descriptions of situations and emotions that at times approach the salacious, with the pious for its moral rectitude—but by adding to the realism of Defoe a power of minute mental analysis which Defoe did not possess, it set a new fashion in fiction, the novel of sensibility.

For all its success, and its importance as both one of the first epistolary novels and the prototype of the novel of sentimental analysis, *Pamela* is not without its faults. Although Richardson makes dramatic use of the letter-writing technique, the device demands an annoying degree of almost priggish self-righteousness on the part of the heroine. Further, the morality of the "lesson" taught is not above suspicion. Pamela defends her virtue valiantly, but not without an eye to the main chance, and in the end is rewarded handsomely by an offer of marriage from her master and would-be seducer.

Richardson's next novel, *Clarissa, or The History of a Young Lady,* avoids both these weaknesses. The story, which tells of the "Distresses that may attend the Misconduct both of Parents and Children in Relation to Marriage," is a truly tragic one. Not only is the characterization in this novel superbly handled, and always believable, but the central dilemma is more genuinely a moral one than in *Pamela;* the problem is not whether Clarissa will be seduced, but whether she can forgive her seducer. But the heroine is no pale, self-righteous prude. Indeed, in this novel Richardson rises to the heighth of his powers as a novelist, both in his ability to present moving and convincing situations and in his power to describe minutely human emotions at times of extreme stress.

Richardson's last novel, *Sir Charles Grandison,* is an attempt to depict a model good man and fine gentleman combined. Like the others, it is in epistolary form; and although the characterization and analysis of emotions are still excellent, it lacks the intense central dilemma that holds the attention in the first two books, and tends to make tedious reading.

After *Sir Charles Grandison* Richardson wrote little more of any importance. He continued to prosper in business, grew rich, was elected Master of the Stationers' Company, was employed to print the journals of the House of Commons, and was eventually appointed Law Printer to the king. Full of years and honors, he died in Parson's Green, London, on July 4, 1761.

Colorless as Richardson was personally, and pedestrian and prolix as his style often became, his importance in the history of the novel should not be underestimated. His books have an extraordinary power which at first attracts and in time holds the reader, and his ability to describe and his insight into the workings of the female heart are unusual. Although English fiction which came after him followed slightly different lines, it is impossible to deny Richardson the credit for inaugurating the novel of sensibility, which for a time became the fashion even more on the Continent than in England.

BIBLIOGRAPHICAL REFERENCES: There are two modern editions of Richardson's novels, that edited by Ethel M. M. McKenna, 20 vols., 1902, and the Blackwell Edition, 19 vols., 1930. The basic source for all biographical studies is *The Correspondence of Samuel Richardson,* edited by Anna L. Barbauld, 6 vols., 1804. The definitive biography is now T. C. D. Eaves and B. I. Kimpel, *Samuel Richardson,* 1971. See also Alan D. McKillop, *Samuel Richardson, Printer and Novelist,* 1936; Clara L. Thomson, *Samuel Richardson,* 1900; Austin Dobson, *Samuel Richardson,* 1902; Brian W. Downs, *Richardson,* 1928; Paul Dottin, *Samuel Richardson, imprimeur de Londres,* 1931; and William M. Sale, Jr., *Samuel Richardson, Master Printer,* 1950. Two companion books to Richardson studies are W. M. Sale, *Samuel Richardson: A Bibliographical Record of His Literary Career,* 1936; and Francesco Cordasco, *Samuel Richardson: A List of Critical Studies Published from 1896 to 1946,* 1948. Recent studies are Ira Konigsberg, *Samuel Richardson and the Dramatic Novel,* 1968; and John Carroll, ed., *Samuel Richardson: A Collection of Critical Essays,* 1969.

CONRAD RICHTER

Born: Pine Grove, Pennsylvania
Date: October 13, 1890

Died: Pottsville, Pennsylvania
Date: October 30, 1968

Principal Works

NOVELS: *The Sea of Grass,* 1937; *The Trees,* 1940; *Tacey Cromwell,* 1942; *The Free Man,* 1943; *The Fields,* 1946; *Always Young and Fair,* 1947; *The Town,* 1950; *The Light in the Forest,* 1953; *The Lady,* 1957; *The Waters of Kronos,* 1960; *A Simple Honorable Man,* 1962; *The Grandfathers,* 1964; *The Trees, The Fields, The Town,* published in one volume as *The Awakening Land,* 1966; *A Country of Strangers,* 1966; *The Aristocrat,* 1968.

SHORT STORIES: *Early Americana,* 1936.

PHILOSOPHICAL STUDY: *The Mountain on the Desert: A Philosophical Journey,* 1955.

JUVENILE: *Over the Blue Mountain,* 1967.

Our leading specialist in early Americana, Conrad (Michael) Richter was born on October 13, 1890, in Pine Grove, Pennsylvania, a town which his great-grandfather, a major in the War of 1812 and a local store and tavern keeper, helped to name. His father was a minister, as were his grandfather, a great-uncle, and an uncle; he feels that his interest in the American past goes back beyond them to earlier ancestors who were soldiers, country squires, traders, farmers. During his boyhood, as his father moved from charge to charge, he became familiar with sections of the state where old habits of living and speech still survived, and these early impressions are reflected in his books. In those days it was expected that he would study for the ministry, but at fifteen he finished high school and went to work driving a wagon over the mountains of central Pennsylvania.

A variety of jobs followed—work in a machine shop, in a coal breaker, on a farm, reporting for Johnstown and Pittsburgh papers. At nineteen he was editor of a country weekly. For two years he worked as a private secretary in Cleveland, Ohio. After a brief mining venture in the Coeur d'Alenes he returned to Pennsylvania to set up a small publishing business of his own. During the next decade his writing was divided between magazine fiction and several nonfiction books of scientific-philosophical theorizing such as *Human Vibration* (1925) and *Principles of Bio-physics* (1927). *Brothers of No Kin,* a collection of short stories, was published in 1924. He married Harvena M. Achenbach in 1915. The Richters had one daughter, Harvena, a poet and short story writer.

In 1928 Conrad Richter sold his business and moved his family to New Mexico. Interested from childhood in stories of pioneer days, he found in the American Southwest a region not long removed from the everyday realities of the frontier experience. Out of the files of old newspapers, diaries, letters, land deeds, account books, and from tales heard at first hand from older settlers in the Southwest, he filled his notebooks with material which eventually became the short stories collected in *Early Americana.* Chronologically and technically, these stories make a good introduction to the whole body of his fiction because they reveal the working of a specialized point of view. Projected by memory or time into a middle distance where his people act freely, away from the distractions and confusion of the present, the rigors and dangers of the frontier do not enlarge upon life for pictorial or dramatic effect; they are its actual substance. If the present intrudes briefly on the past, as it does in several of the stories, it is only because the lives of his people extend into our own time. In these stories the reader may trace the development of a narrative method. It is not the simple pastness of the past that is important but the effect gained by a useful frame of reference.

In *The Sea of Grass*, his first novel, the story of the passing of the great ranges is told long after the events have taken place by an observer who has reflected on the meaning of deeds of betrayal and violence viewed years before. On a domestic level the account of Colonel Jim Brewton and his cattle empire, of the wife who deserted him for a self-seeking politician, and of their outlaw son parallels a picture of the spacious land ravaged by conflict and greed. The same mold of reminiscence shapes *Tacey Cromwell*, in which the vividly realized atmosphere of an Arizona mining town in its boom days is the background for the story of a dance-hall fancy woman, her gambler lover and his small half-brother, and the miner's orphan whom she adopts. Her attempts at respectability fail when the children are taken from her by the town's prim housewives and her lover deserts her to make a proper marriage. Tacey's story is moving but never sentimentalized, realistically presented by a boy innocent of the social implications but candidly observant of the results. *Always Young and Fair*, also told by an observer, presents a small-town heiress who after the death of her lover in the Spanish-American War renounces the world as represented by the Pennsylvania community in which she lives. In his other, more objective, novels Richter has limited his story to the point of view and the idiom of his period. *The Free Man* tells of Henry Dellicker, a Palatine redemptioner who ran away from his Philadelphia master and as Henry Free made a new life for himself among the freedom-loving Pennsylvania German settlers resisting British authority on the farming frontier beyond the Blue Mountains. *The Light in the Forest* deals with a white boy reclaimed from his Indian captors. His efforts to return to the wild forest life and his friendship with a young Indian uncover deeper meanings, the Emersonian idea that for everything given in human society something fundamental is taken away. *The Lady* marks a return to Richter's earlier method; this story of some events surrounding an unsolved disappearance in the New Mexico Territory is told by a youthful observer and participant.

Conrad Richter's major work is the trilogy made up of *The Trees, The Fields,* and *The Town,* novels tracing the history of a pioneer family in the Ohio Valley from the wilderness years of the eighteenth century to the period of the Civil War. The story, following the life of Sayward Luckett from girlhood in the woods to matriarchal old age in the town of Americus, Ohio, begins with a picture of the hardship and waste which frontier life imposed on those who subdued the savage land and ends with its characters involved in the political, social, and moral problems of modern society. These books are wholly in the American grain; on a deeper level than that of action and character they touch upon matters complex and still obscure in the national consciousness: the restlessness, the violence, the communal guilt and shame, the inner loneliness, the secret fears. That Richter sees in his writing undertones of symbolism and myth is indicated by *The Mountain on the Desert,* a book written to extend the themes of his novels and to define his vitalistic philosophy. This deeper texture makes the past a necessary condition of his work, not to create a painted backdrop for appropriate action, as in most historical novels, but to effect a dimension which gives spatial depth to his perspective of meaning.

The Waters of Kronos, which received The National Book Award for fiction in 1961, and *A Simple Honorable Man* are the first two volumes of another trilogy which the author did not live to complete. In these novels he returned to the Pennsylvania of his ancestors and wrote two quietly beautiful stories of the Donner family and the past recaptured. Both books received the highest critical praise. His last two novels, *The Grandfathers* and *The Aristocrat,* were generally held to be good but not as impressive as his earlier work.

BIBLIOGRAPHICAL REFERENCES: Conrad Richter's article, "The Early American Quality," *Atlantic Monthly,* CLXXXVI (September, 1950), 26–30, provides insight into his literary point of view and historical interests. For criticism see Edwin W. Gaston, *Conrad Richter,* 1965; Robert J. Barnes, *Conrad Richter,* 1968; Bruce Sutherland, "Conrad Richter's Americana," *New Mexico Quarterly,* XV (1945), 413–422; Dayton Kohler, "Conrad Richter: Early Americana," *College English,* VIII (1947), 221–227; Frederic I. Carpenter, "Conrad Richter's Pioneers: Reality and Myth," *College English,* XII (1950), 77–82; and John T. Flanagan, "Folklore in the Novels of Conrad Richter," *Midwest Folklore,* II (1952), 5-14.

LYNN RIGGS

Born: Claremore, Oklahoma
Date: August 31, 1899

Died: New York, N. Y.
Date: June 30, 1954

Principal Works

PLAYS: *Big Lake*, 1927; *Sump'n Like Wings*, 1928; *A Lantern to See By*, 1928; *Roadside*, 1930; *Green Grow the Lilacs*, 1931; *Russet Mantle*, 1936; *Cherokee Night*, 1936; *Toward the Western Sky*, 1951.

To the public, Lynn Riggs is only remotely associated with *Oklahoma*; in fact, his *Green Grow the Lilacs* on which the musical is based proved to be the playwright's only popular success. He was, however, a very good poet whose true field was that type of folk play which often lacks widespread appeal.

Riggs was born August 31, 1899, at Claremore, Oklahoma, into the life he portrayed so well in his best work. His father was a rancher, and the family was on good terms with the Rogers family of Claremore. He attended the local schools and the state university, sandwiching his education with a variety of jobs, some associated with writing. His poems were published in national magazines before any of his plays were accepted commercially. *Borned in Texas,* produced as *Roadside* in 1930, was an instant failure on Broadway despite the fact that Arthur Hopkins, Barrett Clark, and others believed in it.

Green Grow the Lilacs, which followed, received an excellent Theatre Guild production in 1931. This same group insisted that Rodgers and Hammerstein revise the play as a musical; out of this collaboration *Oklahoma* was born. In the meantime, Riggs went right on writing, occasionally appearing as visiting lecturer in universities, and assisting in productions, mostly non-professional, of his later works. He died in New York City on June 30, 1954.

Second only to Paul Green in the provocative use of folklore in drama, Riggs was never a popular playwright, yet he continued to write and produce individually excellent plays. No one else has yet taken his place, and criticism has not yet evaluated his minor but significant contribution to the American drama.

BIBLIOGRAPHICAL REFERENCES: Lynn Riggs received little critical attention. In the absence of full studies, survey volumes must be consulted: Richard D. Skinner, *Our Changing Theatre,* 1931; Montrose J. Moses and John Mason Brown, eds., *The American Theatre as Seen by Its Critics, 1752-1934,* 1934; John Mason Brown, *Two on the Aisle,* 1938; and Alan S. Dawson, ed., *The American Drama and Its Critics,* 1965, 116–127. See also Stanley Vestal, "Lynn Riggs: Poet and Dramatist," *Sewanee Review,* XV (Autumn 1929), 64–71—an important article; R. L. Lowe, "The Lyrics of Lynn Riggs," *Poetry,* XXXVIII (1931), 347–349; and Lee Mitchell, "A Designer at Work," *Theatre Arts Monthly,* XVIII (1934), 874–877.

RAINER MARIA RILKE

Born: Prague, Czechoslovakia
Date: December 4, 1875

Died: Valmont, Switzerland
Date: December 29, 1926

Principal Works

POEMS: *Leben und Lieder*, 1894 (*Life and Songs*); *Traumgekrönt*, 1897 (*Dreamcrowned*); *Mir zur Feier*, 1899 (*For My Rest*); *Das Buch der Bilder*, 1902 (*The Book of Pictures*); *Das Stundenbuch*, 1905 (*Poems from the Book of Hours*); *Die Weise von Liebe und Tod des Cornets Christoph Rilke*, 1906 (*The Tale of the Love and Death of Cornet Christopher Rilke*); *Neue Gedichte*, 1907–1908 (*New Poems*); *Fünf Gesänge*, 1914 (*Five Songs*); *Duineser Elegien*, 1923 (*Duino Elegies*); *Die Sonette an Orpheus*, 1923 (*Sonnets to Orpheus*).

PLAYS: *Ohne Gegenwart*, 1898 (*Without the Present*); *Tägliche Leben*, 1902 (*Everyday Life*).

ESSAYS: *Worpswede*, 1903; *Auguste Rodin*, 1903.

STORIES AND TALES: *Am Leben Hin*, 1899 (*To a Lost Life*); *Zwei Prager Geschichten*, 1899 (*Two Prague Stories*); *Geschichten vom Lieben Gott*, 1900 (*Stories of God*).

NOVEL: *Aufzeichnungen des Malte Laurids Brigge*, 1910 (*The Notebook of Malte Laurids Brigge*).

LETTERS: *Briefe an einen jungen Dichter*, 1929 (*Letters to a Young Poet*); *Briefe an eine junge Frau*, 1930; *Gesammelte Briefe*, 1939–1941; *Selected Letters of Rainer Maria Rilke, 1902–1926*, 1946.

In his poetry, Rainer Maria Rilke, born at Prague on December 4, 1875, transcended the cloying limitations of Romanticism, devoting his creative energies to what has been called an eternal "struggle for clarity and coherence." It is somewhat ironic, in view of his search for a static and depersonalized system of images, that his own life—and, still more ironically, his death—should have conformed so perfectly to the stereotyped romantic image of The Poet. He was, in fact, all of those things that a Romantic Poet should be: a sickly, sensitive, and misunderstood young man, constantly harassed and frequently crushed by the unfeeling demands of a cruel materialistic society; a wanderer searching hopelessly for a land of peace and of truth; and, most aptly, a passionate but faithless lover, a true worshipper of the muse in her earthly as well as in her sublime incarnations.

On this latter point, it has been said that "women always played a decisive part in determining Rilke's life." The course of this life can be plotted by a consideration of the decisive parts that, successively, these women played. First there was the mother and the familiar Byronic rejection theme. At ten the spoiled but unloved Maria was packed off to military school where he remained until, broken in health, he was allowed to exchange the rigors of military discipline for the dreariness of a business education. This phase he endured until the second woman in his life appeared upon the scene. She was a young governess with whom he eloped. When Rilke repented his rash action and returned to Prague, he discovered that his mother had moved to

Vienna and that his father had disowned him. Here an uncle, one Jaroslav Rilke, came to his rescue, providing him with tutors and supporting him while he attended the University of Prague.

His attendance there was short-lived, however, because of his uncle's untimely death. But at this point a second mistress, his "bright flame," Valery David-Rhonfeld, exerted her influence. The result was his first collection of poems, *Life and Songs,* published at her expense, and his transfer to the more congenial atmosphere of the University of Munich.

It was at Munich that he began earnestly to pursue his vocation as a poet, and it was from Munich that his long and restless wanderings began. With the publication of his fifth volume of verse, *For My Rest,* his artistic abilities were firmly established, but his desire for a "spiritual homeland" was unsatisfied. He left Munich for Russia, where he visited Tolstoy and met Clara Westoff, a talented young sculptress, a pupil of Rodin, who was then working at the artists' colony at Worpswede. She and Rilke were married in 1901, and for a time the two lived happily in a productive partnership of their respective creative endeavors.

Financial pressure finally destroyed their artistic idyl. Rilke was forced to find work. He had by this time become reconciled with his father, who obligingly offered him a job in a bank. The younger Rilke was horrified. He accepted, instead, a commission to write a critical biography of his wife's great master, Auguste Rodin. In Paris he met the great sculptor, who immediately became his idol. Rilke remained with Rodin for over a year, publishing his monograph, *Auguste Rodin,* and then, after traveling for his failing health first into Italy and next to Denmark, the land of his other great idol, Peter Jacobsen, he returned to France to become Rodin's secretary, an occupation hardly compatible with his poetic temperament. After a year Rilke returned to his literary works.

A productive period which ended with the second volume of *New Poems,* called "his first really mature poetry," was followed by the resumption of his wanderings and the influence of still another woman, the Princess Marie von Thurn und Taxis-Hohenlohe, who allowed him the use of her castle overlooking the Adriatic and who inspired him to renewed creative activity. But soon again he was wandering, not stopping until the war interrupted both his travels and his writing. After the war he settled down in Switzerland, where he produced his final and his greatest poetic triumphs, his *Duino Elegies* and his *Sonnets to Orpheus,* and where he met the last woman who was to influence his life. It is not known who she was, but she was beautiful enough to inspire the ill and aging Rilke to pick a rose for her. The rose pricked his finger. A fatal infection set in. The poet died, symbolically wounded fatally by the eternal poetic symbol of love, at Valmont, Switzerland, on December 29, 1926.

BIBLIOGRAPHICAL REFERENCES: Rilke's major works are now available in translation, the most recent being *Poems, 1906-1926,* translated by J. B. Leishman, 1957. For biographical and critical studies see Lou Andreas-Salomé, *Rainer Maria Rilke,* 1928; Federico Olivero, *Rainer Maria Rilke,* 1929; F. Gundolf, *Rainer Maria Rilke,* 1936; Katharina Kippenberg, *Rainer Maria Rilke,* 1935; E. M. Butler, *Rainer Maria Rilke,*

1941; Nora Wydenbruck, *Rilke, Man and Poet,* 1949; F. W. van Heerikhuizen, *Rainer Maria Rilke: His Life and Work,* translated 1952; William Laurens Graff, *Rainer Maria Rilke: Creative Anguish of a Modern Poet,* 1956; Heinz F. Peters, *Rainer Maria Rilke: Masks and the Man,* 1960; Pricilla Washburn Shaw, *Rilke, Valéry and Yeats: The Domain of the Self,* 1964; and Siegfried Mandel, *Rainer Maria Rilke: The Poetic Instinct,* 1965. *Rainer Maria Rilke: Aspects of His Mind and Poetry* was edited by William Rose and G. Craig Houston, 1938. For brief studies see also Frank Wood, "Rainer Maria Rilke: Paradoxes," *Sewanee Review,* XLVII (1939), 586–592, and "Rilke and D. H. Lawrence," *German Review,* XV (1940), 213–223; Barker Fairley, "Rainer Maria Rilke: An Estimate," *University of Toronto Quarterly,* XI (1942), 1–14; and Ernst Rose, "Rainer Maria Rilke and the Heroic," *German Review,* XVIII (1943), 266–276.

ARTHUR RIMBAUD

Born: Charleville, France
Date: October 20, 1854

Died: Marseilles, France
Date: November 10, 1891

PRINCIPAL WORKS

POEMS: *Une Saison en Enfer,* 1873 (*A Season in Hell*); *Les Illuminations,* 1886 (*Illuminations*); *Reliquaire,* 1891 (*Reliquary*); *Poésies complètes,* 1895; *Le Bateau ivre,* 1920 (*The Drunken Boat*); *Les Stupra,* 1923 (*Debaucheries*).
LETTERS: *Lettres de Jean-Arthur Rimbaud, Égypte, Arabie, Éthiopie,* 1899; *Lettres de la vie littéraire,* 1931.

The life of (Jean Nicolas) Arthur Rimbaud was brief, lasting a scant thirty-seven years, and his life as a poet was briefer still, ending with the completion of *A Season in Hell* in 1873, only a little over three years after his first stormy entrance into Paris in 1870. Yet in this brief tenure as a poet he managed to compose enough verse to fill a sizable volume, and, what is much more important than quantity, he managed to write with such power and such vision that he changed the whole course of the French Symbolist movement and exerted an influence that is still being felt in literature today.

His vision was a dual one, angelic and diabolic at the same time. He followed it compulsively and agonizingly, or, rather, he was driven by it from one excess to another, and from one country to another over two continents, until finally his spiritual agony became a physical one and he was consumed by it completely.

The story of his life has been called a saint's legend in reverse. Like the saint, he was seeking complete truth, a perfect communion with God: that was the angelic side of his vision. Like the saint, he knew that he would have to put aside completely the things of this world, but he would do so not through deprivation but through excess. That was the diabolic side of his experience, the descent into hell. That is one way of looking at the facts. Another would be to say simply that he was the victim of a compulsive neurosis and that in one stage of his progressive disease he was compelled to write some brilliant poetry. But whatever it was, vision or neurosis, he was driven, and his life was one of pain.

Born in Charleville, France, on October 20, 1854, he was writing poems by the time he was fifteen, and by sixteen, through the guidance of a rhetoric professor named Georges Izambard, he had already become an anticlerical revolutionary. When he was sixteen he left the college in Charleville and made his first pilgrimage to Paris. This started out by train, but because he did not have enough money for his fare he was thrown in jail upon arrival. Shipped back to Charleville, he refused to return to his studies but set off again for the capital, this time on foot.

On this second trip to Paris he met Verlaine. Some of Rimbaud's early poems had been printed in *La Revue* and *La Charge,* and Verlaine, having read them, was anxious to meet their young author. The two were introduced by Bretagne—who also introduced Rimbaud to occultism—and their tempestuous and abnormal relationship began. Verlaine had only recently been married, but he found the handsome younger poet more attractive than his pregnant wife. Mme. Verlaine objected to the association. Rimbaud returned home for a time, composed a number of poems at Charleville, and then traveled to Brussels, where Verlaine, leaving his wife and newborn child, met him. The two continued to London, remaining there for almost a year while Rimbaud wrote his first *Illuminations.*

He left Verlaine for the second time in April, 1873. His career as a poet was almost over when he returned to France and began *A Season in Hell.* But the relationship with Verlaine was not entirely finished; Rimbaud went once more to Brussels, where Verlaine was staying, reunited with his wife. The three met and an altercation ensued in which Verlaine wounded Rimbaud in the wrist with a bullet from the pistol he had bought to take his own life. Verlaine was sentenced to two years in prison and Rimbaud left Brussels.

Once more in Charleville, he resumed his writing, finishing his *Illuminations* and *A Season in Hell* and finding, with the latter, that there was no more in poetry for him. With the end of his writing career, his wanderings began again. Driven by a form of madness, he traveled throughout Europe, mostly on foot, searching for the true action that would mean life to him. Not finding it, he joined the Dutch colonial army, but soon deserted and traveled home once more. Finally, in April, 1880, he left for Africa, and there, for eleven years, he remained as an exporter, a gun-runner, and even, it has been suggested, a trader in slaves. However deep he went into the back country, he could not travel far enough to fulfill his haunted vision or relieve his compulsion. He died shortly after his thirty-seventh birthday, after a rheumatic infection of the right leg had sent him to Marseilles for treatment. When his condition grew worse, the leg was amputated, but the infection spread. Rimbaud died, feverish and tormented, on November 10, 1891.

The influence of Rimbaud on French poetry is as obvious now as it ever was. Many have taken over where he left off, but it is doubtful whether any have surpassed him in the ability to call forth images of startling new intensity. No serious discussion of French poetry of either the nineteenth or the twentieth century can proceed very far without Rimbaud's name being evoked.

BIBLIOGRAPHICAL REFERENCES: Rimbaud's *Œuvres complètes,* with a critical preface by Paul Claudel, appeared in 1929. H. de Bouillane de Lacoste has edited three critical editions of the poet's work: *Poésies complètes,* 1939; *Une Saison en Enfer,* 1941; and *Les Illuminations,* 1949. There is also Wallace Fowlie, editor and translator, *Complete Works, Selected Letters,* 1966. The best single book on Rimbaud in English is Enid Starkie, *Rimbaud,* 1947 (rev. ed.). For biography and criticism see also D. Berrichon, *Vie de Arthur Rimbaud,* 1897; J. M. Carré, *La Vie aventureuse d'Arthur Rimbaud,* 1926; Benjamin Fondane, *Rimbaud le voyau,* 1933; C. A. Hackett, *Le Lyrisme de Rimbaud,* 1938; H. de Bouillane de Lacoste, *Rimbaud et le problème des Illuminations,* 1949; Jacques Gengoux, *La Pensée poétique de Rimbaud,* 1950; also, in English, Edgell Rickword, *Rimbaud, the Boy and the Poet,* 1963; and Wallace Fowlie, *Rimbaud,* 1965.

ELIZABETH MADOX ROBERTS

Born: Perryville, Kentucky
Date: October 30, 1881

Died: Orlando, Florida
Date: March 13, 1941

Principal Works

NOVELS: *The Time of Man,* 1926; *My Heart and My Flesh,* 1927; *Jingling in the Wind,* 1928; *The Great Meadow,* 1930; *A Buried Treasure,* 1931; *He Sent Forth a Raven,* 1935; *Black Is My Truelove's Hair,* 1938.
SHORT STORIES: *The Haunted Mirror,* 1932; *Not by Strange Gods,* 1941.
POEMS: *Under the Tree,* 1922; *Song in the Meadow,* 1940.

Among the writers who have given new perspectives to Southern life and character in fiction, Elizabeth Madox Roberts is notable for her sympathetic portrayal of humanity and the poetic qualities of her style. To the folk materials of her region she added the techniques of the modern novel of sensibility. As a result the final effect of her writing is quite different from anything found in the older local colorists whose stories demonstrate an art based on pictures of the quaint and strange enclosing sentimental or melodramatic plots. Local in her choice of setting but never provincial in outlook, she transformed her Kentucky background into a landscape of the imagination and the spirit, filled it with living figures realistically and regionally true to its manners and its climate but recognizable as part of the greater human world as well.

Elizabeth Madox Roberts was born in Perryville, October 30, 1881, in the Pigeon River country where her family had settled generations before. Among her earliest recollections were a grandmother's stories of ancestors who came over Boone's Trace in the 1770's; thus the history of Kentucky became for her a personal account of family tradition. Ill during much of her early life, she lived for several years in the Colorado Rockies after her graduation from high school. *In the Great Steep's Garden,* an uneven but promising first book of poems, appeared in 1915. Two years later she entered the University of Chicago, from which she was graduated in 1921. During her undergraduate days, a member of a literary group that included Glenway Wescott and Yvor Winters, she wrote poetry and prose, winning the McLaughlin Prize for essay writing and the Fisk Prize for a group of poems which, expanded, became *Under the Tree,* published in 1922.

Miss Roberts came to the writing of fiction after several false starts during the years of her literary apprenticeship in New York. One novel had been started but abandoned in despair and another was left unfinished when she began *The Time of Man,* which brought her critical recognition and public fame in 1926. Working on her second novel during a stay in California, she wrote day after day in her Santa Monica apartment, watched from her windows the rolling surf of the Pacific, and grew eager to return to Kentucky. Perhaps that is why the limits of the state expand to become a satirical symbol of American civilization in her third novel, *Jingling in the Wind,* rewritten from an unfinished version preceding *The Time of Man.* When these books appeared, however,

Miss Roberts had already returned to Kentucky to make her permanent home in Springfield. Having found in the tradition and life of her own region those roots and ties which the writer must possess if his work is to draw any meaning from man's relation to his time and place, in her life as in her books she made a segment of the Kentucky landscape her measure of the larger world.

This was a child's world in *Under the Tree*, a poetic anthology of childhood impressions. But the same world has grown vast and strangely cruel to Ellen Chesser in *The Time of Man* as she scrawls her name with a fingertip upon empty air and ponders the mystery of her identity. Among her people pioneering impulses have dwindled to the restlessness of the tenant farmer; her life is a series of removals through a tragic cycle of love, desertion, marriage, and the beginning of another pilgrimage when her children have begun to repeat in legend fashion the story of her earlier migrations. A work of poetic realism, the novel is as timeless as a pastoral or a folk ballad and seemingly as effortless in design. Darkness of the spirit hangs over *My Heart and My Flesh*, in which the aristocratic, futile world of Theodosia Bell dissolves in hunger, madness, and the emotional shock of murder. *Jingling in the Wind*, a less successful effort, brings *Candide* and *Alice in Wonderland* into Kentucky, and attempts a travesty on the Babbitts, professional optimists, and brisk salesmen of our industrial civilization. *The Great Meadow*, a re-creation of the historic past, is a prose monument to the pioneer; in the story of Diony Hall, her heroine, Miss Roberts tried to catch the spirit and even the accents of her grandmother's tales of the settlement of Kentucky.

A Buried Treasure is an old morality story retold, presenting the situation which arises when a pot of hidden gold brings unexpected wealth to those who do not know what to do with it. The short stories of *The Haunted Mirror* represent further crystallization of experience, a compression of inarticulate lives into moments of significance and perception: an awakening to life in "The Sacrifice of the Maidens," the terror of love in "The Scarecrow," the candid spectacle of death in "Death at Bearwallow," the tragedy of violence in "Record at Oak Hill." *He Sent Forth a Raven*, set against the first two decades of the present century, dramatizes in mystic and poetic fashion the conflict between the outer realities of man's world and darker passions of the human spirit.

The cloudy mysticism which critics and readers found puzzling in *He Sent Forth a Raven* does not appear in her last novel, *Black Is My Truelove's Hair*. As simple in outline as the folk song from which its title was taken, it is saved from thematic bareness by Miss Roberts' richly colored landscapes and her sensitive perceptions of her people. The novel is a prose ballad of love betrayed, a ballad with a happy ending, however, and it is written in prose that sings.

Elizabeth Madox Roberts never forgot that she was a poet before she became a novelist. From time to time, in the intervals between books, her poems appeared in various magazines. In 1940 the best of these were printed in *Song in the Meadow*, a collection of lyrics in which she spoke in her own person as a poet. *Not by Strange Gods*, a second book of short stories, was her last published work. She died of anemia in Orlando, Florida, on March 13, 1941.

BIBLIOGRAPHICAL REFERENCES: There is no authorized biography. The first extended critical study is Harry M. Campbell and Ruel E. Foster, *Elizabeth Madox Roberts: American Novelist,* 1956. For criticism in books and periodicals see also Harlan Hatcher, *Creating the Modern American Novel,* 1935; Edward Wagenknecht, *Cavalcade of the American Novel,* 1952; Earl H. Rovit, *Herald to Chaos: The Novels of Elizabeth Madox Roberts,* 1960; Frederick P. W. McDowell, *Elizabeth Madox Roberts,* 1963; Glenway Wescott, "Elizabeth Madox Roberts: A Personal Note," *Bookman,* LXXI (1930), 12–15; Mark Van Doren, "Elizabeth Madox Roberts: Her Mind and Style," *English Journal,* XXI (1932), 521–528; J. Donald Adams, "Elizabeth Madox Roberts," *Virginia Quarterly Review,* XII (1936), 80–90; Francis L. Janney, "Elizabeth Madox Roberts," *Sewanee Review,* XLV (1937), 388–410; Alex M. Buchan, "Elizabeth Madox Roberts," *Southwest Review,* XXV (1940), 463–481; Dayton Kohler, "Elizabeth Madox Roberts: A Regional Example," *Mountain Life and Work,* XXII (Fall, 1946), 5–8; Earl H. Rovit, "Recurrent Symbols in the Novels of Elizabeth Madox Roberts," *Boston University Studies in English,* II (Spring, 1956), 35–54; and Robert Penn Warren, "Elizabeth Madox Roberts: Life Is from Within," *Saturday Review,* XLVI (9 March 1963), 20–21, 38.

KENNETH ROBERTS

Born: Kennebunk, Maine
Date: December 8, 1885

Died: Kennebunk
Date: July 21, 1957

Principal Works

NOVELS: *Arundel,* 1930; *The Lively Lady,* 1931; *Rabble in Arms,* 1933; *Captain Caution,* 1934; *Northwest Passage,* 1937; *Oliver Wiswell,* 1940; *Lydia Bailey,* 1947; *Boon Island,* 1956; *The Battle of Cowpens,* 1958.
AUTOBIOGRAPHY: *I Want to Write,* 1949.

For nearly thirty years, Kenneth Roberts was the scourge of academic historians. A novelist with a journalism background, Roberts loved the history of early America and, more specifically, the history of his native New England. Nothing infuriated him more than the distortion of historical fact, and, as far as he was concerned, no single group of writers distorted history more than the professional historians who, he claimed, mindlessly perpetuated errors of fact and of interpretation.

Roberts' own conviction was that history should be written neutrally, without romantic mythmaking. His two major novels reflect this attitude clearly. In *Arundel,* which chronicles Benedict Arnold's attack on Quebec, the character of the archetypal American traitor is drawn dispassionately, almost sympathetically. *Northwest Passage* is considered by many critics to be Roberts' masterpiece, and his depiction of Robert Rogers shows Rogers as the author believed him to be, partially the romantic hero of history texts, and partially an unscrupulous adventurer.

Kenneth Roberts was a big and vital man. His novels reflect these qualities and are, as several critics have pointed out, most exciting when describing sprawling scenes of violent action. The novels are less successful when their writer depicts more mundane matters, and one senses that the author himself found such scenes tedious and was anxious to get to more interesting matters.

Above all, Kenneth Roberts possessed enthusiastic love for history. His novels are infused with his enthusiasm, which expresses itself in myriad carefully sketched details uncovered during a lifetime of ceaseless reading and research. His work has been credited with fostering public interest in early American history, as the citation for the special Pulitzer Prize awarded him in 1957 stated. By the end of his life, he had even won the grudging esteem of professional historians, who had been forced by his irascibility to reëxamine their own assumptions.

BIBLIOGRAPHICAL REFERENCES: There is little material on Roberts available. See the collection of articles in "For the Quinquennial of Kenneth Roberts," *Colby Library Quarterly,* VI (September, 1962), 83–132; and Ruth Stemple, "Kenneth Roberts: A Supplementary Checklist," *Bulletin of Bibliography,* XXII (1959), 228–230.

For a review of *Northwest Passage* see Frank N. Magill, *Masterplots:* Comprehensive Library Edition, 1968, 3308–3310. For a review of *Boon Island* see *ibid.*, *Survey of Contemporary Literature,* 1971, 476–479.

THOMAS WILLIAM ROBERTSON

Born: Newark, England
Date: January 9, 1829

Died: London, England
Date: February 3, 1871

PRINCIPAL WORKS

PLAYS: *David Garrick*, 1864; *Society*, 1865; *Ours*, 1866; *Caste*, 1867; *School*, 1869; *M.P.*, 1870.

Thomas William Robertson, born at Newark, England, on January 9, 1829, was born also into the theatrical world, for his father and mother were both members of the profession. Because his parents were on the road with a company a great deal, Robertson was cared for much of the time by a distant relative, his great-uncle's widow. Robertson himself made his first appearance on the stage at the age of five. As early as 1843, when but fourteen, he left school to become a stagehand and prompter with his father's players, the Lincoln Company. In 1848, following the dissolution of the Lincoln Company, Robertson went to London, where he found work in the smaller theaters.

His career as a dramatist began with *A Night's Adventure* (1851), but during the 1850's his success as a playwright was slight. During those years he acted with provincial touring companies, wrote, and tried unsuccessfully to enlist in the British Army. In 1856 he married Elizabeth Burton, an actress. Upon the death of their second child in 1858, Robertson returned to London with his family. There he worked as an editor, free-lance writer, and translator. Still his success was so slight that he seriously considered opening a tobacco shop. His fortunes changed, however, when *David Garrick* was produced in 1864. There followed a whole series of successful plays, produced at London's Prince of Wales Theatre: *Society*, *Caste*, his most famous play, and others. Most of Robertson's plays combine sentiment and a superficial worldliness in a fashion which caused critics in his time to dub them "cup-and-saucer drama." Robertson's health failed in 1870, and he made a journey to Torquay to recuperate in December of that year. The effort to restore his health failed, however, and he died in London, February 3, 1871.

BIBLIOGRAPHICAL REFERENCES: The best edition of Robertson's plays is *Principal Dramatic Works*, 2 vols., 1889, with a memoir by his son, T. W. S. Robertson. *Caste* and *Society* were edited by T. Edgar Pemberton, 1905. The standard biography is by T. Edgar Pemberton, *Life and Writings of T. W. Robertson*, 1893. Valuable information from his actress-manager appears in Sir Squire and Lady Bancroft, *Recollections of Sixty Years*, 1909. The only full critical study is Maynard Savin, *Thomas William Robertson: His Plays and Stagecraft*, 1950. Of basic importance is Sir Arthur Wing Pinero, "The Theatre of the 'Seventies," in *The Eighteen-Seventies*, edited by H. Granville-Barker, 1929. See also J. H. Friswell, *Modern Men of Letters*, 1870; and C. F. Armstrong, *Shakespeare to Shaw*, 1913.

EDWIN ARLINGTON ROBINSON

Born: Head Tide, Maine
Date: December 22, 1869

Died: New York, N. Y.
Date: April 6, 1935

Principal Works

POEMS: *The Torrent and the Night Before*, 1896; *The Children of the Night*, 1897; *Captain Craig*, 1902; *The Town Down the River*, 1910; *The Man Against the Sky*, 1916; *Merlin*, 1917; *Lancelot*, 1920; *The Three Taverns*, 1920; *Avon's Harvest*, 1921; *Roman Bartholow*, 1923; *The Man Who Died Twice*, 1924; *Dionysus in Doubt*, 1925; *Tristram*, 1927; *Fortunatus*, 1928; *Three Poems*, 1928; *Sonnets 1889–1927;* 1928; *Cavender's House*, 1929; *Modred, a Fragment*, 1929; *The Glory of the Nightingales*, 1930; *Matthias at the Door*, 1931; *Nicodemus*, 1932; *Talifer*, 1933; *Amaranth*, 1934; *King Jasper*, 1935; *Collected Poems*, 1937.

Edwin Arlington Robinson has been called the last American writer in the nineteenth century tradition of rationalism and psychological understanding, a figure more akin in spirit to the novelists Henry James and Edith Wharton than to any other American poet of his time. Dedicated to his craft of verse and unwilling to disperse his energies in other fields, he became that **rarity in literature, a professional poet** who was critically admired (especially after the publication of *The Man Against the Sky* in 1916) and financially successful after the sales of *Tristram* in 1927.

As a boy Robinson showed no distinctive talents. Born in Head Tide, Maine, on December 22, 1869, he went to Harvard for two years without intending to take a degree and then **returned to Gardiner, Maine, the Tilbury Town** of his early poems, where his father's declining business was located. An apparent failure in life like his own characters Miniver Cheevy and Mr. Flood, Robinson nevertheless wrote steadily and in 1896 privately published his first book, *The Torrent and the Night*. A year later he published *The Children of the Night*, containing "Luke Havergal," later widely known in anthologies, and "The Clerks," two poems marking the appearance of his brief dramas of insight into personality, written in a lucid style of intellectual seriousness.

When his third book, *Captain Craig*, was published in 1902, Robinson was working in New York as a train checker on the subway. During this period Theodore Roosevelt became interested in him and not only offered him a custom house sinecure in 1905 but also wrote a critical commendation of the poet's work for *The Outlook*. Four years later, under the Taft administration, Robinson resigned from the post Roosevelt had found for him in the New York custom house.

The remaining events of Robinson's life were undistinguished except by the fulfillment of his talent in frequent publications of his books. Regularly, after 1911, he divided his time between New York in the winter and the MacDowell Colony in New Hampshire during the summer, supported in part by a legacy and a trust fund established by his friends. Gradually honors came to him: a fiftieth birthday celebration by the New York *Times Book Review* in 1911, three Pulitzer prizes for the 1921 edition of *Collected Poems*, *The Man Who Died Twice*, and *Tristram*;

various poetry prizes, honorary degrees from colleges and universities, the Gold Medal of the National Institute of Arts and Letters in 1929, and the posthumous award of the Medal of the International Mark Twain Society following his death in New York City on April 6, 1935.

Robinson was a poet of major ambition who seemed to combine New England moral integrity and dryness of manner with something of Browning's psychological curiosity and Hardy's involvement with fate. The fact that his work should suggest a Puritan sensibility dissolved in the mainstream of English narrative verse, combined with a mastery of formal techniques, has resulted in divided critical opinion. At the same time his tendency toward prolixity in blank verse and a sort of romantic realism relying on cleverness made him accessible to a public not usually eager for poetry; indeed, such later long works as *Matthias at the Door*, *Talifer*, and *Amaranth* were written with a novelist's awareness of his readers.

It is in his short poems and those of medium length that Robinson is most compelling. "For a Dead Lady," from *The Town Down the River*; "Eros Turannos," a perfect match of wit in form with stark understanding of life, from *The Man Against the Sky*; "The Wandering Jew," from *The Three Taverns*, and "The Sheaves," one of his finest sonnets, from *Dionysus in Doubt*, are all among the clearest examples of his literary cultivation and mastery of purpose. In these he demonstrates his ability to make symbolic thought and the play of ideas poetic with little sensuous imagery. Other poems in *The Man Who Died Twice* and *Nicodemus*, his last impressive volume, also develop his concern with failure and defeat, especially the plight of the potential artist, to the point of unflinching awareness.

The Arthurian trilogy (comprising *Merlin*, a study of romantic love; *Lancelot*, a study of the modern doubter, and *Tristram*, a detailed story of defeated passion based largely on Malory) is his most famous group of poems. But it is doubtful if Robinson's attempt at a major achievement here did more than diffuse his narrative power for the sake of full expression. In his work he was always shifting between the long poem in blank verse and the shorter self-contained stanza forms; since his attitude toward man and destiny was not passionate but skeptical and intellectually firm, it is the laconic expression of his mind in a verse form that is most convincing. The long works of his later years, concluding in 1935 with *King Jasper*, a modern allegory of industrial civilization, did not add much to a reputation already firmly grounded in the philosophical qualities which made his poetry a moral criticism of society and the age.

BIBLIOGRAPHICAL REFERENCES: There are various editions of Robinson's *Collected Poems* dating from 1921; the standard text is *The Collected Poems of Edwin Arlington Robinson*, 1937, containing additions from his later work. Collections of his letters are the *Selected Letters*, edited by Ridgely Torrence, 1940; *Letters of Edwin Arlington Robinson to Howard George Schmitt*, edited by Carl J. Weber, 1943; and *Untriangulated Stars: Letters of Edwin Arlington Robinson to Harry de Forest Smith, 1890–1905*, 1947. Biographies are Hermann Hagedorn, *Edwin Arlington Robinson: A Biography*, 1938; Emery Neff, *Edwin Arlington Robinson*, 1948; and

Chard Powers Smith, *Where the Light Falls,* 1965.

For criticism and analysis see Lloyd Morris, *The Poetry of Edwin Arlington Robinson,* 1923; Ben Ray Redman, *Edwin Arlington Robinson,* 1926; Mark Van Doren, *Edwin Arlington Robinson,* 1927; L. M. Beebe, *Edwin Arlington Robinson and the Arthurian Legend,* 1927; Charles Cestre, *An Introduction to Edwin Arlington Robinson,* 1930; R. W. Brown, *Next Door to a Poet,* 1937; Robert P. T. Coffin, *New Poetry of New England: Frost and Robinson,* 1938; Estelle Kaplan, *Philosophy in the Poetry of Edwin Arlington Robinson,* 1940; Yvor Winters, *Edwin Arlington Robinson,* 1946; Barnard Ellsworth, *Edwin Arlington Robinson,* 1952; Wallace L. Anderson, *Edwin Arlington Robinson,* 1967; and Louis Coxe, *Edwin Arlington Robinson: The Life of Poetry,* 1969. Briefer estimates include Percy H. Boynton, *Some Contemporary Americans,* 1924; Thomas K. Whipple, *Spokesmen,* 1928; Alfred Kreymborg, *Our Singing Strength,* 1929; E. E. Pipkin, "The Arthur of Edwin Arlington Robinson," *English Journal,* XIX (1930), 183–195; Floyd Stovall, "The Optimism behind Robinson's Tragedies," *American Literature,* X (1938), 1–24; C. E. Van Norman, "Captain Craig," *College English,* II (1941), 462–475; Louise Dauner, "Avon and Cavender: Two Children of the Night," *American Literature,* XIV (1942), 55–65; and Richard Crowder, "Men Against the Sky," *College English,* XIV (1953), 269–276.

For other bibliographical listings see also Lillian Lippincott, *A Bibliography of the Writings and Criticisms of Edwin Arlington Robinson,* 1937; supplemented by Charles B. Hogan, "Edwin Arlington Robinson: New Bibliographical Notes," *Papers of the Bibliographical Society of America,* XXXV (1941), 115–144.

HENRY CRABB ROBINSON

Born: Bury St. Edmonds, England
Date: March 13, 1775

Died: London, England
Date: February 5, 1867

Principal Works

PERSONAL PAPERS: *Reminiscences and Correspondence of H. Crabb Robinson*, ed. Thomas Sadler, 1869; *Henry Crabb Robinson on Books and Their Writers*, 3 vols., 1938; *The Correspondence of Crabb Robinson with the Wordsworth Circle*, ed. Edith Morley, 1927; *Henry Crabb Robinson in Germany*, ed. Edith Morley, 1929.

The son of a tanner, Henry Crabb Robinson attended local schools until he began the study of law at the age of fifteen. His future in life changed when, in 1798, he inherited enough money to allow him to leave the law office. In 1800 Robinson journeyed to the Continent and took up residence in Germany, where he began the serious study of German. When he had acquired competence in the language he traveled throughout Germany, much of the time on foot, meeting a number of outstanding men of the time, including Goethe and Schiller. In 1802 he enrolled at the University of Jena, studying there until he returned to England in 1805. Unsuccessful at finding employment with the British diplomatic service, Robinson became a journalist with the London *Times,* first as a correspondent on the Continent and, later, as the foreign editor. In 1808 he was a war correspondent in Spain for several months. In order to insure his financial independence, he returned to the study of law in 1809 and was admitted to the bar in 1813. By 1828 he had accomplished his goal of becoming financially independent, whereupon he retired from legal practice, as he had promised himself he would.

Robinson's significance to literature and history came about as a result of his friendships with many prominent persons, including such famous writers as Coleridge, Wordsworth, Charles Lamb, and Robert Southey. He accompanied Wordsworth on tours in Scotland and Wales, as well as to Switzerland. He kept careful records of his friends and his journeys, conscientiously putting down information he hoped would someday be useful. He was also a champion for his friends and their literary work, especially Wordsworth, when those friends, as young writers, needed help. When he died in his ninety-second year, he left a diary in thirty-five closely written volumes, thirty volumes of correspondence, thirty volumes of journals from tours, plus five additional handwritten volumes of reminiscences and anecdotes. Portions of these volumes have been published over the years, with the first appearing in 1869, just two years after the writer's death. In his own time Robinson was also significant as one of the founders of University College, London, and the Athaeneum Club.

BIBLIOGRAPHICAL REFERENCES: Recent selections from Robinson's writings include *The London Theatre, 1811–1866: Selections from the Diary of Henry Crabb Robinson,* edited by Eluned Brown, 1966; and *The Diary of Henry Crabb Robinson: An Abridgement,* edited by Derek Hudson, 1967.

Good biographies are E. J. Morley, *The Life and Times of Henry Crabb Robinson*, 1935; and J. M. Baker, *Crabb Robinson of Bury, Jena, the Times and Russell Square*, 1937. For a discussion of Robinson's years in Germany see Hertha Marquardt, *Henry Crabb Robinson und seine deutschen Freunde: Brücke zwischen England und Deutschland im Zeitalter der Romantik,* 2 vols., 1964, 1967.

THEODORE ROETHKE

Born: Saginaw, Michigan
Date: May 25, 1908

Died: Seattle, Washington
Date: August, 1963

Principal Works

POEMS: *Open House,* 1941; *The Lost Son and Other Poems,* 1948; *Praise to the End,* 1951; *The Waking: Poems 1933–1953,* 1953; *Words for the Wind,* 1958; *I Am! Says the Lamb,* 1961; *The Far Field,* 1964; *Collected Poems,* 1966.
LETTERS: *The Selected Letters of Theodore Roethke,* 1968.
CRITICISM: *On the Poet and His Craft: Selected Prose,* 1965.
NOTEBOOKS: *Straw for the Fire: From the Notebooks of Theodore Roethke,* selected and arranged by David Wagoner, 1972.

Theodore Roethke was born in Saginaw, Michigan, on May 25, 1908. Much of his childhood was spent in and around the greenhouse owned jointly by his father and his uncle. It is not surprising that all his poetry shows a familiarity with and knowledge of growing things equaled only by his reverence for life in all forms, large and small. He went to the University of Michigan, where he earned distinction as an athlete, and later, like so many of our country's leading poets, did a stint of graduate work at Harvard. His livelihood for many years was teaching. He held positions at Lafayette, Penn State, Bennington, and was Professor of English at The University of Washington. While at Bennington he met and married his wife who was a student there and who is celebrated in some of the most moving love poems of our times. His first book of poems, *Open House* (1941), received little attention or notice, but with *The Waking* twelve years later he received the Pulitzer Prize, the first of a series of major honors and awards culminating in the National Book Award, given posthumously to *The Far Field.* Roethke was a big man who looked more like a football player than the conventional image of the poet, but his appearance of great physical strength was modified by a surprising gentleness. In his last years he gave readings at many colleges and was extremely popular with his student audiences. He died suddenly in August, 1963—his creative powers at a peak and his earned reputation at its highest—survived by his wife, Beatrice, to whom the literary world owes its gratitude for assembling the last poems which make up *The Far Field.*

BIBLIOGRAPHICAL REFERENCES: The first full-scale biography is Allan Seager, *The Glass House: The Life of Theodore Roethke,* 1968. For comment on the poetry see William J. Martz, *The Achievement of Theodore Roethke: A Comprehensive Selection of His Poems with a Critical Introduction,* 1966; Karl Malkoff, *Theodore Roethke: An Introduction to the Poetry,* 1966; Ralph J. Mills, Jr., *Theodore Roethke,* 1963; Arnold Stein, editor, *Theodore Roethke: Essays on the Poetry,* 1965; and William Heyen, editor, *A Profile of Theodore Roethke,* 1971.

FERNANDO DE ROJAS

Born: Puebla de Montalbán (?), Spain
Date: 1475?

Died: Near Talavera (?), Spain
Date: April, 1541

Principal Work

NOVEL: *Comedia de Calisto y Melibea* (*La Celestina*), 1499 (second edition, 1501).

The author of Spain's first realistic novel, *La Celestina*, one of the gems of its national literature, remains a shadowy figure. Even proof that he wrote this novel in dramatic form lies mainly in an acrostic of the 1501 Sevilla edition of twenty-one acts, which gives his home as Montalbán. He may have been born there, about 1475, or in Toledo, if scholars are right in assuming that city as the location of his only known work. A prefatory letter declares that while a student at the University of Salamanca he found the first act and finished the other fifteen acts of the Burgos edition, 1499, at the rate of an act a day during a vacation period.

Modern scholarship has turned up a few more facts and made some deductions. In 1525, Alvaro de Montalbán, accused of relapses into the practice of Jewish faith, claimed that his daughter had married the "converso" Fernando de Rojas, author of *La Celestina*. "Converso" need not mean that Rojas was a new convert; indeed, it is probable that the author of this dialogue-novel was born and brought up in the Christian faith and studied under Nebrija. At all events, when he died in April, 1541, he was a member of the religious order of La Concepción de la Madre, and in his will he directed that his body be buried in the church of the Monastery of Talavera. In 1584 his grandson sought documents to prove he was an *hidalgo*, or man of pure Spanish blood traceable back through his great-grandfather.

Whoever he was, Rojas wrote a novel that critics like Cervantes praised as divine, in spite of its basically human tone, and one that all admire for its realistic character drawing. Not only are those of the lower class true to life, including the go-between Celestina, but even flowery Calisto, the lover, is a typical Petrarch-inspired *galán*. Why Rojas did not boldly claim the book can only be surmised. Perhaps as a lawyer he did not want to be known as a dabbler in fiction. Certainly he did not fear the Inquisition as a Jew, since documents proved he was respected, nor as an author, since the censors never questioned his novel until 1640, long after his death. *La Celestina* went through 120 editions in thirty-five years, with translations into Italian (1506), German (1520), and French (1527). It was the first Spanish volume put into English, in 1530.

BIBLIOGRAPHICAL REFERENCES: See C. L. Penny, *A Book Called Celestina*, 1954; Dorothy C. Clarke, *Allegory, Decalogue, and Deadly Sins in* La Celestina, 1968; also the Preface to the Clásicos Castellanos Edition, 1913; Foulché-Delbosc, "Observations sur La Célestine," in *Revue Hispanique*, VII, 28–80, IX, 171–199; R. E. House, "Notes on the Authorship of the Celestina," in *Philological Quarterly*, II, 38-47, III, 81-91; and Ruth Davis, "New Data on Authorship of Act I of Calisto and Melibea," in *University of Iowa Studies* (1928); and Otis H. Green, "The Judaism of Rojas," in *Hispanic Review*, XV, 3 (1947).

ROMAIN ROLLAND

Born: Clamecy, France
Date: January 29, 1866

Died: Vézelay, France
Date: December 30, 1944

Principal Works

NOVELS: *Jean-Christophe,* 1904–1912; *Colas Breugnon,* 1919; *Clérambault,* 1920; *Pierre et Luce,* 1920; *L'Âme enchantée,* 1922–1933 (*The Soul Enchanted*).

PLAYS: *Aërt,* 1898; *Les Loups,* 1898 (*The Wolves*); *Le Triomphe de la raison,* 1899; *Danton,* 1900; *Le Quatorze Juillet,* 1902 (*The Fourteenth of July*); *Le Jeu de l'amore et de la mort,* 1924 (*The Game of Love and Death*); *Robespierre,* 1939.

BIOGRAPHY: *Vie de Beethoven,* 1903; *Vie de Michel-Ange,* 1906; *Vie de Tolstoi,* 1911; *Handel,* 1901; *Mahatma Gandhi,* 1924; *Beethoven, Les Grandes époqués créatrices,* 1929 (*Beethoven the Creator*); *Goethe et Beethoven,* 1930; *Charles Péguy,* 1944.

AUTOBIOGRAPHY: *Le Voyage intérieur,* 1942 (*The Journey Within*).

POLEMICS: *Au-dessus de la mêlée,* 1915 (*Above the Battle*).

LETTERS: *Les Cahiers des Romain Rolland et Malwida von Meysenbug, 1890–1891,* 1933.

Romain Rolland, Nobel Prize novelist, biographer, and playwright, is known primarily as the author of *Jean-Christophe,* the ten-volume story of a German musician. Rolland was born on January 29, 1866, in Clamecy, France, the son of a notary. His mother was religious and a lover of music. As a boy Rolland experienced poor health, but he amused himself with music and reading, becoming an admirer of Shakespeare.

He attended the collège in Clamecy until he was fourteen, and then continued his education at the schools St. Louis and Louis-le-grand in Paris. In 1886 he entered the École Normale Supérieure, at that time distinguished by its faculty and its scientists in residence, among them Louis Pasteur. He specialized in history with Gabriel Monod. During that period he began to make the acquaintance of distinguished writers and critics, including Ernest Renan, whose influential *Histoire des Origines du Christianisme* (1863–1883) had made him one of the most eminent of French historians, and Leo Tolstoy, author of *War and Peace.* Rolland wrote to Tolstoy because he was depressed by the materialistic life around him and wanted to discuss the matter with Tolstoy. He was also interested in Tolstoy's aesthetic theories.

In 1889 he received his bachelor's degree and went on to the École Française d'Archeologie et d'Histoire in Rome, where he studied history and archaeology. During the next two years he studied, traveled in Italy and Sicily, and formed a close friendship with the aging Malvida von Meysenbug, author of *Memoirs of an Idealist* and friend of Mazzini, Wagner, Nietzsche, and other eminent men of the period.

Rolland then returned to Paris and married Marie Bréal, daughter of Michel Bréal, the philologist. Rolland's doctorate was granted in 1895; his thesis was *The Origins of the Opera in Europe: Before Lully and Scarlatti.* His first published drama, succeeding a considerable number of unpublished dramas on the Italian Renaissance period, was *Saint Louis* (1897). While teaching at the École Normale Supérieure he became a friend of Richard Strauss, Gabriele d'Annunzio, and Eleonora Duse. In 1898 he wrote an important play, *The Wolves,* which had as its subject the Dreyfus affair. Soon afterward his friend Charles Péguy founded a fortnightly publication entitled *Cahiers de la Quinzaine,* in which, from 1900 on, Rolland published most of his important work, including *Jean-Christophe.*

Jean-Christophe established Rolland's reputation in the literary world; in it he used his hero as a device for the criticism of the materialistic emphasis in France, and the dramatic values of the work made poignant the telling analysis of contemporary culture. Upon the completion of the novel, Rolland was awarded the Grand Prize in Literature by the French Academy (1913), and two years later he received the Nobel Prize in Literature, after a recommendation by Anatole France for the French Academy.

In the meantime he suffered extreme criticism from France for the pacifist articles he wrote from Switzerland during the first World War. While in Switzerland he worked for the Red Cross and argued for peace by writing a series of careful apologetic articles. These were published as *Above the Battle* in 1915. His courageous and reasoned defense of his position against war later won him praise from many of France's outstanding intellectuals. After the war he spent two years in Paris. He then returned to Switzerland with his father and sister to live at Villeneuve, where he resided until 1938. While there he commenced an intensive study of India and made the friendship of Gandhi, subject of a biography he published in 1924.

His next important novel was the seven-volume *The Soul Enchanted.* Although this novel enhanced Rolland's reputation, it did not eclipse the standing of *Jean-Christophe* as the novelist's masterpiece.

Over a period of years Rolland advocated a people's theater, and in defense of his humanitarian philosophy wrote a series of plays on themes of revolutionary heroism. From 1900 to 1939 he wrote eight of a projected cycle of twelve plays. Before the turn of the century he had written other series of plays, among them *Les Tragédies de la foi.* He also achieved considerable distinction with his biographies, particularly with his studies of Beethoven, Michelangelo, Tolstoy, and Gandhi.

Rolland made a trip to Moscow in 1935 as the guest of Maxim Gorky, shortly before Gorky's death. While in Russia he met Stalin and other leaders of the government in Moscow. Politically, however, Rolland was bitterly opposed to totalitarian forms of government and regarded himself as a republican with socialist tendencies. During the occupation in World War II he was under house arrest by the Vichy government, but he continued to work and produced his biography of Charles Péguy. He died on December 30, 1944, at his home in Vézelay, France.

BIBLIOGRAPHICAL REFERENCES: For critical studies of Rolland in English see Stefan Zweig, *Romain Rolland, the Man and His Work,* translated 1921; Helen Whitman Machau, *The Popular Theatre Movement in France: Romain Rolland and the Revue d'art dramatique,* 1950 (pamphlet); and William Thomas Starr, *Romain*

Rolland and a World at War, 1956; also *ibid., Romain Rolland*, 1971. See further Rollo Myers, ed., *Richard Strauss and Romain Rolland: Correspondence Together with Fragments from the Diary of Romain Rolland*, 1968. See also Paul Seippel, *Romain Rolland, l'homme et l'œuvre*, 1913; P. J. Jouve, *Romain Rolland vivant, 1914–1919*, 1920; Christian Sénéchal, *Romain Rolland*, 1933; A. R. Levy, *L'idéalisme de Romain Rolland*, 1946; Maurice Descotes, *Romain Rolland*, 1948; and René Arcos, *Romain Rolland*, 1950.

O. E. RÖLVAAG

Born: Dønna, Helgeland, Norway
Date: April 22, 1876

Died: Northfield, Minnesota
Date: November 5, 1931

Principal Works

NOVELS: *Amerika-breve*, 1912 (*Letters from America*; as Paul Mørck); *Paa glemte veie*, 1914 (*On Forgotten Paths*; as Paul Mørck); *To tullinger*, 1920 (*Two Simpletons*); *Længselens baat*, 1921; *I de dage*, 1924 (*In Those Days*); *Riket grundlægges*, 1925 (*The Kingdom Is Founded*); *Giants in the Earth*, 1927 (translated from *I de dage* and *Riket grundlægges*); *Peder Seier*, 1928 (*Peder Victorious*); *Pure Gold*, 1930 (translation of *To tullinger*); *Their Father's God*, 1931 (translation of *Den signede dag*, 1931); *The Boat of Longing*, 1933 (translation of *Længselens baat*).

ESSAYS: *Omkring fædrearven*, 1925 (*Concerning Our Heritage*).

O(le) E(dvart) Rölvaag was born on April 22, 1876, on the Island of Dønna off the coast of Norway. Although his father was a veterinarian, the family was one of peasant fishermen stock, and for a time young Rölvaag also secured his livelihood from the sea. His formal education was slight, for he had only a few weeks' schooling a year. In 1896, determined to come to America, he refused the command of a fishing boat and emigrated to South Dakota. There he worked for a year on an uncle's farm to earn enough money to attend college.

At home Rölvaag had been regarded as a poor student but an avid reader, particularly the novels of Cooper, Dickens, Haggard, Marryat, Dumas, and Verne, as well as those of such Scandinavian writers as Topelius, Lie, and Bjørnson. In this country he added to his love of reading a strong incentive to learn and during the next six years achieved a brilliant record in scholarship. He first attended Augustana College, a small preparatory school in Canton, South Dakota, and from there went to St. Olaf College at Northfield, Minnesota, graduating with honors in 1905. He then returned to Norway for a year of graduate study at the University of Oslo prior to accepting a position in the Department of Norwegian at St. Olaf.

His relations with St. Olaf continued until a few months before his death a quarter of a century later. He settled in Northfield, married Marie Bergdahl in 1908, and became a citizen of the United States in 1908. In 1910 he received a Master of Arts degree from St. Olaf and eventually was honored with a full professorship. His career as a writer began somewhat obscurely during these years of scholastic activity. Upon his return to St. Olaf he had written his first novel, *Nils og Astri, eller Brudstykker av Norsk-Amerikansk Folkeliv . . . Fragments of Norwegian-American Popular Life*), but this work had gone unpublished. He continued his literary efforts now with *Letters from America* which was printed in Norwegian under a pseudonym in 1912. It was Rölvaag's belief that close relationships between the American immigrants and their fellows in the homeland should be maintained, and his early novels were an attempt to secure this relationship. Written in Norwegian, they depicted the trials and the triumphs of pioneers in the New World.

Rölvaag's interest in the preservation

of his homeland culture caused him some difficulty with the rise of strong national feeling during World War I, but criticism and abuse only increased his determination. He continued to write in Norwegian and to advocate the maintenance of Scandinavian folkways in the face of all opinion to the contrary. This was his belief and practice throughout his life, but eventually he was to exchange his native Norwegian for his adopted English in his creative work. This change was brought about through the help of the journalist Lincoln Colcord. Rölvaag had published two novels in Norwegian, *I de dage* and *Riket grundlægges*, both of which dealt with the struggles of the nearly Norwegian settlers in the Dakotas. Colcord, appreciating the power of these two works, persuaded Rölvaag to turn them into English, working with him to help the novelist capture American idiom in its clearest form. The result was *Giants in the Earth*, Rölvaag's great "Saga of the Prairie," published in 1927.

Three more novels in English, *Peder Victorious*, *Pure Gold*, and *The Boat of Longing*, followed his first work in his adopted language, but no other could match the strength or scope of his masterpiece, and it is on *Giants in the Earth* that his reputation as a novelist still rests. The book, praised by such critics as Vernon Parrington and such fellow Midwestern writers as Carl Sandburg, has been lauded as "the finest and most powerful novel that has been written about pioneer life in America."

The success of Rölvaag's writings in English failed to diminish his interest in his native language or old-world traditions. He was made a Knight of St. Olaf by King Haakon in 1926 and was a guest of the Norwegian government at the Ibsen centennial celebration in 1927–1928. Although there were many such demands on his time, he continued his teaching in spite of the fact that he suffered from angina pectoris, a disease to which he finally succumbed at Northfield on November 5, 1931, three months after his retirement from St. Olaf.

BIBLIOGRAPHICAL REFERENCES: There is no collected edition of Rölvaag's work. The authorized biography is Theodore Jorgensen and Nora O. Solum, *Ole Edvart Rölvaag: A Biography*, 1939. The best brief account of his career is the essay by Einar Haugen in the *Dictionary of National Biography*. Perhaps the best introduction to the novels is Vernon L. Parrington, *Main Currents of American Thought*, III, 1930.

For criticism see also Julius E. Olson, "Rölvaag's Novels of Norwegian Pioneer Life in the Dakotas," *Scandinavian Studies and Notes*, IX (1926); George L. White, Jr., "Ole Edvart Rölvaag: Prophet of a People," *Scandinavian Themes in American Fiction*, 1937; Percy H. Boynton, *America in Contemporary Fiction*, 1940; Joseph E. Baker, "Western Man Against Nature: *Giants in the Earth*," *College English*, IV (1942), 19–26; Richard Beck, "Rölvaag, Interpreter of Immigrant Life," *North Dakota Quarterly*, XXIV (1956), 26–30; Robert Steensma, "Rölvaag and Turner's Frontier Thesis," *North Dakota Quarterly*, XXVII (1959), 100–104; and Carroll D. Laverty, "Rölvaag's Creation of the Sense of Doom in *Giants in the Earth*," *South Central Bulletin* 27, iv (1967), 45–50.

PIERRE DE RONSARD

Born: Vendômois, France
Date: September 11, 1524

Died: Touraine, France
Date: December 26 (?), 1585

Principal Works

POEMS: *Odes,* Books I–IV, 1550; Book V, 1552; *Amours de Cassandre,* 1552; *Hymnes,* 1555; *Elégies, mascarades et bergeries,* 1565; *La Françiade,* 1572.

The most important literary movement in sixteenth-century France centered around the "Pléiade," a group of seven poets. Although the manifesto of the group, *Défense et Illustration de la Langue Française,* was written by Du Bellay, Pierre de Ronsard remains the most famous of the coterie. He was born September 11, 1524, at his family's Château de la Poissonnière near Vendôme, the son of an official of the household of Francis I. After a short period at the College of Navarre in Paris, he was appointed a royal page. Later he spent three years in Great Britain and was sent on various diplomatic missions. He was a special favorite of Charles IX, who called Ronsard his "master of poetry."

The aim of the Pléiade was to reform French verse by adhering more closely to classic models: "Follow the Ancients" was their motto. This program led to a violent literary quarrel.

During the next two centuries Ronsard's reputation waned. He was revived by the Romanticists; but the standard French criticism is still that the Pléiade "over-classicized" French poetry. However, the charm of Ronsard's nature-verse and the magnificence of his language and metrics are admitted and admired. Ronsard died at the priory of St.-Côme near Tours and was buried December 27, 1585.

BIBLIOGRAPHICAL REFERENCES: The best studies of Ronsard in English are D. B. Wyndham Lewis, *Ronsard,* 1944, and an earlier study by Humbert Wolfe, *Ronsard and French Romantic Poetry,* 1935; also, Elizabeth Armstrong, *Ronsard and the Age of Gold,* 1968. For biographical and critical studies in French see P. Champion, *Ronsard et son temps,* 1905; P. de Nolhac, *Ronsard et l'humanisme,* 1921; and P. Laumonier, *Ronsard,* 1923.

CHRISTINA ROSSETTI

Born: London, England
Date: December 5, 1830

Died: London
Date: December 29, 1894

Principal Works

POEMS: *Goblin Market and Other Poems*, 1862; *The Prince's Progress and Other Poems*, 1866; *Sing Song*, 1872; *A Pageant and Other Poems*, 1881; *Verses*, 1893; *New Poems*, 1896.

DEVOTIONAL STUDIES: *Speaking Likenesses*, 1874; *Seek and Find*, 1879; *Called Be the Saints*, 1881; *Letter and Spirit*, 1882; *Time Flies*, 1885; *The Face of the Deep*, 1892.

Christina (Georgina) Rossetti, born in London on December 5, 1830, was the sister of Dante Gabriel Rossetti, and the youngest child of a Neapolitan political refugee who had settled in England and who became, eventually, Professor of Italian at King's College, University of London. She began to write poetry very early in her life, and when she was seventeen a small volume of her work was printed at her grandfather's private press. A year later, in 1848, one of her lyrics was published in *The Athenaeum*. When Dante Gabriel Rossetti founded the Pre-Raphaelite magazine, *The Germ*, in 1850, she became one of its frequent contributors, using the pseudonym Ellen Alleyn. Twelve years later her first volume, *Goblin Market and Other Poems*, appeared publicly. She continued to write until the end of her life, but only four more volumes, including her poems for children, were published during her lifetime.

Although her creative life extended over a long period, her output, in terms of quantity, was not extensive for two reasons. The first had to do with the form of the poetry she wrote and the fact that she was essentially a composer of brief lyrics. Like precious gems, they were small but clear and of exceeding value; but since she wrote only when she felt the possibility of perfection, her work was understandably limited. The other reason for her small poetic output was her extreme religious devotion. As she grew older she turned more and more from her poetry to the writing of her religious prose, expending her creative energy on this less artistic genre. Yet it cannot be said that her religious interests worked against her poetry, for the poetry itself is imbued completely with her religious feelings. Some lyrics, such as "Three Enemies," "Weary in Well-Doing," and "A Better Resurrection" are specifically religious in theme and subject matter. In all she wrote, at the root if not in stalk and branch, is her religious preoccupation.

This preoccupation was dominant in her personality as well. Sickly most of her life, and an actual invalid during her last years, she turned more and more from the world until she became almost a complete recluse. In her youth she had refused two different suitors because they did not conform to her Church of England beliefs and had chosen instead to remain with her equally devout mother. Having channeled all of her emotional energies into her religion, nevertheless in the end she was tormented by doubt, not of her beliefs but of her own worthiness. It was in this spirit that she cried out,

"My life is like a faded leaf/My harvest dwindled to a husk," taking no consolation in the fact that the pure freshness of some of her lyrics will remain green for centuries. She died in London on December 29, 1894.

BIBLIOGRAPHICAL REFERENCES: The standard edition of the *Poetical Works* was edited by William Michael Rossetti, 1904 (rev. ed., 1924). The most important study is Lona M. Packer, *Christina Rossetti,* 1963. For further biography and criticism see H. T. M. Bell, *Christina Rosetti: A Biographical and Critical Study,* 1898; Justine de Wilde, *Christina Rossetti, Poet and Woman,* 1923; M. F. Sandars, *The Life of Christina Rossetti,* 1930; Dorothy M. Stuart, *Christina Rossetti,* English Men of Letters Series, 1930; Fredegond Shove, *Christina Rossetti: A Study,* 1931; Eleanor W. Thomas, *Christina Georgina Rossetti,* 1931; and Georgina Battiscombe, *Christina Rossetti,* 1965. For background studies of the Rossetti family and the period see also R. D. Waller, *The Rossetti Family, 1824–1854,* 1932; and Frances Winwar, *Poor Splendid Wings: The Rossettis and Their Circle,* 1933. Virginia Woolf has an essay on Christina Rossetti in *The Common Reader, Second Series,* 1932. See also Winston Weather, "Christina Rossetti: The Sisterhood of Self," *Victorian Poetry,* III (Spring 1965), 81–89.

DANTE GABRIEL ROSSETTI

Born: London, England
Date: May 12, 1828

Died: Birchington, England
Date: April 9, 1882

PRINCIPAL WORKS

POEMS: *Poems*, 1870; *Ballads and Sonnets*, 1881; *Collected Works*, 1886.
TRANSLATIONS: *Early Italian Poets*, 1861 (retitled *Dante and His Circle*, 1874).

Dante Gabriel Rossetti was born in London, May 12, 1828, the son of Gabriele Rossetti, a political refugee from Naples, and the brother of Christina, the poet, and of William Michael Rossetti, later to be the historian of the Pre-Raphaelites. He attended King's College School in London and then various art schools, finally becoming a pupil of Ford Madox Brown. It was in 1848 that Rossetti, Millais, and Holman Hunt founded the Pre-Raphaelite Brotherhood that was to be a storm center in English art for many years. In 1850 they began their magazine, *The Germ*, in which Rossetti published some of his early poems. The paintings of the group were bitterly attacked by Dickens and by the conventional critics; it was only through the influence of Ruskin, then the aesthetic dictator of art and culture, that the public finally accepted the Pre-Raphaelites and their work.

In 1851 Rossetti became engaged to Elizabeth Siddall, whose peculiar beauty had fascinated him and who had become his model; but they were not married until 1860. She was consumptive; their marriage was unhappy because of Rossetti's increasing indifference, and in 1862 she died of an overdose of laudanum, probably a suicide. Then followed the melodramatic gesture of Rossetti's burying the only manuscript of his poems in her coffin and the gruesome sequel of their exhumation in 1869.

Very early, Rossetti came under the influence of Percy's *Reliques* (1765), the poems of Scott, and various medieval romances; and these influences, plus the avowed medievalism of the Pre-Raphaelites, gave to his poetry its special tone. He excelled in the imitation or adaption of the border ballads; his "Sister Helen" has been considered one of the best literary ballads of the nineteenth century. To the stark language of the old poems he added the luxuriant coloring and mysticism of the Pre-Raphaelites. His sonnet-sequence, "The House of Life," inspired by his love for Elizabeth Siddall and Jane Morris, has also been highly praised. Pre-Raphaelite poetry is out of fashion now, being considered overly-decorated and artificial; yet at the time it was a relief from the didacticism of much Victorian verse.

After 1868 Rossetti became subject to fits of melancholia aggravated by the attack on him in 1871 by Robert Buchanan, in an anonymous essay, "The Fleshly School of Poetry." His failing eyesight eventually made him abandon painting for poetry. His last years were made bearable only through the devoted attention of his brother. He died April 9, 1882, at Birchington, near Margate.

BIBLIOGRAPHICAL REFERENCES: Biographical and critical studies of Rossetti are extensive, and there are numerous collections of his letters. Of particular interest is

D. G. Rossetti's Family Letters, edited by William M. Rossetti, 1895, who also edited *Pre-Raphaelite Diaries and Letters*, 1900, and *Rossetti Papers, 1862–1870*, 1903. The definitive edition of the *Letters* is that of Oswald Doughty and John R. Wahl, eds., 4 vols., 1965–1967. Biographical and critical studies include William M. Rossetti, *Ruskin, Rossetti: Pre-Raphaelitism*, 1899; F. G. Stephens, *D. G. Rossetti*, 1894; A. C. Benson, *Rossetti*, in the English Men of Letters Series, 1904; Evelyn Waugh, *Rossetti: His Life and Work*, 1928; R. L. Mégroz, *Dante Gabriel Rossetti*, 1929; Viola Hunt, *The Wife of Rossetti*, 1932; Frances V. Winwar, *Poor Splendid Wings*, 1933; idem, *The Rossettis and Their Circle*, 1934; William Gaunt, *The Pre-Raphaelite Tragedy*, 1942; O. Doughty, *A Victorian Romantic: D. G. Rossetti*, 1949; Gordon Hough, *The Last Romantics*, 1949; J. Heath-Stubbs, *The Darkling Plain*, 1950; and Rosalie Glynn Grylls, *Portrait of Rossetti*, 1964. See also W. Stacy Johnson, "D. G. Rossetti as Painter and Poet," *Victorian Poetry*, III (1965), 9–18.

EDMOND ROSTAND

Born: Marseilles, France
Date: April 1, 1868

Died: Paris, France
Date: December 2, 1918

Principal Works

PLAYS: Les Romanesques, 1894 (The Romancers); La Princesse lointaine, 1895 (The Faraway Princess); La Samaritaine, 1897 (The Woman of Samaria); Cyrano de Bergerac, 1897; L'Aiglon, 1900 (The Eaglet); Chantecler, 1910; Le Bois sacré, 1909 (The Sacred Wood); La dernière nuit de Don Juan, 1921 (Don Juan's Last Night).

POEMS: Les Musardises, 1890.

This descendant of Corneille and Hugo, the last great romanticist of the theater, was born in Marseilles, April 1, 1868, the son of a prominent journalist and economist. Like so many other dramatists, his education was in law, although his interest was in poetry. Again, like many other writers, his first publication was a book of verse, Les Musardises, which appeared in 1890. The fact that he lived in comfortable means made it possible for him to write as little as he pleased, though he did put a polish of romance and a luster of history—and histrionics—on all his theater pieces.

In 1890 he married the poetess Rosemonde Gérard and settled in Paris as a professional writer. While he never sought praise or even approval—indeed his inclinations and interests and tastes ran counter to the feeling of the times —he won both in the 1894 Comédie Française production of The Romancers, a slight comedy in which the young lovers take their cues from Romeo and Juliet. For Sarah Bernhardt he wrote several plays; in The Faraway Princess she played the title role, falling in love with a troubadour; in L'Aiglon the Divine Sarah essayed the role of Napoleon's ineffectual son.

Edmond Rostand's penchant for writing starring roles for outstanding actors gave the world its most famous poetic drama, the historical romance, Cyrano de Bergerac, starring the great Coquelin. Before the year of its production ended, the play had been translated into several languages, and it has been produced everywhere in the civilized world. The swashbuckling hero, a romanticized version of the historical personage bearing that same name, is a household word standing for the idealist who refused to give in to the demands of the world.

So great was the young playwright's reputation that in 1900 he was appointed an Officer of the Legion of Honor, and in 1901 he became a member of the French Academy. His health failing in that same year, he built a villa in southern France where he lived most of the time until his death in Paris, December 2, 1918. His writing was affected by ill health and diminished energy, but he did write one more play which has, especially here in America in the last ten years, received more and more attention. Chantecler was also written for Coquelin, who died before it was finished; Lucien Guitry, however, took on the role of the famous rooster who thought that he was the one who brought the sun up in the morning. The slight fable-satire has some of Rostand's best writing in it, and it perfectly expresses its author's disillusioned point of view:

Chantecler finds that while he does not control the world he can at least tend valiantly his own henyard.

Few critics consider Rostand much more than a one-play author, but a consideration of his last play, based on the Don Juan theme of self-delusion, would lead one to think that his best plays might have been yet to come. In this and other plays he shows himself a master of language, subtle irony, magnificent spectacle, and ingenious manipulation. In a time when sordid realism seemed to win the day, theatergoers everywhere were grateful for the light touch of fantasy and romance; and while Rostand did not change the temper or the times, he at least managed to make time stand still in the romantic world of his creation.

BIBLIOGRAPHICAL REFERENCES: *The Plays of Edmond Rostand*, translated by Henderson Daingerfield and published in 1921. A good edition of *Cyrano de Bergerac* is that translated by Brian Hooker, with an introduction by Clayton Hamilton, Modern Library, 1951. There is no standard biography in English, but a brief life is found in the first chapter of Hobart Ryland, *The Sources of the Play "Cyrano de Bergerac,"* 1936. This book also contains a brief bibliography in addition to its main critical contents. Biographies in French include Paul Faure, *Vingt Ans d'Intimité avec Edmond Rostand*, 1928; M. J. Premsela, *Edmond Rostand*, 1933; and Rosemonde Gerard, *Edmond Rostand*, 1935. Essays in books include those by Edward Everett Hale, Jr., in *Dramatists of Today*, 1910; G. K. Chesterton, *Twelve Types*, 1910; B. H. Clark, *Contemporary French Dramatists*, 1915; A. Duclaux, *Twentieth Century French Writers*, 1919; Eugène Évrard, *Nos Mandarins*, 1920; F. W. Chandler, *The Contemporary Drama of France*, 1921; W. L. Phelps, *Essays on Modern Dramatists*, 1921; Hugh Allison Smith, *Main Currents of Modern French Drama*, 1928; George Jean Nathan, "Rostand," *The Magic Mirror*, 1960, 177–180; and Samuel Moskowitz, *Explorers of the Infinite*, 1963, 17–32. Short critical essays are the Count de Soissons "Edmond Rostand," *Contemporary Review*, CXV (1919), 188–195; Stark Young's review of Walter Hampden in *Cyrano de Bergerac*, *New Republic*, XXXVII (1923), 18–19; Philip Lewis, "The Idealism of Rostand," *Contemporary Review*, CLXXIV (1948), 34–37; C. D. Brenner, "Rostand's *Cyrano de Bergerac*: An Interpretation," *Studies in Philology*, XLVI (1949), 603–611; and J. A. Kilker, "Cyrano without Rostand: An Appraisal," *Canadian Modern Language Review*, XXI, iii (1965), 21–25.

HENRY ROTH

Born: Austria-Hungary
Date: February 8, 1906

Principal Works

NOVEL: *Call It Sleep,* 1934.
SHORT STORIES: In *The New Yorker:* "Broker," November 18, 1939; "Somebody Always Grabs the Purple," March 23, 1940; "Petey and Yotsee and Mario," July 14, 1956.
"PARABLES": In *Commentary:* "At Times in Flight," July, 1959; "The Dun Dakotas," August, 1960.

Henry Roth, born in Austria-Hungary in 1906, wrote his single novel in the early 1930's. Published in 1934 and rediscovered in 1964, *Call It Sleep* vividly evokes the childhood traumas of a sensitive Jewish immigrant boy in the hostile—and sometimes gentle—New York ghetto. Though not strictly autobiographical, the novel derives much from Roth's own boyhood in turbulent New York City. So do his three short pieces published in *The New Yorker.*

Roth began writing at City College, where he majored in English and was graduated in 1928. His chief mentor was Eda Lou Walton of New York University. Her encouragement and support enabled him to devote almost four years to completing *Call It Sleep.* Published in 1934, the novel drew reviewers' praise but made little impact on the public or on most literary scholars. Its subject and style reminded critics of Farrell, Joyce, and Dreiser. Psychologically truthful and unified by skillfully-handled themes and motifs, the book demonstrated Roth's considerable skill in the art of fiction.

Roth received an advance from Maxwell Perkins of Scribner's for a second novel, which was to deal with a Midwest worker who becomes a Communist. But he never got beyond the first 150 pages. Since *Call It Sleep* he has published three short stories and two short autobiographical "parables." Particularly in the stories Roth shows his sense of form and economy and his power of evoking the life of the city.

Between the late 1930's and the mid-1960's, Roth largely abandoned writing for a variety of other occupations: high school teacher in the Bronx, precision metal grinder, teacher in a one-room school in Maine, orderly and supervisor in a mental hospital, breeder of ducks and geese, tutor in Latin and mathematics.

In 1964, *Call It Sleep* was reissued, with considerable critical fanfare. Interviewers who sought out Roth found him a sensitive and thoughtful man who had gone his own way, on a Maine farm, after the fashion of a modern Thoreau. He is an admirer of Robinson Jeffers and a man who rejects the notion that the world is absurd.

Roth received an award from the National Institute of Arts and Letters in 1965. With his children grown and his talent now acknowledged widely, he is cautiously starting to write again.

BIBLIOGRAPHICAL REFERENCES: Essential and perhaps sufficient are the introductory essays by Harold U. Ribalow, Maxwell Geismar, and Meyer Levin in the 1960 reissue of *Call It Sleep* (Pageant Books). See also Walter Allen's six-page afterword in the 1964 edition; Leslie Fiedler, "Henry Roth's Neglected Masterpiece," *Commentary*, XXX (1960), 102–107; Walter Rideout, *The Radical Novel in America* (1956), 185–190; Jane Howard, "The Belated Success of Henry Roth," *Life*, LVIII (1965), 75–76; Irving Howe, "Life Never Let Up," New York *Times Book Review*, October 25, 1964, I, 60–61; and A. Sidney Knowles, Jr., "The Fiction of Henry Roth," *Modern Fiction Studies*, XI (1965), 393–404.

JEAN JACQUES ROUSSEAU

Born: Geneva, Switzerland
Date: June 28, 1712

Died: Ermenonville, France
Date: July 2, 1778

Principal Works

NOVELS: *Julie ou La Nouvelle Héloïse,* 1760 (*The New Héloïse*); *Émile, ou de l'éducation,* 1762 (*Émile*).

MEMOIRS: *Les Confessions,* 1784.

ESSAYS AND STUDIES: *Discours sur les arts et sciences,* 1750; *Discours sur l'inégalité des conditions,* 1754; *Lettre à d'Alembert sur les spectacles,* 1758; *Contrat social,* 1762; *Lettres de la montagne,* 1763; *Rêveries d'un promeneur solitaire,* 1782; *Dialogues,* 1784.

Jean Jacques Rousseau, French philosopher, novelist, and essayist, was born June 28, 1712, in Geneva. The fact that his mother died at his birth he referred to as the first of his misfortunes. When he was twelve years old his father, a watchmaker of restless disposition, abandoned him, and he was placed by an uncle under the tutelage of a pastor of Boissy. Himself a man of many moods and little stability, Rousseau's life was made up of wanderings and positions held for very short periods of time until he settled, more or less, to a life as a writer.

At fourteen he was apprenticed to an engraver; at sixteen he ran away and contacted a Catholic priest who sent him to Madame Louise de Warens at Annecy. She in turn sent him to the seminary of Turin, where it is reported he was converted to Catholicism in nine days. For brief periods he was a lackey in two aristocratic households but returned eventually to Annecy. His study for the priesthood lasted two months. He studied music and gave a very unsuccessful concert, but he did obtain a few pupils. Next he tried to find employment in Paris but failed and returned to Madame de Warens. He also turned down the position she obtained for him as clerk in the census bureau. This was at the age of nineteen. For the next eleven years he lived as Madame de Warens' protégé, lover, and intendant. At her small farm he began his first serious reading and studying for a musical and literary career.

When he was thirty years old, he met two influential ladies in Paris and through them many writers, musicians, and scientists. Diderot became an intimate friend. Through his associations he became secretary to the Comte de Montaigu, French ambassador in Venice, but he was dismissed from his post following a quarrel after one year. About 1744 he took as his mistress a servant, Thérèse Levasseur. Reportedly they had five children whom he consigned to a foundling home. They were married twenty years later.

Rousseau achieved sudden fame in 1750 with his prize winning *Discours sur les arts et sciences* given before the academy of Dijon. To the academy's contest question, "Have the arts and sciences contributed to improve morals?" Rousseau answered impassionately in the negative. Quite the contrary, wrote Rousseau, in that the arts and sciences, the results of institutions and civilization, tended to corrupt man's natural goodness. Furthermore, only countries (no examples cited) which are strong and virtuous are able to retain primitive simplicity. His third main point was that the rewards of progress are corruption and military defeat.

Three years later he competed for another prize at Dijon, the subject being the origin of inequality among men, and whether it is authorized by natural law. In his *Discours sur l'inégalité des conditions* he said that in mankind's march from the original state of nature to modern society, the tribal state is the happiest one; in this, the natural, primitive state, there are no inequalities of social position, rank, or inherited wealth. Furthermore, all development beyond this tribal period he condemned for the introduction of private property, an inequality resulting in a handful of the mighty and the rich as against millions living in squalor and obscurity.

Rousseau preached that the trouble with the world was that selfish laws and customs and spiritual bigotry—absolutism in state and church—had changed man's natural bent and cut him off from the heritage of equality, reason, and benevolence.

Although these ideas were not new, nor his alone by any means, their very real significance lay in the fact that Rousseau presented them concretely at one of those culminating points of history. His ideas became the battle cry of a new age and found powerful expression in the French Revolution, and they also permeated nineteenth century literature. Rousseau has been called the "father of Romanticism" because of the influence he exerted on Wordsworth and Shelley in England and on Herder, Schiller, and Kant in Germany.

He tended to break the hold of all external sanctions in state, church, literature, and society. Individual freedom he exalted; constituted authority he condemned. By temperament and training he was averse to control and restraint. He believed in natural impulse as opposed to discipline, in emotion as against reason. He established the predominance of feeling over the patient investigation of fact.

His *The New Héloïse* and *Émile* further exemplify his chief paradox that a barbarian (the natural man) is superior to a modern European. *The New Héloïse* is the story of Julie, a baron's daughter who marries a count after she has had a scandalous affair with a young man of the middle class. The count asks the young man to join them in "a union of hearts." Noteworthy in the rather tedious work is Rousseau's interest in the common people coupled with his glorifications of nature. *Émile* has given him the title of "father of modern education." It would seem that his ideal system of education was the one that least hindered the development of the pupil's native or natural bent.

In *Contrat social* ("Man is born free and everywhere he is in chains"), he developed the theories of Hooker and Locke that all government rests upon the consent of the governed. His ideal government was one which least checks the individual and gives to the individual the maximum of direct control in all state affairs.

The deistic doctrine expressed in *Émile* (Rousseau is termed an "emotional" deist) was opposed by the Catholic Church. To avoid arrest Rousseau went to Berne and to Prussia. His reply to the attack made upon *Émile* by the Archbishop of Paris was his famous *Lettre à M. de Beaumont* (1763).

Expelled from Geneva, his house stoned, Rousseau went to England at the invitation of David Hume, whom he later suspected of conspiring with his enemies. He returned to France and finally settled in Paris in 1770. There he completed his *Confessions* and in 1776 wrote a series of dialogues with himself. *Rêveries d'un promeneur solitaire* also belongs to this period. He died at Ermenonville, near Paris, of apoplexy, on July 2, 1778.

BIBLIOGRAPHICAL REFERENCES: For a general study of the period see Will and Ariel Durant, *Rousseau and Revolution,* 1967. The standard biography is John Morley's *Rousseau,* 1873. Other biographical and critical studies in English include Frederika Macdonald, *Jean Jacques Rousseau,* 2 vols., 1906; Irving Babbitt, *Rousseau and Romanticism,* 1919; Matthew Josephson, *Jean-Jacques Rousseau,* 1931; Roland Grimsley, *Jean-Jacques Rousseau: A Study in Self-Awareness,* 1961; J. H. Broome, *Rousseau: A Study of His Thought,* 1963; Joan McDonald, *Rousseau and the French Revolution,* 1965; and Roger D. Masters, *The Political Philosophy of Rousseau,* 1968. In French, E. Ritter, *La Famille et jeunesse de Rousseau,* 1896; Jules Lemaître, *Jean-Jacques Rousseau,* 1907; L. Ducros, *Jean-Jacques Rousseau de Genève à l'Hermitage, 1712–1757,* 1908; and Albert Schinz, *La Pensée de Jean-Jacques Rousseau,* 1929. See also the *Annales de la Société Jean-Jacques Rousseau,* 1905 ff.

JUAN RUIZ DE ALARCÓN

Born: Taxco, Mexico
Date: c. 1581

Died: Córdoba, Spain
Date: August 4, 1639

PRINCIPAL WORKS

PLAYS: *El tejedor de Segovia,* (*The Weaver of Segovia*); *Las paredes oyen,* (*Walls Have Ears*); *La verdad sospechosa,* (*Truth Suspected*).

One of the four great dramatists of Spain's Golden Age, Juan Ruiz de Alarcón y Mendoza, the most modern in spirit, was born at Taxco, Mexico, about 1581, and educated in Mexico before he went to Spain in 1600 for postgraduate study. Back in Mexico in 1608, Ruiz de Alarcón hoped to teach in the University. Rejected because of his hunchback, he left Mexico forever in 1613.

How much of his dramatic technique is due to his Mexican upbringing has been much discussed, for few of his twenty-four recognized comedies mention his homeland. As a dramatist he was more interested in character and less in plot than was Lope de Vega, and his thesis plays, illustrating moral truths through a character personifying a vice, greatly influenced Corneille, Molière, and the Italian Goldoni.

Because playwriting was only an avocation, beyond his regular work on the Council of the Indies, the professional dramatists hated and reviled Ruiz de Alarcón, and performances of his plays were frequently interrupted by unexplained accidents on the stage. Discouraged, he did little writing during the last ten years of his life. Collections of his plays were printed in 1628 and 1634. He died in Córdoba, Spain, on August 4, 1639.

BIBLIOGRAPHICAL REFERENCES: Ruiz de Alarcón's *Comedias escogidas* (*Selected Comedies*) were published in Madrid, 2 vols., 1867, and in *Classicos Castellanos,* 1918. For studies in English see James Fitzmaurice Kelly, *Chapters on Spanish Literature,* 1908, Dorothy Schons, "The Mexican Background of Alarcón," *Publications of the Modern Language Association,* LVII (1942), 89–104; and Alice M. Pollin, "The Religious Motive in the Plays of Juan Ruiz de Alarcón," *Hispanic Review,* XXIX (1961), 33–44; in Spanish, Rodríguez Marín, *Data para la biografía de Ruiz de Alarcón,* 1912; Pedro Henríquez Ureña, *Don Juan Ruiz de Alarcón,* 1915 (Havana); Julio Jiménez Rueda, *Ruiz de Alarcón y su tiempo,* 1939 (Mexico); Antonio Castro Leal, *Ruiz de Alarcón, su vida y su obra,* 1943 (Mexico); and Genaro Fernández MacGregor, "La Mexicanidad de Alarcón," in *Letras de Mexico,* II, 8 (August 15, 1939).

JUAN RULFO

Born: Apulco, Jalisco, Mexico
Date: May 16, 1918

Principal Works

SHORT STORIES: *El Llano en Llamas,* 1953.
NOVEL: *Pedro Páramo,* 1955.

In spite of his limited literary production, Juan Nepomuceno Carlos Rulfo, born on one of his father's haciendas near Sayula, Mexico, is at the present considered one of the most original and authentic Hispanic-American writers of fiction.

During his childhood he lived in San Gabriel, a town not too far from his native place. When he was six years old, an assailant killed his father, a landowner, and four years later, his mother died. In the same town, he attended the primary school. He went later to Guadalajara, in pursuit of a degree in law, pushed by his grandfather, a lawyer himself. Feeling uneasy at the University of Guadalajara, he moved to Mexico City and entered the National University, where, more prone to letters than to law, he preferred to be an irregular student at the Faculty of Philosophy and Letters.

He later left the university for a more casual way of living. He has worked as a tax collector, an immigration chief officer, a salesman for a rubber tire company—jobs that have taken him to many points of Mexican life and geography. He has worked at the National Institute of Indian Affairs and has held the office of subdirector of the Mexican Center of Writers.

Rulfo started to write in a rhetorical style. His first works, not yet published, looked like political manifestos, filled with complicated phrases. He has declared that he wanted to say something, but in a way different from those already used. He intended to elevate his style, but, paradoxically, he fell into a complete simplicity, choosing simple characters who speak in a simple way.

Since, according to him, he cannot write about facts, his work is based solely on his imagination. This quality makes Rulfo share the literary trend called "magic realism." His first work, *El Llano en Llamas* (*The Valley in Flames*), a collection of fifteen short stories that take place in the rural setting of the Jalisco State, was greeted as a remarkable and original piece of fiction, because of its depth in the complex, esoteric and, at the same time, primitive souls of his rural characters. In a timeless world, static and paralytic, the men appearing therein live a life of pessimism and fatalism, expressed in a slow, repetitive, regional language. Throughout the stories, the characters act under a tragic contempt of death, the inevitability of events, the instinctive force of passions, and a complete absence of consciousness. Though many of these short stories appear to be told in an autobiographical fashion, the characters have not the attitudes of reflexive but of impassive and apathetic persons.

Rulfo's only published novel, *Pedro Páramo,* originally titled *Los Murmullos* (*The Murmurs*), has almost the same traits as his short stories—passion, violence, pessimism—but with one difference: this world is inhabited by souls, by shadows, by voices. All the characters speak the language of death; from the tomb everyone remembers his life. The paralysis of action appears again—time has stopped everybody and everything. The main character, Pedro Páramo, an unscrupulous rural boss, lover of many women and breeder of many children, dominates the novel; the other characters, Susana San Juan, one of his wives; Juan Preciado, one of his sons and the main narrator of the story; Abundio Martínez, another of Páramo's sons and his murderer; Father Rentería, a priest who could not absolve his parishioners because he was also a sinner; and many other souls in pain, are related to Pedro Páramo by passion and violence. In Comala, a ghost town, only the reminiscences of the dead live. In this book, Rulfo has created a world of nightmare, in which we meet static, tragic, close to naught characters, void of time and freedom.

BIBLIOGRAPHICAL REFERENCES: Sergio Fernández, *"El Llano en llamas* de Juan Rulfo," *Filosofía y Letras,* nos. 53–54 (January–June, 1954), 259–269; Emma Susana Speratti Piñero, "Un narrador de Jalisco," *Buenos Aires Literaria,* II, 17 (February, 1954); Emmanuel Carballo, "Arreola y Rulfo, cuentistas," *Universidad de México,* VIII, 7 (March, 1954), 28–29, 32; Claudio Esteva Fabregat, "Juan Rulfo en la novela mexicana," *Armas y Letras,* XII, 9 (September, 1955), 1–7; Carlos Blanco Aguinaga, "Realidad y estilo de Juan Rulfo," *Revista Mexicana de Literatura,* no. 1 (September–October, 1955), 59–86; Alí Chumacero, "El *Pedro Páramo* de Juan Rulfo," *Universidad de México,* IX, 8 (April, 1955), 25; Mariana Frenk, "*Pedro Páramo* inicia en Alemania su viaje por el mundo," *México en la Cultura,* no. 504 (November, 1958), 7; José de la Colina, "Notas sobre Juan Rulfo," *Casa de las Américas,* IV, 26 (October–November, 1964), 133–138; Julieta Campos, "El mundo absorto de Juan Rulfo," in *La imagen en el espejo,* 1965, 167–171; Hugo Rodríguez Alcalá, *El Arte de Juan Rulfo, Historia de vivos y difuntos,* Mexico City, 1965.

JOHN RUSKIN

Born: London, England
Date: February 8, 1819

Died: Brantwood, Coniston, England
Date: January 20, 1900

Principal Works

ART CRITICISM: *Modern Painters,* Vols. I-V, 1843–1860; *The Seven Lamps of Architecture,* 1849; *Pre-Raphaelitism,* 1850; *The Stones of Venice,* Vols. I-III, 1851–1853; *Lectures on Art,* 1870; *Aratra Pentelici,* 1871; *The Eagle's Nest,* 1872; *Ariadne Florentina,* 1873–1876; *Val d'Arno,* 1874; *Mornings in Florence,* 1875–1877; *St. Mark's Rest: The History of Venice,* 1877–1884; *The Bible of Amiens,* 1880–1885; *Lectures on Landscape,* 1898.

SOCIAL CRITICISM: *The Construction of Sheepfolds,* 1851; *Unto This Last,* 1860, 1862; *Munera Pulveris,* 1862; *Sesame and Lilies,* 1865; *The Ethics of the Dust,* 1866; *The Crown of Wild Olive,* 1866; *Time and Tide,* 1867; *Fors Clavigera,* 1871–1884.

NATURE STUDIES: *Proserpina,* 1875–1886; *Love's Meinie,* 1873–1878; *Deucalion,* 1875–1883.

NOVELLA: *The King of the Golden River,* 1851.

AUTOBIOGRAPHY: *Praeterita,* 1885–1889.

During his lifetime John Ruskin acted in several capacities as a man of letters, writing as an aesthetician, an art historian, a poet, a writer of a fairy tale, and as the author of works on reform and economics. Born in London, February 8, 1819, he was the only child of parents who could and did lavish upon him a great deal of wealth and affection. In addition to study at King's College, in London, and at Christ Church College, Oxford, he traveled extensively through Europe. As early as 1837–1838 he wrote a series of articles on "The Poetry of Architecture" for *London's Architectural Magazine.* A defense of Turner's painting led him to write the voluminous *Modern Painters,* which appeared volume by volume from 1843 to 1860. The work became a treatise on art in general, a defense of painting being done at the time, and a formulation of the five categories Ruskin believed conveyed by art: power, imitation, truth, beauty, and relation.

In 1848 Ruskin married Euphemia Chalmers Gray, then nineteen years old, for whom he had written his novel-fairy tale, *The King of the Golden River,* in 1841. The marriage was unsuccessful and was annulled in 1854, with Miss Gray later marrying Millais, the artist, in the following year. Millais and other Pre-Raphaelite artists were friends of Ruskin, who supported their movement, especially in *The Stones of Venice.* After 1857 Ruskin became interested in writing as a social reformer, his most famous works in this vein being *Unto This Last.* As a reformer Ruskin also helped found the Working Men's College in London in 1854, and he gave lessons in drawing and lectured to groups at that institution. During the 1860's Ruskin wrote much and lectured, despite mental illness. One important book of this period was *Sesame and Lilies,* a collection of essays on aesthetic topics addressed primarily to young people. From 1870 to 1890 he wrote and traveled between increasingly severe attacks of mental illness, and the last decade of his life has been described, because of his condition, as a living death. He died at Brantwood, Coniston, England, on January 20, 1900.

BIBLIOGRAPHICAL REFERENCES: The *Works* of Ruskin have been edited by E. T. Cook and Alexander Wedderburn, 39 vols., 1903–1912; this includes an extensive bibliography. A useful selection is P. C. Quennell's edition of *Selected Writings*, 1952. The *Diaries* were edited by Joan Evans and J. H. Whitehouse, 3 vols., 1956–1959; the *Letters to Lord and Lady Mount-Temple* by J. L. Bradley, 1964. The most thorough biography is E. T. Cook, *The Life of John Ruskin*, 2 vols., 1911. Three briefer biographical studies are Frederick Harrison, *John Ruskin*, English Men of Letters Series, 1902; A. Williams-Ellis, *The Exquisite Tragedy: An Intimate Life of John Ruskin*, 1928; and P. C. Quennell, *Ruskin: The Portrait of a Prophet*, 1949. A valuable handbook is R. H. Wilenski, *John Ruskin: An Introduction to Further Study of His Life and Work*, 1933. Advanced readers may consult H. A. Ladd, *The Victorian Morality of Art: An Analysis of Ruskin's Esthetic*, 1932. A provocative essay on Ruskin appears in Virginia Woolf, *The Captain's Death Bed and Other Essays*, 1950. Also important is John D. Rosenberg, *The Darkening Glass: A Portrait of Ruskin's Genius*, 1961.

W. CLARK RUSSELL

Born: New York, N. Y.
Date: February 24, 1844

Died: Bath, England
Date: November 8, 1911

Principal Works

novels: *John Holdsworth, Chief Mate,* 1875; *The Wreck of the Grosvenor,* 1877; *My Watch Below,* 1822; *Round the Galley Fire,* 1883; *The Romance of a Midshipman,* 1898.

poems: *The Turnpike Sailor,* 1907.

W(illiam) Clark Russell, though of English parentage, was born in New York City, February 24, 1844. His father, Henry Russell, a well-known singer, was playing in America at the time. His mother, Isabella Lloyd Russell, was a distant relative of Wordsworth and herself a writer. W. Clark Russell entered the maritime service at the age of thirteen and remained until 1865. Prior to sea service he had been educated at Winchester School, in England, and abroad. After retiring from the sea he worked for several British newspapers, including the Newcastle *Daily Chronicle* and the London *Daily Telegraph,* staying with the latter until 1889. In 1874 Russell began writing, intending a career as a popular novelist, and during the remainder of his life produced the very remarkable total of fifty-seven volumes. His output included novels of life at sea, lives of Dampier (1889), Nelson (1890), and Collingwood (1891), several collections of short stories, and a volume of light, entertaining poetry

Although his works have never had serious scholarly consideration, they were read and admired by a whole generation of British readers. His best-known work, and the only one with a lasting body of readers, is *The Wreck of the Grosvenor,* one of his earliest novels. During the late nineteenth century many reforms came about in the British merchant marine, and part of the credit has usually been bestowed upon Russell and his books, which brought public attention to the need for improving what were admittedly deplorable conditions. Russell, who was the father of Sir Herbert Russell, a well-known writer on naval subjects, died at Bath, November 8, 1911.

bibliographical references: There is no authorized biography, almost no criticism. See W. J. Ward's memoir, "A National Asset," printed as an introduction to *Fathers of the Sea,* 1911. For a study of Russell in relation to his time and literary generation see also R. R. Bowker, "London as a Literary Center," *Harper's,* LXXVII (1888), 3–26.

VIKTOR RYDBERG

Born: Jönköping, Sweden
Date: December 18, 1828

Died: Stockholm, Sweden
Date: September 22, 1895

Principal Works

NOVELS: *Fribytaren på Ostersjön*, 1857 (*The Freebooter of the Baltic*); *Singoalla*, 1858; *Den siste Athenaren*, 1859 (*The Last Athenian*); *Vapensmeden*, 1891 (*The Armorer*).
ESSAYS: *Romerskadagar*, 1875–1876 (*Roman Days*).
POEMS: *Dikter*, 1882.

(Abraham) Viktor Rydberg, born at Jönköping into a lower class Swedish family on December 18, 1828, had a difficult childhood. It may have been this hard period which turned him toward the later romantic writing for which he became famous. Influenced in his early youth by contemporary liberal pressures, he studied at the University of Lund and in 1854 turned to journalism.

In 1855 he joined the staff of the leading newspaper of the city of Göteborg, and his romantic novels first appeared as serials in the columns of this newspaper. The first of these works, *The Freebooter of the Baltic*, won him some acclaim; it contains evidences of the idealism that was to be more fully developed in his later novels. Of his novels, *The Last Athenian* is the most famous. By the time it appeared in 1859, Rydberg was generally regarded in the first rank of Swedish novelists.

Turning to religion, he produced the first Swedish modern critical study of the Bible, *The Bible's Teaching about Christ* (1862). Besides his work in the novel and in theological criticism he also produced a great deal of material in the fields of aesthetics, philosophy, and psychology. His translation of Goethe's *Faust* in 1876 shows the profound influence that the earlier German writer had upon Rydberg's romanticism.

Rydberg appeared on the Swedish literary scene after a relatively barren period. Historically, he was one of the last of the Romanticists, and certainly one of the few idealists of the period, but his romantic idealism has survived the opposing naturalism that was soon to follow in Scandinavian literature. He died in Stockholm on September 22, 1895.

BIBLIOGRAPHICAL REFERENCES: There is almost no helpful criticism of Rydberg in English. The most comprehensive study is K. Warburg, *Viktor Rydberg, en levnadsteckning*, 2 vols., 1900. See also Ö. Lindberger, *Prometeustanken hos Viktor Rydberg*, 2 vols., 1938. A brief study of his verse is Charles Wharton Stork's essay, "The Poetry of Viktor Rydberg," in *Schelling Anniversary Papers*, edited by A. C Baugh, 1923.

HANS SACHS

Born: Nuremberg, Germany
Date: November 5, 1494

Died: Nuremberg
Date: January 19, 1576

Principal Works

PLAYS: *Die Wittenbergisch Nachtigall,* 1523 (*The Wittenberg Nightingale*); *Lucretia,* 1527; *Der farendt Schüler im Paradeis,* 1550 (*The Wandering Scholar from Paradise*); *Das heisse Eisen,* 1551 (*The Hot Iron*); *Die ungleichen Kinder Evä,* 1553; *Das Narrenschneiden,* date uncertain.

Lovers of Wagner will recognize the *meistersinger* Hans Sachs, the greatest of his time, as the principal character in *Die Meistersinger.* Surprisingly, his present fame does not rest on his songs and poems but on the 208 dramas which helped keep the German theater alive in the sixteenth century.

Sachs was born and died in Nuremberg, a contemporary and disciple of Martin Luther, having been born November 5, 1494. He forsook his early training as a shoemaker to become a wandering troubador, the highest calling in a day when the arts were revered with more than lip service. His apprenticeship over, he became master of his guild in 1517. After fifty years of composition he was said to have composed, before he died on January 19, 1576, more than four thousand songs, two thousand tales in verse, and 208 plays, thirty-four volumes in all exclusive of the songs which were not collected for publication. His plays were in the folk tradition of the *Fastnachtspiel,* the humorous plays for Shrovetide, a form paralleling the development of drama in England at the same time. But Germany was torn by strife over the Reformation and consequently had little patience with delightful trifles. Even Sachs, who wrote a poem of tribute to Luther, was forbidden to write for some few years until his own town sided with the reformer.

The avidity with which Hans Sachs wrote, the propitious times in which he lived, and the care with which his works were preserved all contribute to the great knowledge we have of this man and his work. Wagner was justly paying tribute to one of the men on whose shoulders he stood.

BIBLIOGRAPHICAL REFERENCES: There are various editions of the works of Hans Sachs in German. For critical commentary see Francis M. Ellis, *Hans Sachs Studies,* 1941; and John Gassner, *Masters of the Drama,* 1945. For more specialized study see Eli Sobel, *The Tristan Romance in the Meisterlieder of Hans Sachs,* 1963.

THE MARQUIS DE SADE

Born: Paris, France
Date: June 2, 1740

Died: Charenton Asylum, France
Date: December 2, 1814

Principal Works

NOVELS: *Justine*, 1791; *Les 120 Journées de Sodome* (*The 120 Days of Sodom*), written 1785, published 1904; *Aline et Valcour*, 1795; *La Philosophie dans le Boudoir* (*Philosophy in the Boudoir*), 1795; *Juliette*, 1798; *Les Crimes de l'Amour* (*Crimes of Love*), 1800.

PLAYS: *Le Misanthrope par Amour* (*The Misanthrope in Love*), 1790; *Oxtiern, ou les Malheurs du libertinage* (*Oxtiern, or the Sorrows of Libertinism*), 1799.

COMPLETE WORKS: *Oeuvres Complètes*, 1966–1967.

Donatien Alphonse François Sade was born in Paris in 1740, heir to the title of Count de Sade; in his family the heir carried the title of Marquis. At his father's death, he succeeded to the title of Count, as well as to the governorship of the provinces of Bresse, Bugey, and Valromey, but the earlier title remains associated with him. He was educated by his uncle, the Abbé de Sade, at the Benedictine monastery of Saint Léger d'Ebreuil. In 1754, at the age of fourteen, he embarked on a military career and fought through the Seven Years' War; in 1766, by which time he had achieved the rank of captain, he resigned from the army and married Mademoiselle de Montreuil, who bore him two sons.

Shortly after his marriage de Sade became involved in the extraordinary sexual adventures which have made *sadism* the standard term for cruelty inflicted on a supposed object of love. For these perverted exploits, he was imprisoned at various times in eleven different prisons, for a total of twenty-nine years; at one point, in 1772, he was even sentenced to die for acts of sodomy and poisoning, but was granted a reprieve.

During his terms of imprisonment, first at Vincennes, then at the Bastille, and finally at Charenton Asylum, de Sade wrote an enormous number of novels, plays, and journals; most of his fiction is a thinly-disguised vehicle for his philosophy of perversion. *Justine* and *Juliette* are chronicles of sexual experimentation and violence; the first details the sufferings of virtue under persecution, and the second portrays the triumph of depravity. *Aline et Valcourt* is clearly autobiographical; it is here that de Sade, self-portrayed as Valcourt, professes an indebtedness to Rousseau, whose ideas of personal liberty the later author pursued to extremes.

De Sade's plays are generally less objectionable than his novels, because they were written to be performed by the Théâtre-Français, whose eight-member board of directors voted on each play submitted to them. Nevertheless, *Oxtiern* revolves around the theme of physical violence.

De Sade died in 1814 at Charenton. His works, long condemned as obscene, have recently begun to attract serious critical attention for the light they shed on one rather dark aspect of Romantic philosophy and for their subterranean influence on nineteenth century literature.

BIBLIOGRAPHICAL REFERENCES: Mario Praz, *The Romantic Agony*, 1933, has a chapter ("The Shadow of the 'Divine Marquis' ") devoted to the influence of de Sade. See also Geoffrey Gover, *The Life and Ideas of the Marquis de Sade*, 1963; Norman Gear, *The Divine Demon*, 1963; and Gilbert Lély, *The Marquis de Sade*, translated by Alec Brown, 1970.

CHARLES AUGUSTIN SAINTE-BEUVE

Born: Boulogne-sur-Mer, France
Date: December 23, 1804

Died: Paris, France
Date: October 13, 1869

Principal Works

CRITICISM: *Tableau historique et critique de la poésie française au XVIe siecle*, 1827; *Portraits littéraires*, 1832–1839; *Histoire de Port Royal*, 1840–1848; *Portraits littéraires* (Second Series), 1844; *Portraits de femmes*, 1844; *Portraits contemporains*, 1846; *Châteaubriand et son groupe*, 1849; *Causeries de lundi*, 1851–1862 (*Monday Chats*); *Étude sur Virgile*, 1857; *Nouveaux lundis*, 1863–1870; *Premiers lundis*, 1874–1875.

POEMS: *La vie, les poésies et les pensées de J. Delorme*, 1829 (*The Life, Poems, and Thoughts of Joseph Delorme*); *Consolations*, 1830; *Pensées d'août*, 1837 (*Harvest Thoughts*).

NOVEL: *Volupté*, 1832.

Charles Augustin Sainte-Beuve, the greatest literary critic since Aristotle, was born to humble conditions, a posthumous child whose mother could ill-afford the education his brilliance demanded. After beginning his education in Boulogne, where he was born on December 23, 1804, he completed his studies in the Collège Charlemagne and the Collège Bourbon, in Paris. When a former teacher invited his bright student to write reviews for *Le Globe*, Sainte-Beuve abandoned the study of medicine, begun a year before, and devoted his time to writing.

Although he wrote for the influential *Globe*, and so gained the attention of Goethe and Victor Hugo, and for *La Revue de Paris* as well, his early reputation was largely bound in with *La Revue des Deux Mondes*. The columns he wrote for these papers he collected in seven volumes of *Portraits*. During this period of his life he fell in love with Adèle, wife of Victor Hugo, an affair which caused a separation from his old friend and fellow writer. In 1844 he was elected to the French Academy; he was received there by Hugo, with whom he had become reconciled. Through an error in posting, he was accused of receiving money for intelligence work in the 1848 revolution; consequently, he resigned his post in the Mazarin Library and went to teach French literature at the University of Liége. Another teaching post he held was at the École Normale Superieure from 1858 to 1862; he had previously resigned the chair in Latin poetry at the Collège de France after a few lectures.

Sainte-Beuve, who prided himself on his workaday journalism, produced his greatest series of critical articles in his *Monday Chats*, written for *Le Constitutionnel* and later for *Le Moniteur*. These, when collected, eventually filled fifteen volumes. Thirteen additional volumes were accumulated from his final series, *Nouveaux lundis*. Of all the literary figures of the period, he alone continued to write and prosper under the Empire, and he was made a senator in 1865. In the last year of his life he severed his connection with the official government journal, *Moniteur*, as the result of a political dispute. He died, unable longer to write even for the cause of the new freedom, in Paris on October 13, 1869.

Although he wrote poetry and a

novel, Sainte-Beuve's reputation rests on his literary portraits of French authors and his analysis of their works. His classic definition of a literary classic is included in every compilation of criticism; his books are familiar to students everywhere. Attempts to discredit him, begun during his lifetime, have never been successful because his position is virtually unassailable.

BIBLIOGRAPHICAL REFERENCES: The most recent critical biographies in English are Sir Harold Nicolson, *Sainte-Beuve*, 1957; and Arthur G. Lehmann, *Sainte-Beuve: A Portrait of the Critic*, 1962. An earlier study that is still useful is George McLean Harper, *Sainte-Beuve*, 1909. See also Lewis Freeman Mott, *Sainte-Beuve*, 1925. For biography and criticism in French see Gabriel D'Haussonville, *Sainte-Beauve, sa vie et ses œuvres*, 1875; Gustave Michaut, *Sainte-Beuve*, 1921; L. F. Choisy, *Sainte-Beuve, l'homme et le poète*, 1921; Victor Giraud, *La vie secrète de Sainte-Beuve*, 1935; Maxime Leroy, *La pensée de Sainte-Beuve*, 1940, and *Vie de Sainte-Beuve*, 1947; André Billy, *Sainte-Beuve, sa vie et son temps*, 1952; and Maurice Allemand, *Portrait de Sainte-Beuve*, 1954. For briefer studies see, further, Mary Fisher, *A Group of French Critics*, 1897; and Gustav Pollak, *International Perspective in Criticism*, 1914. See also Norman H. Barlow, *Sainte-Beuve to Baudelaire: A Poetic Legacy*, 1964.

ANTOINE DE SAINT-EXUPÉRY

Born: Lyons, France
Date: June 29, 1900

Died: Southern France
Date: July 31 (?), 1944

Principal Works

NOVELS: *Courrier sud*, 1928 (*Southern Mail*); *Vol de nuit*, 1931 (*Night Flight*).
ESSAYS: *Terre des hommes*, 1939 (*Wind, Sand, and Stars*); *Pilote de Guerre*, 1942 (*Flight to Arras*); *Lettre à un otage*, 1944 (*Letter to a Hostage*); *Citadelle*, 1948 (*The Wisdom of the Sands*).
JUVENILE: *Le petit prince*, 1943 (*The Little Prince*).

Antoine de Saint-Exupéry, born in Lyons, France, on June 29, 1900, joined the French Army Air Force in 1921. After serving as a pilot, he left the Air Force in 1926 and became a commercial pilot flying the routes from France to West Africa and South America. At the same time he began to write about flying, producing first a novel, *Southern Mail*, in which a young French aristocrat, full of impossibly romantic notions, first faces the realities of life and an unhappy love affair through the discipline of flying. In his next novel, *Night Flight*, Saint-Exupéry further developed the importance of flying by establishing a conflict between the "night flight" representing danger, achievement, and man's purpose on the one hand, and the life of home and domesticity on the other. These novels also showed his mastery of a rich, dense, powerfully poetic style well-suited to convey his ideas about flying and man.

For several years during the mid-thirties, Saint-Exupéry had difficulty getting a job flying. He then became a foreign correspondent, covering the May Day celebration in Moscow in 1935 and the 1937 siege of Madrid for *Paris-Soir*, and the outbreak of the Spanish Civil War, in 1936, for *L'Intransigeant*. These experiences deepened both his political and religious interests so that by the time he was ready to write *Wind, Sand, and Stars* he had switched from the novel to a form of personal essay or autobiography. It was André Gide, always a strong admirer of Saint-Exupéry, who is supposed to have suggested this change in form. *Wind, Sand, and Stars* is more political and religious, more thoughtful and metaphysical, than his earlier work, yet it still reflects his direct experiences, particularly his account of a plane crash in the Sahara Desert, and flying still provides both the form for the book and the necessary function for the author.

When World War II began, Saint-Exupéry returned to the Air Force. Shot down, he managed to escape through Portugal to the United States. He then wrote *Flight to Arras*, an account of his wartime experiences widely read in the United States as evidence that not all Frenchmen had succumbed to complacency and indifference in the face of the Nazi invasion and Vichy collaboration. He remained in the United States, writing, voicing his convictions about his responsibilities for his fellow human beings and his feelings of unity with his flight crew, his country, and all men, until he was able to help organize and rejoin the French forces. In his last days he wrote *The Wisdom of the Sands*, published posthumously in 1948. This book, though not always smooth or coherent, stands as the most complete account of his ideas. It is a long "poem" in prose, full of meditations on God and death and love and man's fate, stressing (in a manner some critics have called Nietzschean) man's need for the discipline and creativity afforded by an activity like flying.

Saint-Exupéry was widely admired for his rich, poetic style and his insight. He received the Prix Femina-Vie Heureuse in 1931 and the Grand Prize of the French Academy in 1939. In the United States and England he was even more famous as a spirited, authentic, and articulate voice of the French resistance, and as a writer who used in creative forms the sense of purpose and discipline wrought by human technology.

His death remains a mystery of the war. It is thought that he was shot down over Southern France on July 31, 1944.

BIBLIOGRAPHICAL REFERENCES: Saint-Exupéry's books are available in translation; there is no collected edition. Two recent studies in English are Richard Rumbold and Lady Margaret Stewart, *The Winged Life*, 1953; and Maxwell Austin Smith, *Knight of the Air: The Life and Works of Antoine de Saint-Exupéry*, 1956. Recent biographies in French include René Delange, *La vie de Saint-Exupéry*, 1948; Armand Bottequin, *Antoine de Saint-Exupéry*, 1949; Jules Roy, *Passion de Saint-Exupéry*, 1951; and Jean Bruce, *Saint-Exupéry, pilote légendaire*; in German, Walter Bauer, *Der Gesang von Sturmvogel*, 1949. See further André Maurois, "Antoine de Saint-Exupéry," *From Proust to Camus*, 1966, 201–223; W. M. Frohock, "Saint-Exupéry: The Poet as Novelist," *Style and Temper; Studies in French Fiction, 1925–1960*, 1967, 31–34; and Henri Peyre, "Antoine de Saint-Exupéry," *French Novelists of Today*, 1967, 154–179.

SAKI
Hector Hugh Munro

Born: Akyab, Burma
Date: December 18, 1870

Died: Beaumont Hamel, France
Date: November 14, 1916

PRINCIPAL WORKS

SHORT STORIES: *Reginald*, 1904; *Reginald in Russia*, 1910; *The Chronicles of Clovis*, 1911; *Beasts and Super-Beasts*, 1914; *The Square Egg*, 1924; *The Complete Short Stories of Saki*, 1930.
NOVELS: *The Unbearable Bassington*, 1912; *When William Came*, 1913.

Hector Hugh Munro, an English short story writer and journalist, was born December 18, 1870, in Akyab, Burma, where his father was a colonel in the Bengal Staff Corps and Inspector General of the Police. Because of his mother's death he was reared in England with his elder brother and sister by his grandmother and two aunts in Pilton, near Barnstable, North Devon. He went to grammer school at Exmouth and Bedford, and during his youth was interested in drawing and art. When his father retired from the army he took over the boy's education and accompanied him on a tour of Europe.

In 1893 Munro returned to Burma to join the police force—a position which was the result of his father's influence. But the young man suffered so severely from fever that he returned to England in 1894 to try to make a living from writing. Employed by the *Westminster Gazette*, he wrote the political sketches called *Alice in Westminster*, which were published in book form in 1902. It was during this period that he first used his pen name, Saki. Derived from *The Rubáiyát of Omar Khayyám*, Saki is the name of the cupbearer. In 1902 his *Not So Stories*, written in a satiric vein, were published anonymously. From 1902 to 1908 he traveled as foreign correspondent for the *Morning Post* to the Balkans, Russia, Poland, and France. His serious volume entitled *The Rise of the Russian Empire*, a history of Russia at the time of Peter the Great, had already been published in 1900.

In 1904 *Reginald*, the first volume of his inimitable short stories, was published. It was followed by *Chronicles of Clovis* and *Beasts and Super-Beasts*, both successful. In 1912 appeared *The Unbearable Bassington*, an excellent short novel of social satire written in the clever epigrammatic style of Oscar Wilde.

Saki's short stories, his chief claim to fame, are still widely read and enjoyed. They are likely to retain their popularity because of their sparkling wit and clever humor. Notable for the unexpected phrase, many of his tales are concerned with unusual animals or witty sophisticated young men. Dealing frequently with unconventional subjects or practical jokes, they are not likely to be true to life. Yet they often have a morbid fascination.

In 1910, when Munro returned to England from the continent, he bought a cottage in Surrey, where he did much of his story-writing. Meanwhile he was writing also for the *Bystander* and the *Daily Express*. In 1913 he published *When William Came*, an imagined picture of what British life would be like under German rule. In 1914 he refused a commission and enlisted in the First World War. He was killed on November 14, 1916, near Beaumont Hamel in France. *The Toys of Peace* (1919) and *The Square Egg* were published after his death.

BIBLIOGRAPHICAL REFERENCES: A biographical sketch by Ethel M. Munro, included in *The Square Egg*, 1924, was reprinted in *The Complete Short Stories of Saki*, 1930. A memoir by Rothay Reynolds was printed in *The Toys of Peace*, 1919. See also Victor Sawdon Pritchett, "The Performing Lynx," *The Living Novel and Later Appreciations*, 1964, 219–224; and Graham Greene, "The Burden of Childhood," *Collected Essays*, 1969, 127–131.

J. D. SALINGER

Born: New York, N. Y.
Date: January 1, 1919

Principal Works

NOVEL: *The Catcher in the Rye,* 1951.
SHORT STORIES AND NOVELLAS: *Nine Stories,* 1953; *Franny and Zooey,* 1961; *Raise High the Roof Beam, Carpenters,* and *Seymour—An Introduction,* 1963.

Jerome David Salinger was born in New York City on January 1, 1919, the son of a Scotch-Irish mother and a Jewish father in the food importing business. In 1936 he was graduated from the Valley Forge Military Academy, at Valley Forge, Pennsylvania, where he wrote for school publications and for the drama group. In 1938 he entered Ursinus College at Collegeville, Pennsylvania, but he left in December before the end of the first semester. There he had written a series of nine columns for the college weekly newspaper. In the spring and fall of 1939 he was a student in the Extension Division of Columbia University in New York City. While there he was a member of Whit Burnett's class in short story writing. The next year, in Burnett's magazine, *Story,* Salinger first appeared professionally.

His early military service was in the Army Air Corps, but in 1943 he was transferred to his permanent assignment with a counter intelligence unit of the 12th Infantry Regiment of the 4th Infantry Division. There he served in five campaigns from D-Day to VE-Day, questioning captured Germans and French civilians. He went through the Battle of the Bulge and was in Germany when the war ended. During his two and a half years' service in the European Theater of Operations he continued to write when he could and to publish short fiction in magazines such as *Collier's, Esquire,* and *The Saturday Evening Post.*

In 1946, the year he first appeared in the pages of *The New Yorker,* his brief marriage to a European woman physician ended in divorce. In 1948 he published three stories in *The New Yorker.* The next year there was another and one in *Harper's.* These, like the story which appeared the following year, were later to be collected in a volume of short stories. All his short fiction since then has appeared in *The New Yorker.*

His only novel, *The Catcher in the Rye,* was published in 1951. It became an immediate success. This story, with its appealing protagonist, sixteen-year-old Holden Caulfield, used characters and situations which Salinger had first employed in his shorter fiction. The volume of short stories, called simply, *Nine Stories,* came out in 1953. It further consolidated his enormous popularity, which was particularly strong among college students. Following his return from the war he resided in Westport, Connecticut, but in keeping with his growing reputation for privacy he later moved to Cornish, New Hampshire, a small town on the Vermont border.

In 1954, as in 1952, he published nothing new, but in 1955 two new stories about members of his fictitious Glass family appeared. In that same year he married English-born Claire

Alison Douglas. No new Salinger fiction came out in 1956, but in 1957 he published "Zooey," a long story about another Glass sibling. Two years later appeared "Seymour: An Introduction," further exploring the character of Zooey's deceased older brother. Salinger has published no new fiction since "Seymour: An Introduction," but his large public has warmly welcomed the publication in book form of stories which appeared earlier in magazine form: *Franny and Zooey* in 1961 and *Seymour* and *Raise High the Roof Beam, Carpenters* in 1963. Doubtless there will be further fictional treatments of the Glass family in time.

BIBLIOGRAPHICAL REFERENCES: Extended studies include Frederick L. Gwynn and Joseph L. Blotner, *The Fiction of J. D. Salinger*, 1958; Henry A. Grunwald, editor, *Salinger: A Critical and Personal Portrait*, 1962; William F. Belcher and James W. Lee, editors, *J. D. Salinger and the Critics*, 1962; Warren French, *J. D. Salinger*, 1963; and two pamphlets, James E. Miller, Jr., *J. D. Salinger*, 1965, and Kenneth Hamilton, *J. D. Salinger: A Critical Essay*, 1967.

Salinger is discussed in most books on modern American fiction. Of special interest are David D. Galloway, *The Absurd Hero in American Fiction: Updike, Styron, Bellow, Salinger*, 1966; Jonathan Baumbach, *The Landscape of Nightmare: Studies in the Contemporary American Novel*, 1965; Max F. Schulz, *Radical Sophistication: Studies in Contemporary Jewish/American Novelists*, 1969; and Helen Weinberg, *The New Novel in America: The Kafkan Mode in Contemporary Fiction*, 1970.

Modern Fiction Studies XII, No. 3 (1966) was a special Salinger issue, including a number of important articles and a critical checklist.

FELIX SALTEN
Siegmund Salzmann

Born: Budapest, Hungary
Date: September 6, 1869

Died: Zurich, Switzerland
Date: October 8, 1945

PRINCIPAL WORKS

NOVELS: *Der Hund von Florenz,* 1921 (*The Hound of Florence*); *Bambi,* 1923; *Florian,* 1933 (*Florian, the Emperor's Stallion*); *Perri,* 1938; *Bambis Kinder,* 1939 (*Bambi's Children*).

Felix Salten (pseudonym of Siegmund Salzmann), who was internationally known in his later years for his animal stories that delighted children and adults alike, was born in Budapest on September 6, 1869. His family was poor and, according to his own account, he was largely self-taught. A journalist at seventeen, he was for many years associated with the Viennese *Neue Freie Presse,* the most influential newspaper in Austro-Hungary before World War I. He began his literary career as a writer of historical, romantic, and satirical novels widely read throughout Central Europe. President of the Austrian P.E.N. Club at the time of the Nazi invasion, he took refuge in Switzerland in 1939 and died at Zurich, after a long illness, on October 8, 1945.

Bambi, translated in 1928, became a popular children's book and brought its author wide fame when it was made into a feature-length cartoon by Walt Disney. This lucidly written and moving story of a red deer growing up in the innocence of the great forest describes also the threat by humans (creatures of the "third arm") to the freedom of life in the wilds. By delicately transferring human ideals to his animals, the writer succeeds in a kind of allegory which preserves a delicate balance between a world of reality and one of fancy. Salten once referred to Gottfried Keller as a primary influence on his work.

The Hound of Florence had been Salten's first children's book. After *Bambi, Florian, the Emperor's Stallion,* and *Perri,* the story of a squirrel, appeared. This is perhaps as haunting a book as his story of the deer; in it he created the character of an inarticulate three-year-old girl who understands animals better than humans. With *Good Comrades* (1942) and *Forest World* (1942), Salten's peculiar talent was confirmed as that of an imaginative observer who could sometimes capture the flow of sympathy between the natural orders of humans and animals. *Jibby the Cat* (1948) and *Little World Apart* (1948), both published after his death, added little to his achievement.

He also wrote travel books about America and Palestine and nearly forty novels, most of them hack work and untranslated, as well as short stories, dramas, and essays. *The Private* (1899), an anti-militaristic play, was his most notable writing for the theater.

BIBLIOGRAPHICAL REFERENCES: There is no comprehensive biographical study and almost no criticism. For discussions of the novels, see the *Book Review Digest,* 1928 ff.

FLORENCIO SÁNCHEZ

Born: Montevideo, Uruguay
Date: January 17, 1875

Died: Milan, Italy
Date: November 7, 1910

PRINCIPAL WORKS

PLAYS: *M'hijo el dotor*, 1903 (*My Son, the Lawyer*); *La gringa*, 1904 (*The Foreign Girl*); *Barranca abajo*, 1905 (*Retrogression*); *Los Muertos*, 1905 (*The Dead*).

The theater of the River Plate region was just beginning to deal with local types when Florencio Sánchez was born, in Montevideo, Uruguay, January 17, 1875, the first of eleven children of a middle class family. His father's political activities kept the family on the move and prevented the children from receiving much of a formal education. Florencio worked as secretary and in various jobs on newspapers. His first play was written for the entertainment of a club of political protesters to which he belonged. His second attempt was censored by city officials of Rosario, where he was a newspaper reporter, but when its performance was prevented, he worked all night setting it in type and had it ready for the public to read the next morning. He rewrote his first play as a musical comedy, *Canillita* (1902), which takes its title from its newsboy hero. The success of the play put that word into the Argentine language as a nickname for all newsboys.

A desire to show his sweetheart that he amounted to something forced Sánchez into the writing of his first important play, *My Son, the Lawyer* in 1903. During its rehearsal, the theater doorkeeper refused admission to the stoop-shouldered, shabbily dressed author with Indian features, because he looked like a tramp. Following the success of this tragedy, came a total of twenty plays, eight long dramas and twelve one-act sketches, products of the six years that comprised Sánchez' activities as a dramatist. He wrote rapidly, often on telegraph blanks, and did his best work in noisy bars and among crowds.

He reported that it took only one day to complete the four-act *The Foreign Girl*, called by one critic "the tragedy of the Argentine race." The play has technical flaws in starting slowly and ending twice, for the third act really answers the question whether the easy-going Argentine can withstand the industrious Italians and the final act merely restates the problem and provides a happy ending, with its preachment that the country's hope lies in work and an amalgamation of native and foreigner. The emotions of the play, however, and the realistic pictures of people and life on the pampas have made it Sánchez' most popular play.

Technically better is *Retrogression* (sometimes called *Down the Ravine*), the tragedy of a good gaucho driven to despair and suicide by the unworthy and nagging women about him. In general, the author has neither interest in nor sympathy with the women of his plays. They are hardly more than puppets to develop his ideas and story.

From 1905 on, Sánchez turned his attention to the city, writing nine plays about the lower classes and five tragedies about the middle and upper classes. These works are characterized by social problems and realistic treatment tending toward naturalism. But Sánchez was no follower of Zola. He saw a "tragic fatality of character and circumstance," but he also had sympathy for his creations as the victims of the society in which they live. In wanting to make them over, he followed Ibsen, thereby gaining his nickname, "El Ibsen criollo."

Having dominated the Argentine and Uruguayan theater, Sánchez longed for a hearing in Europe. Several of his plays had already been translated and played in Italian. In 1909 he persuaded his government to send him to Italy. But after he arrived, his long years of irregular living demanded a reckoning. He contracted tuberculosis, and in 1910 the dramatist who had helped introduce realism into the theater of the River Plate died on November 7, and was buried in Milan. In 1921 the Uruguayan government brought home the ashes of its most distinguished playwright.

Perhaps Florencio Sánchez is not great compared to masters of the theater who have exerted great influence outside their own countries. His writing is uneven, with some of his situations trite and weak. He did inspire writers in his own land, however, and his many good qualities have made his theater a cultural heritage of the River Plate region, where he has had few equals and no superiors.

BIBLIOGRAPHICAL REFERENCES: For critical studies see Isaac Goldberg, *The Drama of Transition*, 1922; Ruth Richardson, *Florencio Sánchez and the Argentine Theatre*, 1933; Julio Imbert, *Florencio Sánchez, vida y creación*, 1954 (Buenos Aires); and Willis K. Jones, "The *Gringa* Theme in River Plate Drama," *Hispania*, XXV (1942), 326–332.

GEORGE SAND
Amandine Lucile Aurore Dupin Dudevant

Born: Paris, France
Date: July 1, 1804

Died: Nohant, La Châtre, France
Date: June 8, 1876

PRINCIPAL WORKS

NOVELS: *Indiana*, 1832; *Valentine*, 1832; *Lélia*, 1833; *Lavinia*, 1833; *Le Secrétaire intime*, 1834 (*The Private Secretary*); *Léone Léoni*, 1834; *Jacques*, 1834; *André*, 1835; *Simon*, 1836; *Mauprat*, 1837; *Les Maîtres mosaïstes*, 1837 (*The Masters of Mosaic*); *La Dernière Aldini*, 1837–1838 (*The Last of the Aldini*); *Les Sept Cordes de la Lyre*, 1839 (*The Seven Strings of the Lyre*); *Le Compagnon du tour de France*, 1841 (*The Journeyman-Joiner*); *Horace*, 1841–1842; *Consuelo*, 1842–1843; *La Comtesse de Rudolstadt*, 1843–1844 (*The Countess of Rudolstadt*); *Jeanne*, 1844; *Le Meunier d'Angibault*, 1845 (*The Miller of Angibault*); *Le Péché de M. Antoine*, 1845 (*The Sin of Monsieur Antoine*); *La Mare au diable*, 1846 (*The Devil's Pool*); *Lucrezia Floriani*, 1846; *François le Champi*, 1847–1848 (*François the Waif*); *La Petite Fadette*, 1848–1849 (*Little Fadette*); *Mont-Revêche*, 1852; *La Filleule*, 1853 (*The Goddaughter*); *Les Maîtres sonneurs*, 1853 (*The Master Bell-Ringers*); *Adriani*, 1854; *Le Diable aux champs*, 1855–1856 (*The Devil in the Fields*); *La Daniella*, 1857; *Les Beaux Messieurs de Bois-Doré*, 1857–1858 (*The Gentlemen of Bois-Doré*); *L'Homme de neige*, 1858 (*The Snow Man*); *Elle et Lui*, 1859 (*She and He*); *Jean de la Roche*, 1859; *Le Marquis de Villemer*, 1860 (*The Marquis of Villemer*); *La Famille de Germandre*, 1861 (*The Germandre Family*); *Valvèdre*, 1861; *Tamaris*, 1862; *Antonia*, 1862; *Mademoiselle La Quintinie*, 1863; *Laura*, 1864; *La Confession d'une jeune fille*, 1864 (*The Confession of a Young Girl*); *Monsieur Sylvestre*, 1865; *Le Dernier Amour*, 1866 (*The Last Love*); *Cadio*, 1867; *Pierre qui roule*, 1869 (*Rolling Stone*); *Nanon*, 1872; *Ma Soeur Jeanne*, 1874 (*My Sister Jeanne*); *Flamarande*, 1875; *La Tour de Percemont*, 1875–1876 (*The Tower of Percemont*).

PLAYS: *Cosima*, 1840; *François le Champi*, 1849; *Claudie*, 1851; *Le Mariage de Victorine*, 1851; *Mauprat*, 1853; *Maître Favilla*, 1855; *Le Marquis de Villemer*, 1864; *L'Autre*, 1870 (*The Other One*).

MISCELLANEOUS: *Lettres d'un Voyageur*, 1834–1836 (*Letters of a Traveler*); *Lettres à Marcie*, 1837 (*Letters to Marcie*); *Un hiver à Majorque*, 1841 (*A Winter at Majorca*); *Histoire de ma Vie*, 1854–1855 (*Story of My Life*).

In Amandine Lucile Aurore Dudevant, nee Dupin, known to posterity as George Sand, were united two quite dissimilar lines of heredity. On the mother's side her origins were obscure; Sophie Delaborde, a humble Parisian modiste, was a bird-trainer's daughter. On the father's side her pedigree was brilliant; Maurice Dupin was a dashing officer only a few generations removed from royalty, being the son of M. Dupin de Francueil (who had numbered among his friends Jean Jacques Rousseau) and of Marie Aurore, a granddaughter of Augustus the Strong of Saxony. Maurice Dupin and his wife Sophie were married in the late spring of 1804, and their child Aurore was born in Paris on July 1. In 1808 Dupin was killed in a fall from horseback. Submitting to necessity, Sophie turned the little girl over to the haughty Mme. Dupin de Francueil, who undertook the responsibility of the child's education. Reared at the family estate of Nohant, Aurore was privately tutored and, at thirteen, was sent for schooling to the Convent des

Dames Anglaises at Paris, where she remained three years. At eighteen, her grandmother having died, she was married to Casimir Dudevant, and she soon bore a son and a daughter. In 1831 she left her husband and took up residence in Paris.

Fully aware of her literary genius, she resolved to maintain herself by writing and to carve out a place of eminence in the world of letters. Her first intimate association, dating from 1831, was with a young advocate, Jules Sandeau, with whom she collaborated on two novels, both signed "J. Sand." The next novel, *Indiana*, she wrote alone, but she issued it in 1832 under the name "Georges Sand"; this, anglicized soon afterward, became her invariable pseudonym. Having quarreled with Sandeau, she entered upon a liaison with Alfred de Musset and accompanied him to Italy. In Venice she fell ill; while recovering, she had an affair with her physician, Dr. Pietro Pagello. The consequent rift between herself and Musset was never closed. In 1837, Franz Liszt arranged an introduction between George Sand and Frédéric Chopin, whose love she succeeded in winning, though after some difficulty. The next winter she escorted Chopin, who was in fragile health, to the island of Majorca, where for a few months they lodged in a half-ruined monastery. The nine-year period of their alliance was for both a time of splendid artistic productivity. She manifested strong political interests in the 1840's while engaged, paradoxically, in the writing of her pastoral novels. A few years later, she retired to her childhood home at Nohant and passed the remainder of her life there, dying on June 8, 1876.

George Sand's novels may be classified as belonging to four main periods of development. In her first or feminist period, from 1832 to about 1837, they reflected her emotional rebellion against the bonds of marriage. In her second period, ending about 1845, they acquired a larger consciousness of social and philosophical problems; and this awareness gave rise not only to the socialist novels—*The Journeyman-Joiner, Horace, The Miller of Angibault,* and *The Sin of Monsieur Antoine*—but also to *Consuelo* and *The Countess of Rudolstadt.* Some of these works influenced the American poet, Walt Whitman. In her third or pastoral period, ending about 1856, her novels presented chiefly rural scenes and peasant characters; such was the case with *The Devil's Pool, François the Waif, Little Fadette,* and *The Master Bell-Ringers.* In her final period, up to 1876, her fiction explored a large variety of themes in an increasingly vigorous style. Among the best of her later novels are *The Marquis of Villemer* and the anticlerical *Mademoiselle La Quintinie.*

BIBLIOGRAPHICAL REFERENCES: The best work on George Sand in English is the biography by Andre Maurois, *Lélia*, translated from the French in 1953. In French there is the monumental work by Marie Louise Pailleron, *George Sand, histoire de sa vie*, 3 vols., 1938–1953. See also Magdeleine Paz, *La Vie d'un grand homme, George Sand*, 1947; Jeanne Galzy, *George Sand*, 1950; Pierre Salamon, *George Sand*, 1953; A. J. George, "The Major Romantics: George Sand," *Short Fiction in France, 1800–1850*, 1964, 150–153; and Albert Thibaudet, "George Sand," *French Literature from 1795 to Our Era*, 1968, 212–215.

CARL SANDBURG

Born: Galesburg, Illinois
Date: January 6, 1878

Died: Flat Rock, North Carolina
Date: July 22, 1967

Principal Works

POEMS: *Chicago Poems*, 1916; *Cornhuskers*, 1918; *Smoke and Steel*, 1920; *Slabs of the Sunburnt West*, 1922; *Good Morning, America*, 1928; *The People, Yes*, 1936; *Complete Poems*, 1950; *Wind Song*, 1960; *Honey and Salt*, 1963; *Complete Poems*, revised and enlarged edition, 1970.

BIOGRAPHY: *Abraham Lincoln: The Prairie Years*, 1926; *Steichen the Photographer*, 1929; *Mary Lincoln, Wife and Widow*, 1932 (with Paul M. Angle); *Abraham Lincoln: The War Years*, 1939.

NOVEL: *Remembrance Rock*, 1948.

AUTOBIOGRAPHY: *Always the Young Strangers*, 1952.

CHILDREN'S STORIES: *Rootabaga Stories*, 1922; *Rootabaga Pigeons*, 1923; *Potato Face*, 1930.

MISCELLANEOUS: *The American Songbag*, 1927; *A Lincoln and Whitman Miscellany*, 1938; *Storm over the Land*, 1942; *Home Front Memo*, 1943; *New American Songbag*, 1950.

"As American as Carl Sandburg"— this phrase may well become a part of our language, for in spite of his universal appeal Sandburg seems a writer who could only have sprung from America, the land where big men rise from small beginnings, where people are restless, inventive, jacks of all trades. The Sandburg story began in Galesburg, Illinois, on January 6, 1878. Carl (August) was the second child of August and Clara Anderson Sandburg. Legend says that his father, a blacksmith, changed his name from Johnson to Sandburg to avoid confusion with the other August Johnsons in Galesburg, but Carl himself (perhaps to increase confusion) quoted his mother as saying the name was originally Danielson.

The restlessness of America came early. His schooling was fitful and at thirteen he began the first of many jobs that sound almost like a poetic cataloging from one of his own works: newsboy, milkman, bottle washer, scene shifter, potter's helper, hobo, icehouse worker, painter's apprentice. The tour as a hobo (which included the traditional sock on the jaw by a brakeman) took him through Kansas, Nebraska, Colorado. When he came back to Galesburg in 1898, he began wearing out his hands by sandpapering wood for a painter, but the *Maine* went down in Havana harbor and the restless Carl joined Company C, Sixth Infantry Regiment of Illinois Volunteers. The war took him to Puerto Rico and almost, but not quite, into battle.

Returning once more to Galesburg, Carl decided to enter Lombard College there. About the same time he began to write. He was editor-in-chief of the school paper and, to sustain his versatility, captain of the basketball team. Leaving Lombard without graduating (though the college later awarded him one of his many honorary degrees), he again roamed the United States, finally settling in Milwaukee as an organizer for the Wisconsin Socialist Democratic

Party. In 1904 he published *In Restless Ecstasy*, a pamphlet of twenty-two poems which reveal the beginnings of his famous style. In 1908 he married Lillian Steichen, sister of the outstanding photographer. After several years as secretary to the mayor of Milwaukee, Sandburg moved to Chicago, his "City of the Big Shoulders," and with this move he became a newspaperman. But the poet was there, too; in 1914 he published in Harriet Monroe's *Poetry: A Magazine of Verse* his poem "Chicago," a rugged, hard-punching tribute. With this success he produced his volumes of verse at regular intervals: *Chicago Poems, Cornhuskers, Smoke and Steel, Slabs of the Sunburnt West, Good Morning, America,* and *The People, Yes.* Although some of the poems are weak and misty, these books contain America, the ugliness and the beauty, all sung by a man who can "tear his shirt" on one page and on the next steal softly in "on little cat feet."

Sandburg continued to make his living as a newspaperman. During World War I he was Stockholm correspondent for the Newspaper Enterprise Associates and later an editorial writer for the Chicago *Daily News.*

In 1920 still another Sandburg emerged, the lecturer and singer of folk songs. Equipped with a voice as powerful and wide-ranging as his poetry, Sandburg gave performances in which he talked philosophy, read his poems, and sang the ballads of our country. With these ballads he filled *The American Songbag* in 1927.

Sandburg is known as a biographer of Lincoln, but this flat statement is a pale inadequacy. Without sacrificing his own individuality, Sandburg has become, by combining admiration and research, almost a latter-day Lincoln, a man who looks at things as Lincoln did. Author and subject seem to blend in the poetic prose of *Abraham Lincoln: The Prairie Years* and *Abraham Lincoln: The War Years.* In 1954 he condensed these six volumes into one. His biography brought him a Pulitzer Prize in 1940, making some of his admirers wonder whether it will be Sandburg the poet or Sandburg the biographer who will be long remembered.

Long remembered he is likely to be, for there are still other sides to this versatile, inventive writer. His *Rootabaga Stories* and *Potato Face*, full of the fanciful repetition that is so much a part of childhood, have become classic stories for childern. Because there seemed to be so few literary forms left to conquer, Sandburg tried a novel and in 1948 produced *Remembrance Rock,* a rambling saga of Americans from Plymouth days to the present. With some readers and critics Sandburg's encounter with the novel came out, at best, as a draw; but his triumph is clearcut when it comes to autobiography, for *Always the Young Strangers* is an account of his early years that is written with the charm, strength, and twinkle only he can blend so persuasively.

Honors came late to Sandburg, but they were many. Among them were his selection as a Phi Beta Kappa poet at Harvard and the Litt.D. that university later awarded him. One of his most triumphant days came in 1953 on his seventy-fifth birthday. At a dinner in his honor the tributes included one from the homeland of his parents when he received Sweden's Commander Order of the Northern Star. As a part of the general celebration, Sandburg returned to his birthplace, Galesburg, and read the poems and sang the ballads that had made him famous. Radio and television widened his audience even more; his deep voice and his craggy face overhung by hair that looked like a slab of the sunburnt west penetrated the American living room. This man did so many things (in 1934 a lecturer at the University of Hawaii and next a raiser of goats at his home in Flat Rock, North Carolina) and wrote so well in so many forms (think of the *Rootabaga Stories* and then of *The People, Yes,* a poetic compendium of our tall tales and our slangy speech) that he became, if it can be said of one man, the voice of America.

BIBLIOGRAPHICAL REFERENCES: The standard texts of Sandburg's poetry are *The Complete Poems of Carl Sandburg,* 1950, and *Selected Poems of Carl Sandburg,* edited by Rebecca West, 1926, with a valuable critical introduction. There is no fully detailed biographical study, although several have been reported in preparation. Sandburg has told the story of his early years in *Always the Young Strangers,* 1952. The *Letters* were edited by Herbert Mitgang, 1968. Studies of significance are Karl W. Detzer, *Carl Sandburg: A Study in Personality and Background,* 1941; and Richard Crowder, *Carl Sandburg,* 1964. The most recent bibliography is the checklist by Frances Cheney in Allen Tate, *Sixty American Poets, 1890–1944,* 1945.

Earlier estimates of Sandburg's writing include Conrad Aiken, "Poetic Realism: Carl Sandburg," in *Scepticisms,* 1919; Stuart P. Sherman, *Americans,* 1922; Harry Hansen, *Midwest Portraits,* 1923; Percy H. Boynton, *Some Contemporary Americans,* 1924; Paul Rosenfeld, "Carl Sandburg," in *Port of New York,* 1924; and Bruce Weirick, *From Whitman to Sandburg in American Poetry: A Critical Survey,* 1924. The commentary on the Lincoln biographies is extensive and important. For criticism of *The Prairie Years* consult the *Book Review Digest,* 1926. A collection of reviews of *The War Years,* by Charles A. Beard, Robert E. Sherwood, and others, was reprinted in the pamphlet, *The Lincoln of Carl Sandburg,* 1940. See also Allan Nevins, "Abraham Lincoln in Washington," *Saturday Review of Literature,* XXI (December 2, 1939), 3–4+; Joseph Auslander, "A Poet Writes Biography," *College English,* I (1940), 649–657; and Oscar Cargill, "Carl Sandburg: Crusader and Mystic," *ibid.,* XI (1950), 367–372. *Carl Sandburg's "Remembrance Rock,"* n.d., contains a selected critical commentary on Sandburg's novel. For later estimates of the poems see also Thomas K. Whipple, *Spokesmen,* 1928; Newton Arvin, "Carl Sandburg," in *After the Genteel Tradition,* edited by Malcolm Cowley, 1936; Babette Deutsch, *Poetry in Our Time,* 1952 (rev. ed., 1956); William Carlos Williams, "Carl Sandburg's Complete Poems," in *Selected Essays,* 1954; Charles H. Compton, "Who Reads Carl Sandburg?" *South Atlantic Quarterly,* XXVIII (1929), 190–200; Morton Dauwen Zabel, "Sandburg's Testament," *Poetry,* XLIX (1936), 33–45; and Babette Deutsch, "Poetry for the People," *English Journal,* XXVI (1937), 265–274.

GEORGE SANTAYANA

Born: Madrid, Spain
Date: December 16, 1863

Died: Rome, Italy
Date: September 26, 1952

Principal Works

PHILOSOPHY: *The Sense of Beauty,* 1896; *The Life of Reason,* 1905–1906 (*Reason in Common Sense,* 1905; *Reason in Society,* 1905; *Reason in Religion,* 1905; *Reason in Art,* 1905; *Reason in Science,* 1906); *Scepticism and Animal Faith,* 1923; *The Realms of Being,* 1927–1940 (*The Realm of Essence,* 1927; *The Realm of Matter,* 1930; *The Realm of Truth,* 1938; *The Realm of Spirit,* 1940).

ESSAYS AND CRITICAL STUDIES: *Interpretations of Poetry and Religion,* 1900; *Three Philosophical Poets: Lucretius, Dante, and Goethe,* 1910; *Winds of Doctrine,* 1913; *Character and Opinion in the United States,* 1920; *Soliloquies in England and Later Soliloquies,* 1922; *Dominations and Powers,* 1951.

POEMS: *Sonnets and Other Verses,* 1894; *A Hermit of Carmel and Other Poems,* 1901; *Poems,* 1922.

NOVEL: *The Last Puritan: A Memoir in the Form of a Novel,* 1935.

PLAY: *Lucifer: A Theological Tragedy,* 1899.

AUTOBIOGRAPHY: *Persons and Places,* 1944; *The Middle Span,* 1945; *My Host the World,* 1953.

George Santayana, whose fame derives from his role as an urbane and skeptical philosopher endowed with an excellent literary style, was born in Madrid, December 16, 1863, of nominally Catholic parents, Augustín Ruiz de Santayana and Josefine Borráis. He was christened Jorge Augustín Nicholas Ruiz de Santayana y Borráis.

Until he was nine years of age, he knew no English; his parents, although well-educated in the arts, spoke Spanish in the home. In 1872 Santayana's mother returned to the United States to fulfill an agreement with her former husband, George Sturgis, to educate the three Sturgis children in the United States. In 1872 George Santayana, then nine, joined her and the Sturgis children in Boston. His father, who brought him to the United States, returned to Spain after spending one winter in Boston.

Santayana was educated at the Brimmer School, the Boston Latin School, and Harvard University. In 1883 he returned to Spain to visit his father and there expressed his dissatisfaction with academic life. However, since neither military nor diplomatic service seemed advisable, he decided to continue his work at Harvard. He received his B.A. and a fellowship in 1886 and spent the following two years at the University of Berlin. He then returned to Harvard and in 1889 received the M.A. and Ph.D. in philosophy.

At that time Harvard University was enjoying its greatest philosophical period; on the faculty were William James, Josiah Royce, and George H. Palmer. Although Santayana became a member of that august faculty in 1889 and was to some extent naturally influenced by the ideas about him, he remained for the most part solitary and independent in his work. Santayana ascribed his preference for isolation and his inability to feel at home in America to his Spanish-Catholic background; he adopted the lifelong attitude of following his particular interests, but wished others happiness in their own individual pursuits.

While he was teaching at Harvard, he had as students a number of persons who later achieved their own kinds of fame, among them T. S. Eliot, Conrad Aiken, Felix Frankfurter, and Walter Lippmann.

In 1912, having received a legacy which made retirement possible, Santayana left the faculty at Harvard and returned to Europe, where he spent the remainder of his life. He stayed for a brief time in Spain and France and spent five years in England. Later he settled in Rome where he felt most at ease as a solitary and contemplative writer of philosophical works and critical essays. During World War II he found sanctuary in the grounds of a convent in Rome. There during the last years of his life his work quietly proceeded, interrupted only occasionally by walks and brief talks with visitors. He died at the convent of the Little Company of Mary on September 26, 1952.

Santayana achieved popular notice with his novel, *The Last Puritan*, and near the end of his life with his autobiography, *Persons and Places*. Perhaps his most controversial work was his *Interpretations of Poetry and Religion*, in which he expressed his conviction that religion is primarily a work of the imagination.

George Santayana is regarded by professional philosophers as a careful and sometimes illuminating thinker whose primary virtue nevertheless consists in the fine literary use he has made of his ideas. Technically, he would be regarded as a naturalist and critical realist, as one who regards knowledge as a construction from the basic elements of experience, the sense data, which show by their essence, their character, the changeless, universal relationships in the realm of essence. His most important philosophical works are *Scepticism and Animal Faith*, *The Realms of Being*, and *The Life of Reason*. *The Realms of Being* is composed of four books, separately published: *The Realm of Essence*, *The Realm of Matter*, *The Realm of Truth*, and *The Realm of Spirit*.

BIBLIOGRAPHICAL REFERENCES: The standard collected edition is the Triton Edition of *The Works of George Santayana*, 14 vols., 1936–37. *The Letters of George Santayana* were edited with introduction and commentary by Daniel Cory, 1955. George W. Howgate's critical biography, *George Santayana*, 1938, is acceptable if not definitive; more recent is Willard E. Arnett, *George Santayana*, 1968. Critical books are Van Meter Ames, *Proust and Santayana: The Aesthetic Way of Life*, 1937; Paul Arthur Schilpp, ed., *The Philosophy of George Santayana*, 1940, containing Santayana's autobiography and a bibliography to 1940; Mary C. E. Kinney, *A Critique of the Philosophy of George Santayana in the Light of Thomistic Principles*, 1942; W. E. Arnett, *Santayana and the Sense of Beauty*, 1955; Irving Singer, ed., *Essays in Literary Criticism of George Santayana*, with an introduction, "Santayana as a Literary Critic," 1956; and Irving Singer, *Santayana's Aesthetics*, 1957. See also the essay by A. A. Bowman in *A Sacramental Universe*, 1939. Articles in magazines include Daniel Cory, "A Study of Santayana," *Journal of Philosophic Studies*, II (1927), 349–364; G. W. Howgate, "Santayana and Humanism," *Sewanee Review*, XLIII (1935), 49–57; Q. D. Leavis, "The Critical Writings of George Santayana," *Scrutiny*, III (1935), 278–295; Daniel Cory, "The Later Philosophy of Mr. Santayana," *Criterion*, XV (1936), 379–392; and D. C. Williams, "Of Essence and Existence in Santayana," *Journal of Philosophy*, LI (1954), 31–42.

SANTÔ KYÔDEN

Born: Edo, Japan
Date: 1761

Died: Edo
Date: 1816

PRINCIPAL WORKS

Santô Kyôden has more than ninety-two works of prose fiction to his credit. Some of the best known are Chûshin Suiko-den, 1789 (*A Tale of the Forty-seven Loyal Retainers*); Fukushû Kidan Asaka no Numa, 1803 (*Murder and Revenge of Swamp of Asaka*); Udonge Monogatari, 1804 (*Fortune's Wheel*); Inazuma-byôshi, 1806 (*Trouble in the House of Sasaki*), and its sequel, Honchô Sui-bodai Zenden, 1809.

Santô Kyôden was born at Edo in 1761, the eldest son of Iwase Nobuaki, who himself was the adopted son of a pawnbroker in Edo (later Tokyo). In 1773 his father left the pawnbroker's family to strike out on his own, and later he became a minor city official. Kyôden was apprenticed to a print artist, Kitao Shigemasa, and also studied chanting and playing the samisen. As an artist's apprentice he learned to paint well, and also became acquainted with writers of his day. By the time he was seventeen he also knew the pleasure quarters of the city, but he seems to have been a modest spender, and a contemporary system of "Dutch treat" bears his name. As a wood block print artist he became famous in the last twenty years of the eighteenth century. He produced some excellent work, more or less in the manner of his instructor, Shigemasa, but showing flashes of individual technique, power, composition, and use of color. His favorite subjects were the inmates of the Yoshiwara. Some of the most interesting were the illustrations he did for his own writings. After ten years he seems to have become so busy with his writing that he gave up painting before he might have reached further development.

His first published work was Kaichô Riyaku no Meguri-ai, 1778 (*The Way the Cards Fall*), which he published at the age of seventeen. But he won popular acclaim with his Edo-umare Uwaki no Kabayaki, 1785 (*Vanity and Disillusion*). His first attempt to write a type of short story then current and dealing with the gay quarters was Musuko-beya, 1785 (*Guide Book to Behavior in the Gay Quarters*). This was a form in which he excelled, but in 1791 he was sentenced to house confinement in handcuffs for fifty days for this type of writing. From this time Kyôden turned to the production of more legitimate fiction, such as *A Tale of the Forty-seven Loyal Retainers* which he had already published two years previously, but in this field he was not quite the equal of Kyokutei Bakin (1767–1848). Both his wives were former inmates of the Yoshiwara, and much to everyone's surprise, both of them turned out to be excellent wives. After his father's death in 1799, Kyôden succeeded to the family business as handbag merchant and had a modest success with handbags made of cloth or paper, decorated with his own illustrations. He also made and sold patent medicines. He died at Edo in 1816.

BIBLIOGRAPHICAL REFERENCES: Most of the works and all of the biographies of Santô Kyôden are still in Japanese. Of the former, two works have been translated into non-Japanese languages: *Fortune's Wheel* (*Udenge Monogatari*) in *The Japan Magazine*, XVIII, XIX, and XX (1928–1929); and *Der treue Ritter Uto Yasugata* (*Utô Yasukata Chûgi-den*) in *Deutsche Gesellschaft für Natur-und Völkerkunde Ostasiens*, 5 (Tokyo, 1891). A brief description of his life and works appears in W. G. Aston, *A History of Japanese Literature*, 1937.

SAPPHO

Born: Eresos, Lesbos
Date: Unknown; fl. c. 600 B.C.

Died: Sicily (?)
Date: Unknown

Extant Poems

Ode to Aphrodite; fragments of 8 (or 9) books of lyric poetry.

Sappho, or "Psappho" as she called herself, was born on the Greek Island of Lesbos, in the Aegean Sea, west of Turkey, and flourished in the sixth century B.C. The tenth century Byzantian lexicographer Suïdas gave her father's name as Scamandronymus, and her mother was Cleis. Hers must have been an aristocratic family because her brother Larichus was a cupbearer in the prytaneum of Mytilene, a duty assigned to only those of noble birth. Another of her brothers, Charaxus, is mentioned in her poetry as being in love with a slave girl whom he bought and freed.

Sappho is supposed to have exchanged love poetry with her fellow countryman Alcaeus, who died about 580 B.C. She married Cercylas of Andros, and had a daughter named Cleis. She lived for some years in Sicily and a statue was erected in her honor at Syracuse. There is no foundation for the legend that she became so enamored of the youthful fisherman Phaon that she threw herself from the Leucadian rock when he ignored her.

Regard for her poetry caused the ancients to rank her with Homer and Archilochus and moved Plato in *Phaedrus* to call her the "Tenth Muse." All except seven stanzas of an ode to Aphrodite and a few fragments of lesser lyrics were lost for centuries. Recently papyrus rolls turned up in Egypt to provide mutilated but authentic samples. Some appear to have been written for a society of aristocratic girls, others to friends.

Sappho wrote in the Aeolic dialect, pure but simple love poems, full of passion, with vivid phrasing and a variety of meters. The so-called Sapphic stanza comprising three long and one short lines was much used by Catullus and Horace. Ovid and Swinburne, who translated her, also show her influence. It is thought that she died in Sicily.

BIBLIOGRAPHICAL REFERENCES: There are translations by Francis Fawkes in A. Chalmers, *Works of English Poets,* 1810. See also E. M. Cox, *Poems of Sappho,* 1924; and Edgar Lobel, *Sapphous Mele: Fragments of the Lyrical Poems of Sappho,* 1925.

Books about Sappho are largely conjectural. See Mary M. Patrick, *Sappho and the Island of Lesbos,* 1912; David M. Robinson, *Sappho and Her Influence,* 1924; A. E. P. Weigall, *Sappho of Lesbos,* 1932; Margaret Goldsmith, *Sappho of Lesbos: A Psychological Reconstruction of Her Life,* 1938; and Kenneth Rexroth, "Sappho," *Classics Revisited,* 1968, 41–46.

WILLIAM SAROYAN

Born: Fresno, California
Date: August 31, 1908

Principal Works

SHORT STORIES: *The Daring Young Man on the Flying Trapeze*, 1934; *Inhale and Exhale*, 1936; *Three Times Three*, 1936; *The Gay and Melancholy Flux*, 1937; *Little Children*, 1937; *Love, Here Is My Hat*, 1938; *The Trouble with Tigers*, 1938; *Peace, It's Wonderful*, 1939; *My Name Is Aram*, 1940; *The Assyrian and Other Stories*, 1950; *The Bicycle Rider in Beverly Hills*, 1952; *Love*, 1955; *Whole Voyald and Other Stories*, 1956.

NOVELS: *The Human Comedy*, 1943; *The Adventures of Wesley Jackson*, 1946; *Rock Wagram*, 1951; *The Laughing Matter*, 1953; *Mama, I Love You*, 1956; *Papa, You're Crazy*, 1957; *Boys and Girls Together*, 1963; *One Day in the Afternoon of the World*, 1964.

PLAYS: *My Heart's in the Highlands*, 1939; *The Time of Your Life*, 1939; *Love's Old Sweet Song*, 1940; *The Beautiful People*, 1941; *Razzle Dazzle*, 1942; *The Human Comedy*, 1943; *Get Away, Old Man*, 1944; *Plays*, 1950; *The Cave Dwellers*, 1957; *The London Comedy*, 1961; *Making Money and 19 Other Very Short Plays*, 1969.

MEMOIRS: *The Adventures of William Saroyan*, 1950; *Not Dying*, 1963; *Letters from 74 rue Taitbout*, 1969; *Days of Life and Death and Escape to the Moon*, 1971.

William Saroyan is interesting to students of American literature because he illustrates, in his generation, the same sort of self-conscious simplicity and naïveté that has been the stock-in-trade of American writers ever since Artemus Ward and Mark Twain. Saroyan's simplicity is, to be sure, marked with his awareness of his Armenian ancestry and it is suffused with his own sense of the basic goodness of all persons, particularly those who are obscure and naïve, and the undeniable value of being alive. To Saroyan there is no problem, political or international, that could not be solved by an appeal to the basic good will present in all men.

Saroyan was born on August 31, 1908, in the Armenian section of Fresno, California, one of what he calls the tribe of "proud and angry Saroyans." His elementary school days were marked by truancy and punishment by the principal. Formal education held no attraction for Saroyan; out of sheer boredom he left high school at fifteen after, as he says, he had read every book in the Fresno Public Library. He then went into his uncle's law office, where he read law and learned shorthand and typing.

Although he wrote voluminously during his early years (some four hundred short stories and essays) at the same time that he worked at a dozen different jobs, "The Daring Young Man on the Flying Trapeze," published in *Story* in 1933, was his first published writing. In it Saroyan revealed his impetuous "love for life" and what he calls his "jump in the river and start to swim immediately" technique. The next few years saw the steady publication of his short stories, all marked by an impressionistic manner and a sentimental exaltation of characters ranging from Armenian-American workers to middle-class businessmen. As might be expected from the fact that he is a self-made writer, most of his characters are optimistically associated with the glory of the American dream.

Saroyan's exuberance is not diminished in his plays, three of which were produced on Broadway within a little over a year. In his dramas he also gives us his special version of the American dream, the idea that worldly success means nothing and that only purity and brilliance of aspiration count. The glory of America is that it is the place where such aspirations are possible and, at least in the America Saroyan knows, are cheerfully accepted. *My Heart's in the Highlands* deals with an unsuccessful poet and his son; *The Time of Your Life* shows the essential goodness of man when a wealthy drunkard gives money to a forlorn group of people in a San Francisco bar, people who wish only to pursue their hopes and dreams. For this play Saroyan was awarded the Drama Critics' Circle Award and the Pulitzer Prize for 1940; he refused the Pulitzer award on the grounds that the play was "no more great or good" than anything else he had written. Saroyan's next two plays—*Love's Old Sweet Song*, a farce-comedy set on a California farm, and *The Beautiful People*, similar in theme to *The Time of Your Life*—seemed less attractive, possibly because they marked no advance of ideas or technique. What is true of his plays is true also of his later novels and short stories; from them one gets chiefly a sense of repetition, though even the most banal of his works continue to be enlivened by occasional flashes of poetry and insight. Nowhere is Saroyan's ardent belief in the fundamental goodness of people better illustrated than in his most typical novel, *The Human Comedy*: The "comédie humaine" of Balzac is a parade of greed, lust, and lost illusions, but Saroyan's "human comedy" is, if it be true, a cause for rejoicing because baser motives can always be transformed into noble ones, and human brotherhood is diffused.

BIBLIOGRAPHICAL REFERENCES: The only full length study is Howard R. Floan, *William Saroyan*, 1966. For criticism see further Harlan Hatcher, "William Saroyan," *English Journal*, XXVIII (1939), 169–177; George Jean Nathan, "Saroyan: Whirling Dervish of Fresno," *American Mercury*, LI (1941), 303–308; Philip Rahv, "William Saroyan: A Minority Report," *ibid.*, LVII (1943), 371–377; Edwin B. Burgum, "The Lonesome Young Man on the Flying Trapeze," *Virginia Quarterly Review*, XX (1944), 392–403; and William J. Fisher, "What Ever Happened to Saroyan?" *College English*, XVI (1955), 336–340, 385. Saroyan is also included in the group of California writers discussed by Edmund Wilson in *The Boys in the Back Room*, 1941.

JEAN-PAUL SARTRE

Born: Paris, France
Date: June 21, 1905

Principal Works

PHILOSOPHICAL ESSAYS: *L'Imagination*, 1938; *L'Imaginaire*, 1940; *Esquisse d'une théorie des émotions*, 1940 (*Essay on the Emotions*); *L'Être et le Néant*, 1943 (*Being and Nothingness*); *L'Existéntialisme est un humanisme*, 1946 (*Existentialism and Humanism*).

NOVELS: *La Nausée*, 1938 (*Nausea*); *Les Chemins de la Liberté*, 1945– (*The Roads to Freedom*): *L'Âge de Raison*, 1945 (*The Age of Reason*); *Le Sursis*, 1945 (*The Reprieve*); *La Mort dans l'Âme*, 1949 (*Troubled Sleep*); *La dernière chance*, in preparation.

SHORT STORIES: *Le Mur*, 1939 (*The Wall*).

PLAYS: *Les Mouches*, 1942 (*The Flies*); *Huis-Clos*, 1944 (*No Exit*); *Les Mains sales*, 1948 (*The Red Gloves*; also *Dirty Hands*); *Le Diable et le bon Dieu*, 1951 (*Lucifer and the Lord*); *Les séquestrés d'Altona*, 1960 (*The Condemned of Altona*).

AUTOBIOGRAPHY: *Les mots*, 1964 (*The Words*).

Jean-Paul Sartre, the leading French existentialist, was born in Paris on June 21, 1905. His father died in Indo-China while Sartre was yet a child. The boy was educated at the Lycée de la Rochelle and then, during the first World War, at the Lycée Henri IV. He entered the École Normale Supérieure in 1925 and took his *Agrégation de Philosophie* with high honors in 1928. He then became a teacher in Laon, and later in Le Havre and Neuilly. During the next five years he made several tours, visiting Egypt, Greece, and Germany. During his stay in Berlin he spent a short time as a *pensionnaire* at the Institut Français, where he studied the philosophies of Edmund Husserl, Martin Heidegger, and Søren Kierkegaard, all important influences in the development of his atheistic existentialism.

As a teacher in Paris in 1935 he began work on his theories of the imagination and the emotions. His first novel, *Nausea*, emphasized the breakdown of meaning and the nausea resulting from a sudden apprehension of the existence of things. This concern with the recognition of existence as a starting point in a man's creative life was shown further in a volume of short stories, *The Wall*, which appeared the following year.

Drafted into the French army as a private, he left his teaching position at the Lycée Pasteur at Neuilly in September, 1939. He was sent to the Maginot Line, and in June, 1940, was taken prisoner by the Germans and held until repatriation nine months later. In the meantime critics were acknowledging Sartre's psychological acumen and ingenuity as shown in his recently published books on the imagination and the emotions.

After returning to France in 1941 Sartre took a writer's role in the resistance. He wrote for *Combat*, the lively intellectual underground paper then edited by Albert Camus. At the same time he continued his teaching at the Lycée Pasteur and then at the Lycée Condorcet.

His first play, *The Flies*, a carefully executed expression of the right of a man to reject old gods and to define himself by independent action, was performed in Paris during the German occupation in 1942. Received as a moving play in support of man's freedom, it naturally had poignant significance to French audiences during the occupation. Another play, *No Exit*, presented Hell as a rather dull living room where persons who had failed to act in life had to put up eternally with one another's presence and conversation. These plays and the later *The Red Gloves* aroused considerable interest in New York audiences when they were produced in the United States.

Being and Nothingness, a long philosophical work published in 1943, assured Sartre's status as a responsible and creative philosopher, although some critics assumed that the popularity of existentialism could be accounted for only by supposing its leader to be superficial. During the latter half of the 1940's Sartre and other intellectuals made the Café de Flore in Paris the center of the growing existentialist movement. He visited the United States in 1945–1946 and lectured at American colleges and universities. In 1946 he founded the review *Les Temps Modernes* in which his essays and fiction have since been appearing. An attack on Albert Camus in Sartre's journal led to a schism between the two former philosophical friends, primarily because of Sartre's advocacy of Communist programs.

Sartre's most sustained effort in fiction has been his four-volume series *The Roads to Freedom*, of which three novels, *The Age of Reason*, *The Reprieve*, and *Troubled Sleep* have appeared in this country. He continues to be one of France's most stimulating writers.

BIBLIOGRAPHICAL REFERENCES: The Sartre bibliography is extensive and any listing at this time must be highly selective. The basic study in English is Iris Murdoch, *Sartre, Romantic Rationalist*, 1953. Other books on this controversial figure include Herbert Read, *Existentialism, Marxism, and Anarchism*, 1949; Peter J. Dempsey, *The Psychology of Sartre*, 1950; Maurice Natanson, *A Critique of Jean Paul Sartre's Ontology*, 1951; Alfred Stern, *Sartre: His Philosophy and Psychoanalysis*, 1953; Wilfrid Desan, *The Tragic Finale*, 1954; Arland Ussher, *Journey Through Dread: A Study of Kierkegaard, Heidegger, and Sartre*, 1955; René Marill Albérès, *Jean-Paul Sartre: Philosopher without Faith*, 1961; Maurice W. Cranston, *Jean-Paul Sartre*, 1963; Mary Warnock, *The Philosophy of Sartre*, 1965; and Henri Peyre, *Jean-Paul Sartre*, 1968. See also C. E. Magney, *Les Sandales d'Empédocle*, 1945; R. Campbell, *Jean-Paul Sartre ou une littérature philosophique*, 1945; F. Jeanson, *Le Problème moral et la pensée de Sartre*, 1947; C. Varet, *L'Ontologie de Sartre*, 1948; Nelly Cormeau, *Littérature existéntialiste: le roman et la théâtre de Jean-Paul Sartre*, 1950; Henri Paissac, *Le dieu de Sartre*, 1950; and Hans Heinz Holz, *Jean Paul Sartre*, 1951. See also Hazel E. Barnes, "Jean Paul Sartre and the Haunted Self," *Western Humanities Review*, X (1956), 119–128; and Robert G. Olson, "The Three Theories of Motivation in the Philosophy of Jean-Paul Sartre," *Ethics*, LXVI (1956), 176–187.

SIEGFRIED SASSOON

Born: Brenchley, Kent, England
Date: September 8, 1886

Died: Warminster, England
Date: September 2, 1967

Principal Works

POEMS: *The Old Huntsman and Other Poems*, 1917; *Counter-Attack and Other Poems*, 1918; *War Poems*, 1919; *Picture Show*, 1920; *Recreations*, 1923; *Selected Poems*, 1925; *Satirical Poems*, 1926; *The Heart's Journey*, 1927; *Poems of Pinchbeck Lyre*, 1931; *Vigils*, 1935; *Rhymed Ruminations*, 1940; *Poems Newly Selected 1916–1935*, 1940; *Collected Poems*, 1947; *Sequences*, 1956; *Path to Peace* (selected poems), 1960; *Collected Poems, 1908–1956*, 1961; *An Octave: 8 September 1966*, 1966.

NOVELS: *The Memoirs of George Sherston*, 1937 (comprising *Memoirs of a Fox-Hunting Man*, 1928; *Memoirs of an Infantry Officer*, 1930; *Sherston's Progress*, 1936).

AUTOBIOGRAPHY: *The Old Century and Seven More Years*, 1938; *The Weald of Youth*, 1942; *Siegfried's Journey 1916–1920*, 1945.

BIOGRAPHY: *Meredith*, 1948.

The literary reputation of Siegfried (Lorraine) Sassoon will rest, to a considerable extent, on his vigorous war poems, written at the front between 1914 and 1918. Like those of Wilfred Owen, whom Sassoon influenced and encouraged, they testify bitterly to the ingloriousness of modern warfare. Such pieces as "The Rear-Guard" and "Counter-Attack" express the aversion and horror which led Sassoon, then an officer in the British Army, to become a pacifist and to refuse further military duty. To a later generation, he is better known for the autobiographical novels which relate what he has called his "mental history," the chronicle of his youth and of the spiritual crisis produced on the battlefield. Of these works the three earliest, *Memoirs of a Fox-Hunting Man*, *Memoirs of an Infantry Officer*, and *Sherston's Progress* mask their author under the alias "George Sherston"; fictional in form, they nevertheless present a reflective survey of personal events recorded voluminously in Sassoon's diaries. His more formal autobiographies, *The Old Century and Seven More Years*, *The Weald of Youth*, and *Siegfried's Journey 1916–1920*, re-examine much of the same ground from a later point of view undisguisedly his own. *Memoirs of a Fox-Hunting Man*, awarded both the Hawthornden Prize and the James Tait Black Memorial Prize in 1929, is delightful for its spare, restrained style, conveying in understatement a strong nostalgia for prewar society. Sassoon has used the pseudonyms Pinchbeck Lyre, Sigmund Sashûn, and Saul Kain.

The Sassoons have been eminent chiefly in the realm of English finance. However, Siegfried Sassoon, born at Brenchley, September 8, 1886, and reared by his artist mother in rural Kent (his parents had separated in his childhood), grew up in an atmosphere determined by literature, painting, and summonses to fox meets. He attended Clare College, Cambridge, for two years, until defeated by apathy toward the History Tripos. In the years preceding World War I, he published anonymously several collections of imitative verse, and also tried playwriting. During this period, a narrative poem written in Masefield's manner shows great technical exactitude.

During the war Sassoon received the Military Cross for heroism in action. While recuperating at home from a throat wound, he issued in 1917 a manifesto denouncing the prolongation of the conflict. Although he desired court-martial in order to spread his views, friends had him certified temporarily insane, and subsequently he was placed in a sanatorium in Edinburgh, where he met Wilfred Owen. Later he volunteered to rejoin the forces, served in Palestine and again in France, and suffered a second wound. He was promoted to the rank of captain in the Royal Welsh Fusiliers. He later disowned pacifism, and in the 1951 Honors List was designated a Commander of the British Empire.

BIBLIOGRAPHICAL REFERENCES: The best source for information on Sassoon is his autobiography as told in *The Old Century and Seven More Years*, *The Weald of Youth*, and *Siegfried's Journey*. His fiction is discussed at some length in F. J. H. Darton, *From Surtees to Sassoon*, 1931. For criticism of his poetry see Harold Monro, *Some Contemporary Poets*, 1930; Thomas S. Moore, *Some Soldier Poets*, 1920; Edmund Blunden, "Siegfried Sassoon's Poetry," *London Mercury*, XX (1929), 156–166; and Alexander H. Sackton, "Two Poems on War: A Critical Exercise," *University of Texas Studies in English*, XXXI (1951), 120–124. Quite recent is Michael Thorpe, *Siegfried Sassoon: A Critical Study*, 1966.

FRIEDRICH SCHILLER

Born: Marbach, Germany
Date: November 10, 1759

Died: Weimar, Germany
Date: May 9, 1805

Principal Works

PLAYS: *Die Raüber*, 1781 (*The Robbers*); *Don Carlos*, 1787; *Wallenstein*, 1798–1799; *Maria Stuart*, 1800; *Die Jungfrau de Orleans*, 1801 (*The Maid of Orleans*); *Die Braut von Messina*, 1803 (*The Bride of Messina*); *Wilhelm Tell*, 1804.

NOVELS: *Der Verbrecher aus verlorener Ehre*, 1786 (*The Criminal, in Consequence of Lost Reputation*); *Der Geisterseher*, 1787–1789 (unfinished).

POEMS: *Xenien*, 1796 (with Goethe); *Gedichte*, 1800–1803.

HISTORY: *Geschichte des dreissigjährigen Krieges*, 1790–1792 (*History of the Thirty Years' War*).

ESSAYS AND STUDIES: *Über den Grund des Vergnügens an tragischen Gegenständen*, 1792; *Über die tragische Kunst*, 1792; *Über das Pathetische*, 1793; *Über Anmut und Würde*, 1793 (*On Grace and Dignity*); *Über naive und sentimentalische Dichtung*, 1795–1796 (*On Naïve and Sentimental Poetry*).

(Johann Christoph) Friedrich von Schiller, born on November 10, 1759, at Marbach, Germany, was the son of an officer in the army of the Duke of Württemberg. His parents intended that Johann should enter the ministry of the Lutheran Church, and to this end sent him to the Latin school at Ludwigsburg, then the ducal residence. Duke Karl Eugen of Württemberg, in common with other semi-independent German princelings, had delusions of grandeur, and he tried to imitate the "grand style" of the Bourbons by making his court into a kind of Bavarian Versailles. He lived lavishly, if crudely, ruling largely through sycophants and irresponsible adventurers. At Ludwigsburg young Schiller saw much of the ways of the world and learned early to hate social and political tyranny.

Among the duke's many projects was a military school, established to train the sons of his officers for the public service. When he was fourteen Schiller was offered a scholarship at the academy, a princely favor not to be rejected by his parents, even though it meant giving up their plans for his future. He began as a student of law, but did badly, and when the school was moved to Stuttgart two years later, he transferred to the study of medicine. But in spite of his formal education, young Schiller's true interests did not seem to lie in divinity or law or medicine, but in literature. Although the strict discipline of the academy prevented easy access to contemporary writing, contraband works of the revolutionary "Sturm und Drang" authors found their way into his hands and were avidly read. Under the influence of this reading, and possibly of his own reaction to the world of Ludwigsburg, Schiller began his first play, *The Robbers*, a wild, romantic melodrama of social injustice and rebellion.

In 1780, Schiller was honorably dismissed from the academy, although without a doctor's degree, and was assigned as army doctor to a regiment of invalid soldiers at Stuttgart. To augment his meager income he decided to borrow money and publish his play. As a book, *The Robbers* was largely ignored, but it came to the attention of Dalberg, director of a theater at Mannheim, who in 1782 produced a revised version which was a tremendous success. Dissatisfied with an unpleasant job, and flattered by his sudden notoriety into the conviction that he was born to be a writer of tragedy, Schiller deserted the Württemberg army and fled to Mannheim in a neighboring principality. Dalberg was at first reluctant to associate himself with a refugee from another state, but by 1783 it was apparent that the Duke of Württemberg had ignored the desertion, and Schiller received a one-year contract as theater-playwright. In the following year two new plays were produced at Mannheim, neither of which enjoyed anything like the success of *The Robbers*, but which were, like that play, characterized by a vehement, high-keyed prose and radical sentiments.

Schiller's contract with Dalberg was not renewed, and in 1784 he moved to Leipzig and then to Dresden, where he published his journal, *Die rheinische Thalia*, and worked in a desultory manner on a new play, *Don Carlos*. This tragedy, finished in 1787, represents in many ways the midpoint in Schiller's development as a dramatist. As is true of the earlier Mannheim plays, the language is often high-pitched and the action confusing; like them, the plot deals with an idealist, the Marquis Posa, who is destroyed by his own fanaticism, but, as in the later plays, the form is poetic and the thought mature.

After the completion of *Don Carlos* there was a hiatus of ten years in Schiller's dramatic output. In 1787 he went to Weimar, where he made the acquaintance of the poet Herder, and finally settled in Jena. In his reading for *Don Carlos*, Schiller had become interested in the Spanish-Dutch conflict of the sixteenth century, and as a result decided to devote himself to the writing of history. In 1788 he published his *Geschichte des Abfalls der vereinigten Niederlande* (*History of the Defection of the Netherlands*), and during the next four years wrote the impressive *History of the Thirty Years' War*. Although Schiller's success as a historian led to his appointment as professor at the University of Jena, his work in that field is more notable for its literary qualities than for its historical accuracy or scientific objectivity. He instinctively sided with the oppressed and rebellious, and his republican sympathies colored his prose as well as his plays.

While at Jena, Schiller divided his time between history and philosophy. His concern was primarily with the study of aesthetics, although that is never, in his thinking, entirely divorced from ethics. His best-known essays in this field are *On Grace and Dignity* and *On Naïve and Sentimental Poetry*.

Schiller first met Goethe in Jena, and from 1794 on they were close friends and literary allies. Partly through Goethe's influence, Schiller's interest in writing poetry revived. Together they made a study of the epic style, and out of this interest grew a number of ballads and romanzas which are still among Schiller's most popular works. During this period Schiller also wrote several reflective lyrics expressing the humane idealism and high ethical aspirations which characterized his thought. Goethe was also at that time the director of the small theater at Weimar, where Schiller moved in

1799, and the two friends often worked together selecting and adapting plays for production there. The renewed contact with the stage quite naturally reawakened Schiller's love for the drama, and the remaining years of his life were spent writing poetic plays for the Weimar theater. With a burst of energy he wrote in rapid succession his five greatest plays: the *Wallenstein* trilogy, made up of *Wallenstein's Camp* (1798), *The Piccolomini* (1799), and *Wallenstein's Death* (1799); *Mary Stuart, The Maid of Orleans, The Bride of Messina,* and *William Tell.* The last, undoubtedly Schiller's most popular play, is an intensely human drama dealing with the rebellion of the Swiss people against their Austrian rulers. In the midst of writing still another historical play, *Demetrius,* Schiller contracted the illness which led to his premature death on May 9, 1805.

Schiller has always been considered among the greatest of German dramatists. Although poetic in form, his last plays are by no means lyrical, their force lying in their sonorous, sometimes rhetorical language, and in the intense sincerity of the playwright's idealism. His characteristic themes are those of persecution and tyranny, for Schiller, writing at the height of German Romanticism, was in both philosophy and politics the representative dramatist of his age.

BIBLIOGRAPHICAL REFERENCES: A comprehensive edition of Schiller's works is the *Säkularausgabe,* edited by E. von der Hellen, 16 vols., 1904–1905. The pioneer study of Schiller in English is Thomas Carlyle, *The Life of Friedrich Schiller,* 1845, still useful in spite of the difficulties of the style. For more recent estimates see J. G. Robertson, *Schiller after a Century,* 1906; H. B. Garland, *Schiller,* 1949; William Witte, *Schiller,* 1949; and E. L. Stahl, *Friedrich Schiller's Drama, Theory, and Practice,* 1954. For biographical and critical studies in German see C. von Wolzogen, *Schillers Leben,* 1830; Reinhard Buchwald, *Schiller,* 2 vols., 1937, and *Schiller und Beethoven,* 1946; Ernst Müller, *Der junge Schiller,* 1943; Kurt May, *Friedrich Schiller: Idee und Wirklichkeit im Drama,* 1948; Bernhard Martin, *Schiller und Goethe,* 1949; and Melitta Gerhard, *Schiller,* 1950. Some recent more specialized studies are Ronald D. Miller, *The Drama of Schiller,* 1963; Edmund Kostka, *Schiller in Russian Literature,* 1965; and R. M. Longyear, *Schiller and Music,* 1966.

ARTHUR SCHOPENHAUER

Born: Danzig (free city)
Date: February 22, 1788

Died: Frankfurt-am-Main, Germany
Date: September 21, 1860

Principal Works

PHILOSOPHICAL TREATISES: *Die Welt als Wille und Vorstellung*, 1818 (*The World as Will and Idea*); *Über den Willen in der Natur*, 1836 (*On the Will in Nature*); *Die beiden Grundprobleme der Ethik*, 1841 (*The Two Fundamental Problems of Ethics*); *Parerga und Paralipomena*, 1851 (*Essays*).

Arthur Schopenhauer, the unacademic, pessimistic, woman-hating, self-glorifying philosopher, was born on February 22, 1788, into a rich merchant family living in the free city of Danzig. His father, Heinrich Schopenhauer, was a liberal thinker, a Voltairian, who admired England and feared that Prussia would annex Danzig. When his fears were realized in 1793, the Schopenhauers hurriedly moved to Hamburg. Arthur lived there with his family for four years, and then at the age of nine was placed with a French family in Le Havre in order that he might learn the French language for its commercial value.

In 1803, when he was fifteen, he was placed with an English cleric's family and attended the boarding school there. He was disturbed by the cant and hypocrisy of his instructors and consequently was irritated by the daily rounds of prayers. After three months he returned and was sent on a European tour, having promised that upon his return he would enter his father's business. True to his word, but against his inclinations, he became a clerk in a commercial house in Hamburg.

In 1805 the death of his father, presumably as a suicide, freed Schopenhauer from the business career he disliked. His mother, a popular novelist, had been handicapped by domestic ties, although there is reason to believe she had not wholly respected them; she moved to Weimar and established a literary salon which attracted many intellectuals, artists, and lovers. The most distinguished member of her circle was the elderly Goethe. Although Arthur was impressed by his mother's friends, he thought them romantic and flighty, and he disapproved of his mother's love affairs. He quarreled with her violently, and they parted; loathing each other, they maintained their hatred until their deaths.

Schopenhauer then studied the classics at the Gymnasium at Gotha, before going on to the University of Göttingen, where he studied Plato, Kant, and other philosophers under Schulze. Two years later he moved to Berlin, where he studied the natural sciences and, with distaste, heard Fichte lecture. At Jena, to which he hurried when Prussia declared war against France, he completed his doctorate, and his thesis, in 1813, became his first book, *Über die vierfache Wurzel des Satzes vom Zureichenden Grunde* (*On the Fourfold Root of the Principle of Sufficient Reason*).

In 1818, in his most important work, *The World as Will and Idea*, he presented his basic philosophy to the effect that everything is a manifestation of the will, and that since life is misery, man's objective should be to eliminate the will. The work, disregarded at the time, did not become popular or famous until after Schopen-

hauer had published his later books.
During the 1820's he had a brief and unsuccessful phase as a lecturer at the University of Berlin, withdrawing when he failed to obtain a professorship. From 1831 until his death he lived in solitude at Frankfurt-am-Main, convinced of his own genius and devoting his time to his writing and to his poodle Atma (meaning, the world-soul). He died of a heart attack following pneumonia on September 21, 1860.

BIBLIOGRAPHICAL REFERENCES: The principal works of Schopenhauer are available in English translations by various hands. For the general reader a good introduction to his philosophy is *The Living Thoughts of Schopenhauer*, edited by Thomas Mann, 1940. For biography and analysis see Helen Zimmern, *Arthur Schopenhauer*, 1876; Kuno Fischer, *Schopenhauer*, 1877; Wilhelm Gwinner, *Schopenhauer*, 1878; William Wallace, *Life of Schopenhauer*, 1902—a basic book among the biographical studies; Georg Simmel, *Schopenhauer and Nietzsche*, 1907; André Fauconnet, *L'Esthétique de Schopenhauer*, 1913; V. J. McGill, *Schopenhauer: Pessimist and Pagan*, 1931; Frederic Copleston, *Arthur Schopenhauer, Philosopher of Pessimism*, 1946; Arthur Hübscher, *Arthur Schopenhauer, ein Lebensbild*, 1949; Hugo Busch, *Das Testament Arthur Schopenhauers*, 1950; and Patrick Gardiner, *Schopenauer*, 1963.

OLIVE SCHREINER

Born: Cape Province, Africa
Date: March 24, 1855

Died: Cape Town, South Africa
Date: December 12, 1920

Principal Works

NOVELS: *The Story of an African Farm*, 1883; *Trooper Peter Halket of Mashonaland*, 1897; *From Man to Man*, 1926; *Undine*, 1928.
SHORT STORIES: *Dreams*, 1891; *Dream Life and Real Life*, 1893.
LETTERS: *The Letters of Olive Schreiner*, 1924.

Olive (Emilie Albertina) Schreiner, born at the Wittebergen Mission Station in the African Cape Province on March 24, 1855, was the daughter of a Methodist missionary of German descent and English background. She was largely self-educated, for her family lived too far away from any schools for her to attend. At the age of fifteen she became a governess for a Boer family living on the edge of the Karoo Desert, and while still in her teens she began working on what was to be her famous novel, *The Story of an African Farm*. When it was completed, unable to find a publisher, she invested her limited savings in a trip to England to find a publisher. When the book appeared in 1883, under the pseudonym "Ralph Iron," the author's true identity soon became known, and, since the novel was critical of Christianity and feministic, it created a kind of notoriety for its writer. Olive Schreiner remained in England for eight unhappy years before returning to her native Africa; during this time she became a close friend of Havelock Ellis.

In 1894 she married S. C. Cronwright (who later added Schreiner to his name), a Boer farmer and lawyer, with whom she collaborated in writing *The Political Situation*, 1895. As her literary executor he saw also to the publication of her posthumous books. They had one child, a daughter who died in infancy. During the Boer War, Olive Schreiner was strongly pro-Boer (her second novel, *Trooper Peter Halket of Mashonaland*, had satirized Cecil Rhodes), but a pacifist during World War I. She died at Cape Town on December 12, 1920. Although she wrote much in later life, relatively little was published until after her death. Two novels, a collection of short fiction, and an edition of her letters appeared posthumously.

BIBLIOGRAPHICAL REFERENCES: The fullest biographical account is *The Life of Olive Schreiner*, written by her husband, S. C. Cronwright-Schreiner, 1924. See also Margaret Lawrence, *The School of Femininity*, 1936; V. Buchanan Gould, *Not Without Honour*, 1948; and Lyndall Gregg, *Memories of Olive Schreiner*, 1957.

MICHAEL SCOTT

Born: Cowlairs, Scotland
Date: October 30, 1789

Died: Glasgow, Scotland
Date: November 7, 1835

PRINCIPAL WORKS

NOVELS: *Tom Cringle's Log*, 1829–1833; *The Cruise of the Midge*, 1834–1835.

Son of a Glasgow merchant, Michael Scott was born at Cowlairs, Scotland, on October 30, 1789, and educated at the high school in Glasgow and at the University of Glasgow. He went to Jamaica in 1806, sent there as an estate manager. In 1810 he founded his own business at Kingston. Many of the incidents recorded in his fiction occurred on trips that he took about the West Indies as a businessman. Scott returned to Scotland for a time in 1817. While there he married Margaret Bogle, of Glasgow; they had several children in later years. Scott returned to Jamaica, to remain from 1818 to 1822. Although he remained a merchant until his death, he apparently began to write seriously during the early 1820's.

Tom Cringle's Log began appearing as a series of sketches in *Blackwood's Magazine* in 1829 and ran intermittently until its completion in 1833. As the numbers appeared, the story became very popular, although the identity of its author was not known until some time after Scott's death, which occurred at Glasgow on November 7, 1835.

Tom Cringle's Log did not appear in book form under that title until it was printed in France in 1834, as a volume in Baudry's "European Library." The book's effectiveness and popularity undoubtedly stemmed from the exotic setting and the fact that Scott wrote humorously and a first hand of life in the West Indies. Scott's second novel, *The Cruise of the Midge,* also appeared serially and anonymously. Like the first, it ran in *Blackwood's Magazine,* 1834–1835. Critics were not as lavish in their praise of the second book as they had been of the first, and readers found its humor forced. The novel first appeared in book form in France in 1836. Scott never loomed large on the literary scene, and his work has gone relatively unnoticed by literary scholars.

BIBLIOGRAPHICAL REFERENCES: There is no full-length biography and almost no criticism available. Apart from brief sketches in the standard biographical dictionaries, the best source of information on Michael Scott will be found in Sir George Douglas, *The Blackwood Group,* 1897.

ROBERT F. SCOTT

Born: Devonport, England
Date: June 6, 1868

Died: Antarctica
Date: c. March 29, 1912

Principal Works

JOURNALS OF EXPLORATION: *The Voyage of the* Discovery, 1905; *Scott's Last Expedition,* 1913.

Robert Falcon Scott was born June 6, 1868, at Devonport, England. His early education was acquired at Stoke Damerel and Stubbington House, Fareham; at twelve years of age he was passed into H. M. S. *Britannia.* He became a midshipman in 1882. He served on various ships, rising steadily in rank, and was promoted to first lieutenant in 1897. In 1899 he was offered, and accepted, the command of the National Antarctic Expedition. The party, consisting largely of naval personnel but sailing under the merchant flag, embarked aboard the ship *Discovery* in 1901. They explored the Antarctic ice barrier, discovered King Edward VII Land, and established a camp in McMurdo Sound which remained the expedition base for approximately two years. Various scientific activities were carried out during this period; and Scott, accompanied by Shackleton and Wilson, made two notable sledge journeys southward into the interior of the continent.

On his return from Antarctica in 1904 Scott was promoted to Captain; his achievements were acclaimed, and publication of his journal in two volumes the following year assured his international reputation. In 1909 he was appointed naval assistant to the second Sea Lord of the Admiralty. At this time he was engaged in planning a second Antarctic expedition in which an attempt would be made to reach the South Pole.

His party sailed aboard the *Terra Nova* in June, 1910, and upon arrival at McMurdo Sound a number of supply depots were established along the overland route Scott planned to follow. A similar expedition headed by the Norwegian Roald Amundsen arrived at the Bay of Whales during this period. Scott and four companions set out for the Pole November 1, 1911; after severe hardships and the longest sledge journey ever undertaken—1,842 miles—they reached their destination on January 18, 1912, only to find that Amundsen had been there December 14. Scott's return journey was an unremitting series of disasters. Blizzards, frostbite, and exhaustion took their inevitable toll. Scott was the last of the five men to succumb, and the final entry was made in his journal on March 29. The other tasks of the expedition were pursued by the members who had remained at the base camp. Much valuable exploration and scientific work was carried out by this group.

When the expedition returned to civilization in 1913, the achievements of Scott and the circumstances of his death became generally known. His courage and the heroic manner in which he died created a worldwide sensation. His journal, published posthumously the same year, has remained a classic in the literature of exploration. It is an account of epic struggle and tenacity, of indomitable spirit, and of quiet courage when the end becomes inevitable; the concluding pages, which consist of messages to the families and friends of himself and his companions, betray no weakness but only a deep concern for others. This nobility, perhaps, has done more than any other factor to insure his hold upon the public imagination.

BIBLIOGRAPHICAL REFERENCES: Good biographical materials may be found in Harry Ludlam, *Captain Scott: The Full Story,* 1965; Reginald Pound, *Scott of the Antarctic,* 1966; William Bixby, *Robert Scott: Antarctic Pioneer,* 1970; and William Lashly, *Under Scott's Command: Lashly's Antarctic Diaries,* edited by A. R. Ellis, 1969.

SIR WALTER SCOTT

Born: Edinburgh, Scotland
Date: August 15, 1771

Died: Abbotsford, Scotland
Date: September 21, 1832

Principal Works

NOVELS: *Waverley*, 1814; *Guy Mannering*, 1815; *The Antiquary*, 1816; *The Black Dwarf*, 1816; *Old Mortality*, 1816; *Rob Roy*, 1818; *The Heart of Midlothian*, 1818; *The Bride of Lammermoor*, 1819; *A Legend of Montrose*, 1819; *Ivanhoe*, 1820; *The Monastery*, 1820; *The Abbot*, 1820; *Kenilworth*, 1821; *The Pirate*, 1822; *The Fortunes of Nigel*, 1822; *Peveril of the Peak*, 1823; *Quentin Durward*, 1823; *St. Ronan's Well*, 1824; *Redgauntlet*, 1824; *The Betrothed*, 1825; *The Talisman*, 1825; *Woodstock*, 1826; *Chronicles of the Canongate*, 1927 (*The Two Drovers, The Highland Widow, The Surgeon's Daughter*); *The Fair Maid of Perth*, 1828; *Anne of Geierstein*, 1829; *Count Robert of Paris*, 1831; *Castle Dangerous*, 1831.

POEMS: *The Lay of the Last Minstrel*, 1805; *Marmion*, 1808; *The Lady of the Lake*, 1810; *The Vision of Don Roderick*, 1811; *The Bridal of Triermain*, 1813; *The Lord of the Isles*, 1815; *Rokeby*, 1815.

MISCELLANEOUS: *The Life and Works of John Dryden*, 1808; *The Life and Works of Jonathan Swift*, 1814; *The Life of Napoleon Buonaparte*, 1827.

In spite of physical handicaps Walter Scott lived a full, varied life and created an impressive body of writings. Stricken with infantile paralysis before he was two years old, and alternating between periods of physical vigor and serious ailments throughout his life, he loved and practiced outdoor sports for most of his sixty-odd years.

Born in Edinburgh, August 15, 1771, he was a product of the eighteenth century as well as of the romantic nineteenth. As a child he was a voracious reader and avid listener to tales and legends, particularly those of his native Scotland. His copious reading was stored in a retentive memory and used to advantage in his writings; and his interest in folklore led to his collection and publication of Scottish ballads. Although not a brilliant student, he was praised for his ability to enjoy and understand the Latin poets. He entered the University of Edinburgh in 1783, but after a year at college he suffered one of his severe illnesses and had to return home. He spent his convalescence with a sympathetic uncle, Captain Robert Scott, who encouraged his literary interests.

He studied law in his father's office; and in spite of a disinclination for the profession, he was admitted to the bar in 1792. He made use of his legal experiences in his novels, especially *Redgauntlet*, in which his friend William Clerk served as model for Darsie Latimer, and Scott himself for Allan Fairford. When he was twenty he cast his eye on a lovely fifteen-year-old girl, Williamina Belsches. After an unsuccessful courtship of five years he lost her to a rival and indulged his sorrow for a time with melancholy self-dramatization out of keeping with his usual behavior.

In 1797, when the fear of a Napoleonic invasion seized Great Britain, Scott was the moving force in forming a volunteer home-guard unit, in which he held the position of quartermaster. In spite of his crippled leg he was a bold and expert horseman, and apparently was disappointed at not engaging Napoleon's forces. In the same year, on a tour of the Lake Country with his brother John and his friend Adam Ferguson, he met Charlotte Carpenter (Charpentier), daughter of a French royalist and ward of an English nobleman. This time his courtship was both short and successful, and he married his Charlotte on Christmas Eve, 1797. Their first child died in infancy, but four children reached maturity, two sons and two daughters.

In 1799 Scott was appointed Sheriff-depute of Selkirkshire; the position brought him a steady income and not-too-onerous duties. Seven years later he became Clerk of the Session in Edinburgh, adding to his steady income and increasing his routine labors considerably.

Although he translated for publication Gottfried Bürger's *Lenore* (1799) and Goethe's *Goetz von Berlichingen* (1799) and collected and edited—often revised—ballads in his *Minstrelsy of the Scottish Border* (1802–1803), he won his first recognition as a poet in 1805 with *The Lay of the Last Minstrel* and became a major literary figure in England with *Marmion* and *The Lady of the Lake*. His subsequent long poems added little to his reputation. Shortly after the publication of *The Lay of the Last Minstrel* he formed a partnership (Scott to be a silent partner) with the printer James Ballantyne, an old school friend. During his poetic career Scott completed two major works of scholarship, an eighteen-volume edition of Dryden and a nineteen-volume edition of Swift, either of which would have made a reputation for a professional scholar.

In 1814, with the anonymous publication of *Waverley*, Scott began a new literary career and his most illustrious, for he is now considered primarily a historical novelist, more than either poet or scholar. Scott gave reasons for not acknowledging the authorship of his novels; but at least one reason was a childish delight in mystification, a puckish joy in throwing dust into the public eye. Between 1814 and his death in 1832, he completed about thirty novels and novelettes, several long poems, a large mass of miscellaneous writings, and a nine-volume *Life of Napoleon*.

Scott was the first baronet created by George IV (1820). By this time he had bought acres of land and was sinking a fortune in Abbotsford. One friend who helped plan Abbotsford and stock its library was Daniel Terry, the actor-manager who produced dramatic versions of several of Scott's works, making an especial hit as Bailie Jarvie in *Rob Roy*. Scott's publishing ventures were in bad circumstances which grew worse; in 1826 Constable and Ballantyne failed. Instead of taking refuge in bankruptcy, Scott undertook to write himself and his colleagues out of debt. Few men have displayed more fortitude under adversity. To cap the material loss he suffered a severe spiritual one in the death of his beloved wife. His grief was profound, but he continued to write. In 1830, apparently as a result of his Herculean labors under stress, he suffered his first stroke of apoplexy. He recovered and continued work until recurring strokes paralyzed him and practically destroyed his mind. He died September 21, 1832, still in debt; but his son-in-law, John Gibson Lockhart, cleared the debts with the proceeds of his superb biography of the baronet.

Scott's merits as man and writer

entitle him to a position much nearer his former reputation than he now holds. One of his admirers called him a combination of Shakespeare and Samuel Johnson. Those who think of him only as a cloak-and-sword romancer overlook his remarkable gift of creating comic characters and his broad view of human nature in all walks of life. He was greatly admired by Balzac and Dumas; and wise critics from Goethe to the present have been impressed with his humane wisdom.

BIBLIOGRAPHICAL REFERENCES: There is no recent scholarly edition of Scott's works. The Border Edition of the *Waverley Novels*, 48 vols., 1892–1894, contains notes by Andrew Lang. John Gibson Lockhart's *Memoirs of the Life of Sir Walter Scott, Bart.*, 1837–1838, is basic; the definitive modern biography is Edgar Johnson, *Sir Walter Scott: The Great Unknown*, 1969. See also John Buchan (Lord Tweedsmuir), *Sir Walter Scott*, 1932; Sir Herbert Grierson, *Sir Walter Scott, Bart.*, 1938; Hesketh Pearson, *Sir Walter Scott*, 1954; F. R. Hart, *Scott's Novels*, 1966; David Daiches, *Sir Walter Scott and His World*, 1971; and Paul N. Landis, "The Waverly Novels, or a Hundred Years After," *Publications of the Modern Language Association*, LII (1937), 461–473.

MADELEINE DE SCUDÉRY

Born: Le Havre, France
Date: 1607

Died: Paris, France
Date: June 2, 1701

PRINCIPAL WORKS

NOVELS: *Ibrahim, ou l'illustre bassa*, 1641; *Artamène, ou le grand Cyrus*, 1646–1653; *Clélie*, 1654–1661; *Almahide, ou l'esclave reine*, 1661–1663.
ESSAY: *Le Discours de la gloire*, 1671.

Madeleine de Scudéry was the sister of Georges de Scudéry, a famous dramatist and poet of seventeenth century France. Born in Le Havre in 1607, she went to Paris to live with her brother and soon became well-known in French literary circles as a member of the group known as the Rambouillet coterie. Being a forceful personality, she became a person of consequence in Paris, succeeding Mme. de Rambouillet as the leading hostess of literary Paris in the late 1640's. The salon she established was called the *Société du samedi*, the Saturday Club. As a result of her efforts, Madeleine de Scudéry became the first "bluestocking" of the European literary world. She enjoyed the friendship of Louis XIV and other royalty, as well as that of such famous literary figures as Boileau.

She began to publish prose romances in 1641, when *Ibrahim, ou l'illustre Bassa* appeared. In an age when French romances earned notoriety for their length, hers were longer than most; *Artamène*, was published in ten volumes. It was followed by *Clélie*, and *Almahide*. Though they ostensibly presented an Oriental setting and Oriental heroes and heroines, these romances used the language and action of seventeenth century France, the characters often being recognizable people of the writer's fashionable circle. The romances were published anonymously or under her brother's name, but there is little doubt that she wrote them herself. They were outstandingly popular at the time, at least in aristocratic circles. A writer of essays and other prose studies as well as fiction, Mlle. de Scudéry was the first winner of the prize for French eloquence with her *Discours de la gloire* in 1671. She died in Paris on June 2, 1701.

BIBLIOGRAPHICAL REFERENCES: For biography and criticism see Claude Aragonnés, *Madeleine de Scudéry, reine de tendre*, 1934; and Maurice Magendie, *Le Roman français au XVIIᵉ siècle*, 1932.

LUCIUS ANNAEUS SENECA

Born: Corduba (now Córdoba), Spain
Date: c. 4 B.C.

Died: Near Rome, Italy
Date: A.D. 65

Principal Works

PHILOSOPHICAL TREATISES: *De consolatione ad Marciam,* c. 40–41 (*Consolation Addressed to Marcia*); *De ira,* c. 41–44 (*On Anger*); *De brevitate vitae,* c. 49 (*On the Briefness of Life*); *De clementia,* c. 55 (*On Clemency*); *De vita beata,* c. 58 (*On the Happy Life*); *De beneficiis,* c. 62–64 (*On Benefits*); *Naturales quaestiones,* c. 62–64 (*Natural Questions*); *Epistulae morales,* c. 63.

PLAYS: *Hercules furens, Troades, Phoenissae, Medea, Oedipus, Phaedra, Agamemnon, Thyestes, Hercules Oetaeus.*

SATIRE: *Apocolocyntosis,* c. 55 (*Pumpkinification*).

Lucius Annaeus Seneca, born about 4 B.C., was the son of Annaeus Seneca, a famous rhetorician of Córdoba. The family possessed wealth and high rank, and at an early age Seneca was sent to Rome to be educated. As a student of rhetoric and philosophy, the young man came to the notice of the Emperor Caligula, under whose patronage he entered the Roman senate and gained fame as an orator. Accused by the Empress Messalina of a love affair with Caligula's sister, Seneca was banished to Corsica by the Emperor Claudius. Many of Seneca's philosophical writings were written during his exile, but his conduct while in Corsica apparently exhibited little of the stoicism he advocated. Unhappy in his banishment, he begged to be recalled to Rome. In 49 Agrippina, the new wife of Claudius, procured his return and made him a tutor to her eleven-year-old son Domitius, later the Emperor Nero.

Seneca and Sextus Afranius Burrus, prefect of the Praetorian guard, exercised great influence over Nero and were, according to Tacitus, responsible for the mildness which marked the early years of that monarch's reign. Through Nero, Seneca was for a time virtually the ruler of Rome, but after the death of Burrus in 62, his position as an adviser became dangerous because of the restraints he tried to impose on his debauched and brutal master. New advisers to Nero, who cared little for good government or justice, were at the emperor's ear. Nero was constantly in need of money, and Seneca was wealthy, enormously so. Moreover, enemies had pointed out to the emperor that Seneca was Nero's greatest rival at oratory and poetry, that Seneca was very popular with the Romans, and that he had disparaged Nero's poetry and horsemanship. Seneca, learning of the dangerous situation, went to Nero and asked permission to retire from public life. Although Nero refused to grant permission, Seneca appeared less and less at court and spent much of his time in the privacy of his estate near Rome.

In 65 Seneca was accused of plotting against Nero. Ordered by the emperor to commit suicide, Seneca cut the veins of his wrists and while entertaining friends at his villa near Rome allowed himself to bleed to death. Although some authorities in the past have thought Seneca was a Christian, there is no accepted evidence that he was.

It is difficult to associate Seneca's

writings with his life, for too little information has been saved which relates the two. In his philosophical writings, Seneca delineated a stoicism that he himself apparently failed to practice. In addition to his philosophical writings, Seneca left nine tragedies, probably designed to be read rather than to be viewed on the stage. During the period between 1580 and 1640, Seneca's plays greatly influenced Elizabethan and Jacobean dramatists; stage devices like ghosts, murders, and long-winded harangues by the chief characters were borrowed directly from Senecan drama. Some authorities have maintained that the Senecan plays are an adjunct to his philosophical writings, each play illustrating a point of Stoic doctrine, *Thyestes*, for example, dealing with retribution. Dating of the plays is next to impossible.

BIBLIOGRAPHICAL REFERENCES: The principal works of Seneca, in translations by various hands, are available in the Loeb Classical Library. The plays, translated by F. J. Miller and by Ella Isabel Harris, are in *The Complete Roman Drama*, edited by George E. Duckworth, 2 vols., 1942. See also W. C. Summers, *The Silver Age of Latin Literature*, 1920; Francis C. Holland, *Seneca*, 1920; F. L. Lucas, *Seneca and Elizabethan Tragedy*, 1922; T. S. Eliot, *Selected Essays*, 1932; André de Bovis, *La Sagesse de Sénèque*, 1948; N. T. Pratt, "Tragedy and Moralism, Euripedes and Seneca," in Stallknecht *et al*, eds., *Comparative Literature: Method and Perspective*, 1961, 189–203; and Clarence V. Boyer, "Seneca." *The Villain as Hero in Elizabethan Tragedy*, 1964, 13–20.

MADAME DE SÉVIGNÉ

Born: Paris, France
Date: February 5, 1626

Died: Grignan, Provence, France
Date: April 17, 1696

Principal Works

LETTERS: *Lettres*, 1697; 1725–1726; 1734–1737; 1862–1865; 1876.

Madame de Sévigné was born Marie de Rabutin-Chantal in Paris on February 5, 1626. Her father was Celse-Bénigne de Rabutin, Baron de Chantal, the son of a great noble family whose titles went back at least to the twelfth century. Madame de Sévigné's paternal grandmother, Jeanne-Françoise, who as a widow had given the care of her family to her own parents, had withdrawn from the world in 1610 to embrace the religious life under the direction of the man who was to become one day Saint-François de Sales. She herself was cannonized in 1767 for her exemplary life and work in establishing the Order of the Visitation of Saint Mary. Madame de Sévigné's mother, Marie de Coulanges, was the daughter of a noble but somewhat less illustrious family.

In 1627, just a year after her birth, Madame de Sévigné's father was killed in battle against the English. Six years later, in 1633, her mother also died, and the seven-year-old girl was sent to be cared for by her maternal grandparents. But the child's misfortunes were not yet over. Her grandmother died in 1635, and her grandfather followed his wife in 1636. The ten-year-old girl was then sent to her maternal uncle, Christophe de Coulanges, Abbé of Livry. Here at last she found security.

The Abbé took the girl's up-bringing and education quite seriously. He gave her the best teachers, from whom she learned, among other things, Latin, Spanish, and Italian; and he himself gave her a firm Christian education by the tenets of which she lived her entire life, a respected and virtuous woman. Throughout the rest of his life (until 1687) the Abbé, whom Madame de Sévigné called "Kindness Itself," was a faithful friend and counselor of his niece.

In 1644, at the age of eighteen, Marie married Henri Marquis de Sévigné. It was a "good" but unhappy match. The young Marquis was a gambler, a fighter, and a rake. After badly damaging his own and his wife's fortunes, he was killed in 1651 in a duel over another woman. He left his widow with two small children, a daughter born in 1646, and a son born in 1648. Madame de Sévigné, who, as she said, loved but did not esteem her husband, never remarried. She was much sought after for her person, her wit, and her fortune, by both honorable and not so honorable men.

After her husband's death, Madame de Sévigné spent several years on her estates reorganizing her children's patrimony. That task accomplished, she returned to Paris in 1654 and made a brilliant showing in the high society of the capital. She often appeared at the Hotel de Rambouillet, as well as at other aristocratic salons, and she was one of the most illustrious of the circle of elegant and cultured women who set the intellectual fashions of Paris. Among her many friends and admirers were La Rochefoucauld, Madame de Lafayette, and the great Finance Minister Fouquet (who sought to make her his mistress). Nevertheless, for the most part she devoted herself to the upbringing and education of her two children, the elder of whom, her daughter Françoise-Marguerite, she idolized.

In 1669, Madame de Sévigné arranged the marriage of her daughter to the Comte de Grignan, who, much to the doting mother's distress, was soon appointed Governor of Provence. It is to the enforced separation of Madame de Sévigné and her idolized daughter that we owe the majority of the over 1,500 letters about the life and society of Paris on which rests Madame de Sévigné's literary reputation. She had begun writing characteristically vivid and brilliant letters to her friends before her marriage, and her circle of correspondence always remained wide. But it is in the hundreds of letters to her distant daughter that we see her at her best. Madame de Sévigné, who was visiting her daughter for only the third time since 1671, died of smallpox at her daughter's château in Provence on April 17, 1696.

BIBLIOGRAPHICAL REFERENCES: The standard edition is *Lettres de Madame de Sévigné*, edited by L. J. N. Monmerqué and Adolphe Regnier, 14 vols., 1862–1868, supplemented by *Lettres inedites*, edited by Charles Capmas, 2 vols., 1876. A modern collection is *Lettres*, edited by E. Gerard-Gailly, 3 vols., 1953–1957. Translations include *Letters from Mme. la Marquise de Sévigné*, translated by Violet Hammersley with a preface by Somerset Maugham, 1955; and *Selected Letters*, translated and edited by H. T. Barnwell, 1960.

For biography and criticism see Charles A. Walckenaer, *Mémoires touchant la vie et les écrits de Marie de Rabutin-Chantal . . . marquise de Sévigné*, 5 vols., 1843–1856; J. Lemoine, *Mme. de Sévigné, sa famille et ses amis*, 1926; Gabriel Brunet, "Mme. de Sévigné" in his *Evocations litteraires*, 1930; Arthur A. Tilley, *Mme. de Sévigné, Some Aspects of Her Life and Character*, 1936; Lida Kauffman, *Die Briefe der Mme. de Sévigné*, 1954; Auguste Bailly, *Mme. de Sévigné*, 1955; and Harriet R. Allentuch, *Mme. de Sévigné*, 1963.

WILLIAM SHAKESPEARE

Born: Stratford-upon-Avon, England
Date: April (23?), 1564

Died: Stratford-upon-Avon
Date: April 23, 1616

PRINCIPAL WORKS

PLAYS: *Henry VI*, Parts I, II, and III, 1589–1591; *Richard III*, 1592–1593; *The Comedy of Errors*, 1592–1594; *Titus Andronicus*, 1593–1594; *The Taming of the Shrew*, 1593–1594; *Two Gentlemen of Verona*, 1594–1595; *Love's Labour's Lost*, 1595; *Romeo and Juliet*, 1594–1596; *Richard II*, 1595–1596; *A Midsummer Night's Dream*, 1595–1596; *King John*, 1596–1597; *The Merchant of Venice*, 1596–1597; *The Merry Wives of Windsor*, 1597–1601; *Henry IV*, Parts I and II, 1597–1598; *Much Ado About Nothing*, 1598–1599; *Henry V*, 1598–1599; *Julius Caesar*, 1599–1600; *As You Like It*, 1599–1600; *Twelfth Night*, 1599–1600; *Hamlet*, 1600–1601; *Troilus and Cressida*, 1601–1602; *All's Well That Ends Well*, 1602–1604; *Othello*, 1604; *Measure for Measure*, 1604–1605; *King Lear*, 1605; *Macbeth*, 1606; *Antony and Cleopatra*, 1606–1607; *Coriolanus*, 1607–1608; *Timon of Athens*, 1605–1608; *Pericles*, 1608; *Cymbeline*, 1609; *The Winter's Tale*, 1610–1611; *The Tempest*, 1611; *Henry VIII*, 1612–1613 (with Fletcher).

POEMS: *Venus and Adonis*, 1593; *The Rape of Lucrece*, 1594; *The Passionate Pilgrim*, 1599; *The Phoenix and the Turtle*, 1601; *Sonnets*, 1609.

William Shakespeare, greatest of English poets and dramatists, was born at Stratford-upon-Avon in 1564 and died there in 1616. The biographical data, though sufficient to demolish the Baconian and other heresies, are not helpful in other respects. The view that Shakespeare attended Stratford Grammar School, though inherently probable, remains a surmise, and little is known of his activities prior to 1590, save that he married Anne Hathaway in 1582 and had three children by her.

Most of Shakespeare's working life was spent in London, and allusions, friendly and otherwise, show that by 1592 he was a dramatist of recognized achievement. Francis Meres, in *Palladis Tamia* (1598), virtually establishes that his supremacy in comedy, tragedy, and narrative poetry was generally acknowledged, and this view is endorsed by later testimony, notably that of Ben Jonson. From 1594 on Shakespeare was associated exclusively with the Lord Chamberlain's company, which became the King's company in 1603. This was the most stable and prosperous of the Elizabethan dramatic companies. It built the Globe Theatre in 1599, and acquired the Blackfriars private theater in 1608.

So far as can be ascertained, Shakespeare's career as a dramatist covers the period c. 1590 to c. 1612. His early years show him working in all categories. Chronicle histories are a conspicuous feature of the years 1590–1599, and these reflect England's self-awareness at a time when the threat from Spain was still acutely felt. The same period saw the maturing of his comic genius, through such minor masterpieces as *Love's Labour's Lost* and *A Midsummer Night's Dream*, to the three great comedies, *The Merchant of Venice*, *Much Ado about Nothing*, and *As You Like It*. Two early tragedies, *Titus Andronicus* and *Romeo and Juliet*, promise far more than they actually perform, and *Julius Caesar*, though flawless in conception and execution, lacks urgency and depth. By the end of the century Shakepeare's achievement had equalled, but not surpassed, that of Chaucer, the greatest of his predecessors. The foremost lesson so far learnt was that human and poetic truth, as embodied in Falstaff, is greater than the historical truth of Hal and Hotspur.

After 1600, Shakespeare bade farewell to romantic comedy in the incomparable *Twelfth Night,* and appears to have devoted one or two years to earnest contemplation of both life and art. *Hamlet* is the first of the great tragedies and also the first of a group of deeply contemplative dramas, often referred to as "problem plays," comprising *Troilus and Cressida, All's Well that Ends Well,* and *Measure for Measure,* which furnish an ample background to Shakespeare's whole output. When the tragic hero emerges again in *Othello,* his appeal is more directly emotional than Hamlet's, and this impassioned conception prevails in *King Lear* and *Macbeth.* In these titanic masterpieces man's response to the workings of a relentless and malign destiny is explored and exploited to the full, and the terrible logic of the action is communicated in language of ever-increasing urgency and intensity. *Antony and Cleopatra,* despite its superlative poetry, fails to secure a comparable tragic effect, but looks forward to the regenerative pattern of the late romances. *Timon of Athens* is excessive in its pessimism, and was left unfinished, but *Coriolanus* triumphantly affirms Shakespeare's capacity for recovery. Though outwardly uninviting in both matter and manner, its emotional impact proves terrific, and its psychology is penetrating. The plays of Shakespeare's final period are dramatic romances which present improbable persons and incidents and draw freely upon the musical and spectacular elements popular in the Court masques of the period. Here the themes of atonement and reconciliation, earlier treated in *All's Well that Ends Well* and *Measure for Measure,* are co-ordinated in a general pattern of regeneration symbolized by the heroines. *Pericles* and *Cymbeline* are uncertain in their handling of complicated plot material, but *The Winter's Tale* is magnificent and intense and *The Tempest* confers perfection on these endeavors. *Henry VIII,* last of the canonical plays, is thought to have been written in collaboration with Fletcher. *The Two Noble Kinsmen* purports to be the product of the same partnership, but the alleged Shakespearian scenes have been denounced by many competent critics. Attempts to claim other dramatic works of the period for Shakespeare have, in the main, proved abortive, though it has now been established, beyond reasonable doubt, that *The Book of Sir Thomas More* (British Museum MS. Harley 7368) contains three pages of his work in autograph.

Dryden justly claimed that Shakespeare "was the man who of all Modern, and perhaps Ancient Poets, had the largest and most comprehensive soul." He is the supreme interpreter of human relationships, the supreme percipient of human frailties and potentialities. It is often alleged that he is no philosopher, that his mind is neither mystical nor prophetic, that the beatific vision of Dante is beyond his scope. Even so, his thought, governed by the Christian neo-Platonism of his day, is earnest and profound, and his writings as a whole reveal a consistent, coherent, and possibly distinctive philosophical system. The comedies move ultimately to an acute awareness of the mutability of human affairs, and this sense of time's implacability is crystallized in the Sonnets and communicated, with inexpressible poignancy, in *Twelfth Night*. In the historical plays the curse which falls upon the commonwealth through the deposition and murder of an anointed king is pursued through successive manifestations of violence and anarchy, of which Falstaff is made finally the most potent symbol, until expiation is complete in Henry Tudor. Here the manipulation of history is determined by a clearly-ordered conception of political morality no less than by an artistic conscience. The same outlook is more flexibly presented in *Hamlet*, and Ulysses' great exposition of degree in *Troilus and Cressida* summarizes the acquired political wisdom of a decade. But there is no break in continuity, and Ulysses' speech is equally applicable to the great tragedies, in which Shakespeare contemplates the chaos that ensues when "degree is suffocate." Cognate with the doctrine of degree, and informing the histories and tragedies at all stages, is the concept of absolute justice. Portia, in *The Merchant of Venice*, pleads that mercy is above justice, and this is exemplified, in strenuous and practical terms, in *Measure for Measure*. The conflict between justice and mercy is a conspicuous feature of the great tragedies, notably *King Lear*, and is ultimately resolved, in its tragic context, in *Coriolanus*, when the hero spares Rome and gains his greatest victory—that over himself. *Cymbeline* and *The Winter's Tale*, albeit artificially, plunge into chaos comparable to the chaos of the tragedies, but the resolution now is in terms of reconciliation and regeneration instead of sacrifice and waste. Music, the prime function of the Creation, becomes increasingly prominent in these final romances, each of which looks clearly towards the harmony and unity of the Golden Age. The Platonic vision of the Many and the One, which informs these plays and carries them nearly into mysticism, though dramatically new, is something which Shakespeare had earlier achieved in certain of the *Sonnets* and in the concentrated intricacy of *The Phoenix and the Turtle*, published in Robert Chester's *Love's Martyr* in 1601.

Criticism has often erred in emphasizing particular aspects of Shakespeare's art. With him, action, thought, character, and language are not separable elements; and our response, in theater and study alike, must be to a complex unity in which dramatic conceptions are simultaneously natural and poetic, and language, unique and infinitely creative. The greatest Shakespeare critics—Dryden, Johnson, Coleridge and Bradley—can always be read with profit and delight, and the enormous mass of twentieth century criticism contains much that is of value; but if we have ears to hear and a heart to understand we shall always find that Shakespeare is his own best interpreter.

BIBLIOGRAPHICAL REFERENCES: Because of the extensive range of Shakespeare studies since 1900, even a tentative bibliography would fill a number of pages and would require separate listings for the individual plays. Only general areas of study and criticism can be indicated here. Standard editions are the *Cambridge Shakespeare,* edited by W. G. Clark and W. A. Wright, 9 vols., 1863–1866; the *New Variorum,* edited by H. H. Furness and others, 1871 ff.; the *Arden Shakespeare,* edited by W. J. Craig and R. J. Case, 39 vols., 1899–1924; the *New Cambridge,* edited by J. Dover Wilson, 1921 ff.; the *Kittredge Shakespeare,* edited by G. L. Kittredge, 1936; and the *New Arden,* under the general editorship of Una Ellis-Fermor, 1951 ff.

For biography see J. Q. Adams, *A Life of William Shakespeare,* 1923; E. K. Chambers, *William Shakespeare: A Study of Facts and Problems,* 2 vols., 1930; Leslie Hotson, *Shakespeare versus Shallow,* 1931; *idem, I, William Shakespeare,* 1937; J. Dover Wilson, *The Essential Shakespeare,* 1932; Hazleton Spencer, *The Art and Life of William Shakespeare,* 1940; Ivor Brown, *Shakespeare,* 1949; Marchette Chute, *Shakespeare of London,* 1949; and F. E. Halliday, *The Life of Shakespeare,* 1961.

General background studies include *Shakespeare's England,* edited by Walter Raleigh, 2 vols., 1916; E. K. Chambers, *The Elizabethan Stage,* 4 vols., 1923; Muriel St. C. Byrne, *Elizabethan Life in Town and Country,* 1925; Hardin Craig, *The Enchanted Glass,* 1936; G. B. Harrison, *Elizabethan Plays and Players,* 1940; G. E. Bentley, *The Jacobean and Caroline Stage,* 2 vols., 1941; Theodore Spencer, *Shakespeare and the Nature of Man,* 1942. For criticism see A. C. Bradley, *Shakespearean Tragedy,* 1904; *idem, Oxford Lectures on Poetry,* 1909; M. W. MacCallum, *Shakespeare's Roman Plays,* 1910; E. K. Chambers, *Shakespeare: A Survey,* 1925; G. Wilson Knight, *The Wheel of Fire,* 1930; W. W. Lawrence, *Shakespeare's Problem Comedies,* 1931; E. E. Stoll, *Art and Artifice in Shakespeare,* 1933; Caroline F. E. Spurgeon, *Shakespeare's Imagery,* 1936; Mark Van Doren, *Shakespeare,* 1939; Harley Granville-Barker, *Prefaces to Shakespeare,* 2 vols., 1946; Lily B. Campbell, *Shakespeare's "Histories,"* 1947; R. B. Heilman, *This Great Stage,* 1948; T. M. Parrott, *Shakespearean Comedy,* 1949; Donald Stauffer, *Shakespeare's World of Images,* 1949; and Karl J. Holzknecht, *The Backgrounds of Shakespeare's Plays,* 1950.

Valuable aids for the student are The Norton Facsimile of *The First Folio Shakespeare,* prepared by Charlton Hinman, 1968; Oscar James Campbell and Edward G. Quinn, eds., *The Reader's Encyclopedia of Shakespeare,* 1966; and Marvin Spevack, *A Complete and Systematic Concordance . . . of Shakespeare,* 8 vols. projected, 1967—.

KARL SHAPIRO

Born: Baltimore, Maryland
Date: November 10, 1913

Principal Works

POEMS: *Poems,* 1935; *Person, Place and Thing,* 1942; *The Place of Love,* 1942; *V-Letter and Other Poems,* 1944; *Essay on Rime,* 1945; *Trial of a Poet and Other Poems,* 1947; *Poems 1942–1953,* 1953; *Poems of a Jew,* 1958; *The Bourgeois Poet,* 1964; *Selected Poems,* 1968; *The White-Haired Lover,* 1968.
CRITICISM: *Beyond Criticism,* 1953; *In Defense of Ignorance,* 1960; *A Prosody Handbook* (with Robert Beum), 1964.
NOVEL: *Edsel,* 1971.

Karl Jay Shapiro was born in Baltimore, Maryland, and was educated at the University of Virginia and The Johns Hopkins University. In World War II he served in the U. S. Army for three years. During this absence from the United States, his fiancée, Evelyn Katz, saw two of his books through the presses, including *V-Letter and Other Poems,* which won the Pulitzer Prize for Poetry in 1945. In 1946 and 1947 he served as Consultant in Poetry to the Library of Congress; for the next three years he taught at Johns Hopkins. From 1950 until 1956 he edited *Poetry* magazine in Chicago; he then went to the University of Nebraska and edited *Prairie Schooner* until 1967, when he joined the English faculty of the University of California at Davis.

Shapiro's early poetry established him firmly among the best poets of his generation; *Person, Place and Thing* contains such familiar poems as "Haircut" and "Auto Wreck"; "Elegy for a Dead Soldier" and "The Leg" appeared in *V-Letter.* These poems are characterized by an immediacy of experience and a freedom from the irony and conceptualizing which typified much that was being written at that time.

Having written some of the best war poems of the decade, Shapiro found himself out of the army and in the midst of the literary "establishment"; here it seems to have been difficult for him to carry on his earlier style. He has been casting about ceaselessly ever since, looking for a stance and a style which will be appropriate to what he wishes to say.

Some of these explorations, such as *In Defense of Ignorance* and *The Bourgeois Poet,* constitute extreme reactions against the intellectual tradition fostered by T. S. Eliot; others, like *Poems of a Jew* are attempts to establish a positive state of consciousness from which to speak.

More recently, as in *The White-Haired Lover,* he has returned to traditional verse forms. Out of all these attitudes have come some significant poems, and some useful criticism; but the poems Shapiro wrote before the end of World War II are still his best, and they are among the best poems of the last forty years.

BIBLIOGRAPHICAL REFERENCES: Articles of interest on Shapiro's poetry include Dayton Kohler, "Karl Shapiro: Poet in Uniform," *College English,* VII (February, 1946), 243–249; C. I. Glicksberg, "Karl Shapiro and the Personal Accent," *Prairie Schooner,* XXII (1948), 44–52; Edwin Fussell, "Karl Shapiro: The Paradox of

Prose and Poetry," *Western Review,* XVIII (1954), 225–244; J. G. Southworth, "The Poetry of Karl Shapiro, *English Journal,* LI (1962), 159–166; and Louis D. Rubin, Jr., "The Search for Lost Innocence: Karl Shapiro's *The Bourgeois Poet,*" *The Hollins Critic,* I (1964), 1–16.

BERNARD SHAW

Born: Dublin, Ireland
Date: July 26, 1856

Died: Ayot St. Lawrence, England
Date: November 2, 1950

PRINCIPAL WORKS

PLAYS: *Widowers' Houses*, 1893 [1892]*; *Plays, Pleasant and Unpleasant*, 1898 (Pleasant: *Arms and the Man* [1894], *Candida* [1897], *The Man of Destiny* [1897], *You Never Can Tell* [1899]; Unpleasant: *Widowers' Houses*, *Mrs. Warren's Profession* [1902], *The Philanderer* [1905]); *Three Plays for Puritans*, 1901 (*The Devil's Disciple* [1897], *Caesar and Cleopatra* [1901], *Captain Brassbound's Conversion* [1900]); *Man and Superman*, 1903 [1905]; *John Bull's Other Island*, 1907 (*John Bull's Other Island* [1904], *How He Lied to Her Husband* [1904], *Major Barbara* [1905]); *Press Cuttings*, 1909; *The Doctor's Dilemma*, 1911 (*The Doctor's Dilemma* [1906], *Getting Married* [1908], *The Shewing-up of Blanco Posnet* [1909]); *Misalliance*, 1914 (*Misalliance* [1910], *The Dark Lady of the Sonnets* [1910], *Fanny's First Play* [1911]); *Androcles and the Lion*, 1916 (*Androcles and the Lion* [1913], *Overruled* [1912], *Pygmalion* [1913]); *Heartbreak House*, 1919 (*Heartbreak House* [1920], *Great Catherine* [1913], *Playlets of the War*); *Back to Methuselah*, 1921 [1922]; *Saint Joan*, 1924 [1923]; *The Apple Cart*, 1929; *Too True to Be Good*, 1934 (*Too True to Be Good* [1932], *A Village Wooing* [1934], *On the Rocks* [1933]); *The Simpleton of the Unexpected Isles*, 1936 (*The Simpleton of the Unexpected Isles* [1935], *The Six of Calais* [1934], *The Millionairess* [1936]); *Geneva*, 1939 [1938]; *In Good King Charles's Golden Days*, 1939; *Buoyant Billions*, 1951 [1949].

NOVELS: *Cashel Byron's Profession*, 1886; *An Unsocial Socialist*, 1887; *Love among the Artists*, 1900; *The Irrational Knot*, 1905; *Immaturity*, 1930.

SHORT STORIES AND TALES: *The Adventures of the Black Girl in Her Search for God*, 1932; *Short Stories, Scraps, and Shavings*, 1934.

ESSAYS AND STUDIES: *The Quintessence of Ibsenism*, 1891; *The Sanity of Art*, 1895; *The Impossibilities of Anarchism*, 1893; *The Perfect Wagnerite*, 1898; *Dramatic Opinions and Essays*, 1906; *Common Sense about the War*, 1914 (reprinted as *What I Really Wrote about the War*, 1931); *The Intelligent Woman's Guide to Socialism and Capitalism*, 1928; *The League of Nations*, 1929; *Major Critical Essays*, 1930; *Our Theatres in the Nineties*, 1932 (3 vols.); *Music in London, 1890–1894*, 1932 (3 vols.); *Essays in Fabian Socialism*, 1932; *Pen Portraits and Reviews*, 1932; *London Music in 1888–1889*, 1937; *Everybody's Political What's What*, 1944.

AUTOBIOGRAPHY: *Shaw Gives Himself Away: An Autobiographical Miscellany*, 1939; *Sixteen Self Sketches*, 1949.

LETTERS: *Letters from George Bernard Shaw to Miss Alma Murray*, 1927; *Ellen Terry and Bernard Shaw: A Correspondence*, 1931 (with Ellen Terry); *Some Unpublished Letters of George Bernard Shaw*, 1939; *Bernard Shaw and Mrs. Patrick Campbell: Their Correspondence*, 1952.

(George) Bernard Shaw, dramatist, essayist, and critic, was born of Irish Protestant parents in Dublin on July 26, 1856. From his unsuccessful father and a "wicked uncle" he inherited his Shavian sense of fun and anticlimax and his "superficial blasphemy," from his mother a deep love and knowledge

* Dates of first performances which differ from dates of book publication are set within brackets.

of music, which, with his keen interest in the spoken and written language, was to prove his most enduring love and one of the greatest influences on his work.

In 1876 Shaw left Ireland for good. Though not susceptible to its "Celtic twilight," he was to its natural beauty, the joy of which, he declared, was to remain with him all his life. His work retains what G. K. Chesterton called "the virginity and violence of Ireland. . . . a strange purity and a strange pugnacity." Before he left, he had made his first excursion into print, in a form that was to remain with him to the end a favorite means of expression: a letter to the press. This first one, written to *Public Opinion* in April 1875 on the advent of the famous "firm of American evangelists," Moody and Sankey, deals maturely enough with the unsavory effect on individuals of sudden conversion. True religion is not to be had on the cheap.

In London, where his mother had preceded him, having left her unloved husband to devote herself to music-teaching, young Shaw soon abandoned clerking and turned to literature by writing five novels between 1879 and 1883. All were commercially rejected or unsuccessful; the best are *Love Among the Artists* and *Cashel Byron's Profession*. Written for the most part in an early Shavian prose bearing traces of strained Victorian elegance, they are insufficiently enlivened by the virile colloquialism he later added to form the supple and athletic prose of his prefaces and plays. The genuine Shavian style was developed the hard way, by "a teeming and tumultuous life spent on many platforms, from the British Association to the triangle at the corner of Salmon's Lane in Limehouse." From this vital public speaking experience (1883–1895), Shaw learnt both how easy it is to lose an audience and yet how very much people are prepared to take in the way of serious thought and provocative ideas if entertainingly and strategically presented in dialectically dramatic form leavened with humor. He also acquired the great virtue of courtesy in debate and respect for his adversary's opinions, and to this his plays owe much—not least the great Trial Scene in *Saint Joan*, in which he is, if anything, "too fair" to the Inquisition.

An encounter (1882) with Henry George and the reading of Karl Marx had turned his thoughts towards socialism, and while any direct propagation of it is absent from his plays, his faith in it is the backbone of all his subsequent work. As he himself said, an understanding of economics was to him what a knowledge of anatomy was to Michelangelo, and it stood him in good stead not only as a local government councilor in St. Pancras (in North London) but on the Executive Committee of the small but influential Fabian Society, to which he devoted himself selflessly (1884–1911) and for which he edited *Fabian Essays* (1889) and wrote many well-known socialist tracts.

Political and public speaking activities did not prevent Shaw's taking proudly to journalism (he welcomed it as another platform), and it was as "Corno di Bassetto," music critic for the new *Star* newspaper (1888–1890), that he made what was, perhaps, his first indelible mark on the intellectual and artistic consciousness of his times. In this and in his later music criticism for *The World* (1890–1894) and, above all, in his dramatic criticism for the *Saturday Review* (1895–1898), he was in fact attempting, as De Quincey said of Wordsworth, to create the taste by which he was to be appreciated. To this period also belong *The Quintessence of Ibsenism* and *The Perfect Wagnerite,* tributes to fellow "artist-philosophers" and revelatory as much of the author as of their subjects.

The rest of Shaw's life, especially after his marriage (1898) to the wealthy Charlotte Payne-Townshend, is mainly the history of his plays. Those written between 1892 and the end of the century may be said to be the extension of his theater criticism in more directly dramatic form. The first of these, *Widowers' Houses,* was actually begun in 1885 in collaboration with his great friend and fellow-Ibsenite, William Archer, but was finished quite independently in 1892 as the result of the challenge he felt to produce the drama he had been advocating. Into the earliest plays, which include *Mrs. Warren's Profession, Arms and the Man,* and *Candida* (one of the first of Shaw's remarkable gallery of marvelous feminine portraits), creeps already the Shavian theme of conversion—from dead system and outworn morality towards a more creatively vital approach to life—and it is further developed in *Three Plays for Puritans* written between 1897 and 1899: *The Devil's Disciple, Caesar and Cleopatra,* and *Captain Brassbound's Conversion.* These also develop Shaw's scathing attitude to the routineers and slaves of petty bourgeois morality and his fondness for the exponents of original virtue and for those, true to their own faiths, who live in defiance of accepted codes.

His quest for a new religion or purer ethical approach to life reaches its first apotheosis in the Hell Scene of *Man and Superman,* "a Comedy and a Philosophy" in which Don Juan advocates, against the barren worldliness of Everyman and the more eloquent hedonistic desires of the Devil, the ecstasy of philosophical thought and the true joy of man's unceasing creative evolutionary urge for world betterment as well as for his own self-improvement. This theme was further developed, refined, and possibly enfeebled in *Back to Methuselah,* the longest if not the greatest of all Shaw's attempts, in play and preface, to expound the gospel of Creative Evolution and the Life Force, which he had taken over from Butler and Bergson and to which he added his own more Shavianly socialistic and naturalistically mystical yearnings.

With the turn of the century, Shaw found fame at last, first on the Continent and in the United States, and then, with the important advent in his life of the actor-director-playwright, Granville Barker, in England itself during the Court Theater season of 1904–1907. Notable plays of this "second period" include *John Bull's Other Island, Major Barbara,* and *The Doctor's Dilemma,* which with the two more purely disquisitory plays, *Getting Married* and *Misalliance,* testify to the growing encyclopedic range of the Shavian drama. In 1909 Shaw was "investigated" by the Joint Select Committee on Stage Censorship and declared all his plays to be "conscientiously immoral." Every advance in thought and conduct is made by immoralists and heretics, and from now on Shaw's attitude to men and affairs, manners and customs, and to current morality becomes ever more astringent, his religious views ever more "catholic and comprehensive," anti-Fundamentalist and non-anthropomorphic. In a long line of plays, from *The Shewing-up of Blanco Posnet* the same year, through *Androcles and the Lion* (his "religious pantomime"), *Heartbreak House, Saint Joan,* and onwards to the very end, he is seeking to distill the pure elixir of religion from the muddy faiths of mortal men, desperately trying not to empty out the baby with the dirty bath-water. The stern Shavian morality of complete individual responsibility, self-discipline, heroic effort without thought of reward or "atonement," and unsentimental and non-sexual regard for one's fellow beings is detectable in even a delightful "potboiler" like *Pygmalion.* In *Saint Joan,* whom Eric Bentley has said Shaw would have had to invent had she never existed, is synthesized the aspiring religious greatness of all Shaw's noblest characters and his impassioned devotion to what Bentley calls his "Both/And" view of life.

In 1925 Shaw was awarded the Nobel Prize for literature, but gave away the money to start the Anglo-Swedish Literary Foundation. In 1931 he visited Russia, and in 1932, with Mrs. Shaw, made a world tour which included the United States and a memorable address on political economy at the Metropolitan Opera House. Greater perhaps than any of the plays written in the last years of his life are the two prose works, *The Intelligent Woman's Guide to Socialism and Capitalism,* and *The Adventures of the Black Girl in Her Search for God.* The later plays, except for *The Apple Cart,* have scarcely received adequate public stage presentation, and those such as *Too True To Be Good* and *The Simpleton of the Unexpected Isles* show signs of striking a newer and even more experimental dramatic note altogether.

Shaw sought to be not only a great radical reformer, like Dickens (by whom he was much influenced, not least in his humor and characterization), but a synthesizer of all that was best in the thought of his times as well. His plays, *sui generis,* are richly endowed with striking characterization, colorful situation, and intellectual but dramatic argument. His importance lies in providing a bridge between the old and the new and in showing a way forward that need not be unduly contemptuous of all that is best in what went before. He is the Socratic gadfly that questions all things, yet steadfastly holds fast to that which is good. His clean astringent style is a healthy example to all who would write of serious matters without solemnity (he is the Mozart of literature), and his personal and professional pride in fine workmanship is an inspiration beyond the merely literary to those who study his life and work. Leaving no school and few, if any, avowed disciples, his influence is wide wherever his plays are performed or his works read. And that, in spite of some not unnatural decline in his personal popularity in the British Isles after his death at the age of ninety-four on November 2, 1950, seems to be everywhere.

BIBLIOGRAPHICAL REFERENCES: There are two collected editions of Shaw's *Works,* the limited Ayot St. Lawrence Edition, 30 vols., 1930, and the Standard Edition, 36 vols., 1931 ff. The Bodley Head edition will reach Vol. III in 1973. Excellent one-volume collections are the *Complete Plays,* 1931 (enlarged eds., 1934, 1938), and the *Complete Prefaces,* 1934 (enlarged ed., 1938). The authorized biography is Archibald Henderson's monumental *George Bernard Shaw: Man of the Century,*

1956. Stanley Weintraub has edited an "autobiography" from Shaw's autobiographical sketches: *The Playwright Years*, 1970, and *The Crucial Years*, 1971. The best critical study is Eric Bentley's *Bernard Shaw*, 1947 (rev. ed., 1957).

Shaw studies are so extensive that any listing must be highly selective. For biography and criticism see H. L. Mencken, *George Bernard Shaw: His Plays*, 1905; Holbrook Jackson, *George Bernard Shaw*, 1907; G. K. Chesterton, *George Bernard Shaw*, 1909; Julius Bab, *Bernard Shaw*, 1909; John Palmer, *Bernard Shaw: An Epitaph*, 1915; H. C. Duffin, *The Quintessence of Bernard Shaw*, 1920 (enlarged ed., 1939); Edward Shanks, *Bernard Shaw*, 1924; Archibald Henderson, *Table Talk of G.B.S.*, 1925; idem, *Bernard Shaw, Playboy and Prophet*, 1932; J. S. Collis, *Shaw*, 1925; Frank Harris, *Bernard Shaw*, 1931; André Maurois, *Poets and Prophets*, 1935; Hesketh Pearson, *G.B.S.: A Full-Length Portrait*, 1942; idem, *G.B.S.: A Postscript*, 1951; Stephen Winsten, ed., *G.B.S., 90*, 1946; idem, *Days with Bernard Shaw*, 1948; C. E. M. Joad, *Shaw*, 1949; A. C. Ward, *Bernard Shaw*, 1950; Blanche Patch, *30 Years with G.B.S.*, 1951; Desmond MacCarthy, *Bernard Shaw*, 1951; and Louis Kronenberger, ed., *George Bernard Shaw: A Critical Survey*, 1953, an anthology of Shaw criticism written by various hands, 1901–1951.

See also C. L. and V. M. Broad, *A Dictionary to the Plays and Novels of Bernard Shaw*, 1929; X. Heydet, *Shaw-Kompendium* (in German), 1936; and Raymond Mander and Joe Mitchenson, *Theatrical Companion to Shaw: A Pictorial Record of the First Performances of the Plays of George Bernard Shaw*, 1954. In 1958 Dan H. Laurence had in preparation an authoritative Shaw bibliography.

MARY WOLLSTONECRAFT GODWIN SHELLEY

Born: London, England
Date: August 30, 1797

Died: Bournemouth, England
Date: February 1, 1851

Principal Works

NOVELS: *Frankenstein,* 1818; *Valperga,* 1823; *The Last Man,* 1826; *Lodore,* 1835; *Falkner,* 1837.

TRAVEL SKETCHES: *The Journal of a Six Weeks' Tour,* 1814; *Rambles in Germany and Italy,* 1844.

Authorship of *Frankenstein* was not the only claim to distinction possessed by Mary Wollstonecraft Shelley. The daughter of a radical philosopher and and an early feminist, the wife of an unconventional boy genius, she early came to know life as something of a roller-coaster; and her masterpiece of fictional horror was only one of the more important incidents in an existence heavily underscored with drama.

The future novelist and mate of Percy Bysshe Shelley was born in London, August 30, 1797, the child of William Godwin and Mary Wollstonecraft. Bereaved of her mother almost immediately, she was reared in a bewildering clutter of family which included a stepmother, a stepbrother, a stepsister, a half-brother, and a half-sister. As Mary grew up she increasingly idolized her dead mother, for whose loss she was inclined to blame herself. The depth of this feeling was one of the important factors in her girlhood, the other being the atmosphere of intellectual discussion and debate which enveloped her father and his many visitors.

One of these visitors was a twenty-one-year-old youth whose mental accomplishments had made quite an impression upon William Godwin. The impression darkened when, a month before her seventeenth birthday, Mary Godwin eloped with Percy Bysshe Shelley, casually disregarding the fact that he was already in possession of a wife. More than two years passed before the suicide of Harriet Shelley allowed Shelley and Mary to legalize their marriage. All evidence available points to a reasonably happy union, though Mary's mind, clear and penetrating as it was, experienced times of bafflement in dealing with the unpredictable Shelley. On the other hand, Mary sometimes succumbed to periods of melancholy, which the death of her first three children did much to deepen.

Frankenstein was written in the Shelleys' first Italian days, during their companionship with Byron. So remarkable an achievement is it, especially for a girl of twenty, that it undoubtedly owes much of its sustained quality to the intellectual stimulation provided by the Shelley circle. The author's only novel to attain permanent reputation, it is an appealing combination of strangeness and reality, skillful in its plot structure and enlivened by sharp character contrasts. Published in 1818, *Frankenstein* was an immediate sensation; and its repeated dramatizations have given its title the familiarity of a household word. Other novels of Mary Shelley were to follow, but the author never regained the touch that would lift her fiction above the level of mediocrity. After Shelley's death, his widow's life became a struggle to secure bread and ensure the proper education of the only surviving Shelley child, Percy Florence. Nevertheless, *The Last Man* is interesting for its expression of Mary Shelley's liberal social and political views, and *Lodore* has the fascination of a veiled autobiography.

After her husband's death, Mary refused various offers of marriage: among her suitors were Shelley's friend Trelawny, John Howard Payne and—reportedly, at least—Washington Irving. After the death of Sir Timothy Shelley in 1844, her financial situation became somewhat easier. One of the disappointments of her later years was the discovery that she lacked the strength to complete a long-planned biography of her husband. She died on February 1, 1851, at the age of fifty-three, and was buried at Bournemouth.

BIBLIOGRAPHICAL REFERENCES: There is no edition of Mary Shelley's works. Frederick L. Jones has edited *The Letters of Mary W. Shelley*, 2 vols., 1944, and *Mary Shelley's Journal*, 1947. The standard biography is Mrs. Julian Marshall, *The Life and Letters of Mary Wollstonecraft Shelley*, 2 vols., 1889. Other more recent and less formal studies are R. G. Grylls, *Mary Shelley, A Biography*, 1938; Muriel Spark, *Child of Delight*, 1951; Elizabeth Nitchie, *Mary Shelley, Author of "Frankenstein,"* 1953; and Eileen Bigland, *Mary Shelley*, 1959. See also W. E. Peck, "The Biographical Element in the Novels of Mary Wollstonecraft Shelley," *Publications of the Modern Language Association*, XXXVI (1923), 196–219.

PERCY BYSSHE SHELLEY

Born: Field Place, Sussex, England
Date: August 4, 1792

Died: Off Viareggio, Italy
Date: July 8, 1822

Principal Works

POEMS: *Queen Mab,* 1813; *Alastor, or The Spirit of Solitude,* 1816; *The Revolt of Islam,* 1818; *Rosalind and Helen,* 1819; *Epipsychidion,* 1821; *Adonais,* 1821; *Hellas,* 1822; *Posthumous Poems,* 1824; *Poetical Works,* 1839.
PLAYS: *The Cenci,* 1820; *Prometheus Unbound,* 1820.
TRACTS AND STUDIES: *The Necessity of Atheism,* 1811; *An Address to the Irish People,* 1812; *A Refutation of Deism,* 1814; *A Defence of Poetry,* 1840.

Percy Bysshe Shelley, English poet, was born at Field Place, near Horsham, Sussex, August 4, 1792, the eldest son of a landed country squire. After some tutoring he was sent to Syon House Academy, where his shyness exposed him to brutal bullying. Entering Eton in 1804, he lived as much apart as possible, a moody, sensitive, and precocious boy with the nickname of "mad Shelley." Here he wrote *Zastrozzi* (1810), a wild Gothic romance, *Original Poetry by Victor and Cazire* (1810), and another inferior Gothic romance, *St. Irvyne, or The Rosicrucian,* published in 1811.

Shelley matriculated at University College, Oxford, in 1810. He and Thomas Jefferson Hogg were expelled the following year for publishing and sending to bishops and heads of colleges their pamphlet, *The Necessity of Atheism.* At this time Shelley fell in love with Harriet Westbrook, daughter of a retired hotel-keeper. They eloped, and despite Shelley's open break with the conventions of the Christian religion and particular scorn for the marriage ceremony, they were married in Edinburgh in August, 1811. Both fathers contributed to their support for the next three years, spent wandering in southern England, Ireland, and Wales.

In 1813 their first child was born in London and Shelley's first long poem, *Queen Mab,* was published. Meanwhile, marriage with Harriet was proving a failure. In May, 1814, Shelley met Mary, the daughter of William and Mary Wollstonecraft Godwin. Mary shared his belief that marriage was only a voluntary contract. Harriet left for her father's home, and Shelley and seventeen-year-old Mary eloped to Switzerland, accompanied by Claire Clairmont, Mary's half-sister. When they returned to England in September, Shelley proposed to Harriet that she come live with Mary and him; however, there was no reconciliation.

Mary bore a son in 1816 (the year of *Alastor, or The Spirit of Solitude*). They, with Claire, spent the summer in Switzerland and became close friends of Byron. Soon after they returned to England in the autumn, they heard Harriet had drowned herself. Shelley was now free to marry Mary Godwin (December 30, 1816), but a court order denied him the custody of his two children by Harriet.

After he had completed *The Revolt of Islam,* revised version of his earlier *Laon and Cythna,* the Shelleys and Claire Clairmont, with her child by Byron, went to Italy. There Shelley remained the rest of his life, wandering from Lake Como, Milan, Venice, Este, Rome, Florence, and Pisa to other cities and sections. Much time was spent with Byron. *Julian and Maddalo* (1818) is a poem in the form of a conversation between Shelley (Julian) and Byron (Maddalo). Next followed *The Masque of Anarchy* (1819), a revolutionary propaganda poem; *The Cenci*, a realistic tragedy; and *Prometheus Unbound*, a lyric tragedy completed in 1819 and published in 1820. Earlier in the same year, at Pisa, he wrote some of his most famous lyrics, "The Cloud," "Ode to the West Wind," and "Ode to a Skylark."

The chief productions of 1821 were *Epipsychidion*, a result of his platonic relationship with Countess Emilia Viviani; an uncompleted prose work, *A Defence of Poetry*, published after his death, and *Adonais*, an elegy inspired by the death of John Keats. From his wide reading, he was most greatly influenced by Plato, Lucretius, Spinoza, Rousseau, Hume, and Southey. Godwin's influence lasted until Shelley's death.

His final poem, *The Triumph of Life*, was incomplete at the time he was drowned, July 8, 1822, while sailing off Viareggio. His body was first buried in the sand, then cremated. The ashes were buried in the Protestant cemetery at Rome, January 21, 1823.

The nineteenth century notion of the sensitive poetic soul owes a great deal to the ideal young man (*Alastor*—"the brave, the beautiful—the child of grace and genius") built up largely by Shelley of Shelley. Yet in the history of English literature, Shelley is not as important as Wordsworth or as influential as Byron (more popular as a poet), or Keats. The public was shocked at his defiance of the conventions of life. Today he has many admirers, but for those who dislike Romantic poetry in general, Shelley is a particularly vulnerable target. Unquestionably he could give a song-like character to his verse, for his was the light, lyrical tone. He was a lover of unusual colors, blurred outlines, and large effects. He was also a lover of startling and frank realism and had an obvious passion for the mysterious and far away. In technique he illustrated something more concrete by the less concrete. What Shelley starts to define often results in vague though pretty images. He offers emotion in itself, unattached, in the void.

Because of his sensibility, perhaps, he was at war with the conventions of society from childhood. As a political dreamer he was filled with the hope of transforming the real world into an Arcadia through revolutionary reform. As a disciple of Godwin he directed *Queen Mab* against organized religion. The queen shows the human spirit that evil times, in the past and present, are due to the authority of Church and State. In the future, however, when love reigns supreme, the chains of the human spirit will dissolve; mankind will be boundlessly self-assertive and at the same time temper this self-assertion by a boundless sympathy for others. Then a world will be realized in which there is neither inferior nor superior classes or beings. The end of *Prometheus Unbound* gives this vision of humanity released from all evil artificially imposed from without (one of Rousseau's main tenets), a humanity "where all things flow to all, as rivers to the sea," and "whose nature is its own divine control."

Shelley sets up a humanity glorified through love; he worships in the sanctuary left vacant by "the great absence of God." (His youthful atheism lacked warmth and in the end he turned to a type of pantheism.) Love, as exemplified in his personal life, is a passionate kind of sensuality which becomes his simple moral code with no duty, blame, or obligation attached. The reign of love when no authority was necessary was his millennium.

BIBLIOGRAPHICAL REFERENCES: The best editions of Shelley are the Julian Edition of the *Complete Works*, edited by Roger Ingpen and Walter E. Peck, 10 vols., 1926–1930; and the *Complete Poetical Works*, edited by Thomas Hutchinson, 1933. The standard biography is Newman I. White, *Shelley*, 2 vols., 1940. See also Thomas Medwin, *The Life of Percy Bysshe Shelley*, 1847 (rev. ed., 1913); Edward Dowden, *The Life of Percy Bysshe Shelley*, 2 vols., 1886; André Maurois, *Ariel*, 1923; Edmund Blunden, *Shelley: A Life Story*, 1946; and Jean O. Fuller, *Shelley: A Biography*, 1968. Of great importance are K. N. Cameron, gen. ed., *The Esdaile Notebooks: A Volume of Early Poems*, 1964; and *idem*, gen. ed., *Shelley and His Circle, 1773–1822*, 1961– (4 vols. by 1971). See also Louise Schultz Boas, *Harriet Shelley: Five Long Years*, 1962.

For criticism see H. L. Hoffman, *An Odyssey of the Soul: Shelley's Alastor*, 1933; C. H. Grabo, *The Magic Plant*, 1936; Carlos Baker, *Shelley's Major Poetry*, 1948; R. H. Fogle, *The Imagery of Keats and Shelley*, 1949; K. N. Cameron, *The Young Shelley*, 1950; Sylva Norman, *Flight of the Skylark: The Development of Shelley's Reputation*, 1954; and Neville Rogers, *Shelley at Work*, 1957; also David L. Clark, "Shelley and Shakespeare," *Publications of the Modern Language Association*, LIV (1939), 261–287; E. K. Gibson, "*Alastor*: A Reinterpretation," *ibid.*, LXII (1947), 1022–1046; and Bennett Weaver, "*Prometheus Bound* and *Prometheus Unbound*," *ibid.*, LXIV (1949), 115–133.

RICHARD BRINSLEY SHERIDAN

Born: Dublin, Ireland
Date: October (?), 1751

Died: London, England
Date: July 7, 1816

Principal Works

plays: *The Rivals*, 1775; *Saint Patrick's Day*, 1775; *The Duenna*, 1775; *The School for Scandal*, 1777; *The Critic*, 1779.

Richard Brinsley (Butler) Sheridan, the playwright who with Goldsmith effected the revival of English comedy after the coma into which it had lapsed at the hands of Cibber and Steele, led a more romantic life in actuality than most romantic novelists could invent for fiction. He achieved his striking dramatic successes while still in his twenties; then turned his remarkable talents and energies from the theater to politics.

He was born to a heritage of genius. His paternal grandfather had distinguished himself in the classics at Trinity College, Dublin, had taken Holy Orders, and had set up a school in Dublin which for a time produced nearly £1,000 a year. Thomas Sheridan, his father, took his M.A. at Trinity College and at the Theatre Royal in Dublin achieved fame as an actor second only to David Garrick. Sheridan's mother was an accomplished writer of popular novels, and the author of three plays, one of which Garrick pronounced "one of the best comedies he ever read."

Richard Sheridan, the son of this tradition who brought it to its height, was born in 1751 in Dublin. He went at seven years of age under the tutelage of Mr. Samuel Whyte, but after a year moved with his family to England where, in 1762, he was sent to Harrow. There he was under the tutelage of two remarkable scholars, Dr. Robert Sumner and Dr. Parr. He gained a reputation for pranks for which his masters, though they knew he was responsible, could not bring him to account. In spite of these pranks, however, and in spite of his indolence and carelessness, Sheridan at Harrow achieved both the esteem of his schoolfellows and the admiring attention of his masters. Dr. Parr wrote of him: "He would have done little among the mathematicians at Cambridge; he would have been a rake, or an idler, or a trifler at Dublin, but ... at Oxford he would have become an excellent scholar."

Sheridan was brought home from Harrow to London when he was eighteen. In London for a time he received private tuition from Mr. Lewis Kerr. He had already at Harrow distinguished himself in poetry. In 1771 he published jointly with a friend some translations of "Aristaenetus" which were treated favorably by the critics, but ignored by the public.

About this time one of the most colorful romances in or out of fiction began when Sheridan met, while residing at Bath, the celebrated Maid of Bath, Elizabeth Ann Linley, then eighteen years old. Remarkably blessed with personal beauty and charm and with extraordinary musical talents, all enhanced by the publicity her profession as a singer had gained her, Miss Linley had almost innumerable hearts and fortunes at her feet. Of them all, Sheridan's gained the most attention.

Himself handsome, dashing, somewhat rakish, yet entirely a gentleman, his wit and elegance and devotion presented in his now-famous love verses —these things won her favor. But one Major Mathews, a married man and a friend of the girl's family, had for some time taken advantage of the familiarity his age and position granted him to be indiscreetly attentive to Miss Linley in public and to make shameful proposals to her in private. Repulsed, he is said to have threatened to ruin her reputation if he could not undermine her virtue. She confided in Sheridan, and was persuaded to run away with him to France where they were secretly married.

They were searched out and brought home by the girl's father (the marriage still secret), and Sheridan forthwith dueled with Mathews and forced him to retract publicly some vicious publications he had made about the eloped lovers. Mathews, to regain his reputation, called Sheridan out a second time. In a fierce and bloody duel in which both men broke their swords after wounding each other, Sheridan was this time sorely hurt. Hearing of his wounds, his wife confessed their secret marriage, and they were again married by license in Bath. The year was 1773.

Sheridan, pridefully and delicately rejecting all thoughts of profiting from his wife's already proved talents, set about seeking an independence by his own unproved merits. Under these circumstances he began his dramatic career.

Between 1775 and 1779 Sheridan produced five plays, on two of which his reputation rests. The least important pieces need little comment. *The Duenna* was a comic opera which broke all previous records for full-length plays with seventy-five performances during its first season. Its plot and the music account for its popularity, not the wit of its lines. In 1777 Sheridan made a sterilized adaptation of Vanbrugh's *The Relapse* in *A Trip to Scarborough;* the adaptation was competent and effective. His last original play, *The Critic,* is the least important of the three major works he produced. Appearing in 1779, it follows in the tradition of the Duke of Buckingham's *Rehearsal* and Henry Fielding's *Tom Thumb.* It was successful because it had topical interest, and because it was full of "robust good fun." But it is with *The Rivals* and *The School for Scandal* that Sheridan has made his place in the drama.

The Rivals, the first of Sheridan's plays, represents the short step upward from Goldsmith's *She Stoops to Conquer* to witty and elegant comedy in the maner of Congreve, but purged of his impurities. Because of poor acting and because of the unfortunate offense taken by the Irish gentry to Sir Lucius O'Trigger, the play was soundly damned at its first performance. Withdrawn from the stage, emended, and properly rehearsed, the play returned after eleven days to take the town. The excessively romantic young Lydia Languish is delightfully charming and funny. And Mrs. Malaprop is one of the best comic characters in English literature. From her comes our word "malapropism," and there has been no greater mistress of such than she herself. Her projected schooling for girls is representative of her "nice derangement of epitaphs":

"I would send her, at nine years old, to a boarding school, in order to learn a little ingenuity and artifice. Then,

Sir, she should have a supercilious knowledge of accounts;—and as she grew up, I would have her instructed in geometry that she might know something of the contagious countries;—but above all, she should be mistress of orthodoxy, that she might not misspell, and mis-pronounce words so shamefully as girls usually do."

Two years later, in 1777, *The School for Scandal* appeared. Meanwhile Sheridan had become part owner and manager at Drury Lane. He was thus able to cast his own players, and the result was a tremendous success. For Horace Walpole, "there were more parts performed admirably . . . than I almost ever saw in any play." Sheridan had also learned much about his craft from his close association with the theater, for a comparison of the earlier drafts of the play with its finished form reveals his mastery of the art of revision: "The dialogue . . . was set down with such exquisite Congreve-like precision that it enforced excellence of delivery." The play has poise, dignity, and a "dazzling glitter of wit"; indeed, it has been urged, a surfeit of wit. However, "audiences seldom balk at too much wit; only critics do that."

If Sheridan sought to discredit sentimentalism, this play accomplished his aim, "but sentimentalism is only an ingredient in the rich sauce of his satire. He gives us the quintessence of a scandal-loving society. . . . He can be serious, but not too serious," and he "enlivens the whole with incessant sparkling wit."

Shortly thereafter Sheridan turned from the theater of the drama to the theater of politics, where he played a leading role for more than thirty years. Whether or not that was a loss to letters we shall never know, for he distinguished himself in both occupations. He died in London, July 7, 1816. It must be said, moreover, that he and Goldsmith did not stop sentimental comedy: it lived on; it lives yet. But of all the plays writen from 1660 to our own day, *The Rivals* and *The School for Scandal* are among the half dozen most popular. And as long as men can laugh at themselves they will hold that popularity.

BIBLIOGRAPHICAL REFERENCES: The collected edition is *The Plays and Poems of Richard Brinsley Sheridan*, edited by R. Crompton Rhodes, 3 vols., 1928. This editor is also the author of the standard biography, *Harlequin Sheridan: The Man and the Legends*, 1933. Other biographical and critical studies include Walter Sichel, *Sheridan*, 2 vols., 1909; Lewis Gibbs, *Sheridan: His Life and His Theatre*, 1948; and W. A. Darlington, *Sheridan, 1751-1816*, 1951. C. J. L. Price edited the *Letters*, 3 vols., 1961. For criticism see, further, Ernest Bernbaum, *The Drama of Sensibility*, 1915; and Allardyce Nicoll, *A History of Late Eighteenth Century Drama*, 1927. See also Madeleine Burgham, *Sheridan*, 1972.

ROBERT C. SHERRIFF

Born: Kingston-on-Thames, England
Date: June 6, 1896

Principal Works

PLAYS: *Journey's End*, 1929; *Badger's Green*, 1930; *Windfall*, 1933; *Home at Seven*, 1950; *The White Carnation*, 1953; *The Long Sunset*, 1955; *Telescope*, 1958; *A Shred of Evidence*, 1961; *The Wells of St. Mary's*, 1962.

AUTOBIOGRAPHY: *No Leading Lady*, 1968.

NOVELS: *The Fortnight in September*, 1931; *Greengates*, 1936; *The Hopkins Manuscript*, 1939; *Chedworth*, 1944; *Another Year*, 1946; *King John's Treasure*, 1954.

The versatility of Robert C(edric) Sherriff goes unrecognized by those who know him only as the author of *Journey's End*, one of the most successful war dramas of modern times, for he has gained fame also as a writer for motion pictures and as a novelist. Born at Kingston-on-Thames, near London, on June 6, 1896, he entered an insurance office at seventeen and, apart from service in World War I, in which he was wounded at Ypres and reached the rank of captain, worked for ten years as an insurance adjuster. His introduction to a literary life was accidental. In 1921 he was asked to contribute a dramatic piece to be presented at Kingston for the benefit of the School Chapel Restoration Fund. After he had written other plays for the Kingston Rowing Club, his heightened interest in drama led to *Journey's End*; this, through the good offices of Bernard Shaw, was produced in 1929. After the London production of a second play, *Badger's Green*, in 1930, Sherriff interrupted his career to read for a bachelor's degree at New College, Oxford.

Sherriff has published eight other plays and an equal number of novels. In addition he has been responsible for a number of screenplays, of which perhaps the most distinguished were *The Road Back* (1932) and *Lady Hamilton* (1941).

BIBLIOGRAPHICAL REFERENCES: There is no full-length biographical or critical study. See W. A. Darlington, "Keying Down: The Secret of *Journey's End*," *Theatre Arts Monthly*, XIII (1929), 493–497; Ernest Short, *Theatrical Cavalcade*, 1942; and Stark Young, *Immortal Shadows*, 1948. "Persons and Personages," *Living Age*, CCCXXXIX (1931), 590–592, contains an interview with Sherriff.

ROBERT E. SHERWOOD

Born: New Rochelle, New York
Date: April 4, 1896

Died: New York, N. Y.
Date: November 14, 1955

Principal Works

PLAYS: *The Road to Rome*, 1927; *Waterloo Bridge*, 1930; *Reunion in Vienna*, 1931; *The Petrified Forest*, 1934; *Idiot's Delight*, 1936; *Abe Lincoln in Illinois*, 1938; *There Shall Be No Night*, 1940; *The Rugged Path*, 1945.
NOVEL: *The Virtuous Knight*, 1931.
BIOGRAPHY: *Roosevelt and Hopkins: An Intimate History*, 1948.

Robert E(mmet) Sherwood's association with the Democratic Party during the 1930's and the 1940's can be regarded, like his plays, as an expression of liberal sympathies and hopes; his theater is full of those who resist the imposition of tyranny of persons and superior power and the tyranny that results when outworn ideas continue to be cherished.

The events of Sherwood's life suggest that he moved freely in the world and had reasons for feeling that he knew whereof he spoke. Born in New Rochelle, New York, on April 4, 1896, he was the son of Arthur Murray Sherwood, an investment broker and devotee of the theater, and Rosina Sherwood, a well-known painter and illustrator. Sherwood was educated at Milton Academy and at Harvard, where his first play, *Barnum Was Right*, was produced by the Hasty Pudding Club. During World War I, after being rejected by the U.S. Army because of his height (he was six feet seven inches tall, he joined the famous Canadian Black Guard, and was gassed and wounded at Vimy Ridge. Discharged from the service in 1919, he became the dramatic editor of *Vanity Fair*, but he left this magazine in protest against the dismissal of Dorothy Parker for an unfavorable review. He moved to the old *Life*, then a humorous magazine, as co-editor and motion picture critic, becoming the first conscientious movie reviewer on the staff of any major American magazine. After 1928 he devoted his time to writing plays and scenarios. With Maxwell Anderson, S. N. Behrman, Sidney Howard, and Elmer Rice, he formed the Playwrights' Company in 1938; this action was a protest against the Theatre Guild's production of too many plays by European dramatists. Later, during World War II, he was an influential adviser to Franklin D. Roosevelt. Out of this experience came a book that is one of Sherwood's claims to fame, *Roosevelt and Hopkins: An Intimate History*, which required some thirty months of writing and culling from the forty filing cases of Harry Hopkins' papers. Critical reaction at once observed that Sherwood had not written for the popular market. The book was labeled Sherwood's "finest drama and the most titanic in scale that he has so far written" and "the delight of the journalist and the arsenal of the historian." (This book won Sherwood his fourth Pulitzer Prize; the other three had been for his plays, *Idiot's Delight, Abe Lincoln in Illinois,* and *There Shall Be No Night.*)

Sherwood's drama, from the farcical *Road to Rome* onward, is concerned with a small set of recurrent problems: What are the impersonal forces that shape history; do these forces interfere unjustly with private happiness; and does the thoughtful man have any chance to dominate the tyranny of impersonal power and outworn rule? Thus, in *Idiot's Delight* the love affair of two vaudeville "artists" is played out against the backdrop of power politics; at the end, even though bombs are dropping, the human spirit has some kind of triumph. Earlier, in *The Petrified Forest*, Sherwood had told much the same story, except that here the lovers had faced not bombs but an inhuman killer. Sherwood again was concerned with the assertion of man's dignity in a world that showed little concern for it. This same regard for human dignity appears in Sherwood's play about Lincoln and in his last significant drama, *There Shall Be No Night*, a play in which the exigencies of altering diplomatic alignments have resulted in transfers of setting from Finland to Greece and finally, in 1957, to Hungary. The setting changes but the story does not; against these national backgrounds enlightened, "decent" people confront the dragon of force and perversion of truth; they go down in material defeat, but the moral victory is theirs. This is a view of human destiny which Sherwood shared with many men of his generation: Man is still the master of his own destiny if he wishes to be, for he can be truly defeated only by his own desire for defeat. Sherwood's theater is a deft and sometimes illuminating expression of this typical twentieth century insight. He died in New York City on November 14, 1955.

BIBLIOGRAPHICAL REFERENCES: Two recent studies are available: R. Baird Schuman, *Robert E. Sherwood*, 1964; and John Mason Brown, *The World of Robert E. Sherwood, Mirror to His Times, 1896–1939*, 1965. For articles in books and periodicals see Louis Nizer, *Between You and Me*, 1948; John Mason Brown, *Still Seeing Things*, 1950; Edith J. R. Isaacs, "Robert Sherwood: Man of the Hours," *Theatre Arts Monthly*, XXIII (January, 1939), 31–34, 37–40; John Mason Brown, "On a Larger Stage," *Saturday Review of Literature*, XXXI (November 13, 1948), 54–58; John Gassner, "Robert Emmet Sherwood," *Atlantic Monthly*, CLXIX (January, 1942), 26–33; and Maxwell Anderson, "Robert E. Sherwood," *Theatre Arts Monthly*, XL (February, 1956), 26–27.

SHIH NAI-AN

Born: China
Date: Unknown; fl. fourteenth century

Died: China
Date: Unknown

Principal Work

NOVEL: The *Shui Hu Chuan* (*All Men Are Brothers*).

Nothing is definitely known about Shih Nai-an, the man who has been generally accepted as the author of *All Men Are Brothers* ever since Chin Sheng-t'an wrote in 1644 his seventy-chapter version of the novel with a preface of his own composition and forged Shih's name to it, though an equally good claim can be made for Lo Kuan-chung (*q.v.*). Until the early 1930's all that could be said of Shih was that he probably flourished in the middle decades of the fourteenth century and was perhaps an older contemporary of Lo. Then a census taker reported that he had come upon two documents in the archives of a Shih clan in the Tung-t'ai district of Kiangsu. These give the information that Shih Nai-an's real name was Erh or Tzu-an, that he was born in 1226 and died in 1370, that he passed his *chin-shih* examinations in 1331, and that after serving two years as a magistrate of Ch'ien-t'ang in Chekiang, he resigned because of the usual disagreement with superiors and devoted the rest of his life to writing. A list of his writings is given, which include not only the *Shui Hu Chuan* (under a slightly different title) but also several additional historical romances generally attributed to Lo, with the remark that he was helped in his work by his pupil Lo Kuan-chung. At first the report was hailed as a great literary find, but soon doubts began to be voiced. It would seem at this date that either the census taker had been imposed upon by the Shih family or else we have been imposed upon by him.

Actually neither Shih nor Lo could be the author of the extant versions of the novel, of which there are at least five (in 100, 110, 115, 120, and 124 chapters respectively) which antedate Chin's version. Historical and legendary romances such as the *Shui Hu* and *San Kuo* lived first in the oral tradition of professional storytellers. After a time some of them were set down in crude, sketchy form and were used largely as prompt-books. Shih and Lo were probably famous storytellers of their time; it is also possible that they wrote some of these prompt-books, which have since been lost. It is only natural that when literary hacks began to make up more elaborate reading versions of these romances from about the middle of the sixteenth century on, they should appropriate the Shih-Lo names rather than give their own, since it was not to one's credit in those days to be responsible for such "trash."

BIBLIOGRAPHICAL REFERENCES: The most familiar version of the *Shui Hu Chuan* in English is the translation by Pearl Buck, *All Men Are Brothers*, 1933. Critical studies include Richard G. Irwin, *The Evolution of a Chinese Novel: Shui Hu Chuan*, 1953; and Ho Hsin, *Shui-hu Yen-chiu* (*A Study of the Shui-hu*), 1954 (Shanghai).

JAMES SHIRLEY

Born: London, England
Date: Baptized September 7, 1596

Died: London
Date: October 29, 1666

Principal Works

PLAYS: *Love Tricks, or the School of Compliment*, 1625; *The Maid's Revenge*, 1626; *The Wedding*, c. 1627; *The Witty Fair One*, 1628; *The Grateful Servant*, 1629; *The Traitor*, 1631; *Love's Cruelty*, 1631; *Hyde Park*, 1632; *The Young Admiral*, 1633; *The Bird in a Cage*, 1633; *The Gamester*, 1634; *The Example*, 1634; *The Opportunity*, 1634; *The Lady of Pleasure*, 1635; *The Royal Master*, c. 1637; *The Doubtful Heir*, c. 1639; *The Gentleman of Venice*, 1639; *The Humorous Courtier*, 1640; *The Cardinal*, 1641.

MASQUES: *The Triumph of Peace*, 1634; *Cupid and Death*, 1653; *The Contention of Ajax and Ulysses*, 1659.

Another in the long line of preacher-writers, James Shirley, born in London in September, 1596, received his education at the Merchant Taylors' School, St. John's College, Oxford, and St. Catherine's College, Cambridge. After receiving his M.A. he became a parish priest and teacher at St. Albans; he left this post because of scruples which led to his becoming a Roman Catholic.

About 1625 he lodged in Gray's Inn and began to write plays, mostly for the Queen's Company. Until the closing of the theaters in 1642 he wrote over forty plays still extant. He then returned to teaching but continued to write occasional "entertainments" and masques. Severely burned in the Great Fire of London, he and his wife fled to St. Giles' parish. They died there a day later, October 29, 1666, and were buried in the same grave.

Shirley, coming late in the great age, was no innovator, but he wrote excellent tragedy, sprightly comedy, and masques with some surprising twists. *The Cardinal* is often reprinted as one of the best romantic tragedies, the last of the Jacobean Age. His comedy, *The Gamester*, looks forward to the realistic comedy of manners, and the *Lady of Pleasure* is a highly entertaining, fast-paced comedy in the older tradition.

BIBLIOGRAPHICAL REFERENCES: The standard edition is *The Dramatic Works and Poems of James Shirley*, edited by Alexander Dyce, 6 vols., 1833. The best biographical and critical study is A. H. Nason, *James Shirley, Dramatist*, 1915. See also Edmund Gosse, *James Shirley*, 1888; R. S. Forsythe, *The Relation of Shirley's Plays to Elizabethan Drama*, 1914; C. F. Brooke, ed., *English Drama, 1580–1642*, 1933; and Thomas Marc Parrott and Robert Hamilton Ball, *A Short View of Elizabethan Drama*, 1943; also Robert Read, "James Shirley and the Sentimental Comedy," *Anglia*, LXIII (1955), 149–170.

MIKHAIL SHOLOKHOV

Born: Kruzhlino, Russia
Date: May 24, 1905

Principal Works

novels: *Aloyshkino Serdtse*, 1925 (*The Heart of Aloyshka;* also *Alexander's Heart*); *Dvukhmuznaya*, 1925 (*The Woman with Two Husbands*); *Lazorevaya Steppe*, 1926 (*The Blue Steppes*); *Tikhiy Don*, 1928–1938 (*And Quiet Flows the Don* and *The Don Flows Home to the Sea;* combined as *The Silent Don*, 1942); *Podnyataya Tselina*, 1932–1933 (*Seeds of Tomorrow;* in England, *Virgin Soil Upturned*); *Oni srazhalis za rodinu*, 1944 (*They Fought for Their Country*); *Podniataia Tselina*, 1957 (*Harvest on the Don*); *Sud'ba Cheloveka*, 1959 (*Destiny of Man*).

short stories: *Donskiye Razkazy*, 1925 (*Tales of the Don*); *Early Stories*, translated 1966; *Fierce and Gentle Warrior*, translated 1967.

Mikhail (Aleksandrovich) Sholokhov, epic novelist of the Cossacks, was born in Kruzhlino, a small village near Veshenskaya on the River Don. When he was born, on May 24, 1905, his parents were unmarried, but in 1912 the marriage ceremony was performed and the child was legitimatized. His father was a farmer, a cattle buyer, a clerk, and later the owner of a power mill. The family was poor, but the parents nevertheless managed to send the boy to school near Moscow. Sholokhov's mother, half-Turkish and half-Cossack, was an illiterate woman of strong determination; she learned to read and write in order to be able to correspond with her son while he was away at school.

Sholokhov, forced to leave his school at Voronezh because of the German invasion, returned to his home when he was fifteen. His plans to teach school upset by the revolution, he was assigned by the Bolsheviks to various jobs, among them an assignment in a statistical bureau, as a freight handler, as a food inspector, and as a mason. In 1922, during bandit raids in the region, he participated in some of the fighting.

When he was eighteen he began to write for various newspapers and magazines, and he wrote some short fiction before beginning his long novel and eventual masterpiece, the Don Cossack tetralogy, which was translated into English as *And Quiet Flows the Don* (1934) and *The Don Flows Home to the Sea* (1940) before the whole was combined as *The Silent Don* in 1942. This monumental work, composed over a ten-year period, appeared in Russia in four separate volumes in 1928, 1929, 1933, and 1938. With the first volume of the novel, the author became famous. His analysis in depth into the lives of the Cossacks, showing how history was forcing them into new social roles, became popular because it was an intimate portrait of realistic regional life. Also, the novel expresses something of the power and human dignity of the human beings whose lives it portrays. Ivan Dzerzhinsky, the Soviet composer, used the Don novels as the basis of a highly popular opera, and it was a successful film. Largely on the basis of this work, Sholokhov received the Stalin Prize in 1941. Over a million copies of the book were sold in the U.S.S.R. during its first year of publication, and before Volume IV appeared, the novel had gone through seventy-nine editions, had been translated into thirty-eight languages, and had sold over four and a half million copies.

Sholokhov's work on *The Silent Don* was not continuous. In 1932 he completed the first volume of a two-volume work, *The Seeds of Tomorrow;* the second volume appeared the following year. This novel, dealing with the building of a *kholkoz*, or collective farm, was also a great success in Russia and in other countries. Like the Don novel, it was filmed and made into an opera by Dzerzhinsky. It was also presented as a four-act play by Krashen-inikova at the Simonov Studio Theatre.

Until 1941, Sholokhov lived a quiet life in the Veshenskaya region, where he wrote, farmed, hunted, fished, and entertained his friends. When the Nazis invaded Russia in 1941, he became one of Russia's "fighting correspondents," settling in Moscow where he now lives.

In 1937 he was elected Deputy to the Supreme Soviet. He is a member of the Academy of Sciences of the U.S.S.R. and of the Praesidium Union of Soviet Writers. In 1955, during an official state celebration of his fiftieth birthday, he received the Order of Lenin. During World War II he worked on a war novel and on short stories. He is married to Maria Petrovna and has four children.

Sholokhov has been criticized as a Communist apologist, but most readers of his works agree in regarding him as an artist who has managed to triumph over the propagandist; and he is valued as an epical writer who has portrayed a significant aspect of contemporary Russian life.

BIBLIOGRAPHICAL REFERENCES: A brief introductory sketch to Sholokhov is Isidor Schneider, "The Quiet Don Flows Home," *Soviet Russia Today*, IX (1941), 10–11+. More extensive studies are V. Goffenshefer, *Mikhail Sholokhov*, 1940; and I. G. Lezhnëv, *Mikhail Sholokhov*, 1948. See also George Reavey, *Soviet Literature Today*, 1946; and Gleb Struve, *Soviet-Russian Literature*, 1951. Recent studies are David H. Stewart, *Mikhail Sholokhov, A Critical Introduction*, 1967, and C. G. Bearne, *Sholokhov*, 1969.

JOSEPH HENRY SHORTHOUSE

Born: Birmingham, England
Date: September 9, 1834

Died: Birmingham
Date: March 4, 1903

PRINCIPAL WORKS

NOVELS: *John Inglesant*, 1880; *The Little Schoolmaster Mark*, 1883–1884; *Sir Percival*, 1886; *The Countess Eve*, 1888; *Blanche, Lady Falaise*, 1891.
SHORT STORIES: *A Teacher of the Violin*, 1888.
ESSAYS: *The Platonism of Wordsworth*, 1882; *The Royal Supremacy*, 1899.

Joseph Henry Shorthouse was born into a Quaker family of Birmingham on September 9, 1834. In his childhood he developed a stammer which embarrassed him all his life, and because of that speech impediment he was, except for a brief stay at Tottenham College at the age of fifteen, educated by tutors at home. At the age of sixteen he entered his father's business, a manufacturing concern in Birmingham. In business, despite his handicap, he proved very successful. Although born a Quaker, he had apparently less sympathy for his parents' religion than for others. Throughout his life he evidenced an interest in spiritualism, however, and after his marriage to Sara Scott, in 1857, he became a convert to the Church of England.

An attack of epilepsy in 1862, while Shorthouse was still in his twenties, forced him to turn to literary study and writing which afforded him the quiet, restful existence he needed. For ten years, from 1866 to 1876, Shorthouse worked on his novel, *John Inglesant*. It lay in manuscript for three years before Shorthouse printed it privately in 1880 for distribution to friends. At the suggestion of Mrs. Humphry Ward, the writer, it was published for the trade in 1881 and became very popular. Other novels, none so successful, by Shorthouse are *The Little Schoolmaster Mark*, *Sir Percival*, and *The Countess Eve*. He also wrote an essay on *The Platonism of Wordsworth* and a volume of stories, *A Teacher of the Violin and Other Tales*. Shorthouse's *John Inglesant* aroused surprise, and it remains a still amazing work because of its vivid descriptions of Italy, a land the author did not know at first hand, and its quality of mysticism not ordinarily associated with writings by men of business. Shorthouse died at Edgbaston, Birmingham, on March 4, 1903.

BIBLIOGRAPHICAL REFERENCES: The collected edition of *The Novels of Joseph Henry Shorthouse* is in 6 vols., 1891–1894. The official, and only, biography is *The Life, Letters, and Literary Remains*, edited by Sarah Shorthouse, 2 vols., 1905. Two excellent views of Shorthouse appear in P. E. More, *Shelburne Essays, III*, 1906; and Sir Edmund Gosse, *Portraits and Sketches*, 1912.

Special studies of *John Inglesant* are available: H. E. West, "*John Inglesant*" and "*Sartor Resartus*," *Two Phases of Religion*, 1884; J. Durham, "*Marius the Epicurean*" and "*John Inglesant*," 1905; W. K. Fleming, "Some Truths About John Inglesant," *Quarterly Review*, CCXL (1925), 130–148; M. Polack, *The Historical Philosophical, and Religious Aspects of "John Inglesant,"* 1934–the most valuable work on the subject; and Joseph Ellis Baker, "Joseph Henry Shorthouse, Quaker-Catholic," *The Novel and the Oxford Movement*, 1965, 183–199.

SHUDRAKA

Born: India
Date: c. 100 B.C.

Died: India
Date: Unknown

Principal Work

PLAY: *Mrcchakatikā* (*The Little Clay Cart*).

Shudraka (also spelled "Sūdraka" or "Çudraka") is possibly a legendary prince who never really existed. Tradition has it that he lived in the first or second century before Christ, and *The Little Clay Cart*, a Sanskrit drama of political intrigue and romantic comedy has been attributed to him by tradition. The *Sutradhara*, a later Sanskrit manuscript, ascribes the play to him and describes him as a student of the *Vedas*, a mathematician, and an expert on women and elephants. Shudraka's authorship of the play is disputed, however, and some scholars believe that its author was Dandin (fl. 7th century), a Sanskrit author best known for a picaresque narrative entitled *Dasakumāracharita* (*The Adventures of the Ten Princes*). It may well be, however, that neither Shudraka nor Dandin actually wrote the play, for it seems to date from the fifth century of the Christian era, six or seven centuries after Shudraka's supposed dates and about two centuries before Dandin's lifetime. It seems likely that *The Little Clay Cart* was written at the beginnings of a golden age of Sanskrit drama under the Gupta kings of Kanauj, who ruled over the greater part of India during the fourth and fifth centuries of the Christian era. The play would belong then to that great age of Sanskrit drama which includes the anonymous *Mudrārākṣasa* (*The Prime Minister's Ring*) and Kalidasa's famous *Sakuntala*.

BIBLIOGRAPHICAL REFERENCE: For an excellent background study of Indian drama see A. Bernedale Keith, *The Sanskrit Drama in Its Origin, Development, Theory and Practice*, 1924.

SIR PHILIP SIDNEY

Born: Penshurst, England
Date: November 30, 1554

Died: Arnhem, Netherlands
Date: October 17, 1586

PRINCIPAL WORKS

POEMS: *Astrophel and Stella*, 1591.
PROSE ROMANCE: *Arcadia*, 1590.
CRITICAL ESSAY: *Defence of Poesie*, 1595 (also called *Apologie for Poetry*).

Although Philip Sidney came from a noble family, he received no title until 1583, when he was knighted. His father, Sir Henry Sidney, was a member of a highborn family, and most of Philip Sidney's near relatives were titled; but for most of his life Sidney was poor. A man of steadfast character, he was affected somewhat by the vicissitudes of his life, but his influence on English literature was that of a chivalrous, courtly gentleman.

Born at Penshurst, in Kent, on November 30, 1554, he was entered at Shrewsbury School, near Ludlow Castle, in 1564, and from there he went to Oxford in 1568; he also studied at Cambridge. In 1572 he started an extended tour of Europe. Throughout his life Sidney was intensely interested in learning. He studied the writers of the past but was not bound to them, having an independent spirit. He was generally recognized as a young man of charm, intelligence, and good judgment.

He returned to England in 1575 and remained at court until he was sent to Austria and Germany in 1577. While in England, he labored sedulously to defend his father's policies and position. By 1578 he was becoming known in the world of letters. In that year he wrote *The Lady of the May*, a masque performed before the queen. But his success at court was short-lived; he was disgraced along with the Earl of Leicester, in whose affairs he had become involved. His virtual banishment to the home of his sister, the Countess of Pembroke, at Wilton, may well have been a blessing, for it was there that he began writing the *Arcadia* for his sister's amusement. This work, first begun in 1580, was later revised and added to by Sidney, and the later version is usually considered to be better.

Sidney, permitted to return to court, wrote the great sonnet sequence, *Astrophel and Stella*, which is perhaps best known. The "Stella" in this largely autobiographical and very sincere poetic narrative was Penelope Devereux, daughter of the Earl of Essex, and an early love of Sidney's. The lady had been forced into a marriage of convenience with Lord Rich, and some of Sidney's disappointment may be sensed in these sonnets.

In 1583 Sidney was knighted, and in the same year he married Frances, the daughter of Sir Francis Walsingham. Before and during these events Sidney had been producing what was probably the most truly influential piece of writing he ever did. This was his *Defence of Poesie*, which raised an almost wholly new set of standards for English poetry. By poesie Sidney meant any form of imaginative writing.

Sir Philip Sidney was more than a courtier or literary figure; he was also a man of affairs. A champion of the Protestant cause in Europe, with his primary animosity directed against Spain, in 1585 he was given a command in Holland and made governor of Flushing. He engaged valiantly in several battles during that year. On September 22, 1586, he was severely wounded in a cavalry charge. The famous story is often told, as an example of Sidney's fine sense of humanity and chivalry, of how he refused a cup of water and ordered it to be given to a soldier near him on the battlefield. Sidney died of his wound on October 17, 1586. Following his death he was universally mourned and widely elegized.

Because none of his writing was actually published during his lifetime, most of Sidney's widespread influence was posthumous; nevertheless it was considerable: His *Arcadia*, although essentially a romance, achieves epic qualities and contains some richly developed passages; his *Astrophel and Stella*, perhaps the most fully written sonnet sequence in English, shows a marked improvement in poetic technique over its forerunners; and, with the writing of *Defence of Poesie*, he injected into the rich blood of English literature a necessary impetus toward imaginative but restrained writing. The influence of his genius was felt throughout English writing of the following centuries.

BIBLIOGRAPHICAL REFERENCES: Sidney's writings have been collected in *The Complete Works of Sir Philip Sidney*, edited by A. Feuillerat, 4 vols., 1912–1926, including both versions of the *Arcadia*. The best edition of the *Poems* is that of W. A. Ringler, 1962. The most important studies of his life and works in English are J. A. Symonds, *Sir Philip Sidney*, English Men of Letters Series, 1886; M. W. Wallace, *The Life of Sir Philip Sidney*, 1915; Mona Wilson, *Sir Philip Sidney*, 1932; and A. H. Hill, *Astrophel*, 1937. Of particular importance, in French, is Michael Poirier, *Sir Philip Sidney, le chevalier poète élizabéthain*, 1948. A more specialized study is K. O. Myrick, *Sir Philip Sidney as a Literary Craftsman*, 1940. For complete references see S. A. Tannenbaum, *Sir Philip Sidney: A Concise Bibliography*, 1941.

Recent studies include R. L. Montgomery, *Symmetry and Sense, the Poetry of Sir Philip Sidney*, 1961; W. R. Davis and Richard Lanham, *Sidney's Arcadia*, 1965; A. G. D. Wiles, "Parallel Analyses of the Two Versions of Sidney's Arcadia," *Studies in Philology*, XXXIX (1942), 167–206; F. L. Townsend, "Sidney and Ariosto," *Publications of the Modern Language Association*, LXI (1946), 97–108; P. A. Duhamel, "Sidney's *Arcadia* and Elizabethan Rhetoric," *Studies in Philology*, XLV (1948), 119–133; and Michael F. Krouse, "Plato and Sidney's *Defence of Poesie*," *Comparative Literature*, VI (1954), 138–147.

HENRYK SIENKIEWICZ

Born: Wola Okrzejska, Poland
Date: May 5, 1846

Died: Vevey, Switzerland
Date: November 15, 1916

Principal Works

NOVELS: *Ogniem i mieczem*, 1884 (*With Fire and Sword*); *Potop*, 1886 (*The Deluge*); *Pan Wołodyjowski*, 1887–1888 (*Pan Michael*); *Bez dogmatu*, 1891 (*Without Dogma*); *Rodzina Połanieckich*, 1895 (*Children of the Soil*); *Quo Vadis?* 1896; *Krzyżacy*, 1900 (*The Teutonic Knights*).

Poland's greatest novelist was born on May 5, 1846, near Lukow, in Russian Poland, of a family that belonged to the country gentry. Educated by a tutor who shared his interest in history with his charge, Henryk Sienkiewicz attended the University of Warsaw. There, as one of the Young Positivist admirers of Auguste Comte, he became convinced that all knowledge can be observed through the human senses, including not only colors and sounds, but also their interrelationship. Although he and the other Positivists did not follow their master in scorning the microscope as an attempt to peer beyond human observation, they were interested in the how, rather than the why, of changes. This group largely revolutionized Poland's literary life following the 1863 revolt against Russia; then, and throughout his life, Sienkiewicz was noted for his hatred of Russia.

He began his literary career with his humorous *A Prophet in his Own Country* (1872). Four years later, motivated by his anti-Russian feelings as well as by a spirit of adventure, he emigrated from Poland as a member of a socialistic colony that settled at Anaheim, near Los Angeles. He remained in the United States until 1878, studying the life of Polish immigrants and sending articles back to newspapers in Warsaw. The differences in culture between Poland and the United States, as well as the unwillingness of the colonists to co-operate brought failure to the project. Sienkiewicz returned to Warsaw to make his living as a journalist.

Reading Scott and Dumas inspired him to do something similar for his own land. Discarding his Positivist theories, he began a trilogy dealing with seventeenth century Poland as it tried to establish national unity through wars with the Swedes, Turks, and Cossacks. In *With Fire and Sword*, *The Deluge*, and *Pan Michael*, the central character, Zagloba, has been likened to Falstaff and to Ulysses because of his combination of heroism and buffoonery.

Interested also in psychology and modern social problems, Sienkiewicz wrote about contemporary Poland in *Without Dogma*, and *Children of the Soil*. After these works he apparently realized that his real talent lay in the romantic field, for he returned to the manner of his earlier successes and in *Quo Vadis?* re-created in colorful detail Roman life under Nero. The best developed character in the novel is the epicure Petronius Arbiter. Since one of the purposes of Sienkiewicz's writing was "to strengthen the heart and to help maintain the Polish national spirit," he included in his Roman picture two Polish countrymen, the heroine Lygia and the giant Ursus. The popularity of the novel was enormous. Translated into thirty languages, it is undoubtedly the best known work of Polish literature, far better known than the same author's four-volume *The Teutonic Knights,* also known as *The Knights of the Cross.* The narrowness of Sienkiewicz's intellectual sympathies is frequently blamed for some of the flaws in this and his other novels, yet his ability to write with dash and fire has never been questioned; his award of the Nobel Prize for literature in 1905 was universally acclaimed.

Because of his literary status and his anti-Russian sentiments, Sienkiewicz was frequently sought by the patriots to lead them in their movement for the liberation of Poland. During the First World War, he and the pianist Paderewski organized a committee to help Polish war victims. While working for the Polish Red Cross in Switzerland, Sienkiewicz died at Vevey on November 15, 1916. In 1924 his body was taken to Cracow, former capital of Poland, for burial in the ancient cathedral.

BIBLIOGRAPHICAL REFERENCES: Most of Sienkiewicz's novels are available in translation. The most comprehensive biographical study in English is Monica M. Gardner, *The Patriotic Novelist of Poland, Henryk Sienkiewicz,* 1926. See also Waclaw Lednicki, *Henryk Sienkiewicz,* 1946, and *Bits of Table Talk,* 1956; Mieczyslaw Giergielewicz, *Henryk Sienkiewicz,* 1968; W. L. Phelps, *Essays on Modern Novelists,* 1910; and L. E. Van Norman, "Henryk Sienkiewicz's Poland," *Bookman,* XLIV (1917), 412–426.

FRANS EEMIL SILLANPÄÄ

Born: Hämeenkyrö, Finland
Date: September 16, 1888

Died: Helsinki, Finland
Date: June 3, 1964

Principal Works

NOVELS: *Hurskas kurjuus,* 1919 (*Meek Heritage*); *Hiltu ja Ragnar,* 1923 (*Hiltu and Ragnar*); *Nuorena nukkunut,* 1931 (*The Maid Silja;* also *Fallen Asleep While Young*); *Miehen tie,* 1932 (*A Man's Road*); *Ihmiset suviyössä,* 1934 (*People in a Summer Night*); *Elokuu,* 1941 (*Harvest Month*).
SHORT STORIES: *Töllinmäki,* 1925.
MISCELLANEOUS: *Kerron ja kuvailen,* 1954 (tales, sketches, meditations).

Frans Eemil Sillanpää, winner of the Nobel Prize for literature in 1939, began life as a peasant's son in the Finnish town of Hämeenkyrö, September 16, 1888. As a child he displayed a great aptitude for science; consequently he was sent to the Imperial Alexander University at Helsingfors. But at the university he found more excitement in the company of writers, artists, and musicians (among whom, at that time, was the composer Sibelius) than he did in the laboratory. As a result of this new interest, he faced a great emotional crisis in his life. Having decided that his vocation was writing, he left the university without taking his examinations for a degree and returned home on Christmas Eve of 1913. Since that time his interests followed no other course.

He published his first novel in 1916 and in that same year married a servant girl who was to bear him seven children. His second novel, *Meek Heritage,* concerned with the clash of the Reds and the Whites in the Finnish Revolution, won him fame in his own country and a government pension for life. Translated into a number of languages, the novel also helped to establish his international reputation. *The Maid Silja,* published in 1931, was equally popular at home and abroad. In 1936 Sillanpää was made an honorary doctor of philosophy by the Finnish government. Three years later he was awarded the Nobel Prize.

BIBLIOGRAPHICAL REFERENCES: For brief studies of Sillanpää in English see L. Viljanen, "Sillanpää," *American-Scandinavian Review,* XXVIII (1940), 49–53; R. Beck, "Sillanpää—Finland's Winner of the Nobel Prize," *Poet Lore,* XLVI (1940), 358–363; and Agnes Rothery, "Novels from Finland," *Virginia Quarterly Review,* XVI (1940), 296–299. For more extended studies see T. Vaaskivi, *Frans Eemil Sillanpää,* 1937; Edwin J. H. Linkomies, *Sillanpää,* 1948; and Rafael Koskimies, *Sillanpää,* 1948.

IGNAZIO SILONE

Born: Pescina dei Marsi, Italy
Date: May 1, 1900

Principal Works

NOVELS: *Fontamara, 1933; Pane e vino,* 1936 (*Bread and Wine*); *Il Seme sotto la neve,* 1940 (*The Seed Beneath the Snow*); *Una manciata di more,* 1952 (*A Handful of Blackberries*); *Il segreto di Luca,* 1956 (*The Secret of Luca*); *La volpe e le camelie,* 1960 (*The Fox and the Camellias*).
PLAYS: *Ed egli si nascose,* 1945 (*And He Hid Himself*); *L'avventura d'un povero cristiano,* 1968 (*The Story of a Humble Christian*).
SATIRE: *La scuola dei dittatori,* 1938 (*The School for Dictators*).
ESSAYS: *Uscita di sicurezza,* 1965 (*Emergency Exit*).

Ignazio Silone was born on May 1, 1900, in Pescina dei Marsi in the Abruzzi district of the Italian Apennines. His real name, Secondo Tranquilli, later was dropped to save his family from Fascist persecution. Born the son of a small landowner, he became active in the labor movement as a young boy. In 1917, as secretary for the land workers of the Abruzzi district, he was brought into court on charges of organizing an anti-war demonstration. One of the founders of the Italian Communist Party, by 1921 he was editor of a weekly newspaper in Rome and a daily in Trieste. Even after Mussolini's rise to power, Silone remained in Italy, printing illegal newspapers and carrying out other assignments. He also made trips to Moscow in 1921 and 1927 for the Italian Communist Party. Before he broke with the Party in 1930 and became anti-Communist, he had lost a brother who had died in a Fascist prison and he himself had been imprisoned and then expelled in various European countries.

Taking up residence in Switzerland in 1930, he set to work on his first novel, published in 1933 as *Fontamara.* It describes the systematic destruction by the Black Shirts of a small Italian town which has attempted to resist the Facists. A propagandistic novel which is nonetheless powerful and affecting, it ends with a plea for action against the scourge. Silone's finest book, *Bread and Wine,* tells the story of Pietro Spina, a revolutionist who returns to the Abruzzi district for refuge while he tries to regain his health. Disguised as a priest, he finds the best aspects of his youthful religiousness returning. Carrying out his undercover work, he achieves a kind of regeneration, attempting a fusion of the best of both Christianity and Marxism. *The School for Dictators* was a book of satiric dialogues against Fascism. His third novel, *The Seed Beneath the Snow,* followed the further activities of Pietro Spina among the peasants and small landowners of Silone's native district. With the Allied invasion of Italy, Silone slipped back into Italy disguised as a priest and spent the remainder of the war as a member of the underground.

In 1945 Silone published a drama, *And He Hid Himself,* which was based on the activities of Pietro Spina. At the war's end he became manager of the newspaper *Avanti!* and, as a member of the Constituent Assembly, the leader of the left wing of the Italian Democratic Socialist Party. In 1952, two years after he had retired from political life to devote himself to literature, Silone published *A Handful of Blackberries*. This novel, set in postwar Italy, was the powerful story of an ex-Communist's attempt to break away from the Party, despite its retributory attempts against him and his sweetheart, and to resume his work for the peasants against the great landowners. Silone is now active in Italian and international writers' associations. Recent novels are a philosophical tale, *The Secret of Luke*, and a political tale, *The Fox and The Camellias*. His play, *The Story of a Humble Christian*, deals with the life of Celestine V who abdicated the Papacy in 1294. Critics are sharply divided on its merits.

BIBLIOGRAPHICAL REFERENCES: Aside from reviews of individual books, there is very little helpful criticism of Silone in English. See Edmund Wilson, "Two Survivors: Malraux and Silone," *New Yorker*, XXI (September 8, 1945), 74–78+; James T. Farrell, "Ignazio Silone," *Southern Review*, IV (1939), 771–783; and Julien Steinberg, *Verdict of Three Decades*, 1950. See also articles in R. W. B. Lewis, *The Picaresque Saint: Representative Figures in Contemporary Fiction*, 1959; and William R. Mueller, *The Prophetic Voice in Modern Fiction*, 1959.

WILLIAM GILMORE SIMMS

Born: Charleston, South Carolina *Died:* Charleston
Date: April 17, 1806 *Date:* June 11, 1870

Principal Works

NOVELS: *Guy Rivers*, 1834; *The Partisan*, 1835; *The Yemassee*, 1835; *Mellichampe*, 1836; *Pelayo*, 1838; *Richard Hurdis*, 1838; *The Damsel of Darien*, 1839; *The Border Beagles*, 1840; *The Kinsmen*, 1841 (*The Scout*, 1854); *Beauchampe*, 1842; *Helen Halsey*, 1845; *Count Julian*, 1845; *Katherine Walton*, 1851; *The Golden Christmas*, 1852; *As Good as A Comedy*, 1852; *Vasconselos*, 1853; *The Sword and Distaff*, 1853 (*Woodcraft*, 1854); *The Forayers*, 1855; *Eutaw*, 1856; *Charlemont*, 1856; *The Cassique of Kiawah*, 1859.

SHORT STORIES: *The Wigwam and the Cabin*, 1845–1846.

HISTORY: *A History of South Carolina*, 1840; *South Carolina in the Revolution*, 1854.

POEM: *Atalantis*, 1832.

William Gilmore Simms, born in Charleston, South Carolina, on April 17, 1806, was known in his lifetime as a novelist, short story writer, poet, historian, and journalist; but his reputation rests today on his novels.

Simms's childhood was an unusual one. His mother died while he was still an infant, and his father left the baby in the care of its maternal grandmother. Under her care he seems to have had but casual schooling, but he read widely and listened intently to his grandmother's stories of the Revolutionary War as it had occurred in the South. In 1816, when the boy was ten years old, his father, a frontiersman who had gone westward toward the Mississippi River, paid a visit to Charleston, and eight years later the boy went to visit his father on his plantation in what is now Mississippi. Upon his return to Charleston after that visit Simms published some poems, most of them with a Byronic flavor. In 1828 he entered upon the editorship of a short-lived magazine entitled *The Tablet*. After its failure he became editor of the Charleston *City Gazette*, which opposed the election of John C. Calhoun. Because of the political animosity he incurred as a result, plus the deaths of his wife, grandmother, and father, Simms left for the North, where he found friends and a future.

Some early work was published shortly after he left Charleston, but his first important success came with the publication of *Guy Rivers* in 1834. A story of gold-mining in northern Georgia, the novel, packed with action, is a romantic piece of writing, but one with a realistic, native theme. His next work was *The Partisan*, which was probably inspired by his grandmother's accounts of the Revolutionary War. In the same year appeared *The Yemassee*, destined to remain his most popular book. It is an exciting tale of early days in South Carolina, especially important because of the realistic portrayal of the Indians. Indeed Simms's portrayal of the Indians has been adjudged by scholars to be essentially better than the more popular, idealized pictures given by James Fenimore Cooper in his novels. Simms's realism was a little too much for his own day. Two of his novels, *Beauchampe* and

Charlemont, both about a celebrated Kentucky murder case, were considered in his lifetime too realistic for what was then called good taste, although they seem tame enough for today.

Following his second marriage in 1836, Simms's life began to change. Filling the position of a wealthy planter on his wife's plantation and rearing a family of fifteen children made him an outstanding spokesman for the Southern notion of Greek democracy in America, a concept which implied a defense of slavery. Simms's theories on slavery were found in his *History of South Carolina*. His viewpoint and his reputation as an author made him a great man in the South, but they caused unpopularity in the North. While his works were in vogue before the Civil War, they were neglected afterward. All Simms's important writing came before that war, for while the war ruined his reputation in the North, it also destroyed his home and way of life in the South.

Simms's reputation has been slow in returning. For a half century his books were out of print, except for *The Yemassee*. A frequent comparison of Simms to Cooper as a novelist generally is without critical foundation and really unfair to Simms. His novels are vigorous, and the materials he used and the realism he employed were his own. He wrote about South Carolina during the eighteenth century and about the pre-Civil War frontier, then east of the Mississippi River. He celebrated little-known elements of American history and culture. In three kinds of fiction he excelled: the border romance, of which *Guy Rivers* is his best; the novel of Indian warfare, of which *The Yemassee* is a classic; and the romance about the American Revolution, of which *The Partisan* is a good example. In addition to fiction, poetry and history, Simms also wrote biographies of Francis Marion, Captain John Smith, and Nathaniel Greene.

Simms died in Charleston, June 11, 1870.

BIBLIOGRAPHICAL REFERENCES: *The Works of William Gilmore Simms*, 20 vols., 1853–1866 is not complete. *The Letters of William Gilmore Simms* have been edited by Mary C. Simms Oliphant, Alfred T. Odell, and T. C. D. Eaves, 5 vols., 1952–1956. The standard biography is William P. Trent, *William Gilmore Simms*, 1892. Alexander Cowie's 1937 edition of *The Yemassee* includes an introduction and an excellent bibliography. Outstanding studies of Simms appear in Vernon L. Parrington, *Main Currents in American Thought*, Vol. II, 1927; Van Wyck Brooks, *The World of Washington Irving*, 1944; and Jay B. Hubbell, *The South in American Literature, 1607–1900*, 1954, the latter the leading work on the subject of Southern literature. See further E. W. Parks, *William Gilmore Simms as Literary Critic*, 1961; and J. V. Ridgely, *William Gilmore Simms*, 1962.

MAY SINCLAIR

Born: Rock Ferry, Cheshire, England
Date: 1865 (?)

Died: Aylesbury, England
Date: November 14, 1946

Principal Works

NOVELS: *Audrey Craven*, 1897; *Two Sides of a Question*, 1901; *The Divine Fire*, 1904; *The Helpmate*, 1907; *The Creators*, 1910; *The Three Sisters*, 1914; *Tasker Jevons*, 1916 [*The Belfry*]; *The Tree of Heaven*, 1917; *Mary Olivier*, 1919; *Mr. Waddington of Wyck*, 1921; *Anne Severn and the Fieldings*, 1922; *The Life and Death of Harriet Frean*, 1922; *A Cure of Souls*, 1924; *The Rector of Wyck*, 1925.
SHORT STORIES: *The Judgment of Eve*, 1908 [*The Return of the Prodigal*]; *Uncanny Stories*, 1923; *The Intercessor*, 1931.
POEM: *The Dark Night*, 1924.
BIOGRAPHY: *The Three Brontës*, 1912.

May Sinclair is an unusual British author in that her work found a wider, more enthusiastic audience in America than it did in her native England. Born in Cheshire, probably in 1865, she was educated at home and at Ladies' College, Cheltenham. As a girl she wrote poetry and philosophical criticism, some of which was published. Her first published short story appeared in 1895, and her first novel, *Audrey Craven*, in 1897. But real fame as a novelist waited for almost a decade, until the publication of *The Divine Fire* in 1904. A biography, *The Three Brontës*, published in 1912, was followed by another successful novel, *The Three Sisters*, which showed the influence of her Brontës studies.

During World War I May Sinclair, who was then and throughout her life unmarried, served with an ambulance unit on the front in Belgium and worked with the Hoover Relief Commission. After World War I she lived a quiet life that was unbroken except for several visits to the United States. Miss Sinclair worked steadily, producing more than a dozen books, until invalidism made writing impossible. Outstanding among her later books are *Mary Olivier* and *Anne Severn and the Fieldings*. *Uncanny Stories* is a volume of short fiction reflecting her interest in the supernatural and spiritualism. Her lifelong interest in philosophy, especially idealism, resulted in a study, *The New Idealism* (1922). In the 1920's she wrote several light satirical comedies of manners; *Mr. Waddington of Wyck* and *A Cure of Souls* belong to this genre. *The Dark Night* is a long narrative poem.

As early as the writing of *Mary Olivier*, May Sinclair had begun utilizing the subconscious in her fiction, very much in the manner of Dorothy Richardson, and she has been termed one of the pioneers in the stream-of-consciousness technique. As a young woman she was a suffragette, and throughout her life she maintained an interest in feminist movements. She died on November 14, 1946, at Aylesbury, England.

BIBLIOGRAPHICAL REFERENCES: May Sinclair has received very little critical attention. See Frank Swinnerton, *The Georgian Literary Scene*, 1934; W. C. Frierson, *The English Novel in Transition*, 1942; C. A. Dawson Scott, "May Sinclair," *Book-*

man, LII (1920), 246–249; and Jean de Bosschere, "Charity in the Work of May Sinclair," *Yale Review*, XIV (1924), 82–94.

UPTON SINCLAIR

Born: Baltimore, Maryland
Date: September 20, 1878

Died: Bound Brook, New Jersey
Date: November 25, 1968

Principal Works

NOVELS: *The Journal of Arthur Stirling,* 1903; *The Jungle,* 1906; *The Metropolis,* 1908; *King Coal,* 1917; *100%,* 1920; *They Call Me Carpenter,* 1922; *Oil! A Novel,* 1927; *Boston,* 1928; *Mountain City,* 1930; *Roman Holiday,* 1931; *Co-op,* 1936; *Little Steel,* 1938; *World's End,* 1940; *Between Two Worlds,* 1941; *Dragon's Teeth,* 1942; *Wide Is the Gate,* 1943; *Presidential Agent,* 1944; *Dragon Harvest,* 1945; *A World to Win,* 1946; *Presidential Mission,* 1947; *One Clear Call,* 1948; *O Shepherd, Speak!,* 1949; *Another Pamela; or, Virtue Still Rewarded,* 1950; *The Return of Lanny Budd,* 1953; *What Didymus Did,* 1954; *It Happened to Didymus,* 1958; *Affectionately Eve,* 1961.

PLAYS: *Plays of Protest,* 1912; *Singing Jailbirds,* 1924; *Bill Porter,* 1925; *Oil!,* 1925; *Depression Island,* 1935; *Marie Antoinette,* 1939; *The Enemy Had It Too,* 1950.

ESSAYS AND STUDIES: *Our Bourgeois Literature,* 1905; *The Profits of Religion,* 1918; *The Brass Check: A Study in American Journalism,* 1919; *The Goose-Step: A Study of American Education,* 1923; *The Goslings: A Study of the American Schools,* 1924; *Mammonmart,* 1925; *The Cup of Fury,* 1956.

AUTOBIOGRAPHY: *My Lifetime in Letters,* 1960; *The Autobiography of Upton Sinclair,* 1962.

Upton (Beall) Sinclair was one of the most prolific writers, one of the most widely read, and one of the least recognized writers of his time. The trouble lies probably in the tractarian nature of his writings, for from the beginning of his career Sinclair was a reformer. His book, *The Cup of Fury,* published in 1956, is an analysis of the effect of alcohol, with the conclusion that other writers, had they abstained from liquor like Upton Sinclair, would have been greater writers and would have written much more. The book is, in effect, an old-fashioned temperance tract, an attempt to reform.

Born in Baltimore, Maryland, on September 20, 1878, Sinclair began his career as a prodigy. He finished secondary school when he was twelve and became a student at the City College of New York at the age of fourteen. From the age of fifteen he supported himself in part by writing stories for the pulp magazines. After finishing college, he married in 1900 and, while threatened with poverty, began to write serious novels. His first five books, published between 1901 and 1906, gave him little encouragement, for they produced together less than a thousand dollars. Before leaving college Sinclair had become a Socialist, and his political views influenced his writing. His first fame came with the publication of *The Jungle,* an exposé of the Chicago stockyards which, in its final chapters, becomes a mere Socialist tract. With the proceeds of this book, which was a best seller that still finds readers, Sinclair founded Helicon Hall, a cooperative community at which Sinclair Lewis was temporarily a furnace man. Upton Sinclair continued to write at a furious pace, also becoming a publisher during 1918–1919 with *Upton Sinclair's Magazine.* Beginning with *The Profits of Religion,* in 1918, he wrote a series of non-fictional works on the effects of capitalism in America, from the viewpoint of a Socialist. The series, which has the collective title of *The Dead Hand,* reviewed such phases of American culture as the schools, the colleges, newspapers and publishing, art, and literature.

In private life, as well as in public life, Upton Sinclair had difficulties. He was divorced in 1911 and remarried in 1913. In 1915 he and his second wife, Mary Craig Kimbrough, a poetess, moved to California. In 1923 Sinclair founded the California chapter of the American Civil Liberties Union. Several times he ran for political office, seeking seats in the U.S. House of Representatives and the Senate. He also ran for the governorship of California, twice as a Socialist and once, in 1934, as a Democratic nominee.

In his novels of the period 1917–1940, Upton Sinclair exploited many areas of contemporary life. *King Coal* described conditions in the Colorado coal fields. *Oil!* described life in the oil fields of California, with looks also at the young motion picture industry. *Little Steel* described conditions and strikes in the steel mills during the 1930's.

During the thirteen years between 1940 and 1953, Upton Sinclair labored at a series of novels relating the events of the whole world from 1913 to 1950, including World War I, the peace negotiations after that war, the rise to power of Hitler and Mussolini, the Spanish Civil War, the Munich debacle, Roosevelt's election and re-elections, World War II, and the aftermath of World War II. The whole series is tied together picaresquely and romantically by the character of Lanny Budd, son of a wealthy munitions manufacturer. Lanny Budd, a young man with Socialist leanings, travels far and wide, meets many people, happens usually to be at the right spot at the right time, and even serves as a special agent for Franklin D. Roosevelt.

More recent works by Sinclair include *Another Pamela* (1950), a twentieth-century version of Richardson's novel about virtue rewarded; *The Enemy Had It Too,* a play about the atomic age; and *A Personal Jesus* (1952), Sinclair's own interpretation of the Christ.

Probably no contemporary American writer of fiction has been read by so many people in this country and abroad or been translated into so many languages. Upton Sinclair has been a best seller in other countries when he was not one at home, but that popularity probably rests on social and political bases, rather than on any artistic values. At times Sinclair employed pseudonyms, among them Clarke Fitch, Frederick Garrison, and Arthur Stirling.

BIBLIOGRAPHICAL REFERENCES: There are two convenient compilations of Sinclair's work, *An Upton Sinclair Anthology,* edited by I. O. Evans, 1934; and *Upton Sinclair Anthology,* edited by Irving Stone and Lewis Browne, 1947. Of primary interest is Sinclair's autobiography, *American Outpost: A Book of Reminiscences,* 1932 (published in England as *Candid Reminiscences: My First Thirty Years*). A significant early evaluation is Floyd Dell, *Upton Sinclair: A Study in Social Protest,* 1927. A range of critical estimates may be found in Van Wyck Brooks, *Emerson and Others,* 1927; Harry Hartwick, *The Foreground of American Fiction,* 1934; Harlan Hatcher, *Creating the Modern American Novel,* 1935; and A. H. Quinn, *American Fiction,*

1936. See also Walter Lippmann, "Upton Sinclair," *Saturday Review of Literature,* IV (1928), 641–643; and George J. Becker, "Upton Sinclair: Quixote in a Flivver," *College English,* XXI (1959), 133–140.

ISRAEL JOSHUA SINGER

Born: Bilgoraj, Poland
Date: November 30, 1893

Died: New York, N. Y.
Date: February 10, 1944

Principal Works

NOVELS: *The Brothers Ashkenazi,* tr., 1936; *East of Eden,* tr., 1939.
SHORT STORIES: *Pearl,* 1922; *The River Breaks Up,* 1938.
PLAY: *Yoshe Kalb,* 1932 (*The Sinners*).

Israel Joshua Singer, Yiddish writer, was born on November 30, 1893, in Bilgoraj, Poland. The son of a rabbi, he studied the Talmud as a boy, but at seventeen developed more worldly interests which led him finally to newspaper work. In 1922 he became the Warsaw representative of the *Jewish Daily Forward.* The paper sent him to Russia in 1926 and made him an editor when he emigrated to the United States in 1934.

Pearl, his first volume of stories, was highly successful in Europe and it was followed by more stories and a book about Russia, but Singer's reputation rests on two novels: *The Brothers Ashkenazi,* translated in 1936 and sent through eleven editions before 1939, and *East of Eden,* translated in 1939. The first shows the social, economic, and political forces which affect an industrial town in Poland in the course of the nineteenth century and focuses on the contrasting fortunes of twin brothers. The more somber *East of Eden* traces the desperate careers of a poor, dispossessed family and particularly of the son who turns hopefully to communism, only to be bitterly disillusioned. A dramatic adaptation of a third novel, *The Sinners,* added to Singer's fame when it was produced in New York in 1932.

Singer died in New York on February 10, 1944.

BIBLIOGRAPHICAL REFERENCES: There is no full-length biographical or critical study. See John Cournos, "Three Novelists: Asch, Singer and Schnéour," *Menorah Journal* XXV (1937), 81–91; and Charles Madison Allen, "I. J. Singer: Novelist of Satirical Pessimism," *Yiddish Literature,* 1968, 449–478.

ELSIE SINGMASTER

Born: Schuylkill Haven, Pennsylvania Died: Gettysburg, Pennsylvania
Date: August 29, 1879 Date: September 30, 1958

Principal Works

NOVELS: *Katy Gaumer,* 1915; *Basil Everman,* 1920; *Ellen Levis,* 1921; *Bennett Malin,* 1922; *The Hidden Road,* 1923; *Keller's Anna Ruth,* 1926; *What Everybody Wanted,* 1928; *Swords of Steel,* 1933; *The Magic Mirror,* 1934; *The Loving Heart,* 1937; *Rifles for Washington,* 1938; *A High Wind Rising,* 1942; *I Speak for Thaddeus Stevens,* 1947; *I Heard of a River,* 1948.

SHORT STORIES: *Gettysburg,* 1913; *Bred in the Bone,* 1925; *Stories to Read at Christmas,* 1940.

JUVENILES: *Emmeline,* 1916; *John Baring's House,* 1920; *A Boy at Gettysburg,* 1924; *"Sewing Susie,"* 1927; *Virginia's Bandit,* 1929; *You Make Your Own Luck,* 1929; *Stories of Pennsylvania* (I-IV), 1937–1940; *The Isle of Que,* 1948.

REGIONAL STUDY: *Pennsylvania's Susquehanna,* 1950.

The fiction of Elsie Singmaster may be clearly charted in geography and time. She is the novelist of Pennsylvania, more particularly of the Pennsylvania German region from the colonial period to the present. First in time are her stories of the early settlements in *A High Wind Rising* and *I Heard of a River,* set against the years when French and Indian raiders swept over the Warrior Road and Carlisle and Lancaster stood on a disputed frontier between the French lands on the Ohio and English territory along the Schuylkill and the Delaware. Later the history of the state widens into the history of the nation in her Revolutionary War novel, *Rifles for Washington,* and again in *I Speak for Thaddeus Stevens* and in her stories of the three bloody days at Gettysburg in 1863. For a later time she has written novels and tales of small-town and country life. These are regional rather than historical, for in them she makes vivid and real the Pennsylvania German countryside of red barns and fieldstone houses, the landscape of her sturdy, patriarchal Mennonites, Dunkers, and Amish, with their strange religious dress, their slow unchanging ways of conduct and belief, their simple pieties and old superstitions. This is her own region as well, and she has brought to it her whole vision and understanding as a writer.

Elsie Singmaster was born on August 29, 1879, in the Lutheran parsonage at Schuylkill Haven, Pennsylvania. Her father, the Reverend John Alden Singmaster, had among his ancestors one who studied under Martin Luther and another who was the first Lutheran minister ordained in this country. Part of her childhood was spent at Macungie, the Millerstown of her fiction, where her father had been called to a pastorate of six churches between Allentown and Reading, and she gathered impressions of this locality as she drove about with him when he went to preach to the different congregations in his charge. English was always spoken in the Singmaster home, Mrs. Singmaster being a Quaker of English descent, but from playmates and neighbors the younger Singmasters learned the hybrid mixture of English and German known as Pennsylvania Dutch. This was the only language known to the first teacher who taught her rhetoric.

If her early education was at best rudimentary, there were always good books to read in her father's library. By the time she was eleven she had begun to write stories of her own. Later, at Cornell and Radcliffe, she continued to write sketches of Pennsylvania life and character, partly to set down her observations clearly and partly to explain a foreign-seeming group of people whom she thought misunderstood. She sold her first story in 1905. By the time of her graduation from Radcliffe in 1907 she had already contributed to *Scribner's, Century,* and the *Atlantic Monthly.* In 1912 she married Harold Lewars, a musician, and went to live in Harrisburg. After his death in 1915 she made her permanent home in Gettysburg, where her father was the president of the Lutheran theological seminary.

Elsie Singmaster had already written a number of stories and several books for children when she published *Katy Gaumer,* her first novel, in 1915. Katy is one of Miss Singmaster's typical heroines, a Pennsylvania German girl eager to acquire the learning which will prepare her for life in a larger world. *Basil Everman,* its scene a college town which may be identified as Gettysburg, deals with the influence a young writer of genius has on a group of people of the college and the town many years after his death. *Ellen Levis* and *Keller's Anna Ruth* are stories of gentle, self-sacrificing young women, handicapped by environment, who in the end win for themselves a better future according to their natures and their needs. *Bennett Malin,* darker in mood and implications, tells of a man who builds a false, bright world about himself on a shaky foundation of literary theft. *What Everybody Wanted* shifts its scene to Maryland to present a light and amusing account of human vanity and desire. *The Magic Mirror,* making a return to a more familiar Pennsylvania setting, brings to life a community, a countryside, and a strange but rich way of life through the experiences of Jesse Hummer, whose ambition is to tell the story of his people after he becomes a writer.

Her later novels reveal a renewed interest in historical themes. In *Rifles for Washington* she presents the events and battles of seven years of war from a boy's point of view because she wanted to stress the element of action, the sense of things happening, which would make the deepest impression on a boy's mind. Like many of her stories, this book is juvenile fiction only in the sense that it deals with a youthful hero. *A High Wind Rising* is a regional chronicle dealing with the early settlements and the part played by the Pennsylvania Germans under Conrad Weiser in holding the land for the English during the French and Indian wars. *I Speak for Thaddeus Stevens* is a biographical novel throwing new light on the powerful political figure of the Civil War period. *I Heard of a River* is another story of the early settlements. Of Miss Singmaster's short stories, the most vivid and moving are the Civil War tales in *Gettysburg,* the most amusing her stories of the Mennonite Shindledecker sisters in *Bred in the Bone.* Much of her magazine fiction has never been collected.

A writer of quiet but satisfying richness and depth within her chosen field, Elsie Singmaster has never attracted a wide reading public or the attention of popular criticism. One reason may be that as examples of work done within a clearly defined regional tradition, her books have owed almost nothing to literary fashion. For much the same reason they will lose little when fashions change.

BIBLIOGRAPHICAL REFERENCES: There is no extended biographical or critical study. See Harry R. Warfel, *American Novelists of Today,* 1951; Edward Wagenknecht, *Cavalcade of the American Novel,* 1952; also Dayton Kohler, "Elsie Singmaster," *Bookman,* LXXII (1931), 621–626, and "Elsie Singmaster and the Regional Tradition," *Commonwealth,* I (September, 1947), 15–18.

EDITH SITWELL

Born: Scarborough, England
Date: September 7, 1887

Died: London, England
Date: December 9, 1964

Principal Works

POEMS: *Clowns' Houses,* 1918; *The Wooden Pegasus,* 1920; *Façade,* 1922; *The Sleeping Beauty,* 1924; *Troy Park,* 1925; *Rustic Elegies,* 1927; *Gold Coast Customs,* 1929; *Collected Poems,* 1930; *Poems New and Old,* 1940; *Street Songs,* 1942; *Green Song and Other Poems,* 1944; *The Song of the Cold,* 1945; *The Shadow of Cain,* 1947; *The Canticle of the Rose: Poems 1917–1949,* 1949; *Gardeners and Astronomers,* 1953; *Collected Poems,* 1957; *The Outcasts,* 1962; *Music and Ceremonies,* 1963.

NOVEL: *I Live Under a Black Sun,* 1937.

BIOGRAPHY: *Alexander Pope,* 1930; *The English Eccentrics,* 1933; *Victoria of England,* 1936; *Fanfare for Elizabeth,* 1946; *The Queens and the Hive,* 1962.

CRITICISM: *Poetry and Criticism,* 1925; *Aspects of Modern Poetry,* 1934; *A Poet's Notebook,* 1943; *A Notebook on William Shakespeare,* 1948.

AUTOBIOGRAPHY: *Taken Care Of,* 1965.

Edith Sitwell, one of the century's foremost poets and a flamboyant exponent of experimentation in verse, was the oldest child of Sir George Sitwell, fourth baronet of Renishaw Park, the family seat for six hundred years. Much of the extravagant personality of Edith and her brothers, Osbert and Sachaverell, is readily understandable to the reader of the memoirs of their fabulous and outrageous father, written by Sir Osbert Sitwell in *Left Hand, Right Hand.*

Educated in secret (as she said), Edith Sitwell first became known in 1916 as the editor of an anthology, *Wheels,* which stridently featured for six years her own work, that of her brothers, and other authors whose voices were to be heard frequently in the 1920's. One of the highlights of the 1925 season in London was the premiere of Miss Sitwell's *Façade,* in which she chanted her early fanciful and rythmical verse to similarly exciting musical settings provided by William Walton. For the performance Miss Sitwell spoke through an amplifying mask behind a screen, another device to provide artificiality for the exotic occasion. The London Hall was an uproar of Miss Sitwell's admirers and detracters, as the staid English audience itself came close to a performance more appropriate to Paris or Dublin than to London. Twenty-five years later, the work was similarly performed in New York's Museum of Modern Art, but so far had modern taste and Miss Sitwell's reputation advanced, that the last occasion was almost regal in dignity, as befitted its central performer who was given the accolade of Grand Dame of the Cross of the British Empire in 1954.

Miss Sitwell's flair for self-dramatization for a long time made students of literature uneasy about the seriousness of her poetry. Standing six feet in height, she always appeared in extravagant and archaic costumes and headgear, often medieval, spangled with ostentatious rings and necklaces. "I have always had a great affinity for Queen Elizabeth," she said once. "We were born on the same day of the month and about the same hour of the day."

Although her Dadaist stunts were calculated to express her love of being flamboyant and of irritating the stuffy ("Good taste," she claimed, "is the worst vice ever invented"), her interest in poetry was serious as was her talent. Her keenness for verbal experimentation found a fit subject in the extraordinary *Gold Coast Customs* (1929), her own version of Eliot's *The Waste Land* and one of the remarkable poems of that remarkable decade.

For ten years afterwards Miss Sitwell wrote little verse, devoting herself to critical essays and non-fiction, including a biography of Pope, but mainly taking care of a friend, Helen Rootham, through her fatal illness.

With the coming of World War II, Miss Sitwell returned to poetry, still with her dazzling technical equipment but now with a rich store of traditional Christian imagery. (Miss Sitwell became a Roman Catholic in 1955.) The agonies of the bombardment of London, and the terror of the atomic bomb evoked from Miss Sitwell some of the most moving poetry ever written about the cruelty of war.

Along with her delight in self-dramatization, Miss Sitwell was renowned, from the publication of *Wheels* all through her life, for her championship of younger writers. Dylan Thomas is but one of the best known of the young men whose verbal experimentation she praised and championed early in his career.

BIBLIOGRAPHICAL REFERENCES: Biographical studies include Miss Sitwell's autobiography, *Taken Care Of*, 1965; her brother Osbert's memoirs, *Left Hand, Right Hand*, 5 vols., 1944–1950; her secretary Elizabeth Salter's *The Last Years of a Rebel: A Memoir of Edith Sitwell*, 1967; and John Lehmann's *A Nest of Tigers: Edith, Osbert and Sacheverell Sitwell in Their Times*, 1968. Lehmann and Derek Parker edited *Selected Letters, 1919–1964*, 1970.

For criticism of the work see Ralph J. Mills, Jr., *Edith Sitwell: A Critical Essay*, 1966; Geoffrey Singleton, *Edith Sitwell: The Hymn to Life*, 1960; J. Brophy, *Edith Sitwell: The Symbolist Order*, 1968; Louis Untermeyer, *Lives of the Poets*, 1960; C. M. Bowra, *Edith Sitwell*, 1947; ibid., *Poetry and Politics 1900–1960*, 1966; and Sister M. Jeremy, "Clown and Canticle: The Achievement of Edith Sitwell," *Renascence*, III (Spring, 1951), 135–136. Also of interest are R. L. Megroz, *Three Sitwells: A Biographical and Critical Study*, 1927, reprinted, 1969; and *A Celebration for Edith Sitwell*, edited by José García Villa, 1948.

Additional references may be found in Richard Fifoot, *A Bibliography of Edith, Osbert, and Sacheverell Sitwell*, 1963; and Lois D. Rosenberg, "Edith Sitwell, A Critical Bibliography, 1915–1950," *Bulletin of Bibliography*, XXI, no. 2 (1953), 40–43; XXI, no. 3 (1954), 57–60.

JOHN SKELTON

Born: Norfolk (?), England
Date: 1460(?)

Died: Westminster, England
Date: June 21, 1529

Principal Works

POEMS: *The Bowge of Court*, c. 1499; *Phyllyp Sparrow*, c. 1505; *The Tunning of Elinor Rumming*, c. 1517(?); *Speke, Parrot*, c. 1521; *Collyn Clout*, c. 1521; *Why Come Ye Not to Courte*, 1522; *The Garlande of Laurell*, 1523.
PLAY: *Magnyfycence*, 1516.

John Skelton was born about 1460. The facts about his early life are few. He seems to have attended Cambridge University when quite young, but there is no record of his receiving a degree. When the noted printer Caxton spoke of him in 1490, Skelton had already established his position as writer and scholar. He was "laureated" by the universities of Oxford, Cambridge, and Louvain; the precise nature of this honor is still being debated.

He won royal favor for his accomplishments and was made tutor to Prince Henry, later King Henry VIII, about 1496. He was ordained to the priesthood in 1498. His observations on the life around him inspired his satire on royal hangers-on, *The Bowge of Court*.

The death of Arthur, Prince of Wales, in 1502 brought an abrupt end to Skelton's career as tutor. While his gifts were considered suitable for the education of a future Archbishop of Canterbury, they were apparently not what Henry VII thought fitting for the heir to the throne. Skelton was made rector of Diss in Norfolk, presumably as a reward for his services, and he lived there for several years performing the duties of parish priest.

After Henry VIII's accession to the throne in 1509, Skelton sent him several gifts, hoping to remind him of their past association and thereby win his patronage. His efforts were eventually successful, and in 1512 he returned to Westminster as *orator regius*. As court poet he commemorated notable events in both Latin and English verse, writing elegies for Henry VII and his mother, Lady Margaret Beaufort, who had been Skelton's patroness when he was tutor to Prince Henry, and celebrating the English victory over James IV of Scotland at Flodden.

Skelton soon exceeded his responsibility as *orator regius* by attacking Cardinal Wolsey, who was rapidly becoming the most powerful man in England. Skelton's play, *Magnyfycence*, probably written in 1516, uses the traditional form of the Tudor Interlude, the contest between figures representing virtues and vices for the possession of a hero, to attack the influence of the cardinal on the young king. It was perhaps fortunate for the poet that he was then residing on the grounds of Westminster Abbey and therefore in sanctuary, for he faced sure arrest for his satire. Some accord between the two men was apparently reached about 1522, for Skelton felt free to spend Christmas at the home of the Countess of Surrey in York that year. He dedicated *The Garlande of Laurell* to Wolsey in 1523.

Skelton lived and wrote in Westminster for the last years of his life and died there June 21, 1529.

BIBLIOGRAPHICAL REFERENCES: The standard edition is still Alexander Dyce, *The Poetical Works of John Skelton*, 2 vols., 1843. Philip Henderson edited *The Complete Poems of John Skelton, Laureate* in 1931. *Poems*, selected and edited by Robert S. Kinsman offers a good old-spelling text of many of the works along with excellent critical, biographical, and bibliographical materials.

See also William Nelson, *John Skelton, Laureate*, 1939; I. A. Gordon, *John Skelton, Poet Laureate*, 1943; H. L. R. Edwards, *Skelton; the Life and Times of an Early Tudor Poet*, 1949; Arthur R. Heiserman, *Skelton and Satire*, 1961; Maurice Pollet, *John Skelton: Contribution à l'histoire de la Prérenaissance anglaise*, 1962; E. Schulte, *La poesia di John Skelton*, 1963; S. E. Fish, *John Skelton's Poetry*, 1965; William O. Harriss, *Skelton's "Magnyfycence" and the Cardinal Virtue Tradition*, 1965; and Nan D. Carpenter, *John Skelton*, 1967.

CHRISTOPHER SMART

Born: Shipbourne, England
Date: April 11, 1722

Died: London, England
Date: May 21, 1771

PRINCIPAL WORKS

POEMS: *The Seatonian Poems,* 1750–1756; *A Song to David,* 1763; *Poems by Mr. Smart,* 1763; *Poems on Several Occasions,* 1763.

TRANSLATIONS: *The Works of Horace,* 1756; *A Translation of the Psalms of David,* 1765.

HYMNS: *A Hymn to the Supreme Being,* 1756.

Christopher Smart's life is the record of a very considerable talent profoundly affected by personal misfortunes. He was frail as a child, and, according to the rules of eighteenth-century medicine, he was treated with "cordials" which probably began his lifelong alcoholism. From what witnesses such as Dr. Johnson said, it would appear that Smart suffered from delirium tremens and later from a form of insanity which manifested itself in religious mania. His earlier life did not intimate so tragic an ending: he began writing as a child, attracted some literary attention as a young man, and was sent to Cambridge. At the university his talents and his troubles seem to have had their maturation. He won a reputation as a poet, but his personal difficulties, including a habit of running into debt that was to become perennial, forced him to leave the university.

The next part of Smart's career took place in London, where he spent his time writing, composing music, and publishing his own and other men's literary work. Smart was married in 1752 and enjoyed a short period of happiness and sanity. Within a few years, however, his troubles began in earnest. He was unable to face up to the problems of his domestic life, his literary life, and of the business affairs upon which he had entered. In his middle thirties he became more and more liable to attacks of madness, many of them violent, and all of them, at least by the treatment of his time, incurable. Much of Smart's poetry seems to reflect a disengagement from reality. It indicates, without doubt, his quest for spiritual and psychological security. If his deep emotions found no cure they did find impressive expression in the Hymns and in *A Song to David.*

The madness of Smart did not necessitate his complete confinement; after some years of treatment (1757–1763) he was able to emerge and take his place in the literary society of London. His talents won important friends like Dr. Johnson and Thomas Gray, men who recognized his ability and made allowances for his condition. He was aided by Fanny Burney and her father, who did what they could, personally and financially, to ease his life. Yet Smart, although far from the totally insane man he is often incorrectly pictured as being, was also far from being able to lead a life even remotely normal. His financial condition was as precarious as it had been years before at Cambridge, and the last months of his life witnessed his confinement in debtor's prison. Although he was what may too easily be called a failure, Smart's very weakness enabled him to reach his own form of success. His religious poetry, written in an age of dominant rationalism, supplied men with a strong and valuable sense of the mystical. He reinvigorated the English tradition of holy poetry, a tradition which had been allowed to wither for many years. His madness, one should admit, allowed him a vision of things denied to most of the men around him.

BIBLIOGRAPHICAL REFERENCES: Good editions of Smart's work include the *Collected Poems*, edited by Norman Callan, 2 vols., 1949, and *Poems*, edited by R. E. Brittain, 1950. There are a number of biographical and critical studies, most of them written in the past decade. See E. G. Ainsworth and C. E. Noyes, *Smart: A Biographical and Critical Study*, 1943; K. A. McKenzie, *Smart: sa vie et ses oeuvres*, 1925; C. Devlin, *Poor Kit Smart*, 1961; G. Grigson, *Christopher Smart*, 1961; S. Blaydes, *Smart as a Poet of His Times: A Reappraisal*, 1966; Arthur Sherbo, *Christopher Smart: Scholar of the University*, 1967; and Moira Dearnley, *The Poetry of Smart*, 1968.

See also George Gray, *A Bibliography of the Writings of Smart*, 1903; John Middleton Murry, *Discoveries*, 1924; Roland Botting, "Christopher Smart in London," *Research Studies, State College of Washington*, 1939; Patricia M. Spacks, *Poetry of Vision: Five Eighteenth-Century Poets*, 1967; and William Powell Jones, *The Rhetoric of Science: A Study of Scientific Ideas and Imagery in Eighteenth-Century English Poetry*, 1966.

ADAM SMITH

Born: Kirkcaldy, Scotland
Date: June 5, 1723

Died: Edinburgh, Scotland
Date: July 17, 1790

Principal Works

ESSAYS AND TREATISES: *Theory of Moral Sentiments,* 1759; *An Inquiry into the Nature and Causes of the Wealth of Nations,* 1776; *Considerations Concerning the First Formation of Languages,* 1790; *Essays on Philosophical Subjects,* 1795.

Born at Kirkcaldy in Fifeshire, Scotland, on June 5, 1723, Adam Smith studied at the University of Glasgow, where he came under the influence of the famous professor of moral philosophy, Francis Hutcheson. Smith then studied at Balliol College, Oxford, for six years before returning to Scotland to lecture in rhetoric and polite literature at the University of Edinburgh. His lectures were popular and, unlike those of many of his contemporaries, attracted listeners from the town as well as from the university.

Smith returned to the University of Glasgow in 1751 as professor of logic; in the same year he was appointed to the chair in moral philosophy. At this time Smith was strongly under the influence of his close friend, the historian and philosopher David Hume, and shared in a milder form much of Hume's skepticism. (For example, Smith never took holy orders, an unusual circumstance for a professor of moral philosophy in Scotland at that time.) In 1759, Smith published his *Theory of Moral Sentiments,* in which he claimed that sympathy or feeling was the foundation for all our moral sentiments or judgments. He felt that evil or wrongdoing was punished by remorse in the individual, and that certainly remorse was the most painful of the human sentiments. His position was not very far from that of current philosophers who claim that ethical principles are merely statements of our own emotions.

Even at this early date Smith was highly interested in economics. He often talked of trade and political economy in his lectures, and he urged both students and young businessmen from the growing commercial city and port of Glasgow to attend his lectures. Many criticized him, and one of his colleagues later sneered that "he had converted the chair of moral philosophy into a professorship of trade and finance."

Smith's unconventional lectures attracted a good deal of notice. Late in 1762, the wealthy Duke of Buccleuch became interested in Smith and hired him as his private tutor. Smith left the university and traveled with his patron to France, where he lived for more than two years and met physiocratic economic philosophers like Turgot, Helvétius, and Quesnay. Becoming more and more convinced of the need for coherent study of the principles of political economy, Smith returned from France and spent ten years studying and writing his famous *Wealth of Nations.* Classic statement of the doctrine of laissez faire, this book established the idea that national progress could be best achieved with private initiative and enterprise limited only by the bounds of justice. Although a good deal of Smith's theorizing was borrowed from his French associates, his copious illustrations and his applications of his principles to current problems in England and Scotland insured him a wide and interested audience.

Although he wrote little after the *Wealth of Nations,* the book and its author were both famous. Smith made frequent trips to London where he had a good deal of influence on the Prime Minister, William Pitt, and his opinion was sought on almost all tax legislation passed by Parliament after the disastrous Stamp Act. Widely honored, he was made commissioner of customs for Scotland in 1777 and in 1787 was elected rector of the University of Glasgow. He died in Edinburgh on July 17, 1790.

In later life, Adam Smith came to represent a kind of calm, rational, principled Augustan. He was intimate with many of the great of his age, Hume, Gibbon, and Dr. Johnson (although the last apparently never forgave him for an unkind review of his famous dictionary in the *Edinburgh Review*); and he enjoyed discussing philosophy, semantics, history, politics, and economics in the various London clubs. He was a man apparently without fanaticism or a doctrinaire approach. Despite his advocacy of free trade and unrestricted operation of the law of supply and demand, he did acknowledge the necessity for government control in such matters as education and the public highways. Interested in many phases of the intellect, he was the first to synthesize and articulate many of the economic principles and problems that grew out of the rapid industrial and commercial expansion of his age.

BIBLIOGRAPHICAL REFERENCES: For biography and critical commentary see F. W. Hirst, *Adam Smith,* 1904; A. W. Small, *Adam Smith and Modern Sociology,* 1907; W. R. Scott, *Adam Smith as Student and Professor,* 1937; Charles Ryle Fay, *Adam Smith and the Scotland of His Day,* 1956; Joseph Cropsey, *Polity and Economy: An Interpretation of the Principles of Adam Smith,* 1957; and A. L. Macfie, *The Individual in Society: Papers on Adam Smith,* 1967.

BETTY SMITH

Born: Brooklyn, N. Y.
Date: December 15, 1897

Died: Shelton, Connecticutt
Date: January 17, 1972

Principal Work

NOVELS: *A Tree Grows in Brooklyn*, 1943; *Maggie Now*, 1958; *Joy in the Morning*, 1968.

Betty Smith, like Francie Nolan, was born in Brooklyn (December 15, 1897) and went to college in Michigan. Enrolled as a part-time student at the University of Michigan, she studied writing, particularly playwriting, almost exclusively. In 1930 she published two short plays in a volume written by drama students at Michigan, and in 1931 she won the first prize of $1,000 in the Avery Hopwood competition, mainly for her work in fiction. Even then she was developing the material she used later in her popular novel; one of her winning stories was called "Death of a Singing Waiter."

She continued her studies at the Yale School of Drama and was awarded playwriting fellowships by the Rockefeller Foundation and the Dramatists' Guild. Although she has published or produced over seventy one-act plays, it was not until she wrote *A Tree Grows in Brooklyn* that she received widespread public recognition. The novel was praised mainly for its lyrical treatment of naturalistic subject matter and for its realistic dialogue. She collaborated with George Abbott to write a musical version for the stage.

She again turned from her interest in drama to write novels, returning to the Irish section of Brooklyn for her settings. But she never equaled her first success, which, many critics felt, overshadowed her subsequent books.

BIBLIOGRAPHICAL REFERENCES: For critical comment on Miss Smith's novels see the *Book Review Digest*, 1943, 1948; and Harold Charles Gardiner, "Most Artful Dodger," *In All Conscience*, 1959, 102–104.

HOMER W. SMITH

Born: Denver, Colorado
Date: January 2, 1895

Died: New York, N. Y.
Date: March 25, 1962

Principal Works

NOVELS: *Kamongo,* 1932 (revised paperback edition, 1956); *The End of Illusion,* 1935.

SCIENTIFIC AND PHILOSOPHICAL: *The Kidney: Structure and Function in Health and Disease,* 1951; *Man and His Gods* (with Foreword by Albert Einstein), 1952; *From Fish to Philosopher,* 1953; *Principles of Renal Physiology,* 1956.

For thirty-four years Dr. Homer W. Smith was associated with the New York University Medical School, both in teaching and administrative capacities, and he served as chairman of its Department of Physiology. He had an eminent career as a physiologist, and his major work on the kidney is regarded as an important contribution to the literature on that subject.

He wrote two novels. The second, *The End of Illusion,* generally considered rather contrived and even mechanical in its formulations of plot and ideas, deals with a young man who goes to Malaya to enjoy complete freedom and discovers that the freedom he seeks is nothing but an illusion. The first novel, *Kamongo,* is more successful in its handling of theme. It has a slender story line; its chief interest lies in the detailed account by an American naturalist to an Anglican priest—as they journey homeward on a French steamer through the Red Sea and the Suez Canal—of his capture of the African lung-fish, a relic of the Devonian Age when it unsuccessfully sought to sustain itself on land. The naturalist's narrative, graphic and vivid in the telling, forms only a section of the novel; the remaining portion is the long debate between the two men on various issues of skepticism and faith, with Joel, the scientist, triumphantly demolishing the beliefs of the priest.

The novel, though without formal plot, does contain some excellent descriptive passages; and Smith's style, even when it deals with scientific matters that generally are of interest only to the specialist, is always lively and colorful. Upon its initial publication, *Kamongo* attracted wide popular attention and was a selection of the Book-of-the-Month Club in 1932. In 1935 the late Alexander Woollcott included it in one of his anthologies of current literary favorites, and in 1950, eighteen years after publication, it was a Natural History Book Club choice for its readers.

Two other works by Dr. Smith are worthy of notice. *Man and His Gods* is a vigorous discussion of religion, in which the author, after examining its origin in myth and superstition, decides that man's sense of scientific truth cannot permit him to embrace a belief in supernatural authority. Man must find within his own resources the will to bring about his "fulfillment." The book has been compared to Sir James Frazer's *The Golden Bough* and has been praised as a suitable condensation of the British author's famous many-volume study. *From Fish to Philosopher* is an original examination of man's origin and physical development told largely in terms of the kidney's growing adaptability to varying qualities of environment. Both books are written in engaging, at times brilliant, prose; not the least of Dr. Smith's virtues as a writer was his ability to maintain the interest of his reader. Under the author's touch both biology and anthropology seem at times to read like fiction.

BIBLIOGRAPHICAL REFERENCES: The final chapter of Dr. Smith's *Man and His Gods* gives interesting biographical materials. For discussion of his contributions see Herbert Chasis and William Goldring, editors, *Homer William Smith, His Scientific and Literary Achievements*, 1965; R. F. Pitts, "Homer William Smith," *National Academy of Sciences, Biographical Memoirs*, XXXIX (1967), 445–470; and Alexander Woollcott, *The Woollcott Reader*, 1935

TOBIAS SMOLLETT

Born: Dalquhurn, Scotland
Date: March, 1721

Died: Antignano, Italy
Date: September 17, 1771

Principal Works

NOVELS: *Roderick Random*, 1748; *Peregine Pickle*, 1751; *Ferdinand, Count Fathom*, 1753; *Sir Launcelot Greaves*, 1760-1762; *The Expedition of Humphry Clinker*, 1771.

TRANSLATIONS: *Gil Blas*, 1749; *Don Quixote*, 1755; *The Works of Voltaire*, 1761-1769.

MISCELLANEOUS: *A Complete History of England*, 1757-1758; *The Reprisal*, 1757; *The Modern Part of an Universal History*, 1759-1766; *A Continuation of the Complete History of England*, 1760-1761; 1765; *Travels in France and Italy*, 1766; *The Present State of All Nations*, 1768-1769; *The Adventures of an Atom*, 1769.

Tobias Smollett, born in March, 1721, at Dalquhurn near Bonhill, Scotland, had the ill fortune in his own time and today to be in competition with Henry Fielding. The result is that Smollett's moon has been obscured by Fielding's sun. This is a great pity, for, despite the unattractive behavior of many of his characters and the general brutality of his novels, there is much pleasure to be found in the pages of Smollett.

A poor and hot-tempered Scot, Smollett was a real-life replica of one of his own literary creations. After study at Glasgow University, he went to London to seek his fortune. After a hitch in the navy as surgeon's mate, he remained for a time in the West Indies, where he fell in love with Nancy Lascelles, daughter of a Jamaica planter, whom he later married. In 1744 he was back in London doctoring and writing. His first novel, *Roderick Random*, was a picaresque work which strung together a series of episodes through which the hero ultimately finds love and wealth. Many readers have been repelled by Roderick's selfishness and coarseness; but, as in all of Smollett's novels, there is a plentitude of delight to be found in the minor characters, who are treated as humor types. Lieutenant Tom Bowling, eccentric sea dog, and Morgan, a Welsh surgeon, are two such figures. Because of his interest in naval life, Smollett has been called the father of the nautical novel. The picture of shipboard life and the account of the disastrous attack on Cartagena in *Roderick Random* are among the earliest literary protests against naval abuses.

Peregrine Pickle, his next novel, mined the vein of *Roderick Random*. Again, a young man with roguish tendencies achieves security after a series of adventures and amours. Commodore Hawser Trunnion, Smollett's finest picture of an old salt, graces this novel. *Ferdinand, Count Fathom*, published in 1753, is a novel remarkable chiefly for the baseness of its hero, a thoroughly villainous ingrate who is made to undergo an unconvincing reformation. This was followed by *Sir Launcelot Greaves*, a lackluster imitation of *Don Quixote*.

Then in the year of his death Smollett published *The Expedition of Humphry Clinker*, at once his masterpiece and his happiest book. This epistolary novel employs a trip through the British Isles as the framework for the exhibition of a brilliant set of humor characters. Chief among them is Matthew Bramble, a kindhearted man who unsuccessfully tries to hide his goodness behind a gruff manner. Bramble is accompanied by his sister Tabitha, a grotesque virago who finally succeeds in marrying Lieutenant Obadiah Lismahago, a terrible-tempered Scot. The novel takes its title from a starveling whom Bramble befriends and who turns out to be Bramble's natural son. The episode of the discovery of Humphry's identity is unsurpassed in the English novel.

In addition to his novels, Smollett labored prodigiously at a number of literary projects in which he was sometimes the coördinator of the work of several hack writers. He translated *Gil Blas, Don Quixote,* and *The Works of Voltaire.* He edited *The Critical Review* (1756–63), *The British Magazine* (1760–67), and *The Briton* (1762–63). He also wrote or edited a group of multiple-volume works: *A Complete History of England, A Continuation of the Complete History of England, A Compendium of Voyages* (1756), *The Modern Part of an Universal History,* and *The Present State of All Nations.* In the field of poetry he wrote "The Tears of Scotland" (1746?, 1753), "Advice, a Satire" (1746), "Reproof, a Satire" (1747), and "Ode to Independence" (1773). Smollett was very ambitious for a stage success; after the failure of his tragedy *The Regicide* (1749) he enjoyed a small hit with a farce, *The Reprisal.*

Ill health sent Smollett abroad, and out of his trips came *Travels in France and Italy,* a curious mixture of laughter and anger. *The Adventures of an Atom* is a scurrilous political satire in which events attributed to Japan stand for occurrences in England.

It is difficult to avoid the conclusion that despite his obvious lapses in taste Tobias Smollett possessed one of the most remarkable talents in all of English literature. He died at Antignano, near Leghorn, Italy, on September 17, 1771.

BIBLIOGRAPHICAL REFERENCES: The *Letters* were edited by Lewis M. Knapp in 1971. The most authoritative study of Smollett is Lewis M. Knapp's *Tobias Smollett: Doctor of Men and Manners,* 1949. See also Lewis Melville, *The Life and Letters of Tobias Smollett,* 1927; Lewis M. Kahrl, *Tobias Smollett, Traveler-Novelist,* 1945; F. W. Boege, *Smollett's Reputation as a Novelist,* 1947; also Howard S. Buck, *A Study in Smollett, Chiefly "Peregrine Pickle,"* 1925; Louis L. Martz, *The Later Career of Tobias Smollett,* 1942; and Rufus Putney, "The Plan of *Peregrine Pickle,*" *Publications of the Modern Language Association,* LX (1945), 1051–1065. Of importance is *Bicentennial Essays,* edited by G. S. Rousseau, 1971.

SNORRI STURLUSON

Born: Odda (?), Iceland
Date: 1179

Died: Reykjaholt, Iceland
Date: September 23, 1241

Principal Works

HISTORY: The *Prose Edda*, c. 1220; *Heimskringla*, c. 1230–35 (*Sagas of the Norwegian Kings*).

Snorri Sturluson (or Sturleson), Iceland's best-known writer and historian of the Norse kings, was born at or near Odda in 1179, the scion of a family of powerful Icelandic chiefs. He received an ecclesiastical education at the home of his foster-father at Odda, a cultural center, and read volumes of history and poetry at an early age. Eager for wealth and power, he made a highly advantageous marriage, which brought him several great estates, and became a lawyer, eventually rising to the position of president of the Icelandic legislative assembly and of the highest court of the land. Still seeking power and adventure, Snorri journeyed to Norway and became a favorite of King Haakon, who made him a court chamberlain. Returning to Iceland as Haakon's vassal several years later, he became embroiled in quarrels with other nobles, including some of his own relatives. He was killed at Reykjaholt on September 23, 1241, by agents of the Norwegian king, against whom he had turned traitor in the course of his scheming for self-aggrandizement.

For all his ambition and avarice, Snorri was apparently regarded by his contemporaries as a pious and patriotic man. Certainly the *Heimskringla* indicates his diligent striving after historical accuracy and his desire to immortalize the deeds and characters of the great Norse kings "from the beginning" (i.e. the days of the legendary migrations from Asia) through the reign of Sverri, which ended in 1177. His sources are many: the writings of Ari Torgelson the Wise, the early eleventh century priest-historian; the oral collections of traditions as handed down in ballad form by the scalds or bards, and the legendary biographies of the two King Olafs. To all this material Snorri added much knowledge gleaned from his own studies and observations in Norway.

Although he takes his chronology and many of his facts from Ari, Snorri's style is completely his own. He sets forth his critical standards in the preface to his work, saying that he trusts most sources which are closest in time to the events described, and that even these things may not be true but are only "believed to be true by old and wise men." Only in his account of the miracles of St. Olaf does he abandon his scientific approach to history.

Snorri's history is set forth in the form of a series of brilliant biographies, from which every irrelevant detail which does not contribute to the characterization has been carefully rejected. He borrows from Thucydides and Plutarch the device of putting into his characters' mouths speeches, not as they were actually spoken, but as they might have been. In "The Life of St. Olaf," the only section of the *Heimskringla* which has survived unabridged, he describes not only the king's great deeds but also details of his everyday life which give the character depth and reality.

Snorri is also credited with the *Prose Edda*, a "primer for young poets" which describes the creation and the rise of paganism, the Norse mythological system and legends attributable to the god of poetry, and lays out the rules and theories of ancient verse forms. Although in prose, the language of the *Edda* is highly poetical.

BIBLIOGRAPHICAL REFERENCES: The translation of the *Heimskringla* by Samuel Laing is available in Everyman's Library. *The Stories of the Kings of Norway*, translated from the Icelandic by William Morris and Eríkr Magnússon, 3 vols., 1893–1905, is supplemented by a fourth volume containing a *Life* by Magnússon. See also S. Nordal, **Snorri Sturluson,** 1920; and Fredrik Paasche, **Snorre Sturlason og Sturlungerne,** 1922.

C. P. SNOW

Born: Leicester, England
Date: October 15, 1905

Principal Works

NOVELS: *Death Under Sail,* 1932; *New Lives for Old,* 1933; *The Search,* 1934, revised edition, 1958. *Strangers and Brothers,* a series of eleven volumes including: *Strangers and Brothers,* 1940; *The Light and the Dark,* 1947; *Time of Hope,* 1949; *The Masters,* 1951; *The New Men,* 1954; *Homecomings,* 1956; *The Conscience of the Rich,* 1958; *The Affair,* 1960; *Corridors of Power,* 1964; *The Sleep of Reason,* 1968; *Last Things,* 1970; *The Malcontents,* 1972.
ESSAYS: *The Two Cultures and the Scientific Revolution,* 1959; *Science and Government,* 1961; *Appendix to Science and Government,* 1962; *The Two Cultures, a Second Look,* 1964; *Variety of Men,* 1967; *Public Affairs,* 1971.
PLAY: *View over the Park,* 1950.

Charles Percy Snow was trained as a physicist. A director of the English Electric Company from 1947 to 1964, he was also Parliamentary Secretary to the Ministry of Technology in the British Government from 1964 to 1966. He is, both in governmental career and in appearance, a stolidly bureaucratic administrator.

He is also one of England's leading novelists and a lecturer on the dangers of a gap between the "two cultures" of science and the humanities. His life's work as a novelist has been the eleven volume series *Strangers and Brothers,* although he has occasionally published other fiction and collections of essays. For his joint achievements in government and in literature, he was named Commander of the British Empire in 1943, knighted in 1957, and created a Baron in the life peerage in 1964.

Lord Snow's success has not, however, been unilateral. *Strangers and Brothers* has been attacked, most bitterly by F. R. Leavis. Lionel Trilling dismissed *The Two Cultures and the Scientific Revolution* as a "denial of the actuality of politics" and called it "specious." For these critics—and for many others—C. P. Snow as a novelist and scientific thinker remains a stolidly bureaucratic administrator.

Part of the difficulty lies in Snow's choice of the multi-volume novel for his fictional vehicle. Comparisons are inevitable with the masterpiece of Marcel Proust, *Remembrance of Things Past,* and with Galsworthy's *The Forsyte Saga.* Lord Snow's work is neither as intellectually conceived as Proust's, nor as widely popular as Galsworthy's. His characters are far less lifelike, his prose style less interesting, his imagination less fertile.

It is unfair, however, to compare Snow's series of novels with similar works. His purpose in *Strangers and Brothers* is radically different from that of Proust or Galsworthy: *Strangers and Brothers* traces the life and career of Lewis Eliot, a lawyer who rises from humble origins to become a member of the Establishment, a powerful man in his own right. The novels are not, however, picaresque in the usual sense. Rather than a journey through life, they explore and describe, in sometimes repititious detail, the workings of power and the functioning of political strivings in a series of closed worlds clearly meant as microcosms of the larger society outside. Thus *The Masters* and *The Affair* depict academic politicking at a Cambridge college, *The Conscience of the Rich* explores the disintegration of a wealthy Anglo-Jewish banking family, and *Strangers and Brothers* (the first novel, whose title has been given to the entire series) shows the machinations of a lawyer in a small, provincial English town.

To use the serial form was also to invite criticism. The form had been declared dead by numerous critics; nevertheless, Lord Snow kept on writing, and his novels have been modest successes.

In spite of the many attacks on his work and on his prose style, C. P. Snow has demonstrated that the carefully and often intricately plotted multi-novel series can still be written, and that it still has an audience. His success in that respect is unquestioned, and makes his work noteworthy.

BIBLIOGRAPHICAL REFERENCES: Studies of Snow's life and work include William Cooper, *C. P. Snow*, 1959, revised edition, 1962; Jerome Thale, *C. P. Snow: The Man and His Work*, 1965; Robert G. Davis, *C. P. Snow*, 1965; Robert Graecen, *The World of C. P. Snow*, 1962; Frederick R. Karl, *C. P. Snow, The Politics of Conscience*, 1963; Frank R. Leavis and Michael Yudkin, *Two Cultures: The Significance of C. P. Snow*, 1963; and D. K. Cornelius and E. St. Vincent, *Cultures in Conflict: Perspectives in the Snow-Leavis Controversy*, 1964.

See also Bernard Bergonzi, "The World of Lewis Eliot," *Twentieth Century*, CLXVII (1960), 214–225; and Rubin Rabinovitz, *The Reaction Against Experiment in the English Novel, 1950–1960*, 1968, which includes an extensive bibliography on pages 196–211.

SOCRATES

Born: Athens, Greece
Date: c. 470 B.C.

Died: Athens
Date: 399 B.C.

Socrates did not make a written record of his teachings. What is known of his philosophy comes from the *Dialogues* of Plato (q.v.) in which Socrates is the central figure.

What is known of Socrates, the great Greek philosopher, comes primarily from two of his pupils, Xenophon and Plato. The account of Socrates by Plato in the *Dialogues* is generally taken as being, on the whole, the more reliable report, both of the character and the teachings of Socrates.

Socrates, born in Athens about 470 B.C., was the son of Sophroniscus, a sculptor, and Phænarete, a non-professional midwife. The family was neither poor nor wealthy, and Socrates received the usual elementary education in gymnastics and music, to train the body and the mind. He may have planned to follow his father's occupation, and there are some reports that he actually did produce some works of sculpture; but he apparently decided that he was more at ease with ideas than with stone. He had a reflective, almost mystical temperament at times, and throughout his lifetime had the habit of assuming some immobile position, a kind of trancelike state, during which he sometimes believed himself to hear a supernatural voice that warned him against certain acts he was considering. He claimed that when he disregarded the voice, he got into trouble.

He is pictured as a short, snub-nosed person with widely spaced, perhaps protruding eyes, and broad nostrils. The comic dramatists of the time, Aristophanes, Amipsias, and Eupolis, made him the subject of satirical dramas in which his physical traits as well as his dialectical habits were exaggerated. He lived simply, wearing the same garment winter and summer and traveling barefoot in all seasons. He ate and drank moderately, although he could drink more wine than most men without being affected. He was married to Xanthippe, a woman who seemed to suit him, although later critics tried to give her a shrewish reputation; she bore Socrates at least two children.

Socrates began his philosophical studies with the ideas of Pythagoras, Parmenides, Heraclitus, Anaxagoras, Anaximander, Zeno, and others. Because of the conflicting and sometimes fantastic ideas he found in these philosophies concerning the nature of the universe, he came to the conviction that more was to be gained by a study of justice and goodness. He combined his interest in ethics and the philosophy of politics with a faith in the capacity of the mind to clarify itself by working out the inconsistencies in various notions through a conversational technique which has come to be known as the "Socratic method." He claimed that if there were any truth in the report that the Oracle at Delphi had called him the wisest man in Greece, it was only because, unlike others, he recognized his own ignorance. He believed that he had a mission in life to make men aware of the limitations and defects in their beliefs and thus, by knowing themselves, to prepare for knowledge.

He wandered the streets and market

places of Athens, and when young men, politicians, or other bystanders became involved in conversation with him about justice, honor, courage, or some other matter with which philosophy could be concerned, Socrates would adroitly question them, leading them to an awareness of the inadequacy or falsity of their ideas. Since his ability was obvious and his insight undeniable, those who knew his method began to regard his profession of ignorance as either ironic or sophistical, and opinion was divided as to whether he was a beneficial genius or a dangerous nuisance.

Before he was forty Socrates had established himself as a remarkable teacher and philosopher; he was known and respected by many of the leading philosophers, politicians, and sophists of his time, including Protagoras, with whom Socrates had one of his most famous debates. Others who at various times came to be companions of Socrates during his conversational tours of Athens were Crito, Charmides (Plato's uncle), Critias (Plato's mother's cousin), Plato, Xenophon, Alcibiades, Adimantus and Glaucon (Plato's brothers), Callias (son of the wealthiest Athenian of the time), and Nicias (an outstanding Athenian democrat).

Socrates' role as "gadfly" (his own term) to the Athenian people irritated the democratic leaders more and more, particularly because he was closely associated with Alcibiades, who in 415 B.C. led the Sicilian expedition that ended in defeat for Athens, and with Critias, leader of the Thirty Tyrants imposed on the city by the Spartans after the defeat of the Athenians ended the Peloponnesian War in 404 B.C. That defeat was blamed in part on the new ideas with which, so it was charged, Socrates had corrupted the youth of the city. In 399 B.C., after the democracy was restored, and despite the commendable military record he had made during the war, Socrates was brought to trial on the charges of impiety and corrupting the young. In an eloquent and dignified defense he argued that he had been fulfilling a mission to goad the Athenians into searching for truth, that he was no man's master, and that he would accept acquittal only if it could be had without a sacrifice of his principles. When he was found guilty and was asked to propose a punishment, he claimed that he deserved to be rewarded for his services to Athens, but that he would agree to pay a fine. Condemned to death, he died after drinking hemlock, having refused the opportunity to escape and go into exile.

Plato's dialogues about Socrates' trial and death, the *Apology*, the *Crito*, and the *Phaedo*, together constitute one of the most moving portraits of all dramatic literature and are probably fairly reliable historically.

Socrates is famous for his questioning method, for his belief that if one knows the good he will seek it, for his theory of knowledge as the recollection of ideas, for his conception of the soul and his attempted proofs of the soul's immortality, and for the theory of Ideas which Plato adopted and expanded. He is also remembered as much for his courage and his clear idealism as for his philosophy, and he remains one of the greatest figures in Western history.

BIBLIOGRAPHICAL REFERENCES: The primary sources of our knowledge of the life and teachings are the *Dialogues* of Plato and the *Memorabilia* of Xenophon. See in particular the *Euthyphro, Apology, Crito,* and *Phaedo,* translated by John Burnet, 1924. A. E. Taylor is the author of two books on Socrates: *Varia Socratia,* 1911, and *Socrates,* 1951. See also G. C. Field, *Plato and His Contemporaries,* 1930; Constantin Ritter, *Sokrates,* 1931; R. W. Livingston, *Portrait of Socrates,* 1940; Arthur Hübscher, *Sokrates,* 1950; Cora Mason, *Socrates, the Man Who Dared to Ask,* 1953; A. D. Winspear, *Who Was Socrates?,* 1960 (2nd. ed.); Herbert Spiegelberg, *The Socratic Enigma: A Collection of Testimonies through Twenty-four Centuries,* 1964; and W. K. C. Guthrie, *Socrates,* 1971.

ALEKSANDR SOLZHENITSYN

Born: Rostov on the Don, Russia
Date: December 11, 1918

Principal Works

NOVELS: *Odin den' Ivana Denisovicha,* 1962 (*One Day in the Life of Ivan Denisovich,* 1963); *V Kruge pervom,* (*The First Circle,* 1968); *Rakovyi korpus,* (*The Cancer Ward,* 1968); *August 1914,* 1971.
PLAY: *Etyudy i Krokhotnyye rasskazy,* 1966 (*The Love Girl and the Innocent,* 1969).
MISCELLANEOUS: *Stories and Prose Poems,* translated 1971.

Aleksandr Isayevich Solzhenitsyn was born into an intellectual family in 1918. He took a degree in mathematics from the University of Rostov on the Don, and took correspondence courses in literature from the University of Moscow. In 1941, he joined the army, attended artillery school, and was commissioned in 1942. He served as an artillery captain on the front lines during World War II, and was twice decorated for bravery. At the end of the war, however, he was arrested for having made derogatory remarks about Stalin, and sentenced to forced labor camps from 1945 until 1953. Following these eight years in Stalin's labor camps, he was exiled to Siberia until 1957, when he was officially rehabilitated. While he was in exile, he contracted cancer, which was later arrested; upon his return, he taught mathematics in a secondary school in Ryazan, where he currently resides.

Solzhenitsyn's first novel, *One Day in the Life of Ivan Denisovich,* caused a stir within and outside Russia; it was the first book about Stalin's forced labor camps which the Central Committee allowed to be published.

As its title suggests, the novel spans only one day, but a usual day in a forced labor camp gives the author room to depict all the horror and degradation inflicted on the thousands who endured this type of punishment. Ivan Denisovich is a simple, innocent peasant whose imprisonment is the result of chance. His dogged persistence at survival, and his courage and meekness in the face of despair, lift the book from the ranks of documentary to the level of literature that probes the foundations of the human condition.

The First Circle takes its title from Dante's *Inferno,* in which the first circle of hell is reserved for pre-Christian philosophers not condemned to physical torment. Metaphorically, a research prison, staffed by scientists brought there from forced labor camps, becomes this first circle of hell. Nerzhin, a scientist, struggles with conflicts within himself, trying to decide whether to continue as a researcher, or to defy the regime and be forced to return to a lower circle—a labor camp. Paradoxically, Nerzhin's refusal to bow to inhuman bureaucratic pressures gains him an inner freedom.

The Cancer Ward, set in a Soviet hospital, explores the ideals and beliefs of several patients and doctors, all rendered honest to the point of recklessness by the pervasive sense of impending death. The novel is concerned, like most of Solzhenitsyn's work, with the life of the individual in a collective society; denial of individualism, the author suggests, is a form of malignant disease which can destroy the society. Neither *The First Circle* nor *The Cancer Ward* has been published in Russia, and in 1969 the author was expelled from the Writers' Union.

In 1970, Solzhenitsyn was awarded the Nobel Prize in Literature; the citation praised "the ethical force with which he has pursued the indispensable traditions of Russian literature." The government, however, did not allow him to receive the prize.

BIBLIOGRAPHICAL REFERENCES: For biography see Michael Scammell, *Solzhenitsyn,* 1972; and Leopold Labedz, *Solzhenitsyn, A Documentary Record,* 1971. For critical studies see Abraham Rothberg, *Aleksandr Solzhenitsyn: The Major Novels,* 1971; Vera Alexandrova, *A History of Soviet Literature 1917–1962,* 1963, 353–354; and *The Complection of Russian Literature,* compiled by Andrew Field, 1971, 297–298. See further György Lukács, *Solzhenitsyn,* translated from the German, 1971.

SOPHOCLES

Born: Colonus, near Athens, Greece
Date: c. 496 B.C.

Died: Athens
Date: 406–405 B.C.

Extant Plays

Antigone, 441; *Ajax* (?); *Women of Trachis* (?); *Oedipus Tyrannus,* c. 429; *Electra,* c. 411; *Philoctetes,* 409; *Oedipus at Colonus,* 401.

Few facts of Sophocles' biography are known. He was born about 496 B.C. at Colonus in Attica, near Athens, and his father's name was Sophillus, said by tradition to have been a carpenter, a blacksmith, or a sword-cutler. Perhaps he owned slaves skilled in these trades. At least Sophocles moved in the best society and was not lampooned by the comic writers for low birth, as was his rival Euripides. He married legitimately a woman named Nicostrate, who bore him a son Iophon. His second wife, a woman of Sicyon, was, according to Athenian law, not legally a wife. She bore him illegitimate children, including a son Ariston, whose son, Sophocles, was legitimized, wrote tragedies, and staged his grandfather's *Oedipus at Colonus* immediately after the latter's death. In his old age the poet kept a mistress, Archippe, whom he named his heiress, but she was cheated of her legacy.

It is reported that as a boy he was handsome and well educated in the conventional music and gymnastics, that he was chosen to lead the chorus that celebrated the victory of Salamis in 480 B.C. He studied music under Lampros, an outstanding professional musician (the term is broader than today), and he learned the art of writing tragedy from Aeschylus, with whom he was eventually to compete and sometimes defeat. His first production was offered in 468 B.C. but the names of the tragedies then presented are not certainly known. It is generally agreed that the *Antigone* was the first of his surviving plays to be produced. This is dated by the fact that its popularity is credited with getting him elected to the board of ten generals (another of whom was Pericles), whose term of office occurred during the Samian war of 441–439 B.C.

Sophocles was already a public figure. He had been elected to the board of Hellenotamiai, the treasurers of the Athenian League, in 443. This was the year in which the tribute list was revised, and therefore the office was exceptionally responsible. He held the generalship again some years later. Of his qualities as a general we know only that Pericles once said to him, "You may know how to write poetry, but you certainly don't know how to command an army."

An uncertain tradition connects Sophocles with the introduction of the worship of Asclepius, the god of healing, at Athens, makes him a priest of a mysterious healer god Alon (or Alkon), and has the Athenians decree him heroic honors under the name Dexion (Receiver) after his death. This tradition may reflect his interest in Ionian medicine. He certainly knew the historian Herodotus, and from the language of his plays, as well as from other sources, we are fairly certain that he was aware of the growing interest in the technical aspects of language, from which the sciences of grammar, rhetoric, and logic took their start.

Sophocles' personality impressed his contemporaries with its gentleness and even temper. He lived, of course, through the great Periclean Age of Athens—until 406 or 405—and came to symbolize to a later generation the largeness, serenity, and idealism of that time. His dramas reflect these qualities in the idealized aspect of their heroes, the ease and skill of their dramatic construction, and the calm beauty of many of their choral odes. They have, however, something more than these qualities. The hero of a Sophoclean tragedy is at bottom intransigent. He is destroyed by circumstances, only partly, if at all, of his own making, which would crush into nothingness a lesser man. Yet, though destroyed he is not crushed. For us, as spectators, he retains in his ruin the integrity of his nature. Sophocles' dramatic skill consists in his ability to reveal this quality through speeches of the characters and songs by the chorus. His heroes are intelligent. Though they do not foresee their approaching doom, they recognize it when it is at hand for what it is. The action of most of the tragedies consists in showing by dialogue or monologue the steps by which this awareness is achieved. Sophocles uses the chorus well to heighten this effect. The chorus sympathizes with the hero, but feels terror at his suffering. They would be crushed by it. They often give expression to pessimism about life as a result of being close observers of the tragic fate of the hero. This pessimism is often wrongly attributed to Sophocles himself.

Not all of the extant tragedies—seven out of some one hundred twenty he wrote—exactly fit this pattern. Sophocles had a variety of things to say, but he is most Sophoclean in the plays that do fit it to a greater or less degree. Antigone, the daughter of Oedipus, is the starkest tragic figure in her self-isolation in the cause of her brother's burial. *Oedipus Tyrannus* shows the hero weaving for himself an involuntary net of dire circumstance to discover his own undoing. Even in his last play, *Oedipus at Colonus,* Sophocles shows us the same hero, still maintaining his integrity and ending in the awe-filled isolation of a mysterious death. *Ajax* is a variation on the theme. The hero has in madness disgraced himself. Suicide and its consequences in regard to his burial raise the problem of the place of the hero in a world of politicians and small minded men. Herakles in the *Women of Trachis* literally goes through fire to purge away his human weakness. Only the *Philoctetes* mutes the theme. Though the hero suffers and stands firm, a happy ending is brought about by the intervention of a god. *Electra,* dealing with the old theme of the punishment of the murderers of Agamemnon, is more a melodrama than a tragedy. Orestes and Electra do the bloody deed and rejoice at the end. They, too, preserve their integrity, but at the cost for the spectators of appearing devoid of human feeling. This statement could not be made of any other Sophoclean heroes that we know.

Sophocles is said by Aristotle, in the *Poetics,* to have introduced a third actor. This device made possible more varied scenes, with three viewpoints possible at one time. He also is said to have invented scene-painting.

Sophocles lacks Aeschylus' brooding and dark grandeur, his cosmic background to man's fate, the grim, majestic gods who tread his stage. Perhaps for this reason Sophocles gave up the practice of presenting three plays on a single subject. For him the gods who appear on the stage are dramatic devices. The real motive forces are less tangible; they are gods ultimately, but working through an oracular screen and in man's inner character. Sophocles' language, therefore, is tenser and more ironic than Aeschylus', his poetry is more metaphor and allusion and less verbal ornament. Finally, he was probably more rationally intelligent than Aeschylus, less direct in feeling. He once said to Aeschylus, "Even if you do the right thing, you don't know why." Sophocles certainly knew why.

BIBLIOGRAPHICAL REFERENCES: The standard edition in English is R. C. Jebb, *Sophocles, The Plays and Fragments*, containing critical commentary and full notes, 7 vols., 1885–1896. For translations see also F. Storr, *Sophocles, with an English Translation*, in the Loeb Classical Library, 2 vols., 1919; and Whitney J. Oates and Eugene O'Neill, Jr., *The Complete Greek Drama*, 2 vols., 1938. For general studies and criticism see also A. E. Haigh, *The Tragic Drama of the Greeks*, 1896; J. T. Sheppard, *Aeschylus and Sophocles*, 1927; Gilbert Norwood, *Greek Tragedy*, 1928; Edith Hamilton, *The Greek Way*, 1930; R. C. Flickinger, *The Greek Theater and Its Drama*, 1936 (3rd edition); W. N. Bates, *Sophocles: Poet and Dramatist*, 1940; P. W. Harsh, *A Handbook of Classical Drama*, 1944; C. M. Bowra, *Sophoclean Tragedy*, 1945; Moses Hadas, *A History of Greek Literature*, 1950; Bernard Knox, *The Heroic Temper, Studies in Sophoclean Tragedy*, 1964; and Thomas M. Woodard, ed., *Sophocles: A Collection of Critical Essays*, 1966.

ROBERT SOUTHEY

Born: Bristol, England
Date: August 12, 1774

Died: Greta Hall, Keswick, England
Date: March 21, 1843

PRINCIPAL WORKS

POEMS: *Ballads*, 1796-1798; *Joan of Arc*, 1796; *Thalaba the Destroyer*, 1801; *Madoc*, 1805; *The Curse of Kehama*, 1810; *Roderick, the Last of the Goths*, 1814; *The Vision of Judgment*, 1821.
BIOGRAPHY: *Life of Nelson*, 1813; *Life of Wesley*, 1820; *Sir Thomas More*, 1829.
HISTORY: *History of Brazil*, 1810; *History of the Expedition of Orsua and Crimes of Aguirre*, 1821; *History of the Peninsular War*, 1823.
TRANSLATIONS: *Amadis de Gaul*, 1805; *Palmerin of England*, 1807; *Chronicle of the Cid*, 1808.

One of the hardiest of English poet laureates, Robert Southey held that post for the last thirty years of his life, from 1813 to 1843. During that time he also held a firm grip on the attention of the English reading public, though the twentieth century has removed him from the pedestal that it still allows Wordsworth and Coleridge. Nevertheless, he was a man of many parts and much energy, and even today it is impossible to dismiss him as a factor in the literary scene of the Romantic era.

Son of a Bristol linen draper, Southey was born in Bristol on August 12, 1774. At the age of three he was surrendered to the care of a maternal aunt, Elizabeth Tyler, of Bath, a lady distinguished by both her personal attractiveness and imperious temper. The latter found employment against her nephew's school, Westminster, when young Robert was expelled for an article about flogging, which he had written for the school paper. Another sympathetic relative, the Reverend Herbert Hill, sent him on to Oxford where, after Christ Church rejected him because of the Westminster incident, he was accepted at Balliol in November, 1792.

At Oxford, according to Southey's own confession, his chief interests turned out to be boating and swimming. He did, however, briefly espouse the cause of the French Revolution; at Oxford, too, he first met Coleridge, who promptly converted him to Unitarianism and Pantisocracy. The two youths jointly sponsored an idealistic scheme to establish a perfect community on the banks of the Susquehanna in Pennsylvania. The venture died stillborn, for lack of funds, but not before Southey and Coleridge had equipped themselves with helpmates in the persons of the Fricker sisters. Another even more dubious byproduct of their scheme was Southey's sudden loss of his aunt's patronage; that strong-minded person, accidentally hearing of the Utopian project, promptly dismissed him from her house and her affections.

After various temporary employments, Southey settled at Keswick in 1803, where his family shared a double house with the Coleridges. Here he devoted himself completely to literature, forming a connection with the *Quarterly Review* and turning out a steady stream of books, poems, and articles. Of these, comparatively few are read today. Modern taste does not respond to the ambitious epic poems which were Southey's chief stock in trade, though *Thalaba the Destroyer*,

Madoc, and *The Curse of Kehama* achieved considerable contemporary success. A few shorter poems, such as "The Battle of Blenheim" and "The Inchcape Rock," have survived the blight which has overtaken most of Southey's poetry; but modern criticism prefers the author's prose to his verse, especially as regards such outstanding biographies as his *Life of Nelson* and a *Life of Wesley.*

Though the laureateship, in 1813, brought added recognition to Southey, its effect was offset by a series of family tragedies. The deaths of his much-loved son and a daughter were followed by an additional blow, the loss of his wife's sanity. Mrs. Southey died in 1837, and two years later Southey was married again, to Caroline Bowles; but his health had already broken under the strain. Four years after his second marriage, he succumbed to an attack of brain fever, dying at Keswick on March 21, 1843. Wordsworth attended his funeral, and memorials were placed in Westminster Abbey and Bristol Cathedral.

BIBLIOGRAPHICAL REFERENCES: Southey's letters provide valuable source material. Of the various editions, the first and most complete is *The Life and Correspondence of the Late Robert Southey,* edited by his son, Charles Cuthbert Southey, 6 vols., 1849–1850. See also John Dennis, *Robert Southey: The Story of His Life Written in His Letters,* 1894; and more recently Kenneth Curry, ed., *New Letters,* 1965. The best brief biography is Edward Dowden's *Southey,* in the English Men of Letters Series, 1879. See also W. Haller, *The Early Life of Robert Southey, 1774–1803,* 1917; Jack Simmons, *Robert Southey,* 1945; and Geoffrey Carnall, *Robert Southey and His Age,* 1960.

MURIEL SPARK

Born: Edinburgh, Scotland
Date: 1918

Principal Works

NOVELS: *The Comforters,* 1957; *Robinson,* 1958; *Memento Mori,* 1959; *The Ballad of Peckham Rye,* 1960; *The Bachelors,* 1960; *Voices at Play,* 1961; *The Prime of Miss Jean Brodie,* 1961; *The Girls of Slender Means,* 1963; *The Mandelbaum Gate,* 1965; *The Public Image,* 1968; *The Driver's Seat,* 1970; *Not to Disturb,* 1972.
SHORT STORIES: *The Go-Away Bird,* 1958; *Collected Stories, I,* 1967.
POEMS: *The Fanfarlo and Other Verse,* 1952; *Collected Poems, I,* 1967.
PLAY: *Doctors of Philosophy,* 1963.
CRITICISM: *Tribute to Wordsworth* (joint editor), 1950; *Selected Poems of Emily Bronte* (editor), 1952; *Child of Light: A Reassessment of Mary Shelley,* 1951; *John Masefield,* 1953; *Emily Bronte, Her Life and Work,* 1953; *The Bronte Letters* (editor), 1954; *Letters of John Henry Newman* (joint editor), 1957.

Muriel Spark's numerous novels pose a major critical problem: they might be termed "metaphysical satire," and they leave the reader unsure whether the author intends metaphysics or satire to be their primary impact. Mrs. Spark herself provides no clues, either in the novels or through personal statements. A canny Scotswoman, she has said that her novels speak for themselves and do not need her elaboration.

Muriel Spark was born in Edinburgh and educated at James Gillespie's School for Girls, an experience which bears certain resemblances to the setting of her best-known work, *The Prime of Miss Jean Brodie.* She was primarily known as an interesting, if minor, poetess who edited *The Poetry Review* in the late 1940's, and wrote a series of critical evaluations. As was the case with her poetry, the criticism was competent but little more.

In 1957, Mrs. Spark published a surprising novel which demonstrated not only a sure grasp of the fictional form, but also probed deeply into the human experience. *The Comforters* was an extraordinary work, and a major triumph for a first novel. Since then, her fiction has become increasingly interesting and increasingly sophisticated.

A Roman Catholic convert, Mrs. Spark deals ultimately in her novels with problems of faith. Her characters are, at a climactic moment in the plot, faced with a moral choice, and each novel's interest revolves about the manner in which they make that choice. The characters in *Memento Mori,* for example, are asked to accept the fact of approaching death, while Barbara Vaughn (of *The Mandelbaum Gate*) must decide whether human love or religious orthodoxy is most important in her life.

Part of Mrs. Spark's power lies in the centrality of metaphysical concerns to all her books. The surface details of her situations, always incisively and wittily sketched, create a disturbing tension when confronted by terrifying, otherworldly elements. Her vision of life, which she finds faintly comic, is invariably oblique; further, the very suspense of the novels adds to their tension. The complexity of her plots has been criticized: some reviewers found *The Driver's Seat* little more than a pretentious detective story masquerading as a moral fable.

Mrs. Spark has been favorably compared to both Waugh and Golding, and with validity. She has managed to combine mysticism with satire, eccentricity with pathos, and as a result her novels, if not without flaws, are among the most satisfying of contemporary English fiction.

BIBLIOGRAPHICAL REFERENCES: The most extensive commentary is in Derek Stanford, *Muriel Spark: A Biographical and Critical Study*, 1963. See also Karl Malkoff, *Muriel Spark*, 1968; J. Wildman, "Translated by Muriel Spark," *Nine Essays in Modern Literature*, edited by Derek Stanford, 1965; George Greene, "A Reading of Muriel Spark," *Thought*, XLIII (1968), 393–407; Charles Shapiro, editor, *Contemporary British Novelists*, 1965; and Frank Kermode, *Continuities*, 1968.

STEPHEN SPENDER

Born: London, England
Date: February 28, 1909

Principal Works

POEMS: *Nine Entertainments,* 1928; *Twenty Poems,* 1930; *Poems,* 1933; *Poems,* 1934; *Vienna,* 1935; *The Still Centre,* 1939; *Ruins and Visions,* 1942; *Poems of Dedication,* 1947; *Returning to Vienna,* 1947; *The Edge of Being,* 1949; *Collected Poems, 1928–1953,* 1955; *The Generous Days,* 1971.

CRITICISM: *The Destructive Element,* 1936; *The Creative Element,* 1954; *The Struggle of the Moderns,* 1963.

PLAYS: *Trial of a Judge,* 1938.

ESSAYS: *Forward from Liberalism,* 1937; *Life and the Poet,* 1942, *Citizens in War and After,* 1945; *Shelley,* 1952; *The Making of a Poem,* 1955; *The Year of the Young Rebels,* 1969.

TRAVEL SKETCHES AND IMPRESSIONS: *European Witness,* 1946; *Learning Laughter,* 1953.

AUTOBIOGRAPHY: *World Within World,* 1951.

SHORT STORIES: *The Burning Cactus,* 1936.

NOVELS: *The Backward Son,* 1940; *Engaged in Writing,* and *The Fool and the Princess,* 2 vols. in one, 1958.

Stephen (Harold) Spender was born on February 28, 1909, in London, the son of an English father, journalist Edwin Harold Spender, and a German-Jewish mother, Violet Schuster Spender. After attending University College School and University College, Oxford, which he left in 1931 without taking his degree, he became associated in London with the vocal and promising group of young poets which included Christopher Isherwood, W. H. Auden, Louis MacNeice, and C. Day Lewis. As early as 1928 he had published a book of verse called *Nine Entertainments,* which was followed by *Twenty Poems* two years later. It was not until 1933, however, with the publication of *Poems,* that he began to receive widespread recognition. Critics applauded the lyrical, Shelleyan quality of his poetry which was infused, however, with the Marxist views of the decade. Although he was always an individualist and never a doctrinaire Communist, much of his poetry was based upon a criticism of capitalism and espousal of the cause of the proletariat and revolutionary movements. *Vienna* showed his awareness of the events which were producing the ominous political tensions of Europe, and in 1937, while he was attending the leftist International Writers' Congress in Spain, he found himself in the midst of the Spanish Civil War. A drama, *Trial of a Judge,* was not as successful as his lyric writing had been.

In 1939, the year he published *The Still Centre,* Spender became cofounder with Cyril Connolly of the influential literary magazine, *Horizon,* only to break with Connolly over political policy in 1941. From 1941 through 1944 he served as a member of the London Auxiliary Fire Service, still managing to continue his work, however, and to publish *Ruins and*

Visions in 1942. Like many other disillusioned artists and intellectuals, but considerably later than some, he broke with communism after the war, recording his struggle in *The God That Failed*. In postwar years his reputation as a poet has declined somewhat (unlike that of his friend and colleague Auden) while his stature as a critic and prose writer has grown. In 1936 he had published *The Burning Cactus,* a book of short stories, and in 1940 the novel, *A Backward Son. World Within World* was a sensitive, reflective, and at times lyrical autobiography which further showed his versatility as a mature man of letters. *Collected Poems, 1928–1953,* which was published in 1955, emphasized the fact that though he might not be a twentieth century Shelley, he is an influential and a major modern poet. In addition to editing three anthologies of English poetry, he has translated two volumes of the work of Rainer Maria Rilke and one of the poetry of Federico García Lorca. Since 1953 co-editor of *Encounter,* he continues as a prolific poet-critic-editor whose career has in many ways been typical of that of the literary artist of his generation.

BIBLIOGRAPHICAL REFERENCES: For biographical detail the most reliable work is the poet's autobiography, *World Within World,* 1951. Most of the books dealing with English literature of the 1930's contain material on Spender; see in particular Francis Scarfe, "Stephen Spender: A Sensitive," in *Auden and After,* 1942. See also James G. Southworth, "Stephen Spender," *Sewanee Review,* XLV (1937), 272–284; C. I. Glicksberg, "Poetry and the Social Revolution," *Dalhousie Review,* XVII (1938), 493–503; and Willis D. Jacobs, "The Moderate Poetical Success of Stephen Spender," *College English,* XVII (1956), 374–378.

EDMUND SPENSER

Born: London, England
Date: c. 1552

Died: Westminster, London
Date: January 13, 1599

Principal Works

POEMS: *The Shepheardes Calender*, 1579; *The Faerie Queene*, 1590–1596; *Daphnaïda*, 1591; *Complaints*, 1591; *Colin Clout's Come Home Again*, 1595; *Astrophel*, 1595; *Amoretti*, 1595; *Epithalamion*, 1595; *Fowre Hymns*, 1596; *Prothalamion*, 1596.

POLITICAL TRACT: *View of the Present State of Ireland*, 1633 (written in 1596).

Edmund Spenser was one of three children born, probably in 1552, to John and Elizabeth Spenser. He tells us in *Prothalamion* that London was his birthplace. With his brother he attended the Merchant Taylors' School under the famous educator Richard Mulcaster, whose progressive theories included even education for women, though he was unable to put this practice into effect. Under Mulcaster the principal studies were Hebrew, Greek, Latin, French, English, and music; the students also had experience in acting, which the master thought of considerable educational value.

When Spenser was still in his teens, his first published poetry appeared in *A Theatre wherein be represented . . . the miseries & calamities that follow voluptuous Worldlings* (1569). In the same year he entered Pembroke College, Cambridge. At college he was apparently a wide reader rather than a profound scholar. Among his favorite classical authors were Plato, Aristotle, and Vergil; among his later favorites, Chaucer and Ariosto. At Cambridge began his lasting friendship with Gabriel Harvey, the pedantic target of much Elizabethan wit and barbed satire. Also at Cambridge he imbibed Puritan leanings. As both Mulcaster and Harvey were stanch advocates of English composition rather than Latin specialization, Spenser was a worthy protégé of both men. He received his M.A. degree from Cambridge in 1576, and left to visit some of his family in Lancashire.

His first trip to Ireland, the scene of much of his mature life, was probably made in 1577. In 1578 he was in London as secretary of Dr. John Young, Bishop of Rochester. In 1579 the first major event of his literary career took place, the publication of *The Shepheardes Calender*. Looking back over the great peaks of *Paradise Lost* and the Elizabethan drama, the modern reader can hardly realize the impact the *Calender* must have had on the poetic circle of its day. A good preparation for a modern reader would be a retirement of several weeks spent with the poetry written and published between 1500 and 1579; after this Spenser would be a revelation. The *Calender*, published anonymously, was dedicated to Sir Philip Sidney, and was furnished with notes by a mysterious E. K.—supposedly a close friend of the author—with great inside knowledge, but with very convenient ignorance about any matter which might have political repercussions. In general it has been assumed that E. K. was Spenser's friend Edward Kirke, but that most of the notes were furnished or inspired by Spenser himself. Obviously the pastoral names of the characters sometimes cloak actual individuals, but some may have been entirely fictitious. For example, much throwing about of brains has gone into the identification of Rosalind, Colin Clout's beloved. Was she an early sweetheart? Was she an aristocratic patroness treated with the conventional love-fiction that Queen Elizabeth received from her courtiers? Or was she a fictional mistress? There are several answers, but no certain one. Colin Clout remained Spenser's poetic nom de plume in the autobiographical *Colin Clout's Come Home Again* and in the sixth book of *The Faerie Queene*.

As the dedication of the *Calender* indicates, by 1579 Spenser was acquainted with Sir Philip Sidney; and he also knew Sidney's uncle, the Earl of Leicester, who had a distinguished career as a patron (see Eleanor Rosenburg, *Leicester, Patron of Letters*, 1955). For some reason the Earl did not take the interest in Spenser that the latter hoped for—or, indeed, that his ability justified. It is ironical that today Leicester is more remembered for his half-hearted patronage of Spenser than for his whole-hearted patronage of many others.

In 1580 Spenser went to Ireland as a secretary of Lord Grey de Wilton, the Lord Deputy of Ireland, whose policies he defended in verse and prose for many years to come. For about eight years he lived in or near Dublin. During this period the friendship between Spenser and Lodowick Bryskett developed. Bryskett's *Discourse of Civil Life* (1606) contains an account of a courtly conversation with Spenser in a literary company. Bryskett also contributed poems to Spenser's *Astrophel*, the memorial volume on the death of Sir Philip Sidney. He was Clerk of the Council of Munster, in which province Spenser lived from 1588 to 1598, serving for part of that time as Bryskett's deputy.

In 1589 Sir Walter Raleigh visited Spenser in Munster. The visit was recorded in *Colin Clout's Come Home Again*, the dedicatory letter of which is dated 1591. Spenser returned Raleigh's visit and brought with him to London three books of *The Faerie Queene*, on which he had been working for about a decade. To his great disappointment the visit did not lead to an eminent position in the Court; but he did gain a pension of fifty pounds, by no means a contemptible amount—if, as J. B. Fletcher stated, the poet ever collected it. The first three books of *The Faerie Queene* were published in 1590. The next six years were productive ones, climaxed by the publication in 1596 of the first six books of the masterpiece, bringing it to the halfway point. Only a scant surviving fragment takes the poem any further toward completion. These productive years of writing and publishing were filled with turmoil and disappointment. For ten years Spenser was harassed by lawsuits instigated by Lord Roche of Fermoy, who earned thereby an unenviable immortality.

The final decade of Spenser's life was not, however, a period of unmitigated gloom: in 1594 he married Elizabeth Boyle and celebrated his love and marriage by publishing his sonnets, *Amoretti*, and his magnificent marriage hymn, *Epithalamion*. Some skeptics believe the sonnets were originally written to another girl; but the general view is that the sequence is unique in the Tudor period in being written and addressed to the poet's wife. The couple had three children (a fourth one believed in formerly has now been attributed to gossip alone).

In 1598, in Tyrone's rebellion,

Spenser's Irish home, Kilcolman Castle, was sacked. He and his family escaped first to Cork and then to England; but within a month after his return to his native land he died. He was buried near Chaucer's tomb in what is now known as Poets' Corner in Westminster Abbey.

Probably no poet of comparable merit and former reputation in English literature suffers a comparable neglect today. Perhaps in the future, readers will regain the taste for allegory and the skills for deciphering it with pleasure. If so, they will find that Spenser is far more than a mere painter with words and that he is thoroughly relevant to modern times.

BIBLIOGRAPHICAL REFERENCES: The foundation of all modern Spenser studies is *The Works of Edmund Spenser*, 10 vols., 1932–1945, a variorum edition edited by Edwin Greenlaw, Charles G. Osgood, Frederick M. Padelford, and Roy Heffner. See also J. C. Smith and E. de Sélincourt, *The Poetical Works of Edmund Spenser*, 1912. Other biographical and critical studies include C. H. Whitman, *A Subject-Index to the Poems of Edmund Spenser*, 1918; W. L. Renwick, *Edmund Spenser*, 1925; H. S. V. Jones, *A Spenser Handbook*, 1930; B. E. C. Davis, *Edmund Spenser*, 1933; Janet Spens, *Spenser's Faerie Queene*, 1934; C. S. Lewis, *The Allegory of Love*, 1938; A. C. Judson, *The Life of Edmund Spenser*, 1945; L. Bradner, *Spenser and the Faerie Queene*, 1948; Jefferson B. Fletcher, "Edmund Spenser," *Encyclopedia Americana*, Vol. XXV (1955); Josephine W. Bennett, *The Evolution of "The Faerie Queene,"* 1960; and A. C. Hamilton, *The Structure of Allegory in "The Faerie Queene,"* 1961. There is also the *Annotated Bibliography 1937–1960*, edited by Waldo F. McNeir and Foster Provost, 1962.

BENEDICTUS DE SPINOZA

Born: Amsterdam, Netherlands
Date: November 24, 1632

Died: The Hague, Netherlands
Date: February 20, 1677

PRINCIPAL WORKS

PHILOSOPHICAL TREATISES: *Renati des Cartes principia philosophiae*, 1663 (*Principles of Descartes' Philosophy*), with *Cogitata metaphysica* (*Metaphysical Thoughts*); *Tractatus theologico-politicus*, 1670 (*Theological-Political Treatise*); *Opera posthuma*, 1677 (*Posthumous Works*): *Ethica ordine geometrico demonstrata* (*Ethics*), *Tractatus politicus* (*Politics*), *De intellectus emendatione* (*On the Improvement of the Understanding*), *Epistolae doctorum quorundam virorum ad B.D.S. et auctoris responsiones* (*Letters and Replies*), *Compendium grammatices linguae Hebraeae* (*Hebrew Grammar*); *Tractatus de Deo et homine eiusque felicitate*, 1862 (*A Short Treatise on God, Man, and His Well-being*).

Benedictus de Spinoza, the great Dutch philosopher who tried to demonstrate the existence and nature of God in a geometrically precise fashion, was christened Baruch, the son of Michael and Hannah Deborah de Spinoza, descendants of Jews who, having been forced into the Catholic faith and having practiced their Jewish religion in secret, fled from Spain and Portugal during the Inquisition. Michael Spinoza was a merchant, only moderately prosperous, and Baruch, born in Amsterdam on November 24, 1632, was the third child of his second wife. Baruch's mother died when he was six years old, and Baruch was probably left in the care of Rebecca, the remaining child of Michael Spinoza's first marriage.

He attended a local Hebrew school where his education began with the Hebrew alphabet and proceeded through the Old Testament and the Talmud. When he was eight years old his father married for the third time, and the family soon moved to better quarters as the father's business improved. The boy's studies continued; his work was so promising that he went on to advanced studies at a Hebrew academy, Etz Hayim, and remained there from 1645 to 1652.

Sometime in the course of his studies Spinoza began to doubt the truth of what he was being taught. Although he followed the Hebrew tradition, at the same time he began to study philosophy and gradually to convince himself that he was not interested in being a rabbi. His questioning attitude became apparent to his fellow students, and in 1656, two years after his father's death, he was excommunicated by the Jews. Feeling against him was intense; at one time before the excommunication someone had tried to assassinate him. Spinoza, believing himself to be right in his doubts, quietly settled in Amsterdam and took up the trade of grinding lenses. The work was arduous and painstaking, and the dust irritated his lungs, but he was able to devote his nights to study, particularly to the reading of Descartes. Fascinated with Descartes' method of building up proofs from ideas that could not be doubted, he began to consider constructing an account of reality that would have geometrical exactness.

He changed his name from Baruch to Benedictus, the Latin form of Baruch, which means "blessed," and thereby completed his liberation from the traditions of his fathers. He studied Latin with the Dutch scholar Van den Enden, and there were rumors that he was attracted to his tutor's daughter. If he was, nothing came of it; and Spinoza finally left Amsterdam and moved to the village of Rijnsburg. While he was there he wrote his first philosophical work, *Principles of Descartes' Philosophy*, an attempt to put into geometric form the philosophy of Descartes. At the same time he was working on other projects, the most important being his *Ethics;* and he was spending a considerable amount of time corresponding and helping visiting students who came to him from Amsterdam. He moved to The Hague, and in 1670 his second book appeared, the *Theological-Political Treatise*. It caused a furor, for the philosopher's conception of God and reality was quite different from the orthodox Christian and Jewish views. The Dutch Synod prohibited the work; the Catholics put it on the Index, and its anonymous author was condemned as the devil. When Spinoza became known as the author, the criticism abated to some extent because of his quiet manner and scholarly reputation, but it never wholly died down during his lifetime.

Offered the chair of philosophy at Heidelberg, he refused the post in order to be free both in his opinion and in his time to write. He continued to grind lenses during the day and to write philosophy at night. Pleasant in his personal relationships, he had many good friends. His death came at The Hague on February 20, 1677 from tuberculosis, probably as the result of having breathed glass dust over the years. As he had planned it, his principal works were published after his death; and the quality of them is such that Spinoza has become one of the most famous and respected of philosophers.

BIBLIOGRAPHICAL REFERENCES: The Spinoza *Opera* appeared in 4 vols. in 1926. Abraham Wolf edited the *Correspondence* in 1928. For biographical and analytical studies see H. H. Joachim, *A Study of the Ethics of Spinoza*, 1901; Abraham Wolf's commentary on *A Short Treatise on God, Man, and Well-being*, 1910; J. A. Gunn, *Benedict Spinoza*, 1925, with a bibliography; R. P. Mackeon, *The Philosophy of Spinoza*, 1928; Leon Roth, *Spinoza*, 1929; H. F. Hallett, *Aeternitas: A Spinozistic Study*, 1930; Lewis Browne, *Blesséd Spinoza*, 1932; H. A. Wolfson, *The Philosophy of Spinoza*, 2 vols., 1934; David Bidney, *The Psychology and Ethics of Spinoza*, 1940; Stuart Hampshire, *Spinoza*, 1951; Ruth L. Saw, *The Vindication of Metaphysics: A Study in the Philosophy of Spinoza*, 1951; Paul Siwek, *Au cœur du spinozisme*, 1952; G. H. R. Parkinson, *Spinoza's Theory of Knowledge*, 1954; Robert J. McShea, *The Political Philosophy of Spinoza*, 1968; Edwin M. Curley, *Spinoza's Metaphysics*, 1969; and Dan Levin, *Spinoza, the Young Thinker Who Destroyed the Past*, 1970.

MADAME DE STAËL

Born: Paris, France
Date: April 22, 1766

Died: Paris
Date: July 14, 1817

Principal Works

NOVELS: *Delphine*, 1802; *Corinne*, 1807.

ESSAYS: *Lettres sur le caractère et les écrits de J. J. Rousseau*, 1788; *De l'Influence des passions*, 1796 (*The Influence of the Passions*); *De la littérature considerée dans ses rapports avec les institutions sociales*, 1800 (*The Influence of Literature on Society*); *De l'Allemagne*, 1810 (*Germany*); *Considérations sur la révolution française*, 1818 (*Considerations on the Principal Events of the French Revolution*).

A leader of the movement to destroy the classical influence on French literature and thought, Anne Louise Germaine de Staël, nee Necker, brought Romantic thought to the forefront of French consciousness. A friend of writers, scientists, and statesmen since childhood, she grew up in an atmosphere of intellectual freedom. Her salon provided a meeting place for literary and political radicals and her literary work introduced the current of German Romanticism into French culture.

Born in Paris on April 22, 1766, the daughter of Jacques Necker, finance minister of Louis XVI, she married the Swedish ambassador to Paris, the Baron de Staël-Holstein, largely because he would be too ineffectual to disturb her love affairs; she divorced him in 1797. To escape the Reign of Terror, she fled to Coppet, Switzerland, where she bore the Comte de Narbonne's son. She visited England and returned to Paris, where she began her famous love affair with Benjamin Constant. Napoleon exiled her for her political activities in 1803, and she set up her salon at Coppet. During her long exile she traveled widely and wrote her most important book, *Germany*, which became a source book for French Romanticism. In 1811 she married Albert de la Rocca, who survived her by one year.

Apart from her books on literature and society, Madame de Staël wrote two romantic novels, *Delphine* and *Corinne*, and introduced the popular figure of the misunderstood heroine into French literature. A believer in the inevitability of progress, she set the themes for much of the literature of nineteenth century France and England. She died in Paris on July 14, 1817.

BIBLIOGRAPHICAL REFERENCES: The most comprehensive biographical studies are Lady Blennerhasset, *Madame de Staël et son temps*, 1887-1889; and D. G. Larg, *Madame de Staël*, 2 vols., 1926-1928. More recent studies are Olga Taxis-Bordogna, *Madame de Staël*, 1949; and Wayne Andrews, *Germaine: A Portrait of Madame de Staël*, 1963. See also Paul Gautier, *Madame de Staël et Napoleon*, 1903; also Pierre Kohler, *Madame de Staël et la Suisse*, 1918, and *Au château de Coppet*, 1952.

STATIUS
Publius Papinius Statius

Born: Naples, Italy
Date: c. 45

Died: Naples
Date: c. 96

Principal Works

POEMS: *Thebais; Achilleid; Silvae.*

Publius Papinius Statius, born in Naples about 45, was a poet of the court of the Emperor Domitian (81–96) and wrote adulatory poetry for that emperor who had no taste for verse. Statius' father had been a poet and the son began early and competed frequently, and usually successfully, in poetic contests in Naples. One clue to his success may be his public acknowledgment that the public never saw his verse until it had been approved by the Divine Emperor.

Victor at Domitian's festival at Alba, where he was awarded the coveted gold wreath from Domitian's hands, he entered the quinquennial Capitoline competition in 94, but failed to win the oakleaf crown. Discouraged, he returned to Naples and died in that city about A.D. 96.

It took Statius twelve years to complete the twelve books of his Vergilian poem, the *Thebais*. Only fragments remain of his epic about the early life of Achilles. In his own time, and through the Middle Ages, Statius was overesteemed as an epic poet. His *Silvae* are pleasant occasional verses about his friends, the emperor, and his wife Claudia. He also wrote a birthday ode to Lucan, valuable because of its comments on earlier writers.

BIBLIOGRAPHICAL REFERENCES: See *Works of Statius,* translated by D. A. Slater, in Oxford Library of Translations, 1908; and J. H. Mozley, *Statius with English Translations,* 2 vols., 1928. Some special studies are Thomas M. Greene, "Virgil," *The Descent from Heaven, a Study in Epic Continuity,* 1963, 74–103; A. J. Gossage, "Virgil and the Flavian Epic" in Donald R. Dudley, ed., *Virgil,* 1969, 67–93; and A. B. Wise, *The Influence of Statius upon Chaucer,* 1967.

SIR RICHARD STEELE

Born: Dublin, Ireland
Date: March, 1672

Died: Near Carmarthen, Wales
Date: September 1, 1729

Principal Works

PLAYS: *The Funeral, or Grief-à-la-Mode,* 1701; *The Lying Lover,* 1703; *The Tender Husband,* 1705; *The Conscious Lovers,* 1722.
ESSAYS: *The Tatler,* 1709–1710, and *The Spectator,* 1711–1712 (with Addison); *The Plebiean,* 1718; *The Theatre,* 1720.
ETHICAL TREATISES: *The Christian Hero,* 1701.

Sir Richard Steele was born in Dublin in March, 1672, the son of an attorney. Both his parents died when he was a child, and he became the ward of a prominent uncle, Henry Gascoigne. Through his uncle's influence he entered the Charterhouse School in 1684, where he met and became the lifelong friend of Joseph Addison. In 1689 he followed Addison to Oxford University, but while Addison remained to take his M.A. and to become a fellow, Steele left without a degree in 1694 to enlist as private in a regiment of guards under the command of his uncle's employer, the Duke of Ormond. On the strength of a poem which he published anonymously, he became in the following year an ensign in Lord Cutts' regiment.

By 1700 he was Captain Steele, stationed at the Tower, and the friend of Sir Charles Sedley, Vanbrugh, Congreve, and other wits and writers of the day. In that same year Dryden died, and Congreve published his last important play, these two latter events marking the sunset of Restoration comedy.

His life as a soldier stationed at the Tower led Steele into excesses of which he repented, and which caused him to publish in 1701 a little book, *The Christian Hero,* to prove "that no principles but those of religion are sufficient to make a great man." The sentiments expressed in this little volume lost him his popularity among his fellow soldiers, and to regain that popularity he wrote his first comedy, *The Funeral, or Grief à-la-Mode,* for "Nothing can make the town so fond of a man as a successful play."

This play, which met with "more than expected success," illustrates the tendency of the age to react against libertine elegance and to return to bourgeois respectability. In it Steele attacks the mockery of grief in the person of Sable the undertaker; the mockery of justice in Puzzle the lawyer; and the popular dramatic disregard for women in the persons of Lady Sharlot and Lady Hariot. This staunch stand for morality is readily seen as unusual when compared with that in the plays of Etherege, Congreve, and even Vanbrugh. The "more than expected success" of this play led Steele to write *The Lying Lover* in 1703; this work was, however, "dam'd for its piety," as Steele himself said. Steele tried again in 1705 with *The Tender Husband* which had somewhat more success than its predecessor, but even so, Steele wrote no more plays for seventeen years.

He entered, instead, into politics (quite actively from 1707 to 1710), and he began to write periodical essays, most significantly in collaboration with his old friend Addison. These two men, with some little help from other writers now forgotten except by scholars, published first *The Tatler,* which appeared three times weekly from 1709–1710, and later *The Spectator,* which appeared daily from 1711–1712. Of both papers Steele was the fathering genius.

In both these forerunners of the modern newspaper, Steele, writing on subjects ranging from descriptions of London and of life in the country to articles on dueling and the question of immortality, preached the gospel of reformed gentility and true gentle manliness to oppose the artificial elegance symbolized by Etherege's Dorimant; and he preached in a style supple and precise, warm and penetrating, a style later used by Benjamin Franklin as a model when he was teaching himself to write. In the dedication to the first collected volume of *The Tatler* (1710), Steele wrote, "The general purpose of this paper, is to expose the false arts of life, to pull off the disguises of cunning, vanity, and affectation, and to recommend a general simplicity in our dress, our discourse, and our behavior."

It is indicative of the trend toward "rational conduct" that these papers were imminently successful in an age when journals, like the lilies of the field, bloomed today and were cast tomorrow in the fire. It is moreover indicative of the influence they had—or the trend they reflected—that when Steele's last play, *The Conscious Lovers,* appeared at Drury Lane in 1722, it ran for eighteen nights and was a great success.

In this play, the contrast with the Restoration is complete. The characters are not fine ladies and gentlemen, but frankly middle class. The lovers do not fence verbally through four acts about their affection before they dare to confess it in the fifth; their mutual love is clear throughout the play, though no amorous words pass between them. Young Bevil, the hero, is not even tainted with rakishness, but is thoroughly upright and worthy; and the solution to the plot which occurs in the last act just in time to show virtue rewarded with wealth, and consequent lifelong happiness, appeared then not at all incongruous, but achieved its purpose of moving the audience to compassion.

Though the play has a well-knit structure—even the startling denouement is handled with sureness and restraint—and though the expression is easy and natural, it celebrates the funeral of Restoration comedy and the coming of age of sentimental comedy. True dramatic comedy is dead, for whatever the faults of Restoration comedy, and they were many, it was dramatic, it was brilliant, and it was funny. Reformation was required, not revolution. But *The Conscious Lovers* banished vice and for a time, at least, theatrical immorality was dead. That dramatic comedy was dead as well seemed at the time unimportant. One imagines Steele would have been pleased, not offended, at Hazlitt's apt remark: "It is almost a misnomer to call them comedies; they are rather homilies in dialogues."

In any case, Sir Richard Steele had temporarily achieved the purpose he set forth in *The Tatler.* In that respect, he must have gone peacefully to his death. He died September 1, 1729. He lies buried in St. Peter's Church, Carmarthen, Wales.

BIBLIOGRAPHICAL REFERENCES: The standard edition of *The Tatler* was edited by George A. Aitken, 4 vols., 1898–1899. There are two modern editions of *The Spectator*, that edited by G. Gregory Smith, 8 vols., 1897–1898, reissued in Everyman's Library, 1907; and the edition by George A. Aitken, 8 vols., 1898. Aitken also edited Steele's *Dramatic Works*, 1894 and 1903; but this has been supplanted by *Plays*, edited by Shirley S. Kenny, 1970. Rae Blanchard has edited several volumes of the miscellaneous works: *The Christian Hero*, 1932; the *Correspondence*, 1941; *Tracts and Pamphlets*, 1944; *Occasional Verses*, 1952; and *The Englishman*, 1955.

The fullest biography is G. A. Aitken, *Life of Richard Steele*, 2 vols., 1889, with a bibliography. More recent are Willard Connely, *Sir Richard Steele*, 1934; Calhoun Winton, *Captain Steele*, 1964; and idem., *Sir Richard Steele, M.P.*, 1970. Still useful is Austin Dobson, *Richard Steele*, 1886. See also the Addison bibliography for studies on the development of the periodical and the periodical essay.

JOHN STEINBECK

Born: Salinas, California
Date: February 27, 1902

Died: New York, N. Y.
Date: December 20, 1968

Principal Works

NOVELS: *Cup of Gold,* 1929; *To a God Unknown,* 1933; *Tortilla Flat,* 1935; *In Dubious Battle,* 1936; *Of Mice and Men,* 1937; *The Grapes of Wrath,* 1939; *The Moon Is Down,* 1942; *Cannery Row,* 1945; *The Wayward Bus,* 1947; *Burning Bright,* 1950; *East of Eden,* 1952; *Sweet Thursday,* 1954; *The Short Reign of Pippin IV: A Fabrication,* 1957; *The Winter of Our Discontent,* 1961.

SHORT STORIES: *The Pastures of Heaven,* 1932; *Saint Katy the Virgin,* 1936; *The Red Pony,* 1937; *The Long Valley,* 1938; *The Pearl,* 1947.

MISCELLANEOUS: *The Forgotten Village,* 1941; *Sea of Cortez,* 1941; *Bombs Away,* 1942; *A Russian Journal,* 1948; *Once There Was a War,* 1958; *Travels with Charley; In Search of America,* 1962; *Letters to Alicia,* 1965; *Journal of a Novel: The East of Eden Letters,* 1969.

PLAY: *Burning Bright; A Play in Three Acts,* 1951.

John (Ernst) Steinbeck's career as a novelist allows us to view a man who has enjoyed great popularity and, for long periods of time, serious literary acclaim. This double success is in part due to the fact that his books gave expression to the social and economic tensions that were at work during the period of his greatest success. *The Grapes of Wrath,* in particular, appeared at an opportune moment when the fate of the "Okies" in his novel seemed also to reflect the fate of the nation.

Steinbeck once wrote inquirers for biographical data: "Please feel free to make up your own facts about me as you need them. I can't remember how much of me really happened and how much I invented. . . . Biography by its very nature must be half-fiction." Nevertheless, the records show that he was born in Salinas, California, on February 27, 1902. His father was active in local politics, and his mother was a schoolteacher in the Big Sur country. At nineteen Steinbeck went to Stanford University, where intermittent enrollment and part-time jobs for six years did not lead to a degree. From California he went to New York via the Panama Canal by freighter and continued to live by casual jobs as newspaperman, hod carrier on the construction of New York buildings, chemist, and day laborer. In retrospect, this drifting career seems admirably designed to fit him to be the novelist of the submerged classes and to speak for those who were not able to speak for themselves.

Steinbeck's first three books sold fewer than three thousand copies, but after the popular attention given *Tortilla Flat* in 1935 he moved rapidly into the literary spotlight. *In Dubious Battle* is a study of the confused currents of self-interest and generous emotion involved in a strike of California fruit pickers. In it one sees, as one has seen ever since, Steinbeck's generous social sympathies qualified by his personal skepticism about the possibility of reform and social progress. This same sympathy played over two itinerant farm hands in *Of Mice and*

Men. In these novels phases of life that more conventionally trained writers would be powerless to handle took on vivid reality.

Steinbeck's full critical acclaim came in 1939 with *The Grapes of Wrath,* awarded the Pulitzer Prize in 1940 and hailed as the twentieth century *Uncle Tom's Cabin.* Social dislocation, the indifference of large-scale economy to private well-being, the havoc wrought by uninformed prejudice—all these important themes find expression in this work. The chief family in the novel, the Joads, became as famous as Sinclair Lewis' Babbitt of twenty years before; both are almost common nouns in our language. Critics were able to point out that the Joads are the "noble savages" of the twentieth century, endowed with much the same dignity and purity of intent that Rousseau and his followers once imagined existed in the American Indian. Critics also pointed to literary sophistication in the novel; interchapters of general comment have a Whitmanesque note, and the conclusion that some readers found shocking is a carefully contrived passage of symbolism.

No subsequent book of Steinbeck's has made a similar impact on the national consciousness, but in novels like *Cannery Row* Steinbeck underlined his claims to a class and a region as his proper subject matter. Certain veins of inverse sentimentality are easy to distinguish in both *Cannery Row* and *The Wayward Bus;* it is a self-evident truth that in Steinbeck's world the virtues of generosity and kindness are found only on the lower rungs of the social ladder, among those very persons whom more fortunate persons call "sinners." It is also apparent that Steinbeck resented the increasing mechanization of our culture and, in romanticizing the dignity of the poor and the outcast, he defended the proper dignity of all men.

East of Eden is a story which, in a sense, is about Steinbeck's own people, one that comes into a focus in a study of the reaction two brothers give to past scandal in their family; the ne'er-do-well brother survives the shock of discovering his mother's profession, but the brother who has lived for conscious purity and uprightness disintegrates when confronted by the truth. In this novel Steinbeck appeared once more as the advocate of unconscious, spontaneous patterns of behavior. The posthumously published *Journal of a Novel* gives an account of the writing of this book.

Steinbeck's career, subsequent to his initial success, was one which mingled travel, journalism, and public utterance on questions of the day. At his best he touched the conscience of his generation and, incidentally, showed us how that conscience works.

BIBLIOGRAPHICAL REFERENCES: There is no authorized biography. Four critical studies important for general reference on the man and his books are Harry T. Moore, *The Novels of John Steinbeck: A First Critical Study,* 1939; Peter Lisca, *The Wide World of John Steinbeck,* 1957; F. W. Watt, *John Steinbeck,* 1962; and Joseph Fontenrose, *John Steinbeck: An Introduction and Interpretation,* 1963. See also Lewis Gannett, *John Steinbeck, Personal and Bibliographical Notes: A Pamphlet,* 1939. A useful introduction to the work is *The Portable Steinbeck,* edited by Pascal Covici, with an introduction by Lewis Gannett, 1943 (enlarged, 1946).

For briefer studies see Percy H. Boynton, *America in Contemporary Fiction,* 1940; Edmund Wilson, *The Boys in the Back Room,* 1941; Maxwell Geismar, *Writers in*

Crisis, 1942; W. M. Frohock, *The Novel of Violence in America,* 1950; John S. Kennedy, "John Steinbeck: Life Affirmed and Dissolved," in *Fifty Years of the American Novel,* edited by Harold C. Gardiner, S.J., 1952; Charles Child Walcutt, *American Literary Naturalism, A Divided Stream,* 1957; Claude E. Jones, "Proletarian Writing and John Steinbeck," *Sewanee Review,* XLVIII (1940), 445–456; Frederic I. Carpenter, "The Philosophical Joads," *College English,* II (1941), 315–325; Lincoln R. Gibbs, "John Steinbeck, Moralist," *Antioch Review,* II (1942), 172–184; Woodburn Ross, "John Steinbeck: Earth and Stars," *Missouri Studies in Honor of A. H. R. Fairchild,* 1946; and Frederick Bracher, "Steinbeck and the Biological View of Man," *Pacific Spectator,* III (1949), 302–310. The most ambitious treatment of Steinbeck criticism to date is *Steinbeck and His Critics: A Record of Twenty-five Years,* a collection of comprehensive and significant essays edited by E. W. Tedlock, Jr., and C. V. Wicker, 1957.

STENDHAL
Marie Henri Beyle

Born: Grenoble, France
Date: January 23, 1783

Died: Paris, France
Date: March 23, 1842

Principal Works

novels: *Armance*, 1827; *Le Rouge et le noir*, 1830 (*The Red and the Black*); *La Chartreuse de Parme*, 1839 (*The Charterhouse of Parma*); *Lamiel*, 1889; *Lucien Leuwen*, 1894, 1926–1927 (I, *The Green Huntsman*; II, *The Telegraph*).
novellas: *L'Abbesse de Castro*, 1839; *Romans et nouvelles*, 1854; *Nouvelles inédites*, 1855.
autobiography: *Journal*, 1923–1924.

Stendhal, born Marie Henri Beyle at Grenoble, France, on January 23, 1783, was the most "unromantic" figure of France's Romantic period (1830–1848), yet he ranks with Hugo, Balzac, Flaubert, and Zola as one of the greatest French novelists of the nineteenth century. Always of an independent nature, he left his Grenoble birthplace at an early age to seek his fortune in Paris. There he obtained a position in the Ministry of War and, in 1800, became a dragoon in the army of Napoleon. He accompanied the army in the Italian, Prussian, and Russian campaigns, serving with distinction until the fall of Napoleon in 1814. Still a young man, he spent the next seven years in Milan, scene of *The Charterhouse of Parma*, one of his two masterpieces. The rest of his life was spent as an independent and stubborn consular officer of France, mainly in Trieste and in Civitavecchia. Tempestuous love affairs occupied a considerable amount of his time, and some of the events connected with these are to be found in his writings. He died at Paris on March 23, 1842.

Stendhal's writing career began in 1814 in Milan. There he produced two studies, *Haydn, Mozart and Métastase* (1814) and *Rome, Naples and Florence* (1817). He also contributed several critical essays to British literary journals during this period, and his name was better known in England then than it was in France. Stendhal's first novel, *Armance*, appeared in 1827. Five years earlier, he had written a searching study of one of his own love affairs under the title *De l'Amour*. None of these early writings received significant attention. In 1830 appeared the first of Stendhal's two unquestioned masterpieces, *The Red and the Black*. The title indicates the strife between the Napoleonic spirit of the military and the power of the clergy, whom Stendhal detested. The protagonist of the novel, Julien Sorel, has come to typify the post-Revolutionary *arriviste* in France. Much of Stendhal is in this character. Sorel is a poor tutor who makes love to his student's mother in order to further his own ambitions. When this woman, his first mistress, betrays him to a second, he attempts to kill her and is condemned to die. In addition to giving a profound psychological study of Sorel, *The Red and the Black* also furnishes an excellent representation of the social upheaval which France had undergone during the years since the Revolution. Sorel epitomizes the uprooted peasant, the man of mediocre talent who is intelligent enough to wish above all to avail himself of the limitless opportunities offered those like him under the Republic.

During the years 1831–1838, Stendhal wrote (but did not publish) two autobiographical works (*Souvenirs d'égotisme* and *La Vie d'Henri Buclard*) and one novel, *Lucien Leuwen*. Stendhal's greatest novel, *The Charterhouse of Parma*, was published in 1839. This is the story of Fabrice del Dongo (roughly the equivalent of Julien Sorel) and his relations with a duchess and a highwayman. The story is laid in nineteenth century Italy, although the most famous passage is a realistic description of the Battle of Waterloo as seen through the young hero's eyes. Stendhal, who professed to love Italy better than France, succeeds admirably in painting a true picture of life in a petty Italian principality, and his study of the loves and intrigues of his characters is again brilliant. This work, like *The Red and the Black*, shows Stendhal at his best: careless of form, but willing to put his brilliant energy and his stubborn and egotistical mind to the task of recording, with effective economy of detail, the minutiae and grandeur of life. Stendhal is not above using improbable characters and situations, but his study of both is brutally exact. Thus he is called both romantic and realist.

In his own day Stendhal was not appreciated, and only Balzac saw much worth to his novels. But in the late 1880's, with the appearance of his unpublished works, there occurred a curious literary revival; he was praised by both the naturalists and the psychologists. His reputation grows with each year, and his journals, recently published, have enjoyed a great success. Stendhal, it has been said, went further than any other writer of France in reconciling the two great literary traditions of that country, classical simplicity and romantic imagination.

BIBLIOGRAPHICAL REFERENCES: Stendhal's *Œuvres Complètes* were published in 79 vols., 1927–1937. His most important works are available in English translation; the most recent to appear was Robert Sage's translation of *The Private Diaries of Stendhal*, 1953. The growing literary stature of Stendhal as a novelist has produced a variety of biographical and critical studies. There are several good introductions in English to his personality and work: F. C. Green, *Stendhal*, 1939; Matthew Josephson, *Stendhal, or the Pursuit of Happiness*, 1946; Howard Clewes, *Stendhal: An Introduction to the Novelist*, 1950; and John Atherton, *Stendhal*, 1965. Studies in French include Leon Blum, *Stendhal et le Beylisme*, 1914; Paul Arbelet, *La Jeunesse de Stendhal*, 2 vols., 1919; Armand Caraccio, *Stendhal, l'homme et l'œuvre*, 1951; Henri Martineau, *L'œuvre de Stendhal*, 1951; Jean Prévost, *La Création chez Stendhal*, 1951; Jules Alciatore, *Stendhal et Helvetius*, 1952; and *Stendhal et Maine de Biran*, 1954.

For briefer studies see also Lytton Strachey, *Books and Characters*, 1922; Stefan Zweig, *Adepts in Self-Portraiture*, 1928 (trans., 1929); François Mauriac, *Petits essais de psychologie religieuse*, 1933; Meyer Levin, *Toward Stendhal, Pharo III*, 1945; Irving Howe, "Stendhal: The Politics of Survival," in *Politics and the Novel*, 1957; and Victor Brombert, "Stendhal: Creation and Self-Knowledge," *Romantic Review*, XLIII (1952), 190–197.

JAMES STEPHENS

Born: Dublin, Ireland
Date: February 2, 1882

Died: London, England
Date: December 26, 1950

PRINCIPAL WORKS

POEMS: *Insurrections*, 1909; *The Lonely God and Other Poems*, 1909; *The Hill of Vision*, 1912; *The Rocky Road to Dublin*, 1915; *Songs from the Clay*, 1915; *Green Branches*, 1916; *Reincarnations*, 1918; *The Outcast*, 1929; *Theme and Variations*, 1930; *Strict Joy*, 1931; *Collected Poems*, 1954.
NOVELS: *The Charwoman's Daughter*, 1912 [*Mary, Mary*]; *The Crock of Gold*, 1912; *The Demigods*, 1914; *Deirdre*, 1923; *In the Land of Youth*, 1924.
SHORT STORIES: *Here Are Ladies*, 1913; *Etched in Moonlight*, 1928.
PLAY: *Julia Elizabeth*, 1929.

James Stephens, born to a poor Irish family on February 2, 1882, grew up in the slums of Dublin and for the most part educated himself by reading widely. To earn a living he taught himself stenography. While working as a stenographer, he began to write poems and stories, some of which were praised by George W. Russell (Æ), who read them in manuscript. But the praise of an established writer was still insufficient to secure publication, and Stephens found editors and publishers uninterested in his work. His first success did not come until he was thirty, when *The Crock of Gold* was published. *The Crock of Gold*, although never exceptionally popular, has become a minor classic because a respectable number of readers have found it appealing through more than four decades, its splendidly written fantasy appealing to literary appetites tired of realism and naturalism. The book won the Polignac Prize for 1912. A series of novels attempting to create a new mythology for Irish literature followed, the best-known being *Deirdre,* awarded the Tailteann Gold Medal.

Among Stephens' lifelong interests was almost every phase of Gaelic culture, language, art, and literature. As an authority on Gaelic art, he served for some years as an assistant curator of the Dublin National Gallery. Among his amusements was singing Irish folk songs, playing an accompaniment on the concertina.

As an adult Stephens spent much time away from his native city and land. He visited the United States a number of times, for both short and long periods, coming to the United States for the first time in 1925. Just a decade later he spent most of a year on the West Coast, lecturing on literature and Gaelic culture at the University of California. In other ways than lecturing Stephens left an imprint on American higher education. Two anthologies which he edited with E. L. Beck and R. H. Snow have been standard college textbooks for almost a quarter of a century: *English Romantic Poets* (1933) and *Victorian and Later English Poets* (1934). Between the two world wars Stephens also spent a great deal of time in France, especially Paris. In spite of his travels abroad, Stephens remained an ardent Irish nationalist, belonged to the Sinn Fein movement, ardently supported Eamon De Valera, the Irish political leader and president of Eire. During World War II, however, he felt obliged to go counter to Irish neutrality and he declared himself a supporter of the Allies. The British government granted him a pension in 1942.

In addition to his novels and poetry, none of which has had any truly wide popularity in America, Stephens tried his hand at other literary forms. *Here Are Ladies* and *Etched in Moonlight* are collections of stories. *Irish Fairy Tales* (1920) is a volume for children. *Julia Elizabeth* is an attempt in drama. *On Prose and Verse* (1928) is a critical study of literature.

Stephens was married and had two children. He died on December 26, 1950, in London, where he had resided for a number of years.

BIBLIOGRAPHICAL REFERENCES: There are two recent biographical and critical studies: Birgit Bramsbäck, *James Stephens: A Literary and Bibliographical Study,* 1959; and Hilary Pyle, *James Stephens: His Work and an Account of His Life,* 1965. See also Æ (George W. Russell), *Imagination and Reveries,* 1916; Iola A. Williams, *John Collings Squire and James Stephens,* 1922; Ernest Boyd, *Portraits: Real and Imaginary,* 1924; Edward Davison, *Some Modern Poets,* 1928; Cornelius Weygandt, "The Riddling of James Stephens," in *Tuesdays at Ten,* 1928; David Morton, *The Renaissance of Irish Poetry,* 1929; Frank Swinnerton, *The Georgian Literary Scene, 1910–1935,* 1935; and Groff Conklin, "James Stephens, Metrist," *English Journal,* XXV (1936), 268–277.

LAURENCE STERNE

Born: Clonmel, Ireland
Date: November 24, 1713

Died: London, England
Date: March 18, 1768

PRINCIPAL WORKS

NOVEL: *The Life and Opinions of Tristram Shandy, Gent.,* 1759-1767.
TRAVEL MISCELLANY: *A Sentimental Journey through France and Italy,* 1768.
SATIRE: *A Political Romance,* 1759.
SERMONS: *The Sermons of Mr. Yorick,* 1760-1769.
LETTERS AND JOURNALS: *Letters from Yorick to Eliza,* 1773; *Sterne's Letters to His Friends on Various Occasions,* 1775; *Letters of the Late Rev. Mr. Sterne to His Most Intimate Friends,* 1775; *Journal to Eliza,* 1904.

Laurence Sterne, the most delightfully eccentric of English novelists, was born in Clonmel, Ireland, on November 24, 1713, the son of an Irish woman and an ensign in the English army whose regiment had just been transferred to Ireland from Dunkirk. Though his parentage was undistinguished, Sterne's father came from an old family in Yorkshire, where a great-grandfather had been an archbishop. A childhood spent in the rigors of camp-following undoubtedly had a harmful effect on the novelist's frail constitution; but the experience provided him with details of barracks life and campaign reminiscences that ultimately enriched his great novel with such authentic creations as Uncle Toby and Corporal Trim.

Between 1723 and 1731, the year of his father's death, Sterne was in school at Halifax, Yorkshire. In 1733, after two years of idleness at Elvington, he was enrolled as a sizar in Jesus College, Cambridge, through the grudging benevolence of relatives. At Cambridge he indulged in the easy, convivial university life of the time. Not surprisingly he discovered an incapacity for mathematics and a contempt for formal logic. Nevertheless, he did considerable reading, developing a deep admiration for John Locke, whose philosophy was to be the most important single influence on his thinking. He also formed a close friendship with John Hall-Stevenson, later the hypochondriac author of *Crazy Tales* (1762). Cambridge granted Sterne a B.A. in 1737 and an M.A. in 1740.

As a matter of expediency rather than religious conviction, he took holy orders. He was ordained deacon in 1737 and inducted into the vicarage of Sutton on the Forest in 1738. Two years later he received a prebendal stall in the York Cathedral. In 1744 he acquired the parish of Stillington, near Sutton.

In 1741, after a "sentimental" courtship he married the homely but well-connected Elizabeth Lumley. A daughter, Lydia, was born in 1747. The Sternes, however, were never really compatible. Not only was Mrs. Sterne ill-tempered but she also suffered aberrations which, according to gossip, were not allayed by her husband's "small, quiet attentions" to various ladies. Actually, there is evidence that Sterne treated his wife with commendable patience. And though he was not averse to paying attention to other women, his philandering was chiefly sentimental—as was, for example, his affair with Catherine ("Kitty") Fourmantelle, a singer from London who came to York in 1759.

In Sutton, Sterne spent twenty years of relative obscurity, serving two parishes with some conscientiousness, unsuccessfully farming his glebe, and making occasional trips to York to preach his turn in the cathedral or to dabble in diocesan politics. He found amusement in hunting, skating, fiddling, and painting, as well as in social gatherings at Newburgh Priory, the seat of Lord Fauconberg, and in the ribald carousals of the "Demoniacks" at Hall-Stevenson's Skelton Castle. He later immortalized his role of "heteroclite parson" in his portrait of Yorick.

In 1759 his participation in local church politics produced a satire called *A Political Romance* (later renamed *The History of a Good Warm Watch-Coat*). Though all but a few copies were burned to prevent embarrassment to the diocese, its success among Sterne's friends gave him the impetus to embark on *Tristram Shandy,* the first two volumes of which came out in York in December of the same year. Introduced to London through the enthusiasm of David Garrick, the novel so impressed the capital with its whimsicality, eccentric humor, and indecorum that it was immediately successful. In fact, when Sterne journeyed down to London in the spring of 1760, he found himself a social lion. Never had the city seen such a witty, hedonistic priest whose lustrous eyes and ebulliently secular conversation so enchantingly belied his black garb, his pale face, thin body, and hollow chest.

But disapprobation soon followed success. Literary men like Walpole, Goldsmith, and Richardson condemned the book for various evils ranging from tediousness to indecency; and a flood of hostile articles, pamphlets, and bad imitations poured from the press. When the author brought out the first two volumes of the *Sermons of Mr. Yorick* (1760), the comminatory chorus grew—chiefly because the title bore the name of "a *Jester.* . . . in an obscene romance."

Returning to Yorkshire, Sterne received from Lord Fauconberg the living of Coxwold, to which "sweet retirement" he moved his family. Here for the rest of his life his home was a rambling gabled house that he called Shandy Hall. In January, 1761, he was again in London to see two more volumes of *Tristram* published. Though the critical reception was now unfavorable, the books sold well. Sterne returned to Coxwold, completed two more volumes, and was back in November for their publication. This time his reputation soared again. The story of Le Fever, Trim's animadversions on death, and Uncle Toby's campaigns had won universal applause.

Weakened by a serious hemorrhage from chronically weak lungs, Sterne set out for France in 1762 in a "race with death." Recovering in Paris, he was brilliantly lionized by the cream of French intellectual society. He later settled with his family in Toulouse. Back in Coxwold in 1764, he completed volumes seven and eight of Tristram Shandy, including an account of his tour through France and the affair of Uncle Toby and the Widow Wadman. These came out in January, 1765. Two more volumes of sermons followed in January, 1766.

Once again on the Continent in 1766, Sterne had a "joyous" winter in France and Italy. Though hemorrhages were becoming more frequent, he returned during the year to his desk in Coxwold, and by January, 1767, he was on hand in London for the appearance of the ninth volume of *Tristram Shandy*. During this winter he indulged in his famous sentimental affair with Eliza Draper, the young wife of an official of the East India Company, for whom he kept the *Journal to Eliza* after her departure for Bombay.

Late in February, 1768, Sterne brought out *A Sentimental Journey through France and Italy*. Its triumphant reception he was permitted to enjoy only briefly. An attack of influenza that developed into pleurisy proved more than his disease-wracked body could bear. He died in London on March 18, 1768, and was buried at St. George's, Hanover Square.

Sterne's work, like his life, is marked with a refreshing unconventionality. Though the *Sermons* (1760-69) lack religious conviction and orginality of material, they preach a warm benevolence and a comfortable morality in a style that can be at once graceful and dramatic. *A Sentimental Journey*—in which Sterne substituted his traveler's sentimental adventures for the conventional accounts of nations, peoples, and memorable sights in travel books—is a nearly perfect small masterpiece.

The humor of *Tristram Shandy* is plainly in the tradition of Rabelais, Cervantes, and Swift; and its borrowings range from Robert Burton to miscellaneous curiosa. Superficially, the novel may seem merely like an engaging hodge-podge full of tricks, including black, marbled, and blank pages, omitted chapters, unorthodox punctuation and typography, and numerous digressions. But *Tristram Shandy* is far from planless. By insisting on the importance of opinions about action rather than on that of action itself Sterne opened unexplored avenues into the inner lives of his superbly ingratiating characters and achieved a new architectonic principle based on the mind as Locke had illuminated it in the *Essay on Human Understanding*. At the same time he achieved a new concept of time in fiction, a fascinating awareness of the life process itself, and a fresh concept of comedy based on the idea of individual isolation in a world where each person is a product of his own peculiar association of ideas.

BIBLIOGRAPHICAL REFERENCES: The standard edition is the *Life and Works of Laurence Sterne*, edited by Wilbur L. Cross, 12 vols., 1904. See also *Letters*, edited by L. P. Curtis, 1935; and *Tristram Shandy*, edited by James A. Work, 1940. The standard biography is Wilbur L. Cross, *The Life and Times of Laurence Sterne*, 2 vols., 1929. Other full-length biographical and critical studies include Walter Sichel, *Sterne: A Study*, 1910; Lodwick Hartley, *This is Lorence*, 1943; L. V. Hammond, *Sterne's "Sermons of Mr. Yorick,"* 1946; E. N. Dilworth, *The Unsentimental Journey of Laurence Sterne*, 1948; and Arthur H. Cash and John M. Stedman, eds., *The Winged Skull* (essays by various hands), 1971.

See also Edward Wagenknecht, *Cavalcade of the English Novel,* 1943; Walter Allen, *The English Novel,* 1954; Herbert Read, The Sense of Glory, 1929; Virginia Woolf, "The 'Sentimental Journey'" in *The Second Common Reader,* 1932; W. B. C. Watkins, "Yorick Revisited," in *Perilous Balance,* 1939; Theodore Baird, "The Time-Scheme of Tristram Shandy and a Source," *Publications of the Modern Language Association,* LI (1936), 803–820; Walter L. Myers, "O, the Hobby Horse," *Virginia Quarterly Review,* XIX (1943), 268–277; Lodwick Hartley, "Tristram and the Angels," *College English,* IX (1947), 62–69; Louis D. Rubin, Jr., "Joyce and Sterne: A Study in Affinity," *Hopkins Review,* III (1950), 1–15; and Wayne Booth, "Did Sterne Complete Tristram Shandy?" *Modern Philology,* XLVIII (1951), 172–183.

JAMES STEVENS

Born: Albia, Iowa
Date: November 15, 1892

Principal Works

TALES AND SKETCHES: *Paul Bunyan,* 1925; *Homer in the Sagebrush,* 1928; *Saginaw Paul Bunyan,* 1932; *Paul Bunyan's Bears,* 1947.
NOVELS: *Brawnyman,* 1926; *Mattock,* 1927; *Big Jim Turner,* 1948.
BOOKS ON FORESTRY: *Tree Treasure: A Conservation Story,* 1950; *Green Power: The Story of Public Law 273,* 1958.

James (Floyd) Stevens, born in Monroe County, Iowa, on November 15, 1892, has always been drawn to the great outdoors, the rivers and forests of America. His novels, short stories, and journalistic writings constitute, on the whole, a partial autobiography and an account of the realistic and mythic heroes of the lumberman, fisherman, and pioneer laborer.

Stevens' strongest claim to a place in literary history is his first book, *Paul Bunyan,* published in 1925. Although one reviewer said that it "converted folklore to farce," most critics were laudatory: "James Stevens merits to be known by this epical work as the prose Homer of American mythology"; "No one but Mark Twain has been able to set down tall tales with such winning conviction." By 1948, the book had sold over 200,000 copies and Stevens issued a new edition, adding a chapter which described a fabulous log run up the Columbia River with tame whales doing the work.

Paul Bunyan was followed by *Brawnyman,* which describes in a ragged, raw style the life of a hobo laborer, Jim Turner, who hops freights from job to job. *Mattock* is based on Stevens' fourteen months in France as an infantryman in World War I. It is Private Parvin Mattock's vernacular account of a farm boy's shocking experiences in the AEF; it closes with the first convention of the American Legion.

Homer in the Sagebrush, a collection of magazine stories of the Northwest frontier was criticized for being too raw, lacking artistic form. His next collection, *Saginaw Paul Bunyan,* seemed, on the other hand, "too prosy and correct . . . a saga in pseudo-literary style." Stevens continued to produce novels and stories, the most significant being *Big Jim Turner,* an autobiographical social chronicle of the early 1900's—railroading and lumber, labor agitation, the IWW, Eugene V. Debs. Although picturesque and often forceful, his later books have never quite fulfilled the expectations aroused by *Paul Bunyan.*

BIBLIOGRAPHICAL REFERENCES: Harry R. Warfel, *American Novelists of Today,* 1951, gives a biographical sketch. Studies are: Stuart Sherman, *The Main Stream,* 1927; Elizabeth Montgomery, *The Story Behind Modern Books,* 1949; and Daniel Hoffman, *Paul Bunyan,* 1952. See also Stevens' "Medicine Men," *American Mercury,* XXVIII (1933), 487–497, and his "Folklore and the Artist," *ibid.,* LXXX (1950), 343–349; also Warren L. Clare, "James Stevens: The Laborer and Literature," *Research Studies* (Washington State University), XXXII (1964), 355–367.

WALLACE STEVENS

Born: Reading, Pennsylvania
Date: October 2, 1879

Died: Hartford, Connecticut
Date: August 2, 1955

Principal Works

POEMS: *Harmonium*, 1923; *Ideas of Order*, 1935; *Owl's Clover*, 1936; *The Man with the Blue Guitar*, 1937; *Parts of a World*, 1942; *Notes Toward a Supreme Fiction*, 1942; *Esthétique du Mal*, 1945; *Transport to Summer*, 1947; *Three Academic Pieces*, 1947; *A Primitive Like an Orb*, 1948; *The Auroras of Autumn*, 1952; *Collected Poems*, 1954.

ESSAYS: *The Necessary Angel: Essays on Reality and the Imagination*, 1951.

MISCELLANEOUS: *Opus Posthumous*, 1957.

The life of Wallace Stevens has been called a "double life," split between the seemingly antithetical professions of poet and insurance lawyer. However, as Frank Kermode notes, "Stevens did not find that he must choose between the careers of insurance lawyer and poet. The fork in the road where he took the wrong turning is a critic's invention. . . ."

Stevens was born in Reading, Pennsylvania, in 1879, of Pennsylvania Dutch ancestry. This fact becomes important in some of his verse, notably "Dutch Graves in Bucks County," wherein "the old flag of Holland/ Flutters in tiny darkness" and Stevens' "semblables," or forefathers, "are crusts that lie/ In the shrivellings of your time and place," dead to the present "new glory of new men" on their way to war and destruction. Even here, however, Stevens does not approach autobiographical writing; his symbols are impersonal and comprehension of his work does not depend closely on a knowledge of his life.

Stevens attended Harvard from 1897 until 1900, and there his first poems appeared in *The Harvard Advocate*. He left Harvard before graduating and planned to go to Paris to write, but instead he took a job as reporter on the *New York Herald Tribune*, following which he entered law school at New York University. He received a degree in law in 1903 and was admitted to the New York Bar Association, practicing law in New York City from 1904 until 1916. During this period, Stevens continued to write poetry and made several friends among the writers then living in Greenwich Village—William Carlos Williams, Marianne Moore, Harriet Monroe, and others. According to Williams, who was like Stevens in devoting himself to two professions, Stevens was always reserved, shy, "unwilling to be active or vocal. . . . He was always the well-dressed one, diffident about letting down his hair. Precise when we were sloppy. Drank little. . . . But we all knew, liked, and admired him."

During his New York sojourn, Stevens published in Harriet Monroe's *Poetry* as well as in Alfred Kreymborg's *Others*, at first under the pseudonym, "Peter Parasol." Two plays appeared in *Poetry*, including "Three Travellers Watch the Sunrise," which won a verse-play competition, but more importantly the journals of Harriet Monroe and Kreymborg offered an outlet for some of Stevens' best early verse—for example, "Sunday Morning" and "Peter Quince."

In 1916 Stevens went to work on the legal staff of the Hartford Accident and Indemnity Company, becoming vice president of the firm in 1934. Like Crispin in "The Comedian as the Letter C," Stevens in Hartford seems to have found the end of his journey, establishing "a nice shady home" and raising a "daughter with curls"—Holly Bright Stevens, offspring of Stevens' marriage to Elsie Kachel of Reading. As a "romantic poet," in other words, Stevens made Hartford his "ivory tower," looking down on a reality made up of insurance law, Key West, and Connecticut, and, at times, "an exceptional view of the public dump" which any public man must face. Nevertheless, neither business, family life, self-scrutiny, nor social scrutiny appear as important keys to Stevens' verse. They function merely as "parts of a world"—three more "porpoises" and "apricots" in an "inscrutable" reality which is romantic poetry, and in romantic poetry which creates reality.

Stevens' first volume of verse was *Harmonium*; it appeared in 1923 and was not widely noticed. There followed twelve years in which he published little, but then came *Ideas of Order* (1935) and *The Man With the Blue Guitar* (1937) which contained, besides the title poem, the long poem, "Owl's Clover," published separately the year before. Subsequent volumes include *Parts of a World* (1942), *Transport to Summer* (1947), *Three Academic Pieces* (1947), *The Auroras of Autumn* (1950), *The Necessary Angel* (1951), *The Collected Poems* (1954), and *Opus Posthumous* (1957), edited by Samuel French Morse. At no time did Stevens relish public appearances and readings, but later on in his career he lectured in verse and read prose lectures which sounded like poetry—as the contents of *Necessary Angel,* containing both prose and verse, testify. Furthermore, when asked to be Charles Eliot Norton Professor at Harvard for 1955–56, Stevens declined the offer, feeling, as he was well on in years, that acceptance of the position would entail his retirement from Hartford Accident.

For *Auroras of Autumn* Stevens won the National Book Award in 1951, winning it again, along with a Pulitzer Prize for Poetry, in 1955 for *The Collected Poems.* Stevens was also recipient of the Yale Library Bollingen Prize in poetry in 1949. He died suddenly, in 1955, following an operation.

BIBLIOGRAPHICAL REFERENCES: The standard edition, although not definitive, is *The Collected Poems of Wallace Stevens,* 1954. *Opus Posthumous,* containing additional poems, aphorisms, essays, and dramatic sketches, was edited by Samuel French Morse, 1957.

There is no authorized biography. The major critical studies are William Van O'Connor, *The Shaping Spirit: A Study of Wallace Stevens,* 1950; Frank Kermode, *Wallace Stevens,* 1961; Joseph N. Riddel, *The Clairvoyant Eye: The Poetry and Poetics of Wallace Stevens,* 1965; and William A. Burney, *Wallace Stevens,* 1968. Of bibliographical importance is Samuel French Morse, *Wallace Stevens: A Preliminary Checklist of His Published Writings,* 1954. For critical articles in periodicals see Gorham Munson, "The Dandyism of Wallace Stevens," *Dial,* LXXIX (1925), 413–417; Morton Dauwen Zabel, "The Harmonium of Wallace Stevens," *Poetry,* XXXIX

(1931), 148–154; R. P. Blackmur, "Examples of Wallace Stevens," *Hound and Horn,* V (1932), 223–255; Hi Simons, " 'The Comedian as the Letter C': Its Sense and Significance," *Southern Review,* V (1940), 453–468, "The Humanism of Wallace Stevens," *Poetry,* LXI (1942), 448–452, and "The Genre of Wallace Stevens," *Sewanee Review,* LIII (1945), 566–579; Wylie Sypher, "Connoisseur in Chaos: Wallace Stevens," *Partisan Review,* XIII (1946), 83–94; Marius Bewley, "The Poetry of Wallace Stevens," *Partisan Review,* XVI (1949), 895–915; Harold H. Watts, "Wallace Stevens and the Rock of Summer," *Kenyon Review,* XIV (1952), 122–140; Donald Davie, " 'Essential Gaudiness': The Poems of Wallace Stevens," *Twentieth Century,* CLIII (1953), 455–462; Elder Olson, "The Poetry of Wallace Stevens," *College English,* XVI (1955), 395–402; R. P. Blackmur, "The Substance That Prevails," *Kenyon Review,* XVII (1955), 94–110; Randall Jarrell, "The Collected Poems of Wallace Stevens," *Yale Review,* XLIV (1955), 340–353; William Carlos Williams, "Wallace Stevens," *Poetry,* LXXXVII (1956), 234–239; and Howard Nemerov, "The Poetry of Wallace Stevens," *Sewanee Review,* LXV (1957), 1–14.

The Wallace Stevens Number of the *Harvard Advocate,* CXXVII, No. 3 (December, 1940), contained essays and statements by Marianne Moore, F. O. Matthiessen, Robert Penn Warren, William Carlos Williams, and others.

ROBERT LOUIS STEVENSON

Born: Edinburgh, Scotland
Date: November 13, 1850

Died: Apia, Samoa
Date: December 3, 1894

Principal Works

NOVELS: *Treasure Island,* 1883; *Prince Otto,* 1885; *The Strange Case of Dr. Jekyll and Mr. Hyde,* 1886; *Kidnapped,* 1886; *The Merry Men,* 1887; *The Black Arrow,* 1888; *The Master of Ballantrae,* 1888; *The Wrong Box,* 1889 (with Lloyd Osbourne); *The Wrecker,* 1892 (with Lloyd Osbourne); *Catriona,* 1893 [*David Balfour*]; *The Ebb-Tide,* 1894 (with Lloyd Osbourne); *Weir of Hermiston,* 1896 (unfinished); *St. Ives,* 1897 (completed by Arthur Quiller-Couch).

SHORT STORIES AND SKETCHES: *The New Arabian Nights,* 1882; *More New Arabian Nights,* 1885 (with Mrs. Stevenson); *Island Nights' Entertainments,* 1893.

TRAVEL SKETCHES AND IMPRESSIONS: *An Inland Voyage,* 1878; *Travels with a Donkey,* 1879; *The Silverado Squatters,* 1883; *Across the Plains,* 1892; *The Amateur Emigrant,* 1895; *In the South Seas,* 1896.

POEMS: *A Child's Garden of Verses,* 1885; *Underwoods,* 1887; *Ballads,* 1890.

ESSAYS AND STUDIES: *Virginibus Puerisque,* 1881; *Familiar Studies of Men and Books,* 1882; *Memories and Portraits,* 1887; *Father Damien,* 1890.

Robert Louis (Balfour) Stevenson, born in Edinburgh on November 13, 1850, has achieved fame by his romantic life nearly as much as by his romantic fiction, for his life displays the same dualism between romantic adventure and grim reality that the discerning reader finds in much of his writing. Stevenson's brief forty-four year life was a nearly constant journey in search of adventure and relief from the agonies of tuberculosis, with which he was afflicted from early childhood. His father, Thomas Stevenson, a successful Edinburgh lighthouse engineer, hoped for a law career for his only son; but, though Robert did study to be a barrister, he soon commenced a life of traveling that took him to Switzerland, France, the United States, and, finally, the South Seas. In each place Stevenson found adventure; and when he did not find it ready-made, he created it for himself out of his teeming imagination.

Although Stevenson is best known for his fiction, he was a prodigious essayist. The vivid impressions made by the places he visited are found recorded in such brilliant travel sketches and essays as *An Inland Voyage,* which tells of a canoeing trip through Belgium and France, and *Travels with a Donkey in the Cévennes,* which deals with his journeys in southern France. In these books Stevenson shows his fine eye for color and vivid impressions, that sort of sensitivity that was to add so much to the popularity of his fiction.

He had always been ambitious to write and had prepared himself laboriously for a literary career. His famous statements about how he copied the style of great writers such as Lamb, Hazlitt, Defoe, and Hawthorne, and about how he was always writing, polishing, and correcting are evidence of this ambition. So, too, is the delicate, precise, but rich style that his fiction achieves.

Stevenson fell in love with Mrs. Fanny Osbourne in France and went to California in 1879 to marry her after she had secured a divorce from her husband. This trip caused a break with

Stevenson's family, who were opposed to the alliance, and he suffered many hardships until he acquired a measure of fame and prosperity with the publication of his first major work, *Treasure Island*, written chiefly for the entertainment of his stepson, Lloyd Osbourne. This most famous and loved of adventure stories demonstrated Stevenson's ability at colorful narration and his technique of using a relatively minor character as observer and narrator. *Kidnapped* was immediately popular, but it never attained the following of *Treasure Island*. A striking contrast to these tales of romantic adventure is *The Strange Case of Dr. Jekyll and Mr. Hyde*, perhaps the most famous of all Stevenson's fiction; this grim story of dual personality is moralistic and filled with Stevenson's concern for ethical problems.

Again in search of improved health, Stevenson left California and traveled in the United States, his longest stay being in Saranac Lake, a health resort in the Adirondacks. He stayed there during 1887–1888. While at Saranac Lake he wrote *The Master of Ballantrae*, a tale of the Jacobite struggle, the same subject dealt with in the earlier *Kidnapped*. In *The Black Arrow* he went farther back in time to the Wars of the Roses; this book contains a lively picture of late medieval times.

In a final desperate effort to regain his health, Stevenson moved to the South Seas and settled on the island of Samoa. There he found a serenity that encouraged his literary efforts. He was considered a truly great man by the natives, and he took an active interest in Samoan politics. In his last years he was very productive, turning out *The Wrecker* with Lloyd Osbourne, his stepson, and *David Balfour*, a sequel to *Kidnapped* but a more able literary performance.

Stevenson died suddenly of apoplexy on December 3, 1894, leaving unfinished his *Weir of Hermiston*, the work that is generally regarded as his masterpiece. In this fragment Stevenson manifests the culmination of his constant efforts to improve his style and displays again his conviction that the romance of life is, to the individual, more real than what critics and other materialistic novelists of his period were praising as detached objectivity. Criticism is still sharply divided over the whole body of his work, but he holds a firm place in the favor of all children and of all adults who believe that romance is a valid part of life.

BIBLIOGRAPHICAL REFERENCES: Complete editions of Stevenson's works are the Swanston Edition, 25 vols., 1911–1912, with an introduction by Andrew Lang, and the Tusitala Edition, 35 vols., 1923–1924. There is also the *Collected Poems*, edited by J. Adam Smith, 1950. Sir Sidney Colvin has edited the *Letters* in 4 vols., 1911. The standard bibliography is by W. F. Prideaux, *A Bibliography of the Works of Robert Louis Stevenson*, 1903, revised by F. V. Livingston, 1917. Good biographies are J. C. Furnas' *Voyage to Windward*, 1951; and Charles Neider's edition of *Our Samoan Adventure*, 1955, which includes a previously unpublished three year diary and rare photographs. See also Dennis Butts, *R. L. Stevenson*, 1966. Important critical works are Frank Swinnerton, *Robert Louis Stevenson: A Critical Study*, 1923; J. A. Steuart, *Robert Louis Stevenson: Man and Writer. A Critical Biography*, 2 vols., 1924; David Daiches, *Robert Louis Stevenson*, 1946, *Stevenson and the Art of Fiction*, 1951; Robert Kiely, *Robert Louis Stevenson and the Fiction of Adventure*, 1964; and Edwin M. Eigner, *Robert Louis Stevenson and the Romantic Tradi-*

tion, 1966. Informative essays include H. W. Garrod's "The Poetry of Robert Louis Stevenson" in his *The Profession of Poetry,* 1929, and "The Poetry of Stevenson" in *Essays Presented to Sir Humphrey Milford,* 1948.

JAMES STILL

Born: Double Creek, Alabama
Date: July 16, 1906

Principal Works

NOVEL: *River of Earth*, 1940.
SHORT STORIES: *On Troublesome Creek*, 1941.
POEMS: *Hounds on the Mountain*, 1937.

A Kentuckian by adoption, James Still was born on Double Creek, Chambers County, Alabama, on July 16, 1906. His boyhood ambition was to be a veterinarian like his father, and among his earliest recollections are the nights he spent with his father while they nursed a sick animal on some neighbor's farm. When he was seventeen he entered Lincoln Memorial University at Harrogate, Tennessee. There he worked in a rock quarry and in the school library to pay his expenses. After his graduation in 1929 he completed work for his M.A. degree at Vanderbilt University in 1930 and spent a year at the University of Illinois Library School. For the next six years he was librarian at the Hindman Settlement School in Knott County, Kentucky. One of his duties was to carry boxes of books, twenty to the carton, over mountain trails to supply one-room schools without libraries of their own. During those years he tramped over every ridge and hollow mentioned in his books, which have their settings in the region of hill farms and coal camps scattered along the branch waters of Little Carr and Troublesome creeks.

In 1937 he published *Hounds on the Mountain*, a book of poems highly praised for their regional freshness and the lyric beauty of their style. In the meantime, at work on his first novel, he went to live in a log cabin between Deadmare Branch and Wolfpen Creek.

River of Earth appeared in 1940. Covering two years in the life of a mountain family, it is a simple but moving chronicle of the hill country presented through the eyes of a boy growing into a realization of the strange, bewildering world of human relationships and of man's responsibilities within that world. The story, which falls easily into a pattern of memory, loses nothing in the episodic manner of its telling, and the whole is tuned to a clear colloquial style that holds echoes of old proverbs and hillborn wisdom as well as the occasional incorrectness of folk speech in its idiom. *River of Earth* was selected for the Southern Authors' Award in 1941. *On Troublesome Creek* is a collection of short stories in much the same pattern and mood, set against a landscape where the lives of men and women follow the round of the seasons in an almost timeless cycle of birth, growth, seed-time, and death.

During World War II James Still served with the U. S. Army Air Force in Africa and the Middle East. He was a Guggenheim fellow in 1946, and in 1947, in recognition of "his gift of style and mastery of character and scene," he received a special award from the Academy of Arts and Letters and the National Institute of Arts and Letters. More recently he has been the librarian at the Hindman school and a member of the faculty at the annual writers' conference sponsored by Morehead State College. He remains an unhurried and scrupulous writer whose tales of the Kentucky mountains appear from time to time in magazines and short story anthologies.

BIBLIOGRAPHICAL REFERENCES: There is no extended biographical or critical study. See Dayton Kohler, "Jesse Stuart and James Still: Mountain Regionalists," *College English,* III (1942), 523–533; Archer Taylor, "Proverbial Comparisons and Similes in *On Troublesome Creek,*" *Kentucky Folklore Record,* VIII (1962), 87–95; Leonard Roberts, "Additional Notes on Archer Taylor's *On Troublesome Creek,*" *ibid.,* 142-144; and Dean Cadle, *"Man on Troublesome," Yale Review,* 57 (1967), 236-255; also the *Book Review Digest,* 1937, 1940, 1941.

BRAM STOKER

Born: Dublin, Ireland
Date: 1847

Died: London, England
Date: April 20, 1912

Principal Work

NOVEL: *Dracula*, 1897.

Born in Dublin, Ireland, in 1847, Bram (Abraham) Stoker, famous for his sensational novel, *Dracula*, was a sickly child, so weak that he was unable to stand up alone until the age of seven. He outgrew his childhood weakness, however, and became a champion athlete while at Dublin University, from which he was graduated in 1867. For the next ten years he drudged away as an Irish civil servant. From 1871 to 1876 Stoker served as an unpaid drama critic for the Dublin *Mail*, work which won for him the friendship of Henry Irving, the actor. As a result of their friendship, Stoker served as Irving's manager for many years.

After touring America with Irving, Stoker wrote a series of lectures about life in the United States to deliver to English audiences. The success of the lectures when printed in pamphlet form caused Stoker to consider other kinds of writing. *Dracula* appeared in 1897. Negligible as literature, the book is really no more than a *tour de force* combining werewolves, vampires, hypnotism, and unhappy spirits. It is horrifying, and yet it is compelling, and it has achieved notoriety, if not fame, as a novel, a stage play, and several motion picture versions. The work represents a late nineteenth century development of the earlier Gothic novel, and its marked success stimulated other authors to imitate the type. Other works by Stoker worth noting are *The Jewel of Seven Stars* (1904), a novel; and *Personal Reminiscences of Henry Irving* (1906), the latter recording Stoker's life with Irving and with the Lyceum Theatre. During his last years Stoker was also on the literary staff of the London *Telegraph*. He died in London on April 20, 1912.

BIBLIOGRAPHICAL REFERENCES: The only biographical study is Harry Ludlam, *A Biography of Dracula: The Life Story of Bram Stoker*, 1962. An excellent study of the Gothic novel and its writers is Dorothy Scarborough, *The Supernatural in Modern English Fiction*, 1917.

PHIL STONG

Born: Keosauqua, Iowa
Date: January 27, 1899

Died: Washington, Connecticut
Date: April 26, 1957

Principal Works

NOVELS: *State Fair*, 1932; *Stranger's Return*, 1933; *Village Tale*, 1934; *Week-End*, 1935; *Buckskin Breeches*, 1937; *The Long Lane*, 1939; *Return in August*, 1953.

Following graduation from the public schools of Keosauqua, Iowa, where he was born on January 27, 1899, Phil (ip Duffield) Stong went to Drake University, from which he was graduated in 1919. After some graduate study at Columbia University (1920–1921) and at the University of Kansas, (1923–1924) Stong wrote editorials for the Des Moines *Register* and later taught courses in journalism and speech at Drake University. In 1925 he went to New York City, working successively for the Associated Press, the North American Newspaper Alliance, *Liberty*, *Editor and Publisher*, and the New York *World*. In 1931 he began to devote all his time to creative writing.

Stong's first published novel, *State Fair*, was an immediate success, bringing him economic security and a strong reputation. The novel was made into a motion picture, with Will Rogers in one of the lead roles; after World War II the story was again filmed, this time in color. One of the immediate results of the first motion picture version was that the author was able to repurchase the farmstead which had belonged to his maternal grandfather. After 1932 Stong published a number of novels, but none has achieved the popularity of his first. Most of his fiction is about Iowa and the people from the rural areas and small towns of that state. In his work Stong presented Midwest farm life as a full and pleasant one, not the horror which some other writers, following Hamlin Garland's example, have portrayed. *Stranger's Return* relates the return to happy farm life of a young woman who went East to marry a newspaperman. *Village Tale* presents life and an episode of unusual violence in a small Iowa railroad town. *Week-end* exposes the shams of supposedly sophisticated New Yorkers. *Farmer in the Dell* (1935) drew upon Stong's experience in Hollywood and presents an Iowa farmer's brief experience as a Hollywood actor. In 1937 Stong reached back into history for *Buckskin Breeches*, which tells of one family's migration from Ohio to Iowa early in the nineteenth century.

Later novels draw upon different kinds of materials. *The Iron Mountain* (1942), a study of a Finnish woman's impact on a Scandinavian and Balkan community in the famous Mesabi country of Minnesota makes skillful use of dialects. *Our Destiny* (1942) is a topical novel describing the effect of the Pearl Harbor attack and World War II on an Iowa farm family and their way of life. *Jessamy John* (1947) is a fictional presentation of John Law and the fabulous Mississippi Bubble. None of these later novels, all well-done pieces of fiction, has achieved great popularity or won critical acclaim; Stong remained for most readers the author of a single novel, *State Fair*.

In addition to these novels, Stong turned out a host of other volumes, including a number of books for children. One of them, *The Hired Man's Elephant* (1939), won the New York

Herald Tribune prize for juvenile fiction in that year. Also in 1939 appeared Stong's study of the horse in America, Horses and Americans. Other non-fictional items include Hawkeyes (1940), a history of Iowa; If School Keeps (1940), an autobiographical volume; and Marta of Muscovy (1947), a biography of the wife of Peter the Great. Stong's last novel was Return in August, a sequel to State Fair which picks up Margy Drake twenty years after the first volume left her and her romance.

BIBLIOGRAPHICAL REFERENCES: For autobiographical material see Stong's If School Keeps, 1940. Elizabeth Rider Montgomery, The Story Behind Modern Books, 1949, is useful. The pamphlet, "Buckskin Breeches by Phil Stong, a Selection of the Discoverers," 1937, was reprinted as prefatory material in the limited edition of his Buckskin Breeches. See also Harry R. Warfel, American Novelists of Today, 1951.

HARRIET BEECHER STOWE

Born: Litchfield, Connecticut
Date: June 14, 1811

Died: Hartford, Connecticut
Date: July 1, 1896

PRINCIPAL WORKS

NOVELS: *Uncle Tom's Cabin, or Life Among the Lowly,* 1852; *Dred: A Tale of the Great Dismal Swamp,* 1856; *The Minister's Wooing,* 1859; *The Pearl of Orr's Island,* 1862; *Agnes of Sorrento,* 1862; *Oldtown Folks,* 1869; *Pink and White Tyranny,* 1871; *My Wife and I,* 1871; *We and Our Neighbors,* 1875; *Poganuc People,* 1878.
SHORT STORIES AND SKETCHES: *Sam Lawson's Oldtown Fireside Stories,* 1872.
TRAVEL SKETCHES: *Sunny Memories of Foreign Lands,* 1854.

Harriet (Elizabeth) Beecher Stowe presented two regional backgrounds in her fiction: the South before the Civil War and the rural area of New England (Maine). Her novels of the antebellum South, were less authentic as well as more melodramatic in style. They were more popular, however, because of the timeliness of their theme and the antislavery feeling they created.

Born in Litchfield, Connecticut, on June 14, 1811, Harriet Elizabeth Beecher was the daughter of a famous minister, the Reverend Lyman Beecher, and sister of Henry Ward Beecher. She was educated in the school of her older sister Catherine, who encouraged her inclination to write. The family moved to Cincinnati when Harriet was eighteen. There she married Calvin Ellis Stowe, a professor in the Lane Theological Seminary, and spent eighteen years across the river from a slave state.

Uncle Tom's Cabin, written after the Stowes had moved to Maine, brought its author immediate worldwide fame. The literature of the period generally was influenced by a humanitarian impulse, and Mrs. Stowe had a ready audience for her romantic, even melodramatic history of the relations of a group of southern white families and their slaves. Of her material, she said, "Two nations, the types of two exactly opposite styles of existence, are here struggling; and from the intermingling of these two a third race has arisen, and the three are interlocked in wild and singular relations, that evolve every possible combination of romance." She added, "It is the moral bearings of the subject involved which have had the chief influence in its selection."

The success of her first novel encouraged Mrs. Stowe to write a second on the same theme. The Dred Scott decision, stating that the Negro is not a human being, served as the catalyst for *Dred,* a novel in which her purpose of showing the general corruption of Christian principles brought on by slavery remained the same. Attacked by the critics, like the first novel, for artistic faults, mainly those of artificiality of language, contrived plotting, and sentimental characterizations, the book was less popular than its predecessor.

Turning next to her New England background, Mrs. Stowe wrote four novels in a manner that did not increase her fame but did raise her position on the ground of literary merit. These novels were *The Minister's Wooing, The Pearl of Orr's Island, Oldtown Folks,* and *Poganuc People.*

She also wrote society novels and in *Agnes of Sorrento* produced a didactic historical romance. Mrs. Stowe was the first writer to use New England dialect for the sake of realism, becoming a pioneer in the tradition of Mary E. Wilkins Freeman and Sarah Orne Jewett. But her constant interpolation of Christian aphorisms and her use of routine plots kept these novels on the level of conventional nineteenth century romance and local color fiction. A daughter of the transcendental period, she was the most famous sentimental novelist of her time. She died at Hartford, Connecticut, July 1, 1896.

BIBLIOGRAPHICAL REFERENCES: The collected edition is *The Writings of Harriet Beecher Stowe*, 16 vols., 1896. There are several authorized biographies: Annie A. Fields, *Life and Letters of Harriet Beecher Stow*, 1897; Charles E. Stowe, *Life of Harriet Beecher Stowe: Compiled from her Journals and Letters*, 1899; and Charles E. Stowe and Lyman Beecher Stowe, *Harriet Beecher Stowe: The Story of her Life*, 1911. There are two recent biographies: Catherine Gilbertson, *Harriet Beecher Stowe*, 1937; and Forrest Wilson, *Crusader in Crinoline: The Life of Harriet Beecher Stowe*, 1941—the most valuable single work. A useful critical study is Charles H. Foster, *The Rungless Ladder: Harriet Beecher Stowe and New England Puritanism*, 1954. See also Constance Rourke, *Trumpets of Jubilee*, 1927; Jay B. Hubbell, *The South in American Literature*, 1954; John R. Adams, *Harriet Beecher Stowe*, 1963; and Alice C. Crozier, *The Novels of Harriet Beecher Stowe*, 1969.

LYTTON STRACHEY

Born: London, England
Died: March 1, 1880

Died: Wiltshire, England
Date: January 21, 1932

Principal Works

BIOGRAPHY: *Eminent Victorians,* 1918; *Queen Victoria,* 1921; *Elizabeth and Essex,* 1928; *Portraits in Miniature,* 1931.

ESSAYS AND STUDIES: *Landmarks in French Literature,* 1912; *Books and Characters, French and English,* 1922; *Characters and Commentaries,* 1933.

The new movement in biography as a literary form began in England with (Giles) Lytton Strachey as World War I came to an end. Its chief characteristic was debunking and its main flaw parochialism, but at his best Strachey managed to exude a maximum of the first with a minimum of the second. Born in London on March 1, 1880, Strachey came from a family distinguished in the army, the civil service, and literature. His mother, Lady Jane Strachey, was a respected essayist and an amateur student of French literature; Lionel Strachey, a cousin, had established a literary reputation in the United States; another cousin, John St. Loe Strachey, was the brilliant editor of the *Spectator* from 1898 to 1925, and his children, John Strachey and Mrs. Amabel Williams-Ellis, were both writers.

A delicate child of marked but rather special talents, Lytton Strachey was limited in his choice of profession. At Trinity College, Cambridge, he distinguished himself in his studies, composed verses, and won the Chancellor's Medal with his poem, "Ely." Fearing that he lacked true creative power, however, he dallied with literature in the critical essays which he wrote while living with his mother on an independent income. Almost feminine in outlook, he was sociable but catty. When aroused, usually by some sign of weakness in another, he became feline, verbally dissecting his victim. Eventually this habit was channelized into written sketches of the great and the near-great of the Victorian Age, and some of these were in turn published as *Eminent Victorians* in 1918. As biography, his style was new to the English public but it caught their fancy and the book sold well. Actually Strachey had been strongly influenced by French biographers, especially Sainte-Beuve—his first publication was *Landmarks in French Literature* in 1912—and their naturalistic approach suited his predilection for accentuating the negative in personal relations. Bothered by his own physique, he laid emphasis on others' weak points, especially among the famous in politics or letters.

Consciously or not, he was effecting in his attitude a new realism to which his readers reacted, not in terms of scorn but rather with greater insight and sympathy. With flaws the sacrosanct Victorian figures became more human and thus more lovable. Especially true was this in the reaction to his *Queen Victoria.* While this biography was just as iconoclastic as the others in its portrait of the queen, the very style of the book, witty and concise, brought her to life as a woman as no similar work or public eulogy had ever done. Emphasizing personality rather than idea, he brought his subject down to the human level. His greatest popular success, *Elizabeth and Essex,* was the most obvious in its revelation that the author was judging the world by what was within himself, a man much different from what his exterior signified.

Never marrying, he moved with his mother to Bloomsbury, London, on a whim. By chance there were other literary people in the neighborhood, and they were welcomed at the Strachey home. Among them were Virginia Woolf and E. M. Forster. Though known later as the Bloomsbury Group, their only tie besides sociability was a desire to reveal the warm current of fallibility beneath the façade of conventionality in English life. Among the members of the so-called Bloomsbury Group Strachey found his spiritual home and his friends, who shared his interest in the excercise of clarity, restraint, and precision as the basis of literary style. These qualities are all apparent in the portrait gallery of minor, even obscure, figures whom Strachey presents in his *Portraits in Miniature,* the best book of his lifetime. He died on January 21, 1932, at Ham Spray House in Wiltshire, a country residence he had bought with his royalties from *Queen Victoria.*

BIBLIOGRAPHICAL REFERENCES: Lytton Strachey's books have been reprinted in the *Collected Works,* 6 vols., 1948. The standard biography has been Charles Richard Sanders, *Lytton Strachey: His Mind and Art,* 1957; but this is now superseded by Michael Holroyd, *Lytton Strachey* (Vol. I, *The Unknown Years, 1880–1910;* Vol. II, *The Years of Achievement, 1910–1932*), 1968. For further biography and criticism see also Mark Longaker, *Contemporary Biography,* 1934; André Maurois, *Prophets and Poets,* 1935; Edgar Johnson, *One Mighty Torrent,* 1937; Cyril Clemens, *Lytton Strachey,* 1942; Max Beerbohm, *Lytton Strachey: The Rede Lecture,* 1943; George Carver, *Alms for Oblivion,* 1946; George Gordon, *The Lives of Authors,* 1950; also D. S. Mirsky, "Mr. Lytton Strachey," *London Mercury,* VIII (1923), 175–184; Desmond MacCarthy, "Lytton Strachey as a Biographer," *Life and Letters,* VIII (1932), 90–102; Vincent Sheean, "Lytton Strachey: Cambridge and Bloomsbury," *New Republic,* LXX (1932), 19–20; Guy Boas, "Lytton Strachey," *English Association Pamphlets,* No. 93, (1935); Leonard Bacon, "An Eminent Post-Victorian," *Yale Review* XXX (1941), 310–324; and Charles Richard Sanders, "Lytton Strachey's Conception of Biography," *Publications of the Modern Language Association,* LXVI (1951), 295–315.

AUGUST STRINDBERG

Born: Stockholm, Sweden
Date: January 22, 1849

Died: Stockholm
Date: May 14, 1912

Principal Works

PLAYS: *Mäster Olof*, 1872–1881; *Lycko-Pers resa*, 1882 (*Lucky Peter's Travels*); *Fadren*, 1887 (*The Father*); *Fröken Julie*, 1888 (*Miss Julie*); *Komraterna*, 1888 (*The Comrades*); *Fordringsägare*, 1888 (*Creditors*); *Paria*, 1888–1889 (*Pariah*); *Den Starkare*, 1889 (*The Stronger*); *Bandet*, 1893 (*The Link*); *Till Damaskus*, I and II, 1898 (*To Damascus*); *Advent*, 1898; *Brott och Brott*, 1899 (*Crimes and Crimes*); *Gustavus Vasa*, 1899; *Erik XIV*, 1899; *Gustavus Adolphus*, 1900; *Påsk*, 1900 (*Easter*); *Kronbruden*, 1901 (*The Bridal Crown*); *Carl XII*, 1901; *Dödsdansen*, 1901 (*The Dance of Death*); *Svanevit*, 1901 (*Swanwhite*); *Ett Drömspel*, 1901 (*The Dream Play*); *Kristina*, 1903 (*Queen Christina*); *Till Damaskus*, III, 1904; *Spöksonaten*, 1907 (*The Spook Sonata*).

NOVELS: *Röda rummet*, 1879 (*The Red Room*); *Hemsöborna*, 1887 (*The Dwellers of Hemsö*); *Den romantiske klockaren på Rånö*, 1888 (*The Romantic Sexton of Rånö*); *I Havsbandet*, 1890 (*By the Open Sea*); *Fagervik och Skamsund*, 1902 (*Fairhaven and Foulstrand*); *Swarta Fanor*, 1904 (*Black Banners*).

SHORT STORIES: *Giftas*, I and II, 1886–1888 (*Married*).

AUTOBIOGRAPHICAL FICTION: *Tjänstekvinnans son*, 1886–1909 (*The Son of a Servant*); *En dåres försvärstal*, 1887 (*A Fool's Defense*); *Inferno*, 1897; *Legender*, 1897–1898 (*Legends*); *Einsam*, 1903 (*Alone*).

August Strindberg, greatest of Swedish writers and one of the few real geniuses among modern dramatists, was born in Stockholm on January 22, 1849. He barely escaped illegitimacy, for his father, a bankrupt shipping agent, married his servant-mistress just before August's birth; three boys had been born before the marriage, and of the numerous children born later, four survived to crowd the tiny flat of the impoverished family. The over-sensitive boy was unhappy at home and unhappier at school, where he felt himself tormented because of his vulgar origins and where he was exasperated by a school system geared to the most stupid children. Upon the death of his mother, whom August idealized, his father married his young housekeeper, much to August's pain and humiliation.

At secondary school he was stimulated by the study of science, and to the end of his life he was a student of geology, astronomy, biology, and chemistry. He attended Uppsala University but was unhappy there, poor, lonely, confused. Leaving the university without taking a degree, he engaged in a bewildering series of activities, becoming at various times a teacher, a tutor, an actor, a journalist, a political radical, a landscape painter, a medical student, a playwright, a librarian, a Sinologist, a poet, a chemist, a novelist, and an autobiographer.

Most of all he was a dramatist who gradually attained fame over all Europe, though at home his genuine distinction was difficult for his compatriots to discern through the clouds of scandal surrounding his melodramatically unsuccessful marriages, the shocking notoriety resulting from his frankly autobiographical books, subjective novels, and short stories, and his bizarre conduct during periods of near-insanity and frightening religious mania. Although none of the many studies of Strindberg has succeeded in making him a completely understandable human being, nearly half a century after his death the "mad genius" strikes us more and more as a great genius, less and less as a madman. In fact, five years preceding his death, on May 14, 1912, Strindberg ended his Continental exile and again lived in Stockholm, where he was associated with an intimate theater for the presentation of his plays and where he became a respected public figure. But he was still frustrated and tormented in his search for certainty, and his literary record of volcanic adventures of mind and spirit made him a violent and controversial figure to the end.

Just how important a figure Strindberg is in modern drama no American or British critic can say with authority, largely because most of his plays have never been translated into English. (The translations are slowly being done, thanks to Bernard Shaw, who gave his Nobel Prize money for this purpose.) The consensus of critics is, however, that he is one of the greatest playwrights of the modern movement. A few, including the late Eugene O'Neill, consider him the greatest dramatic genius of the past century.

The sweep of his dramatic output is breathtaking: historical verse plays, fairy plays, romances, dozens of realistic and naturalistic plays, moralities, religious dramas, plays of complete cynicism and pessimism, and the earliest expressionistic plays. Not only was he far more versatile than any other modern playwright, but he attained distinction in every genre he attempted. The reader is sharply conscious of the dynamic intellect on every page of Strindberg. His plays, except for *The Father* and *Miss Julie*, are infrequently performed in America, although he is receiving increased attention in the more and more significant theaters off Broadway, where at least six of his plays were performed in 1956 and 1957.

Strindberg's historical and religious dramas and his social-reform or crusading plays have little interest for the British and American critics, who feel that Strindberg reached his full stature in his revolutionary naturalistic and expressionistic plays. The former reflect, if not a pathological misogyny, at least the most ferocious anti-feminism ever to appear in drama. *The Father, Comrades, The Dance of Death,* and *Creditors* have as their central theme the duel of the sexes, in each of which the woman is more unscrupulous, selfish, and conscienceless than the man. *The Father* is one of the most terrifying tragedies ever written, partly because Strindberg poured into it experience from his own shattered marriage, partly because there is no alleviation of hope, and partly because of the superb construction and swift tempo which sweep the playgoer or reader along in breathless horror to the tragic and cynical final curtain. Present in this work are echoes of Greek tragedy (the Omphale motif) and of Shakespeare (Iago cleverly planting the seeds of doubt), but *The Father* is modern in its sharp study of a crumbling mind. *The Comrades* is not a tragedy but is no less an intense expression of Strinberg's misogyny, his contempt for Ibsen's and Nora Helmer's ideal of marriage as a companionship of equals. To Strindberg, woman has neither the integrity nor the intelligence to succeed as a comrade or partner. *The Dance of Death* exploits the same theme, that the underside of love is hate and only tragedy can result from their inseparableness.

Almost as famous and well known as *The Father* is *Miss Julie,* a powerful story of an aristocratic girl who gives herself to an impudent, attractive servant and who in disgust takes her own life immediately afterward. Here Strindberg makes the man as odious as the woman, although Julie is somewhat more aggressive. *Miss Julie* is a classic naturalistic tragedy in its careful presentation of character as a product of heredity and environment.

Strindberg stands as the father of expressionistic drama, which was carried to its greatest success in Germany after World War I and which went into decline as a dramatic form in the 1930's. But echoes of expressionism are still heard in many modern plays, where its techniques have been utilized to some extent by O'Neill, Rice, Williams, Miller, Millar, Anouilh, Priestley, and others. *To Damascus* is the first real expressionistic drama. In it Strindberg abandoned traditional dramatic techniques in order to dramatize his own inferno of soul in his search for religious certainty. His other two great expressionistic dramas are *The Dream Play* and *The Spook Sonata.* This latter play Eugene O'Neill admired extravagantly, and its influence is to be found in a number of his plays.

BIBLIOGRAPHICAL REFERENCES: The collected works of Strindberg were edited by J. Landquist, 55 vols., 1911–1921. In translation, *Plays by August Strindberg,* 4 vols., 1912–1916, contains valuable introductions by Edwin Bjorkman. For biography and criticism see Nils Erdmann, *August Strindberg,* 1924; C. E. W. L. Dahlström, *Strindberg's Dramatic Expressionism,* 1930; V. J. McGill, *August Strindberg: The Bedeviled Viking,* 1930; A. Jolivet, *Le Théâtre de Strindberg,* 1931; G. A. Campbell, *Strindberg,* 1933; Martin Lamm, *August Strindberg,* 1942; Elizabeth Sprigge, *The Strange Life of August Strindberg,* 1949; Eugen Diem, *August Strindberg: Leben und Werk,* 1949; Maurice Gravier, *Strindberg et le théâtre moderne,* 1949; Karl Jaspers, *Strindberg und van Gogh,* 1949; Brita M. Mortensen and Brian W. Downs, *Strindberg: An Introduction to His Life and Work,* 1949; Nils Norman, *Den unge Strindberg och bäckelserörelsen,* 1953; also see John Gassner, *Masters of the Drama,* 1945; Eric Bentley, *The Playwright as Thinker,* 1946; Barrett H. Clark and George Freedley, *A History of the Modern Drama,* 1947; Walter Johnson, *Strindberg and the Historical Drama,* 1963; and *Strindberg: A Collection of Critical Essays,* edited by Otto Reinert, 1971.

L. A. G. STRONG

Born: Plympton, Devonshire, England
Date: March 8, 1896

Died: Guilford, England
Date: August 17, 1958

Principal Works

NOVELS: *Dewer Rides*, 1929; *The Jealous Ghost*, 1930; *The Garden*, 1931; *The Brothers*, 1932; *Sea Wall*, 1933; *Corporal Tune*, 1934; *The Seven Arms*, 1935; *The Last Enemy*, 1936; *The Swift Shadow*, 1937; *Laughter in the West*, 1937; *The Open Sky*, 1939; *The Bay*, 1941; *Trevannion*, 1948; *The Hill of Howth*, 1953; *Deliverance*, 1955.

SHORT STORIES: *Doyle's Rock and Other Stories*, 1925; *The English Captain*, 1929; *The Big Man*, 1931; *Don Juan and the Wheelbarrow*, 1932; *Tuesday Afternoon*, 1935; *Sun on the Water*, 1940; *Travellers*, 1945; *Darling Tom*, 1952.

POEMS: *Dallington Rhymes*, 1919; *Dublin Days*, 1921; *Twice Four*, 1921; *Says the Muse to Me, Says She*, 1922; *Eight Poems*, 1923; *The Lowery Road*, 1923; *Seven*, 1924; *Difficult Love*, 1927; *At Glenan Cross*, 1928; *Northern Light*, 1930; *Selected Poems*, 1931; *March Evening*, 1932; *Call to the Swan*, 1936; *The Body's Imperfection*, 1957.

BIOGRAPHY: *The Minstrel Boy*, 1937; *John McCormack*, 1941; *Maude Cherrill*, 1950; *Dr. Quicksilver*, 1955.

CRITICISM AND BELLES-LETTRES: *Common Sense About Poetry*, 1932; *A Letter to W. B. Yeats*, 1932; *Life in English Literature*, 1932 (with Monica Redlich); *The Hansom Cab and the Pigeons*, 1935; *The Sacred River*, 1949; *The Writer's Trade*, 1953.

L(eonard) A(lfred) G(eorge) Strong was born, March 8, 1896, in Devonshire. Of three-fourths Irish descent, he spent part of his childhood in the vicinity of Dublin. Retaining stanch ties with his Irish Protestant heritage, he has drawn upon early memories in much of his fiction. He was educated on scholarships at Brighton College and at Wadham College, Oxford. Exempted from military service on account of disability, he began to teach at Summer Fields, a preparatory school near Oxford, in 1917. Here he remained twelve years; in 1930 he moved to London to devote his full time to writing. Interested in speech and its development, he has taught oral interpretation of drama and has broadcast for the B.B.C. In addition, owing apparently to his mixed cultural background, he has maintained an interest in regional dialects, expert knowledge of which he reveals in his poems of rustic life.

Strong became known first for his poems, some of which show affinities with the work of Hardy and the poet of Spoon River. His succinct lyric portrayals of provincial life express satire, pathos, and laughter of delight. Outstanding among his poems are "An Old Woman, Outside the Abbey Theatre," which is epigrammatically ironic in a manner worthy of Yeats, and "The Mad Woman of Punnet's Town," which depicts vitality and joy. After deciding to live by his writing, he concentrated in the main on works of prose; most of his novels, short stories, and essays have been published in rapid succession. As a novelist, he is at his best in treatments of rural domestic scenes. He excels in his realistic handling of conversation; his descriptive style tends to be somewhat dry. Of late years, he has written several crime stories, featuring the character of Ellis McKay, a Scotland Yard detective indifferently successful at solving cases by induction. In these short novels, Strong, like his friend Nicholas Blake (C. Day Lewis), holds to the British tradition of "playing fair" with the reader.

With the English public he has achieved great celebrity as the author of short stories; but, though many of these are available in collected editions, they seem to be little known in America. For the collection entitled *Travellers*, in 1945, Strong was awarded the James Tait Black Memorial Prize. His other works include juveniles and several penetrating critical studies, notably his study of James Joyce in *The Sacred River*.

BIBLIOGRAPHICAL REFERENCES: There is no extensive criticism of Strong and his work. See R. L. Mégroz, *Five Novelist Poets of Today*, 1933; and Dayton Kohler, "L. A. G. Strong," *Bookman*, LXXIII (1931), 570–575.

JESSE STUART

Born: W-Hollow, Riverton, Kentucky
Date: August 8, 1907

Principal Works

NOVELS: *Trees of Heaven,* 1940; *Taps for Private Tussie,* 1943; *Foretaste of Glory,* 1946; *Hie to the Hunters,* 1950; *The Good Spirit of Laurel Ridge,* 1953; *Daughter of the Legend,* 1965; *Mr. Gallion's School,* 1967.

SHORT STORIES: *Head o' W-Hollow,* 1936; *Men of the Mountains,* 1941; *Tales from the Plum Grove Hills,* 1946; *Clearing in the Sky,* 1950; *Plowshare in Heaven: Tales True and Tall from the Kentucky Hills,* 1958; *Save Every Lamb,* 1964; *My Land Has a Voice,* 1966; *Come Gentle Spring,* 1969; *Come Back to the Farm,* 1971.

POEMS: *Man with a Bull-Tongue Plow,* 1934; *Album of Destiny,* 1944; *Kentucky Is My Land,* 1952; *Hold April,* 1962.

AUTOBIOGRAPHY: *Beyond Dark Hills,* 1938; *The Thread That Runs So True,* 1949; *The Year of My Rebirth,* 1956; *To Teach, To Love,* 1970.

JUVENILES: *Mongrel Mettle,* 1944; *The Beatinest Boy,* 1953; *A Penny's Worth of Character,* 1954; *Red Mule,* 1955; *Rightful Owner,* 1960; *Andy Finds a Way,* 1961.

"Kentucky is my land," says Jesse Stuart. His life and work make good his claim. Hill-born, he writes about his region with the assurance of one whose familiarity with a place and its people was bred in the bone. All this is as it should be. His forebears had been Kentuckians for generations: the Hiltons, rebels, Democrats, country preachers, lovers of book learning and bright colors, and the Stuarts, hardy fighters, Republicans, heavy drinkers, good workers, tellers of tales. Lustiest of the clan was old Mitch Stuart, the Civil War veteran and mountain feudist celebrated in "Elegy for Mitch Stuart," the first poem his grandson sold to a magazine of national circulation. From stories of these people and their mountain neighbors Jesse Stuart absorbed the background of folk wisdom, family legend, and community experience which gives his writing its local coloring and flavor.

A son of Mitchell and Martha (Hilton) Stuart, the unlettered but earthwise parents to whom he has paid tribute in his autobiographical studies, Jesse (Hilton) Stuart was born on August 8, 1907, in a one-room log cabin overlooking W-Hollow, near Riverton, Kentucky. He had his first schooling at nearby Plum Grove, but he never finished a complete term because he was needed to help with the clearing and cropping on the seven rented farms on which he lived as a boy. At the age of nine he began to hire out to the other farmers of the neighborhood for twenty-five cents a day. When he was eleven he left school, and for the next four years he harvested corn and worked on a paving gang in the summertime and cut timber in the winter. He entered the Greenup County High School when he was fifteen. During vacations throughout his high school years he took charge of the farm so that his father would be free to work for the C&O Railway. About the same time he discovered the poetry of Robert Burns and began to write poems of his own on whatever was at hand—scraps of paper, tobacco sacks, even poplar leaves. Restless after finishing school, he ran away with a carnival. Fired, he got a job as a blacksmith in a steel mill.

This experience convinced him that an education was more important than anything else. In 1926, with $30 he had saved, he went to Lincoln Memorial University at Harrogate, Tennessee. There he worked in the hay fields, in a rock quarry, and in the college kitchen to pay his fees. He ran track, edited the college paper, and wrote about 500 poems. Some of these were later printed in *Harvest of Youth* (1930), a book long out of print and now almost unavailable. Graduated in 1929, he went home and taught in public schools for two years before beginning graduate work at Vanderbilt University in 1931. After a dormitory fire destroyed his clothes, his thesis, some poems, and part of a novel, he managed to get along on one meal a day until the end of the session. He never rewrote his thesis and so failed to qualify for a degree, but he wrote a book-length term paper which his professor called "crudely written and yet beautiful, tremendous, and powerful." He returned to teaching, becoming superintendent of the Greenup County schools and later principal of McKell High School. In the early 1930's his crusade to improve the conditions of secondary education in his county made him a number of enemies, exposed him to physical violence, and involved him in thirty-two lawsuits; but in the end he and his backers won their fight. This is the story he has told in *The Thread That Runs So True*. His book of regional poems, *Man with a Bull-Tongue Plow* appeared in 1934, *Head o' W-Hollow*, a collection of short stories, two years later. In 1937 he went to Europe on a Guggenheim fellowship and in Scotland rewrote his Vanderbilt term paper, published in 1938 as *Beyond Dark Hills*. He married Naomi Deane Norris in 1939; they have one daughter, Jessica Jane. Their W-Hollow home, remodeled from an old house once rented by Mitchell Stuart, is part of a timbered farm covering 785 acres over which Jesse Stuart has tramped, worked, and hunted all his life. His longest period of time away from his homeplace came when, enlisting as an apprentice seaman early in 1944 and commissioned several months later, he served in the Naval Reserve during World War II.

Jesse Stuart's writing is never far away from the poetry with which he began. *Man with a Bull-Tongue Plow*, a collection of 703 sonnets re-creating in lyric language and mood the Kentucky landscape in all lights and seasons and bringing roaringly to life his people of the hills, has been followed by two more books of poems, *Album of Destiny* and *Kentucky Is My Land*. In his prose the same poet's imagination blends with the realist's sharp eye and the gusty, tall story humor of the fabulist. There is a sense in which Stuart's early novels and short stories mark the late flowering of an old tradition in American literature rather than the beginning of a new one. Certainly his talent for anecdote and character drawing goes back through Mark Twain, the Sut Lovingood papers, and Augustus Longstreet's *Georgia Scenes* to the anonymous frontier storytellers who in comic elaborations of character and drawling reminiscence dramatized the pioneer experience with shrewd appraisal and salty enjoyment. *Trees of Heaven* is filled with tags of frontier realism and rough humor in its account of the grudge fight between settler and squatter as personified by patriarchal Anse Bushman and shiftless Boliver Tussie. *Taps for Private Tussie*, winner of the Thomas Jefferson Southern Award in 1943, tells what happens after the same Tussie clan comes into $10,000 of government insurance money when soldier Kim Tussie is reported killed overseas. *Mongrel Mettle*, which goes back to the manner of the old beast fables, has a dog for its central figure. Although it was written as a book for younger readers, adults continue to read it as folk allegory. *Foretaste of Glory* deals with the agitation caused in a small Kentucky town by a prophecy that the world will end in September, 1941. *Hie to the Hunters* is the story of a city boy who finds a new life among the fox hunters and tobacco growers of the hill country. If this novel and *The Good Spirit of Laurel Ridge* seem more restrained in treatment and style than Stuart's earlier fiction, the reason is that the patterns of mountain life are in a process of change. Paved roads, the automobile, good schools, radio, the movies, and two world wars have brought urban ways into the hills; Jesse Stuart's books are a documentation of this transition.

The same shift in emphasis and tone may be traced through his collections of short stories and his tales for younger readers.

Of his more recent novels, *Daughter of the Legend* received high praise; but the reaction to *Mr. Gallion's School* was, at most, lukewarm. The feeling was that the novel fell far short of the author's autobiographical sketch, *The Thread That Runs So True*, which also dealt with teaching experience.

Always in demand as a lecturer, Jesse Stuart had just concluded a talk before a college audience at Murray, Kentucky, in October, 1954, when he was stricken with a coronary occlusion. Part autobiography, part regional chronicle, *The Year of My Rebirth* tells the story of his gradual recovery. Late in his convalescence he received a tribute of affection and respect from his friends and neighbors in Greenup County. October 15, 1955, was proclaimed Jesse Stuart Day by the governor of the state and at Greenup a monument honoring him as poet, novelist, and educator was unveiled in recognition of this writer whose books have given shape and life to the Kentucky hills.

BIBLIOGRAPHICAL REFERENCES: Jesse Stuart's four autobiographical books are valuable for the outline of his life and the light they throw on his background and personality. For biographical and critical studies see E. L. Blair, *Jesse Stuart: His Life and Works*, 1967; Mary W. Clarke, *Jesse Stuart's Kentucky*, 1968; and R. E. Foster, *Jesse Stuart*, 1968. For brief biographical and critical studies see Harry R. Warfel, *American Novelists of Today*, 1951; Charlotte Salmon, "Jesse Stuart," *Southwest Review*, XXI (1936), 163–168; Dayton Kohler, "Jesse Stuart and James Still: Mountain Regionalists," *College English*, III (1942), 523–533; Marguerite Shelburne, "Jesse Stuart, Young Man of the Mountains," *Holland's*, LXVI (December, 1947), 8–9; and William D. Moore, "Jesse H. Stuart, Teacher," *Educational Forum*, XXI (1956), 75–80.

WILLIAM STYRON

Born: Newport News, Virginia
Date: June 11, 1925

Principal Works

NOVELS: *Lie Down in Darkness*, 1951; *The Long March*, 1953; *Set This House on Fire*, 1960; *The Confessions of Nat Turner*, 1967.

William Styron was born in Newport News, Virginia, on June 11, 1925, and began writing seriously in William Blackburn's class at Duke University. After spending two and one half years in the Marine Corps during World War II, he returned to Duke and received an A.B. degree in 1947. He then went to New York and studied with Hiram Haydn at the New School. *Lie Down in Darkness* was finished under Haydn's guidance and published in 1951.

This first novel established Styron as an important contemporary novelist at the age of twenty-six. The book was awarded the Prix de Rome of the American Academy of Arts and Letters for 1952. A story of the dissolution of a Virginia family, it has been called a masterpiece of psychological fiction. Set in the locale of Styron's youth, the novel is an ambitious attempt to explore the failures of three members of the Loftis family. Milton Loftis is the good-intentioned husband and father who finds himself unable to salvage his crumbling world. Helen, his wife, is a victim of pride and hatred, while Peyton, the product of their unhappy marriage, is emotionally crippled and incapable of dealing with life and its demands. The technical problems Styron encountered are visible in the complex structure of the novel and in the time sequences, which consist of a series of flashbacks within flashbacks. Because of the difficult task Styron set for himself, the focus is somewhat dissipated. However, the writing itself is rich in imagery, especially metaphor, and symbolism. Styron's impressive talent is most obvious in the section in which the reader sees the world through the eyes of Peyton Loftis' deranged mind.

In 1950 during the Korean crisis, Styron was recalled to the Marine Corps. Out of this military experience came *The Long March,* his short novel of conflict between a man and a system. Published in 1953, the work showed further evidence of Styron's talent, although his initial character does not quite reach tragic proportions. From 1952, Styron lived in Europe, spending most of his time in France and Italy. In 1953 he married the former Rose Burgunder and was also made a fellow of the American Academy of Arts and Letters in Rome.

Styron was one of the founders and editors of the *Paris Review,* and in 1959 he edited a volume entitled, *Best Stories from Paris Review*. In 1960, *Set This House on Fire* was published. In this novel of an American artist in Europe, Styron has again written an impressive work, although critical opinion of his third piece of fiction has not been entirely favorable. Again, the central character fails to reach tragic dimensions and the promise of the writer's first literary endeavor is not wholly fulfilled. Still, Styron maintains the position of an important contemporary writer.

In 1963, he was elected to the Board of Directors of the Inter-American Foundation of the Arts and the following year was made a fellow of Silliman College, Yale. Styron, too, has had an impressive journalistic career. He has contributed articles and stories to *Esquire, Nation, New Republic, Harper's Bazaar* and other publications. His work has been translated into twelve languages.

The author has since returned to America and resides in Roxbury, Connecticut, with his wife and three children. His most recent work is *The Confessions of Nat Turner,* a novel about the Negro slave who led an uprising against white landholders in Virginia in 1831.

BIBLIOGRAPHICAL REFERENCES: Biographical and critical works include Robert Fossom, *William Styron,* 1968; Cooper R. Mackin, *William Styron,* 1969; and Richard Pearce, *William Styron,* 1971.

There are essays on Styron's work in many volumes on modern American fiction. See Jonathan Baumbach, *The Landscape of Nightmare,* 1965; Louise Y. Gossett, *Violence in Recent Southern Fiction,* 1965; David D. Galloway, *The Absurd Hero in American Fiction,* 1966; Frederick J. Hoffman, *The Art of Southern Fiction,* 1967; William Van O'Connor, "John Updike and William Styron: The Burden of Talent," *Contemporary American Novelists,* edited by Harry T. Moore, 1964; Gunnar Urang, "The Voices of Tragedy in the Novels of William Styron," *Adversity and Grace: Studies in Recent American Literature,* edited by Nathan A. Scott, Jr., 1968; and John W. Aldridge, *Time to Murder and Create,* 1966.

Also of interest are *William Styron's "The Confessions of Nat Turner,"* a critical handbook edited by Melvin J. Friedman and Irving Malin, 1970; *William Styron's "Nat Turner": Ten Black Writers Respond,* edited by J. H. Clark, 1968; and *Configuration Critique de William Styron,* edited by M. Friedman and A. J. Nigro, 1967.

SIR JOHN SUCKLING

Born: Twickenham, England
Date: February, 1609

Died: Paris, France
Date: 1642

Principal Works

POEMS: *Fragmenta Aurea*, 1646; *The Last Remains*, 1659.
PLAYS: *Aglaura*, 1638; *Brennoralt*, 1639.

Sir John Suckling is typical of the Cavalier poets, who flourished at the court of Charles I and Queen Henrietta Maria during the decade before the outbreak of the Civil War, serving the King, writing polished, witty verses, and entertaining the court ladies with their gallantries. Suckling was born in 1609 in Twickenham, a suburb of London, into a family with close court connections. His father, Sir John Suckling, was a member of parliament, Secretary of State, and Comptroller of the Household under James I, and he became a member of the Privy Council of Charles I. The poet's mother, who died when he was four, was the sister of Lionel Cranfield, James's Lord Treasurer from 1622 to 1626, the one man who almost succeeded in curbing the royal extravagances for a brief period.

Suckling may have attended the Westminster school before he entered Trinity College, Cambridge, in 1623. He left the university without a degree and went on to London to Gray's Inn, ostensibly to study law. However, at this period the Inns of Court were as much the playground for rich young noblemen as institutions of learning, and Suckling probably sought amusement where he could find it. When his father died in 1627, he began at once to squander his newly-acquired fortune, which was substantial.

The young nobleman left Gray's Inn in 1628 for a two-year tour of France and Italy. Knighted by Charles I at Theobalds when he came back to England in 1630, he soon joined a group of English soldiers who fought under King Gustavus Adolphus of Sweden in the following year. His extravagance on his return to London in 1632 was legendary; the story is told that his sisters wept for fear he would gamble away their dowries. He lived chiefly at court, where he was named Gentleman of the Privy Chamber, and where he composed many of his clever, cynical lyrics addressed to mournful lovers and faithless ladies.

Suckling's interests were not exclusively frivolous; he numbered among his friends the noted philosopher Lucius Cary, Lord Falkland, and the scientist Robert Boyle, as well as many of the poets of his time. He himself composed a philosophical tract, "An Account of Religion by Reason," which was published with his poetry in *Fragmenta Aurea*, in 1646.

A number of Suckling's best works were written between 1635 and 1640; one of the wittiest of them, "A Session of the Poets," contains satirical portraits of his literary acquaintances. His play *Aglaura* was lavishly produced for the court at his own expense in 1637, and *Brennoralt*, a dramatic commentary on the Scottish rebellion, appeared in the following year.

When Charles I raised an army to invade Scotland in 1639, Suckling furnished a unit that was distinguished for its magnificent finery, if not for its military ability, an act which earned him considerable ridicule from his countrymen. He became a member of the Long Parliament in 1640, but his public career ended abruptly with his involvement in a plot to free Thomas Wentworth, Earl of Strafford, who had been sentenced to death by Parliament for treason. To escape arrest Suckling fled to France, where he died in 1642, by a self-administered dose of poison, according to the gossipy seventeenth century biographer, John Aubrey. Another report says that a servant caused his death. While his death was untimely, the world in which he had delighted no longer existed; there was no place in Cromwell's Commonwealth for the dilettante man of letters who played at being a soldier when it suited his fancy.

BIBLIOGRAPHICAL REFERENCES: Currently at press is a 2 volume edition, *The Works of John Suckling, The Non-Dramatic Works*, edited by Thomas Clayton, and *The Plays*, edited by L. A. Beaurline. For criticism see F. O. Henderson, "Traditions of Precieux and Libertin in Suckling's Poetry," *English Literary History*, IV (1937), 274–298; K. M. Lynch, *Social Mode of Restoration Comedy*, 1926; K. A. McEuen, *Classical Influences upon the Tribe of Ben*, 1939; Douglas Bush, *English Literature in the Earlier Seventeenth Century*, 1945; R. Skelton, *The Cavalier Poets*, 1960; and H. M. Richmond, *The School of Love: The Evolution of the Stuart Love Lyric*, 1964.

RUTH SUCKOW

Born: Hawarden, Iowa
Date: August 6, 1892

Died: Claremont, California
Date: January 23, 1960

Principal Works

NOVELS: *Country People*, 1924; *The Bonney Family*, 1929; *The Kramer Girls*, 1930; *The Folks*, 1934; *New Hope*, 1942; *The John Wood Case*, 1959.
SHORT STORIES: *Iowa Interiors*, 1926; *Children and Other People*, 1931; *Some Others and Myself*, 1952.

Ruth Suckow was the grandchild of German immigrants, on both sides of her family. Western Iowa was, when she was born, but recently settled. Her father was a liberal Congregational minister whose career took his family to a number of Iowa communities during his daughter's childhood.

After high school Ruth Suckow spent three years at Grinnell College and a year at the Curry Dramatic School, in Boston. She took her A.B. degree in 1917, at the University of Denver. While in Colorado she learned beekeeping, in order to have a way of earning a living, and following her graduation from college she operated the Orchard Apiary, at Earleville, Iowa, as a livelihood while she served her apprenticeship as a writer. Her beekeeping allowed her to spend some months during the winters in New York City. Her first published work was a story in *Midland*, a periodical for which she later became an associate editor. The editor of *Midland* encouraged her to submit some manuscripts to H. L. Mencken, who liked her work, and she became a contributor to *Smart Set, American Mercury*, and other periodicals during the 1920's. Her *Country People* (1924) was first published by Carl Van Doren in the *Century* as a serialized novel. Both her stories and novels of the 1920's set the pattern of her work. As a regionalist she drew upon the people and the countryside and the towns of the Midwest, especially the families of German immigrants; thus she utilized the region and the people she knew closely from her own early life. *The Bonney Family* (1929) is a novel of life in a minister's home, reflecting Ruth Suckow's own family and its experiences. In the early 1930's she began working on a novel, *The Folks*, which appeared in 1934. This book, which reputedly had greater advance sale than the highly popular *Anthony Adverse*, is usually considered her most typical and best work. It describes the average small-town Midwestern family, one which is a single generation removed from the farm and two generations removed from genuine pioneer experience.

Following her marriage to Ferner Nuhn in 1929, she lived at various times in New York City, Washington, D. C., California, Vermont, New Mexico, and Iowa. She considered Cedar Falls, Iowa, where she is buried, as "home." During the 1940's and 1950's her literary fame and reputation dwindled, and she wrote less than she had earlier in life. However, her last novel appeared just a few months before she died, in her sixty-eighth year.

BIBLIOGRAPHICAL REFERENCES: The only full-length study is Leedice Kissane, *Ruth Suckow*, 1969. Relevant articles include Joseph E. Baker, "Regionalism in the Middle West," *American Review*, V (March, 1935), 603–614; A. A. Hamblen, "Protestantism in Three American Novels," *Forum*, III (Fall–Winter, 1960), 40–43; and *ibid.*, "Ruth Suckow and Thomas Wolfe: A Study in Similarity," *Forum* (Houston), III, (Winter, 1962), 27–31.

HERMANN SUDERMANN

Born: Matziken, East Prussia
Date: September 30, 1857

Died: Berlin, Germany
Date: November 21, 1928

Principal Works

NOVELS: *Frau Sorge*, 1887 (*Dame Care*); *Der Katzensteg*, 1889 (*Regina*); *Das hohe Lied*, 1908 (*The Song of Songs*); *Der tolle Professor*, 1926 (*The Mad Professor*); *Die Frau des Steffen Tromholt*, 1927 (*The Wife of Steffen Tromholt*); *Purzelchen*, 1928 (*The Dance of Youth*).

PLAYS: *Die Ehre*, 1889 (*Honor*); *Sodoms Ende*, 1891 (*The Man and His Picture*); *Heimat*, 1893 (*Magda*); *Die Schmetterlingsschlacht*, 1895 (*The Battle of the Butterflies*); *Das Glück im Winkel*, 1895 (*The Vale of Content*); *Morituri*, 1896; *Die drei Reiherfedern*, 1899 (*The Three Herons' Feathers*); *Johannisfeuer*, 1900 (*The Fires of St. John*); *Sturmgeselle Sokrates*, 1903; *Stein unter Steinen*, 1905.

SHORT STORIES: *Im Zwielicht*, 1886; *Geschwister*, 1888; *Die Reise nach Tilsit*, 1917 (*The Excursion to Tilsit*).

AUTOBIOGRAPHY: *Das Bilderbuch meiner Jugend*, 1922 (*Book of My Youth*).

Hermann Sudermann, German novelist and playwright, regarded during his lifetime as one of Germany's great modern dramatists, was born on September 30, 1857, the son of a brewer who worked in the village of Heydekrug. The Sudermann family was Mennonite and from Holland; an ancestor was Daniel Sudermann (1550–1632), a moralistic writer. Hermann Sudermann's birthplace, Matziken, in East Prussia, was a village where German and Lithuanian elements were mixed, and it was from the rich local strain of folk tales and customs that he was able to draw late in his career in order to put new life into his work.

He received his early education at the Realschule in Elbing, but as a result of his family's near-poverty he was compelled to go to work at the age of fourteen as apprentice to a chemist. He then entered the Realgymnasium in Tilsit. His advanced education was received at the university in Königsberg, where he studied philology and history, and at the University of Berlin. While in Berlin, to which he came at the age of twenty, he was tutor of the children of Hans von Hopfen (1835–1904), a writer by whom Sudermann was to some extent influenced in his own creative work.

In 1881 and 1882 Sudermann was an editor of *Deutsches Reichsblatt*, a political journal. At the time his political views were fairly liberal, but after leaving the editorship he became increasingly conservative; he was later charged with allowing considerations of royalties to affect his political convictions.

His writing career began with the writing of short stories, and a first collection, *Im Zwielicht*, appeared in 1886. The following year saw the publication of *Dame Care*, a sentimental example of German romanticism, but skillful enough in its portrayal of persons of various classes to make it one of Sudermann's most successful novels. Neither this book nor *Regina* achieved popular recognition until after the overwhelming reception accorded to his play *Honor*, which opened at the Lessing Theatre in Berlin on November 27, 1889. The play had originally been intended as a tragedy, but following the advice of others Sudermann gave it a happy ending which satisfied the audiences that first saw it. *Honor* shows the influence of Nietzsche on Sudermann; the play is in effect a pseudo-intellectual attack on the morality of the lower classes. With this play Sudermann's highly successful career as a dramatist was launched, and his novels suddenly began to sell in considerable numbers.

Magda, another successful drama, made Sudermann's name known all over Europe, and the play became a favorite vehicle for the leading actresses of the day: Bernhardt, Mrs. Campbell, Duse, and Modjeska. Sudermann wrote his plays at a fortunate time, and he was careful to achieve the kind of technical finish that would make them popular; consequently, although he enjoyed considerable fame for a number of years and was ranked with Gerhart Hauptmann, his plays lost favor when the fashion changed, and neither the audiences nor the critics seemed to care. Sudermann, concentrating on the novel during the last few years of his life, managed to produce enough satisfactory work to establish himself as an important novelist.

The play, *The Man and His Picture*, like *St. John's Fire* provided some critics with evidence to support their claim that Sudermann was a writer with an honest social conscience, that he was freeing German drama from the French influence and replacing romanticism with naturalism. However, Sudermann's portrayals of the vicious social life of fashionable Berlin never quite succeeded in losing the drawing-room comedy touch; perhaps the very features which accounted for his quick success were also accountable for the decline of interest in his plays. Of his novels, *Dame Care* and *The Song of Songs* are now generally regarded as his best, and the short stories in *The Excursion to Tilsit* contain much of his best writing.

Sudermann lived in a villa at Grunewald, a suburb of Berlin, and at his castle at Blankensee, near Trebbin, which he purchased from play royalties. He was married in 1891 to Klara Schultz Lauckner, a widow and a writer. He died in Berlin on November 21, 1928.

BIBLIOGRAPHICAL REFERENCES: For biography and criticism see K. Busse, *Hermann Sudermann, sein Wesen und sein Werke*, 1927; and Irmgard Leux, *Hermann Sudermann*, 1931; also Alfred Kerr, *Das neue Drama*, I, 1917; E. Feise, "Stilverwirrung in Sudermann's 'Frau Sorge,' " *Germanic Review*, V (1930), 225–237; and William F. Mainland, "Hermann Sudermann," *German Men of Letters*, II, 1963, 33–53.

EUGÈNE SUE

Born: Paris, France
Date: January 20, 1804

Died: Annecy, France
Date: August 3, 1857

PRINCIPAL WORKS

NOVELS: *Les Mystères de Paris*, 1842–1843 (*The Mysteries of Paris*); *Le Juif errant*, 1844–1845 (*The Wandering Jew*).

Born in Paris on January 20, 1804, Eugène Sue, whose real name was Marie Joseph Sue, was the son of a distinguished surgeon who had served with Napoleon's armies. At his baptism, Sue's sponsors were Prince Eugène Beauharnais and the Empress Joséphine; it was his godfather's name that Sue adopted as part of his pseudonym. Educated at private schools in Paris, he later studied medicine and became a surgeon. From 1823 to 1829 he served aboard ships of the French Navy as a naval surgeon, taking part in the French campaign against Spain in 1823 and in the battle of Navarino in 1828. At his father's death Sue inherited a large fortune and retired from the navy. Returning to Paris, he became a fashionable young man-about-town, but the life bored him and he turned to writing as an outlet for his energies.

Sue is reputed to have become a novelist by accident when an editor outlined a novel of the sea and suggested that Sue was the man to write the book because of his experience in the navy. *Plick et Plock* (1831) was the first of a series of sea novels which brought him critical praise as "the French James Fenimore Cooper." Sainte-Beuve, the eminent French critic, claimed that Sue was the first Frenchman to exploit the sea for French literature and the first author to make use of the Mediterranean Sea for literature. Anxious to become a serious man of letters, Sue turned to writing historical works, including a history of the French Navy (1837) in five volumes. He then wrote historical romances, the two best-known being *Jean Cavalier* (1840) and *Latréaumont* (1837).

His most famous novels, *The Mysteries of Paris* and *The Wandering Jew* resulted from his interest in social problems. The former, taking the reader through episodes of lower-class and underworld Paris, presented the social misery Sue saw in his city; his attempts at reform were comparable to those of Dickens in England at the time. In *The Wandering Jew*, Sue attempted to allegorize in the wretched man doomed to wander for centuries the long, weary journey of humanity in its search for just social structures. Although both novels are long and rambling, they illustrate the writer's ability to combine dramatic episodes with moral earnestness. Extremely popular in France, the books were also circulated widely in translation. A later work of moral earnestness, though never popular, was *Les Sept péchés capitaux* (1847–1849, *The Seven Cardinal Sins*), with stories illustrating each of the sins.

After the revolution of 1848, Sue stood for a seat in the French assembly representing Paris. He served in that chamber until the *coup d'état* of 1851 aroused his opposition and he went to live in exile in Haute-Savoie. He died there on August 3, 1857.

BIBLIOGRAPHICAL REFERENCES: Recent biographical and critical studies are Paul Ginisty, *Eugène Sue*, 1929; and N. Atkinson, *Eugène Sue et le roman-feuilleton*, 1929. A contemporary literary portrait is that by Eugène de Mirecourt, 1855.

SUETONIUS
Gaius Suetonius Tranquillus

Born: Britain (?)
Date: c. 70

Died: Rome (?), Italy
Date: c. 140

PRINCIPAL WORKS

BIOGRAPHY AND HISTORY: *De viris illustribus*, 106–113 (*Concerning Illustrious Men*); *De vita Caesarum*, c. 120 (*Lives of the Caesars*).

Since his father was military tribune of the XIII Legion, Gaius Suetonius Tranquillus may have been born in Britain or Africa about A.D. 70. He studied in Rome and became a lawyer and teacher of rhetoric. Part of his *De grammaticis* still exists. He also traveled widely. He accompanied Governor Pliny (The Younger) to Bithynia in 112. He also served for a time (119–121) as private secretary to Emperor Hadrian, but lost favor apparently for inattention to the empress while Hadrian was in Britain.

Suetonius' fame rests on his historical biographies of famous men. He collected anecdotes about figures in the public eye and set them down with more attention to their interest than to their accuracy. So he was a chronicler, rather than a historian. He made no attempt at general impression or psychological interpretation, but his stories about Horace and Terence, among other famous men, and his private lives of the twelve Caesars cover ground untouched by any contemporary except Tacitus and Dio Cassius. Many later biographers have taken him as a model. It is believed that he died in Rome about 140.

BIBLIOGRAPHICAL REFERENCES: A translation reissued many times is Philemon Holland, *The History of Twelve Caesars*, 1606 (rev. eds., 1923, 1931). More recent translations include Alexander Thomson, *Lives of the Twelve Caesars*, 1901 (rev. ed., 1914); and J. C. Rolfe, *Suetonius*, 2 vols., 1914. See also D. H. Stuart, *Epochs of Greek and Roman Biography*, 1928.

WILLIAM GRAHAM SUMNER

Born: Patterson, New Jersey
Date: October 30, 1840

Died: Englewood, New Jersey
Date: April 12, 1910

Principal Works

SOCIAL STUDIES: *What Social Classes Owe to Each Other*, 1883; *Folkways*, 1907; *Science of Society* (with A. G. Keller), 1927.
ESSAYS: *Discipline*, 1880's (?); *What Is the "Proletariat"?*, 1886; *What Is Free Trade?*, 1886; *Legislation by Clamor*, 1887; *The Absurd Effort to Make the World Over*, 1894; *Earth Hunger or the Philosophy of Land Grabbing*, 1896; *Advancing Social and Political Organization in the United States*, 1897; *The Conquest of the United States by Spain*, 1899; *The Bequests of the Nineteenth Century to the Twentieth*, 1901 (published in 1933); *War*, 1903; *Economics and Politics*, 1905.
BIOGRAPHIES: *Andrew Jackson as a Public Man*, 1882; *Alexander Hamilton*, 1890; *Robert Morris*, 1892.

William Graham Sumner was born in 1840 in Patterson, New Jersey. His father, Thomas, a Lancashire artisan who came to Patterson in 1836, was a self-educated man who acquired the lessons of the English classical economists through practical experience as a working man. Young Sumner was raised with a profound respect for the man who worked, saved regularly, and expected nothing from the government but to be left in peace. After graduating from Yale in 1863, Sumner studied in Geneva, Gottingen, and Oxford. When he returned home several years later, he entered the ministry and served both in New York and New Jersey. He proved to be an able minister but his interests centered more and more on social and economic questions.

In 1872, Sumner was offered a position as Professor of Political Economy at Yale University. Instead of the safe, orthodox theologist the Yale administration expected, Sumner shocked them by attacking governmental subsidies in the form of protective tariffs, by using Herbert Spencer's *The Study of Sociology* as a class text, and by speaking against American imperialism abroad during and after the Spanish American War. A former student, Thomas Beer, remembered him as

> . . . a prodigious personality, something cold and massive and autocratic. He came stalking into the classroom with a sort of "Be damned to you" air. . . . We respected and admired him, however little we appreciated him. If he had been seriously threatened with expulsion from Yale in 1899, when he blew up imperialism, there would have been an academic revolution.

As great changes in America took place, Sumner began to look less to theological concerns and turned his attention to the public affairs of the post-Civil War period. His faith in his father's concept of the Protestant ethic led him to relate the successful middle class property holder with a moral and natural superiority. He fortified his belief in classical economics with the writings of Spencer and Darwin. It was Spencer who first used the phrase "survival of the fittest" and applied it to economics. Sumner accepted these conclusions and became an outspoken opponent of reform laws, protective tariffs, anti-trust legislation, and any form of socialism. He repeated the idea that that government was best which governed least.

Indeed, for Sumner, the first prerequisite to an understanding of political economy is a willingness to look at the world the way it is, not the way we wish it to be. According to Sumner, state interference is never justified. Social reformers and humanitarians take away honestly earned money from the "forgotten men"—the thrifty, hardworking middle class—and give it to those who pay the least and benefit the most: the poor and the unfit. He was convinced that catering to the poor and the weak would carry "society downward and favors its worst enemies."

Sumner was an avowed critic of American imperialism and war mainly because they represented and required the inflexible and centrally controlled state he opposed. He denounced the Republican platform of 1900 as nonsense and predicted for America in the twentieth century ". . . war, debt, taxation, diplomacy, a grand governmental system, pomp, glory, a big army and navy, lavish expenditures, political jobbery." Some observers today would insist that his predictions have come true.

Sumner's sociological and anthropological study, *Folkways,* was his most significant and influential book. Its direct and honest approach had a great impact on early twentieth century America. But his particular forte, the short, biting essays are still effective, still relevant, still capable of provoking intelligent and rational debate. He died of a stroke in 1910 while giving a public lecture in Englewood, New Jersey.

BIBLIOGRAPHICAL REFERENCES: Little has been written about Sumner the man. The only full-length biography is Harris E. Starr, *William Graham Sumner,* 1925. See also Albert G. Keller, *Reminiscences (Mainly Personal) of William Graham Sumner,* 1933. For critical comment see Maurice R. Davie, *William Graham Sumner,* 1963.

ROBERT SMITH SURTEES

Born: Northumberland, England
Date: May 17, 1803

Died: Brighton, England
Date: March 16, 1864

Principal Works

NOVELS: *Jorrocks' Jaunts and Jollities*, 1838; *Handley Cross, or the Spa Hunt*, 1843, 1854; *Hillingdon Hall, or the Cockney Squire*, 1845; *Hawbuck Grange, or the Sporting Adventures of Thomas Scott, Esq.*, 1847; *Mr. Sponge's Sporting Tour*, 1853; *Ask Mamma, or the Richest Commoner in England*, 1858; *Plain or Ringlets?* 1860; *Mr. Facey Romford's Hounds*, 1865.
TECHNICAL AND SPORTING MANUALS: *The Horseman's Manual*, 1831; *The Analysis of the Hunting-Field*, 1846.

Like Anthony Trollope, Robert Smith Surtees re-created in his novels a limited but significant phase of the social milieu of his time. The world of his fiction, although small, is admirably self-contained and complete in every detail within its boundaries of the kennel and the stable, the hunting fields and the drawing rooms of the English squirearchy. Against this background he presented a cross section of Victorian society: the aristocracy entrenched behind barriers of caste and privilege, the new middle class trying to rise above its origins in trade, tuft-hunters and amiable blackguards aping the gentry and living at the expense of their social betters, sturdy yeoman farmers, the laboring tenantry, comic yokels. These people fill a series of sporting novels lively with humor and pungent with that flavor of satire which was Surtees' master bias as a writer.

Descended from an ancient country family that took its name from the River Tees, Robert Smith Surtees was born at The Riding, Northumberland, on May 17, 1803. His boyhood was spent at Hamsterley Hall, near Durham, a seventeenth century manor bought by his father in 1810. A younger son without prospects of inheritance, he was educated at Ovingham School and at the Durham Grammar School, and in 1822 was articled to a solicitor at Newcastle-on-Tyne in preparation for a career in law. Three years later he transferred to the office of another solicitor in Bow Churchyard, London. Admitted in Chancery in 1828, he abandoned law for journalism a year later and became a hunting correspondent for the *Sporting Magazine*. His first book, combining his knowledge of law with his interest in sport, was *The Horseman's Manual*, published in 1831. In the same year his older brother died and Surtees became the heir to Hamsterley, a change of fortune which probably influenced his decision to join Rudolph Ackermann in founding the *New Sporting Magazine*, which he edited until 1836. For the third issue of the magazine, in July, 1831, he wrote the first of the humorous sketches dealing with John Jorrocks, the sporting Cockney grocer of Great Coram Street. This series, continued until September, 1834, proved so popular that the publishing house of Chapman and Hall planned a similar miscellany which resulted in Dickens' *Pickwick Papers*. Opposed to repeal of the Corn Laws, Surtees stood unsuccessfully for Parliament in 1837.

Following his father's death in 1838, he returned to Hamsterley to lead the life of a country landlord and hunting squire. He married in 1841 and in the following year was appointed a justice of the peace and deputy lieutenant for Durham County. He was also for a time a major in the Durham Militia, an experience he later satirized in his account of the Heavysteed Dragoons. He became high sheriff of Durham County in 1856.

A shy, unsentimental, taciturn man, Surtees, after *The Horseman's Manual*, would not allow his name to be used in connection with his books. Published anonymously, the Jorrocks sketches were collected in 1838 as *Jorrocks' Jaunts and Jollities, or the Hunting, Shooting, Racing, Driving, Sailing, Eating, Eccentric and Extravagant Exploits of that Renowned Sporting Citizen, Mr. John Jorrocks of St. Botolph Lane and Great Coram Street.* On its appearance the book was completely eclipsed by the greater popularity of *Pickwick Papers,* which had been published a year before, so much so that friendly critics were forced to defend the author of *Jorrocks' Jaunts and Jollities* against charges of plagiarism. The third edition of 1843 contained the fifteen colored plates by Henry Alken which have become the familiar illustrations of this humorous classic. The adventures of Jorrocks were continued in *Handley Cross*, also published in 1843 but not expanded to its full proportions until 1854. This book, now considered Surtees' masterpiece, received little attention at the time; the reappearance of Jorrocks as a Master of Fox Hounds gave Surtees every opportunity to ridicule social snobbery and the idea that fox hunting was a fashionable sport to be enjoyed only by the rich, and a snobbish age repaid him with its neglect. Jorrocks made his last appearance in *Hillingdon Hall*, where as a country squire he was allowed to voice Surtees' own views on agriculture and reform. The election of his hero to Parliament at the end of the novel hints that Surtees may have intended to continue the series with an account of the Cockney grocer in politics. If so, the plan was abandoned. Instead, *Hillingdon Hall* was followed in 1846 by *The Analysis of the Hunting-Field*, a collection of sporting sketches of a rather technical nature, and in 1847 by *Hawbuck Grange.*

Surtees' first real success came in 1853 with *Mr. Sponge's Sporting Tour.* Here is the ancient rogue story transformed into a satirical comedy of manners, with a cast that includes aristocratic bores and wastrels, ambitious social climbers, dishonest horse dealers, patronizing masters of hounds, the raggle-taggle of the army and the stage. This was the first of Surtees' books to be illustrated by John Leech, whose drawings for *Mr. Sponge* and later novels are almost as familiar as the author's text. The novel had been serialized in the *New Monthly Magazine*, edited by William Harrison Ainsworth. Ainsworth, anxious to print another work by Surtees, had contracted for the publication of *Young Tom Hall, his Heartbreaks and Horses.* Before many installments had appeared, however, Ainsworth printed an advertisement giving Surtees' name as the author of the new serial. Surtees was angry and Ainsworth tactless; as a result Surtees stopped work on the novel, which promised to be one of his best. Although the book was never completed, it was not a total loss: *Ask*

Mamma and *Plain or Ringlets?* contain a few characters and several episodes he was able to salvage for later use. After *Handley Cross* and *Mr. Sponge's Sporting Tour* these novels are decidedly inferior and reveal too plainly the patchwork of their design. But Surtees was once more at his best in *Mr. Facey Romford's Hounds,* a comic hunting novel and sly satire in which Mr. Sponge and Lucy Glitters, his actress wife, reappear. Surtees did not live to see his last novel in print. At work on an autobiographical work to be called *Sporting and Social Recollections,* he and his wife had gone to Brighton for a short holiday. He died there on March 16, 1864.

Surtees is not one of the eminent Victorians. His field was limited and he had no imagination for anything which lay outside his own experience. But he knew the town as well as the country, and he had seen the agricultural England of his youth transformed by the development of the railway and the growth of factories. Writing of these things, he became what most of the major Victorians, except Thackeray, were not, a social historian and a novelist of manners. His true genius, however, was in creating the comic character; among English novelists he is second only to Dickens in this respect. Jorrocks, in the gallery of great humorous characters, stands only a notch or two below Falstaff, Parson Adams, Mr. Pickwick, and Mr. Micawber. Mr. Sponge and Facey Romford are rogues, but their vulgarity and cunning point to the underlying spirit of an age.

BIBLIOGRAPHICAL REFERENCES: There are several modern editions of Surtees; the most recent, although not definitive, is that issued by the Folio Society, 9 vols., 1949–1956, with reproductions of the original hand-colored illustrations by Leech, Alken, and Hublot K. Browne. *Robert Smith Surtees: Scenes and Characters* is a book of selections edited by Cyril Ray, 1948.

There is no authorized biography. E. D. Cumings, *Robert Smith Surtees, Creator of 'Jorrocks,'* 1924, contains an autobiographical sketch. Later biographical and critical studies include Frederick Watson, *Robert Smith Surtees,* 1933; and Leonard Cooper, *R. S. Surtees,* 1952. See also Hugh S. Gladstone, *Shooting with Surtees,* 1928; F. J. Harvey Darton, *From Surtees to Sassoon,* 1931; Anthony Steel, *Jorrocks' England,* 1932; Una Pope-Hennessy, *Durham Company,* 1941; G. G. French, *John Jorrocks and Other Characters,* 1947; Charles A. Hoyt, "Robert Smith Surtees," *Minor British Novelists,* 1967, 59–78. Moira O'Neill, "Some Novels by Surtees," *Blackwood's,* CXCIII (1913), 535–542, and "The Author of 'Jorrocks,'" *Blackwood's,* CCXC (1924), 857–868; W. C. Rivers, "The Place of Robert Smith Surtees," *London Mercury,* X (1924), 605–613; John Shand, "Squire Surtees," *Atlantic Monthly,* CLXXV (January, 1945), 91–96; and Robert L. Collison, "Robert Smith Surtees: Satirist and Sociologist," *Nineteenth Century Fiction,* VII (1952), 202–207.

EMANUEL SWEDENBORG

Born: Stockholm, Sweden
Date: January 29, 1688

Died: London, England
Date: March 29, 1772

Principal Works

SCIENTIFIC TREATISES: *Opera philosophica et mineralia,* 1734 (*Philosophical and Scientific Works*).

RELIGIOUS TREATISES: *Arcana Coelestia,* 1749–1756 (*Heavenly Secrets*); *Heaven and Hell,* 1758; *Divine Love and Wisdom,* 1763; *The True Christian Religion,* 1771.

Emanuel Swedenborg was born Emanuel Swedberg—at Stockholm, January 29, 1688—the son of Dr. Jesper Swedberg, professor of theology at the University of Uppsala and Bishop of Skara who, raised to the rank of the nobility for services to the Swedish crown, later changed his name to Swedenborg. By Swedenborg's own account, his childhood was unusual in that he spent much time in spiritual thought and in conversation with clergymen on matters of faith. He attended the University of Uppsala, taking his degree in 1709. He then traveled in England, Holland, France, and Germany before returning to Sweden in 1715. During his travels he studied wherever he went, and upon his return he entered Uppsala once again to study science and engineering. Charles XII of Sweden, who had become a friend and admirer of Swedenborg, appointed him assessor on the Swedish board of mines, a post Swedenborg filled until 1747 and for which he received a salary for the rest of his life. In 1724, Swedenborg was offered a post as professor of mathematics at Uppsala, but he declined, saying he did not wish to be limited to theorizing.

Prior to 1720, Swedenborg had published a volume of Latin verse and more than twenty treatises on scientific and mechanical subjects. The scientific works prior to 1721 were largely in Swedish, but the later writings, regardless of subject, were written in Latin. Most of Swedenborg's works were published outside Sweden, the arrangements being made during his many trips abroad. His first major work in philosophy and theology was the *Principia,* which was one volume in the three-volume *Philosophical and Scientific Works,* published in 1734. In the same year he published *Prodromus philosophiae ratiocinantis de infinito et causa finali creationis,* a work dealing with the relations of the finite to the infinite and the body to the soul. During the next few years Swedenborg turned his attention to anatomy, hoping to find the seat of the soul. Two works on anatomy resulted from his studies. These works, to which little attention was paid, anticipated many modern physiological theories.

In addition to being a scientist, Swedenborg was a mystic. According to his report, he experienced God on three occasions between 1743 and 1745. During the third of the spiritual experiences Swedenborg, according to his own account, was called upon to reveal what he called the "Doctrine of the New Jerusalem." He then turned his energies to religious inquiry, dividing his time between stays in Sweden, England, and Holland while he wrote works of Biblical interpretation and

1723

oversaw their publication. Among the important books of this period was *Heavenly Secrets,* an eight-volume work giving a revealed interpretation of the Bible. *Heaven and Hell* describes the future of mankind after death. *The Last Judgment* (1758) tells of a mystical experience in which God revealed to Swedenborg a vision of doomsday. The last of many theological works from Swedenborg's hand was *The True Christian Religion,* in which he set forth his New Church doctrines. Although he did not found a sect or attempt to do so, later adherents to his doctrines did form a sect of their own, the New Jerusalem Church.

Swedenborg died on March 29, 1772, while on one of his visits to England. Temporarily buried in London, his body was later removed and interred in a place of honor in the cathedral at Uppsala.

BIBLIOGRAPHICAL REFERENCES: The Swedenborg bibliography is extensive. For biography and commentary see R. L. Tafel, *Documents Concerning the Life and Character of Emanuel Swedenborg,* 3 vols., 1875–1877; M. Lann, *Swedenborg,* 1915, and *Upplysningstidens Romantik,* 1918–1920; E. Kleen, *Swedenborg,* 1917–1919; George Trobridge, *Swedenborg: His Life, Teaching and Influence,* 1918; *Letters and Memorials of Emanuel Swedenborg,* translated and edited by Alfred Acton, 1948; Signe Toksvig, *Emanuel Swedenborg, Scientist and Mystic,* 1948; and C. S. Sigstedt, *The Swedenborg Epic: The Life and Works of Emanuel Swedenborg,* 1952. See also James Hyde, *A Bibliography of the Works of Emanuel Swedenborg,* 1897. See further William A. Johnson, "Swedenborg as a Modern Thinker: His Influence upon American Thought," *American Swedish Historical Foundation Yearbook* (1966), 23–36.

JONATHAN SWIFT

Born: Dublin, Ireland
Date: November 30, 1667

Died: Dublin
Date: October 19, 1745

Principal Works

SATIRICAL FICTION: *A Tale of a Tub*, 1704; *Travels into Several Remote Nations of the World . . . by Lemuel Gulliver*, 1726 [*Gulliver's Travels*].

ESSAYS AND TRACTS: *A Discourse on the Dissensions between the Nobles and Commons in Athens and Rome*, 1701; *The Battle of the Books*, 1704; *The Sentiments of a Church of England Man*, 1708; *An Argument against Abolishing Christianity*, 1708; *A Project for the Advancement of Religion*, 1709; *The Conduct of the Allies*, 1711; *The Public Spirit of the Whigs*, 1714; *The Drapier Letters*, 1724; *A Modest Proposal for Preventing the Children of Poor People of Ireland from Being a Burden to Their Parents*, 1729.

POEMS: *Petition to Frances*, 1700; *Miscellanies*, 1708–1711; *Cadenus and Vanessa*, 1713; *On Poetry: A Rhapsody*, 1733; *Verses on the Death of Dr. Swift, Written by Himself*, 1739.

Jonathan Swift, with perhaps the keenest mind and sharpest tongue in an age marked by intellectual brilliance, was a mass of contradictions. Dedicated to the ideals of rationality and common sense, he approached the irrational in his contempt for man's failure to live up to his ideal; profoundly distrustful of all "enthusiasm" or fanaticism, he was himself something of an enthusiast in his glorification of "pure reason"; possessed of one of the clearest and most direct styles in the English language, the subtleties of his irony were misunderstood in his own and later ages.

Although biographical details will never adequately explain either the genius or the contradictions of a man life Swift, the combination of extreme pride and a position of dependence on the favors of the rich or powerful does throw some light on the persistent dissatisfaction with life as it is that colors almost all his work. Born in Dublin on November 30, 1667, the son of an impecunious Englishman who had settled in Ireland, Swift was educated at Trinity College with the aid of a wealthy uncle. In 1688 he left Ireland and became secretary to Sir William Temple at Moor Park, Surrey. Temple was not a congenial master, and Swift chafed to be independent in the more exciting world of London. It was the cultured Sir William, however, who gave polish to the somewhat uncouth young man, and introduced him into his own world of wit and polite learning, and it was in his behalf that Swift entered the controversy over the relative merits of the "ancients" and the "moderns" in his *Battle of the Books*. In this brilliant example of neo-classical mock-heroic prose, Swift pours out his contempt on the self-righteous complacency of modern criticism and poetry. During this same period (1696–1698) Swift, on his own behalf, wrote *A Tale of a Tub*, a burlesque history of the Church in which his genius first revealed itself in its full force. Just as important as his tale of the degradation of the Church through selfishness and fanaticism are the numerous digressions on moral, philosophical, and literary subjects. It was also at Moor Park that Swift first met Esther Johnson, possibly Temple's illegitimate daughter, the "Stella" of his later life.

In 1694, dissatisfied with Moor Park, Swift returned to Ireland, where he was ordained an Anglican priest, but after a dreary year in an Irish parish he was back in England. Between 1708 and 1714 he was in London, and during that period he achieved his greatest triumphs, social, literary, and political. He quickly became familiar with the literary lights of the age, Steele, Addison, Pope, Gay, and Arbuthnot. He wrote pieces for Steele's *Tatler,* and entered Church controversies with such essays as his brilliantly ironic *Argument to prove that the Abolishing of Christianity in England, may . . . be Attended with some inconveniences* In 1710, partly from hopes of personal advancement, and partly through a passionate interest in defending the prerogatives of the Church, Swift switched his allegiance from the Whig to the Tory party. This move won him the enmity of Whigs such as Addison and Steele, but gained him even more powerful friends in Robert Harley and Henry St. John, leaders of the new Tory ministry. Swift's political writing, in the Tory *Examiner* (which he edited briefly, from 1710–1711) and in pamphlets attacking Robert Walpole and the Duke of Marlborough, was a powerful aid to the Tory administration in its attempts to discredit the Whig "war party." For his untiring labors Swift hoped, and expected, to be rewarded with ecclesiastical preferment, perhaps a bishopric. But the memories of men who have risen to high places are notoriously short. Finally, in 1713, Swift was made Dean of St. Patrick's Cathedral, Dublin—virtually exiled from England. When the Tory ministry collapsed in 1714, all hope ended, and Swift returned to Ireland for good, disillusioned and bitter. Probably the best picture of Swift's mind during this period of political writing, as well as of the behind-the-scenes intrigue of London politics, is to be found in the charming and frank letters which make up the *Journal to Stella* (1766–1768), his correspondence with his protégée and friend, Esther Johnson. This was also the period in which Esther Vanhomrigh, whom he had met in London, followed him to Ireland. The "Vanessa" of his poem *Cadenus and Vanessa,* she died in 1723.

Bitter as he was, Swift's energy and wit could not long be stifled, and he turned his talents to defending Irish political and economic interests against the English. In such pamphlets as *The Drapier's Letters,* in which he protests against the circulation of debased coinage in Ireland, or his ironic masterpiece, *A Modest Proposal,* in which he suggests that for the Irish to sell their infants as food is their only defense against economic starvation by England, Swift not only continued his war with the Whig administration, but won the love and respect of all Ireland. During this period (1721–1725), he also worked intermittently on his greatest and best-known work, *Travels into Several Remote Nations of the World,* better known to us today as *Gulliver's Travels.*

Gulliver's Travels, Swift's final word on man and human nature, is a witty and at times vitriolic comment on man's abuse and perversion of his God-given reason. Books I and II, the account of voyages to Lilliput and Brobdingnag, deal with the corruption of practical reason, as it operates in the social and political worlds. Books III and IV are concerned with theoretical reason, either in its misuse, as among the Laputans or in the Academy of Lagado, or in its ideal application among the Houyhnhnms. Swift's brutal characterization of man as a despicable Yahoo (Book IV) has led many readers to feel that the intensity of his misanthropy destroys the validity of his work as satire. But bitter as Swift was at man's failure to live up to his ideal of rationality and common sense, the very fact that he wrote *Gulliver's Travels* suggests his recognition of the existence of such a goal, or at least his hope that man could be stimulated to reach it. For those who can rise above the smug satisfaction of having read *Gulliver's Travels* as a children's classic, Swift's satire and irony can scarcely help producing a serious re-evaluation of the principles by which we live.

Swift's health had never been good, and by 1740 mental decay had seriously weakened his mind. In 1742 guardians were appointed for him since he was on the verge of insanity. He died in Dublin on October 19, 1745.

BIBLIOGRAPHICAL REFERENCES: The basic edition is the Dublin edition of the *Works*, published by George Faulkner, 4 vols., 1735, with later editions edited by John Hawkesworth, 12 vols., 1755; Sir Walter Scott, 19 vols., 1814; and Temple Scott, Bohn Classical Library, 12 vols., 1897–1908. The standard modern edition of the *Prose Works* is in preparation by Herbert Davis, 1939 ff. The *Poems* have been edited by Harold Williams, 3 vols., 1937. There are three important collections of letters: Swift's *Correspondence*, edited by F. Elrington Ball, 6 vols., 1910–1914; *Vanessa and Her Correspondence with Jonathan Swift*, edited by Alexander M. Freeman, 1921; and *The Letters of Swift to Charles Ford*, edited by David Nichol Smith, 1935. A useful one-volume edition of selections is *The Portable Swift*, edited by Carl Van Doren, 1948.

The standard biography is Sir Henry Craik, *The Life of Jonathan Swift*, 2 vols., 1894, but this is being supplanted by Irvin Ehrenpreis, *Swift: The Man, His Works, and the Age*, Vol. I, 1962, Vol. II, 1967. The best critical study is Richard Quintana, *The Mind and Art of Jonathan Swift*, 1936. For additional biographical and critical studies see Carl Van Doren, *Swift*, 1930; W. B. C. Watkins, *Perilous Balance*, 1939; G. Wilson Knight, *The Burning Oracle*, 1939; R. W. Jackson, *Swift and His Circle*, 1945; R. C. Churchill, *He Served Human Liberty*, 1946; Herbert Davis, *The Satire of Jonathan Swift*, 1947; Evelyn Hardy, *The Conjured Spirit*, 1949; and J. M. Bullit, *Jonathan Swift and the Anatomy of Satire*, 1953. The *Correspondence* has been edited by Harold Williams, 5 vols., 1963–1965.

The literature on *Gulliver's Travels* is extensive. See W. A. Eddy, *Gulliver's Travels: A Critical Study*, 1923; A. E. Case, *Four Essays on Gulliver's Travels*, 1945; Harold Williams, *The Text of Gulliver's Travels*, 1952; H. M. Dargan, "The Nature of Allegory as Used by Swift," *Studies in Philology*, XIII (1916), 159–179; J. B. Moore, "The Role of Gulliver," *Modern Philology*, XXV (1928), 469–480; Samuel Kliger, "The Unity of Gulliver's Travels," *Modern Language Quarterly*, VI (1945), 401–415; Edward Stone, "Swift and the Horses: Misanthropy or Comedy," *ibid.*, X (1949), 367–376; Ellen D. Leyburn, "Certain Problems of Allegorical Satire in Gulliver's Travels," *Huntington Library Quarterly*, XIII (1950), 161–189; H. D. Kelling, "Some Significant Names in Gulliver's Travels," *Studies in Philology*, XLVIII (1951), 413; K. M. Williams, "Gulliver's Voyage to the Houyhnhnms," *English Literary History*, XVIII (1951), 275–286; Irvin Ehrenpreis, "Swift and

Satire," *College English,* XIII (1952), 309–312; and H. D. Kelling, *"Gulliver's Travels:* A Comedy of Humours," *University of Toronto Quarterly,* XXI (1952), 362–375.

Edith Sitwell's novel, *I Live Under a Black Sun,* 1938, is based on the life of Swift.

ALGERNON CHARLES SWINBURNE

Born: London, England
Date: April 5, 1837

Died: London
Date: April 10, 1909

Principal Works

POEMS: *Poems and Ballads,* 1866 [*Laus Veneris*]; *Songs Before Sunrise,* 1871; *Poems and Ballads: Second Series,* 1878; *Songs of the Springtides,* 1880; *Tristram of Lyonesse,* 1882; *A Midsummer Holiday,* 1884; *Poems and Ballads: Third Series,* 1889; *The Tale of Balen,* 1896.

PLAYS: *The Queen Mother,* 1860; *Rosamond,* 1860; *Atalanta in Calydon,* 1865; *Chastelard,* 1865; *Bothwell,* 1874; *Erechtheus,* 1876; *Mary Stuart,* 1881; *Marino Faliero,* 1885; *Locrine,* 1887.

CRITICISM: *William Blake,* 1868; *Essays and Studies,* 1875; *A Note on Charlotte Brontë,* 1877; *A Study of Shakespeare,* 1880; *A Study of Victor Hugo,* 1886; *A Study of Ben Jonson,* 1889; *Studies in Prose and Poetry,* 1894; *The Age of Shakespeare,* 1908.

Swinburne's fame as a poet rests on several claims: his dexterity in manipulation of verse; his subject matter, which often glorified the life of the senses or argued for the necessity of social change; and certain oddities in his actual career. In all of these claims, we can see a man at odds with his age and yet drawing strength from his surroundings since they incited him to his protests.

Swinburne was descended from English nobility. The mother of the future revolutionary poet was the daughter of the Earl of Ashburnham, and his father was Admiral Charles Henry Swinburne. Algernon Charles Swinburne enjoyed fully the advantages of his background. From his mother he acquired a literary taste, a love of the French and Italian languages and literatures, and a thorough knowledge of the Bible. He was also able to read such critical writers as Victor Hugo and W. S. Landor, both advocates of republicanism and both objects of Swinburne's hero worship. From a grandfather in Northumberland, Swinburne learned hatred of monarchy and disapproval of the hereditary privileges of the House of Lords.

Born in London, April 5, 1837, Swinburne early discovered his poetic vocation. Acquaintance in childhood with Wordsworth and Samuel Rogers confirmed his intent by the time he was fifteen. The next decade brought Swinburne the companionship and encouragement of the leading literary figures of the period: Tennyson, Ruskin, and among the Pre-Raphaelites, William Morris, Edward Burne-Jones, and Dante Gabriel Rossetti. Swinburne's youthful claims to attention led Burne-Jones to welcome him thus: "We have hitherto been three, and now there are four of us." Swinburne modeled for some of Rossetti's paintings and had the painter's personal direction in his writings. Further, his affiliation with the Pre-Raphaelite movement drew attention to his work, which early struck his contemporaries as clever, audacious, and erudite. From *Atalanta in Calydon* and *Chastelard,* published in 1865, Swinburne's place in public awareness was important, and remained so for about fifteen years.

Swinburne's themes—glorification of the senses and the assertion of man's dignity—are but two aspects of his central impatience with restraint; the only restraint that Swinburne ever welcomed was that imposed by rather elaborate and even archaic poetical forms. In *Poems and Ballads* he scandalized his times with outspoken endorsement of sensuality; in *Songs Before Sunrise* he stirred them deeply with apostrophes to the insurgent republicans of Italy. In these years he was also a prose propagandist for the Pre-Raphaelites and a defender of his own literary practices. Against a charge made by the *Saturday Review* that with colors intense and violent he effected an "audacious counterfeiting of strong and noble passion by mad, intoxicated sensuality," Swinburne protested against a literary age which "has room only for such as are content to write for children and girls."

The revolt in Swinburne's own life had to be curbed. In 1879 Theodore Watts-Dunton took Swinburne from London to save him from the effects of acute alcoholic dysentery. Although the move to Putney and simplicity probably extended Swinburne's life, it took the essential fire from his writings. He relinquished the idea of political freedom; he turned from poetry to literary criticism more and more; he was capable, as the young Swinburne with his impassioned seriousness would not have been, of composing parodies on the work of prominent Victorian poets like Tennyson, Rossetti, and himself. The prose of his last years is far removed from his Pre-Raphaelite struggles and contemporary politics; he took up his early enthusiasm for the drama of Elizabethan England, of which he wrote brilliantly in criticism which scholarship finds subject to correction.

Upon his death in London, April 10, 1909, Swinburne was buried near his family at Bonchurch, Isle of Wight— his family from which, at every phase of his career, he had been sharply separated.

Swinburne has been described as a man more "elf-like than human." He was just over five feet tall and thin; he had a massive head thatched with shaggy red hair. His bizarre appearance brought him failure in love and, it can be believed, gave him reason for heightening heretical behavior which led to his removal from Eton and Oxford, behavior that later led him to refuse a degree from the great university that had ejected him. It is not surprising that he welcomed the onslaught of Darwinism; nor did the poet of the senses and political action find admirable Robert Browning's optimism and Tennyson's aspirations toward immortality. Here again, as might be expected, he departed from his era's canons of taste and created his own philosophy and forms.

BIBLIOGRAPHICAL REFERENCES: The definitive edition is *The Complete Works of Algernon Charles Swinburne*, edited by Edmund Gosse and T. J. Wise, 20 vols., 1925–1927. The same editors published a separate edition of the *Letters*, 2 vols., 1919. The standard biography is Edmund Gosse, *The Life of Algernon Charles Swinburne*, 1917, a work supplemented by Sir Herbert Grierson, *Swinburne*, 1953. See also T. E. Welby, *Swinburne: A Critical Study*, 1914; Harold Nicolson, *Swinburne*, 1926; Georges Lafourcade, *La Jeunesse de Swinburne*, 1928; Samuel C. Chew,

Swinburne, 1929; Georges Lafourcade, *Swinburne: A Literary Biography,* 1932; C. K. Hyder, *Swinburne's Literary Career and Fame,* 1933; Humphrey Hare, *Swinburne: A Biographical Approach,* 1949; and John A. Cassidy, *Algernon C. Swinburne,* 1964. See also *Swinburne: The Critical Heritage,* edited by Clyde K. Hyder, 1970; and John D. Rosenberg, "Swinburne," *Victorian Studies,* XI (December, 1967), 131–152. Swinburne's letters were edited by Cecil Lang, 6 vols., 1959–1962.

FRANK SWINNERTON

Born: Wood Green, England
Date: August 12, 1884

Principal Works

NOVELS: *The Merry Heart,* 1909; *The Casement,* 1911; *The Happy Family,* 1912; *Nocturne,* 1917; *September,* 1919; *Coquette,* 1921; *The Three Lovers,* 1922; *Young Felix,* 1923; *The Elder Sister,* 1925; *Summer Storm,* 1926; *A Brood of Ducklings,* 1928; *Sketch of a Sinner,* 1929; *The Georgian House,* 1932; *Elizabeth,* 1934; *Harvest Comedy,* 1937; *The Two Wives,* 1939; *The Fortunate Lady,* 1941; *Thankless Child,* 1942; *A Woman in Sunshine,* 1945; *A Flower for Catherine,* 1951; *A Month in Gordon Square,* 1953; *The Summer Intrigue,* 1955; *Woman from Sicily,* 1957; *Tigress in the Village,* 1959; *The Grace Divorce,* 1960; *Death of a Highbrow,* 1961; *Quadrille,* 1965; *Sanctuary,* 1966.
ESSAYS AND STUDIES: *George Gissing,* 1912; *R. L. Stevenson,* 1914; *Tokefield Papers,* 1927; *A London Bookman,* 1928; *The Georgian Scene,* 1934 (English edition, *The Georgian Literary Scene,* 1935); *The Bookman's London,* 1951; *Background with Chorus,* 1956; *Authors I Never Met,* 1956; *Figures in the Foreground; Literary Reminiscences 1917–1940,* 1963; *Reflections from a Village,* 1969.
AUTOBIOGRAPHY: *Swinnerton, An Autobiography,* 1936.

Frank (Arthur) Swinnerton, born in a London suburb on August 12, 1884, was a precocious boy who avowedly taught himself to read at the age of four. A series of illnesses as a child, including diphtheria, paralysis, and scarlet fever, caused poor health through most of his later boyhood.

He decided early to be a journalist and became an office boy for a newspaper company at the age of fourteen In 1900 having decided to become a man of letters rather than a journalist, he found work with J. M. Dent & Co., British publishers. Six years later he left this firm to join the staff of Chatto & Windus, another British publishing house. Following the publication of a not too successful novel of his own Swinnerton became an editor for the firm, in which position he continued for almost two decades. Before he was thirty Swinnerton had published several books, novels, and critical biographies. His first outstanding success came in 1917 with *Nocturne,* a short but almost perfect Cockney idyl. Since that time he has continued to publish novels and literary essays. *A London Bookman, Tokefield Papers,* and *The Bookman's London* are volumes of essays. *The Georgian Literary Scene* is a work of literary criticism; it is, with *Harvest Comedy,* one of the two books Swinnerton considers his best. From 1937 to 1942 he was chief reviewer of fiction for the London *Observer.* During World War II he served his government as a civil servant in the Ministry of Information. His first wife was Helen Dircks, a poet. His second wife, whom he married in 1924, was Mary Dorothy Bennett; they have one daughter. Critics have never been enthusiastic for Swinnerton's works, though he is considered a competent novelist and a dependable storyteller.

BIBLIOGRAPHICAL REFERENCES: Most of Swinnerton's own story has been told in his autobiography and in collections of essays like *Tokefield Papers, The Bookman's Lon-*

don, and *Background with Chorus.* There is comparatively little criticism. See *Frank Swinnerton,* a pamphlet containing sketches by Arnold Bennett, H. G. Wells, and Grant M. Overton, 1920; A. Rotter, *Frank Swinnerton und George Gissing, eine kritische studie,* 1930; R. C. McKay, *George Gissing and His Critic Frank Swinnerton,* 1933; and Thomas Beer, "Frank Swinnerton," *Bookman,* LVIII (1923–1924), 404–409.

JOHN MILLINGTON SYNGE

Born: Newton Little, Ireland
Date: April 16, 1871

Died: Dublin, Ireland
Date: March 24, 1909

Principal Works

PLAYS: *In the Shadow of the Glen,* 1903; *Riders to the Sea,* 1904; *The Well of the Saints,* 1905; *The Tinker's Wedding,* 1907; *The Playboy of the Western World,* 1907; *Deirdre of the Sorrows,* 1910.
POEMS: *Poems and Translations,* 1910.
TALES AND SKETCHES: *The Aran Islands,* 1907.

Although Synge was long considered the greatest Irish dramatist, his eminence is now challenged by Sean O'Casey, who certainly is not the superior of the older playwright in tragic or comic power, or in beauty of language, but who exhibits far greater versatility and productive powers. Synge's five completed plays all deal with the Irish peasant; about 1900 all literary Ireland was fascinated by the peasant and his primitive culture—William Butler Yeats, Æ., Douglas Hyde, Padraic Colum, Lady Gregory, and others were recording his stories and trying to capture the lilting poetry of his speech. Just before Synge died, however, he told Yeats that he was tired of the peasant on the stage and planned a play of Dublin slum life. Had he not died at the early age of thirty-eight, his dramatic work might have had the sweep of O'Casey's.

John Millington Synge was born in Newton Little, near Dublin, on April 16, 1871, the son of a barrister and grandson of the translator of Josephus. He attended private schools until he was fourteen, then studied for three years with a tutor. Later, while a student at Trinity College, Dublin, he also studied music at the Royal Irish Academy and became a more than competent pianist and violinist. After receiving his degree, he went to Germany to study music and German, then to Italy for further language study, and finally to Paris, where he wrote verse and studied French literature. With his small legacy he might have spent the rest of his life as a minor poet and critic, if William Butler Yeats had not met him in Paris and urged him to go to Galway and the Aran Islands to study the peasants, whose rich if primitive life had never been treated in literature. Synge left his Latin Quarter hotel, went to Wicklow, Kerry, and the Aran Islands, and for some years lived among the peasants, carefully studying their life and speech. With his genius for companionship this association bore rich rewards —articles in British weeklies, a book of great beauty, *The Aran Islands,* and finally his classic folk plays.

At the same time the Irish Literary Revival, which had started in the 1890's, was advancing with spectacular success, its happiest manifestation being the famed Abbey Theatre, founded in 1904 for the production of native plays. For over a decade more good plays were written in tiny Ireland than in the entire United States. Synge's devotion to the Abbey and his close friendship with its other literary advisers made the performance of his own plays there inevitable. Because he failed to idealize the Irish national character or concern himself with passionate nationalism, his plays provoked hostile demonstrations at the Abbey when first produced, but they are now accepted, even by the Irish, as the greatest classics of the Abbey Theatre.

In the Shadow of the Glen, derived from an old folk tale, is sharp with satire, and was at first resented as a slur on Irish womanhood. *Riders to the Sea*, considered the greatest short tragedy in modern drama, has as its themes the eternal conflict of man and nature and man's dignified submission to fate; every line in the play has a solemn music, rhythmical and poetic, yet with genuine folk-flavor. *The Well of the Saints* is a sardonic comedy, a tragic-farce of the flavor of Anouilh's *Waltz of the Toreadors* a half century later. *The Playboy of the Western World* is one of the great modern comedies—satirical, boisterous, exquisitely beautiful in language. The crude humors of *The Tinker's Wedding* are in contrast to the legendary, poetic theme of *Deirdre of the Sorrows*, left unfinished at Synge's death. He died in a nursing home in Dublin, March 24, 1909.

BIBLIOGRAPHICAL REFERENCES: Synge's plays, sketches, and poems have been collected in his *Complete Works*, 1935; but a new and definitive edition edited by Robin Skelton is in progress, 1962–. Also by Skelton are *J. M. Synge and His World*, 1971; and *The Writings of J. M. Synge*, 1971. For further biographical and critical studies see P. P. Howe, *John Millington Synge: A Critical Study*, 1912; Maurice Bourgeois, *John Millington Synge and the Irish Theatre*, 1913; John Masefield, *John M. Synge: A Few Personal Recollections*, 1915; Daniel Corkery, *Synge and Anglo-Irish Literature*, 1931; A. D. Estill, *The Sources of Synge*, 1939; L. A. G. Strong, *John Millington Synge*, 1941; and David H. Green and Edward M. Stephens, *J. M. Synge*, 1959. Synge and his work are also treated briefly in the following: Cornelius Weygandt, *Irish Plays and Playwrights*, 1913; Lady Augusta Gregory, *Our Irish Theatre: A Chapter of Autobiography*, 1913; William Butler Yeats, *Dramatis Personae*, 1936; Una Ellis-Fermor, *The Irish Dramatic Movement*, 1939; John Gassner, *Masters of the Drama*, 1940, 1945; and Ronald Peacock, *The Poet in the Theatre*, 1946.

TACITUS
Cornelius Tacitus

Born: Comum (Como?), Italy
Date: c. 55

Died: Rome (?), Italy
Date: c. 120

Principal Works

BIOGRAPHY: *De vita et moribus Julii Agricolae,* c. 98 (*Life of Agricola*).
HISTORY: *Historiae,* c. 116; *Annales,* c. 119.
TREATISES: *Dialogus de oratoribus,* c. 76–77 (*Dialogue on Orators*); the *Germania,* c. 98.

The life of (Publius or Gaius) Cornelius Tacitus is known only from autobiographical allusions in the remains of his works and from eleven letters written to him by Pliny the Younger. This remarkable republican lived through the reign of nine emperors from Nero to Trajan. As a brilliant lawyer, senator and consul, he was a close observer of public affairs, and his dismay at the degeneration of his age and his fear of tyranny are expressed in pithy language. His *Dialogue on Orators* laments the decay of education and eloquence; the *Life of Agricola* is a fine biography with a sketch of Britain under the Romans; *Concerning the Geography, the Customs and Manners, and the Tribes of Germany,* a valuable classic despite its errors, contrasts the free barbarians with the servile Romans; the *Histories* include a fascinating, prejudical account of the Jews; and the *Annals* provide a philosophy of history.

Despite the "singularly blessed time" of his last years, Tacitus could never shake off the morbid effects of Domitian's reign of terror. Nevertheless, convinced of Rome's corruption, he served loyally and well, receiving in 99 a special vote of thanks from the Roman Senate. He recorded the society more than he cured it, however; and his works collectively give us a vivid panoramic view of the empire in the first century. Many modern historians still subscribe to his dictum that "history's highest function is to rescue merit from oblivion, and to hold up as a terror to base words and actions the reprobation of posterity."

The places and dates of Tacitus' birth and death are not definitely known.

BIBLIOGRAPHICAL REFERENCES: There are numerous editions of Tacitus in modern translation. See in particular *The Complete Works of Tacitus,* edited and with an introduction by Moses Hadas, 1942. Translations of selected works include George Gilbert Ramsay, *The Annals of Tacitus,* 2 vols., 1904–1909; W. Hamilton Fyfe, *Dialogus, Agricola, and Germania,* 1908; *idem, The Histories,* 2 vols., 1912; William Peterson and Maurice Hutton, *Dialogus, Agricola, and Germania,* 1914; and Clifford H. Moore, *The Histories,* 4 vols., 1925–1937. See also M. L. W. Laistner, *Greater Roman Historians,* 1947; Clarence W. Mendell, *Tacitus: The Man and His Work,* 1957; and Ronald Syme, *Ten Studies in Tacitus,* 1970.

HIPPOLYTE TAINE

Born: Vouziers, France
Date: April 21, 1828

Died: Paris, France
Date: March 9, 1893

Principal Works

ESSAYS AND STUDIES: *Essai sur Tite-Live*, 1856 (*Essay on Livy*); *Les philosophes classiques du XIXe siècle en France*, 1857 (*The Classic Philosophers of the Nineteenth Century in France*); *Essai sur La Fontaine et ses fables*, 1860; *Histoire de la littérature anglaise*, 1863–1869; *Philosophie de l'art*, 1865; *Nouveaux essais de critique et d'histoire*, 1865; *De l'idéal dans l'art*, 1867; *Théorie de l'intelligence*, 1870.
HISTORY: *Les Origines de la France contemporaine*, 1875–1894 (*The Origins of Contemporary France*).

Hippolyte (Adolphe) Taine, born at Vouziers, France, on April 21, 1828, was educated at the Collège Bourbon and the Normal School in Paris. After leaving school, he became a teacher at Toulon, but because of his political views he was appointed to successively poorer posts until he left teaching entirely in 1852 and devoted his time to study and writing. In 1853 he completed his *Essay on La Fontaine and His Fables*, written as the thesis for his doctorate at the Sorbonne. He immediately began his *Essay on Livy* which, entered in competition, won him an award from the French Academy in 1855. Early in 1854, however, Taine had suffered a breakdown in health because of his arduous program of writing. After a period of enforced rest he resumed his literary activities by contributing articles on various subjects to periodicals. One series of articles, published as *The Classic Philosophers of the Nineteenth Century in France*, first suggested Taine's theory of the application of scientific methods to psychological and metaphysical research. The book attracted considerable interest and helped to spread the author's critical fame. A revised version of his doctoral essay on La Fontaine was published in 1860.

In 1864, Taine received two appointments, both of which gave him security and left him free to study and write. He became examiner at Saint-Cyr and professor of aesthetics and art history at L'École des Beaux Arts. In the same year he published a study of John Stuart Mill, under the title *Le Positivisme anglais*. In the meantime his famous *History of English Literature* had appeared, a work illustrating how determinism could be applied to the study of literature by utilizing the elements of race, milieu, and moment. During the years from 1864 to 1870 Taine fulfilled his tasks at Saint-Cyr and lectured at L'École des Beaux Arts. At the same time he was engaged in writing his books on aesthetics and art. A general study of the philosophy of art appeared in 1865 and was followed by volumes on various phases of art and the philosophy of art. He married Mlle. Denuelle, the daughter of an architect, in 1868.

The Franco-Prussian War ended that happy period in Taine's life and turned his thinking into new paths. Anxious to ascertain the cause of France's weakness and political instability, and feeling that they were traceable to the French Revolution of 1789, Taine began what was to be his greatest work, his study of the origins of contemporary France. He worked at it constantly, even giving up his professorship in 1884 to avail himself of more time; even so, he left it unfinished when he died in Paris on March 9, 1893. The methods that Taine used in this work were the same quasi-scientific and deterministic methods he had already utilized successfully in his studies of literature and art. The book marked Taine as one of the great intellectual leaders of the nineteenth century, the leader of a generation in France which sought in art, literature, and history to find truth that could be regarded as "objective" and "scientific."

BIBLIOGRAPHICAL REFERENCES: For biography and critical analysis see Gabriel Monod, *Les Maîtres de l'histoire*, 1894; M. E. Boutmy, *Taine, Scherer, Laboulaye*, 1901; F. C. Roe, *Taine et l'Angleterre*, 1924; Victor Giraud, *Hippolyte Taine*, 1928; André Chevrillon, *Taine, formation de sa pensée*, 1932; Maxime Leroy, *Taine*, 1933; Georges Léotard, *L'erreur de Taine*, 1949; and André Cresson, *Hippolyte Taine*, 1951. A recent specialized study is Sholom Jacob Kahn, *Science and Aesthetic Judgment: A Study of Taine's Critical Method*, 1953. See further Vernon Hall, "Taine," in *A Short History of Literary Criticism*, 1963, 104–107; and Albert Thibaudet, "Taine," *French Literature from 1795 to Our Era*, 1968, 306–313.

BOOTH TARKINGTON

Born: Indianapolis, Indiana
Date: July 29, 1869

Died: Indianapolis
Date: May 19, 1946

Principal Works

NOVELS: *The Gentleman from Indiana,* 1899; *Monsieur Beaucaire,* 1900; *The Conquest of Canaan,* 1905; *His Own People,* 1907; *The Flirt,* 1913; *Penrod,* 1914; *The Turmoil,* 1915; *Penrod and Sam,* 1916; *Seventeen,* 1916; *The Magnificent Ambersons,* 1918; *Ramsey Milholland,* 1919; *Alice Adams,* 1921; *Gentle Julia,* 1922; *The Midlander,* 1923; *Growth,* 1927 (*The Turmoil, The Magnificent Ambersons,* and *The Midlander*); *Penrod Jashber,* 1929; *Young Mrs. Greeley,* 1929; *Presenting Lily Mars,* 1933; *Little Orvie,* 1934; *The Heritage of Hatcher Ide,* 1941; *The Fighting Littles,* 1941; *Kate Fennigate,* 1943; *Image of Josephine,* 1945.

SHORT STORIES: *In the Arena,* 1905; *The Fascinating Stranger and Other Stories,* 1923.

PLAYS: *The Guardian,* 1907 (with Harry Leon Wilson); *Mister Antonio,* 1916; *The Gibson Upright,* 1919 (with Harry Leon Wilson); *Clarence,* 1919.

REMINISCENCES: *The World Does Move,* 1928.

(Newton) Booth Tarkington was born in Indianapolis, Indiana, on July 29, 1869. He attended Phillips Exeter Academy and Purdue University and was graduated from Princeton. Primarily interested in art, he preferred to make drawing his career, until financial necessity turned him to writing. After an inauspicious beginning he gradually achieved loyal popularity from readers and considerable acclaim from critics. His first popular success in fiction was *Monsieur Beaucaire,* a romantic novelette that helped call attention to his first novel, *The Gentleman from Indiana,* which had appeared in 1899. Today, Tarkington is perhaps most widely known for his stories of youth and teen-agers: *Penrod, Penrod and Sam, Penrod Jashber,* and *Seventeen.* These are "American Boy" stories, comic but very human and appealing. Perhaps his best novel, *Alice Adams,* appeared in 1921 and won the Pulitzer Prize for fiction in 1922. *The Magnificent Ambersons* had earlier won the same prize. In 1933 Tarkington was awarded the Gold Medal of the National Institute of Arts and Letters.

Tarkington was twice married, to Miss Laurel Louisa Fletcher, of Indianapolis, in 1902, and to Miss Susannah Robinson, of Dayton, Ohio, in 1912. He was a prolific writer, with successful ventures in the short story and the drama, but it is chiefly as a novelist that he is remembered. Among his other representative novels are *The Conquest of Canaan, His Own People, The Flirt, The Turmoil, Ramsey Milholland, Gentle Julia, The Midlander,* and *Young Mrs. Greeley.* A trilogy dealing with the industrial development of the Middle West came out in 1927 under the title of *Growth;* it included *The Turmoil, The Magnificent Ambersons,* and *The Midlander.*

Tarkington, who suffered difficulties with his eyesight for years, became totally blind in 1930, but his sight was partially restored by a series of operations. For the last thirty-five years of his life he divided his time between his home in Indianapolis and his house in

Kennebunkport, Maine. He died May 19, 1946, in Indianapolis.

BIBLIOGRAPHICAL REFERENCES: The only full-length biography is James Woodress, *Booth Tarkington: Gentleman from Indiana*, 1955, a work based extensively on the Tarkington papers at Princeton University. Two other works indispensable to Tarkington studies are the unfinished autobiography, *As It Seems to Me, Saturday Evening Post*, CCXIV (July 5–August 23, 1941); and Dorothy R. Russo and Thelma L. Sullivan, *A Bibliography of Booth Tarkington, 1869–1946*, 1949. See also Robert C. Holliday, *Booth Tarkington*, 1918; Asa D. Dickinson, *Booth Tarkington: A Sketch*, 1926, (pamphlet); and Kenneth Roberts, *I Wanted to Write*, 1949. Two articles are W. T. Scott, "Tarkington and the 1920's," *American Scholar*, XXVI (1957), 181–194; and John D. Seelye, "That Marvelous Boy-Penrod Once Again," *Virginia Quarterly Review*, XXXVII (1960), 591–604.

TORQUATO TASSO

Born: Sorrento, Italy
Date: March 11, 1544

Died: Near Rome, Italy
Date: April 25, 1595

Principal Works

POEMS: *Rinaldo*, 1562; *Gerusalemme Liberata*, 1580–1581 (*Jerusalem Delivered*).
PLAY: *Aminta*, 1573.

Torquato Tasso, born at Sorrento on March 11, 1544, was the son of Bernardo Tasso (1493–1569), a famous Italian poet exiled from Naples during his son's childhood. Tasso spent his early years in Naples with his mother, a woman of wealth and rank who sent him to school to the Jesuits. When he was ten, he joined his father at Pesaro, where he and the heir to the Duke of Urbino were tutored together. In 1557 his father sent him to study law at the University of Padua. Finding the law uninteresting, he turned before long to the study of philosophy and poetry. A few of his poems appeared as early as 1561, but real fame came with the publication of *Rinaldo,* a romantic epic published while the eighteen-year-old author was still a student at Padua.

After a short period of study at the University of Bologna, Tasso returned to Padua, and by 1565 he had found a wealthy patron in Cardinal Luigi d'Este, a member of the noble house of Ferrara that Tasso was to celebrate in his *Jerusalem Delivered*. This was the later title of the epic poem, *Goffredo,* which he had begun at Bologna. The next five years of his life were happy and busy ones, except for the death of his father in 1569. A year later Tasso traveled with the cardinal to Paris, where he met Ronsard and other French writers of the period. A short time later a difference of opinion on religious matters caused him to exchange the cardinal's patronage for that of Duke Alfonso d'Este of Ferrara. *Aminta,* his charming pastoral drama, added to his literary fame after its initial presentation at Ferrara in 1573.

Jerusalem Delivered, Tasso's great masterpiece, was completed the following year and was read publicly to the Duke of Ferrara and the court in 1575. Having chosen Vergil as his model, Tasso followed the Roman poet's strict adherence to unity, style, and form. The subject matter of the poem is the First Crusade, the theme dealing with the efforts of the forces of evil, personified by the beautiful sorceress Armida, to keep the crusaders under Godfrey of Bouillon from capturing the Holy City. Although classic in form, the poem is closer to medieval romance in its use of allegory and in the romantic interest supplied by love affairs between Christian knights and pagan heroines. Following the reading of *Jerusalem Delivered,* Tasso became ill, probably of malaria, and suffered delusions that attempts were being made on his life. When he asked for permission to leave the court, the duke was patient but firm in his refusal; perhaps he feared that Tasso, if angered or allowed to leave Ferrara, might dedicate his poem to the Medici family of Florence. It is thought that Tasso became temporarily insane about this time, for in 1577 he was placed under the medical care of the Franciscans at Ferrara.

In July of that year he escaped in

the disguise of a peasant and went to Sorrento to take refuge with his sister Cornelia. His condition improved and he was in Ferrara again in 1578. After a year spent wandering about Italy he returned to Ferrara and openly accused Duke Alfonso of trying to poison him. He was then confined to an insane asylum for seven years. Although denied liberty of movement, he was permitted to receive visitors and was given spacious apartments in which to live. During this time, in 1580, an inaccurate version of *Goffredo* was printed in Venice. A year later the complete work was published at Ferrara under its present title, *Jerusalem Delivered*. Publication was by order of the duke after Tasso's manuscript had been seized along with his other effects; when the work appeared he received nothing for the poem which made him famous throughout Europe.

Through the effects of friendly Vincenzio Gonzaga, Prince of Mantua, Tasso was released in 1586 and allowed to go to Mantua to live under the protection of the prince. There he wrote *Torrismondo* (1586) before he became a wanderer again. From 1587 to 1594 he traveled aimlessly about Europe, a victim of physical illness, mental weakness, and poverty. *Gerusalemme Conquistata,* a sequel to *Jerusalem Delivered* but a much inferior work, was published in 1593. In 1594 arrangements were made to crown him poet laureate at the court of Pope Clement VIII and to grant him a suitable pension. But honors and money came too late. Before the ceremony could be performed, Tasso retired to the monastery of St. Onofrio, near Rome, and announced that he was entering the monastery to die, as he did less than a month later, on April 25, 1595.

BIBLIOGRAPHICAL REFERENCES: Standard translations of *Jerusalem Delivered* are those by Sir Edward Fairfax, 1600, frequently reprinted, and J. K. James, 1884. The standard biography is A. Solerti, *La Vita di Torquato Tasso,* 3 vols., 1895. For biographical and critical studies in English see Robert Milman, *Life of Tasso,* 2 vols., 1850; William Boulting, *Tasso and His Times,* 1907; and C. P. Brand, *Torquato Tasso: A Study of the Poet and His Contribution to English Literature,* 1965. Recent European studies include Lafranco Caretti, *Studi sulle rime del Tasso,* 1950; Leo Ulrich, *Torquato Tasso: Studien zur Vorgeschichte des Secentismo,* 1951; Benedetto Croce, *Poeti e scrittori del pieno e del tardo Rinascimento,* 1952; and B. T. Sozzi, *Studi sul Tasso,* 1954.

ALLEN TATE

Born: Winchester, Kentucky
Date: November 19, 1899

Principal Works

POEMS: *Mr. Pope and Other Poems*, 1928; *Poems: 1928–1931*, 1932; *The Mediterranean and Other Poems*, 1936; *Selected Poems*, 1937; *The Winter Sea*, 1944; *Poems: 1922–1947*, 1948; *Poems*, 1960; *The Swimmers and Other Selected Poems*, 1971.

NOVEL: *The Fathers*, 1938.

BIOGRAPHY: *Stonewall Jackson: The Good Soldier*, 1928; *Jefferson Davis: His Rise and Fall*, 1929.

CRITICISM: *Reactionary Essays on Poetry and Ideas*, 1936; *Reason in Madness, Critical Essays*, 1941; *On the Limits of Poetry, Selected Essays 1928–1948*, 1948; *The Hovering Fly and Other Essays*, 1949; *The Forlorn Demon: Didactic and Critical Essays*, 1953; *The Man of Letters in the Modern World: Selected Essays, 1928–1955*, 1955; *Collected Essays*, 1959; *Essays of Four Decades*, 1968.

John Orley Allen Tate was born in Winchester, Kentucky, on November 19, 1899, the third son of Eleanor Varnell and John Orley Tate. His early education was somewhat sporadic, but in 1918 he entered Vanderbilt University, where he began to dedicate himself to literature, in the company of such writers as John Crowe Ransom and Robert Penn Warren, with whom he was active in the Fugitive and Agrarian movements. In 1924 he married Caroline Gordon. In 1959 he married Isabella Gardner, and, in 1966, Helen Heinz.

Tate has come to be regarded as the prototype of the twentieth century man of letters. Best known as a poet, he is also the author of biographies of Stonewall Jackson and Jefferson Davis, as well as *The Fathers*, a complex, brilliant novel set against the background of the Civil War. His many critical essays have constituted a shaping force in modern literature. In addition, he served as Consultant in Poetry to the Library of Congress (1943–1944), edited *The Sewanee Review* (1944–1945), and taught at several universities, including Princeton, the University of North Carolina at Greensboro, and the University of Minnesota.

Tate's earlier poetry, best represented by the famous "Ode to the Confederate Dead," is classical in attitude as well as in execution. The *Ode* is a profound meditation which transcends its nominal subject to treat the theme of the self's struggles in a faithless era. Another major poem, *The Mediterranean*, parallels Tate's interest in his own past with Aeneas' search for a home after the fall of Troy. More recently Tate has softened the austerity of his classicism in poems which seek to integrate physical and imaginative vision; these efforts culminate in *The Maimed Man*, *The Swimmers*, and *The Buried Lake*, parts of a long poem in terza rima, still in progress.

As a critic, Tate has been identified with the New Critics, who argued for the autonomous nature of the literary work, the reading of which should not be influenced by knowledge external to the work itself. It should be noted, however, that his approach to literature does not employ the "scientific" method of such New Critics as I. A. Richards. In an almost Socratic fashion, Tate seeks to unravel in detail the terms on which a literary work presents itself to a reader. Allen Tate's essays and poems, each shedding light on the other, stand as major achievements in American literature.

BIBLIOGRAPHICAL REFERENCES: Among the numerous studies of Allen Tate are Willard Burdett Arnold, *The Social Ideas of Allen Tate,* 1955; George Hemphill, *Allen Tate,* 1963; Ferman Bishop, *Allen Tate,* 1967; R. K. Meiners, *The Last Alternatives: A Study of the Works of Allen Tate,* 1963; ibid., *Everything to Be Endured,* 1970; Radcliffe Squires, *Allen Tate: A Literary Biography,* 1971; ibid., editor, *Allen Tate and His Work: Critical Evaluations,* 1971; and M. E. Bradford, *Rumors of Mortality: An Introduction to Allen Tate,* 1969. Of special interest are the essays by John Crowe Ransom and other contemporaries in "Homage to Allen Tate," *Sewanee Review,* LXVII (1959), 528–631.

See also Cleanth Brooks, *Modern Poetry and the Tradition,* 1939; John M. Bradbury, *The Fugitives,* 1958; and John L. Stewart, *The Burden of Time: The Fugitives and Agrarians,* 1965. For additional criticism see W. Thorp and J. Korges, "Allen Tate: A Checklist," *Critique,* X, no. 2 (1968), 17–52; and William C. Pratt, compiler, "Allen Tate," *A Bibliographical Guide to the Study of Southern Literature,* edited by Louis D. Rubin, 1969, 302–305.

EDWARD TAYLOR

Born: Leicestershire, England
Date: c. 1645

Died: Westfield, Massachusetts
Date: June 24, 1729

Principal Work

POEMS: *The Poetical Works of Edward Taylor* (including "God's Determinations" and "Sacramental Meditations"), 1939.

The poetry of Edward Taylor, New England mystic, is a fairly recent, but highly important, literary discovery. The manuscripts which contained some three hundred poems had lain untouched for over two centuries before they were resurrected by Thomas H. Johnson in 1937. Johnson edited a selection of the poems and in 1939 published them, along with a biographical sketch and a critical introduction, in *The Poetical Works of Edward Taylor*. And his efforts proved to be well worth the trouble. Taylor, who wrote in a style imitative of the seventeenth century metaphysicals, demonstrated a fairly high degree of poetical competency, especially in his long, semi-dramatic "God's Determinations," which has been called "perhaps the finest single poetic achievement in America before the nineteenth century."

As for the author of the poems, little is known about him before his arrival in Boston in 1668. It is believed that he was born about 1645 near Sketchley in Leicestershire, that he attended a Non-Conformist school, and that he came to this country because he could not take the oath of conformity then demanded of all English clergymen; but none of these conjectures is certain.

Following his arrival in Massachusetts, however, his activities were well documented. First, he was admitted to Harvard as a sophomore and was given the post of college butler; he was graduated in 1671. Next, he went to the settlement of Westfield as minister and remained there for the rest of his life, marrying twice, begetting fourteen children, quieting the Indians, acting as a physician, and in general caring for the physical as well as the spiritual well-being of his flock.

All this time he was writing his poetry. The masterpiece, "God's Determination," was probably written around 1690, and the "Sacramental Meditations," which are irregular in quality, over an extended period of time after that. The manuscript of the poems was inherited by his grandson, Ezra Stiles, who respected his ancestor's injunction that "his heirs should never publish it." The poems were deposited in the library of Yale College during Stiles' presidency, and they remained there until their discovery in 1937.

Taylor died at Westfield on June 24, 1729.

BIBLIOGRAPHICAL REFERENCES: The *Poems of Edward Taylor* were last edited by Donald E. Stanford, 1960. The best biographical and critical sketch is Thomas H. Johnson, Introduction to *The Poetical Works of Edward Taylor*, 1939. Some extracts from Edward Taylor's diary were also printed in the *Processes of the Massachusetts Historical Society*, XVIII (1881), 4–18, but the original manuscript has apparently been lost. Biographical and critical books are Norman S. Grabo, *Edward Taylor*, 1961; and Donald E. Stanford, *Edward Taylor*, 1965. For critical studies see Thomas H. Johnson, "The Discovery of Edward Taylor's Poetry," *Colophon*,

New Graphic Series I, No. 2, (1939), 101–106; Austin Warren, "Edward Taylor's Poetry: Colonial Baroque," *Kenyon Review*, III (1941), 355–371; Wallace C. Brown, "Edward Taylor, An American Metaphysical," *American Literature*, XVI (1944), 186–197; and Willie T. Weathers, "Edward Taylor: Hellenistic Puritan," *ibid.*, 18–26.

ESAIAS TEGNÉR

Born: Kyrkerud, Sweden
Date: November 13, 1782

Died: Östrabo, Sweden
Date: November 2, 1846

Principal Works

POEMS: *Svea*, 1811 (*Sweden*); *Nattvardsbarnen*, 1820 (*The First Communion*); *Axel*, 1822; *Frithiof's Saga*, 1825.

Esaias Tegnér, born in the Värmland district of Sweden on November 13, 1782, was the son of Esaias Lucasson, a clergyman who changed his name to Tegnerus, after the town of Tegnaby in Småland. The poet subsequently changed his name to Tegnér. Left fatherless in childhood, the boy received some tutoring through the assistance of the crown bailiff and later, with the aid of his brother's employer, was able to enter the University of Lund. After receiving his degree in philosophy in 1802, Tegnér remained at the university as lecturer and professor of Greek for twenty-two years. During this period he slowly made progress toward being recognized as Sweden's leading national poet. After some early failures, he achieved overnight fame in 1808 with his "War Song of the Militia of Scania." Three years later his patriotic poem, *Sweden*, won him the grand prize of the Swedish Academy.

Together with Arvid Afzelius and Erik Geijer, Tegnér developed the Gothic League in opposition to modernist European trends in Swedish literature, and in 1819 he was appointed a life member of the Academy. Drawing principally on Icelandic sagas and Norse folk tales, Tegnér made his great contributions to Swedish literature in *The First Communion*, made famous by Longfellow's paraphrase in *The Children of the Lord's Supper*; *Frithiof's Saga*, now translated into almost every European language, and his long narrative poem, *Axel*.

In 1824 Tegnér was named to the bishopric of Växjö, but his health broke under the burden of diocesan and parliamentary duties and for a time he became mad. He recovered sufficiently, however, to fulfill the duties of his church office from 1841 until his death at Östrabo on November 2, 1846. Two epic poems, *Gerda* and *Kronbruden*, remained unfinished when he died.

BIBLIOGRAPHICAL REFERENCES: An early study of the man and his work is Georg Brandes, *Esaias Tegnér*, 1876. See also F. Böök, *Esaias Tegnér*, 2 vols., 1946–1947.

ALFRED, LORD TENNYSON

Born: Somersby, England
Date: August 6, 1809

Died: Near Haslemere, England
Date: October 6, 1892

PRINCIPAL WORKS

POEMS: *Poems, Chiefly Lyrical,* 1830; *Poems,* 1832; *Poems,* 1842 (2 vols.); *The Princess,* 1847; *In Memoriam,* 1850; *Maud and Other Poems,* 1855; *Idylls of the King,* 1859–1885; *Enoch Arden and Other Poems,* 1864; *The Holy Grail and Other Poems,* 1869; *Ballads and Other Poems,* 1880; *Tiresias and Other Poems,* 1885; *Locksley Hall Sixty Years After,* 1886; *Demeter and Other Poems,* 1889; *The Death of Œnone,* 1892.

PLAYS: *Queen Mary,* 1875; *Harold,* 1876; *The Cup,* 1884; *The Falcon,* 1884; *Becket,* 1884; *The Promise of May,* 1886; *The Foresters,* 1892.

"Man comes and tills the field
and lies beneath."

Thus in one crisp, true line is life summed up by Tennyson. And between his birth on August 6, 1809, and his death on October 6, 1892, no poet in the whole range of English literature ever tilled the field of poetry with more diligence and versatility than Alfred, fourth son of the Rev. G. C. Tennyson, rector of the parish at Somersby in Lincolnshire, where the boy was born. Tennyson's output began at the age of six, with blank verse scribbled on a slate, and culminated some seventy-five years later, with the much-quoted "Crossing the Bar." In between came poetry that is sometimes magnificent, often vapid and mawkish, but always characteristic of an age alternately self-confident and self-conscious, the age of Victoria.

Somersby was a quiet village containing less than a hundred inhabitants. Tennyson's father was talented (a dabbler in poetry, painting, architecture, and music) and his mother, whose maiden name was Elizabeth Fytche, was noted for her gentleness and sweet disposition. In this setting Tennyson's talent developed early. While he was attending Louth grammar school he broke into print with *Poems by Two Brothers,* a collection which actually contained the works of three members of a talented family—Alfred, Frederick, and Charles. This juvenile volume shows the influence of Byron, whom Alfred admired so greatly that when he heard of his death he took a lonely, sad walk and carved into the sandstone, "Byron is dead."

In 1828 Tennyson went to Trinity College, Cambridge. There he took an interest in politics and became a member of The Apostles, a club of young literary men. Among these friends was Arthur Henry Hallam, whose later death, at the age of twenty-three, so affected Tennyson that he published nothing for ten years. Hallam is elegized in *In Memoriam,* a loose collection of philosophical lyrics that seems to be groping for, but never quite reaching, the handhold of faith. At Cambridge Tennyson won the chancellor's medal for his poem, "Timbuctoo," and it was there he brought out in 1830 his first important volume, *Poems, Chiefly Lyrical.* Although some of the reviews of this book were unkind, perhaps justifiably so, and although the influence of another Romantic poet, Keats, is very evident, the volume marked the beginning of a career almost unmatched in popularity afforded a poet during his lifetime.

Two years later came another volume, which included "The Lady of Shalott" and "The Lotus Eaters," two poems in the smooth, melancholy tone of Tennyson at his best. Then came Hallam's death and the ten years of silence. Hallam was Tennyson's close friend and the fiancé of his sister Emily; when Tennyson heard the news of his unexpected death in Vienna, he was dreadfully shocked and shaken. Later he began working on *In Memoriam* a labor that lasted for seventeen years. Not until 1842 did Tennyson publish again, bringing out two volumes, one of which contained "Morte d'Arthur," the beginning of a series on the Arthurian legends which became *Idylls of the King*. Also in 1842 appeared "Locksley Hall," one of Tennyson's most popular poems.

The auspicious year for Tennyson was 1850. After unwise speculation had left him penniless and two bouts with nervous prostration had damaged his health, his affairs took a threefold upsurge: he married Emily Sellwood, he published *In Memoriam*, and he was appointed Poet Laureate to succeed Wordsworth. Outstanding among his "official" poems as laureate is his "Ode on the Death of the Duke of Wellington," a stiff but moving tribute. The laureateship became the first step toward elevation to the peerage, an honor bestowed on him by an admiring queen. Tennyson had twice refused this honor (tendered to him first through Gladstone and then through Disraeli), but he accepted it in 1883, becoming Baron of Aldworth and Farrington. Even before he became a peer, Tennyson's popularity had been great (for example, ten thousand copies of the first series of *Idylls of the King*, published in 1859, were sold within a few weeks) but now this tall, gaunt man, the idealized figure of a poet, became almost a living legend. So popular was he that after his death there set in a natural reaction against his sentimentality and "Victorianism." But poems like "The Lotus Eaters," "Tithonus," and "Ulysses" still ring strong and true.

Tennyson's life was quiet, unhurried. Most of it he spent at his home, Farringford, on the Isle of Wight and, after 1867, at Blackdown in Surrey, where he lived in a house which he named Aldworth. In this later period he tried his hand at poetic dramas, *Queen Mary*, *Harold*, and *Becket*. Only the latter became a success on the stage. In 1889, *Demeter and Other Poems* came out, twenty thousand copies of which were sold within a week. On his eightieth birthday, Tennyson received tributes from all over the world. And though the end was not far away, he still had the strength to write a romantic play, *The Foresters*, a drama on the Robin Hood theme, which was produced at Daly's Theatre in New York in 1892.

Tennyson died at eighty-three at his home, Aldworth House, and was buried in the Poets' Corner of Westminster Abbey. To many readers Tennyson, not Shakespeare, seems more fittingly called the Swan of English literature. The name seems too gentle for the oftentimes fierce Elizabethan, but very appropriate for Tennyson, who experimented widely in the technique of poetry and whose best poems glide with the grace and beauty of a swan moving slowly across an unruffled lake.

BIBLIOGRAPHICAL REFERENCES: The standard edition is *The Works of Lord Tennyson*, edited by Hallam Tennyson, 9 vols., 1908–1910. More recent editions are

Poems of Tennyson, edited by Jerome H. Buckley, 1958; and *Poems,* edited by Christopher Ricks, 1969, probably the definitive edition. The most recent and informing of the many Tennyson biographies is Sir Charles Tennyson, *Alfred Tennyson,* 1949. See also Arthur Waugh, *Alfred, Lord Tennyson,* 1894; Hallam Tennyson, *Alfred, Lord Tennyson: A Memoir,* 2 vols., 1898; A. C. Benson, *Alfred Tennyson,* 1904; T. R. Lounsbury, *The Life and Times of Tennyson,* 1915; A. C. Bradley, *A Commentary on Tennyson's "In Memoriam,"* 1929; T. S. Eliot, " 'In Memoriam,' " in *Essays Ancient and Modern,* 1936; H. G. Nicolson, *Tennyson, Aspects of His Life, Character, and Poetry,* 1949; Jerome H. Buckley, *Tennyson: The Growth of a Poet,* 1960; Joanna Richardson, *The Pre-eminent Victorian: A Study of Tennyson,* 1962; and Ralph W. Rader, *"Maud": The Biographical Genesis,* 1963. A useful short work is J. B. Steane, *Tennyson,* 1966.

TERENCE

Born: Carthage (?)　　　　　　　*Died:* Athens, Greece, or at sea
Date: c. 190 B.C.　　　　　　　　*Date:* 159 B.C.

Principal Works

PLAYS: *Andria,* 166 B.C. (*The Girl from Andros*); *Heautontimorumenos,* 163 B.C. (*The Self-Tormentor*); *Eunuchus,* 161 B.C. (*The Eunuch*); *Phormio,* 161 B.C.; *Hecyra,* 160 B.C. (*The Mother-in-law*); *Adelphi,* 160 B.C. (*The Brothers*).

Publius Terentius Afer (Terence) was probably born in the North African city of Carthage in 190 or 185 B.C. Our sole source of knowledge about his life is the fourth century grammarian and commentator Donatus, who, in his commentary on Terence's plays, preserves a biographical extract from Suetonius' lost *De viris illustribus*. Terence was brought to Rome in childhood as a slave, but was given the education of a gentleman by his master, the senator M. Terentius Lucanus. After having been given his freedom, the young man took the name of his former master and added the cognomen Afer (African).

His intellectual brilliance and personal charm won Terence a place among the aristocratic literary coterie in Rome, a group of young men intent on Hellenizing Roman society and bringing Greek literature and its refinements to the Romans. His personal attractiveness, which secured him the patronage of Caecilius, the poet, and the backing of the literary and aristocratic party, stood Terence in good stead when he was accused of plagiarism and of receiving "help" from his noble friends. Although the elegance and purity of his style and language, surprising in one so young, and a foreigner, indicate that the accusation may have had some basis in truth, he was successful in repelling the charges, and continued to be lionized by Roman society.

Around 160 B.C. Terence spent some time in Greece, probably studying Greek life and institutions for future use in his writing. Tradition has it that he was lost at sea in 159 B.C., as he was returning to Italy bearing a translation of the plays of Menander.

Six plays of Terence have survived: *Andria, Hecyra, Heautontimorumenos, Eunuchus, Phormio,* and *Adelphi,* all produced between 166 and 160 B.C. Like the works of Plautus, they are modeled on Greek comedies, primarily those of Menander, but showing also the influence of Diphilus and Apollodorus. While Terence seems to have taken greater liberties with the plots and characterizations of the Greek originals than did Plautus, often combining scenes from several different plays, he nevertheless remains truer to the spirit and style of his sources. Unlike Plautus, his language is consistently temperate and refined, and he avoids the incongruity of introducing Roman allusions or traditions into his plays. Terence seems to have been less concerned with the applause of the masses than with achieving a fusion of the purity of cultivated Latin with the smoothness of Attic Greek, and he strove to introduce Greek culture and sophistication to a Rome that must have appeared to him vulgar, if not barbaric.

Terence's plays are characterized by complex but careful plot construction and by a sense of the probability of the incidents he portrays. Consistency and moderation in speech and characterization, quite different from the extravagance of Plautus's writing, mark his work. All six comedies deal with the love entanglements of young men, usually involving two love-relationships, one with a wellborn young woman and one with a courtesan, and complicated by the presence of a parent (or parents) and, as in *Phormio*, by a clever parasite. Although the characterization in the early plays follows closely the stock types of Greek comedy, Terence's later plays show considerable development toward a subtle and sympathetic understanding of human psychology.

BIBLIOGRAPHICAL REFERENCES: The standard scholarly text is *P. Terenti Afri comoediae*, edited by S. G. Ashmore, 1910. Among the translations in English are William Ritchie, *The Plays of Terence*, 1927; John Sargeunt, *Terence*, 1931; and G. E. Duckworth, *The Complete Roman Drama*, 2 vols., 1942. See also Gilbert Norwood, *The Art of Terence*, 1923. An excellent background study is William Beare, *The Roman Stage*, 1950. See further T. Dorey and Donald R. Dudley, eds., *Roman Drama*, 1965, 193–226.

WILLIAM MAKEPEACE THACKERAY

Born: Calcutta, India
Date: July 18, 1811

Died: London, England
Date: December 24, 1863

PRINCIPAL WORKS

NOVELS: *Catherine,* 1839–1840; *The History of Samuel Titmarsh and the Great Hoggarty Diamond,* 1841; *Barry Lyndon,* 1844; *Vanity Fair,* 1847–1848; *Pendennis,* 1848–1850; *Henry Esmond,* 1852; *The Newcomes,* 1853–1855; *The Virginians,* 1857–1859; *The Adventures of Philip,* 1861–1862; *Denis Duval,* 1864.

SKETCHES: *The Paris Sketch Book,* 1840; *Comic Tales and Sketches,* 1841; *The Irish Sketch Book,* 1843; *The Book of Snobs,* 1848; *Sketches and Travels in London,* 1856.

CHRISTMAS STORY: *The Rose and the Ring,* 1854.

LECTURES AND ESSAYS: *The English Humorists of the Eighteenth Century,* 1851; *The Four Georges,* 1855; *Roundabout Papers,* 1864.

William Makepeace Thackeray was born at Calcutta, India (where his father was in the service of the East India Company), on July 18, 1811, and died in London on December 24, 1863. At least until 1859, when George Eliot's *Adam Bede* appeared, he was Dickens' only possible rival as the leading Victorian novelist.

Thackeray's father, Richmond Thackeray, died in 1815; his mother thereafter married Captain Henry Carmichael-Smyth, who became the original of Colonel Newcome. In 1822 the boy was sent to the Charterhouse School, whence he proceeded to Trinity College, Cambridge, which he left without taking a degree. He studied law in a desultory fashion and wandered about Weimar and Paris dabbling in art. In 1833, through a combination of folly and ill luck, he lost most of his considerable fortune. His first thought was to make his living as an artist (he later illustrated his own writings), but he soon turned instead to literature.

Thackeray began his career by burlesquing popular contemporary novelists whose work he considered mawkish, absurd, or morally vicious, for *Fraser's Magazine;* the most important outcome of these labors was his *Catherine,* in which he attacked the vogue of the story of crime. A more important enterprise, *Barry Lyndon,* was an eighteenth century rogue story, importantly influenced by Thackeray's admiration for Fielding's *Jonathan Wild;* but the writer did not really catch the public fancy until he published *Vanity Fair* in 1847–1848. From then until the end, though his sales always ran far behind those of Dickens, his reputation was secure. In the 1850's he made two lecture tours in America; from 1860 to 1862 he edited *The Cornhill Magazine.* His domestic happiness was clouded by the insanity of his Irish wife, Isabella Shaw (whom he married in 1836, and who outlived him by many years); in his relations with his daughters he showed all the tenderness of which his kindly, but in some ways weak, nature was capable.

Thackeray was at once a cynic and a sentimentalist. The judgments he makes of his characters are often uncertain and conventional, but he portrays them with a vivid realism which in his time seemed shocking in English fiction. Many of his most successful characters are, in one way or another, rogues. "The Art of Novels," he declared, "*is* to represent Nature; to convey as strongly as possible the sentiment of reality. . . ." The heightening and idealism proper to "a tragedy or a poem or a lofty drama" he ruled out. Not by this alone was he differentiated from Dickens but also by his upper-class point of view, his lack of Dickens' enthusiasm, vitality, and inexhaustible sympathy, and by his more bookish, elegant style. His world, in its main aspects, comprises Mayfair and Bohemia. Though the two great writers did not fail to appreciate each other, Dickens was inclined to resent his rival's somewhat superior and aristocratic air toward "the art that he held in trust." Thus the tone of careless ease in Thackeray's writing is an important element in his charm, but it also indicates an important limitation.

His major novels are few in number and make up a comparatively small portion of the twenty-five odd volumes of his collected works. Probably the most brilliant are *Vanity Fair,* a stunning panorama of a corrupt upper- and middle-class society around the Waterloo crisis, with a heroine, Becky Sharp, who has been for a hundred years the most celebrated female rogue in English fiction, and *Henry Esmond,* a novel in the form of a memoir, presenting Jacobitish and other intrigues in an eighteenth century London in some ways more congenial to Thackeray's mind and spirit than his own time. *Henry Esmond's* cool, autumnal elegance and perfect distinction of style place it forever in the aristocracy of the world's great novels. It has, too, in Beatrix Esmond, one of the most subtly and completely portrayed of all heroines of fiction. *Pendennis* is an attempt to use for fiction the materials of Thackeray's own life in the manner and spirit of Fielding's *Tom Jones. The Newcomes,* a family novel covering three generations, is a wider-scoped *Vanity Fair. The Virginians* gives us Esmond's grandsons in the American Revolution and in London. These are all major novels. But *The Adventures of Philip* is only a minor *Pendennis,* and *Denis Duval,* a brilliant adventure story, which represents for Thackeray a frank capitulation to romance, he unfortunately did not live to finish.

Thackeray's achievement, like that of his master Fielding, is central in the development of the English novel. Though he had neither Scott's imagination nor Dickens' brilliance, he had an unerring sense of the scope and direction of fiction. After a hundred years he still deserves to be called one of our very greatest realists.

BIBLIOGRAPHICAL REFERENCES: An important event in Thackeray biography and criticism occurred in 1945–1946, when the Thackeray family allowed Gordon N. Ray to publish *The Letters and Private Papers of William Makepeace Thackeray,* 4 vols. Ray's *The Buried Life,* 1952, is a critical study; his *Thackeray: The Uses of Adversity,* 1955, and *Thackeray: The Age of Wisdom,* 1958, now make up the definitive biography. Lionel Stevenson, *The Showman of Vanity Fair,* 1947, was the last important book prepared without access to Ray's documents. Recent critical studies include John W. Dodds, *Thackeray: A Critical Portrait,* 1941; and Geoffrey Tillotson, *Thackeray the Novelist,* 1954.

Among the books published before the *Letters and Private Papers,* the most important are the writings of Thackeray's daughter, Lady Ritchie, especially *Chapters from Some Unwritten Memoirs*, 1894, and *Thackeray and His Daughter*, 1924. See also Lewis Melville, *The Life of William Makepeace Thackeray*, 2 vols., 1899; and Malcolm Elwin, *Thackeray: A Personality*, 1932. Miriam M. H. Thrall's *Rebellious Fraser's*, 1934, is important for Thackeray's apprenticeship. See also Geoffrey Tillotson and Donald Hawes, *Thackeray: The Critical Heritage*, 1968; and M. G. Sundell, ed., *"Vanity Fair," Twentieth Century Interpretations*, 1969.

THEOCRITUS

Born: Syracuse (?)
Date: 305 (?), B.C.

Died: Syracuse (?)
Date: c. 250 B.C.

Principal Works

POEMS: The *Bucolics;* the *Epics.*

Theocritus is one of the ancient authors about whom all too little is known to satisfy scholars. Much of what has sometimes passed for fact about him has been inferred from his writings, particularly from the *Charites,* and in some cases doubt has been cast on works attributed to him. It would appear reasonable to assume, however, that he was born about 305 B.C. in Syracuse (though equal claims have been made for Cos) and that he studied as a youth and young man under the Greek master Philetas, in Cos. Becoming certain of his craft as a poet, Theocritus appealed to Hiero the Second, ruler of Syracuse, for Hiero's support as a patron (probably in 275 B.C.), but was refused. Shortly thereafter a similar plea to Ptolemy Philadelphus brought success, and Theocritus took up residence in Alexandria sometime between 275 and 270 B.C. How long he stayed there or where he went afterward is a problem for which we have only conjectures, rather than answers. Probably he went to Cos, perhaps back to Syracuse, where he probably died about 250 B.C.

Much of Theocritus' poetry illustrates the love the ancient Greeks had for their homeland. Apparently the poet, far away from Greece in Alexandria, wrote much of his poetry in the pastoral convention to express the love he had for Greece. His most famous poems, the *Bucolics,* are pastoral poems on mythical subjects. The *Epics,* a later work, include poems to Hiero and Ptolemy, also to their respective spouses. There is also a series of epigrams of doubtful authenticity and equally doubtful date. The poems of Theocritus are often referred to as idylls, a word bestowed upon them by ancient authors. Credit is usually given to Theocritus for being the inventor of bucolic poetry, and he probably was, although modern scholarship, by showing how Theocritus borrowed ideas and fragments from earlier authors, has somewhat diminished the reputation he once enjoyed.

BIBLIOGRAPHICAL REFERENCES: The best translation of Theocritus in prose is that by Andrew Lang, 1901. Verse translations are numerous. See also J. M. Edmonds, *The Greek Bucolic Poets,* 1912; R. J. Cholmeley, Introduction to *The Idylls of Theocritus,* 1919; André Bonnard, *Greek Civilization: From Euripides to Alexandria,* 1961, 229–245; Gilbert Lawall, *Theocritus' Coan Pastorals; A Poetry Book,* 1967; and Thomas G. Rosenmeyer, *The Green Cabinet: Theocritus and the European Pastoral Lyric,* 1969.

DYLAN THOMAS

Born: Swansea, Wales
Date: October 27, 1914

Died: New York, N. Y.
Date: November 9, 1953

Principal Works

POEMS: *18 Poems*, 1934; *Twenty-five Poems*, 1936; *The Map of Love*, 1939; *The World I Breathe*, 1939; *New Poems*, 1943; *Deaths and Entrances*, 1946; *In Country Sleep*, 1952; *Collected Poems, 1934–1952*, 1952.
SHORT STORIES AND SKETCHES: *Adventures in the Skin Trade and Other Stories*, 1955.
AUTOBIOGRAPHY: *Portrait of the Artist as a Young Dog*, 1940.
PLAYS: *The Doctor and the Devils*, 1953; *Under Milk Wood*, 1954.
ESSAYS AND BROADCASTS: *Quite Early One Morning*, 1954.

Dylan (Marlais) Thomas, born in Swansea, Wales, on October 27, 1914, regularly produced and published poetry and short fiction to the age of thirty-five. His last four years were wasted in public readings of earlier works as well as the works of other poets (for the ostensible purpose of earning more but as well to find reassurance in adulation), and new works were produced but occasionally and hurriedly under the pressure of professional commitments. It was during this latter period that Thomas disintegrated psychically to die of acute alcoholism in New York City on November 9, 1953. When the memory of his exuberant personality has dissipated, he will probably be judged the greatest lyric poet of his generation and a fiction writer of original humor and charm.

The total amount of Thomas' work could be contained in one volume; however, he was not so much a slow writer as a careful one, altering some of his poems over two hundred times. He insisted that his work be read at its face value, preferably aloud. (Thomas once said that he wanted to be *read*, not *read into*.) Much of the criticism of the obscurity of his work has been irrelevant for this reason: the reader is not supposed to find answers to anything; rather, he is to allow the words to work on him, which they do tremendously in spite of the many private and esoteric references. While some scholars have traced these to their sources for further enjoyment, the magic of the literature as it stands is the main reward.

Thomas was a tragic figure, a man of effusive good will who dissipated to death in agonies of guilt. While his poetry tortuously worked through to a celebration of the Christian belief, in his prose, as well as in his personal life, he revealed the mind of one who wished to believe, to find faith, but could not, and in not finding it knew life as a nightmare from which there was no escape except death. This was the reason for the number of images depicting horror in his work. If some of it was symbolic, it was because there was nothing in the familiar world that sufficiently expressed the horror that he saw. Extremely sensitive, imbued with an impossible ethical code by his schoolmaster father, he projected his own guilt onto the world at large, its hypocrisy and money-getting, its general inhumanity. Two symptoms of this were his telling the truth beyond the edge of tact and his profligate wastefulness of money, though he was miserable when the first resulted in hurt feelings and the second in poverty.

Thomas was essentially a rural poet, and much of what he had to say was concerned with that world, of its harmony with the rhythm of the earth in its emphasis on birth, marriage, death, rebirth, and a simple faith in God, or else with the lost world of childhood innocence. His readers were of the urban world, however, a world he feared and hated.

Thomas was educated in the Swansea Grammer School in which his father was an English master. The English scholar is often antithetical to works of writers not dead, and Dylan's later scorn of scholars in England and America may indicate that his father belittled his early efforts, just as his anti-social boisterousness indicated an overstrict childhood. However, his early poetry and prose were published frequently in the grammar school literary magazine; and when his first volume, *18 Poems*, appeared, it was received enthusiastically by critics such as Edith Sitwell, though not by the general public, some of whom wrote virulent abuses to the *Sunday Times*. The poetry of this first period was concerned almost entirely with personal problems and was made perhaps deliberately obscure by private imagery and a highly personalized style.

Until World War II Thomas lived in London much of the time. Short but broad, of huge energy, he had experiences that were in many ways those of any proud rural innocent; always scornful of hypocrisy and the unnatural, he found much to reject in the city. At the same time his great warmth and talent made him many friends among its literary leaders. His way of adapting to this life was to mock the conventions with droll acts. During the war he served as an anti-aircraft gunner; the sight of the courage and suffering induced his second creative phase, one which revealed poignant feelings for others. When he also read poetry over the B.B.C., he began to have a general public.

With the printing of *The Collected Poems of Dylan Thomas* in 1952 he became a public figure on the basis of his enthusiastic reception by reviewers and critics. His later poetry had begun to reveal the change in his attitude from one of doubt and fear to faith and hope, with love of God gained through love of man and the world of nature. It also was more verbose. It was at this time that he became unbearably dissatisfied with life, expressing this in such poems as "I Have Longed to Move Away." Part of this feeling may have been due to his growing fear of alienation from his Irish-born wife Caitlin and their three children; part of it may have been the effect of his fear of losing his powers and upon which the first fear would be based. In addition, he was miserable as a public figure. Like all provincials, he was anxious before the stranger; although he was deeply appreciated by the audiences he read to, most of these people were interested in the poet of public fame, not in the private man. For a man with a huge capacity and need to love and be loved, this experience may have been devastating. Whatever the causes, Thomas produced mostly fiction and verse plays the last few years of his life. Of these the unfinished *Adventures in the Skin Trade* deals with his urban experiences, *Under Milk Wood* with his village reminiscences. Both of these works were celebrations of innocence, written at a time when the poet said of himself, "I have seen the gates of hell."

BIBLIOGRAPHICAL REFERENCES: There are two biographies: John Ackerman, *Dylan Thomas: His Life and Work*, 1964; and Constantine FitzGibbon, *The Life of Dylan Thomas*, 1965. See also *ibid.*, ed., *Selected Letters*, 1966. The *Poems* have been edited by Daniel Jones, 1971. Highly subjective and often conflicting details are given in two works combining biography and reminiscence: John Malcolm Brinnin, *Dylan Thomas in America*, 1955; and Caitlin Thomas, *Leftover Life to Kill*, 1957. The basic critical studies are Henry Treece, *Dylan Thomas*, 1949; Elder Olson, *The Poetry of Dylan Thomas*, 1954; and Clark Emery, *The World of Dylan Thomas*, 1971. See also *Dylan Thomas: Letters to Vernon Watkins*, edited, with an introduction, by Vernon Watkins, 1957.

The best brief yet comprehensive study of the poetry and prose is John L. Sweeney's Introduction to *Selected Writings of Dylan Thomas*, 1946. See also Francis Scarfe, "Dylan Thomas: A Pioneer," in *Auden and After*, 1942; Babette Deutsch, "Alchemists of the Word," in *Poetry in Our Time*, 1952; M. W. Stearn, "Unsex the Skeleton: Notes on the Poetry of Dylan Thomas," *Sewanee Review*, LII (1944), 424–440; Robert Horan, "In Defense of Dylan Thomas," *Kenyon Review*, VII (1945), 304–310; Anon., "Salute to a Poet," *London Times Literary Supplement*, LI (Nov. 28, 1952), 776; David Daiches, "The Poetry of Dylan Thomas," *College English*, XVI (1954), 1–8; and Henry W. Wells, "Voice and Verse in Dylan Thomas' Play," *College English*, XV (1954), 438–444.

THOMAS À KEMPIS

Born: Kempen, Germany
Date: c. 1380

Died: St. Agnietenberg, Netherlands
Date: July 25, 1471

Principal Work

THEOLOGICAL TREATISE: *Imitatio Christi,* c. 1400 (*The Imitation of Christ*).

Thomas à Kempis, born Thomas Hammerken (or Hemerken) about 1380, was the son of a peasant whose wife was the keeper of an old-fashioned dame-school for small children. At the age of twelve, Thomas was sent to the chapter school at Deventer, where among his teachers was Florens Radewijns (Florentius Radewyn). Known at Deventer as Thomas from Kempen, the scholar gradually assumed the name by which posterity knows him. When it became apparent to Thomas and his teachers that he was suited for a monk's life, he went in 1399 to the monastery of St. Agnietenberg, near Zwolle, where the prior was his brother John. Thomas entered the Augustinian order in 1406 and was ordained a priest in 1413 or 1414.

The remainder of his long life was spent in that monastery, except for a brief period of exile from 1429 to 1432, during the Utrecht schism. Thomas copied a great deal of material, earning money for his monastery by his labors. He also wrote original material, for which dates of composition are too vague to have any value. Included in his works are biographies of Gerhard Groot, Florentius Radewyn, and the Flemish St. Louise. He also wrote many tracts and a chronicle of the monastery of St. Agnietenberg. The most important of the writings with which his name is associated is *The Imitation of Christ,* written between 1380 and 1410 and first circulated in 1418, a moving religious document that next to the Bible is the most widely known of all religious books. Although Thomas à Kempis' authorship has been disputed, the arguments advanced against his authorship have only seemed to strengthen the belief that the work is really from his pen. Thomas was made subprior of St. Agnietenberg in 1425. He died there on July 25, 1471.

BIBLIOGRAPHICAL REFERENCES: The standard edition is the *Opera Omnia,* edited by M. J. Pohl, 1907–1922. The most recent translations of *Imitation of Christ* are those by L. Shirley-Price, 1953; and Ronald Knox and Michael Oakley, 1959. A good brief biographical study is F. R. Cruise, *Outline of the Life of Thomas à Kempis,* 1904. See also Samuel Kettlewell, *Thomas à Kempis and the Brothers of the Common Life,* 1882; and James Williams, *Thomas of Kempen,* 1910.

DANIEL PIERCE THOMPSON

Born: Charlestown, Massachusetts
Date: October 1, 1795

Died: Montpelier, Vermont
Date: June 6, 1868

Principal Works

NOVELS: *The Green Mountain Boys,* 1839; *Locke Amsden,* 1847; *The Rangers,* 1851.

Born of an old American family that reached Massachusetts early in the seventeenth century, and claiming an ancestor killed at the Battle of Lexington, Daniel Pierce Thompson had reason to be interested in history. Shortly after his birth, at Charlestown, Massachusetts, on October 1, 1795, his family moved to Berlin, Vermont, a frontier settlement with neither school nor library. The chance discovery of a volume of poetry inspired him to get an education. After studying by himself and at a preparatory school, he entered Middlebury College with advanced standing, financing himself by the sale of his sheep and by poems and articles he contributed to magazines.

After graduation, Thompson tutored the son of a rich southern planter and met Thomas Jefferson, who turned the young man's thoughts toward the law. After some study, Thompson returned to Vermont and was admitted to the bar. He codified the laws of Vermont in 1834. His first fiction was the anti-Masonic *Adventures of Timothy Peacock, Esq.* (1835), whom he called a "Masonic Quixote." Association with survivors of the Revolutionary period inspired his novel *The Green Mountain Boys,* first printed on a small newspaper press. Immediately successful, the novel went through fifty editions in twenty years. Its sequel was *The Rangers,* published in 1851. Thompson also edited the anti-slavery *Green Mountain Freeman* (1849–1856).

As a man, Thompson was an old-fashioned Yankee with a keen sense of humor. A contemporary portrait shows him with thin features, a jutting chin, long nose, and a tangled mop of hair. He died at Montpelier, Vermont, June 6, 1868.

BIBLIOGRAPHICAL REFERENCES: Thompson has attracted very little attention; however, there is a full-length study that supplies all the necessary basic information: J. E. Flitcroft, *The Novelist of Vermont, A Biographical and Critical Study of Daniel Pierce Thompson,* 1929. See also L. D. Loshe, *The Early American Novels,* 1907 (rev. ed., 1930); and Van Wyck Brooks's comments in *The Flowering of New England,* 1936.

FRANCIS THOMPSON

Born: Preston, England
Date: December 18, 1859

Died: London, England
Date: November 13, 1907

Principal Works

POEMS: *Poems*, 1893, including "The Hound of Heaven," originally published in *Merrie England*, 1891; *Sister Songs*, 1895 and 1908; *New Poems*, 1897.
ESSAYS: *Health and Holiness: A Study of the Relations Between Brother Ass the Body and His Rider the Soul*, 1905; *Essay on Shelley*, 1909.
BIOGRAPHY: *Life of St. Ignatius Loyola*, 1909; *The Life of John Baptist de la Galle*, 1911.

Francis Thompson, born the son of an homeopathist, was brought up a Catholic and was educated at Ushaw College preparatory to becoming a priest. At the age of seventeen he went to study medicine, following his father's desires, at Owens College, Manchester. But, frail and timid, he found medical study repugnant. After trying for six years to become a doctor, he gave up the attempt. He then went to London. He soon became addicted to opium and sank into the direst depths of destitution, for a time earning his living selling matches or newspapers. In the spring of 1888 he sent two poems to *Merrie England;* they were accepted by the editor, Wilfred Meynell. With the strong urging of his new friends and patrons, Thompson tried to break the opium habit.

His first volume of poetry, called simply *Poems,* contained the famous "Hound of Heaven," which despite its strict Catholic dogma became immediately popular. In addition to the Catholic mysticism which informs his early works, Thompson was tremendously influenced by the English Metaphysical poets of the seventeenth century. Since his memorable poems and prose works are few, Thompson probably never lived up to his potential. He was never able to break his addiction to opium and the complications resulting from it. He died of tuberculosis on November 13, 1907, and was buried under his own very revealing epitaph: "Look for me in the nurseries of Heaven."

BIBLIOGRAPHICAL REFERENCES: Thompson's *Works* were edited by Wilfred Meynell, 3 vols., 1913. An important edition of the poetry is T. L. Connolly, editor, *Poems of Thompson,* 1941. Connolly also edited *Francis Thompson, Literary Criticisms: Newly Discovered and Collected,* 1948.

Recent biographical and critical studies include J. C. Reid, *Francis Thompson: Man and Poet,* 1959; P. Danchin, *Thompson: la vie et l'oeuvre d'un poète,* 1959; Paul van Kuykendall Thomson, *Francis Thompson: A Critical Biography,* 1961; and John Walsh, *Strange Harp, Strange Symphony: The Life of Francis Thompson,* 1967. Earlier biographies of interest are E. Meynell, *The Life of Francis Thompson,* 1913; T. H. Wright, *Francis Thompson and His Poetry,* 1927; and V. Meynell, *Francis Thompson and Wilfred Meynell,* 1952.

See also *The Letters of Francis Thompson,* edited by John Walsh, 1969; G. Krishnamurty, editor, *The Hound of Heaven: A Commemorative Volume,* 1967; and M. P. Pope, *A Critical Bibliography of Works by and About Thompson,* 1959.

JAMES THOMSON

Born: Ednam, Roxburghshire, Scotland
Date: September 7, 1700

Died: Kew Gardens, England
Date: August 27, 1748

Principal Works

POETRY: *The Seasons*, 1730; *Hymn*, 1730; *Liberty*, 1736; *The Castle of Indolence*, 1748.

PLAYS: *Sophonsiba*, 1730; *Agamemnon*, 1738; *Edward and Eleanora*, 1739; *Alfred* (with David Mallet), 1740; *Tancred and Sigismunda*, 1745; *Coriolanus*, 1749.

James Thomson was for more than a century considered a major British poet. His most popular work, *The Seasons*, was among the best-selling poems between 1730 and 1850, and was often ranked with Milton's *Paradise Lost* as the representative British work. He was highly praised by Hazlitt, Coleridge, and Lamb, among others, and his works in translation proved popular in France, Germany, and Spain. It is of some historical interest that *Alfred*, a masque written in collaboration with David Mallet, contains the famous song "Rule, Britannia."

Although a contemporary of Pope, who is known to have made some revisions in Thomson's verse, Thomson wrote most of his work in blank verse. He further departs from the Augustan tradition in his use of nature; his evocative descriptions of nature, expressed in simple language, free of the self-conscious artificiality of his contemporaries, foreshadowed the Romantic movement.

Thomson's affinity with nature can be traced to his early days in the small Scottish village of Ednam. Educated at Edinburgh University, he traveled to London in 1725, and passed through a series of patrons, pensions, and tutorial positions—a frequent pattern among writers in eighteenth century London. The phenomenal success of the individual poems of *The Seasons* (originally published separately) helped make him financially independent, and in 1736 he moved to Kew Gardens, then a rural district outside London, where he spent the remainder of his life.

The Castle of Indolence, an imitation of Spenser's *Faerie Queene*, recounts the enticement of weary pilgrims into the castle of the Wizard Indolence, and the subsequent destruction of the wizard and the castle by the Knight of Arms and Industry. The lush music of the poem's style is more memorable than its allegorical exhortation to cultivate the virtues of Industry.

Thomson was also a popular playwright, and his heroic tragedies were performed regularly at Drury Lane by Garrick and Quin. His major importance, however, rests upon his early mastery of poetic forms—blank verse and the Spenserian stanza—and subjects which were atypical of an age dominated by reason and the heroic couplet.

BIBLIOGRAPHICAL REFERENCES: The standard edition is still *Poetical Works*, edited by J. Logie Robertson, 1908. More recent is *The Castle of Indolence and Other Poems*, edited by Alan D. McKillop, 1961. The standard biography is Douglas Grant, *James Thomson: Poet of "The Seasons,"* 1951. See also *Letters and Docu-*

ments, edited by Alan D. McKillop, 1958. For criticism see Alan D. McKillop, *The Background of Thomson's Seasons,* 1942; Patricia Meyer Spacks, *The Varied God: A Critical Study of Thomson's* "The Seasons," 1969; and Ralph Cohen, *The Unfolding of* "The Seasons," 1970.

HENRY DAVID THOREAU

Born: Concord, Massachusetts
Date: July 12, 1817

Died: Concord
Date: May 6, 1862

Principal Works

NATURE STUDIES AND ESSAYS: *A Week on the Concord and Merrimack Rivers,* 1849; *Walden, or Life in the Woods,* 1854; *Excursions,* 1863; *The Maine Woods,* 1864; *Cape Cod,* 1865; *A Yankee in Canada, with Anti-Slavery and Reform Papers,* 1866; *Early Spring in Massachusetts,* 1881; *Summer,* 1884; *Winter,* 1888; *Autumn,* 1894.
POEMS: *Poems of Nature,* 1895; *Collected Poems,* 1943.
LETTERS: *Letters to Various Persons,* edited by Ralph Waldo Emerson, 1865; *Familiar Letters of Henry David Thoreau,* edited by F. B. Sanborn, 1894.

Henry David Thoreau, defier of labels, was a man born before his time. Thirty or forty years later *Walden* might have surged to success on the tide of nature interest which benefited such writers as John Burroughs and John Muir. As it was, Thoreau was largely ignored by his own generation, which dismissed him as an impractical reformer. It has remained to a later period to recognize him as one of the most original thinkers and one of the best prose writers of his time.

Along with Emerson and Hawthorne, Thoreau is often referred to as a member of the "Concord Group"; of this trio, however, Thoreau alone could claim the town as his birthplace. He was born there July 12, 1817, the second son of John and Cynthia (Dunbar) Thoreau. He grew up in Concord village, attending the local school—apparently an excellent one—in preparation for Harvard College, which he entered at the age of sixteen. Despite financial difficulties during the next four years, he was graduated in 1837, well versed in languages and skillful in the use of his pen. Already a non-conformist, during his Harvard days he disregarded honors, neglected unattractive studies, and deplored the necessity of spending five dollars for a diploma.

Unlike his literary contemporaries, Thoreau never prepared for a profession. After graduation from college he taught school in Concord for a time, together with his brother John. With the latter he made a trip on the Concord and Merrimack Rivers in 1839. John, to whom his brother was devoted, died of lockjaw in 1842. He was ill with tuberculosis at the time, a disease which took the father of the boys and, finally, Thoreau himself.

It was about 1840 that Thoreau decided to become a writer. The decision made no change in his simple manner of life: throughout his career, he preferred to support himself by the labor of his hands. Intermittently he worked at lead pencil making (his father's business), did surveying, or made gardens. It was in the capacity of gardener that he became a member of Emerson's household in 1841, though his services came to include helping Emerson to edit the Transcendentalist journal, *The Dial.* Despite Lowell's contention that Thoreau was the imitator of his employer, it seems equally likely that Emerson's interest in nature and nature lore was gained, at least in part, from Thoreau.

The independence and fearlessness of Thoreau's nature led him to speak out actively against whatever he found reason to regard as wrong. He strongly championed John Brown and the Abolitionists, for example, at a time when such a stand was highly unpopular. In 1845, following the example of Bronson Alcott, he went to jail rather than pay poll tax to a government which, as Thoreau saw it, countenanced war and slavery. He provided a living embodiment of Emerson's doctrines of self-reliance and non-conformity; but it is notable that he did so without forfeiting the love and respect of those who knew him best.

Perhaps the most important activity of Thoreau's life began in 1845, when he retired to a little hut at Walden Pond near Concord. Here, he lived for over two years, cultivating a small plot of ground and attempting to prove that a man need not go beyond his own resources for sustenance and enjoyment. The literary result of this experiment was *Walden*, his best-known work. Published in 1854, this book provided the first and best example of that literary product especially identified with America, the "nature book."

Aside from *Walden*, the only other of Thoreau's books published during his lifetime was *A Week on the Concord and Merrimack Rivers*, of which the public took little notice, only two hundred or so copies being sold. It was not until after his death that the bulk of Thoreau's writing was published, although some articles and addresses had made their appearance in contemporary periodicals, chiefly in *The Dial* and *Putnam's Magazine*. Since his death in Concord on May 6, 1862, the complete journal of Thoreau has been published; and, even though his total writing output is slim in comparison with that of some of his fellow New Englanders, it is sufficient to give him belated recognition as one of the really original and vigorous writers of the century.

The nineteenth century neglect of Thoreau, which continued for a decade or two after his death, was partly the result of the inaccurate estimates of his worth made by such respected critics as Lowell. The nature school, arising at the end of the century, has played a part in his literary revival; nevertheless, Thoreau's essential value as a writer depends only partly on the nature of his subject matter. Clarity of expression, shrewdness, and occasional humor combine to form an individual prose style of compelling charm. The integrity of the man shines through his work, and his positive views on nature and government constitute a continuing challenge to a civilization bowed down by frustrations and complexities.

BIBLIOGRAPHICAL REFERENCES: The complete works of Henry David Thoreau have been posthumously published in the Manuscript Edition, 20 vols., 1906, and in the standard Walden Edition printed from the same plates. Odell Shepherd edited *The Heart of Thoreau's Journals*, 1927. There is also *The Correspondence of Henry David Thoreau*, edited by Carl Bode and Walter Harding, 1958. See also Bartholow V. Crawford, ed., *Henry David Thoreau: Representative Selections*, 1934; Henry Seidel Canby, ed., *The Works of Thoreau*, 1947; and Carl Bode, ed., *The Portable Thoreau*, 1947.

The most extensive biographical study is Henry S. Canby, *Thoreau*, 1939. Other biographical studies include Henry S. Salt, *The Life of Henry David Thoreau*, 1890; Mark Van Doren, *Henry David Thoreau: A Critical Study*, 1916; Leon Bazalgette, *Henry Thoreau: Bachelor of Nature*, 1924; Brooks Atkinson, *Henry D. Thoreau: The Cosmic Yankee*, 1927; and Walter Harding, *The Days of Henry Thoreau*,

1965.

For briefer studies see F. O. Matthiessen, *American Renaissance,* 1941; Carl Bode, Introduction to *The Portable Thoreau,* 1947; Sherman Paul, ed., *Thoreau: A Collection of Critical Essays,* 1962; Norman Foerster, "Thoreau as Artist," *Sewanee Review,* XXIX (1921), 2–13; Raymond Adams, "A Bibliographical Note on *Walden,*" *American Literature,* II (1930), 166–168; *idem,* "Thoreau's Literary Apprenticeship," *Studies in Philology,* XXIX (1932), 617–629; Henry W. Wells, "An Evaluation of Thoreau's Poetry," *American Literature,* XVI (1944), 99–109; Randall Stewart, "The Growth of Thoreau's Reputation," *College English,* VII (1946), 208–214; Madeleine B. Stern, "Approaches to Biography," *South Atlantic Quarterly,* XIX (1946), 362–371; and S. T. Hyman, "Henry Thoreau in Our Time," *Atlantic Monthly,* CLXXVIII (1946), 137–146.

THUCYDIDES

Born: Athens, Greece
Date: 455 (?), B.C.

Died: Thrace (?)
Date: c. 400 B.C.

Principal Work

HISTORY: *History of the Peloponnesian War* (written c. 431–400 B.C.).

Thucydides was the son of Olorus, an Athenian citizen. The date of his birth is uncertain; it has been put as early as 471 B.C. and as late as 455 B.C., the latter date being the more probable. He may have spent part of his youth in Thrace, where his family owned gold-mining rights. He says that he began his history of the Peloponnesian war at the moment when the war broke out, so that he was presumably living at Athens in 431. He was certainly there the following year during the plague, of which he fell ill. In 424 he was appointed, jointly with Eucles, to defend the coastal region bordering on Thrace, and was entrusted with a naval squadron. His failure to prevent the capture of Amphipolis when it was invested by the Spartans provoked the Athenians to send him into exile. He passed the twenty years of his banishment in visiting the cities of the enemy and the principal battlefields of the war, and in collecting from veterans of the war the historical materials needed for his work. He returned to Athens about 403. He did not live to complete his great work, the *History* ending in 411, seven years before the peace was finally made. His death is supposed to have occurred in Thrace at the hands of an assassin about 400 B.C.

Thucydides' *History* is both highly objective and highly dramatic. In the numerous orations which he reports or constructs, he shows his precise understanding of ideological issues. His narratives are marvelously vivid; among the most memorable are his accounts of the plague at Athens and of the Syracusan campaign, which ended with the imprisonment of the expeditionary force in the rock quarries.

BIBLIOGRAPHICAL REFERENCES: The best translation of Thucydides in English is that by Benjamin Jowett, 1881 (rev. ed., 2 vols., 1900). For historical and critical comment see G. B. Grundy, *Thucydides and the History of His Age*, 1911; G. F. Abbott, *Thucydides: A Study in Historical Reality*, 1925; C. N. Cochrane, *Thucydides and the Science of History*, 1929; J. H. Finley, *Thucydides*, 1942; and Joseph Gavorse, Introduction to *The Peloponnesian War*, Modern Library edition, 1934.

JAMES THURBER

Born: Columbus, Ohio
Date: December 8, 1894

Died: New York, N. Y.
Date: November 2, 1961

Principal Works

ESSAYS, STORIES, SKETCHES, AND DRAWINGS: *Is Sex Necessary?*, 1929 (with E. B. White); *The Owl in the Attic and Other Perplexities*, 1931; *The Seal in the Bedroom and Other Predicaments*, 1932; *My Life and Hard Times*, 1933; *The Middle-Aged Man on the Flying Trapeze*, 1935; *Let Your Mind Alone*, 1937; *The Last Flower*, 1939; *My World—And Welcome to It!*, 1942; *Men, Women and Dogs*, 1943; *The Thurber Carnival*, 1945; *The Beast in Me and Other Animals*, 1948; *The Thurber Album*, 1952; *Thurber Country*, 1953; *Thurber's Dogs*, 1955.

FABLES AND FANTASIES: *Fables for Our Time*, 1940; *Many Moons*, 1943; *The Great Quillow*, 1944; *The White Deer*, 1945; *The Thirteen Clocks*, 1950; *Further Fables for Our Time*, 1956; *The Wonderful O*, 1957.

PLAY: *The Male Animal*, 1940 (with Elliott Nugent).

James (Grover) Thurber, born in Columbus, Ohio, on December 8, 1894, came to the East Coast by way of the Chicago *Tribune* and Paris, France, and settled down, finally, with E. B. White to make *The New Yorker* what it is today.

These journalistic meanderings started at Ohio State where Thurber began his writing career as a reporter for the university newspaper. They were interrupted by a year of war duty (unable to get into the Army because of one sightless eye, Thurber served as a code clerk in Washington and Paris) and by a second year which he took off just to read. But they were resumed in 1919, and were continued, after his graduation, on a professional basis with the Columbus *Dispatch*. Next came the *Tribune* and Paris. Thurber served as editor of the *Tribune's* Paris edition until 1929, when he returned to the United States and began his historic relationship with White on the staff of *The New Yorker*.

The story of his beginning with the magazine has become a legend. Reputedly, Thurber was brought by White into the magazine's offices. His object was simply a job. He emerged as managing editor and remained in that capacity for six months. Eventually he joined White in the composition of the "Talk of the Town" and continued in that department until his resignation in 1933.

The resignation did not end his relations with *The New Yorker*, however. His work continued to appear in its pages in the form of frequent essays, fables, tales, and drawings, and almost all the material collected in his books first appeared in the columns of that magazine.

Is Sex Necessary? was written in collaboration with White, its content a blend of Thurber's delightful whimsy, White's spoofing erudition, and, certainly not the least important, illustrations by Thurber himself.

The success of this first collection meant a demand for more. *The Owl in the Attic*, with an introduction by White, appeared in 1931, followed logically enough by *The Seal in the Bedroom*, and by the comically autobiographical *My Life and Hard Times*. Some fifteen additional volumes have appeared since, and with each one

Thurber's reputation as the leading humorist of our age has become more firmly established. There have been numerous efforts to explain and evaluate his very particular brand of humor; no less a figure than T. S. Eliot has analyzed his genius, a quality easier to recognize than to define. Whether narrating the eternal war between the sexes, describing the homicidal effects of a baseball announcer's clichés, reviewing the frustrations brought on by recalcitrant machinery, or capturing with a few sketchy lines the canine quintessence of befuddled dogdom, Thurber is funny—sometimes quietly funny, sometimes hilariously funny, but always, it would seem, funny in a unique and inimitable way. There is whimsy in his humor, but "whimsy" is too limited a word to describe the total effect. His humor is in the American tradition of exaggeration and the tall tale (the uncle who caught the chestnut blight, the draft prospect who served four months undetected as an examiner), but there is a pathos behind it, a sort of subliminal human (or canine) tragedy that makes it something more. T. S. Eliot says that "There is a criticism of life at the bottom of it," and that "His writing and also his illustrations are capable of surviving the immediate environment and time out of which they spring." If this proves to be true, Thurber will certainly rank among the greatest of American humorists, alongside Mark Twain and Oliver Wendell Holmes.

Personally retiring to the point of shyness, Thurber heard his fame reverberate far beyond the quietly sophisticated sphere of *The New Yorker*. His introverted Walter Mitty has been brought to life on the screen by the frenetic Danny Kaye; his *Thirteen Clocks* has been performed on the stage and as a television opera; a New York bar decorated its interior with murals from his drawings. But for all this renown he lived quietly in Connecticut and, in spite of almost complete blindness, continued to write and draw. His death occurred in New York City on November 2, 1961.

BIBLIOGRAPHICAL REFERENCES: Two studies of Thurber have appeared since his death: Robert E. Mossberger, *James Thurber*, 1964; and Richard C. Tobias, *The Art of James Thurber*, 1969; and the basic facts about his career are available in a *Time* cover article, LVIII (July 9, 1951), 88–95. There is an excellent interview by George Plimpton and Max Steele in *The Paris Review*, 11 (Fall 1955), 35–49. See also Walter Blair, *Horse Sense in American Humor*, 1942; "James Thurber: The Comic Prufrock," *Poetry*, LXII (1943), 150–159, an anonymous article; Francis Downing, "Thurber," *Commonweal*, XLI (1945), 518–519; and Gerald Weales, "The World in Thurber's Fables," *ibid.*, LXV (1957), 409–411.

ALEXIS DE TOCQUEVILLE

Born: Paris, France
Date: July 29, 1805

Died: Cannes, France
Date: April 16, 1859

PRINCIPAL WORKS

HISTORY AND POLITICAL SCIENCE: *De la démocratie en Amérique,* 1835, 1840 (*Democracy in America*); *L'Ancien Régime et la Révolution,* 1856.
MEMOIRS: *Memoir, Letters, and Remains of Alexis de Tocqueville,* 2 vols., 1861; *Souvenirs d'Alexis de Tocqueville,* 1893.

Alexis de Tocqueville was born in Paris, July 29, 1805. As a child he displayed great powers of intelligence, and he was fortunate enough to be allowed to develop them through study and travel. His journey to America resulted in his first book, a study of the penal system of both the Old and New Worlds. This book, which appeared in 1832, was based on a long and hard exploration of a year's duration, during which he familiarized himself with the nature of American culture. Another book, one which was to make him famous, was also a consequence of this journey. *Democracy in America* (1835) immediately raised Tocqueville to the status of a great European author, and he was compared to such thinkers as Châteaubriand and Montesquieu.

Democracy in America was the answer of an empiricist to political theories derived largely from speculation. It was based on close study of institutions rather than on a theory of human nature, and it covered in great detail the economics, legal structure, and social structure of the United States. It covered too the dangers of democracy: the probability of increased centralization of power, the encroachment of oligarchy on popular rights. In the years after the publication of this great work Tocqueville took an active part in government and became a fascinated observer of the violent political changes of the 1830's and 1840's. He laid at this time the basis for his future works, which were to culminate in *L'Ancien Régime et la Révolution* (1856).

The preoccupation of Tocqueville during these years was decidedly not with ideas or theories, but with what he called the realities of authority, morality, and religion. He was opposed to revolutionary activities that would, in the name of reform, destroy these positive values. His fear was of too much freedom, of the destruction of the European community by private interests. He wrote of the dangers from two directions: from a plutocracy that would become more and more selfish, considering the working classes as of no more value than the machines they operated, and from the despotism of the working classes themselves.

In his books, letters, and his personal life he consistently stated that institutions which worked badly were preferable to those that did not work at all. He foretold the new despotism of the twentieth century, and he characterized it as the product of a time which had abandoned its past. The ties of caste, class, corporation, and family were essential to his view of orderly government, and he discerned that these ties were rapidly becoming weaker even in his own lifetime. What would replace them was private interest, whether of the mob, the middle classes, or a ruling clique. The one way to stop this danger, he believed, was through freedom. Political freedom, he stated in his last work, was the one agent that could unite the varying interests of the modern state.

BIBLIOGRAPHICAL REFERENCES: The *Oeuvres Complètes d'Alexis de Tocqueville* was published by Madame de Tocqueville and Gustave de Beaumont, 9 vols., 1860–1865. Publication of a new edition, *Oeuvres, Papiers et Correspondances*, edited by J. P. Mayer, began in 1951. One of the several good translations of *Democracy in America* is that of George Lawrence, edited by Mayer, 1966.

Mayer's *Alexis de Tocqueville: A Biographical Study in Political Science*, 1960, is a useful introduction to the author's life and work. See also G. W. Pierson, *Tocqueville and Beaumont in America*, 1938; Seymour I. Drescher, *Dilemmas of Democracy: Tocqueville and Modernization*, 1968; Edward T. Gargan, *De Tocqueville*, 1965; Max Lerner. *Tocqueville and America*, 1969; Jack Lively, *Social and Political Thought of Alexis de Tocqueville*, 1962; Marvin Zetterbaum, *Tocqueville and the Problem of Democracy*, 1967; and Irving M. Zeitlin, *Liberty, Equality, and Revolution in Alexis De Tocqueville*, 1971.

JOHN RONALD REUEL TOLKIEN

Born: Bloemfontein, South Africa
Date: January 3, 1892

Died: Princeton, New Jersey
Date: April 11, 1970

Principal Works

NOVELS: *The Hobbit*, 1937; *Farmer Giles of Ham*, 1949; *The Lord of the Rings* (Vol. I, *The Fellowship of the Ring*, 1954; Vol. II, *The Two Towers*, 1954; Vol. III, *The Return of the King*, 1955).

SHORT STORIES: *Leaf by Niggle*, 1945; *Smith of Wootton Major*, 1964.

POEMS: "The Lay of Aotrou and Itroun," *The Welsh Review*, IV, 245–266 (1945); *The Pearl: A Verse Translation*, 1946; "The Homecoming of Beorhtnoth Beorhthelm's Son," *Essays and Studies*, VI, 1–18 (1953); *The Adventures of Tom Bombadil*, 1962.

SCHOLARLY AND CRITICAL WORKS: *A Middle English Vocabulary*, 1922; *Sir Gawain and the Green Knight* (edited with E. V. Gordon), 1925; *Chaucer as a Philologist*, 1934; "Beowulf: The Monsters and the Critics," *Proceedings of the British Academy*, XXII, 245–295 (1936); "On Fairy-stories," *Essays Presented to Charles Williams*, 1947 (reprinted with revisions in *Tree and Leaf*, 1964): *Ancren Wisse* (edited for the Early English Text Society), 1962.

The phenomenon of an eminent professional scholar who is also a superb creative artist is rare enough to be greeted with heightened respect. J. R. R. Tolkien is such a phenomenon; internationally respected as a linguist and literary scholar, he is also a major creative writer.

He was born of British parents in Bloemfontein, South Africa, in 1892. His father, Arthur Reuel Tolkien, died when the boy was only four. His mother, who returned to England with her two sons, died in 1904. Father Francis Xavier Morgan cared for the orphans. Young Tolkien was educated at the King Edward VI School in Birmingham and at Exeter College, Oxford, receiving his B.A. in 1916 and his M.A. in 1919. During World War I he served with the Lancashire Fusiliers. He married Edith Mary Bratt in 1916; they celebrated their golden wedding in 1966. Their children are three sons and a daughter. Tolkien has lectured at the Universities of Leeds, St. Andrews, and Glasgow, and has held professorships of Anglo-Saxon and of English Language and Literature at Oxford. He holds honorary doctorates from the University College, Dublin, and the University of Liège; he is a Fellow of the Royal Society of Literature and an honorary member of the Icelandic Literary Society. He has produced a distinguished body of scholarly writings and editions.

Publication of *The Hobbit* in 1937 marked the beginning of a second important career for him. It is an adventure story, originally composed to be told aloud to his children. Its plot is based on the Homeric themes of journey and battle, to which the author returned in his masterly *Lord of the Rings*, a three-volume sequel to *The Hobbit* aimed primarily at an adult audience, though it also has great appeal for children. This epic romance, the work of a true myth-maker, is deeply rooted in the past but pertinent to the present. Two of Tolkien's articles are particularly helpful in understanding him as a creative artist: "On Fairy-stories" and "Beowulf: The Monsters and the Critics." He was a member of a circle of about a dozen scholar-writers who called themselves the Inklings; they included the late Charles Williams and C. S. Lewis. As Lewis himself has told us, the members read aloud their works in progress and discussed them critically. Their mutual influence was important and beneficial.

Aristotle would have classified Tolkien as a poet on the strength of his creative fiction; but he is also a poet in the conventional sense. His "Lay of Aotrou and Itroun" is worthy of comparison with Coleridge's *Christabel*; and his "Homecoming of Beorhtnoth Beorhthelm's Son" is a moving poetic sequel to the Anglo-Saxon "Battle of Maldon." *The Adventures of Tom Bombadil* is a collection of poems, some drawn from *The Lord of the Rings*.

A long-awaited sequel to *The Lord of the Rings*, *The Silmarillion* (which deals with earlier events in Middle-Earth), is in progress.

BIBLIOGRAPHICAL REFERENCES: Full-length studies include N. D. Isaacs and R. A. Zimbardo, *Tolkien and the Critics*, 1968; Ian Carter, *Tolkien: A Look Behind* "The Lord of the Rings," 1969; Catherine R. Stimpson, *J. R. R. Tolkien*, 1969; and *The Tolkien Papers, Mankato State College Studies*, Vol. II, no. 1, 1967.

See also Roger Lancelyn Green, *Tellers of Tales*, 1953; Patricia Meyer Spacks, "Ethical Pattern in *The Lord of the Rings*," *Critique*, III (1959), 30–42; W. R. Irwin, "There and Back Again: The Romances of Williams, Lewis, and Tolkien," *The Sewanee Review*, LXIX (1961), 566–578; and Charles Moorman, *The Precincts of Felicity*, 1966. For additional references see B. M. Christensen, "J. R. R. Tolkien: A Bibliography," *Bulletin of Bibliography*, XXVII (July, 1970), 61–67; and Richard C. West, *Tolkien Criticism: An Annotated Checklist*, 1970.

COUNT LEO TOLSTOY

Born: Yásnaya Polyána, Russia
Date: August 28, 1828

Died: Astapovo, Russia
Date: November 7, 1910

PRINCIPAL WORK

NOVELS: *Kazaki*, 1863 (*The Cossacks*); *Voina i mir*, 1865–1869 (*War and Peace*); *Anna Karenina*, 1873–1877; *Smert Ivana Ilyicha*, 1884 (*The Death of Ivan Ilyich*); *Khozyain i rabotnik*, 1885 (*Master and Man*); *Kreitserova Sonata*, 1889 (*The Kreutzer Sonata*); *Voskraeseniye*, 1899 (*The Resurrection*).
AUTOBIOGRAPHY: *Destvo*, 1852 (*Childhood*); *Otrochestvo*, 1854 (*Boyhood*); *Yunost*, 1857 (*Adolescence*); *Ispoved*, 1884 (*A Confession*).
PLAY: *Vlast tmy*, 1886 (*The Power of Darkness*).

Count Leo (Lev) Nikolayevich Tolstoy, Russian author and moral philosopher, was born on August 28, 1828, at Yásnaya Polyána, near Tula, Russia, into a family of aristocratic landowners. He was educated first at home and then at the University of Kazan, which he left without taking a degree. One of his early and enduring influences was that of Rousseau. As if prompted by it he returned from Kazan to his estate with the object of improving the living conditions of his serfs. Frustrated in this task, he left in 1851 for the Caucasus where he joined the army and spent much of his time among the primitive Cossack settlers so wonderfully described in his novel *The Cossacks*, written in 1854 but not printed until 1863. In the Caucasus he finished his first important work, *Childhood*, a delightful string of autobiographic sketches which was followed up by *Boyhood* and *Adolescence*. Tolstoy took part in the Crimean campaign, and his three Sevastopol stories, with their frank realism, established his reputation. Even in these early writings he combined a profound psychological insight with an almost incredible visual and plastic power. He soon gave up the army and for a while divided his time between Moscow and his estate. In 1857 and again in 1860 he traveled extensively abroad where he became rather disappointed with the materialistic trend of Western civilization. This only fostered his sympathy with the Russian peasant masses whose simple ways of life he had admired from the outset. On his estate he actually set up, in 1859, a school for peasant children and he himself taught in it for a while on more or less Rousseauesque lines. In 1862 he married Sophia Andreyevna Behrs. A year later he was already writing his great novel, *War and Peace*, which he finished in 1869.

In this epic of a whole people at the time of a historical crisis Tolstoy depicts, on a very broad canvas, all the strata of the Russian nation in their resistance to Napoleon's invasion in 1812. Yet the backbone of the novel is the interlacing history of two noble families—those of Tolstoy's father and mother—which in the end become united through marriage. Among the many unforgettable characters conjured up by Tolstoy's genius, that of the young Natasha Rostova is particularly wonderful. Yet Tolstoy the moralist and the seeker, quite noticeable in a number of his previous writings, comes also here to the fore. He projected his own quest into Pierre Bezukhov and Prince Andrey, but he did it objectively enough to make both of them independent of their author's views and tendencies.

Tolstoy's own "vexation of the spirit" is felt, however, much more tangibly in Levin, the hero of his next masterpiece, *Anna Karenina,* which he wrote between 1873 and 1877. The novel is a chronicle of three or four families, Tolstoy's own growing family being one of them. But this time the background is that of the 1870's when Russia, no longer in the grip of serfdom, had to cope with the problems of capitalist economy gradually encroaching upon the patriarchal countryside. Too much of a patriarchal squire at heart to welcome anything that smelled of capitalism and town civilization, Tolstoy based the very structure of this novel on the contrast between the unsophisticated countryside on the one hand and the "corrupt" city life on the other. Yet in spite of all the idyllic charms of his family life and his prosperous farming, the squire Levin was unable to escape from his inner crisis which was due to his quest for a meaning of life. Such a meaning was imparted to him at last by a simple God-fearing peasant who lived according to the teaching of the Gospel. In this way Levin anticipated Tolstoy's own conversion so pathetically described in his *A Confession,* written in 1879 and first published (abroad) in 1884.

Such a crisis and conversion had actually been latent in Tolstoy's inner make-up itself. Endowed with a spontaneous and truly pagan love of life, he was yet unable to affirm life without a meaning which he envisaged above all in terms of moral values. Far from being unexpected, his conversion was only a turning point at which the moralizing rationalist in Tolstoy took the upper hand over Tolstoy the artist. After a long quest he discovered the true meaning of life in the Sermon on the Mount which he "corrected" in such a way as to turn it against private property and all social divisions, all laws and authorities; in fact, against all civilized existence as such. The only law he acknowledged was God's commandment of brotherly love instilled in man's conscience. From the beginning of the 1880's Tolstoy wrote one eloquent pamphlet after the other in order to propagate his primitive Christian anarchism. In his brilliantly misleading book, *What is Art* (1897), he condemned all art which failed to foster the moral good among men. In another pamphlet he even made a savage onslaught on Shakespeare. His teaching soon found adherents in all parts of the world, but none of the "Tolstoyan" communities had a long lease of life. Paradoxically enough, in spite of his strange teaching of non-resistance (which was subsequently taken up by his Hindu follower, Gandhi), Tolstoy's virulent criticism of the social evils of our time helped to create in Russia that ferment which led to the revolution of 1917.

Tolstoy himself was too much of an artist to be entirely ousted by the moralist. Even with an eye on the moral "purpose" he still retained his creative power and wrote a number of masterpieces such as the haunting narrative *The Death of Ivan Ilyich, The Kreutzer Sonata, Master and Man,* and his last great novel, *The Resurrection.* Among his posthumous stories, *The Devil, The False Coupon, Father Sergius,* and *Hadji Murat* (all published in 1911) are particularly well told. As for his plays, the satirical comedy *Fruits of Enlightenment* (1891), the naturalistic peasant drama, *The Power of Darkness*, and *The Live Corpse*, unfinished, (1911), have been staged all over the world.

During the last twenty years of his life, Tolstoy became not only the most conspicuous literary figure in the world, but also one of the great moral forces of his time. Even in Russia he was allowed to say what he liked without any fear of the police or censorship. Realizing the responsibility of such a position, he did his best to live up to his own principles. He got rid of his personal property and even wanted to divide his land among the peasants, but his wife (who had to think of her large family) had responsibilities of her own which did not tally with those of her unpractical husband. Quarrels and misunderstandings between the two thus could not be avoided. In the end Tolstoy ran away from his home. During his flight he caught pneumonia and died at the small railway station, Astapovo, on November 7, 1910, at the age of eighty-two.

BIBLIOGRAPHICAL REFERENCES: The most recent Russian edition of Tolstoy's works is *Polnoc Sobranic Sochineniy*, 1940 ff. See in English *The Centenary Edition of Tolstoy's Works*, edited by A. Maude, 1928–1937. See also D. Merezhkovsky, *Tolstoy i Dostoevsky*, St. Petersburg, 1901–1902 (2 vols.); Ivanov-Razumnik, *L. Tolstoy*, 1910; V. Veresayev, *O. Dostoevskom i Tolstom*, 1913; M. Gorky, *Vospominanya o Tolstom*, 1919; P. J. Biryukov, *L. N. Tolstoy*, 1923; N. N. Gusev, *Zhizn Tolstogo*, 1927; V. F. Bulgakov, *Tragediya Tolstogo*, 1928; N. N. Gusev, *Letopis Zhizni i Tvorchertva Tolstogo*, 1937; and I. A. Bunin *Osvobozhdenie Tolstogo*, 1937.

Studies in English include: H. Fausset, *Tolstoy*, 1927; A. Maude, *The Life of Tolstoy*, 1929–1930 (2 vols.); A. I. Nazarov, *Tolstoy, the Inconstant Genius*, 1930; Sofya A. Tolstaya, *The Diary of Tolstoy's Wife*, 1928; A. Maude, *The Final Struggle*, 1936; L. Derrick, *Tolstoy*, 1944; Janko Lavrin, *Tolstoy*, 1946; E. Simmons, *Leo Tolstoy*, 1946, 1949; Isaiah Berlin, *The Hedgehog and the Fox*, 1953; A. L. Tolstaya, *A Life of My Father*, 1953; and Ilya Tolstoy, *Tolstoy, My Father*, 1971. The most important recent works are George Steiner, *Tolstoy or Dostoevsky*, 1959; and the biography by Henri Troyat translated by Nancy Amphoux, 1968.

H. M. TOMLINSON

Born: London, England
Date: 1873

Died: London
Date: February 5, 1958

Principal Works

NOVELS: *Gallions Reach*, 1927; *All Our Yesterdays*, 1930; *The Snows of Helicon*, 1933; *Mars His Idiot*, 1935; *All Hands!* 1937 [*Pipe All Hands!*]; *The Day Before*, 1939; *Morning Light*, 1946; *The Trumpet Shall Sound*, 1957.

ESSAYS AND STUDIES: *Old Junk*, 1918; *London River*, 1921; *Waiting for Daylight*, 1922; *Gifts of Fortune*, 1926; *Under the Red Ensign*, 1926 [*The Foreshore of England*]; *Thomas Hardy*, 1929; *Between the Lines*, 1930; *Norman Douglas*, 1931; *Out of Soundings*, 1931; *The Wind Is Rising*, 1941; *The Turn of the Tide*, 1946; *The Face of the Earth*, 1950; *Malay Waters*, 1950; *The Haunted Forest*, 1951; *A Mingled Yarn*, 1953.

TRAVEL SKETCHES AND IMPRESSIONS: *The Sea and the Jungle*, 1912; *Tidemarks*, 1923; *Below London Bridge*, 1934; *South to Cadiz*, 1934.

H(enry) M(ajor) Tomlinson was born in 1873 in the East End of London and lived his youth around the docks. At the age of twelve he was employed as a shipping clerk. Hating the drudgery of the work, he loved the ships with which his labors brought him in contact. Even while working, however, he found time to read extensively, some of his favorite authors being Whitman, Melville, Emerson, and Thoreau. He also studied geology, entomology, and music.

H. M. Tomlinson started writing early in his life and began submitting his work to editors in hopes of escaping from the shipping office, but he was thirty-one before he was able to leave the job as a clerk. He became a member of the editorial staff of the London *Morning Leader* in 1904, and remained in this position until 1912, when he went on a long tour up the Amazon River on a tramp steamer. This trip and his experiences on it are the source for *The Sea and the Jungle*, his best-known travel book. In 1912 he joined the staff of the London *Daily News*, where he remained until 1917, when he became literary editor of *The Nation and Athenaeum* until 1923. From 1914 until 1917, Tomlinson was a foreign correspondent in France and Belgium. After 1923 he free-lanced as a journalist and novelist.

With the publication of *Gallions Reach* in 1927, Tomlinson achieved success as a novelist, and subsequently he devoted much of his attention to fiction. His first novel, a romance set in the Far East, won the Femina-Vie Heureuse Prize and caused Tomlinson to be associated, as an author, with Joseph Conrad. Perhaps the primary resemblance between them is their devotion to the sea, although Tomlinson seemed to share Conrad's conviction that the human state of mind, the thought process, is more important than action as such.

In his next novel, *All Our Yesterdays*, Tomlinson created a more severe tone, attacking the weaknesses of civilization. He felt that changing people's attitudes is the only hope for society. In these books, as in his later ones, he preferred settings which were unusual and exotic, places far from the main centers of life. His style is also individualistic, having a calmness and a vigor that have won him considerable praise. The books of essays which brought him a large following of readers are *Old Junk, London River,* and *Waiting for Daylight.* In these, as in his novels, a style of impressive imagery and verbal beauty accompanies the writer's gift of poetic introspection. His novels are often autobiographical, and his views of areas of the world such as the tropics border on impressionism. Although he has written much travel literature about far-off places, he was essentially a Londoner. Even so, his ability to create the mood and atmosphere of a distant place for his readers will probably continue to make him a widely read and appreciated writer whose best work has in it something of the force and yet the serenity of the sea. Tomlinson died in London on February 5, 1958.

BIBLIOGRAPHICAL REFERENCES: There is no extended body of criticism on Tomlinson. See Robert Lynd, *Books and Authors,* 1923; S. K. Ratcliffe, Introduction to *Old Junk,* 1920; John Freeman, "Mr. H. M. Tomlinson," *London Mercury,* XVI (1927), 400–408; F. P. Mayer, "H. M. Tomlinson: The Eternal Youth," *Virginia Quarterly Review,* IV (1928), 78–82; Helen and Richard Altick, "Square Rigger on a Modern Mission," *College English,* V (1943), 75–80; Alva A. Gay, "H. M. Tomlinson, Essayist and Traveller," *Studies in Honor of John Wilcox,* A. D. Wallace and W. O. Ross, eds., 1958, 209–217; Edmund C. Blunden, "H. M. Tomlinson," *Edmund Blunden: A Selection of His Poetry and Prose,* 1961, 303–308; Frank A. Swinnerton, "Four Journalists," *Figures in the Foreground,* 1964, 116–135; and Bernard Bergonzi, "Retrospect II: Fiction," *Heroes' Twilight: A Study of the Literature of the Great War,* 1966, 171–197.

JEAN TOOMER

Born: Washington, D. C.
Date: December 26, 1894

Died: Doylestown, Pennsylvania
Date: March 30, 1967

PRINCIPAL WORKS

POETRY AND PROSE: *Cane*, 1923.
PLAY: *Balo, A One-Act Sketch of Negro Life*, 1927.
JOURNALS AND APHORISMS: *Essentials*, 1931; *Portage Potential*, 1932.

Jean Toomer's *Cane*, a collection of poems, stories, and sketches, has come to be regarded as one of the most significant evocations of Negro life to have appeared in this century. The settings range from rural Georgia to the ghettoes of Washington, D. C.; the variety of characters and voices transcends the stereotypes which populated the works of other writers of the period. Objective and free of propaganda, *Cane* is the work of a man whose loyalty to his race was exceeded by his loyalty to literary excellence.

Toomer's parents came from Georgia, and were of mixed ancestry; Toomer claimed to have seven blood mixtures: French, Dutch, Welsh, Negro, German, Jewish, and Indian; at various times he lived as a Negro or as a white man. He spent a comparatively short time thinking of himself as a "Negro writer"; he preferred to draw on all his backgrounds for his own conception of his spiritual makeup.

In 1932 he married Marjory Latimer, a promising novelist; she died in childbirth the following year. In 1934 he married Marjorie Content, the daughter of a New York stockbroker. They moved to Doylestown, in Bucks County, Pennsylvania, where Toomer seems to have avoided his former associations with Negro literary movements; he spent a considerable amount of time writing for *The Friends Intelligencer* and lecturing to groups of Quakers in the area.

Aside from *Cane*, Toomer published two collections of aphorisms and journal entries; these grew out of several experiences, including a brief period of study at the Gurdjieff Institute in France, and a period of psychoanalysis. *Balo*, a play, met with an unfavorable critical reception on its appearance in 1927.

Much of Toomer's work remains unpublished; for example, among his papers, donated to Fisk University in 1963, is a novel, *York Beach*, part of which appeared in 1929 in *New American Caravan*, edited by Alfred Kreymborg. Much remains to be discovered about Toomer's life and work, but it is doubtful that he has left behind any single work as accomplished as *Cane*, which is a landmark in the Negro literature of this century.

BIBLIOGRAPHICAL REFERENCES: A sketch of Toomer's personality is to be found in Paul Rosenfeld, *Men Seen*, 1925, 227–233. For criticism see Eugene Holmes, "Jean Toomer, Apostle of Beauty," *Opportunity*, III (1925), 252–254; Gorham Munson, "The Significance of Jean Toomer," *ibid.*, 262–263; Saunders Redding, *To Make a Poet Black*, 1939, 103–106; Hugh M. Gloster, *Negro Voices in American*

Fiction, 1948, 111, 114, 117, 128–130, 171, 194, 222, 238; Arna Bontemps, "The Negro Renaissance: Jean Toomer and the Harlem of the 1920's" in *Anger and Beyond: The Negro Writer in the United States,* edited by Herbert Hill, 1966, 20–36; and Darwin T. Turner, "The Failure of a Playwright," *College Language Association Journal,* X (1967), 308–318.

ALBION WINEGAR TOURGÉE

Born: Ashtabula, Ohio
Date: May 2, 1838

Died: Bordeaux, France
Date: May 21, 1905

Principal Works

NOVELS: *A Fool's Errand,* 1879; *Bricks Without Straw,* 1880; *A Royal Gentleman,* 1881 (first published 1874 as *Toinette* under the pen name, "Henry Churton"); *Hot Plowshares,* 1883; *Murvale Eastman, Christian Socialist,* 1889–1890.

NONFICTION: *The Code of Civil Procedure of North Carolina,* 1878; *A Digest of Cited Cases,* 1878; *The Invisible Empire,* 1879–1880.

Albion W. Tourgée is one of many writers who have written fiction putting argument above art. Tourgée, a Union soldier in the Civil War, wrote to justify the Radical Republican theory of Reconstruction. Other minor American writers used Reconstruction themes, but unlike Tourgée they were native Southerners, they did not experience Reconstruction directly, and they were not involved in its politics. Tourgée was thus unique.

He grew up in Ohio and was graduated from Rochester College in 1862. His war career lasted less than two years, and in 1865 he moved to North Carolina. As a carpetbag lawyer he wanted to help establish racial equality and generally to improve and enlighten the South. He later realized how radical and naïve these ideas were. Disillusioned, he fictionalized his experiences under the title *A Fool's Errand.*

The book is the best of his more than twenty novels. It is largely autobiographical—the central figure of the "Fool" is an idealistic Michigan lawyer who moves South and finds himself *persona non grata* as he tries to help Negroes obtain their rights. Suspense and violent action help rescue the book from Tourgée's heavy burden of moralizing. Particularly memorable are the vivid accounts of Klan threats and atrocities. Comfort Servosse, the "Fool," finally realizes that the South will not change instantly. He admires the courage and courtesy of Southern aristocrats but hates their stubbornness and prejudice. His sad concluding moral is curiously prescient, calling for federal action to help educate the Negroes and hoping that strong Negro leadership will arise. Tourgée departs from self-portrayal as he idealizes the "Fool" beyond credibility. He himself was frequently intemperate and slanderous, a contrast to the dignified Servosse.

Most of Tourgée's other novels are thought of as pieces of third-rate sentimentalism—bad imitations of his idol, James Fenimore Cooper. Stereotyped characters and wholly implausible situations abound.

But when, as in *A Fool's Errand,* he confined himself to the times and situations he knew, he rose to second-rate status. Novels in this category are *Bricks Without Straw,* dealing with the rise of one Negro, and *A Royal Gentleman,* on a miscegenation theme, showing how one Southern gentleman could not give up his belief in Negro inferiority. *Murvale Eastman, Christian Socialist,* is a sometimes powerful but often artificial novel on a promising theme.

Tourgée's best books were his earliest. While writing, he served variously as superior court judge, codifier of state law, newspaper columnist, magazine editor, and consul to Bordeaux.

BIBLIOGRAPHICAL REFERENCES: Recent biographical-critical studies include Otto H. Olsen, *Carpetbagger's Crusade: The Life of Albion Winegar Tourgée*, 1965; and Theodore L. Gross, *Albion W. Tourgée*, 1963. See also R. F. Dibble, *Albion W. Tourgée*, 1921; Alexander Cowie, *Rise of the American Novel*, 1948; Edmund Wilson, *Patriotic Gore*, 1962; and John Hope Franklin's "Albion Tourgée, Social Critic," in *A Fool's Errand*, 1961, vii–xxviii.

Significant articles are George J. Becker, "Albion W. Tourgée: Pioneer in Social Criticism," *American Literature*, XIX (1947), 59–72; T. L. Gross, "The Fool's Errand of Albion Winegar Tourgée," *Phylon*, XXIV (1963), 240–254; T. N. Weissbuch, "Albion Winegar Tourgée: Propagandist and Critic of Reconstruction," *Oregon Historical Quarterly*, LXX (January, 1961), 27–44; and Dean H. Keller, "A Checklist of the Writings of Albion W. Tourgée (1838–1905)," *Studies in Bibliography*, XVIII (1964).

CYRIL TOURNEUR

Born: Unknown
Date: c. 1575

Died: Kinsdale, Ireland
Date: February 28, 1626

PRINCIPAL WORKS

PLAYS: *The Revenger's Tragedy*, c. 1607; *The Atheist's Tragedy*, c. 1611.
POEMS: *A Funeral Poem upon the Death of the Most Worthy and True Soldier, Sir Francis Vere*, 1609; *A Grief on the Death of Prince Henry*, 1613.
MISCELLANEOUS: *The Transformed Metamorphosis*, 1600; *Character of Sir Robert Cecil, Earl of Salisbury*, 1612.

Cyril Tourneur, about whom little is known, was perhaps the son of Captain Richard Turnor, a follower of Sir Thomas Cecil. The young Tourneur, probably born about 1575, was a follower of the Cecils also, and served the Veres and the Earl of Essex at different times during his career. Much of that career was spent in military or diplomatic service. He probably served with the English forces in The Netherlands in the early years of the seventeenth century.

A verse satire, *The Transformed Metamorphosis*, was published in 1600, and *The Revenger's Tragedy*, which has been ascribed to Tourneur, was published in 1607. Tourneur's literary reputation rests chiefly on this play, although it was not ascribed to him until 1656, some fifty years after its performance, and its authorship has been contested. However, it is generally accepted as his work. His second surviving play, *The Atheist's Tragedy*, was published in 1611. The Stationers' Register contains an entry in 1612 of *The Nobleman*, a tragi-comedy by Cyril Tourneur; but this play and *The Arraignment of London*, for which he wrote one of the acts for Henslowe's company, are both lost.

He was a government courier in 1613 and a campaign soldier again in 1614. Imprisoned in 1617, he was released on Sir Edward Cecil's bond. In 1625 he accompanied Sir Edward on a naval expedition against Spain. As Lord Marshall of the Fleet, Sir Edward appointed Tourneur Secretary to the Council of War and Secretary to the Marshall's Court; but the first appointment was not approved. The expedition failed; Sir Edward's flagship, *The Royal Anna*, was badly damaged, with many of the crew killed or wounded, among them Tourneur. The ship reached port in Kinsdale, Ireland, where Tourneur was put ashore. He died there of his wounds on February 28, 1626.

Unlike many of the Elizabethan and Jacobean dramatists, Tourneur devoted most of his life to his active military career and relatively little of it to writing for the stage. T. M. Parrott considers him "a poet expressing himself in dramatic form rather than a professional playwright." The morbid splendor of his two surviving plays has attracted much critical interest.

BIBLIOGRAPHICAL REFERENCES: There are various editions of the complete and selected works: *The Plays and Poems of Cyril Tourneur*, edited by J. Churton Collins, 1878; *The Works of Cyril Tourneur*, edited by Allardyce Nicoll, 1930, reprinted 1963; *The Best Plays of Webster and Tourneur*, edited by John Addington Symonds, 1888; and *Masterpieces of the English Drama: Webster and Tourneur,* with an introduction by Ashley H. Thorndike, 1912. See also Henry W. Wells, *Elizabethan and Jacobean Playwrights,* 1939; T. M. Parrott and R. H. Ball, *A Short View of Elizabethan Drama,* 1943; and *Dictionary of National Biography,* Vol. 19. Recent studies are Allardyce Nicoll, "The Revenger's Tragedy and the Virtue of Anonimity," *Essays on Shakespeare and Elizabethan Drama,* Richard Hosley, ed., 1962, and Peter B. Murray, *A Study of Cyril Tourneur,* 1964.

ARNOLD TOYNBEE

Born: London, England
Date: April 14, 1889

Principal Works

MISCELLANEOUS: *Nationality and the War,* 1915; *The New Europe,* 1915; *The Western Question in Greece and Turkey,* 1922; *Greek Historical Thought,* 1924; *Greek Civilization and Character,* 1924; *The World After the Peace Conference,* 1925; *Turkey,* 1926 (with K. P. Kirkwood); *A Journey to China,* 1931; *A Study of History,* 1934–1954; *Christianity and Civilization,* 1940; *Civilization on Trial,* 1948; *Prospects of Western Civilization,* 1949; *The World and the West,* 1953; *An Historian's Approach to Religion,* 1956; *Christianity Among the Religions of the World,* 1957; *East to West; A Journey Round the World,* 1958; *Hellenism, the History of a Civilization,* 1959; Vol. XI of *A Study of History* (with Edward D. Myers), 1959; Vol. XII of *A Study of History,* 1961; *Between Oxus and Jumma,* 1961; *The Present-day Experiment in Western Civilization,* 1962; *Between Niger and Nile,* 1965; *Hannibal's Legacy: The Hannibalic War's Effect on Roman Life,* 2 vols., 1965; *Cities on the Move,* 1970; *Surviving the Future,* 1971.

Among philosophers of history Arnold (Joseph) Toynbee is unique in having made a profound appeal to scholars and general readers alike. His most impressive work to date has been his nine-volume *Study of History,* which has received careful attention from historians and philosophers of history and has afforded exciting reading to thousands who know the work through abridgements.

Toynbee, born in London on April 14, 1889, was educated at Winchester and then at Balliol College, Oxford. His academic record enabled him to be a Scholar at both schools. From 1912 to 1915 he was a fellow and tutor at Balliol. Later in his life, when his scholarly activities had given him distinguished status among commentators on history, he was awarded various honorary degrees: an Hon. D.Litt. from Oxford, Birmingham, and Columbia; a Litt.D. from Cambridge, and a D.C.L. from Princeton.

During World War I Toynbee worked at various governmental jobs, including a period with the British Foreign Office in 1918 as a member of the staff in the political intelligence department. He was a member of the Middle Eastern Section of the British Delegation to the Peace Conference in Paris in 1919.

Having engaged in the practical application of his knowledge of Middle Eastern affairs, Toynbee returned to academic life in his position as Koraes Professor of Byzantine and Modern Greek Language, Literature, and History at London University from 1919 to 1924. Recognition of his increasing competence in his fields brought him the distinction of becoming Director of Studies at the Royal Institute of International Affairs and Research Professor of International History at the University of London. He held these posts on a Sir Daniel Stevenson Foundation grant from 1925 until his retirement in 1955.

In the meantime Toynbee had initiated what developed into an impressive series of publications. In addition to writing such books as *The New Europe, The Western Question in Greece and Turkey,* and *Greek Historical Thought,* Toynbee, as both editor and writer, dealt with current international history in a series of yearbooks entitled *Survey of International Affairs* (1920–1946).

During World War II he was a director of foreign research and press services at the Royal Institute of International Affairs, and from 1943 to 1946 was director of the research department of the British Foreign Office. He was once again a member of the British delegation at the Peace Conference in 1946. Since 1934 he has been an editor of the *British Commonwealth Relations*.

Toynbee's monumental work in *A Study of History* had its beginnings in 1922; engaged in other tasks, he worked on the project intermittently until its completion in 1954, a period of study and writing at the Institute for Advanced Study in Princeton, N.J., having enabled him to complete the final volumes. A frequent visitor to the United States, he makes his permanent home in London.

The distinctive feature of Toynbee's study of history has been his claim that civilizations, not nations, are the determining factors in history; and that the life of a civilization is the story of its challenges and responses to environmental conditions. He has provoked considerable critical attack with his contention that history shows how God's influence works.

BIBLIOGRAPHICAL REFERENCES: There is no authorized biography or full-length critical study. For studies in books and periodicals see Pitirim Sorokin, *Social Philosophies of an Age of Crisis*, 1950; P. W. Martin, *Experiment in Depth: A Study of the Work of Jung, Eliot and Toynbee*, 1955; Ashley Montagu, ed., *Toynbee and History: Critical Essays and Reviews*, 1956; Richard Chase, "Toynbee: The Historian as Artist," *American Scholar*, XVI (1947), 268–282; Granville Hicks, "Arnold Toynbee: The Boldest Historian," *Harper's* CXCIV (1947), 116–124; Owen Lattimore, "Spengler and Toynbee," *Atlantic Monthly*, CLXXXI (1948), 104–105; Kenneth Kirkwood, *Arnold J. Toynbee, Philosopher of History*, 1953 (pamphlet), an address given at Karachi; R. P. Blackmur, "Reflections of Toynbee," *Kenyon Review*, XVII (1955), 357–370; K. W. Thompson, "Toynbee's Approach to History Reviewed," *Ethics*, LXV (1955), 287–303, and "Toynbee and the Theory of International Politics," *Political Science Quarterly*, LXXI (1956), 365–386; Crane Brinton, "Toynbee's City of God," *Virginia Quarterly Review*, XXXII (1956), 361–375; R. Coulborn, "Fact and Fiction in Toynbee's Study of History," *Ethics*, LXVI (1956), 235–249; F. Borkenau, "Toynbee and the Culture Cycle," *Commentary*, XXI (1956), 239–249; G. Barraclough, "Misuses of History," *Nation* CLXXXIII (1956), 392–394; M. A. Fitzsimmons, "Toynbee: Criticism and Judgment," *Commonweal*, LXVI (1957), 43–45; R. P. Mohan, "Arnold Toynbee and His Syncretic Faith," in John K. Ryan, ed., *Twentieth-century Thinkers*, 1965, 213–230; and Bruce Mazlish, "Toynbee," in *The Riddle of History*, 1966, 351–380.

THOMAS TRAHERNE

Born: Herefordshire, England
Date: c. 1637

Died: Teddington, England
Date: October, 1674

PRINCIPAL WORKS

POEMS: *Poems,* c. 1655–1674, first published 1903; *Poems of Felicity,* c. 1655–1674, first published 1910.
MEDITATIONS: *Centuries of Meditations,* c. 1660–1674, first published 1908.
TREATISES: *Roman Forgeries,* 1673; *Christian Ethicks,* 1675; *A Serious and Patheticall Contemplation of the Mercies of God,* 1699.

The seventeenth century meditative religious poet, Thomas Traherne, has acquired literary fame only in the last century, for the poems and the prose reflections, *Centuries of Meditations,* on which his reputation rests, were lost for over two hundred years after his death, reappearing finally at a London bookseller's in 1897. Consequently, little is known about the poet's quiet life. Most of the extant information was recorded by Anthony à Wood, a seventeenth century man of letters, in his *Athenae Oxoniensis,* a collection of brief biographical sketches of all the Oxford graduates he considered in any way noteworthy.

Traherne was born about 1637 in Herefordshire; his father, a shoemaker, came from a once-prominent Welsh family. His Celtic heritage links Traherne with Henry Vaughan, another seventeenth century religious poet whose works reveal a mystical concept of the relationship between man and nature, as well as a soul seeking to return to its original state of innocence when it was one with God.

Both Thomas and his elder brother, Philip, were provided with financial support for a good education, apparently by another Philip Traherne, a wealthy innkeeper of their village, who was probably a relative. Thomas entered Brasenose College, Oxford, in 1652. He was granted the degree of Bachelor of Arts in 1656 and created Master of Arts in 1661, after his ordination to the priesthood in the Church of England in December, 1657. He remained a staunch, if somewhat unorthodox, Anglican throughout his life.

Traherne accepted the position of rector of the parish of Credenhill, near Hereford, soon after his ordination, but, according to the custom of the time, he evidently spent at least part of the years of his tenure there in Oxford, studying for the degree of Bachelor of Divinity, which was granted in 1669, and doing research in the Bodleian Library for his scholarly treatise, *Roman Forgeries.*

It was probably during the time at Credenhill that Traherne wrote many of his meditations glorifying the innocence and wonder of childhood and lamenting the corruption that wealth and the desire for it brought upon man. His own desire was to live so simply that he might recapture the closeness to God that had vanished with his youth. He wrote in one of the meditations: "When I came into the country, and being seated among silent trees, and meads and hills, had all my time in mine own hands, I resolved to spend it all, whatever it cost me, in search of happiness, and to satiate that burning thirst which

1788

Nature had enkindled in me from my youth. In which I was so resolute, that I chose rather to live upon ten pounds a year, and to go in leather clothes, and feed upon bread and water, so that I might have all my time clearly to myself, than to keep many thousands per annum in an estate of life where my time would be devoured in care and labor."

By 1669, Traherne had joined the staff of Sir Orlando Bridgeman, Lord Keeper of the Great Seal under Charles II, as chaplain. When Bridgeman retired to Teddington, a London suburb not far from Hampton Court, in 1672, Traherne accompanied him and remained in service there until his death, at the age of thirty-seven, in 1674.

The sophisticated, witty court near which Traherne spent the last few years of his life was a world completely foreign to his temperament. His intensely introspective meditations on innocence, childhood, and the beauties of nature reveal him as the true contemporary not of those urbane Restoration classicists, Waller, Denham, and Dryden, but of poets like Herbert, Vaughan, Blake, and Wordsworth, fellow seekers after a pure and uncorrupted spiritual state.

BIBLIOGRAPHICAL REFERENCES: There are several excellent modern editions of Traherne's works: *Poems, Centuries, and Thanksgivings,* edited by H. M. Margoliouth, 2 vols., 1958; *Poems, Centuries and Three Thanksgivings,* edited by Anne Ridler, 1966; and *Christian Ethicks,* edited by Carol L. Marks and George Robert Guffey, 1968.

Biographical and critical works include G. I. Wade, *Thomas Traherne,* 1944; G. E. Willett, *Traherne: An Essay,* 1919; and K. W. Salter, *Thomas Traherne: Mystic and Poet,* 1964. See also J. B. Leishman, *The Metaphysical Poets,* 1934; Helen C. White, *The Metaphysical Poets,* 1936; Louis L. Martz, *The Paradise Within: Studies in Vaughan, Traherne, and Milton,* 1964; and Joan Webber, *The Eloquent 'I': Style and Self in Seventeenth-Century Prose,* 1968.

For additional references see Edward E. Samaha, Jr., "Richard Crashaw and Thomas Traherne: A Bibliography, 1938–1966," *Seventeenth Century News,* XXVII, no. iii (1969), Item 3.

B. TRAVEN
Traven Torsvan

Born: Chicago, Illinois (?) *Died:* Mexico City, Mexico
Date: 1900 (?) *Date:* March 27, 1969

Principal Works

NOVELS: *Das Totenschiff,* 1926 (*The Death Ship*); *Der Wobbly,* 1926; *Der Schatz der Sierra Madre,* 1927 (*The Treasure of the Sierra Madre*); *Die Brücke im Dschungel,* 1929 (*The Bridge in the Jungle*); *Die weisse Rose,* 1929 (*The White Rose*); *Der Karren,* 1931 (*The Carreta*); *Sonnenschöpfung,* 1936 (*Sun-Creation*); *Der Marsch ins Reich der Caoba,* 1933 (*March to Caobaland,* 1961); *Die Rebellion der Gehenkten,* 1936 (*The Rebellion of the Hanged*); *Die Troza,* 1936; *Ein General kommt aus dem Dschungel,* 1940 (*The General from the Jungle*); *Macario,* 1949.

SHORT STORIES: *Der Busch,* 1930 (*The Bush*); *The Night Visitor and Other Stories,* 1966.

NONFICTION: *Die Regierung,* 1931 (*Government*).
TRAVEL: *Das Land des Frühlings,* 1928.

Almost every statement about B. Traven, the most famous international literary mystery of the twentieth century, must end with a question mark. In a comment on his life and work, Traven said, "Of an artist or writer, one should never ask an autobiography, because he is bound to lie. . . . If a writer, who he is and what he is, cannot be recognized by his work, either his books are worthless, or he himself is." His readers should look for him, he said, along and between the lines of his works.

When a New York publisher rejected his first two novels on the grounds that they lacked commercial possibilities and a finished style, Traven took them to Germany; they were published, and he became famous. From the beginning, he refused to allow his fascinating life and personality to be exploited for publicity. In 1963, he refused a literary prize from Germany. His agents in Mexico City protected him from most of the numerous letters addressed to him, many from editors all over the world.

Until Hitler banned his books for their radical point of view on the exploitation of the worker, Traven would not allow his work to appear in the United States. Finally, Alfred A. Knopf persuaded him to release the American rights, and five novels have appeared in this country; a classic motion picture was made from *The Treasure of the Sierra Madre.* In his native country (he has stated that he *is* an American), his novels are less appreciated than elsewhere; they have sold millions of copies in thirty languages. In Europe he is considered a major figure in contemporary fiction, and in the judgment of twenty or more nations, *The Death Ship* is one of America's greatest novels.

Sorting among the scattered bits of information about Traven, one can be fairly certain of these "facts": he was born about 1900 in Chicago; his parents were poor Norwegian-Swedish immigrant workers. A life of hard work began when he was seven. Though he was truant much of the time, he read a great many borrowed books. At ten he sailed on a tramp freighter as a cabin boy. The port of Mazatlán was one of his first exposures to Mexico, to which he returned again and again before settling in that tropical region where he spent most of his mature life. But for a decade, he sailed the world under several flags and worked at a great variety of laborer's jobs in Mexico. At some time he probably belonged to the IWW Wobblies. Traven wrote and spoke German, French, Spanish, and English fluently; he also spoke two of the unwritten Indian languages of southeast Mexico.

Traven's sixteen novels are concerned with the common man, laboring on ships and in the jungles of Mexico. His characters speak the slang of the early twentieth century with an immigrant accent. There is much description of landscapes and seascapes, and he has a special interest in depicting strong, courageous women, children, and the personalities of certain animals. The hard-core center of most of his realistic fiction is work. Among his books are sociological studies, documentaries, Mexican travel books, illustrated with his own photographs, and Mexican folk tales. His outlook was that of the self-educated worker—sardonic and ironic, expressed, even in crawling misery, with wit and ribald humor. His novels depict men with a great appetite for life struggling to survive, always within the immediate vicinity of death.

One third of Traven's novels are in the first person; all have a strong autobiographical basis. But whether told in the third person or in the first, his novels aggressively state his radical revolutionary sentiments. He is alienated not only from Western civilization in general but from any formal creed or ideology in particular. In *The Death Ship,* Gerald Gales, who reappears in several of the novels, speaks of national and international bureaucracy as the irreconcilable enemy of individual freedom. Though one may be tempted, because of Traven's radical thinking and adventurous life, to associate him with Jack London, he is more a philosophical revolutionary in the tradition of Thoreau, whose love of privacy he shared. Much of his work resembles American proletarian fiction, although most of it was written several years before novels in that genre began to appear. And because of the attitude toward life that he and his characters demonstrate in action and speech, Traven may be regarded as one of the finest of the tough-guy novelists.

BIBLIOGRAPHICAL REFERENCES: There are a number of articles dealing with questions about Traven's life. See Hubert Jannach, "The B. Traven Mystery," *Books Abroad,* XXXV (Winter, 1961), 28–29; *ibid.,* "B. Traven—An American or German Author," *German Quarterly,* XXXVI (November, 1963); R. Recknagel, "B. Traven: Beiträge zur Biographie," 1966; "The Great Traven Mystery," *New Yorker,* XLIII (July 22, 1967), 82+; and Judy Stone, "The Mystery of B. Traven," *Ramparts,* VI (1967), 31–49+.

The B. Traven feature in the Winter, 1963, issue of *The Texas Quarterly,* edited by C. H. Miller and R. E. Pujan, contains the first biographical notes and tell-tale excerpts from his novels to be authorized by Traven himself for publication in the United States. See also John Fraser, "Splendour in the Darkness: B. Traven's *The Death Ship,*" *Dalhousie Review,* XLIV (1964), 35–43; and C. H. Miller, "B.

Traven, Pure Proletarian Writer," *Proletarian Writers of the Thirties,* edited by David Madden, 1968. Miller's introduction to *The Night Visitor and Other Stories* and the bibliography of Traven's work concluding it are also helpful.

For additional material see E. R. Hagemann, "A Checklist of the Work of B. Traven and the Critical Estimates and Bibliographical Essays on Him, Together with a Brief Biography," *Papers of the Bibliographical Society of America,* LIII, 1 (1959), 37–67.

GEORGE MACAULAY TREVELYAN

Born: Stratford-on-Avon, England
Date: February 16, 1876

Died: Cambridge, England
Date: July 21, 1962

Principal Works

HISTORY: *England in the Age of Wycliffe*, 1899; *England Under the Stuarts*, 1904; *Garibaldi's Defence of the Roman Republic*, 1907; *Garibaldi and the Thousand*, 1909; *Garibaldi and the Making of Italy*, 1911; *History of England*, 1926, 1937, 3rd ed. 1945; *England Under Queen Anne*, 3 vols., 1930, 1932, 1934; *English Social History*, 1944; *An Autobiography and Other Essays* 1949.

George Macaulay Trevelyan, the distinguished historian, was the third son of Sir George Otto Trevelyan, himself a historian and author and editor of the *Life and Letters* of his uncle, Lord Macaulay. The younger Trevelyan was born at Stratford-on-Avon, England, on February 16, 1876. His brief autobiography tells us some of the chief events of his life. From the beginning his imagination was stirred by history, and his political bias was Liberal. It is significant that throughout his life he read poetry with pleasure. He speaks of "the poetry of history"—the idea that here on this ground other persons once walked.

Trevelyan was educated at Harrow and at Trinity College, Cambridge, and though he took up an academic career, writing and lecturing and producing his first book, *England in the Age of Wycliffe,* he soon felt that he must leave the college to write independent of scholastic criticism, able as he was to finance such a break. He contracted to write *England Under the Stuarts* as one book in a multi-volume history by various authors. He married, and soon began a three-volume study of Garibaldi. Other books followed, especially his overall survey, the *History of England.*

With these considerable achievements behind him, he then returned to the academy, accepting the Regius Professorship of Modern History at Cambridge. He was awarded the Order of Merit in 1930. Later he became Master of Trinity College.

Meanwhile, other books appeared; especially noteworthy is the short work, *The English Revolution, 1688–89.* Afterward came the large study *England Under Queen Anne.* Finally, there was one more great achievement, the *English Social History: A Survey of Six Centuries.* He wrote two pleasant shorter books, and was deeply committed to the work of the novelist and poet George Meredith. To the autobiography he added lectures and essays on history, as well as expressions of his love of literature. Trevelyan died in 1962.

BIBLIOGRAPHICAL REFERENCES: There is relatively little material available. See John H. Plumb's pamphlet, *G. M. Trevelyan,* 1951; H. R. Winkler, "George Macaulay Trevelyan," *Some Twentieth Century Historians,* edited by Samuel W. Halperin, 1961, 31-55; Sir George Norman Clark, "George Macaulay Trevelyan, 1876-1962," *British Academy, London, Proceedings,* XLIX (1963), 375-386; and "George Macaulay Trevelyan," *Royal Society of London, Biographical Memoirs of Fellows of the Royal Society,* 1963, 315-321. There are also biographical details in

Basil Willey, *Cambridge and Other Memories,* 1968, and S. C. Roberts, *Adventures with Authors,* 1966.

ANTHONY TROLLOPE

Born: London, England
Date: April 24, 1815

Died: Harting, England
Date: December 6, 1882

Principal Works

THE CHRONICLES OF BARSETSHIRE: *The Warden*, 1855; *Barchester Towers*, 1857; *Doctor Thorne*, 1858; *Framley Parsonage*, 1861; *The Small House at Allington*, 1864; *The Last Chronicle of Barset*, 1867.

POLITICAL NOVELS: *Can You Forgive Her?*, 1864; *Phineas Finn, the Irish Member*, 1869; *The Eustace Diamonds*, 1873; *Phineas Redux*, 1874; *The Prime Minister*, 1876; *The Duke's Children*, 1880.

IRISH NOVELS: *The Macdermots of Ballycloran*, 1847; *The Kellys and the O'Kellys*, 1848; *Castle Richmond*, 1860; *The Landleaguers*, 1883.

NOVELS OF SOCIETY: *The Bertrams*, 1859; *Orley Farm*, 1862; *Rachel Ray*, 1863; *The Belton Estate*, 1866; *He Knew He Was Right*, 1869; *The Vicar of Bullhampton*, 1870; *The Way We Live Now*, 1875; *Is He Popenjoy?*, 1878; *Dr. Wortle's School*, 1881.

SHORT STORIES: *Tales of All Countries*, 1861, 1863; *Lotta Schmidt and Other Stories*, 1867; *An Editor's Tales*, 1870; *Why Frau Frohmann Raised Her Prices and Other Stories*, 1882.

MEMOIRS: *Autobiography*, 1883.

Anthony Trollope's father, Thomas Anthony Trollope, was an eccentric barrister who lost his wealth in wild speculations; his mother, Frances Trollope, kept the family together by fleeing to Belgium to escape creditors and by writing a total of 114 volumes, mostly novels. Her best-known work today is *Domestic Manners of the Americans* (1832), a caustic and grossly exaggerated account of the America she observed on an unsuccessful trip to Cincinnati in 1823 to set up a great bazaar. Since his older brother, Thomas Adolphus, was also a writer, Anthony was following a well-established family tradition.

According to his posthumous *Autobiography*, Trollope was born in London on April 24, 1815; he grew into an ungainly, oafish, and unpopular boy who spent miserable and friendless years at Harrow and Winchester, where he learned nothing. When he was nineteen, he sought work in London, first as a clerk and then as a civil servant with the Post Office. He hated his work and his lonely life in the city, and seven years later accepted with relief an appointment as traveling postal inspector in Ireland (1841–1859). Later his duties carried him on brief trips to all the continents of the world. In Ireland, Trollope's pleasant experiences with genial country people and an exhilarating landscape developed his confidence and optimism.

He married Rose Haseltine and at the age of thirty began to write, his first novels being inspired by the ruins of an Irish mansion. His early works were failures, but he persevered under difficult conditions until his fourth book, *The Warden*, found a responsive audience in 1855. This "scene from clerical life," its setting the episcopal establishment of Barchester, presents a detailed account of the day to day events of provincial life in Victorian England. Its sequel, *Barchester Towers*, with its incorrigible comic character, Bertie, was so successful that it was followed by four other novels on the same theme, the whole group constituting the perennially popular "Chronicles of Barsetshire." During this same period, Trollope also wrote other novels, the best of which are *The Three Clerks* (1858), an autobiographical account of the English civil service, and *Orley Farm*, a work which combines a plot involving a forged will with genre pictures of family life in the country.

In 1867, now confident of his powers, Trollope resigned from the Post Office and became interested in politics. He stood as Liberal candidate for Parliament in 1868 but was defeated. Nevertheless, he cut an impressive bearded figure, chatting in the London literary clubs and riding to the hounds in Southern England. All these interests are faithfully embodied in a series sometimes called the "Parliamentary Novels," among them *Phineas Finn, Phineas Redux, The Prime Minister,* and *The Duke's Children*. But Trollope could not compete with Disraeli in this field (just as he was unable to compete with Dickens in depicting city life among the lower and middle classes), and despite their appealing portraits of political life and character, his Parliamentary series was not widely read.

Trollope continued to turn out novel after novel—social manners, mild satires, histories, romances, travelogues, and even, in *The Fixed Period* (1882), a futuristic work about life in 1980. A curiously interesting work is the story of an erring woman, in *Can You Forgive Her?*—a novel as close as he ever came to modern realism. Despite the fact that he wrote some sixty novels in all, it cannot be said of Trollope that he made the world his stage. He surveys generally a rather narrow scene, usually rural and provincial, peopled by mild villains and tame heroes. No powerful philosophical or social conviction charges his writing, and no keen analysis of human psychology opens the inner beings of his characters. "A novel," he said, "should give a picture of common life enlivened by humor and sweetened by pathos." In this endeavor Trollope succeeded so completely that Henry James said of him, "His great, his inestimable merit was a complete appreciation of the usual." He died of paralysis at Harting, Sussex, on December 6, 1882.

Trollope's posthumously published *Autobiography* disappointed his admirers and dampened his reputation, for he candidly confessed (as Arnold Bennett was to do a half-century later) that he wrote 250 words per minute, completing eight to sixteen pages a day. He is said to have earned some £70,000 from his writings. Despite the fact that he was not an inspired writer, he amused a whole generation with pleasant tales, the best of which have considerable value as sociological insights into a mellow and tranquil age now forever past.

BIBLIOGRAPHICAL REFERENCES: Although there is no complete edition of Trollope, several publishing houses have issued sets of selected groups of novels such as the Barsetshire Chronicles and the political series and his most representative titles are now available in Everyman's Library and the World's Classics. Also in progress is "The Oxford Trollope," edited by Michael Sadleir and Frederick Page. Useful one volume editions of selections are *The Trollope Reader,* edited by Esther C. Dunn and Marion E. Dodd, 1947; and *The Bedside Barsetshire,* edited by L. O. Tingay, 1951. Also available are a new edition of the *Autobiography* and *The Letters of Anthony Trollope,* 1951, both edited by Bradford A. Booth.

The standard critical biography is Michael Sadleir, *Anthony Trollope, A Commentary,* 1927 (rev. ed., 1945). Of considerable importance also is Lucy P. Stebbins and Richard P. Stebbins, *The Trollopes: The Chronicle of a Writing Family,* 1945. For additional biography and criticism see T. H. S. Escott, *Anthony Trollope: His Works, Associates, and Literary Originals,* 1913; Hugh Walpole, *Anthony Trollope,* English Men of Letters Series, 1928; Beatrice C. Brown, *Anthony Trollope,* 1950; and A. O. J. Cockshut, *Anthony Trollope: A Critical Study,* 1955. More specialized studies include John T. Wildman, *Anthony Trollope's England,* 1940; W. G. and J. T. Gerould, *A Guide to Trollope,* 1948; Marcie Muir, *Anthony Trollope in Australia,* 1949; and Donald Smalley, ed., *Trollope: The Critical Heritage,* 1969.

For briefer studies see also Henry James, *Partial Portraits,* 1888; James Bryce, *Studies in Contemporary Biography,* 1903; Morris E. Speare, *The Political Novel,* 1923; Lord David Cecil, *Early Victorian Novelists,* 1935; T. A. Sherman, "The Financial Motive in the Barchester Novels," *College English,* IX (1948), 413–418; F. E. Robins, "Chronology and History in Trollope's Barset and Parliamentary Novels," *Nineteenth Century Fiction,* V (1951), 303–316; Robert M. Adams, "*Orley Farm* and Real Fiction," *ibid.,* VII (1953), 27–41; Edd W. Parks, "Trollope and the Defense of Exegesis," *ibid.,* VII (1953), 265–271; and William Coyle, "Trollope as Social Anthropologist," *College English,* XVII (1956), 392–397. Michael Sadleir has compiled *Trollope, A Bibliography,* 1928.

JOHN TOWNSEND TROWBRIDGE

Born: Ogden Township, New York
Date: September 18, 1827

Died: Arlington, Massachusetts
Date: February 12, 1916

Principal Works

novels: *Neighbor Jackwood*, 1856; *Cudjo's Cave*, 1864; *Coupon Bonds*, 1871.
poems: *The Vagabonds and Other Poems*, 1869.

John Townsend Trowbridge was an American novelist who wrote for and found his greatest popularity with teen-age boys, and he himself considered his forty-odd novels as little more than hack work. He believed his only serious and great literary efforts were the series of volumes of didactic narrative poetry which later generations have forgotten, as they have almost forgotten his novels.

Trowbridge was born on a farm in Ogden Township, New York, September 18, 1827, and spent his childhood there. As he grew up, bad eyesight caused him difficulty in school. Because of his handicap, he was largely self-taught, although he acquired a great deal of learning, including a knowledge of French, Latin, and Greek. After completing a year at the academy in Lockport, New York, Trowbridge traveled to the Middle West. He taught school in Illinois in 1845, then moved back to Lockport to teach school there for a year. In 1847 he went to New York City and began to make a reputation for himself as a writer, contributing his work principally to the *Dollar Magazine*.

During the period from 1849 to 1860, Trowbridge edited periodicals and wrote for the *Atlantic Monthly*, the *Youth's Companion*, and *Our Young Folks*. His interest in writing for boys and his success in pleasing their tastes won for Trowbridge the editorship of *Our Young Folks*, a position he held from 1860 to 1873. He made his own a type of adventure fiction popular with adolescent boys and of interest to some adults. *Cudjo's Cave* is an excellent example of the type.

In 1860 Trowbridge married Cornelia Warren, who died four years later, leaving two children. The following year Trowbridge moved his family to Arlington, Massachusetts, near Boston. His second marriage was to Sarah Newton, of Arlington, in 1873. Among Trowbridge's friends were such diverse literary personalities as Oliver Wendell Holmes, Henry Wadsworth Longfellow, and Walt Whitman. He died at Arlington on February 12, 1916.

bibliographical references: The chief source of biographical data is Trowbridge's *My Own Story*, 1903. See also Caroline Ticknor, *Glimpses of Authors*, 1922. The brief sketch in the *Dictionary of National Biography* is by George H. Genzer. See further Edmund Wilson, "Northerners in the South: Frederick L. Olmsted, John T. Trowbridge," in *Patriotic Gore: Studies in the Literature of the American Civil War*, 1962, 219–238.

IVAN TURGENEV

Born: Orel, Russia
Date: October 28, 1818

Died: Paris, France
Date: September 8, 1883

Principal Works

NOVELS: *Rudin*, 1856; *Dvoryanskoe gnezdo*, 1858 (*A House of Gentlefolk*); *Nakanune*, 1860 (*On the Eve*); *Ottsy i deti*, 1862 (*Fathers and Sons*); *Dym*, 1867 (*Smoke*); *Veshniye vody*, 1871 (*Spring Torrents*); *Nov'*, 1877 (*Virgin Soil*).

SHORT STORIES: *Zapiski okhotnika*, 1852 (*A Sportsman's Sketches*).

PLAYS: *Gde tonko tam i rviotsya*, 1847 (*The Weakest Link*); *Nakhlebnik*, 1848 (*The Parasite*); *Kholostyak*, 1849 (*The Bachelor*); *Provintzialka*, 1850 (*The Provincial Lady*); *Mesyats v derevne*, 1850 (*A Month in the Country*).

Ivan Sergeyevich Turgenev, the first of the great Russian novelists to be read widely in Europe, was born at Orel, Russia, on October 28, 1818. He was the second of three sons born to his unhappily married parents: ugly, harsh, and tyrannical Varvara Petrovna Lutovinov, who had inherited large estates at twenty-six after an unhappy childhood, and cold, handsome, philandering Sergey Nikolayeyvich Turgenev, an impecunious young cavalry officer who had married this woman six years his senior only for her money. The child, who was to be known as the most European of the great Russian masters, first saw Europe at the age of four with his family and its entourage. Turgenev spent his earliest years in the elegance of the family mansion on the Spasskoye estate. When the family moved to their Moscow house in 1827, Turgenev began to prepare for the entrance examinations to Moscow University. By the time he entered, in 1834, he had fallen under the influence of Hegel and Schiller. In the same year, however, Colonel Turgenev transferred his son to St. Petersburg University. Then, with his wife away in Italy, the aloof, handsome colonel died.

Turgenev had written since childhood, and at St. Petersburg he continued his attempts, seeing two of his poems published a year after his graduation in 1837. In 1838 he went to Berlin to study intensively for a career as a teacher of literature, returning to St. Petersburg in 1841 to prepare for his M.A. examinations. Under the impact of an unhappy love affair, however, he failed to take his degree. The poem *Parasha* in 1843 signaled Turgenev's escape from romanticism and was praised by critics for its sensitive simplicity. When he resigned shortly thereafter from the civil service job he had taken in 1842, his tyrannical mother sharply reduced his allowance, and from that time on their relationship steadily became more acrimonious. Just then he met Madame Pauline Viardot, the ugly, magnetic opera singer to whom he was to be devoted for the rest of his life, alternately her enchanted and despairing admirer. A successful realistic sketch in *The Contemporary Review* led to others in a similar vein. Then, in February, 1847, he left Russia with Pauline Viardot and her husband despite Madame Turgenev's frantic efforts to prevent him. He left the Viardots at Berlin, and in Paris, Brussels, and Lyons he continued to work on what were to be *A*

Sportsman's Sketches. Taking up residence at Courtavenel, the Viardots' summer home, in the summer of 1848, he stayed into 1849. By the summer of 1850, when he returned home because of his mother's deteriorating health, he had also composed many poems and more than half a dozen plays. For the most part these were comedies conspicuous for their dialogue. Although some were successfully staged, Turgenev was always extremely critical of them.

His mother's death in November, 1850, made him a rich man. In March, 1852, however, he found himself under arrest. A laudatory article upon Gogol shortly after his death, combined with the suspicion created by his sketches as they appeared, caused Turgenev's arrest by the Tsar's political police. He was confined in jail for a month and then placed under house arrest at Spasskoye for a year and a half. *A Sportsman's Sketches,* collected in book form in August, 1852, was an immediate and resounding success. The realistic treatment of Russian life, particularly the plight of the peasants, was so influential that it helped bring about the emancipation of the serfs nine years later. Regaining his freedom, Turgenev worked on his first novel during 1855. Published in *The Contemporary Review* in January and February of 1856, *Rudin* was the story of a Utopian who had eloquence, honesty, faith, and enthusiasm, but who was not strong enough to achieve real love or political usefulness.

He dropped his literary work for a time in 1856 to return to Pauline Viardot in France, but her departure with another man left him desolate, and illness completed his misery. His return to Russia in 1858 was the beginning of three years of fruitful work.

In January *The Contemporary Review* published *A House of Gentlefolk,* into which Turgenev had written many of his emotions arising out of his relationships with Pauline Viardot and his own family. This melancholy novel of infidelity, worldliness, and wasted lives was a resounding success. Now the most celebrated of Russian writers, he immediately set to work, this time in Vichy, on a novel based on a manuscript given him by a young soldier rightly convinced that he would not survive the Crimean War to complete it. It became *On the Eve,* appearing in *The Russian Herald* in January and February, 1860. A depiction on one level merely of a love affair, on another level it was a foreshadowing of the Russia to come, when in the 1860's so many of the nation's youth were to band together against Tsarist autocracy. Acrimonious political controversies, quarrels with Goncharov and Tolstoy, and estrangement from Madame Viardot saddened Turgenev, but he completed *Fathers and Sons,* which was published in March, 1862, in *The Russian Monthly.* This classic novel presented the age-old conflict between generations, but it was also localized in provincial Russia and set in a critical period. And in Bazaroff (often Bazarov), Turgenev created one of the first of the nihilists, men who wanted to sweep away the old and apply the tenets and methods of science to politics and other human affairs. The novel incensed both young and old, extremists and reactionaries. Turgenev, surprised and hurt, was attacked from all sides.

Except for brief visits home, the years between 1863 and 1871 were spent in Baden-Baden, some of them with the Viardot family. During this period he joined the admiring group which included Flaubert and Goncourt. In March, 1867, he published another novel, *Smoke,* in *The Russian Herald.* This love story with its portrayal of aristocrats and young revolutionaries, like *Fathers and Sons,* pleased no one. Sympathizing with neither, castigating political persons and follies, he became in his turn a target for criticism from all quarters. During these years he continued his prolific output of short stories. The best of them, such as "A Lear of the Steppes" and "First Love," bore the same hallmarks of his art as did his novels: the psychological insight, the melancholy realism, the delicate nuances, the subtle creation of mood, and the sensitive pastel landscapes. After spending part of 1870 and 1871 in England and Scotland, he published the short, non-political novel, *Spring Torrents,* in January, 1871, in *The European Herald.* It was a great success and very soon reprinted. In 1874 he moved into a suite of rooms in the house of the Viardots, where Henry James visited him in 1875.

Turgenev spent six years planning and writing his last novel, *Virgin Soil,* published in the January and February issues of *The European Herald* in 1877. This novel, presenting to the reader a wide variety of the types who were to become revolutionaries, portrayed the aristocratic class which did not perceive itself in the process of dissolution; it also predicted with a high degree of accuracy the course that future events were to take in the writer's unhappy country. Although the novel was a best seller in France, England, and the United States, it was a failure in Russia, and Turgenev resolved to renounce fiction. In 1878, however, he began composing his *Poems in Prose,* reflections upon politics, philosophy, and his own intimate concerns. Though he was still a pessimistic agnostic, some of these works showed a lightening and a heartening at examples in man and nature of courage and defiance of death.

Turgenev's brief return to Russia in 1879 was a triumph in which honors and acclaim greeted him, and he was hailed as a pioneer and master. His academic honors conferred in Russia were soon matched by great universities in France and England. By 1882, however, when he had returned to the Viardot household, his health had begun to decline rapidly. Although he was told that he was suffering from angina pectoris, it was actually cancer of the spinal cord which confined him to his bed. In September he had virtually abandoned hope, but he lived on through a year of torment, dying quietly in Paris on September 8, 1883. His funeral in St. Petersburg, attended by delegations from 180 different organizations, was an occasion of national mourning, an acknowledgment of the passing of one of the great masters of Russian literature.

BIBLIOGRAPHICAL REFERENCES: The standard edition of Turgenev's fiction in English is *The Novels of Ivan Turgenev,* translated by Constance Garnett, 17 vols., 1919–1923. Another edition of the *Works* was translated by Isabel F. Hapgood, 7 vols., 1916. M. S. Mandell translated *The Plays of Ivan Turgenev,* 1924. Constance Garnett also translated *Three Plays,* 1934. There are also recent editions of the novels in translations by various hands. A good selected edition is *The Borzoi Turgenev,* translated by Harry Stevens, with a foreword by Serge Koussevitsky and an introduction by Avrahm Yarmolinsky, 1950. *Fathers and Sons* has been published in a Modern Library edition, translated by Constance Garnett and with an introduction by Herbert J. Muller. The best edition of *A Sportsman's Notebook* is that by Charles and Natasha Hepburn, 1950.

There are two standard biographies in English: Avrahm Yarmolinsky, *Turgenev, the Man, His Art, and His Age*, 1926 (reprinted 1961); and David Magarshack, *Turgenev: A Life*, 1954. Critical studies include Edward Garnett, *Turgenev*, with an introduction by Joseph Conrad, 1924; Harry Hershkowitz, *Democratic Ideas in Turgenev's Works*, 1932; and R. A. Gettmann, *Turgenev in England and America*, 1941, with a bibliography. Studies in Russian include those by V. I. Pokrovsky, 1905; E. A. Solovyev, 1922; E. K. Semenov, 1930; and N. O. Antsiferov, 1947; in French, by E. Haumont, 1906; and André Maurois, 1931. Brief critical essays include Janko Lavrin, in *Russian Writers—Their Lives and Literature*, 1954; Irving Howe, "Turgenev: The Politics of Hesitation," in *The Political Novel*, 1957; Henry James, "Ivan Turgenev," *Atlantic Monthly*, LIII (1884), 42–55; Charles Morgan, "Turgenev's Treatment of a Love Story," *Royal Society of London: Essays by Divers Hands*, XXV (1950), 102–119; and Edmund Wilson, "Turgenev and the Life-Giving Drop," *New Yorker*, XXXIII (Oct. 19, 1957), 150–200.

FREDERICK JACKSON TURNER

Born: Portage, Wisconsin
Date: November 14, 1861

Died: Pasadena, California
Date: March 14, 1932

Principal Works

HISTORY: *The Frontier in American History*, 1920; *The Significance of Sections in American History*, 1932.

As a boy, Frederick Jackson Turner attended local schools at Portage, Wisconsin, where his father was a journalist, political figure, and something of a local historian. As a young man he attended the University of Wisconsin, where Professor William Francis Allen had an influence on him. He received his A.B. degree from the University of Wisconsin in 1884. After a few years of interest in journalism and elocution, Turner returned to historical studies, taking an M.A. at Wisconsin in 1888. He began working on manuscripts at the Wisconsin State Historical Society, and from that work came his doctoral dissertation, "The Character and Influence of the Indian Trade in Wisconsin," accepted at The Johns Hopkins University for the Ph.D. in 1890. Turner was a member of the history staff at his alma mater, Wisconsin, from 1889 to 1910, although he had opportunities during that time to move to posts at other universities. He became a significant figure in the study of American history through a paper presented in 1893 to the American Historical Society, when it met at the World's Fair in Chicago. In this famous paper he suggested that the frontier was the factor that made American history unique and that the closing of the frontier in 1890 marked a distinct change in the course of American history and culture.

Turner's work as a historian led to his receiving a number of honorary degrees: an LL.D. from the University of Illinois, 1908; a Litt.D. from Harvard University, 1909; a Ph.D. from Royal Frederick University, Christiania, 1911; and a Litt.D. from the University of Wisconsin in 1921.

In 1909–1910 Professor Turner became president of the American Historical Association. In 1910 he left Wisconsin to accept a professorship at Harvard University, where he taught and worked on his research until his retirement in 1924. His essays, including "The Significance of the Frontier," were published in the volume entitled *The Frontier in American History*, in 1920. Another group of essays appeared as *The Significance of Sections in American History*, in 1932. For the latter volume the author was awarded a Pulitzer Prize shortly after his death.

Following his retirement from Harvard, Turner lived for a time in Wisconsin, but later moved to California, where he became a research associate at the Huntington Library, having his residence at Pasadena. Although his theory of the effect of the frontier is no longer so highly regarded, it had, in its time, an important influence on American historical studies.

BIBLIOGRAPHICAL REFERENCES: Works published after Turner's death include *The United States, 1830–1850*, edited by Avery Craven, 1934, and *Frederick Jackson Turner's Legacy: Unpublished Writings in American History*, edited by Wilbur R.

Jacobs, 1965. Valuable biographical materials are to be found in *Dear Lady: The Letters of Frederick Jackson Turner and Alice Forbes Perkins Hooper, 1910–1932*, edited by R. A. Billington, 1971, and *The Historical World of Frederick Jackson Turner with Selections from His Correspondence*, edited by Jacobs, 1968.

For critical commentary see *Wisconsin Witness to Frederick Jackson Turner: A Collection of Essays on the Historian and the Thesis*, 1949, reprinted 1961; Wilbur R. Jacobs, *Turner, Bolton and Webb, Three Historians of the American Frontier*, 1965; *The Turner Thesis*, edited by G. R. Taylor, 1956; Lee Benson, *Turner and Beard, American Historical Writing Reconsidered*, 1960; and Richard Hofstadter and Seymour Lipset, editors, *Turner and the Sociology of the Frontier*, 1968.

Also of interest are Ray A. Billington, *America's Frontier Heritage*, 1966; Richard Hofstadter, *Progressive Historians*, 1968; and *Pastmasters*, edited by Marcus Cunliffe and Robin W. Winks, 1969.

AMOS TUTUOLA

Born: Abeokuta, Nigeria
Date: 1920

Principal Works

NOVELS: *The Palm-Wine Drinkard and His Dead Palm-Wine Tapster in the Dead's Town,* 1952; *My Life in the Bush of Ghosts,* 1954; *Simbi and the Satyr of the Dark Jungle,* 1955; *The Brave African Huntress,* 1958; *The Feather Woman of the Jungle,* 1962; *Ajaiyi and His Inherited Poverty,* 1967.

Amos Tutuola is a Black African writer born in Nigeria in 1920, the son of Charles and Esther Tutuola. After attending various schools in Nigeria he joined the West African Air Corps (a branch of the Royal Air Force) as a coppersmith, serving in his own country from 1943 to 1945. He began writing after the war and his first novel, *The Palm-Wine Drinkard and His Dead Palm-Wine Tapster in the Dead's Town,* appeared in 1952.

The same influences and conditions that have produced other African Negro writers since World War II have operated upon Tutuola: experiences during the conflict which required a working knowledge of English and prompted a desire to experiment with it; the great upsurge of nationalism that stirred all Africa following the war; and the accompanying need for national and personal self-expression. The first of these new writers came from South Africa, French Africa, and the West Indies. They were all highly literate, effectively demolished the old stereotypes applied to "native writers," and came to be considered a distinct literary movement. Tutuola was the first of the new writers in Nigeria, and among Nigerians he remains a unique talent. Unlike the other new African authors, he has no great literacy in English. His abstract narratives are a series of continuous and uninhibited experiments with the language. Structurally the tales are quite simple: they embody a number of consecutive adventures encountered during a quest, and take place in the mysterious world of Bush country. They are stories of magic, and are filled with elements of transformation, dream, the supernatural and the unknown. To at least some extent they are a recasting of Yoruba myths and folklore, and they are presented in a highly original form of semi-English that carries an odd authority with it. In their blending of the normal and the impossible they are strongly reminiscent of surrealism. It has been suggested that apart from his unique approach to language and the obvious anthropological significance of his work, the deeper value of Tutuola's writing may be its demonstration of the underlying oneness that permeates all human folklore.

In addition to his novels, Tutuola has written many short stories for radio. He is founder of the Mbari Club, an organization for Nigerian writers.

BIBLIOGRAPHICAL REFERENCES: The most detailed study is Harold R. Collins, *Amos Tutuola,* 1969. See also G. Moore, *Seven African Writers,* 1962; Margaret Laurence, *Long Drums and Cannons: Nigerian Dramatists and Novelists, 1952–1966,* 1968; Harold R. Collins, "The Ghost Novels of Amos Tutuola," *Critique,* IV (Autumn–

Winter, 1960–1961); and Bernth Lindfors, "Amos Tutuola's *The Palm-Wine Drinkard* and Oral Tradition," *Critique,* XI (1969), 42–50.

MARK TWAIN
Samuel Langhorne Clemens

Born: Florida, Missouri
Date: November 30, 1835

Died: Redding, Connecticut
Date: April 21, 1910

Principal Works

NOVELS: *The Gilded Age,* 1873 (with Charles Dudley Warner); *The Adventures of Tom Sawyer,* 1876; *The Prince and the Pauper,* 1882; *The Adventures of Huckleberry Finn,* 1884; *A Connecticut Yankee at King Arthur's Court,* 1889; *The American Claimant,* 1892; *Tom Sawyer Abroad,* 1894; *The Tragedy of Pudd'nhead Wilson,* 1894; *Personal Recollections of Joan of Arc,* 1896.

SHORT STORIES: *The Celebrated Jumping Frog of Calaveras County and Other Sketches,* 1867; *Mark Twain's Sketches: New and Old,* 1875; *The Stolen White Elephant,* 1882; *The £1,000,000 Bank-Note,* 1893; *The Man That Corrupted Hadleyburg,* 1900; *A Double Barrelled Detective Story,* 1902; *The $30,000 Bequest,* 1906; *A Horse's Tale,* 1907; *The Mysterious Stranger,* 1916.

REMINISCENCES AND AUTOBIOGRAPHY: *Roughing It,* 1872; *Life on the Mississippi,* 1883; *Mark Twain's Autobiography,* 1924 (2 vols.).

TRAVEL SKETCHES AND IMPRESSIONS: *The Innocents Abroad,* 1869; *A Tramp Abroad,* 1880; *Following the Equator,* 1897.

ESSAYS AND HUMOROUS MISCELLANIES: *How to Tell a Story and Other Essays,* 1897; *My Debut as a Literary Person,* 1903; *Extracts from Adam's Diary,* 1904; *King Leopold's Soliloquy,* 1905; *What is Man?* 1906; *Eve's Diary,* 1906; *Christian Science,* 1907; *Is Shakespeare Dead?* 1909; *Extract from Captain Stormfield's Visit to Heaven,* 1909.

"Mark Twain" was the pen name of Samuel L(anghorne) Clemens, who was born in Florida, Missouri, on November 30, 1835. His father was a dreamy Virginia lawyer and experimenter who, in drifting westward in search of wealth through land speculation, married in Kentucky and settled finally in 1839 in Hannibal, Missouri. In this community, on the Mississippi River between Quincy and St. Louis, the boy grew up amid the scenery and in the atmosphere portrayed in *Tom Sawyer* and *Huckleberry Finn*. At twelve, following his father's death, Sam left school to become a printer; for ten years he set type as a roving journeyman as far east as New York City. In 1857 his plans to visit South America ended when Horace Bixby undertook to teach him to be a steamboat pilot. When the Civil War closed down navigation, Sam soldiered a few months with a Confederate volunteer company. With his brother Orion he went to Nevada as a clerk and then drifted into silver mining and journalism. In 1862 he adopted his pen name, a river term meaning "two fathoms deep." Fame came in 1865 with "The Jumping Frog of Calaveras County," a tall tale. Printed lectures about a journey to the Sandwich—now Hawaiian —Islands increased his popularity, and *Innocents Abroad,* a hilarious book of fun-making at the expense of gawking American travelers in the Holy Land and in Italian art centers, solidified his position as America's leading humorist. Following his marriage in 1870 to Olivia Langdon, he settled in Hartford, Connecticut. Thereafter he alternated between periods of writing and lecturing in America and Europe. Ill-advised investments in a publishing firm and in the development of a mechanical typesetting machine—evidence of a lifelong dream of becoming a millionaire by a lucky turn of the wheel of chance—reduced him to bankruptcy in 1894, but in four years these debts were paid. A native vein of bitterness and pessimism deepened when his wife and two of their three daughters died; some of his last writings, at his wish, were issued several years after his death at his home in Redding, Connecticut, on April 21, 1910.

A humorist pokes fun at human shortcomings: Twain does so by exaggerating instances of gullibility, meanness, inexpertness, and unwise romanticism. His chief characters speak for him; the frontier humor tradition, which he inherited and which he carried to its greatest artistic successes, abetted his alternating moods of boylike playfulness and redheaded anger. His materials, though originating in anecdotes, wisecracks, and personal experience, entered like mosaics into large contexts and pictured—rather than explained in traditional essay form as did Hawthorne and Melville—the problems of his generation. Hidden behind the account of his "slothful, valueless, heedless career" in Nevada in *Roughing It* is a narrative of pioneers' "buffeting and hard striving" to establish civilization in an outpost. *The Gilded Age*, whose love story was written by Charles Dudley Warner, gave its name to, even as it half praised and half scowled on, an era of political and business dishonesty. *Tom Sawyer*, seemingly about a boy's high spirits, is a study of personal conscience set against a milieu characterized by "glaring insincerity." *Huckleberry Finn*, a first-person narrative in Missouri dialect, recounts a nature-loving boy's rebellion against an institution-ridden "sivilization" containing slavery, feuds, and fraud. *A Connecticut Yankee* flays the concept of the divine right of kings who enslave the common people and withhold from them the technological advances by which their lot might be improved; the masses of men, Twain said, can always produce "the material in abundance whereby to govern itself." A priest-led political league which betrayed "Patriotism embodied, concreted, made flesh" in the Maid of Orleans is excoriated in Twain's one biographical-historical novel, *Joan of Arc*. The posthumously published *The Mysterious Stranger* brings Satan in human form among Austrian villagers to ridicule religious and social concepts based upon an alleged "moral sense."

Twain's books reflect his view of man as an almost helpless and therefore comic free agent in a still incompletely formed society uncertain of its direction. Civilization seemed a vulgar parade of hypocrisy, scheming pretense, incompetence, bungling, pork-barrel politics, and boodlery. Yet Twain was not a thinker, not a philosopher as ordinarily fiction writers strove to be or to represent themselves. He solved no problems in his stories, as Howells tried to do; rather, Twain was, like Henry James and Stephen Crane, a pictorial artist with insight into human psychological responses during climactic moments of decision. The ordinary boy-girl or man-woman romantic relationships seldom occur in Twain's books.

A man of feeling, Twain was a sensitive barometer. As with Tom Sawyer, Huck Finn, and Pudd'nhead Wilson, Twain's mental weather fluctuated with every cloud in the social sky. He yielded to self-pity, bragged about and scolded himself, roared defiance and whimpered despondently at fate's blows, curried favors of the great and snarled at co-workers like Bret Harte and G. W. Cable, minced like a spaniel and strutted in his white suit like a king beside the dons at Oxford and Yale, who conferred honorary doctor's degrees upon him. Yet it is exactly this mercurial quality—this unexpected flash of temperament, this alternation of favorable and negative response—which enlivens his writings.

A masterly control over the English language, in its standard and Western dialect forms, made many scenes memorable, like the uproarious visit of Scotty Briggs to the fledgling parson in *Roughing It* and Sherburn's successful defiance of the lynch-hungry mob in *Huckleberry Finn*. His stories move by scenes or episodes rather than by a tightly knit plot structure woven around a clearly stated theme; yet each picture plays its role in the painter's impressionistic manner to give a single effect. In artistic manner, as in language, Twain was wholly American, wholly a product of native forces. If he was, as Dixon Wecter has suggested, "a kind of pocket miner, stumbling like fortune's darling upon native ore of incredible richness and exploiting it with effortless skill—but often gleefully mistaking fool's gold for the genuine article," the gold he found and wrought into great art remains an imperishable possession for the world's enjoyment and enrichment.

BIBLIOGRAPHICAL REFERENCES: The definitive edition, *The Writings of Mark Twain*, edited by Albert Bigelow Paine, 37 vols., 1922–1925, is now out of print. The best one-volume selections are *The Family Mark Twain*, with an Introduction by Albert Bigelow Paine, 1935, and *The Portable Mark Twain*, edited by Bernard DeVoto, 1946.

Mark Twain's Autobiography, edited by Albert Bigelow Paine, 2 vols., 1924, and *Mark Twain's Notebooks*, published by the same editor in 1935, provide valuable source material, though they are not always reliable. The *Autobiography* has been re-edited with previously unpublished chapters by Charles Neider, 1959. Bernard DeVoto, *Mark Twain in Eruption*, 1940, is an important addition to the autobiography. Two useful collections of correspondence are *Mark Twain's Letters*, edited by Albert Bigelow Paine, 2 vols., 1917, and *The Love Letters of Mark Twain*, edited by Dixon Wecter, 1949. The authorized biography is Albert Bigelow Paine, *Mark Twain: A Biography*, 3 vols., 1912 (reissued 1935); but an authoritative modern work is Maxwell Geismar, *Mark Twain: An American Prophet*, 1970. The best of the general Mark Twain studies are Bernard DeVoto, *Mark Twain's America*, 1932; Edward Wagenknecht, *Mark Twain: The Man and His Work*, 1935; and Dixon Wecter, *Sam Clemens of Hannibal*, 1952. See also William Dean Howells, *My Mark Twain: Reminiscences and Criticisms*, 1910; Van Wyck Brooks, *The Ordeal of Mark Twain*, 1920; Clara Clemens, *My Father, Mark Twain*, 1931; Edgar Lee Masters, *Mark Twain: A Portrait*, 1938; Bernard DeVoto, *Mark Twain at Work*, 1940; DeLancey Ferguson, *Mark Twain: Man and Legend*, 1943; Samuel C. Webster, *Mark Twain, Business Man*, 1946; Dixon Wecter, "Mark Twain," in *The Literary History of the United States*, edited by Robert E. Spiller, Willard Thorp, Thomas H. Johnson, and Henry S. Canby, Vol. II, 1948; Kenneth R. Andrews, *Nook Farm: Mark Twain's Hartford Circle*, 1950; Walter Blair, *Mark Twain and Huck Finn*, 1960; Kenneth S. Lynn, *Mark Twain and Southwestern Humor*, 1960; and Henry Nash Smith, *Mark Twain: The Development of a Writer*, 1962.

For criticism and more specialized studies see the extensive bibliography in *The Literary History of the United States,* Vol. III, 1948, 442–450.

NICHOLAS UDALL (WOODALL)

Born: Hampshire, England
Date: 1505

Died: Place unknown
Date: 1556

PRINCIPAL WORKS

PLAYS: *Placidas*, c. 1534; *Ralph Roister Doister*, c. 1552-1554.
TRANSLATIONS: *Apothegms* of Erasmus, 1542.

Born in Hampshire in 1505, Nicholas Udall was educated at Winchester and Corpus Christi College, Oxford, where he served as lecturer from 1526 to 1528. When he was twenty-seven, he assisted in the preparation of verses for Anne Boleyn's coronation. From 1533 to 1547 he was Vicar of Braintree, Essex. According to E. K. Chambers, he was probably the author of a play, *Placidas*, recorded in 1534. From 1534 to 1541 he was headmaster of Eton. In 1538 he was paid for "playing before my Lord." His career at Eton ended in disgrace, for he was accused of theft and other misconduct and dismissed.

For the next fourteen years, before becoming headmaster of Westminster School, he was writer, tutor, and churchman under patronage of members of the royal household. His principles as churchman were flexible enough to permit his serving Edward VI as a Protestant and Mary Tudor as a Catholic. Before the latter he performed or produced various dialogues and interludes. The date of his only surviving play, *Ralph Roister Doister*, is uncertain, probably between 1552 and 1554—possibly in Edward's, possibly in Mary's reign. Written for performance by and before schoolboys, it may have been done when Udall was master at Eton or Westminster. (Sir Edmund Chambers favors 1553-1554 and Westminster.) The printed Epilogue praises "our most noble Queen"; but this might have been an addition for a later performance before Elizabeth I.

Udall died in 1556. After his death, Bishop John Bale in *Scriptores* credited him with several comedies and a translated tragedy. In 1564 (the memorable year of the death of Michelangelo and the birth of William Shakespeare) Queen Elizabeth saw at Cambridge an *Ezekias* by Udall. However, the author's literary reputation rests solely on *Ralph Roister Doister*. Its Prologue defends "mirth with modesty," and the play lives up to the precept quite well. With the elimination of a few words common to the vocabulary of small boys at recess, it could be produced in any modern grammer school without shocking the most staid teacher; and it has a wholesome supply of mirth. Its companion piece in the period anthologies, *Gammer Gurton's Needle*, has copious mirth, but hardly a thimbleful of modesty. *Ralph Roister Doister* is modeled on Plautus's *Miles Gloriosus*; but it shows the influence of English mystery plays and interludes. Its characters are English rather than Roman; and it shows a healthy delight in sheer slapstick. The topsy-turvy reading of Ralph's letter proposing to the Widow Custance foreshadows the mispunctuated prologue delivered by Peter Quince in the interlude of "Pyramus and Thisbe" from *A Midsummer Night's Dream*.

BIBLIOGRAPHICAL REFERENCES: Brief biographical and critical studies are presented in E. K. Chambers, *The Medieval Stage*, Vol. II (1903); and C. R. Baskervill, V. B. Heltzel, and A. H. Nethercot, *Elizabethan and Stuart Plays* (1934).

MIGUEL DE UNAMUNO Y JUGO

Born: Bilbao, Spain
Date: September 29, 1864

Died: Salamanca, Spain
Date: December 31, 1936

Principal Works

ESSAYS: *En Torno al Casticismo*, 1895; *Vida de Don Quijote y Sancho*, 1905; *Del Sentimiento Trágico de la Vida*, 1913; *La Agonía del Cristianismo*, 1925.

NOVELS: *Paz en la Guerra*, 1897; *Amor y Pedagogía*, 1902; *Niebla*, 1914; *Abel Sánchez*, 1917; *San Manuel Bueno, Mártir*, 1933.

POETRY: *Rosario de Sonetos Líricos*, 1911; *El Cristo de Velásquez*, 1920.

DIARY: *Diario íntimo*, 1971.

Before all else, Unamuno was an individualist. A Basque by birth, he advocated the use of Castilian. Professor of Greek at Salamanca, he was a political figure of outstanding distinction. Antagonist to the monarchy, he was persecuted by the Falangists. Early an avid supporter of rationalism, he viciously attacked systems and called himself a "confusionist." As a child, he began to feel the primacy of life, and for his first literary effort he translated Carlyle's *The French Revolution*, a book that reflected his own hatred of hypocrisy and cant. When he became too outspoken, however, the monarchy exiled him. Still, Unamuno visualized himself as Spain's gadfly, the man whose task it was to irritate her into sense.

Deeply concerned with the individual, Unamuno wrote his many essays and novels in order to help make Spain a country where the individual could develop himself to his fullest potentials. He set himself in bitter opposition to anything that inhibited this man of flesh and bone, and with no hesitation attacked the Church, the Monarchy, the Socialists, the Republic. As a result of his unrestrained assaults on political hypocrisy, religious cant, and philosophical jargon, Unamuno became one of the leading existential writers of the twentieth century as well as one of the most influential Spanish thinkers of modern times. Although he was deeply depressed by his country's political disturbance and unrest when he died, he was a voice that has been widely heard and that has greatly influenced younger generations of his countrymen.

BIBLIOGRAPHICAL REFERENCES: Recent books on Unamuno include J. Maráas Aquilera, *Miguel de Unamuno*, 1966; Paul Ilie, *Unamuno: An Existential View of Self and Society*, 1967; Demetrios Basedkis, *Unamuno and Spanish Literature*, 1967; and Allen Lacy, *Miguel de Unamuno*, 1967.

SIGRID UNDSET

Born: Kalundborg, Denmark
Date: May 20, 1882

Died: Lillehammer, Norway
Date: June 10, 1949

PRINCIPAL WORKS

NOVELS: Fru Martha Oulie, 1907; Viga-Ljot og Vigdis, 1909 (Gunnar's Daughter); Jenny, 1911; Vaaren, 1914 (Springtime); Kristin Lavransdatter: Kransen, Husfrue, and Korset, 1920, 1921, 1922 (Kristin Lavransdatter: The Bridal Wreath, The Mistress of Husaby, and The Cross); Olav Audunssøn i Hestviken, 1925 (The Master of Hestviken: The Axe and The Snake Pit); Olav Audunssøn og hans børn, 1927 (The Master of Hestviken: In the Wilderness and The Son Avenger); Gymnedenia, 1929 (The Wild Orchid); Den brændende busk, 1930 (The Burning Bush); Ida Elisabeth, 1932; Den trofaste husfru, 1936 (The Faithful Wife); Madame Dorthea, 1939.

SHORT STORIES: Den lykkelige alder, 1908 (The Happy Age); Splinten av troldspeilet, 1917 (Images in a Mirror); De Kloge jongfruer, 1918 (The Wise Virgins).

AUTOBIOGRAPHY: Elleve år, 1934 (The Longest Year).

ESSAYS IN TRANSLATION: Men, Women, and Places, 1939.

Sigrid Undset, born at Kalundborg, Denmark, May 20, 1882, was the daughter of Ingvald Martin Undset, a distinguished Norwegian archaeologist. As a small child, she and her mother lived with her mother's family while the father was doing archaeological work in Italy. Later her father became a university lecturer and took his family to live in Christiania (now Oslo), Norway. Two other daughters were born to the family. As a child Sigrid Undset took an interest in her father's work, and that fact influenced her own work and interests throughout life, for she had a passionate concern for the past, especially medieval Norway. As a girl she was educated at the private academy of Fru Ragna Nielsen, in Oslo. After her father's death, Sigrid Undset and her sisters continued at the academy, even though they were unable to pay the fees, thanks to the goodheartedness of Fru Nielsen. But at the age of fifteen Sigrid decided that she did not wish to prepare for the university and a scientific career, as her teachers and family had expected her to do. Having been interested in painting since she was a small child, she wished to become an artist, but the family's poverty precluded an artistic career, and she enrolled in a business school.

Finishing business school, Sigrid, still a girl, began doing clerical work, which she found distasteful. As an escape from her distasteful work, she began writing after finishing her day's work, sometimes putting in as many as eighteen hours a day at her office and home. She remained in clerical work for ten years, until her two sisters were self-supporting, but before the time she left office work she had published two novels. Neither of those first two books made any stir in literary circles, and it was not until the appearance of Jenny, published in 1911, that Sigrid Undset had any fame or popularity. The following year, 1912, she married A. C. Svarstad, a Norwegian artist. Three children were born to them before she and her husband separated in 1925. The oldest child, a son, was killed while fighting against the Germans at the time of the German invasion of Norway during World

War II. Although reared a Lutheran, Sigrid Undset early became interested in Roman Catholicism, coming to believe that the only real heroes of history were the Christian saints and that the future of civilization lay with the Roman Church. She became a convert to the Roman Catholic Church in November, 1924.

During the following decade Sigrid Undset's greatest books were published. *The Bridal Wreath,* translated in 1923, *The Mistress of Husaby* (1925), and *The Cross* (1927) became her famous trilogy, *Kristin Lavransdatter,* issued as a single volume in 1929. This trilogy about life in medieval Norway became amazingly popular and was translated into many languages. Sigrid Undset was expected to receive the Nobel Prize for literature in 1925, but no award was made that year. She did receive the Nobel Prize in 1928. Second only to *Kristin Lavransdatter* is Sigrid Undset's tetralogy, *The Master of Hestviken,* composed of *The Axe,* translated in 1928, *The Snake Pit,* (1929), *In the Wilderness,* (1929), and *The Son Avenger,* (1930). Like *Kristin Lavransdatter, The Master of Hestviken* is about life in medieval Norway.

In the late 1930's Sigrid Undset turned to writing fiction about later periods, including her own. She also published a collection of essays, *Men, Women, and Places,* which illustrate her enthusiasm for Roman Catholicism. Her writings, which expressed concern for religious and racial tolerance, made her unpopular with the Nazi German government, but when World War II broke out she remained in her homeland, serving as a censor until the German invasion forced her to flee to Sweden with little more than her life. She came to the United States in 1940 and remained until her homeland was freed in 1945. During her years in America she lectured and continued writing. Upon her return to Norway she was awarded the Grand Cross of St. Olaf by her king, making her the first woman commoner ever to receive the award. During her last years Sigrid Undset lived quietly at Lillehammer, Norway, in a house dating back to Viking times. She collected old lace and other Norse antiques, and spent much of her time studying Norwegian history. She died at Lillehammer after suffering a paralytic stroke, June 10, 1949.

BIBLIOGRAPHICAL REFERENCES: There is very little criticism of Sigrid Undset in English. See Hanna Lastrop Larsen, *Sigrid Undset,* 1929; Joseph Warren Beach, *The Twentieth-Century Novel,* 1932; and Alrik Gustafson, *Six Scandinavian Novelists,* 1940.

JOHN UPDIKE

Born: Shillington, Pennsylvania
Date: March 18, 1932

Principal Works

NOVELS: *The Poorhouse Fair,* 1959; *Rabbit, Run,* 1960; *The Centaur,* 1963; *Of the Farm,* 1965; *Couples,* 1968; *Bech: A Book,* 1970; *Rabbit Redux,* 1971.
SHORT STORIES: *The Same Door,* 1959; *Pigeon Feathers and Other Stories,* 1962; *Olinger Stories: A Selection,* 1964; *The Music School,* 1966.
POEMS: *The Carpentered Hen and Other Tame Creatures,* 1958; *Telephone Poles and Other Poems,* 1963; *Midpoint and Other Poems,* 1969.
ESSAYS: *Assorted Prose,* 1963.
MISCELLANEOUS: *The Magic Flute,* 1963; *Bottom's Dream,* 1969.

Born in 1932, the son of a teacher, John Updike went to the public schools in Shillington, Pennsylvania, which became, he has written, the model for his fictional town of Olinger. After his graduation from Harvard, where he was already known for his considerable literary talent, he attended the Ruskin School of Drawing and Fine Art in Oxford, England. For two years, from 1955 to 1957, he worked in New York as a staff member of *The New Yorker.* In addition to editorial work and contributions to "The Talk of the Town," he wrote short stories, poems, parody, and satire which were published in that magazine. He has been a regular contributor ever since. In addition to his collections of short stories, he has published three collections of poems, including *The Carpentered Hen* (1958) and *Telephone Poles* (1960), and is the author of a number of highly praised novels including *The Poorhouse Fair* (1959), *Rabbit, Run* (1960), and *The Centaur* (1963). He has done some childrens' stories and an adaptation of the story of Mozart's opera, *The Magic Flute.* One of his recent books is a collection of his essays, reviews, parodies and *aperçus* published under the title *Assorted Prose* (1965). He is married, has four children, and lives in Ipswich, Massachusetts. His work from the very beginning has received the highest critical attention and regard, and a number of distinguished critics are on record as naming him to be one of the most important writers of his generation.

BIBLIOGRAPHICAL REFERENCES: Critical studies include Alice and Kenneth Hamilton, *John Updike: A Critical Essay,* 1967; *idem., The Elements of John Updike,* 1970; Charles Samuels, *John Updike,* 1969; and portions of David D. Galloway, *The Absurd Hero in American Fiction,* 1966; John W. Aldridge, *Time to Murder and Create,* 1966; Howard M. Harper, Jr., *Desperate Faith,* 1967; Larry E. Taylor, *Pastoral and Anti-pastoral Patterns in John Updike's Fiction,* 1971; and Rachael C. Burchard, *John Updike: Yea Saying,* 1971.
See also William Van O'Connor, "John Updike and William Styron: The Burden of Talent," *Contemporary American Novelists,* edited by Harry T. Moore, 1964; J. A. Ward, "John Updike's Fiction," *Critique,* V (Spring–Summer, 1962), 27–40; Norris W. Yates, "The Doubt and Faith of John Updike," *College English,* XXVI

(March, 1965), 469–474; and C. Clarke Taylor, *John Updike: A Bibliography*, 1968.

JUAN VALERA Y ALCALÁ GALIANO

Born: Cabrá, Córdoba, Spain
Date: October 18, 1824

Died: Madrid, Spain
Date: April 18, 1905

PRINCIPAL WORKS

NOVELS: *Pepita Jiménez*, 1874; *El comendador Mendoza*, 1877 (*Commander Mendoza*); *Doña Luz*, 1879; *Juanita la larga*, 1895 (*Big Jane*).
CRITICISM: *Sobre los cuentos de Leopardi e del romanticismo en España*, 1854.

In contrast to many Spanish authors who came from humble or middle class families, Juan Valera y Alcalá Galiano, born in the town of Cabrá on October 18, 1824, was an aristocrat, his father being a naval officer and his mother a marquise of Córdoba. His education was thorough, with a degree in philosophy from Málaga (1840) and one in law from Madrid (1846). He was also a linguist who read in many languages and a poet whose first volume *Ensayos poéticos* (*Poetic Attempts*) appeared before he finished the university. For it and other critical and poetic volumes, he was elected to the Spanish Academy in 1861.

Not until he was fifty, and then by accident, did he become a novelist. While studying Spanish mysticism, he was moved to put onto paper his thinking on the differences between human and divine love. Inventing a young theological student to make his thoughts more concrete, he ended with a lengthy bit of fiction, the best psychological novel of Spain, *Pepita Jiménez*. Letters from the vacationing student to his uncle at the seminary make up the first part of the novel, a fortunate inspiration for the beginning novelist whose greatest flaw is making the conversation of his characters resemble his own. The conclusion reached in the novel, that priests are born, not made, may be somewhat biographical, since the author's early education was received in religious schools; but it does not represent Valera's own convictions, since five years later he reversed the theme in *Doña Luz*, where religion conquers carnal love and the young heroine is satisfied with platonic friendship for the priest. The two novels really treat religion as a psychological matter, rather than a social, political, or even moral problem.

Between these two novels, in 1875, came *Las ilusiones del doctor Faustino* (*The Illusions of Dr. Faust*), whose skeptical hero has to get along without magical assistance. It deals with the theme later voiced by the Generation of '98: the failure of intellectuals in modern society, through lack of will power.

More complicated in plot was *Commander Mendoza*, whose skeptical man-of-the-world hero seems to some critics an embodiment of the author. Though still analyzing sentiment and passion, Valera tells the story of the efforts of a man back from Peru to get the daughter of his former mistress married to the man of her choice instead of to the richer but older suitor favored by the fanatical mother. As a novelist, Valera shows weakness in letting the death of the mother contrive the happy ending.

In 1895, old and nearly blind, this Spaniard called "the last Humanist" dictated his final novel, *Big Jane*, which provided a photographic reproduction of the region where he was born. In this work, however, the local color is less important than the character development, and the realism is second to the happy memories of the writer's childhood.

The aristocratic Valera was never a popular author. His "elusive and mystical idealism" did not suit the tastes of the masses, nor did they understand the cosmopolitan outlook of this cultured aristocrat. But Azorín calls him "The best Spanish prose writer of us all"; and he is one of two authors (Hartzenbusch is the other) of whom the Royal Academy declared: "Anything he writes is correct Spanish." Valera died in Madrid, April 18, 1905.

BIBLIOGRAPHICAL REFERENCES: For criticism see J. D. M. Ford, *Main Currents of Spanish Literature*, 1919; S. Fishtine, *Don Juan Valera the Critic*, 1933; César Barja, *Libros y autores modernos*, 1933; P. Romero Mendoza, *Don Juan Valera*, 1940; and José A. Balseiro, *Novelistas españoles contemporáneos*, 1947; also, Cyrus C. de Coster, "Valera: Critic of American Literature," *Hispania*, XLIII (1960), 364–367; and Paul Smith, "Juan Valera and the Illegitimacy Motif," *Hispania*, LI (1968), 804–811.

PAUL VALÉRY

Born: Sète, France
Date: October 30, 1871

Died: Paris, France
Date: July 20, 1945

Principal Works

POEMS: *La Jeune Parque*, 1917; *Album de Vers Anciens, Poemes 1890–1900*, 1920; *Charmes*, 1922.

ESSAYS AND DIALOGUES: *Introduction à la méthode de Léonard de Vinci*, 1895; *La soirée avec Monsieur Teste*, 1896; *L'âme et la danse*, 1923; *Eupalinos*, 1923; *L'Idée fixe*, 1932; *Varieté*, 5 vols., 1924–1944; *Tel quel*, 2 vols., 1941, 1943; *Mon Faust*, 1945.

NOTEBOOKS: *Cahiers*, 29 vols., 1958–1961.

LETTERS: *André Gide-Paul Valéry: Correspondance 1890–1942*, 1955; *Paul Valéry-Gustave Fourment: Correspondance 1887–1933*, 1957.

Son of an Italian mother and a Corsican father, Paul Valéry was born at Sète, France, on October 30, 1871. He first attended school in his home town, and then spent 1884–1888 at the lycée of Montpellier. His career there was undistinguished. Judging himself too untalented in mathematics to attend the Naval Academy, Valéry turned his interest to the arts, especially poetry. Among the chief literary influences on him at this time were Hugo, Gautier, and Baudelaire; by 1889 he had written a number of poems.

During his military service (1889–1890) his tastes began to change toward Symbolist poetry. His reading of Huysmans directed Valéry to the poetry of Verlaine and, particularly, Mallarmé. In 1890 he met Pierre Louys, who put him in touch with Mallarmé, Heredia, and André Gide; and Louys began publishing Valéry's poetry in his literary journal, *La Conque*. In the meantime, Valéry devoted himself to the study of law, again at Montpellier.

Thus things stood until 1892 when the poet, caught up in a personal crisis, went to spend his vacation with his mother's family. In the course of an October night of anxiety and insomnia, he became obsessed with the idea that the emotional and esthetic life distorted and crippled intellectual clarity and activity. He decided to reject writing and the artistic life to devote himself to what he valued most: self-knowledge and the consideration of the intellect and the life of thought. When he returned to school, he gave up most of his books.

In 1894, Valéry went to Paris to seek government service. In 1895 he entered the Ministry of War. Also in 1895 he published his *Introduction to the Method of Leonardo da Vinci*, and *An Evening with Monsieur Teste* appeared in 1896. Valéry left the Ministry of War in 1900 to become the private secretary of his friend, Edouard Lebey, an influential businessman. He held this position for twenty-two years, until the death of Lebey. Nineteen hundred was also the year of Valéry's marriage. His position with Lebey took little time, and Valéry spent many hours each day during these two decades noting his observations of his mental and intellectual activity: he watched the self in thought, in dream, in time, and he examined the relation of thought and language. His metaphor for himself during these years was that of a man caught in the labyrinth of his own thought attempting vainly to find the thread that would guide him out.

In 1912, twenty years after he had given up poetry, Valéry was asked by André Gide and another friend to publish an edition of his early poems, *Album de Vers Anciens,* which appeared in 1920. From his efforts at this project developed, after four years of work, a single new poem: "The Young Fate." The success of this poem led Valéry to write and publish more poetry, most notably his famous "Cemetery by the Sea" (1920). *Charmes,* a collected volume of his poetry written since "The Young Fate," was published in 1922.

Valéry's reputation grew very large very rapidly.

With the death of Lebey in 1922, Valéry devoted himself completely to the life of a man of letters. He was lionized by the reading public, and his essays and prefaces were in great demand. The French Academy elected him to the chair of Anatole France in 1925. Many other honors were paid him in the twenties and thirties, the period when he wrote most of his celebrated dialogues, and in 1937 he took the chair of poetry at the College de France. Continuing to teach during the occupation, Valéry did much to encourage the Resistance. He died in Paris on July 20, 1945, just after the Liberation; and he was buried in the cemetery beside the sea in Sète.

BIBLIOGRAPHICAL REFERENCES: A good recent text is *Œuvres,* edited by J. Hytier, 2 vols., 1957, 1960. J. Mathews is editing an English translation of *The Collected Works of Paul Valéry;* publication of a projected 15 volumes began in 1956.

Criticism in English includes T. S. Eliot, *A Brief Introduction to the Method of Paul Valéry,* 1924; Elizabeth Sewell, *Paul Valéry: The Mind in the Mirror,* 1952; F. Scarfe, *The Art of Paul Valéry,* 1954; W. N. Ince, *The Poetic Theory of Paul Valéry,* 1961; A. E. Mackay, *The Universal Self: A Study of Paul Valéry,* 1961; A. W. Thomson, *Valéry,* 1965; and H. A. Grubbs, *Paul Valéry,* 1968.

In French see M. Raymond, *Paul Valéry et la tentation de l'esprit,* 1946, new edition 1964; Francois Porché, *Paul Valéry et la poésie pure,* 1946; M. Bemol, *La méthode critique de Paul Valéry,* 1950, reprinted 1960; J. Hytier, *La poétique de Valéry,* 1953; P.-O. Walzer, *La Poésie de Valéry,* 1953; F. E. Sutcliffe, *La Pensée de Paul Valéry,* 1955; and L. Tauman, *Paul Valéry ou le mal de l'art,* 1969.

VALMIKI

Born: Ayodhya (?), India
Date: c. 350 B.C.

Died: India
Date: Unknown

Principal Work

POEM: *Ramayana,* c. 350 B.C. (*The Fortunes of Rama*).

Valmiki is one of those ancient authors who tantalize scholars because so little is known or can be known about them. Valmiki may be a legend that people long ago created to account for a great work of literature, for the traditional story is that Valmiki was a wise and holy man who lived in a forest in the north of India. To Valmiki came Narada, the messenger of the gods, who recited to the holy man the virtues and adventures of Rama, the ideal hero and an incarnation of Vishnu. When he had heard the tale, Valmiki mourned that he had no poetic power to pass on the tale to other men, until one day he saw a hunter kill a heron. Moved by his pity for the bird and his anger at the man, Valmiki began to express himself in Sanskrit poetry. While he was reciting *slokas,* the god Brahma appeared and ordered Valmiki to use his new-found poetic power to sing of Rama, his love for Sita, and Rama's victory over the demons. The story of Rama is famous and has been retold many times, regardless of whoever may have composed it first. Later renditions of the *Ramayana* are Kshmendra's *Ramayana-kathasara-manjari,* Bhoja's *Ramayana-champu,* and Tulsi Das's *Ram-charit-manas.* While Valmiki may or may not have ever lived, the poem attributed to him exists and still holds meaning for its readers. Untold millions of people in India have found inspiration and pleasure in the *Ramayana.*

BIBLIOGRAPHICAL REFERENCES: The standard modern translation is *The Ramayana of Valmiki,* by Hari Prasad Shastri, 1952. Aubrey Menen, *The Ramayana,* 1956, is a satirical adaptation of the original. Some articles in the *Journal of the Oriental Institute* (Baroda) are C. Bulcke, "More about Vālmīki," VIII (1959), 346–348; G. H. Bhatt, "On Vālmīki," IX (1959), 1–4; and Maya Prasad Tripathi, "Science of Geography in the Vālmīki Rāmāyana," IX (1959), 53–65.

SIR JOHN VANBRUGH

Born: London, England
Date: January, 1664

Died: London
Date: March 26, 1726

Principal Works

PLAYS: *The Relapse,* 1697; *The Provoked Wife,* 1697; *Aesop,* 1697 (adapted from the French); *Confederacy,* 1705 (adapted from Dancourt's *Bourgeoises à la mode*); *A Journey to London* (completed by Colley Cibber as *The Provoked Husband,* 1728).

John Vanbrugh, architect and playwright, was the son of a London merchant and a daughter of Sir Dudley Carleton. His paternal grandfather had fled to England from the Low Countries to avoid persecution by the Duke of Alva. Vanbrugh was born in London in January, 1664, but very little is known of the events of his early life before he became associated with the theater, except that he seems to have studied architecture in France from 1683 to 1685. He was commissioned as an officer in the British army in 1686 and served for several years. While in France in 1690 he was imprisoned for several months in the Bastille as a suspected English spy. His best play, *The Relapse,* was an original work produced in 1697, as was *The Provoked Wife,* presented in the same year but written about 1691. Other plays which he wrote or collaborated on were adaptations from earlier English or Continental dramatists.

The Relapse was a sequel to Colley Cibber's *Love's Last Shift* (1696). Like other dramatists of the 1690's, Vanbrugh depended on comedy of manners, sex, and lively action to carry along his plays. Social problems are introduced into the plays at times, but usually only for the purpose of making some cynical humor out of them. Notable in *The Relapse* is the sudden conversion of a debauched and faithless husband to marital constancy; such a reformation at the end of an immoral play was the dramatist's reply to charges hurled at the stage at the time that it was presenting immorality. Vanbrugh's plays, popular during his lifetime, were published in a collected edition in 1730, just four years after his death. On the side of notoriety rather than fame, Vanbrugh was one of the dramatists attacked for immorality by Jeremy Collier in his *Short View of the Immorality and Profaneness of the English Stage* (1698).

As an architect, Vanbrugh designed Castle Howard, the Haymarket Theater, Blenheim Palace, and (collaborating with Nicholas Hawksmoor) the Clarendon Building at Oxford. Vanbrugh was knighted in 1723. He was married in 1719 to Henrietta Yarborough, who bore him several children of whom a boy and a girl survived. Vanbrugh's personality and well-constructed, good-humored plays continue to hold interest for many readers in modern times. He died in London on March 26, 1726.

BIBLIOGRAPHICAL REFERENCES: The chief edition is Bonamy Dobrée and Geoffrey Webb, *Complete Works,* 4 vols., 1927–1928; this includes the letters. There are three reliable biographies: G. H. Lovegrove, *The Life, Work, and Influence of Sir John Vanbrugh,* 1902; Laurence Whistler, *Sir John Vanbrugh,* 1938; and Bernard

Harris, *Sir John Vanbrugh*, 1967. An interesting section on Vanbrugh appears in Henry T. E. Perry, *The Comic Spirit in Restoration Drama*, 1925. Of basic importance are the evaluations in Allardyce Nicoll, *History of Restoration Comedy, 1660–1700*, 1923; and Bonamy Dobrée, *Restoration Comedy*, 1924. See also, Paul Mueschke and Jeannette Fleisher, "A Re-evaluation of Vanbrugh," *Publications of the Modern Language Association*, XL (1934), 848–889; and Albert Rosenberg, "New Light on Vanbrugh," *Philosophical Quarterly*, 45 (1966), 603–613.

CARL VAN VECHTEN

Born: Cedar Rapids, Iowa
Date: June 17, 1880

Died: New York, N. Y.
Date: December 21, 1964

Principal Works

NOVELS: *Peter Whiffle*, 1922; *The Blind Bow-Boy*, 1923; *The Tattooed Countess*, 1924; *Firecrackers*, 1925; *Spider Boy*, 1928; *Parties*, 1930.

ESSAYS: *Music after the Great War*, 1915; *Music and Bad Manners*, 1916; *Interpreters and Interpretations*, 1917; *The Merry-Go-Round*, 1918; *The Music of Spain*, 1918; *In the Garret*, 1920; *The Tiger in the House*, 1920; *Red: Papers on Musical Subjects*, 1925; *Excavations: A Book of Advocacies*, 1926; *Sacred and Profane Memories*, 1932.

Carl Van Vechten was born in Cedar Rapids, Iowa, June 17, 1880. Graduated from the University of Chicago in 1903, he became assistant music critic on the *New York Times* in 1906. Although he continued to associate with music criticisms and notes for much of his career, he later became a dramatic critic and finally a novelist.

His career as a novelist began with the signal success of his first novel, *Peter Whiffle*, a satirical work which enjoyed great vogue and popularity during the 1920's. His best-known novels include *The Blind Bow-Boy* and *Firecrackers*, both stories of artistic and society sets in New York; *The Tattooed Countess*, which deals with the return to her Midwestern home of an American woman of the world; *Nigger Heaven* (1926), about life in Harlem; *Spider Boy*, a satire on Hollywood and movie people; and *Parties*, a New York novel of the period. In his books Mr. Van Vechten uses his knowledge of and enthusiasm for many phases of the arts—music, dancing, painting, literature—as topics of commentary. As a cat-lover, Mr. Van Vechten has written some excellent essays in *The Tiger in the House* and as editor has collected other writings on cats in *Lords of the Housetops* (1921). He has established a well-deserved reputation for himself as an "unprofessional" photographer of many figures of the arts in the 1930's and 1940's.

BIBLIOGRAPHICAL REFERENCES: See Carl Van Vechten, "Notes for an Autobiography," *Colophon*, Part III (1930); also Scott Cunningham, *A Bibliography of the Writings of Carl Van Vechten*, 1924. There are two studies of the writer and his work: Edward Lueders, *Carl Van Vechten*, 1965; and Bruce Kellner, *Carl Van Vechten and the Irreverent Decade*, 1968.

HENRY VAUGHAN

Born: Newton, Brecknockshire, England
Date: April 17, 1622

Died: Newton, Brecknockshire
Date: April 23, 1695

Principal Works

POEMS: *Poems,* 1646; *Olor Iscanus,* 1651; *Thalia Rediviva,* 1678.
PROSE: *The Mount of Olives,* 1652; *Hermetical Physick,* 1655.

A number of seventeenth century poets have won new popularity in the last few decades in the wake of the revived interest in the metaphysical poetry of John Donne. Among the writers who have achieved recent fame is Henry Vaughan, whose works reflect the influence of the religious lyrics of Donne and his disciple, George Herbert.

Vaughan came from a middle class Welsh family. He was born in 1622 in Newton, Brecknockshire, and, with his twin brother Thomas, received his early education from Matthew Herbert, a clergyman who lived in a nearby village. The two young men probably entered Jesus College, Oxford, together in 1638; the records of Thomas' matriculation, but not of Henry's, are still extant.

Thomas Vaughan remained in Oxford to receive his degree and was later ordained a priest in the Church of England, but Henry went on to London in 1640 to study law. There is little factual evidence of his activities at that time, but he probably took advantage of the opportunity to become familiar with contemporary literature. His first volume of poetry reveals his knowledge of the works of many of the Cavalier poets of the court of Charles I.

Vaughan seems to have abandoned his legal studies about 1642 with the outbreak of the Civil Wars, and he almost certainly served in King Charles' army before 1646. At some time during the same four-year period he was employed as clerk to Sir Marmaduke Lloyd, Chief Justice of the Brecon Circuit, Vaughan's home district.

Vaughan's first book of poems was published in 1646. The verses included in it, polished love lyrics addressed to his lady, Amoret, are full of classical allusions and Platonic sentiments in the Caroline tradition of Carew, Suckling, and Randolph. He prepared a second similar volume, but it was never published, probably partly because of unpopular political references; the Puritans controlled South Wales after 1646. A second, perhaps stronger, reason was Vaughan's increasing preoccupation with religion. His growing seriousness was apparently intensified by the death of his younger brother William in 1648. His religious thought was also influenced by that of Thomas, who had turned his attention from orthodox Anglicanism to neo-Platonism, mysticism, and the occult sciences. Henry's poetry reflects a neo-Platonic concept of childhood as a state in which man gradually grows away from the union with God that preceded his birth. Man's constant yearning for the renewal of this perfect unity of the human and the divine is the subject of many of his lyrics.

Vaughan settled in his father's home, the village of Newton-on-Usk, in 1646 and married Catherine Wise of Warwickshire soon afterward. At some time in the next decade he began practicing medicine. No evidence to indicate when or where he received his medical training has been discovered.

Mrs. Vaughan died in 1653, leaving her husband with four young children. Two years later he married his wife's sister, Elizabeth, who bore him four more offspring.

Vaughan's prose and poetic works appeared with regularity during the years from 1650 to 1655. The best of his poems appeared in *Silex Scintillans,* published in two parts, in 1650 and 1655, and in *Olor Iscanus,* in 1651. His devotional essays, the *Mount of Olives,* came out in 1652, followed by translations of several religious and medical treatises. He published almost nothing for almost twenty years after this burst of creative activity. His final volume, *Thalia Rediviva,* a collection of his own later poems and of several by his brother, Thomas, who had died in 1666, appeared in 1678. Vaughan lived to a venerable age for his century, dying at the age of seventy-three on April 23, 1695, in Newton.

BIBLIOGRAPHICAL REFERENCES: The standard edition is *The Works of Henry Vaughan,* edited by L. C. Martin, 2 vols., 1914, reprinted in 1957. Another excellent annotated text is *The Complete Poetry of Henry Vaughan,* edited by French Fogle, 1964. F. E. Hutchinson's *Henry Vaughan: A Life and Interpretation,* 1947, is a fine biographical and critical study.

There are many good discussions of Vaughan's poetry, among them Elizabeth Holmes, *Henry Vaughan and the Hermetic Philosophy,* 1932; Ross Garner, *Henry Vaughan: Experience and the Tradition,* 1959; E. C. Pettet, *Of Paradise and Light: A Study of Vaughan's Silex Scintillans,* 1960; and R. A. Durr, *On the Mystical Poetry of Henry Vaughan,* 1962.

See also J. B. Leishman, *The Metaphysical Poets,* 1934; Helen C. White, *The Metaphysical Poets,* 1936; Louis L. Martz, *The Poetry of Meditation,* 1954; Joan Bennett, *Five Metaphysical Poets,* 1964; and George Williamson, *Six Metaphysical Poets: A Reader's Guide,* 1967. For additional references see E. L. Marilla, *A Comprehensive Bibliography of Henry Vaughan,* 1948, and Marilla and James D. Simmonds, *Henry Vaughan: A Bibliographical Supplement, 1946–1960,* 1963.

IVAN VAZOV

Born: Sopot, Bulgaria
Date: June 27, 1850

Died: Sofia, Bulgaria
Died: September 22, 1921

Principal Works

NOVELS: *Pod igoto*, 1893 (*Under the Yoke*); *Nova zemya*, 1894 (*New Country*); *Kazalarskata tsaritsa*, 1903 (*The Empress of Kazalar*).

PLAYS: *Sluzhbogontsi*, 1903 (*The Service-Chasers*); *Borislav*, 1909; *Ivaylo*, 1911.

POEMS: *Izbavlenie*, 1878 (*Liberation*); *Epopeya na zabravenite*, 1879 (*Epic of the Heroes*); *Pod nashete nebe*, 1900 (*Under Our Heaven*); *Pesni za Makedoniya*, 1914 (*Songs for Macedonia*); *Ne shte zagine*, 1920 (*It Will Not Perish*).

Ivan (Minchov) Vazov, for thirty years the outstanding writer in Bulgaria, was Bulgaria's first great writer in the various creative fields of the novel, poetry, and the drama. During his most influential years, from 1890 to 1920, his name was used to characterize the period as "the Vazov period."

Vazov, born on June 27, 1850, received his elementary education in his native town of Sopot and at Plovdiv. Son of a conservative merchant who was financially well-to-do, the boy enjoyed a comfortable childhood. He left Bulgaria when he was nineteen, and his first creative work, which appeared in the 1870's, was poems on patriotic and revolutionary themes, published in Bucharest. During that time he made a business trip to Rumania and met the revolutionary writers Karavelov and Botev. Inspired by them and by Petko Rachev Slaveukov, the pre-revolutionary poet, he decided to give up his schooling at the University of Zagreb and devote his work to the cause of the people.

After the liberation of Bulgaria from Turkish rule in 1878 he returned to his country and served as judge of the circuit court in Berkovitsa and Vidin. From 1886 to 1889 he was a political exile in Odessa, having opposed Stambolov's Bulgarian government. When he returned to Sofia he settled down to a life of prolific writing, achieving his most notable success in 1893 with the novel *Under the Yoke*, a story of the beginnings of the Bulgarian revolt against the Turks.

His novels, plays, and poems were praised for sympathy for the common people apparent in all of his work. On October 2, 1920, he was honored by a national jubilee celebrating his completion of fifty years of creative work. He died of a heart attack in Sofia, on September 22, 1921.

BIBLIOGRAPHICAL REFERENCES: For criticism and comment see T. Minkhov, "Ivan Vazov," in *Bulgarski pisateli*, IV (1929), 3–72; E. Damiani, "Ivan Vazov, poeta della rinascita nazionale," *Nuova Antologia*, CCCLIX (1932), 286–288; and A. Werner, "Ivan Vazov," *Books Abroad*, XXIV (1950), 242–244.

THORSTEIN VEBLEN

Born: Manitowoc County, Wisconsin
Date: July 30, 1857

Died: Palo Alto, California
Date: August 3, 1929

Principal Works

ECONOMIC AND SOCIAL THEORY: *The Theory of the Leisure Class*, 1899; *The Theory of Business Enterprise*, 1904; *The Instinct of Workmanship*, 1914; *An Inquiry into the Nature of Peace and the Terms of Its Perpetuation*, 1917; *The Higher Learning in America*, 1918; *The Place of Science in Modern Civilization and Other Papers*, 1920; *The Engineers and the Price System*, 1921.

Thorstein Bunde Veblen was born to Norwegian-immigrant parents on a farm in Wisconsin when that state was largely on the frontier of the time. He was the sixth of twelve children. In 1865 the family moved to a 290-acre farm in Minnesota, in a Norwegian community where Old World ways and speech were dominant. When young Veblen was seventeen, his father, eager for his children to be educated, took the boy in a buggy to Northfield, Minnesota. In six years young Veblen had finished his preparatory work and a college program at Carleton College. After graduation he went to Madison, Wisconsin, where he taught for a year, 1880-1881, at Monona Academy, after which apprenticeship he went East to do graduate work at The Johns Hopkins University. Failing to receive a fellowship there, he left before the first term's end for Yale, where he took a Ph.D. in philosophy in 1884. That same year two of his writings appeared: an essay on Kant in the *Journal of Speculative Philosophy* and an essay on the surplus Federal revenue of 1837. The latter won the John Addison Porter Prize.

Unable to find a job, despite his publications and his doctorate, Veblen returned to the farm in Minnesota, where he led an unhappy life. After marrying Ellen May Rolfe, whom he had known in college, he moved with her to a farm in Iowa. In 1891 he returned to the East, to Cornell University, where he obtained a fellowship and continued writing for the learned journals. Through a friend he received a teaching fellowship at the new University of Chicago in 1892, where he remained until 1906, being editor of the *Journal of Political Economy* as well from 1896 to 1905. During these years his two best-known works—*The Theory of the Leisure Class* and *The Theory of Business Enterprise*—were published, making him famous outside academic circles. Because of marital problems he moved to the West, where he was at Stanford University for slightly more than two years, leaving because of a love affair in 1909. Returning to the Midwest to teach at the University of Missouri in 1911, he married a second time. He held his academic position at Missouri for seven years, continuing also to write his controversial books. After a brief period as an editor of the *Dial* he became a faculty member at the New School for Social Research in 1919. His thought and writings became more and more bitter and increasingly revolutionary. When his second wife died in 1926 he returned to his mountain cabin near Palo Alto, living with his stepdaughter until his death from heart disease, just after his 72nd birth-

1829

day. His was a stormy life; as a man, he was, in fact, a failure. He was the subject of one of H. L. Mencken's most derisive essays in *Prejudices, First Series,* 1919. Mencken ridiculed Veblen's tortured style and what he considered to be the essential hollowness of the ideas, concluding that Veblen was merely a "geyser of pishposh." Nevertheless, his writings have had a considerable influence on social and economic thought, among those who opposed his theories, as well as among those who admired them.

BIBLIOGRAPHICAL REFERENCES: There are a number of extensive discussions of Veblen, among them Joseph Dorfman, *Thorstein Veblen and His America,* 1934, reprinted 1961; Stanley Daugert, *The Philosophy of Thorstein Veblen,* 1950; David Riesman, *Thorstein Veblen: A Critical Interpretation,* 1953; Bernard Rosenberg, *The Values of Veblen,* 1956; Douglas F. Dowd, editor, *Thorstein Veblen: A Critical Reappraisal,* 1958; ibid., *Thorstein Veblen,* 1964; and William Jaffe, *Theories Economiques et Sociales de Thorstein Veblen,* 1971.

Also of interest are Jay M. Gould, *Technical Elite,* 1966; Howard D. Marshall, *Great Economists,* 1967; and Thomas Reed West, *Flesh of Steel: Literature and the Machine in American Culture,* 1967.

LOPE DE VEGA

Born: Madrid, Spain
Date: November 25, 1562

Died: Madrid
Date: August 27, 1635

Principal Works

HISTORICAL PLAYS: *Peribáñez y el comendador de Ocana*, c. 1605 (*Peribáñez and the Commander of Ocana*); *Fuente ovejuna*, c. 1619 (*The Sheep Well*); *El mejor alcalde el rey*, c. 1623 (*The King, the Greatest Alcalde*).
COMEDIES: *El acero de Madrid*, c. 1613 (*Madrid Steel*); *La dama boba*, 1613 (*The Stupid Lady*); *El perro del hortelano*, c. 1615 (*The Gardener's Dog*); *Amar sin saber a quien*, c. 1620 (*Love for Love's Sake*); *La Moza de cántaro*, c. 1627 (*The Water Seller*).

Architect of the Golden Age of the theater in Spain was Lope Félix de Vega Carpio, who could justly boast that when he started writing plays only two companies of actors were performing, while at the end of his career forty companies employing at least a thousand people were providing the Spanish capital with plays. Modern scholarship sets at about eight hundred his total dramatic output instead of the 1,800 claimed by his exuberant friend, Montalbán. At least 507 are unquestionably his, many in his own handwriting. One of the greatest, *La estrella de Sevilla* (c. 1617, *The Star of Seville*) may possibly be by him, though modern scholarship discredits his authorship. The total body of his work is more than any other dramatist can claim, and though many were written in less than a day, none is wholly bad, none untouched by his genius. Publishers sent shorthand experts to the theater to copy his plays and pirate them. In the provinces managers advertised their offerings as by Lope de Vega to be sure of an audience. So great was his popularity that anything excellent, from food to jewels, was referred to as "of Lope."

This "prodigy of nature" (*monstruo de la naturaleza*), as his contemporaries called him, was the son of a worker in gold and was born in Madrid on November 25, 1562. An ecclesiastical patron entered him in the University of Alcalá, but a love affair with the wife of an actor kept him from taking orders as he had planned. This was the first of many love affairs, all of which he transmuted into important literary works. Friends had only to suggest a form of literature he had not attempted to have him compose for them a good example of it.

The theater was his great love, however. Able to write a play in verse almost faster than a scribe could copy it, he seized on anything as a plot idea. The medical fad of taking iron for the blood inspired *Madrid Steel*. A proverb was the seed of *The Gardener's Dog*. Reports of piratical activity in the Mediterranean inspired The Arabian Nights theme of *La doncella Teodora* (*The Damsel Theodora*).

In his rhymed *Arte nueva de hacer comedias* (1609, *New Art of Writing Plays*), Lope de Vega laid down the rules under which he wrote: "In the first act, state your case; in the second, your events, so that not till the middle of the third does anybody begin to suspect what is going to come of it all. . . . Do not permit the solution till you come to the last scene." His dramas, therefore, were full of suspense. Action, not philosophy, was what his audiences wanted, and he confessed that the audience dictated his plots, chose his characters, and wrote his plays. Though he knew the rules of the classical theater, he admitted that with a half dozen exceptions, he broke them to please the people and to be true to life. Prose and poetry, he hoped, would gain him fame, and he made no secret of the fact that he wrote plays for money. From his plays he earned $400,000, most of which he generously gave to friends in need.

While his genius touched all types of drama, his popularity rested chiefly on the type called *comedias de capa y espada*, or cape-and-sword plays which were full of intrigue and complications, with masked nobles and women disguised as men. The plots commanded the characters and stock impulses motivated the action (love easily transferred, jealousy easily aroused, honor easily offended); and an entertaining and involved plot kept the spectators guessing until matrimony at the final curtain washed away all stains on family honor. The outcome of these plays is not always logical. In his treatise on playwriting Lope de Vega declared: "At times, that which is contrary to logic for that very reason is pleasing." Good examples of this practice are *Madrid Steel*, and the gay *The Stupid Lady*.

He was also successful in religious plays with saints as heroes, in comedies of manners with lower class characters, and in heroic plays with historical or legendary characters, such as *The Sheep Well* and *The King, the Greatest Alcalde*. In addition, he composed several hundred *autos sacramentales*, short plays for the Corpus Christi season and other Church holy days.

Lope de Vega was also fertile in non-dramatic works. Some one has calculated his entire output at 22,300,000 lines; it takes twenty-one quarto volumes to contain writings already published. *The Beauty of Angelica* (1602), an epic poem, runs to 11,000 lines, while he penned 10,000 lines in poetic tribute to Madrid's patron Saint Isidor. The epic, *Jerusalem Conquered* (1609), is twice that long. In 1598 he composed *La Dragontea,* an epic in ten cantos about the misdeeds of Francis Drake, and wrote 2,000 lines about the loves and adventures of a cat in his mock epic *La Gatomaquia* (1634). Fifteen hundred sonnets resulted from his poetic musing. In prose he wrote *La Arcadia* (1598), a pastoral novel. His favorite novel, *La Dorotea,* was inspired by his first love; frequently revised, it was finally published in 1632.

As a man, Lope was less admirable. He was a product of the most corrupt age of Spanish history and moved in the most corrupt circles of that age. As a boy, he showed precocity: "dedicated to the Muses from his birth," composing poetry when he was only five, and writing a play at the age of twelve. No wonder he ran away from school with a companion and toured Spain until a pawnbroker grew suspicious at the wealth they displayed and turned them over to the police.

At the university, he perfected himself chiefly in fencing, singing, and dancing. Studies over, he surrendered to his love for the theater and by fifteen was seeing his plays professionally performed. His love for adventure led him in 1583 to join a naval expedition to the Azores; he returned to an intensive life of writing. Five years later he was banished from Madrid on penalty of death for a criminal libel against his mistress, Elena Osorio, daughter of a theatrical manager for whom he provided plays. From exile in Valencia he wooed Isabel de Urbina and returned boldly to the capital to elope with her. Nineteen days after their marriage, he deserted her to join the Invincible Armada; he used his leisure from military duties to write an epic poem.

Rough seas and the death of his brother made war unattractive, and following the death of his beloved Isabel he spent the next forty years in a succession of love intrigues and scandals. His two favorite children were illegitimate. Friend and associate of the nobility, serving the Duke of Alba, the Marques of Malpica, and the Count of Lemos, he reached the depths as panderer for the dissipated Duke of Sessa.

But he had his moments of repentance. In 1609 he became a *familiar* of the Inquisition. He joined three religious confraternities in two years. When his second wife, Juana, and their son Carlos died almost simultaneously, Lope entered Holy Orders. In 1614 he was ordained priest in Toledo, at a time when he was carrying on a love affair of his own and was providing mistresses for Sessa.

Truly, Lope was a strange compound of sensuality, pettiness, conceit, servility, and genius. Fortunately the last quality outweighs all the rest, and it was that quality which all Madrid recognized on Tuesday, August 28, 1635, in according him funereal honors such as have seldom been equaled for a man of letters. Ironically, when his resting place, San Estéban, was remodeled in the eighteenth century, no distinguishing mark was put on his coffin, so that Lope's present grave is uncertain. But he left his own monument in the Spanish theater.

He established the play of three acts, set down rules of versification for the expression of various emotions and situations, and brought to the stage a richness of poetic inspiration unequaled in Spanish literature. He reflected the life, customs, and ideas of the sixteenth and seventeenth centuries with realistic naturalness and poetic freedom. Inferior to Tirso de Molina in handling comedy, incapable of the poetic heights of Calderón, less careful than Alarcón in character portrayal and analysis, Lope de Vega nevertheless surpassed all his Golden Age contemporaries in skill at blending poetry and life, which he painted in vivid colors, although he did not interpret it deeply. He gave freedom and importance to women and dignity to the lower classes, and produced an enormous number of masterpieces at the time when variety was necessary to encourage a theater-going public and bring to greatness the theater of the Golden Age in Spain.

BIBLIOGRAPHICAL REFERENCES: Biographical and critical studies of Lope de Vega in English include H. A. Rennert, *The Life of Lope de Vega*, 1904 (rev. ed., 1937); R. Schevill, *The Dramatic Art of Lope de Vega*, 1918; Angel Flores, *Lope de Vega: Monster of Nature*, 1930; James Fitzmaurice Kelly, *Chapters on Spanish Literature*, 1908; and Francis C. Hayes, *Lope de Vega*, 1967. See also F. A. de Icaza, *Lope de Vega, sus amores y sus odios*, 1925; Astraña Marín, *La vida azarosa de Lope de Vega*, 1935; and J. de Entrambasaguas, *La vida de Lope*, 1936, and *Estudios sobre Lope*, 1946. The Lope de Vega Number of *The Hispanic Review*, III, 3 (1935) contains articles by contemporary scholars and critics.

GIOVANNI VERGA

Born: Catania, Sicily
Date: August 31, 1840

Died: Catania
Date: January 27, 1922

Principal Works

novels: *I Malavoglia*, 1881 (*The House by the Medlar Tree*); *Mastro-don Gesualdo*, 1889.
short stories: *Vita dei campi*, 1880 (*Life of the Fields*); *Novelle rusticane*, 1883 (*Country Tales*).

The greatest Italian novelist since Manzoni was born in Catania, Sicily, on August 31, 1840, of a family supposed to have come from Aragon in the thirteenth century. The Vergas were a family of patriots. The grandfather was an underground fighter for independence and a deputy to the first Sicilian parliament in 1812. During Giovanni's boyhood his mother encouraged him to read. Although he gave her credit for his decision at the age of fifteen to become a novelist, biographers point out that his teacher Pietro Abato wrote poems and novels and assigned class work that caused the young student to write a 600-page novel, *Love and Country*, about George Washington and the American Revolution. Fortunately Verga knew more about the subjects of his later fiction.

Instead of entering the university in 1860, he persuaded his father to let him use the money to publish another manuscript he had completed in four volumes. *Carbonari della montagna* concerned the adventures of his grandfather. During the next fifteen years Verga lived in Florence and Milan. In these cities, under the influence of the French writers, he wrote passable novels of middle-class life, among them the sentimental *Storia di una capinera* (1869, *Story of a Wren*). In Milan he described adultery in high society, in *Eva* (1873) and *Tigre reale* (1873).

From this distance Verga could look back on his childhood home and draw upon his impressions of Sicilian life. *Nedda*, published in 1874, was a story of a wronged girl of Sicily, a work realistic in treatment in which the writer, in spite of his attitude of scientific observation, revealed warm sympathy for his characters. He scorned being classified. When some found in him the masked pity and underlying pessimism of a Hardy and others called him a supporter of Verism, with its anti-Romanticist reaction, he retorted that "works of art may be born of any -ism. The main thing is for it to be born."

The years 1878 to 1880, after returning to Milan following the death of his favorite sister in Sicily, marked the turning point in his career. His renewed interest in the Sicilian peasants and fishermen as subjects of art was shown in the collection of short stories, *Life of the Fields*, which contained "Cavalleria Rusticana," a tale of primitive passion and violence that he was to dramatize for the great Duse in 1884, and then use as libretto for the Mascagni opera. But his greatest fame came from *The House by the Medlar Tree*, a novel dealing with Sicilian fishermen defeated in their struggle for existence, but with the town as the real protagonist. Verga's home town, under the disguise of Trezza, also figured in his last great novel *Mastro-*

don Gesualdo, which tells of the downfall of a proud, ambitious peasant.

The foreword to *The House by the Medlar Tree* had announced Verga's purpose to write a Sicilian *Comédie Humaine* which he titled *I Vinti* (*The Defeated*), to show "the slow, inevitable flow of the rivers of social life." But writing was hard for him, and during the last twenty years of his life spent in his native town in southern Sicily he wrote and published little. A third novel of the series, *La Duchessa di Leyra,* was planned as a study of the Sicilian aristocracy but was never completed. He died at Catania on January 27, 1922.

The style of Verga's writing, mentioned by all critics, grew from his admiration for a moving story by a sea captain that he read when young, and which appealed to him in spite of its colloquial and illiterate style. Although an aristocrat, Verga tried to make his own writing echo the speech of the simple peasants. For most readers the wealth of detail and the keen observation of the life and customs of the lower class give his novels of Southern Italy their greatest appeal, so that D. H. Lawrence was moved to translate *Mastro-don Gesualdo* and two volumes of short stories in order to give pleasure to readers ignorant of Italian. Verga's own life was uneventful; he lived vicariously in the experiences of the impoverished people whose stories he told so well.

BIBLIOGRAPHICAL REFERENCES: The most authoritative study of Verga in English is T. G. Bergin, *Giovanni Verga,* 1931. For biographical and critical studies in Italian see A. Momigliano, *Giovanni Verga, narratore,* 1923; Luigi Russo, *Giovanni Verga,* 1934; Rosario Verde, *Giovanni Verga, drammaturgo,* 1950; Eurialo de Michelis, *Dostojevskij minore, con un saggio sul Verga europeo,* 1954; and Giorgio Santagelo, *Storia della critica Verghiana,* 1954. *Studi Verghiani,* edited by L. Perroni, 1929, is a collection of brief critical studies. A recent special study is Olga Ragusa, *Verga's Milanese Tales,* 1964.

VERGIL
Publius Vergilius Maro

Born: Andes, Italy
Date: October 15, 70 B.C.

Died: Brundisium, Italy
Date: September 21, 19 B.C.

Principal Works

POEMS: *Eclogues,* c. 40–37 B.C.; *Georgics,* c. 37–29 B.C.; *Aeneid,* c. 29–19 B.C.

Publius Vergilius Maro, author of one of the most familiar epics in all literature, was born in the village of Andes, in northern Italy, October 15, 70 B.C., only a few decades before the end of the Golden Age of the Roman Republic. It is claimed that his father was a potter who by hard work and an advantageous marriage had become a landowner prosperous enough to give his son a superior education. The youth studied under eminent teachers at Cremona and Milan, and under the Greek poet and grammarian Parthenius at Naples. At the age of twenty-three Vergil went to Rome to study not only poetry and philosophy but also mathematics and physics under Siro the Epicurean, whose philosophy affected Vergil's thought and writings throughout his life.

Although he was a shy, rustic, and slow-spoken youth, his personal charm and the literary ability evident in his early poems won Vergil the friendship of some of the most cultivated and powerful men in Rome, among them Octavian, Maecenas, Pollio, Horace, and Cornelius Gallus. His popularity was such that in 41 B.C., when his farm was threatened with seizure, along with surrounding territories to be divided among the victorious soldiers of the triumvirs returning from the battle of Philippi, his friends were able to intercede at Rome to have it saved. Despite his popularity in the capital, however, Vergil spent much time in retirement on his beloved farm, studying Greek and Roman history and literature.

In 42 B.C., at the request of his friend Asinius Pollio, Vergil began work on the *Eclogues,* which were finally completed about 37 B.C. These idyllic pastoral poems were based on the *Idylls* of the third century B.C. Sicilian poet, Theocritus. The setting, structure, and language of the *Eclogues* are highly imitative, but their greater complexity and artificiality reflect a wider range of observation and the background of a more highly developed civilization. They are also original in their extensive use of allegory and their many laudatory references to the author's friends.

After the publication of the *Eclogues,* Vergil took up residence at a country estate near Naples, where he spent most of the rest of his life. It was here that he wrote the *Georgics,* a didactic poem in four books on the subject of husbandry. Written at the request of Maecenas, who wished to revive an interest in the old Roman virtues of industry and a fondness for rustic life, the poems are considered to be the most technically polished and elaborate of all Vergil's work. Unlike the rather dry, strictly didactic *Works and Days* of the Greek poet Hesiod, on which they were based, the *Georgics* were obviously never intended to teach the specific techniques of successful agriculture to anyone who did not know them already. What they aimed to do, and did most successfully, was to interest the reader in the lost art of agriculture by making it attractive and interesting to him. This the author did by means of graceful language, imaginative imagery, concrete illustrations, and digressions on various subjects which added much to the charm, if not to the unity, of the work.

Vergil was forty-one years old before he embarked on his lifelong ambition, the composition of a Homeric epic which would commemorate the glory of Rome and his friend, the Emperor Augustus, and would win back the Roman people, unsettled and corrupted by long civil strife, to their primitive religion and ancient virtues. He worked on the *Aeneid* for ten years. When he died of a fever at Brundisium, Italy, on September 21, 19 B.C., after a trip to Greece, final revisions were not yet completed, but Augustus ordered that the work be preserved.

Vergil chose as his topic the voyage of the Trojan hero Aeneas to Italy after the fall of Troy, because Aeneas was the only character in the Homeric tale whom poets had connected with the legendary founding of Rome. Although Vergil borrowed heavily, not only from Homer, but also from Apollonius, Greek tragedy, and the Latin epic poet Ennius, the total conception and expression were all his own. The skillful handling of the hexameters, the imagery, the characterizations of the central figures were all original, as was the interweaving of numerous old tales and legends into one comprehensive whole. In the character of Queen Dido, particularly, we have a "modern" treatment of romantic love and its effects on the human character largely foreign to Greek classical literature. The *Aeneid* is a literary rather than a "true" epic in that it is the result of conscious artistic effort rather than of natural, gradual evolution. But there is nothing artificial in Vergil's deeply rooted patriotic sentiment nor in his unquestioning belief in the divine origin and destiny of the Roman state. His *Aeneid* remains today one of the most stirring productions of a great civilization.

BIBLIOGRAPHICAL REFERENCES: The most complete modern edition is *P. Vergili Maronis opera*, edited by Frederic A. Hirtzel, 1953. There are many translations of Vergil in English; among the most recent are *Virgil*, translated by H. Rushton Fairclough, 1946; *Virgil's Works*, translated by J. W. Mackail, 1950; and *The Aeneid of Virgil*, translated by C. Day Lewis, 1952. See also John W. Mackail, *Virgil*, 1931; William F. J. Knight, *Roman Vergil*, 1944; Steele Commager, ed., *Virgil: A Collection of Critical Essays*, 1966; William S. Anderson, *The Art of the Aeneid*, 1969; L. Wilkinson, *The Georgics of Virgil: A Critical Survey*, 1969; and Michael C. Putnam, *Virgil's Pastoral Art; Studies in the Eclogues*, 1970.

PAUL VERLAINE

Born: Metz, France
Date: March 30, 1844

Died: Paris, France
Date: January 8, 1896

Principal Works

POEMS: *Poèmes saturniens*, 1866; *Fêtes galantes*, 1869; *La bonne chanson*, 1870; *Romances sans paroles*, 1874; *Sagesse*, 1881; *Jadis et naguère*, 1884; *Amour*, 1888; *Parallèlement*, 1889; *Bonheur*, 1891.
POEMS IN TRANSLATION: *Complete Works*, 1909; *Selected Poems*, 1948.
AUTOBIOGRAPHY: *Confessions*, 1895 (*Confessions of a Poet*).

The son of a former captain of engineers of Napoleon's army, Paul (Marie) Verlaine was born in Metz, March 30, 1844. He was educated in Paris, and then secured a minor position with an insurance company, thus following the tradition of many French artists and writers who have so often attached themselves to humdrum jobs that would provide a small salary and yet leave some spare time for creative work. In 1870 he married a Mlle. Mautet; and in the following year he formed the fatal friendship with Arthur Rimbaud that was to affect his life so adversely and was to be a curious forerunner of the Oscar Wilde-Lord Alfred Douglas affair that rocked England twenty years later. With Rimbaud, a much younger man of savage, indeed almost insane temperament, Verlaine wandered through England, France, and Belgium. He had long been drinking heavily, and the journey ended disastrously when he tried to shoot Rimbaud. This act cost Verlaine two years in prison at Mons, during which time he was converted to Catholicism. When he returned to France in 1875, his wife divorced him; he went to England again to earn his living as a teacher of French.

Verlaine had begun his poetic career as a member of the "Parnassian" school, led by Leconte de Lisle, whose members aimed at a detached severity in poetry; but as early as his second volume he was obviously slipping away from them by means of the eighteenth century fantasies of the *Fêtes galantes*. This phase, charming though it may have been, was not, however, Verlaine's important work. His greatest significance, beginning with *Romances sans paroles*, lies in his contribution to the Symbolist Movement.

The poets included in this general movement were at first known as the "decadents," a term that Verlaine was willing to accept. The name "Symbolists" was suggested by Moréas, and the school derived primarily from Baudelaire's poem "Correspondences," in which nature is described as a "forest of symbols." It was a reaction against the austere impersonality of the Parnassians, and can perhaps best be described by quoting Mallarmé's comment: "To name an object is to suppress three-fourths of the enjoyment of the poem. . . . to suggest it, there is the dream." Thus Symbolist poetry consists largely of vague suggestions, of half-hints, by which the poet tries to express "the secret affinities of things with his soul." "No color," Verlaine said in his poem, "The Art of Poetry," "no color, only the nuance." And again: "Take eloquence and wring its neck"—a protest against the sonorous declamations of poetry such as Hugo's. Symbolist practice led inevitably to poetry that became more and more "private" as each poet developed his own set of symbols, the ultimate, perhaps, being Rimbaud's insistence that for him each vowel had a different color—A, black; E, white; and so on. Poetry, then, finally came to resemble music; its purpose was the evocation of a mood, and the "subject" was unimportant. Behind the Symbolists clearly stood the figure of Poe, whom Baudelaire had introduced to France in the 1860's.

In France, the Symbolist Movement led to Mallarmé and finall to Paul Valéry; in England, it influenced the young William Butler Yeats as well as a number of almost-forgotten poets of the 1890's. Much of the difficulty that many readers experience in dealing with contemporary poetry stems from the Symbolists' practice of developing a "private language."

Although Verlaine regained sufficient respectability to be invited to lecture in England in 1894, his later life was that of the perfect bohemian as the term is popularly understood. He alternated between cafés and hospitals, and finally died in Paris, January 8, 1896.

BIBLIOGRAPHICAL REFERENCES: The definitive French edition is *Œuvres Poétiques* (Pléiade), 1948. There is a bilingual edition translated and edited by Doris Gourévitch, 1970. The standard study of Verlaine is E. Lepelletier, *Paul Verlaine: sa vie et son œuvre*, 1907 (Eng. trans., 1909). An important recent work in English is Joanna Richardson, *Verlaine*, 1971. See also Anatole France, *La Vie littéraire* (Third Series, 1891); E. Delille, "The Poet Verlaine," *Fortnightly Review*, XLIX (March 1891); Arthur Symons, *The Symbolist Movement in Literature*, 1908; Frank Harris, *Contemporary Portraits: First Series*, 1920; and Lawrence and Elizabeth Hanson, *Verlaine: Fool of God*, 1957.

JULES VERNE

Born: Nantes, France
Date: February 8, 1828

Died: Amiens, France
Date: March 24, 1905

Principal Works

NOVELS: *Cinq semaines en ballon*, 1863 (*Five Weeks in a Balloon*); *Voyage au centre de la terre*, 1864 (*A Journey to the Center of the Earth*); *De la terre à la lune*, 1865 (*A Trip to the Moon*); *Vingt mille lieues sous les mers*, 1870 (*Twenty Thousand Leagues under the Sea*); *L'Île mystérieuse*, 1870 (*The Mysterious Island*); *Le Tour du monde en quatre-vingts jours*, 1872 (*Around the World in Eighty Days*); *Michel Strogoff*, 1876; *Le Rayon vert*, 1882.

With the possible exception of Dumas, Jules Verne is probably the best known of all French novelists among English-speaking peoples. Born on February 8, 1828, he lived a quiet childhood in Nantes, where he attended the local lycée before going to Paris to study law. Soon after arriving in Paris, he discovered that he preferred literary work and began to write for the stage; in addition to writing several librettos for operas he also collaborated with the younger Dumas on some ephemeral plays. His first real success came with the publication of a novelette, *Five Weeks in a Balloon*, in 1863. The popularity of that short narrative encouraged Verne to continue writing what seemed at the time extravagant tales of technocracy and technology to which he added carefully prepared scientific and geographical data to provide a background of realism, in much the same way that Daniel Defoe had done in providing realistic background for his novels a century and a half before. The subject matter and lively action of Verne's tales soon gained for him an immense following in France and abroad, for his books coincided with the popular interest in science and invention beginning to sweep people's imagination during the second half of the nineteenth century. His novels, intended at the time for adult readers, still have a wide following in America, at least among youngsters, and the wide popularity of his tales is attested to by the great number of translations and foreign editions. Each novel foretells some scientific or technological development, many of which have now been reached or passed, with the result that some of Verne's devices seem crude to twentieth century readers.

The most famous of Verne's novels is *Twenty Thousand Leagues Under the Sea*, rewritten many times for children. In its own day the novel was a pioneer work introducing the submarine to literature decades before such craft were successfully built and used by any of the world's navies. In this case, as in others, Verne came startlingly close to later technological developments; his fictional *Nautilus* is propelled by electricity and functions on principles very similar to those of modern undersea craft.

Although literary scholars and even modern writers of science fiction have neglected his voluminous works, generations of readers have turned to Verne while forgetting other French authors with more serious intentions. In his own time Verne did not go unhonored. He was made a Chevalier of the Legion of Honor by the French government, and he was acclaimed by the French Academy. He died at Amiens on March 24, 1905, too early to see many of his fictional dreams of technology come true in real life.

BIBLIOGRAPHICAL REFERENCES: Verne's principal works are available in translation. For biography and criticism see Charles Lemire, *Jules Verne,* 1908; F. C. Herne, *Jules Verne: An Appreciation,* 1914; Kenneth Allott, *Jules Verne,* 1940; G. H. Waltz, *Jules Verne,* 1943; and I. O. Evans, *Jules Verne and His Work,* 1966. An interesting biography intended for young people is Catherine Owens Peare, *Jules Verne: His Life,* 1956.

ALFRED DE VIGNY

Born: Loches, France
Date: March 27, 1799

Died: Paris, France
Date: September 17, 1863

Principal Works

NOVEL: *Cinq-Mars*, 1826.

TALES AND SKETCHES: *Servitude et grandeur militaires*, 1835 (*Military Service and Greatness*).

POEMS: *Poèmes antiques et modernes*, 1822; *Éloa, ou la sœur des anges*, 1824; *Poèmes philosophiques*, 1843.

PLAYS: *La Maréchale d'Ancre*, 1831; *Chatterton*, 1835.

ESSAYS AND STUDIES: *Stello, ou les diables bleus*, 1832.

In French literature Alfred (Victor), Comte de Vigny is important as a great pioneer of the romantic movement in the nineteenth century, but to speakers of English he is best known as the author of a single novel, *Cinq-Mars*, a historical romance. Born at Loches on March 27, 1799, he followed a family tradition of generations and began his career as an officer in the French army in 1813, at the age of sixteen. He retired from military life in 1825, after twelve years of peacetime service. Before retiring he had already begun to write, and a volume of his verse, *Poèmes antiques et modernes*, had been published in 1822. This volume was followed by a series of narrative poems, including *Éloa* in 1824. The early poetry of Vigny, collected in 1837, was, according to his own preface to the collected edition, philosophic thought clothed in the form of poetic art. Alfred de Musset, Victor Hugo, and Lamartine, all later and important French romantic poets, were influenced by Vigny's work. In his later poetry he tried to analyze human problems and present them through Biblical symbols, as in *La Colère de Samson* (1839, *Samson's Anger*) and *Le Mont des Oliviers* (1843–1844, *The Mount of Olives*).

In addition to his poetry and his very popular novel, *Cinq-Mars*, Vigny translated Shakespeare into French, wrote studies of the poet in modern society in *Stello*, wrote plays (including one about the English poet Chatterton), and published a volume of sketches and essays on military life, *Military Service and Greatness*.

In private life Vigny was unfortunate. He was married to an Englishwoman, Lydia Bunbury, in 1828, but she shortly afterward became a permanent invalid. From 1831 to 1837 Vigny was the lover of Marie Dorval, a celebrated actress, but the affair ended unhappily. He was elected to the French Academy in 1845. Twice he ran unsuccessfully for the French Assembly, in 1848 and 1849. He died in Paris on September 17, 1863.

BIBLIOGRAPHICAL REFERENCES: This author has received little attention from English and American critics. The best studies are Arnold Whitridge, *Alfred de Vigny*, 1933, which includes a bibliography; and James Doolittle, *Alfred de Vigny*, 1967. See also Anatole France, *Alfred de Vigny*, 1923. For readers of French there is Emile Lauvrière, *Alfred de Vigny*, 2 vols., 1946. S. Harvey Clarke, *The Works of Vigny Judged by His Contemporaries*, 1932, is a collection of critical passages with a slight commentary. Charles W. Bird, *Alfred de Vigny's "Chatterton,"* 1941, is a source study for advanced students.

FRANÇOIS VILLON

Born: Paris, France
Date: 1431

Died: Unknown
Date: Unknown

PRINCIPAL WORKS

POEMS: *Le Petit Testament,* 1456 (*Little Testament*); *Le Grand Testament,* 1461 (*Great Testament*).

Nothing is known of the background and youth of Villon except that he was "almost certainly" born in Paris in 1431, of poor parents. His father apparently died early; his mother was still living in 1461. His name was actually Montcorbier, but he took the name of his patron (and probable relative) Guillaume de Villon, a priest and professor of canon law in Paris. The patron sent young Villon to the University of Paris, at that time one of the greatest in Europe, where he received the degree of bachelor of arts (1449) and master of arts (1452).

Shortly after Villon received his master's degree, there began the long series of embroilments with the law, incidents which scholars have dug out of the Paris archives and which make Villon's life so colorful. On June 5, 1455, he was involved in a street brawl with one Jehan le Mardi and a priest named Phillippe Chermoye, as a result of which Chermoye died of his wounds. Villon fled the city and was banished, but the sentence was remitted. Back in Paris the next year, he was so badly beaten in another brawl that he planned to go to Angers. But before his departure, near the Christmas of 1456, he and some equally disreputable friends robbed the chapel of the College of Navarre. The robbery was discovered in the spring; one of the gang turned king's evidence, and Villon was again banished from Paris. For four years he wandered about France, touching the heights and depths of the medieval world. In 1457 he was a visitor at the court of Charles, Duc d'Orléans, himself one of the great French medieval poets, and was likewise sheltered by Jean II of Bourbon. But he could not keep out of trouble; in 1460 he was sentenced to death in Orléans and was freed only as a result of the general amnesty proclaimed on the state entry of the duke's infant daughter. The summer of 1461 found him in prison at Meung, and again he owed his release to the royal house, for Louis XI passed through the city and prisoners were consequently pardoned.

The autumn of 1462 found him back in Paris and again involved in a complicated web of trouble in which the old robbery figured. He was thrown into the Châtelet prison, tortured, and sentenced to be hanged; but the Parlement de Paris commuted his sentence to ten years' banishment from the city. After this date he vanished completely, and the most diligent research has not solved the mystery of his last years. From what is known of his life, it is likely that his death was neither edifying nor pleasant. Rabelais stated that he found refuge in London, but there is no evidence for this unlikely report.

Villon's *Testaments* are long, rambling poems in eight-line stanzas interspersed with *ballades* and *lais.* It is highly personal poetry, in which the author makes no attempt to hide the details of his sordid career—"in the thirtieth year of my age, when I have drunk so deep of shame." By ironically using the form of a "testament," he was able to include a long list of people with whom he had had dealings, bequeathing to each some appropriate memento, thus paying off old scores and expressing gratitude. The charm of the poems to modern readers lies in the unrivaled picture that is given of France at the close of the Middle Ages, a picture that cannot be gained from the romances of chivalry or the poems of courtly love. We can visualize the swarming city of Paris, the church where his mother went to pray, the taverns, the brothel where he lived with Fat Margot—for Villon had seen all aspects of contemporary life, from the court of Charles d'Orléans to the prison of Le Châtelet. There is also the frank revelation of the fascinating personality of a man who could jest about the gallows he had, more than once, narrowly escaped and the next moment write the *ballade* of his mother praying to the Virgin. Though Villon made the conventional gesture of blaming his ill-luck on Fortune, he clearly knew that his troubles were of his own making, that he was hopelessly enmeshed in vice, that the gibbet was perilously close. The only consolation he could draw was from the favorite theme of the fifteenth century—"the Dance of Death," Death the Leveller, who brings high and low alike to the same end.

Ignored during the neo-classic seventeenth and eighteenth centuries, Villon's poetry was revived by the Romanticists as part of the renewed interest in medieval literature. It appealed particularly to writers of the latter part of the nineteenth century, who, from the safety of Victorian England, enjoyed peering into the turbulent fifteenth century that had produced such contrasts as Jeanne d'Arc and François Villon.

BIBLIOGRAPHICAL REFERENCES: The *Œuvres Complètes* were edited by M. Auguste Longnon, 1892. There are two translations of Villon's poetry, that by John Heron Lepper, including the sundry translations by John Payne and others, 1926, and that of Lewis Wharton, 1935. The best study of Villon in English is D. B. Wyndham Lewis, *François Villon: A Documented Survey*, 1928. See also Gaston Paris, **François Villon**, 1901; P. Champion, *François Villon: sa vie et son temps*, 1913; and, in English, John Fox, *The Poetry of Villon*, 1962.

FRANÇOIS MARIE AROUET DE VOLTAIRE

Born: Paris, France
Date: November 21, 1694

Died: Paris
Date: May 30, 1778

Principal Works

novels: *Zadig,* 1747; *Candide,* 1759; *L'Ingènu,* 1767; *La Princesse de Babilone,* 1768; *L'Homme aux quarante écus,* 1768.

philosophical and critical essays: *Lettres philosophiques sur les Anglais,* 1733; *Temple du goût,* 1733; *Traité sur la tolérance,* 1763; *Théâtre de Pierre Corneille,* 1764; *Dictionnaire philosophique,* 1764; *Droits des hommes,* 1768.

plays: *Œdipe,* 1718; *Brutus,* 1730; *Zaïre,* 1732; *Tancrède,* 1760; *Irène,* 1778.

poems: *La Henriade,* 1724; *Discours en vers sur l'homme,* 1738; *La Pucelle,* 1755.

history: *Histoire de Charles XII,* 1731; *Essai sur les mœurs et l'esprit des nations,* 1754; *Le Siècle de Louis XIV,* 1756.

The man who, under the name of Voltaire, was to be remembered as the foremost spokesman of the Age of Enlightenment, was born François Marie Arouet in Paris on November 21, 1694. The son of a prosperous lawyer who numbered among his friends members of the nobility and the literary aristocracy, young François grew up in an atmosphere of wit and culture. At the age of eleven, already known in Paris as an unusually clever rhymer of verses, he was invited to the salon of the celebrated Ninon de l'Enclos, thus gaining an early entree into a dazzling world of free morals and free thought. Although from a Jansenist family, François received his formal education at the Jesuit Collège Louis-le-Grand, where he acquired a solid classical background, familiarity with poetry and drama, and a number of noble and influential friends who were to serve him well throughout his lifetime.

While still in his school days, he became a member of the cultivated, freethinking, epicurean, and rather debauched "Society of the Temple." Resisting his father's efforts to make him a lawyer, he insisted that he would be a poet, and soon his biting verses mocking those in high places had earned him several brief exiles from Paris and, in 1717, an eleven-month sojourn in the Bastille. He emerged from prison with a finished draft of *Œdipe,* the first of the more than fifty plays he was to write during his lifetime. Some of these plays were failures, others were spectacular successes on the contemporary stage, but none has survived the test of time. Although they are interesting in their frequently exotic settings, their use of characters from French history, and their introduction of some of the elements of the less formal English drama upon the rigorously defined classical stage of France, it is for their historic interest rather than their literary or dramatic merit that they are read today.

A few years later, following another brief term in prison, a three-year exile in England brought François, who by this time had changed his name to Arouet de Voltaire, into the society of such men as Pope, Swift, and Gay, and into contact with the ideas of Bacon, Locke, and Newton. As a result of this sojourn, much of the intellectual activity of Voltaire's most productive period was devoted to synthesizing the two streams of rationalistic, freethinking ideas, French and English. Voltaire returned to France with his Deism and skepticism strengthened, and with a strong desire to cultivate liberal thought in his homeland. One of his first weapons in this cause was the *Lettres philosophiques sur les Anglais* which, in characteristically brief, epigrammatic sentences, described the political liberty, religious tolerance, and commercial enterprise of the British, contrasting them with conditions in France. When this volume was published its implied criticism of French law, religion, and institutions incurred royal wrath which forced Voltaire to flee Paris and take up residence with various wealthy sponsors in the provinces.

At the home of one of these sponsors Voltaire met the Marquise du Châtelet, the brilliant and learned woman who was to be his mistress and intellectual companion for fifteen years. The years he spent with her at Cirey were fruitful ones of intellectual development and consolidation. During that time he was appointed royal historiographer, was elected to the French Academy, wrote numerous plays, worked on several volumes of historical criticism, including the rationalistic, freethinking *Essai sur les mœurs* (1754, *Essay on Manners*), which was not published until 1754, and published the tale *Zadig* in 1747. After the Marquise du Châtelet's death in 1749 Voltaire spent three years at the court of his great admirer and patron, Frederick the Great of Prussia, years which had been intended for the creation in reality of the Platonic ideal of a philosopher-king, but which were marked by increasingly bitter quarrels and disillusionment. Upon his return to France, Voltaire, grown rich from writings, pensions, and shrewd business ventures, purchased and settled on a great estate at Ferney, conveniently close to the Swiss border. It was during his life there that his *Traité sur la tolérance* was written and the first volume of the *Dictionnaire philosophique,* a work which epitomized Voltaire's rationalism and his universal interests, was published. At Ferney he wrote articles for Diderot's *Encyclopédie* and dedicated himself to the extirpation of "L'Infâme," the intolerance and superstition which he believed to be the inevitable accompaniment of any form of organized religion. In the midst of numerous sustained interests and activities, he spent three days writing *Candide,* the work for which he is best remembered.

In *Candide, ou l'Optimisme,* the fantastically improbable travels, adventures, and misfortunes of the young Candide, his fiancée Cunegonde, and his tutor Pangloss are recounted in a terse, dry, understated style. Voltaire, never an unqualified optimist, and progressively disillusioned by his mistress's death, the failure of his schemes for Frederick the Great, the gratuitous horror and suffering of the great Lisbon earthquake of 1755, and his acquaintance with the universal folly and wickedness of mankind derived from his wide reading, makes his exaggerated adventure tale an ironic attack on the optimistic philosophy of Leibniz and Pope, who contended that this was "the best of all possible worlds." By endowing his characters initially with a good fortune and every prospect for happiness, and then leading them through every conceivable misfortune into resigned old age, Voltaire makes the point that only by taking life as it comes and avoiding theoretical speculation about its meaning can man ward off despair. Richly spiced with a wit and humor which are as fresh today as when they were created, *Candide* is nevertheless the thoughtful and embittered product of a mind more concerned with communicating an idea than with skillful characterization or pure entertainment.

Early in 1778 Voltaire entered Paris in triumph to oversee the production of his latest play, *Irène*. There, in his hour of greatest glory, he died on May 30. Characteristically, the man whose clear, direct style made him the greatest spokesman for the anti-clerical and rationalistic ideas of the Age of Enlightenment, had died "in a state of sin," and his body had to be smuggled out of Paris at night to prevent its ignominious burial in a common ditch.

BIBLIOGRAPHICAL REFERENCES: The literature on Voltaire is tremendous. See G. Bengesco, *Bibliographie des Œuvres de Voltaire*, 4 vols., 1882–1890, for a listing of the items credited to him; and for Voltaire criticism Mary H. Barr, *Bibliography of Writings on Voltaire, 1825–1925*, 1926, and *Bibliographical Data on Voltaire from 1926 to 1930*, 1933. An edition of the *Complete Works* was published in Paris, 1877–1885. A useful one-volume edition is *The Portable Voltaire*, edited by Ben Ray Redman, 1949.

For biography and criticism see S. G. Tallentyre, *Life of Voltaire*, 2 vols., 1903, the best of the biographical studies in English; also John Morley, *Voltaire*, 1874; J. C. Collins, *Voltaire in England*, 1886; J. M. Robertson, *Voltaire*, 1922; Richard Aldington, *Voltaire*, 1925; Cleveland B. Chase, *The Young Voltaire*, 1926; H. N. Brailsford, *Voltaire*, 1935; and Nancy Mitford, *Voltaire in Love*, 1957. A good introductory study is Georges Pellissier, *Voltaire philosophe*, 1908. An interesting anthology is *Voltaire's England*, edited by Desmond Flower, 1951. See also Gustave Lanson, *Voltaire*, translated by Robert A. Wagoner, 1966; Wiliam F. Bottiglia, ed., *Voltaire: A Collection of Critical Essays*, 1968; and Norman L. Torrey, *The Spirit of Voltaire*, 1968.

LEWIS WALLACE

Born: Brookville, Indiana
Date: April 10, 1827

Died: Crawfordsville, Indiana
Date: February 15, 1905

Principal Works

NOVELS: *The Fair God,* 1873; *Ben Hur: A Tale of the Christ,* 1880; *The Prince of India,* 1893.

General Lewis (Lew) Wallace, though a successful realist as a soldier and politician, was a successful romantic as a novelist at the time in American literary history when the best novelists were realists. The general American reading public, however, preferred romance and sentiment, and his novel *Ben Hur,* published in 1880, became an outsanding best seller.

Wallace, born at Brookville, Indiana, April 10, 1827, studied for the bar and practiced law until the outbreak of the Mexican War, in which he served. He remained in government service, rose to the rank of major-general during the Civil War, served as president of court in the Andersonville prison trials, acted as governor of the New Mexico Territory from 1878–1881 (during which time he wrote *Ben Hur*), and represented the United States as minister to Turkey (1881–1885). After his retirement from public life he wrote biographies, a tragedy in blank verse, and *The Prince of India.* His first novel, *The Fair God,* a tale of the conquest of Mexico by Cortez, is often considered his best. *Ben Hur* is a dramatization of the story of Christ, sentimentalized in action and language but vivid and memorable in its authentic detail. *The Prince of India* presents the legendary character of the Wandering Jew. Wallace died at Crawfordsville, Indiana, on February 15, 1905.

BIBLIOGRAPHICAL REFERENCES: For the author's own account of his life see *Lew Wallace: An Autobiography,* 1906. A brief sketch is that by Anna Lane Lingelbach in the *Dictionary of National Biography.* See also Caroline Ticknor, *Glimpses of Authors,* 1922.

EDWARD LEWIS WALLANT

Born: New Haven, Connecticut
Date: October 19, 1926

Died: Norwalk, Connecticut
Date: December 5, 1962

Principal Works

NOVELS: *The Human Season,* 1960; *The Pawnbroker,* 1961; *The Tenants of Moonbloom,* 1963; *The Children at the Gates,* 1964.

Edward Lewis Wallant was born October 19, 1926, in New Haven, Connecticut. He was the son of Sol and Ann (Mendel) Wallant. He received his elementary and secondary education in the public schools. From 1944 to 1946 he served in the U. S. Navy as a gunner's mate aboard the U.S.S. *Glennon.* After the war he attended Pratt Institute (1947–1950) and later the New School for Social Research (1954–1955). From 1950 to 1962 he worked as a graphic artist for various advertising agencies. His first novel, *The Human Season,* was published in 1960; it was followed in 1961 by *The Pawnbroker.* Both works received high critical acclaim. Wallant was given the Jewish National Book Award for fiction in 1960, a scholarship from the Breadloaf Writer's Conference the same year, and a Guggenheim grant in 1962. On December 5, 1962, Wallant died suddenly of an aneurysm; his untimely death cut short a career of unusual promise. He left behind two additional novels which were published posthumously.

In spite of the recognition he gained, Wallant's writing did not fit into the styles that are currently fashionable. His profound sense of humor, although it depended to some extent upon absurdities, was not based upon existentialism; and although he was Jewish and was particularly concerned with Jewish themes, he was not one of those who have been typed as "Jewish Writers." His striking and sometimes grotesque characterizations, his caustic wit and sly humor, are peculiarly his own. His world, though full of problems and ridiculous situations, is not the conventionalized blind universe of irrationality, hopelessness, and despair. Wallant admired the human spirit and believed in its infinite possibilities.

BIBLIOGRAPHICAL REFERENCES: Wallant's novels are considered in some depth in Jonathan Baumbach, *The Landscape of Nightmare,* 1965; Louis D. Rubin, *The Curious Death of the Novel,* 1967; Ernest Becker, "*The Pawnbroker*: A Study in Basic Psychology," *Angel in Armor,* 1969; Max F. Schulz, *Radical Sophistication: Studies in Contemporary Jewish/American Novelists,* 1969; and Charles Alva Hoyt, *Minor American Novelists,* 1970.

Articles of interest include Thomas Lorch, "The Novels of Edward Lewis Wallant," *Chicago Review,* XIX (1967), 78–91; Raney Stanford, "The Novels of Edward Wallant," *Colorado Quarterly,* XVII (1969), 393–406; and Nicholas Ayo, "The Secular Heart: The Achievement of Edward Lewis Wallant," *Critique,* XII (1970), 86–94. For additional material see the *Bulletin of Bibliography,* XXVIII, no. 4 (October–December, 1971), 119.

EDMUND WALLER

Born: Hertfordshire, England
Date: March 3, 1606

Died: Hall Barn, England
Date: October 21, 1687

Principal Works

POEMS: *Poems*, 1645; *Divine Poems*, 1685; *The Second Part of Mr. Waller's Poems*, 1690.

PROSE: *The Workes of Edmund Waller in This Parliament*, 1645.

Edmund Waller was born on March 3, 1606. He had private instruction for some years, as did most of the literary figures of his time. Thereafter he was sent to Eton and to Cambridge. Waller was married in 1631, after having served for several years as a member of Parliament. His wife died soon after their marriage and Waller retired to Beaconfield, where he lived the life of a wealthy country gentleman. He wrote at this time some of the poems which were to make him famous, especially those love poems to the lady he called Sacharissa. Whether the relationship was more than literary seems unlikely—she was indifferent to the poems, and he proved to be indifferent to her marriage to another man. She served, it would appear, more as a model for art than as a passion of life.

In Parliament once again, Waller distinguished himself as a speaker. He became known as a moderate, and was therefore out of place in a time and place becoming increasingly revolutionary. After attempting to conciliate the King and the House of Commons, Waller tried to arrange to set the former at liberty. As a result he was placed under arrest and then banished to France. When Cromwell took power Waller was able to return. After the Restoration he managed to dispel a reputation for ingratiating himself with Cromwell, and he became popular with Cromwell's enemies. He continued his service in Parliament and distinguished himself in the cause of religious toleration. At court he was a literary model for the younger men who admired his poetry.

Waller's work consisted of short lyrical poems, for the most part on love. He was an important innovator, giving to the couplet the form, smoothness, and precision that later poets were to admire and imitate. Indeed, he can be thought of as one of the best of the seventeenth century poetic craftsmen. His poems today are no longer admired (they are read only in the universities). Yet Waller's technical work had very great influence; he endowed the poets of the eighteenth century with the couplet, which became its favorite mode of verse. He endowed them too with a diction and an attitude towards poetry that dominated literary life for a considerable time after his death. Classicism in English poetry is attributable not only to the Roman verse that served as its models, but to men like Waller and Denham, who tried to replace the poetry of the early seventeenth century. Under their influence poetry became less intellectual —and also more lyrical. In essence, Waller brought back harmonics to English verse, and laid the groundwork for poets as distinguished as Dryden and Pope.

BIBLIOGRAPHICAL REFERENCES: The best edition is still that of G. Thorn-Drury, 2 vols., 1905. There is a good discussion of Waller's life and work in Samuel Johnson's *Lives of the Poets,* 1779.

The most important critical study is Warren L. Chernaik, *The Poetry of Limitation: A Study of Edmund Waller,* 1968. See also Ruth Wallerstein, "The Rhetoric and Metre of the Heroic Couplet," *Publications of the Modern Language Association,* L (1935), 166–210; R. L. Sharp, *From Donne to Dryden,* 1940; F. W. Bateson, *English Poetry: A Critical Introduction,* 1950; A. W. Allison, *Toward an Augustan Poetic,* 1965; and John Buxton, *A Tradition of Poetry,* 1967. Additional references and brief comment may be found in Douglas Bush, *English Literature in the Earlier Seventeenth Century,* 1945.

HORACE WALPOLE

Born: London, England
Date: September 24, 1717

Died: London
Date: March 2, 1797

Principal Works

NOVEL: *The Castle of Otranto*, 1765.
LETTERS: *Letters*, edited by Peter Cunningham, 1857–1859 (9 vols.); *Letters*, edited by Mrs. Paget Toynbee, 1903–1905 (16 vols.); *The Yale Edition of Horace Walpole's Correspondence*, edited by W. S. Lewis, 1937 ff.
MEMOIRS: *Reminiscences*, 1805; *Memoirs of the Last Ten Years of the Reign of George II*, 1822; *Memoirs of the Reign of George III*, 1845; *Journal of the Reign of George III from 1771 to 1783*, 1859.
PLAY: *The Mysterious Mother*, 1768.
MISCELLANEOUS: *Aedes Walpolianae*, 1747; *A Catalogue of the Royal and Noble Authors of England*, 1758; *Anecdotes of Painting in England*, 1763–1771; *Historic Doubts on the Life and Reign of Richard III*, 1768.

Born in London, September 24, 1717, Horace (christened Horatio) Walpole was the son of Sir Robert Walpole, notorious British prime minister of the eighteenth century. At the age of ten Walpole was sent to Eton, where he formed friendships with boys like Thomas Ashton, Richard West, and Thomas Gray, who all became famous men. Following Eton came an academic career at King's College, Cambridge, from 1735 to 1739. Although he was supposed to enter upon a study of law after leaving the university, Walpole, in the company of Thomas Gray, made a lengthy tour of the Continent, visiting and finding delightful Paris, the Alps, Florence, and Rome. In Florence they met Horace Mann, the famous American who was destined to receive the largest number of Walpole's letters after the English dilettante became the most inveterate and voluminous writer of letters in English literary history.

Following his return to England, Walpole became a member of Parliament, serving from 1741 to 1768. In 1747 he acquired a small house in Twickenham, a residence to become famous as Strawberry Hill; famous as Walpole's home, as the center of the owner's enthusiasm for Gothic architecture and "ruins," as the home of the Strawberry Hill Press, and as a kind of park-museum-showplace. By his work on Strawberry Hill, Walpole—who was something of an expert in society, politics, literature, and painting—was to make a name for himself as a gardener and an architect. For twenty years the house was enlarged and given additional architectural features. The Strawberry Hill Press, which published Gray's great odes, also stimulated Walpole to publication. His *Fugitive Pieces in Verse and Prose* (1758) and his tragic drama, *The Mysterious Mother*, were printed there, although his famous *The Castle of Otranto*, which was published anonymously, was not.

In his second preface to *The Castle of Otranto*, Walpole said that his novel was written to revive the supernatural elements of the earlier French romances, adding some of the aspects of the sentimental novel of the eighteenth century in England. The supernatural elements were designed to provide terror for the readers; if they did at the time, they do so no longer, being regarded often by contemporary readers as merely slightly humorous. Perhaps the chief contribution Walpole made to fiction was a reliance on stage-set backgrounds. Later Gothic writers adopted them in an effort to provide a background against which the reader would accept anything that the novelist wished to include in the action, regardless of how absurd it might be.

Outside the realm of fiction, other facets of Walpole's life loom as much more important. His memoirs, covering the last half of the eighteenth century, were written in a conscious effort to be the historian of his own times. One set covers the reign of George III, and another set covers the last years of the reign of George II. Of even greater importance to the modern student of history is Walpole's tremendous correspondence. In his letters Walpole specialized. To Horace Mann, for example, went letters on politics, while to other selected recipients, he sent letters on other topics. A vast amount of information on the culture and affairs of England and the Continent is contained in the letters; they are a source of historical knowledge which is still far from measured, and they have been compared in value to a thousand of the "documentary" films of the twentieth century.

Walpole became the fourth Earl of Orford in 1791. He never married; perhaps too busy for domestic affairs. Mme. du Deffand, the famous French wit and bluestocking, was in love with him, and Mary Berry, a neighbor whose family was intimate with Walpole, seems to have been in love with him as well. Walpole's most famous aphorism is his statement, "Life is a comedy to those who think, a tragedy to those who feel." He died in London, March 2, 1797. The auction of his Strawberry Hill collection in 1842 was one of the most celebrated sales of the nineteenth century.

BIBLIOGRAPHICAL REFERENCES: The standard modern biography is Robert W. Ketton-Cremer's *Horace Walpole: A Biography,* 1940 (reprinted 1966). For biography and criticism see also Austin Dobson, *Horace Walpole,* 1890; Dorothy M. Stuart, *Horace Walpole,* 1927; K. K. Mehrota, *Horace Walpole and the English Novel,* 1934; Montague Summers, *The Gothic Quest,* 1938; Hugh Honour, *Horace Walpole,* 1957; W. S. Lewis, *Horace Walpole,* 1960; Warren H. Smith, ed., *Horace Walpole: Writer, Politician, and Connoisseur,* (essays by various hands), 1967; and W. S. Lewis, "Horace Walpole Reread," *Atlantic Monthly,* CLXXVI (1945), 48–51.

SIR HUGH WALPOLE

Born: Auckland, New Zealand
Date: March 13, 1884

Died: Keswick, Cumberland, England
Date: June 1, 1941

Principal Works

novels: *The Wooden Horse,* 1909; *Maradick at Forty,* 1910; *Mr. Perrin and Mr. Traill,* 1911 [*The Gods and Mr. Perrin*]; *The Prelude to Adventure,* 1912; *Fortitude,* 1913; *The Duchess of Wrexe,* 1914; *The Golden Scarecrow,* 1915; *The Dark Forest,* 1916; *The Green Mirror,* 1917; *Jeremy,* 1919; *The Secret City,* 1919; *The Captives,* 1920; *The Young Enchanted,* 1921; *The Cathedral,* 1922; *Jeremy and Hamlet,* 1923; *The Old Ladies,* 1924; *Portrait of a Man with Red Hair,* 1925; *Harmer John,* 1926; *Jeremy at Crale,* 1927; *Wintersmoon,* 1928; *Hans Frost,* 1929; *Rogue Herries,* 1930; *Above the Dark Circus,* 1931 [*Above the Dark Tumult*]; *Judith Paris,* 1931; *The Fortress,* 1932; *Vanessa,* 1933; *Captain Nicholas,* 1934; *The Inquisitor,* 1935; *A Prayer for my Son,* 1936; *John Cornelius,* 1937; *The Joyful Delaneys,* 1938; *The Sea Tower,* 1939; *The Bright Pavilions,* 1940; *The Blindman's House,* 1941; *The Killer and the Slain,* 1942; *Katherine Christian,* 1943.

short stories: *The Thirteen Travellers,* 1921; *The Silver Thorn,* 1928; *All Souls' Night,* 1933; *Head in Green Bronze,* 1938.

miscellaneous: *Joseph Conrad,* 1916; *The English Novel,* 1925; *Anthony Trollope,* 1928; *A Letter to a Modern Novelist,* 1932; *The Apple Trees,* 1932.

Hugh (Seymour) Walpole was born in Auckland, New Zealand, March 13, 1884, the son of an English minister sent in 1882 as incumbent of St. Mary's Pro-Cathedral in Auckland. As a boy, Walpole was sent to school in Cornwall, England. His family returned to England and lived in Durham, a Cathedral city; Dr. Walpole was Bishop of Edinburgh from 1910 until his death in 1929.

Walpole was educated at King's College, Canterbury, and Emanuel College, Cambridge. He began writing novels while still an undergraduate, but without success in his early literary ventures. His first journalism took the form of reviews; his first successful novel was *Fortitude,* published in 1913, and his popularity as a writer of fiction on both sides of the Atlantic stems from that year. During World War I Walpole was working in Russia with the Red Cross, and two novels grew out of his experiences there: *The Dark Forest* and *The Secret City,* awarded the James Tait Black Memorial Prize. Most of Walpole's books have a romantic tinge, and many of them have enjoyed very large sales. His most successful ones are parts of a tetralogy covering two hundred years of English social history: *Rogue Herries, Judith Paris, The Fortress,* and *Vanessa.* Other novels include *Mr. Perrin and Mr. Traill, The Duchess of Wrexe, The Captives, The Cathedral, The Old Ladies, Portrait of a Man with Red Hair, Hans Frost, The Inquisitor, John Cornelius, The Sea Tower,* and *The Bright Pavilions.*

At the time of King George VI's coronation, Walpole was knighted and proudly bore his title of Sir Hugh Walpole. Prolific in his fiction, Walpole also wrote short stories, critical studies, plays; did scenarios for films in both Hollywood and Britain; enjoyed great success as public lecturer on numerous lecture tours to the United States and also in Britain. W. Somerset Maugham caricatured him as Alroy Kear in *Cakes and Ale*. Walpole died at his home, Brackenburn, in the Lake District on June 1, 1941.

BIBLIOGRAPHICAL REFERENCES: The authorized biography is Rupert Hart-Davis, *Hugh Walpole*, 1952. See also Clemence Dane, *Tradition and Hugh Walpole*, 1929; Marguerite Steen, *Hugh Walpole: A Study*, 1933; Joseph Hergesheimer, *Hugh Walpole: An Appreciation*, 1919 (pamphlet); J. B. Priestley, "Hugh Walpole," *English Journal*, XVII (1928), 529–536; and Frank Swinnerton, "Hugh Walpole," in *Figures in the Foreground*, 1964, 37–46; *ibid.*, "Maugham and Walpole," 89–94; and *ibid.*, "Walpole in America and Home Again," 95-107.

IZAAK WALTON

Born: Near Stafford, England
Date: August 9, 1593

Died: Winchester, England
Date: December 15, 1683

Principal Works

ESSAYS: *The Compleat Angler, or the Contemplative Man's Recreation,* 1653.
BIOGRAPHY: *The Life of John Donne,* 1640; *The Life of Sir Henry Wotton,* 1651; *The Life of Mr. Richard Hooker,* 1665; *The Life of Mr. George Herbert,* 1670.

Izaak Walton, often called the first professional English biographer, was born of yeoman stock at St. Mary, near Stafford on August 9, 1593. In his youth he was apprenticed to an ironmonger in London and, becoming a freeman in the company in 1618, he prospered as a dealer in ironware until his retirement during the civil war. Although he was a royalist in his sympathies and his interests were literary, he never became involved in the political or literary contention of the times. In retirement, he devoted himself to his favorite pastime, fishing, out of which developed the charming yet authoritative discourse in *The Compleat Angler.*

Largely self-educated, Walton began his literary career in his late forties when he was commissioned by Sir Henry Wotton to collect material for a projected life of John Donne. Walton, who called himself "the poorest, the meanest, of all his friends," had been a member of Donne's parish of St. Dunstan's; therefore, when Wotton died before the biography had been written, Walton undertook the task of writing a brief life of the poet and divine. The result, published as an introduction to the 1640 edition of Donne's *Sermons,* has become an integral part of the great editions of Donne's poetry and prose. A life of Wotton appeared eleven years later, followed by biographies of such worthies as Bishop Sanderson, Richard Hooker, and George Herbert.

In everything he wrote, Walton presented his material from a Christian point of view, and *The Compleat Angler,* more than a study of a man's recreational pursuits, also champions the Christian virtues of peace, friendship, and goodness as opposed to the money-getting scrambling of the city. One of the writer's aims was to show how one may find peace of mind, so that the book typifies a pervading seventeenth century spirit to seek relief from the world's woes in nature and works of God. The effortless charm and clarity of the style and the freshness of the anecdotage make the work especially attractive, just as the personality of Walton himself made for the many friendships which allowed him to gather material for his less well-known biographies. The bucolic appeal of *The Compleat Angler* is universal; the more than three hundred editions printed since 1653 testify to its enduring popularity. Walton died at Winchester on December 15, 1683.

BIBLIOGRAPHICAL REFERENCES: The best modern edition is *The Compleat Walton,* edited by G. L. Keynes, 1929. Of the many editions of *The Compleat Angler,* those by R. B. Marston, 1888, and by Richard Le Gallienne, 1896, may be mentioned in particular. *The Lives,* edited by George Saintsbury, 1927, contain an important introduction by the editor. See also Stapleton Martin, *Izaak Walton and His Friends,*

1904; D. A. Stauffer, *English Biography Before 1700*, 1930; Edgar Johnson, *One Mighty Torrent*, 1937; John R. Cooper, *The Art of The Compleat Angler*, 1968; and John Butt, "Izaak Walton's Methods in Biography," *English Association Essays*, XIX (1933), 67–84.

ROBERT PENN WARREN

Born: Guthrie, Kentucky
Date: April 24, 1905

Principal Works

NOVELS: *Night Rider,* 1939; *At Heaven's Gate,* 1943; *All the King's Men,* 1946; *World Enough and Time,* 1950; *Band of Angels,* 1955; *Cave,* 1959; *Flood; A Romance of Our Time,* 1964; *Meet Me in the Green Glen,* 1972.

SHORT STORIES: *Blackberry Winter,* 1946; *The Circus in the Attic,* 1947.

POEMS: *Pondy Woods and Other Poems,* 1930; *Thirty-Six Poems,* 1935; *Eleven Poems on the Same Theme,* 1942; *Selected Poems, 1923–1943,* 1944; *Brother to Dragons: A Tale in Verse and Voices,* 1953; *Promises: Poems 1954–1956,* 1957; *You, Emperors, and Others; Poems, 1957–1960,* 1960; *Incarnations: Poems, 1966–1968;* 1968.

BIOGRAPHY: *John Brown: The Making of a Martyr,* 1929.

Robert Penn Warren, born at Guthrie, Kentucky, on April 24, 1905, has employed his Southern background in nearly all his writing. Warren's subjects are usually taken from Southern history; and although his plots abound in violent action, his chief concern is with characters engaged in a philosophical quest in which they seek to discover the meaning of their lives and the meaning of their positions in history.

Warren is probably the best educated major American novelist. After graduating from Vanderbilt University, where he was a contributor to *The Fugitive,* he took his M.A. at the University of California and received a B.Litt. from Oxford as a Rhodes Scholar. He has been notably successful at combining writing with an academic career, and was one of the founders of *The Southern Review* while teaching at Louisiana State University.

Warren's first novel, *Night Rider,* published in 1939, draws upon the Kentucky tobacco wars of the early 1900's. *At Heaven's Gate* is a novel about the daughter of a Southern financier who rebels against her father. *All the King's Men,* his best and most successful novel, won a Pulitzer Prize in 1947. It deals with the rise and assassination of a Deep South politician styled after Huey Long. The novel was also made into a play. *The Circus in the Attic* is a collection of novelettes and short stories. *World Enough and Time,* is a novel based on the famous Kentucky Tragedy, a sensational murder case of 1825. His latest novel, *Band of Angels,* relates the story of a girl who is reared as white and then discovers she is a Negro slave.

Warren has published considerable poetry, and he appears to regard himself as much a poet as a novelist. His poems have been collected in several volumes: *Pondy Woods and Other Poems, Thirty-Six Poems, Eleven Poems on the Same Theme,* and *Selected Poems. Brother to Dragons* is a book-length narrative poem on the murder of a slave by his master.

In the field of non-fiction Warren has written *John Brown: The Making of a Martyr* and *Segregation* (1956), and he has contributed to *I'll Take My Stand* (1930) and *Who Owns America?* (1936), two regional symposiums. With Cleanth Brooks he has been a leader of the New Critics, a school of criticism opposed to the historical or biographical approach to literature. Brooks and Warren have edited a number of anthologies and college textbooks.

If he had written just his thoughtful and energetic novels, Robert Penn Warren would have been a central figure in contemporary American literature. But his remarkable success at combining several literary and scholarly careers makes him a figure of still greater influence and prestige. It seems probable that his reputation will continue to mount.

BIBLIOGRAPHICAL REFERENCES: Full-length studies include Leonard Casper, *Robert Penn Warren: The Dark and Bloody Ground,* 1960; Paul West, *Robert Penn Warren,* 1964; and John Lewis Longley, ed., *Robert Penn Warren: A Collection of Critical Essays,* 1965. For briefer articles see Frederick Brantley, "The Achievement of Robert Penn Warren," in *Modern American Poetry,* edited by B. Rajan, 1950; Charles R. Anderson, "Violence and Order in the Novels of Warren," in *Southern Renascence,* edited by Louis D. Rubin, Jr., and Robert Jacobs, 1953; Babette Deutsch, *Poetry in Our Time,* 1956; also Irene Hendry, "The Regional Novel: The Example of Robert Penn Warren," *Sewanee Review,* LIII (1945), 84–102; Robert Heilman, "Melpomene as Wallflower; or the Reading of Tragedy," *ibid.,* LV (1947), 154–166; Oscar Cargill, "Anatomist of Monsters," *College English,* IX (1947), 1–8; J. E. Baker, "Irony in Fiction: *All the King's Men,*" *ibid.,* IX (1947), 122–130; Eric Bentley, "The Meaning of Robert Penn Warren's Novels," *Kenyon Review,* X (1948), 407–424; Arthur Mizener, "Amphibium in Old Kentucky," *ibid.,* XII (1950), 697–701; W. M. Frohock, "Mr. Warren's Albatross," *Southwest Review,* XXXVI (1951), 48–59; Sam Hynes, "R. P. Warren: The Symbolic Journey," *University of Kansas City Review,* XVII (1951), 279–285; and John M. Bradbury, "Robert Penn Warren's Novels: The Symbolic and Textual Patterns," *Accent,* XIII (1953), 77–89. Warren's activity as a New Critic is covered by F. P. McDowell, "Robert Penn Warren's Criticism," *Accent,* XV (1955), 173–196. For an unfriendly opinion see Norman Kelvin, "The Failure of Robert Penn Warren," *College English,* XVIII (1957), 355-364.

JAKOB WASSERMANN

Born: Fürth, Germany
Date: March 10, 1873

Died: Alt-Aussee, Austria
Date: January 1, 1934

Principal Works

NOVELS: *Die Juden von Zirndorf*, 1897 (*Dark Pilgrimage*); *Die Geschichte der jungen Renate Fuchs*, 1900 (*The Story of Young Renate Fuchs*); *Caspar Hauser oder die Trägheit des Herzens*, 1908 (*Caspar Hauser*); *Das Gänsemännchen*, 1915 (*The Goose Man*); *Christian Wahnschaffe*, 1918 (*The World's Illusion*); *Der Wendekreis I: Der unbekannte Gast*, 1920 (*World's Ends*); *Der Wendekreis II: Oberlins drei Stufen, Sturreganz*, 1922 (*Oberlin's Three Stages: Sturreganz*); *Der Wendekreis III: Ulrike Woytich*, 1923 (*Gold*); *Der Wendekreis IV: Faber oder die verlorenen Jahre*, 1924 (*Faber, or the Lost Years*); *Der Aufruhr um den Junker Ernst*, 1926 (*The Triumph of Youth*); *Der Fall Maurizius*, 1928 (*The Maurizius Case*); *Etzel Andergast*, 1931 (*Doctor Kerkhoven*).

PLAYS: *Die ungleichen Schalen*, 1912 (*Unbalanced Scales*); *Lukardis*, 1932.

BIOGRAPHY: *Deutsche Charaktere und Begebenheiten*, 1915 (*German Characters and Events*); *Hofmannsthal der Freund*, 1929 (*Hofmannsthal: A Friend*); *Christoph Columbus, Der Don Quichote des Ozeans*, 1929 (*Christopher Columbus, Don Quixote of the Seas*); *Bula Matari, Das Leben Stanleys*, 1932 (*Bula Matari: Stanley, Conqueror of a Continent*).

AUTOBIOGRAPHY: *Mein Weg als Deutscher und Jude*, 1921 (*My Life as German and Jew*); *Lebensdienst*, 1928 (*In the Service of Life*); *Selbstbetrachtungen*, 1933 (*Self-Contemplation*).

LETTERS: *Briefe an seine Braut und Gattin Julie, 1900–1929*, 1940 (first published in English as *The Letters of Jakob Wassermann to Frau Julie Wassermann*, 1935).

Perhaps no writer of modern times, unless possibly Francis Thompson, has suffered greater indignities than Jakob Wassermann in the struggle to vindicate himself as an artist. He was born of Jewish parentage at Fürth, near Nuremberg, on March 10, 1873. His father was a merchant with a narrow, conservative outlook who allowed his second wife, the boy's unsympathetic stepmother, to regulate the life of the household. In his childhood, Wassermann's literary talents were ruthlessly curbed, on the principle that if he should become a writer he would be poor and therefore worthless. In 1889 he was packed off to Vienna, where his uncle was the proprietor of a factory; but, unable to bear the routine of business, he made a temporary escape to Munich with the plan of studying to enter the university. Lacking money, he had to retreat home. He was then sent to Vienna again, this time to learn the export trade. Less than a year later, he left his new job, disgraced by a gross practical joke played on him by a fellow employee. Being of an age to perform the enforced military duty, he was thrust into the army, where anti-Semitic comrades made him the butt of pranks and insults.

After completing his year of service he held a government job in Nuremberg until, inheriting a small sum of money, he ventured to Munich again and remained as long as his resources allowed. He then obtained employment briefly at Freiburg. Destitute, he roamed as a beggar in the Black Forest. Finding his way to Zurich and then once more to Munich, he kept himself alive through working at odd jobs. A turn in his fortunes occurred, just in time to avert the collapse of his health, when he was engaged as secretary to a writer, Ernst von Wolzogen, in 1895. Shortly thereafter, he was hired as an editorial assistant by the manager of *Simplicissimus*, a periodical then in its first year of publication. Some of his poems and tales appeared in that journal in 1896, and one story gained him a prize of three hundred marks. In 1898 he returned to Austria, to live there the rest of his life. He finally succeeded in supporting himself by writing. *Dark Pilgrimage* and *The Story of Young Renate Fuchs*, both well received, inaugurated the succession of major novels that established his literary reputation. In 1901 he married Julie Speyer, of Vienna, but separated from her in 1919 and obtained a divorce several years later; he afterwards married Marta Karlweis. On New Year's Day, 1934, he died at Alt-Aussee, where he had resided for ten years.

Wassermann was strongly admired by Schnitzler, Hofmannsthal, and Thomas Mann. His work, though sometimes too diffuse, is impressive for the scope of its themes. He was especially exercised by the problems of ethical conduct and was devoted to the ideals of democratic liberalism.

BIBLIOGRAPHICAL REFERENCES: A primary source for biographical material is Jakob Wassermann, *My Life as A German Jew*, translated 1933. Studies in English include J. C. Blankenagel, *The Writings of Jakob Wassermann*, 1942, and "Jakob Wassermann's Views on America," *German Quarterly*, XXVII (1954), 51–57. For studies in German see Julie Wassermann-Speyer, *Jakob Wassermann und sein Werk*, 1923; S. Bing, *Jakob Wassermann*, 1933; and Marta Karlweis, *Jakob Wassermann*, 1935. See also Henry Regensteiner, "Jakob Wassermann in Retrospect," *Revue des Langues Vivantes* (Bruxelles), XXX (1964), 590–601, and "The Status of Education in the Light of Jakob Wassermann," 621–623; and *ibid.*, "The Obsessive Personality in Jakob Wassermann's Novel *Der Fall Maurizius*," *Literature and Psychology*, XIV (1964), 106–115.

HUGO WAST
Gustavo Martínez Zuviría

Born: Córdoba, Argentina
Date: October 23, 1883

Died: Buenos Aires
Date: March 28, 1962

PRINCIPAL WORKS

NOVELS: *Alegre,* 1905; *Flor de durazno,* 1911 (*Peach Blossom*); *Casa de los cuevos,* 1916 (*The House of the Ravens*); *Valle negro,* 1918 (*Black Valley*); *La corbata celeste,* 1920 (*The Blue Necktie*); *Desierto de piedra,* 1925 (*Stone Desert*); *Myriam la conspiradora,* 1926 (*Myriam the Conspirator*); *Lucía Miranda,* 1929.
HISTORY: *Año X,* 1960 (*Year Ten*).

Gustavo Martínez Zuviría, known in literature as Hugo Wast, was born in Córdoba, Argentina, October 23, 1883. While still a university student he wrote his first novel, *Alegre,* published in 1905. Then he went on to become a Doctor of Laws (1907) and joined the University of Santa Fe as Professor of Economics and Sociology. Politics also attracted him, and he served several terms in Congress. For a long time he was Director of Argentina's National Library; later, Minister of Education.

After two juvenile attempts at novel writing, he published a serious novel about unmarried love, *Peach Blossom,* in 1911. Afraid that the critics of Buenos Aires would scorn any work of a provincial author, he signed it with an anagram of his first name, Gustavo, from which he made "Hugo Wast." The novel finally proved a success. During the next forty years, Wast published thirty-three books, many of them through a company that he organized. They have also appeared with Spanish and Chilean imprints to the number of 290 editions, and nearly a million and a half copies have been sold. In addition, seventy translations have appeared in eleven different languages.

Wast's best seller, *The House of the Ravens,* won for him a prize of the Ateneo in 1915. For his *Black Valley* he won the gold medal of the Spanish Academy, which later made him a corresponding member and enlarged its dictionary by the inclusion of words from his writing. *Stone Desert* was awarded the Grand National Prize of Argentine Literature for the year of its appearance.

Wast's novels can be divided into several groups. One series covers the history of his country from the earliest days of exploration and conquest, as told in *Lucía Miranda,* through the struggle for independence shown in *Myriam the Conspirator,* the period of the dictatorship dramatized in *The Blue Necktie,* and into the future in novels like *Juana Tabor* and *666* (1942).

Wast's training in economics and sociology is apparent in his problem novels set in the rural regions—*Black Valley* and *Stone Desert*—and in his fictional treatment of the urban problem in novels like *Fuente Sellada* (1914) and *Ciudad turbulenta, Ciudad alegre* (*Turbulent City, Happy City*), published in 1919. He also had young readers in mind for several novels, especially the amusing *Pata de zorra* (1924), named from the fortune teller who tried to help a university student pass his examination in Roman law.

It is for the number of readers whom Wast's writings have attracted, rather than for any special influence he has exerted on his contemporaries, that he merits a place in Argentine literature. His ideas about writing are included in his *Vocación de escritor* (*A Writer's Calling*) published in 1946. His most recent volumes of gaucho life are *Estrella de la tarde* (*Evening Star*), published in 1954, and its sequel, *¿Le tiraría la primera piedra?* (*Would You Throw the First Stone?*).

BIBLIOGRAPHICAL REFERENCES: Wast's own account of his career is told in *Vocación de escritor*, printed as Vol. XXXI of his *Obras completas*. See also E. H. Hespelt, "Hugo Wast, Argentine Novelist," *Hispania*, VII (1924); Ruth Sedgwick, "Hugo Wast, Argentina's Most Popular Novelist," *Hispanic American Historical Review*, IX (1929), 116–26; and prefaces to his novels translated into English.

EVELYN WAUGH

Born: Hampstead, London, England
Date: October 28, 1903

Died: Taunton, Somerset, England
Date: April 10, 1966

Principal Works

NOVELS: *Decline and Fall*, 1928; *Vile Bodies*, 1930; *Black Mischief*, 1932; *A Handful of Dust*, 1934; *Scoop*, 1938; *Put Out More Flags*, 1942; *Work Suspended*, 1942; *Brideshead Revisited*, 1945; *Scott-King's Modern Europe*, 1947; *The Loved One*, 1948; *Helena*, 1950; *Men at Arms*, 1952; *Officers and Gentlemen*, 1955; *The Ordeal of Gilbert Pinfold*, 1957; *The End of the Battle*, 1962; *Sword of Honor*, 1966 (final version of *Men at Arms*, *Officers and Gentlemen*, and *The End of the Battle*).

SHORT STORIES: *Mr. Loveday's Little Outing and Other Sad Stories*, 1936; *Love Among the Ruins*, 1953; *Tactical Exercise*, 1954.

TRAVEL SKETCHES AND IMPRESSIONS: *Labels*, 1930 [*A Bachelor Abroad*]; *Remote People*, 1931 [*They Were Still Dancing*]; *Ninety-Two Days*, 1934; *Waugh in Abyssinia*, 1936; *When the Going Was Good*, 1946; *Tourist in Africa*, 1960.

BIOGRAPHY: *Rossetti: His Life and Works*, 1928; *Edmund Campion*, 1935.

AUTOBIOGRAPHY: *A Little Learning*, 1964.

Evelyn Waugh, English satirist and Catholic apologist, was born in London, October 28, 1903, the second son of Arthur Waugh, English critic and publisher, managing director of Chapman & Hall, Limited. He was christened Evelyn Arthur St. John Waugh. An older brother is the novelist Alec Waugh.

His first writing effort, as far as his biographers know, was a 500-word novel in nine chapters entitled *The Curse of the Horse Race*, which was written when he was seven. His first published book appeared in 1928: *Rossetti: His Life and Works*.

Between those two efforts Waugh acquired an education and some experience in earning a living. He prepared for the university at Lancing School, where he won a prize for his verses. He then attended Hertford College, Oxford, for several years, but left the university without a degree. After Oxford he studied painting at Heatherley's Art School. Later he was both a schoolmaster and a journalist, working for a time on the *London Daily Express*.

Although he began his writing career with the biography of Rossetti, he found his forte in the witty, satirical style he set in *Decline and Fall*, published in 1928. He had been brought up in the intellectual circles of English middle-class society, but his independent, critical mind enabled him to see the false fronts in the most impressive performances about him. His indignation was fundamentally moral, presaging the disciplined devotion he was later to find in the Roman Catholic Church, but his manner was modern: bitter, humorous, and cutting in the distinctive fashion that Aldous Huxley in his earlier works also exemplified.

In 1928 he married Evelyn Gardner, daughter of Lord Burghclere, but the marriage was short-lived, ending in divorce two years later. He became a Roman Catholic convert in 1930. That same year saw the publication of his second satirical novel, *Vile Bodies*, a work that hinted at but did not quite reveal the growing seriousness with which he faced contemporary society. After one more novel, *A Handful of Dust,* Waugh made his first impressive mark as a distinctively Catholic writer with his biography of *Edmund Campion,* the sixteenth century English Jesuit martyr. The book proved to be a carefully written, impressive portrait, and it won for its author the Hawthornden Prize in 1936. He was married in 1937 to Laura Herbert, the youngest daughter of Aubrey Herbert, M.P.

By this time Waugh had written, in addition to his novels and biographies, several travel or near-travel books. Among them were *Labels: A Mediterranean Journal,* published in the United States under the title *A Bachelor Abroad; Remote People,* published in the United States as *They Were Still Dancing;* and *Waugh in Abyssinia.* Although the books are entertaining and well written, they have not achieved the popularity of his novels.

Waugh received a temporary commission as a second lieutenant in the Royal Marines in the latter part of 1939. During the war he became a major in the commandos, participated in a raid on Bardia, and was one of a military team parachuted into Yugoslavia to observe Tito's campaign against the Germans. In 1942 he was transferred to the Royal Horse Guards. *Put Out More Flags* marked the transition between his satires on decadent modern society with its Bright Young People and his war novels. Other books reflecting the author's war experiences are *Men at Arms,* which won the James Tait Black Memorial Prize, and *Officers and Gentlemen.*

In 1945 Waugh won mixed critical reception but an extensive reading public with his novel *Brideshead Revisited,* a study of the changing fortunes and souls of the members of a Catholic family. The book was a book club selection in the United States. The public response to the novel made a visit to the United States and a lecture tour possible. The book was responsible for Waugh's receiving the 1945 Catholic Literary Award given by the Gallery of Living Catholic Authors.

Waugh returned briefly to his urbane cutting style with the amusing satirical novel, *The Loved One,* a work criticizing American funeral tastes, particularly as revealed by certain immense Hollywood cemeteries, and the vulgarities of love. In this work a confusion of notices from a funeral home for human beings with a similar institution for dogs puts the final ridiculous stamp on Waugh's sophisticated comment.

BIBLIOGRAPHICAL REFERENCES: The most comprehensive study is Christopher Hollis, *Evelyn Waugh,* 1954. See also Frederick J. Stopp, *Evelyn Waugh: Portrait of an Artist,* 1958; and James F. Careus, *The Satiric Art of Evelyn Waugh,* 1966. For additional criticism see Edmund Wilson, *Classics and Commercials,* 1950; Rose Macaulay, "Evelyn Waugh," *Horizon,* XIV (1946), 360–377; Donat O'Donnell, "The Pieties of Evelyn Waugh," *Kenyon Review,* IX (1947), 400–411; Richard J. Voorhees, "Evelyn Waugh Revisited," *South Atlantic Quarterly,* XLVIII (1949), 270–280; Charles Rolo, "Evelyn Waugh: The Best and the Worst," *Atlantic Monthly,* CXCIV (1954), 80–86; and Steven Marcus, "Evelyn Waugh and the Act of Entertainment," *Partisan Review,* XXIII (1956), 348–357.

MARY WEBB

Born: Leighton, Shropshire, England
Date: March 25, 1881

Died: St. Leonard's, England
Date: October 8, 1927

Principal Works

NOVELS: *The Golden Arrow*, 1916; *Gone to Earth*, 1917; *The House in Dormer Forest*, 1920; *Seven for a Secret*, 1922; *Precious Bane*, 1924; *Armour Wherein He Trusted*, 1929.

POEMS AND ESSAYS: *The Spring of Joy*, 1917; *Poems and The Spring of Joy*, 1928.

Mary (Gladys Meredith) Webb, born in Leighton, England, March 25, 1881, was the daughter of an English-Welsh schoolmaster portrayed as a charming, sympathetic man in his daughter's first novel, *The Golden Arrow*. Mary Webb must have known her father well, for she was educated largely at home, although she spent two years at a private school in Southport, England. She began to write when she was a child, trying her hand at stories and poetry, none of which has ever been published. In 1912 she married Henry Bertram Law Webb, also a schoolmaster.

Mrs. Webb's five novels appeared from 1916 to 1924, with almost no recognition at the time of their publication from either readers or critics. Her only award was the Femina-Vie Heureuse Prize for 1924–1925, which she received for *Precious Bane*. An unfinished novel, *Armour Wherein He Trusted*, was published posthumously, following her death at St. Leonard's, Sussex, October 8, 1927. When Mrs. Webb died she was practically unknown, but in 1928 Prime Minister Stanley Baldwin praised her novels at a Royal Literary Fund dinner. After that recognition, her fame began to grow; her five novels were reprinted shortly thereafter, with introductions by Baldwin, G. K. Chesterton, and others. Whether or not that recognition is permanent, it is still too early to say. Critics are of varying opinion about her work.

Mrs. Webb's novels seem to derive from a good many earlier writers, especially George Eliot and Mrs. Gaskell, and they tend to concentrate on inner meanings which sometimes cause her books to stray away from the reality of most contemporary fiction. Her frequent didacticism, too, is contrary to the tastes of many modern readers. In *The Golden Arrow*, Mrs. Webb placed two pairs of lovers, one pair exemplary and one pair foolish. The contrasts are always obvious, and the author frequently invades the narrative with intrusive commentary and unnecessary moralizing. In *The House in Dormer Forest* there is a contrast again, this time between one family that is close to nature and another that is grasping and materialistic. Once more Mrs. Webb is obvious in preferring the former to the latter and asking the reader to do the same. In this novel, as in other of her books, there are stock characters, such as the plain, despised woman of hidden sweetness who is saved from wasting a life by the timely arrival of a husband who is the epitome of masculinity and carries about with him in obvious fashion a set of high, idealistic values. Other novels are *Gone to Earth, Seven for a Secret*, and *Precious Bane*, which is Mrs. Webb's best-known novel. Her unfinished novel, *Armour Wherein He Trusted*, took the author out of the setting she had habitually used—contemporary Shropshire—into medieval times, for the work was to be a historical romance set against the background of the First Crusade. After her death in 1927 there appeared a volume of essays and poetry written during her adult years. This collection, *The Spring of Joy*, had a preface by Walter de la Mare, in which he pointed out that her poetry and prose both contained certain poetic elements and that her prose rhythms derive from such specific seventeenth century authors as Sir Thomas Browne, author of *Religio Medici* and *Urn Burial*.

BIBLIOGRAPHICAL REFERENCES: The most comprehensive studies are Thomas Moult, *Mary Webb: Her Life and Work*, 1932; and Dorothy P. H. Wrenn, *Goodbye to Morning: A Biographical Study of Mary Webb*, 1964. See also Hilda Addison, *Mary Webb*, 1931, and the prefaces to her novels.

WALTER PRESCOTT WEBB

Born: Panola County, Texas
Date: April 3, 1888

Died: Austin, Texas
Date: March 8, 1963

Principal Works

HISTORY: *Growth of a Nation: The U.S.A.* (with E. C. Barker and W. E. Dodd), 1928; *The Story of Our Nation: The U.S.A.* (with E. C. Barker and W. E. Dodd), 1929; *The Great Plains*, 1931; *Our Nation Grows Up* (with E. C. Barker and W. E. Dodd), 1933; *The Texas Rangers*, 1935; *The Great Frontier*, 1952.

MISCELLANEOUS: *Divided We Stand: Crisis of a Frontierless Democracy*, 1937; editor, *The Handbook of Texas*, 1950; *More Water for Texas*, 1954; *Flat Top: A Story of Modern Ranching*, 1960; *Washington Wife: From the Journal of Ellen Maury Slaydon*, 1963.

Walter Prescott Webb grew up in an impoverished area of western Texas, and he had little schooling until 1905, when his family, having had a good crop, moved from their farm to the town of Kent, Texas. In 1906, after a year of school in Kent, the future historian was granted a certificate to teach in rural schools. After a year of teaching he returned for a higher certificate from the normal school, continuing as a public school teacher. He graduated from the University of Texas in 1915, with an A.B. degree, taking his M.A. in 1920 and his Ph.D. in 1932 from the same university. He also did graduate work at the Universities of Wisconsin and Chicago. He became an instructor at the University of Texas in 1918, where he spent his career, rising to the rank of professor by 1933. He also had special appointments: he became a consulting historian for the National Park Service in 1937; he had a Guggenheim Fellowship in 1938; he was Harkness lecturer at the University of London in 1938; he was Harmsworth Professor of American History at Oxford University in 1942-1943. His fellow historians elected him president of the American Historical Association in 1958, the same year in which he received the award of the American Council of Learned Societies. As a writer, as well as a historian, he was honored: his *The Great Plains* earned him the Lonbat Prize from Columbia University. He received an honorary M.A. from Oxford in 1942, and a Litt. D. from Southern Methodist University in 1951.

As a writer Webb wanted to make the Westerner see what lies all about him. His historical theses were not altogether popular, sometimes offending Southerners, sometimes fellow historians, sometimes Chambers of Commerce, sometimes corporations. He himself believed that his greatest work, done during the late 1950's, was establishing the theory of European history (including the western hemisphere), based upon the expansion of Europeans into America, that the prosperity of all European civilization from 1500-1950 resulted from the existence of the American frontier. Webb's death came at the age of 75, the result of an automobile accident. He was at the time a passenger in a car driven by his second wife, just a few months after their marriage; his wife was the widow of Texas senator Maury Maverick.

BIBLIOGRAPHICAL REFERENCES: See Joe B. Frantz, "Walter Prescott Webb," *Turner, Bolton, and Webb: Three Historians of the American Frontier*, 1965; William A. Owens, *Three Friends: Roy Bedichek, J. Frank Dobie, Walter Prescott Webb*, 1969; Walter Rundell, *Walter Prescott Webb*, 1971; and A. M. Young, "Walter Prescott Webb," *Texas Quarterly*, XI (Spring, 1968), 70–79.

JOHN WEBSTER

Born: London (?), England
Date: Unknown

Died: Unknown
Date: Before 1635

Principal Works

PLAYS: *Westward Ho!* 1604 (with Dekker); *Northward Ho!* 1605 (with Dekker); *The White Devil,* c. 1612; *The Duchess of Malfi,* c. 1613; *The Devil's Law Case,* 1623.

PAGEANT: *Monuments of Honour,* 1624.

The important fact in the life of John Webster is that he wrote *The White Devil* and *The Duchess of Malfi.* The scanty biographical information about this remarkable writer is an indication of the slight esteem Renaissance England granted to its great drama; it also reminds the twentieth century of how exceptional is the relatively large amount of information surviving about William Shakespeare.

Since Webster stated in the Epistle to his *Monuments of Honour* that he was born free of the Guild of Merchant Tailors, it is a reasonable assumption that the John Webster who appears in the Guild records in 1571 and 1576 was his father. A John Webster was a member of an Anglo-German acting company in 1596; a John Webster was admitted to the Middle Temple in 1598. Possibly these references are to the dramatist. Thomas Heywood referred to the dramatist as dead in 1635; but he may have died as much as ten years earlier.

The early part of Webster's dramatic career was spent as a collaborator (read "hack"?) in Philip Henslowe's prolific stable of playwrights; Webster's chief collaborators were John Marston and Thomas Dekker. Between 1610 and 1615 he reached his prime with the two celebrated tragedies which make his reputation. In these masterpieces he is a powerful and moving poet and an excellent man of the theater. Nothing in the plays before the masterpieces or in the plays after them indicates a comparable power.

BIBLIOGRAPHICAL REFERENCES: The standard edition is F. L. Lucas, ed., *The Complete Works of John Webster* (1927). Other studies include E. E. Stoll, *John Webster,* 1905; Rupert Brooke, *John Webster and Elizabethan Drama,* 1916; Travis Bogard, *The Tragic Satire of John Webster,* 1955; Clifford Leech, *Webster: The Duchess of Malfi,* 1963; and E. K. Chambers, *The Elizabethan Stage,* Vol. III, 1923.

FRANK WEDEKIND

Born: Hanover, Germany
Date: July 24, 1864

Died: Munich, Germany
Date: March 9, 1918

Principal Works

PLAYS: *Frühlings erwachen,* 1891 (*The Awakening of Spring*); *Erdgeist,* 1895 (*Earth Spirit*); *Die Kammersänger,* 1899 (*The Tenor*); *Der Marquis von Keith,* 1901; *Die Büchse der Pandora,* 1903 (*Pandora's Box*); *Franziska,* 1912.
POEMS: *Die vier Jahreszeiten,* 1905.
NOVEL: *Mine-haha,* 1901.

Frank (Benjamin Franklin) Wedekind, one of the most controversial of fin-de-siècle German writers, was the son of a world-traveler doctor who at sixty-four had married an actress less than half his age. Born in Hanover, Germany, on July 24, 1864, Wedekind was graduated from Lenzburg in Switzerland in 1883. Later he worked as a journalist and as traveling secretary for Herzog's Circus. While he was with the circus he became convinced that man is essentially an animal who is healthiest when he lives entirely by his instincts, uncorrupted by bourgeois education.

After a brief period as secretary to a Parisian art dealer, Wedekind went to Munich and wrote his first play, *The World of Youth* (1890), the story of a girls' boarding school. It was followed by *The Awakening of Spring,* which presents an adolescent youth tormented by sexual drives and ruthlessly curbed by the iron discipline of society—an attempt on Wedekind's part to out-Nietzsche Nietzsche. He also attacked Ibsen and the realists of the preceding generation for being too genteel and middle class. As writer, actor, and director of the Munich Theater, he felt that the stage needed "beasts of prey," and he proceeded to supply them.

Lulu, the heroine of *Earth Spirit* and *Pandora's Box,* is a Dionysiac character who becomes sex incarnate and is finally cut down by Jack the Ripper. The hero of *The Marquis of Keith* conceives of love as sexual orgy, drives his wife to suicide, tries to build a bawdy house with stolen money but fails, and is abandoned by his mistress. These plays are not simply acted; they are mimed, danced, and screamed, as if Wedekind had Caliban within every character. Toward the end of his career, however, Wedekind reformed, thanked the judges who condemned *Pandora's Box,* and expressed a reverence for the Church. His works, like those of Strindberg, were condemned by Hitler and are now being revived as curiosities of morbid emotional and imaginative excess in the modern German theater. Wedekind died in Munich on March 9, 1918.

BIBLIOGRAPHICAL REFERENCES: Wedekind's principal plays are available in translation. For biography and criticism see Paul Fechter, *Frank Wedekind,* 1920; Arthur Kutscher, *Frank Wedekind, sein Leben und seine Werke,* 1922–1924; Fritz Dehnow, *Frank Wedekind,* 1922; and Samuel Eliot, *Tragedies of Sex,* 1923. For briefer studies see also Raimund Pissin, *Frank Wedekind,* in *Modern Essais,* 53, c. 1905; Anita Block, *The Changing World in Plays and Theatre,* 1939; Eric Bentley, *The Playwright as Thinker,* 1946; and Alexander Natan, "Frank Wedekind," *German Men of Letters,* II, 1964, 103–129.

H. G. WELLS

Born: Bromley, England
Date: September 21, 1866

Died: London, England
Date: August 13, 1946

PRINCIPAL WORKS

PSEUDO-SCIENTIFIC NOVELS AND FANTASIES: *The Time Machine*, 1895; *The Wonderful Visit*, 1895; *The Island of Dr. Moreau*, 1896; *The Invisible Man*, 1897; *The War of the Worlds*, 1898; *The Sleeper Awakes*, 1899; *The First Men in the Moon*, 1901; *The Sea Lady*, 1902; *The Food of the Gods*, 1904; *In the Days of the Comet*, 1906; *The War in the Air*, 1908; *The World Set Free*, 1914; *Men Like Gods*, 1923; *Mr. Blettsworthy on Rampole Island*, 1928; *The King Who Was a King*, 1929; *The Autocracy of Mr. Parham*, 1930; *The Shape of Things to Come*, 1933; *The Croquet Player*, 1937; *Star-Begotten*, 1937; *The Camford Visitation*, 1937.

NOVELS OF CHARACTER: *The Wheels of Chance*, 1896; *Kipps*, 1905; *The History of Mr. Polly*, 1910; *Bealby*, 1915; *The Dream*, 1924; *Christina Alberta's Father*, 1925; *The Bulpington of Blup*, 1933; *Brynhild*, 1937; *Apropos of Dolores*, 1938.

NOVELS OF SOCIAL CRITICISM AND THEME: *Love and Mr. Lewisham*, 1900; *Tono-Bungay*, 1909; *Ann Veronica*, 1909; *The New Machiavelli*, 1911; *Marriage*, 1912; *The Passionate Friends*, 1913; *The Wife of Sir Isaac Harman*, 1914; *The Research Magnificent*, 1915; *Mr. Britling Sees It Through*, 1916; *The Soul of a Bishop*, 1917; *Joan and Peter*, 1918; *The Undying Fire*, 1919; *The Secret Places of the Heart*, 1922; *The World of William Clissold*, 1926; *Meanwhile*, 1927; *The Brothers*, 1938; *The Holy Terror*, 1939; *Babes in the Darkling Wood*, 1940; *All Aboard for Ararat*, 1941; *You Can't Be Too Careful*, 1942.

SHORT STORIES: *The Stolen Bacillus and Other Incidents*, 1895; *The Plattner Story and Others*, 1897; *The Vacant Country*, 1899; *The Country of the Blind*, 1911; *The Short Stories of H. G. Wells*, 1927.

ESSAYS AND STUDIES: *The Discovery of the Future*, 1902; *Mankind in the Making*, 1903; *This Misery of Boots*, 1907; *Socialism and Marriage*, 1908; *New Worlds for Old*, 1908; *First and Last Things*, 1908; *The Great State*, 1912 [*Socialism and the Great State*]; *God, the Invisible King*, 1917; *The Salvaging of Civilization*, 1921; *Socialism and the Scientific Motive*, 1923; *After Democracy*, 1929; *The Way to World Peace*, 1930; *The Work, Wealth and Happiness of Mankind*, 1931; *The Science of Life*, 1931 (with Julian Huxley and G. P. Wells); *The Anatomy of Frustration*, 1936; *World Brain*, 1938; *The New World Order*, 1940; *The Common Sense of War and Peace*, 1940; *The Conquest of Time*, 1942; *'42 to '44*, 1944; *Mind at the End of Its Tether*, 1946.

HISTORY: *The Outline of History*, 1920; *A Short History of the World*, 1922.

BIOGRAPHY AND AUTOBIOGRAPHY: *Certain Personal Matters*, 1897; *The Book of Catherine Wells*, 1928; *An Experiment in Autobiography*, 1934.

H(erbert) G(eorge) Wells, one of modern England's most prolific and best-known writers, was born at Bromley, Kent, on September 21, 1866. His background was obscure; his father was an improvident Shopkeeper and professional cricket player, his mother a maidservant and housekeeper. Although he had to work for a living very early in life, Wells was determined to get an education and rise in the world. After a period in which he was a draper's apprentice and a chemist's assistant, he managed to go to school at Midhurst Grammar School, where he made an exceptional academic record.

He then worked for a time in a dry-goods firm in London. In 1884 he won a scholarship at the Royal College of Science, where he studied biology under Thomas Henry Huxley. He was graduated with the bachelor of science degree from London University in 1888. Following graduation, he began tutoring and working on a biology textbook until tuberculosis forced him to give up teaching. While convalescing he began to write essays and stories, and by 1891 he was in sufficiently good health to return to London. Publication of one of his essays in the *Fortnightly Review* in 1891 marked the beginning of his long and active career as a writer. For the next several years he divided his time between instruction in a correspondence school and journalism.

In 1891 Wells married a cousin, Isabel Mary Wells. The two were incompatible, however, and they were divorced in 1895, after a two-year separation. Wells later married Amy Catherine Robbins, by whom he had two sons. After the death of his second wife in 1927, Wells lived mostly in London or France.

Wells's first book of a literary rather than an academic nature was *Select Conversations with an Uncle* (1895), which was overshadowed in the same year by the first of his pseudo-scientific romances, *The Time Machine*. This novel was frequently compared to the work of Jules Verne, but Wells protested that his book was written for political ends, while Verne's was not. Although he was classified nominally as a Socialist, having joined the Fabian Society in 1903, Wells's political Utopia came to be more like Plato's republic than a Socialist or Communist state. Most readers saw only the scientific speculation in such books as *The Wonderful Visit, The Stolen Bacillus and Other Incidents, The Island of Dr. Moreau, The Invisible Man,* and *The War of the Worlds*. The power and excitement still inherent in his fiction were amply demonstrated in 1938, when a radio adaptation of *The War of the Worlds* created a few hours of panic throughout the United States.

In *The Wheels of Chance*, published in 1896, Wells wrote the first of his novels dealing with the attempts of the lower middle class to rise in the world; of this series, *Kipps* and *The History of Mr. Polly* are generally considered the best. Like Dickens, Wells was capable of treating less privileged people generously and sympathetically. From about 1905 to the period of World War I, he was a realistic novelist, using social rather than political ideas in his work and developing real, yet often highly individualized, characters. Other examples of his work from this period are *Ann Veronica* and *Mr. Britling Sees It Through*. During the same period he wrote *This Misery of Boots* and *Socialism and Marriage*, important as Fabian tracts. *New Worlds for Old* was an explanation of Wells's own version of socialism. In *Tono-Bungay*, published in 1909, he began a group of novels using themes from contemporary history, a series including *The New Machiavelli, The Passionate Friends,* and *The Research Magnificent*.

Following World War I, Wells turned to the writing of history, achieving a much-debated but world-wide reputation with his *Outline of History* in 1920. In this work he attempted a chronological survey of the world from its origins to the present era. Immensely popular, the book sold more than two million copies. Such a work was doomed to have shortcomings, as critics pointed out, but it did put into readable form, within two volumes, a history of the world which general readers could, and did, read with considerable profit. It was followed by a briefer account, *A Short History of the World* in 1922.

In his writings and other activities after World War I, Wells made a bid for political recognition. To this period belong *Russia in the Shadows* (1920) and *Washington and the Riddle of Peace* (1922). He himself entered politics in 1922 as a candidate for Parliament on the Labour Party ticket. Defeated, he made a second unsuccessful attempt in 1923. He continued to write during the 1920's, but none of his books attracted the attention that earlier volumes had. *The Science of Life*, published in 1929, is an erudite and monumental work which was written in collaboration with Julian Huxley and George Philip Wells, his son. During the 1930's Wells showed much interest in the New Deal experiments in the United States; his writing during the decade reflected current economic and political problems.

Three years before his death Wells completed a thesis on personality and was awarded the doctor of science degree from London University. One of his last books was *'42 to '44*, an intolerant castigation of the period discussed. He died in London on August 13, 1946.

Although he wrote a great deal, too much to be effective throughout his long career, Wells deserves an important place in contemporary literary history. His ideas, not always worked out in detail, were presented effectively and with sincerity. Although he sacrificed art to propaganda in much of his work, he spoke with eloquence and conviction to a world in crisis. Only at the end of his life did he feel that he had failed in his efforts to improve human society by thought and word.

BIBLIOGRAPHICAL REFERENCES: The standard edition, though not definitive, is *The Works of H. G. Wells*, 28 vols., 1924–1927. For an account of Wells's life, the best source is still his own *Experiment in Autobiography*, 1934. This work should be supplemented by two works by Geoffrey H. Wells, his son, *The Works of H. G. Wells: A Bibliography, Dictionary, and Subject Index*, 1926, and *H. G. Wells: A Sketch for a Portrait*, 1930. Also valuable is Georges A. Connes, *A Dictionary of Characters and Scenes in the Novels, Romances and Short Stories of H. G. Wells*, 1926.

Recent biographical studies include Antonina Valentin, *H. G. Wells: Prophet of Our Day*, 1950; Norman Nicholson, *H. G. Wells*, 1950; and Vincent Brome, *H. G. Wells*, 1951. See also Van Wyck Brooks, *The World of H. G. Wells*, 1915; R. T. Hopkins, *H. G. Wells*, 1922; Sidney Dark, *The Outline of H. G. Wells*, 1922; Ivor Brown, *H. G. Wells*, 1925; Patrick Braybrooke, *Some Aspects of H. G. Wells*, 1928; Montgomery Belgion, *H. G. Wells*, 1953; Mark R. Hillegas, *The Future as Nightmare: H. G. Wells and the Anti-Utopians*, 1967; and Lovat Dickson, *H. G. Wells: His Turbulent Life and Times*, 1969.

Briefer articles in books and periodicals include E. E. Slosson, *Six Major Prophets*, 1917; Stuart P. Sherman, *Contemporary Woodcuts*, 1926; Wilbur T. Cross, *Four Contemporary Novelists*, 1930; André Maurois, *Prophets and Poets*, 1935; Ford Madox Ford, *Portraits from Life*, 1937; George Orwell, *Dickens, Dali, and Others*, 1946; Stanley Kauffman, "Wells and the New Generation," *College English*, I (1940), 573–582; E. K. Brown, "Two Formulas for Fiction: Henry James and H. G. Wells," *ibid.*, VIII (1946), 7–17; Richard H. Costa, "H. G. Wells: Literary

Journalist," *Journalism Quarterly*, XXVIII (1951), 63–68; and William J Hyde, "The Socialism of H. G. Wells," *Journal of the History of Ideas*, XVII (1956), 217–234.

EUDORA WELTY

Born: Jackson, Mississippi
Date: April 13, 1909

Principal Works

SHORT STORIES: *A Curtain of Green,* 1941; *The Wide Net,* 1943; *The Golden Apples,* 1949; *The Bride of the Innisfallen,* 1955; *Thirteen Stories,* 1965.
NOVELS: *The Robber Bridegroom,* 1942; *Delta Wedding,* 1946; *The Ponder Heart,* 1954; *Losing Battles,* 1970; *The Optimist's Daughter,* 1972.
ESSAYS: *Short Stories,* 1950; *Place in Fiction,* 1957.

Eudora Welty, born in Jackson, Mississippi, on April 13, 1909, writes her short stories and novels principally about the Mississippi area where she was born and has lived during most of her life. She has described with imaginative power a wide range of Southern backgrounds, never limiting herself to mere documentation: the span of history along the Natchez Trace in *The Wide Net,* the plantation setting of *Delta Wedding,* the provincial atmosphere of *The Golden Apples,* and the mysterious forest as re-created in her historical fable, *The Robber Bridegroom.* Her art of fiction combines William Faulkner's and Katherine Anne Porter's ability to project regional sentiment into a kind of cultural symbolism, with that subtle shifting between the inner and outer worlds of character which is found also in the novels of Virginia Woolf.

Miss Welty was educated at the Mississippi State College for Women and later studied advertising copywriting. She has had shows as painter and photographer and has worked as a government publicist. Her first volume was *A Curtain of Green,* a collection of short stories. "The Death of a Traveling Salesman" from this book, previously printed in the magazine *Manuscript* as her first published story, established her talent for synthesizing acute observations of character, that of the dying salesman, with an evocative background, the wayside home of a poor farming couple. The other stories unite to develop a view of Southern life continued by her later work, often criticized as eccentric and grotesque. She can also be humorous, as in "Why I Live at the P.O.," "The Petrified Man," and the beautifully sustained mood of *The Ponder Heart.* But whatever her effects, she remains interested in emotions not easily expressed, in fundamental states of mind.

In *The Robber Bridegroom* she reveals an interest in outright fantasy, having based her story on a Psyche-like fable, the love of Jamie Lockhart, the outlaw, for Rosamund. *The Wide Net* is a collection of short fiction containing historical scenes of the great forest; the title story was included in the *O. Henry Prize Stories of 1942.* The stories show a blending of fantasy with reality and a further development of two of her major themes: the mysteries of personality and the essential bonds between people who affect each other's lives. In *The Golden Apples* these themes are again stressed in the story of King MacLain, who periodically vanishes and reappears unaccountably. In almost all the stories the fabulous element in her work is suggested by her titles, "Shower of Gold," "Moon Lake," "Music from Spain."

Delta Wedding is probably her most widely known book. In this novel she handles people with growing assurance as the characters come slowly into focus, viewed through the eyes of a nine-year-old girl describing late summer wedding preparations on a Mississippi plantation where a large and widely scattered family has gathered for the event. In *The Ponder Heart,* a short novel and later a Broadway play about an aging spinster and her uncle, married to a weak-minded young country girl, there is a scene which epitomizes Miss Welty's use of symbolic violence. During a thunderstorm the wife, called Bonnie Dee Peacock in keeping with the author's characteristic preference for suggestive names, is being tickled by Uncle Daniel. She dies of mingled terror and laughter, her head buried under a cushion. The ingenuity, like the writing itself, may be called precious, but Miss Welty's tone and use of idiom to enforce her themes are everywhere authoritative.

A volume of *Selected Stories* was published in 1954. It was followed by a collection of seven new stories, *The Bride of the Innisfallen* in 1955. In these, as in her earlier work, she continues to draw a sophisticated picture of eccentric variety based upon a timeless or at least changeless past. Her sensitivity to language and dialogue, her comic inventions, are entertaining, but rely on a serious conception of the symbolic or the mythic for their fullest effect.

BIBLIOGRAPHICAL REFERENCES: There are two critical studies: Ruth M. V. Kieft, *Eudora Welty,* 1962; and Alfred Appel, *A Season of Dreams: The Fiction of Eudora Welty,* 1965. For brief studies in books or magazines see Katherine Anne Porter, Introduction to *A Curtain of Green,* 1941 (reprinted in *The Days Before,* 1952); Robert Van Gelder, ed., *Writers and Writing,* 1946; Eunice Glenn, "Fantasy in the Fiction of Eudora Welty," in *A Southern Vanguard,* edited by Allen Tate, 1947; Robert Penn Warren, "The Love and Separateness in Miss Welty," *Kenyon Review,* VI (1944), 246-259; John Edward Hardy, "Delta Wedding as Region and Symbol," *Sewanee Review,* LX (1952), 397-418; Granville Hicks, "Eudora Welty," *College English,* XIV (1952), 69-76; Harry C. Morris, "Zeus and the Golden Apples: Eudora Welty," *Perspective,* V (1952), 190-199; Robert Daniel, "The World of Eudora Welty," *Hopkins Review,* VI (1953), 461-468; Audrey Hodgins, "The Narrator as Ironic Device in a Short Story of Eudora Welty," *Twentieth Century Literature,* I (1956), 215-219; and Kurt Opitz, "Eudora Welty: The Order of a Captive Soul," *Critique,* VII, ii (1965), 79-91. For bibliography see Katherine H. Smythe, "Eudora Welty: A Checklist," *Bulletin of Bibliography,* XXI (1956), 207-208.

FRANZ WERFEL

Born: Prague, Czechoslovakia
Date: September 10, 1890

Died: Hollywood, California
Date: August 26, 1945

Principal Works

NOVELS: *Verdi*, 1924; *Barbara oder Die Frömmigkeit*, 1929 (*The Pure in Heart*); *Die Geschwister von Neapel*, 1931 (*The Pascarella Family*); *Die vierzig Tage des Musa Dagh*, 1934 (*The Forty Days of Musa Dagh*); *Der veruntreute Himmel*, 1939 (*Embezzled Heaven*); *Das Lied von Bernadette*, 1941 (*The Song of Bernadette*); *Stern der Ungeborenen*, 1946 (*The Star of the Unborn*).

NOVELLAS AND TALES IN TRANSLATION: *Twilight of a World*, 1937.

PLAYS: *Der Spiegelmensch*, 1920; *Bocksgesang*, 1921 (*Goat Song*); *Juarez und Maximilian*, 1924; *Paulus unter den Juden*, 1926 (*Paul Among the Jews*); *Das Reich Gottes in Böhmen*, 1930 (*The Kingdom of God in Bohemia*); *Jakobowski und der Oberst*, 1944 (*Jacobowski and the Colonel*).

POEMS: *Gedichte aus den Jahren*, 1908–1945.

Franz Werfel was born into a Jewish family of Prague on September 10, 1890. His father, the owner of a glove factory, was intensely interested in art and music, but he saw in his son only a future partner and an heir to the business; consequently, he opposed the boy's early inclinations toward literature. Young Werfel was educated at the local gymnasium and spent two years, 1909–1910, at the University of Prague. Having tasted the pleasure of seeing some of his work in print, Werfel had little interest in an academic career, preferring to spend his time writing and discussing literature with literary friends who included such recognized writers as Gustav Meyrink, Max Brod, and Otokar Březina.

After leaving the university in 1910, Werfel went to Hamburg, Germany. There he took a job in a business firm but at the same time he continued to write. Following a year of compulsory military service, from 1911 to 1912, he settled for a time in Leipzig, where he became a publisher's reader. With the opening of World War I, he took a pacifist stand, publishing pacifist poems like "Der Krieg," "Wortmacher des Krieges," and "Der Ulan," all of which appeared in *Einander* (1915). Despite his attitude toward the war, Werfel was called into the service as an officer in an artillery regiment and served during 1916–1917. In 1916 his adaptation of Euripides' *Trojan Women* had a successful season on the Berlin stage and in other cities. By the time he was thirty, Werfel had made himself a reputation in both poetry and drama; in addition, he already had written and published a short novel, *Not the Murderer* (1919). This and other of his early works have never been translated into English.

During the early 1920's Werfel's work was primarily in drama. *Der Spiegelmensch* opened simultaneously on stages in Düsseldorf, Leipzig, and Stuttgart. Werfel's first play to appear on the American stage was *Goat Song*, produced in New York in 1926. One of his most popular plays was *Juarez and Maximilian*, which after a successful run in Europe was translated into English and produced in New York before being made also into a motion picture. Three religious plays were written somwhat later in Werfel's career: *Paul Among the Jews, The Kingdom of God in Bohemia,* and *The Eternal Road* (1936). The last-named, a presentation of early Jewish history, was translated into English and produced in New York in 1937.

From 1925 on, Werfel was interested primarily in fiction, and a series of stories and short novels preceded his more important novels. In the United States his popularity came with the publication of *The Forty Days of Musa Dagh,* a novel based on the Armenian resistance to the Turks. *Hearken unto the Voice* (1937) showed the author's continued interest in the Jews and their history. *Embezzled Heaven,* also popular in America, illustrates how Werfel's religiosity caused him to become highly sympathetic to Roman Catholicism.

After World War I Werfel lived in Vienna. At the time of the *Anschluss* he fled to Paris, only to become a fugitive once more when the Germans invaded France. Eventually he reached the United States and safety. While escaping from the Germans, he had found a temporary refuge at Lourdes. While there he vowed to write a book about the young woman who had seen a vision of the Virgin Mary at that shrine. *The Song of Bernadette,* an exceptionally popular book in America, fulfilled that vow. A play, *Jacobowski and the Colonel,* was successfully produced in New York in 1944, and a collection of his verse, *Poems,* translated by E. A. Snow, was published in 1945.

Werfel and his wife Anna, who was the widow of Gustav Mahler, the composer, moved to Hollywood, California, where Werfel continued to write despite failing health. His last novel, *The Star of the Unborn,* was completed just a few days before he succumbed to a heart attack on August 26, 1945.

BIBLIOGRAPHICAL REFERENCES: Werfel's *Gesammelte Werke,* 8 vols., were published 1927–1935. The best study of the man and his work is Richard Specht, *Franz Werfel,* 1926. Studies of Werfel as one of Germany's writers-in-exile appear in Harry Slochower, *No Voice Is Wholly Lost,* 1945, and Vernon L. Parrington, *American Dreams,* 1947. See also Elisabeth Hunna, *Die Dramen von Franz Werfel,* 1947; Marysia Turrian, *Dostojewskij und Franz Werfel,* 1950; and Annemarie von Puttkamer, *Franz Werfel, Wort und Antwort,* 1952; in English, Lore B. Foltin, ed., *Franz Werfel, 1890–1945* (collection of articles), 1961; and W. H. Fox, "Franz Werfel," *German Men of Letters,* III (1964), 107–125.

GLENWAY WESCOTT

Born: Kewaskum, Wisconsin
Date: April 11, 1901

Principal Works

NOVELS: *The Apple of the Eye,* 1924; *The Grandmothers,* 1927; *The Pilgrim Hawk,* 1940; *Apartment in Athens,* 1945.
SHORT STORIES: *Goodbye Wisconsin,* 1928; *The Babe's Bed,* 1930.
POEMS: *The Bitterns,* 1920; *Natives of Rock,* 1925.
BELLES-LETTRES: *Fear and Trembling,* 1932; *A Calendar of Saints for Unbelievers,* 1932; *Images of Truth: Remembrances and Criticism,* 1962.

Glenway Wescott, born in Kewaskum, Wisconsin, April 11, 1901, is a Middle Westerner by birth and education. He attended public schools in various Wisconsin towns and spent two years (1917–1919) at the University of Chicago. His family had hoped he would enter the ministry, while he himself entertained some hope of becoming a professional musician. After World War I he spent a year in Germany, then returned to live for a short time in New Mexico. His first book was a volume of poetry, *The Bitterns,* published in 1920; this was followed by a second book of verse, *Natives of Rock,* in 1925. His first novel, *The Apple of the Eye,* was completed during a period of several months that Wescott spent in New York City. Set against a background of rural Wisconsin, the novel relates the conflicts and forces involved in a boy's search for an understanding of the world and sex, a series of problems similiar to those probed by many contemporary novelists, who seem to be fascinated by the problems of the adolescent in the modern world. After the publication of his novel Wescott went again to Europe and during the next eight years was one of a large colony of American writers who lived abroad in the 1920's.

While in Europe he wrote *The Grandmothers,* which has received more acclaim from readers and critics than any of his other novels. It earned for Wescott the Harper Prize Novel Award for the year of publication. The novel, a saga of pioneer life in early Wisconsin, unfolds as it appears to Alwyn Tower, a young man who is very much like the author and who has his curiosity aroused by an old family photograph album. His awakened curiosity leads him to piece together the story of his family and relate the story as he finds it. This novel, like most of Wescott's fiction, interprets humanity through the desires and motives of typical human beings. The novel is illustrative, too, of the flowing, cadenced prose which is one of Wescott's strong points as a writer. The prose approaches the cadences of folk literature, and it was particularly well chosen for a novel about American pioneer life. Other works which appeared during the author's years of expatriation were *Goodbye Wisconsin,* a volume of short stories; *The Babe's Bed,* a long short story; *Fear and Trembling* a volume of essays; and *A Calendar of Saints for Unbelievers.* The most interesting of these works is *The Babe's Bed,* which is a meditation in which a young man dreams about the possible future of a baby nephew.

Returning to America in 1934, Wescott settled on a farm in Hunterdon County, New Jersey. *The Pilgrim Hawk*, published in 1940, is a novel which indicated that the author had managed to weather successfully a period of inactivity such as is sometimes fatal to a writer's reputation. Ineligible for military service during World War II, Wescott sought to aid his country in other ways. An attempt to write a novel which would help Americans understand what had produced Nazism proved unsuccessful, however. An encounter with a Greek underground leader led Wescott to write another novel, *Apartment in Athens*, which describes the effect of the German occupation on one family in Athens, Greece, during World War II. The book was chosen by one of the national book clubs for its list and achieved a rather wide body of readers. Part of its value was, of course, its topicality at the time of publication.

Early in the 1950's Wescott turned to critical writing. He edited *The Maugham Reader* (1950) and *Short Novels of Colette* (1951).

BIBLIOGRAPHICAL REFERENCES: For a critical study see I. Johnson, *Glenway Wescott: The Paradox of Voice*, 1971. For brief criticism see Edmund Wilson, *Classics and Commercials*, 1950; Dayton Kohler, "Glenway Wescott: Legend-Maker," *American Bookman*, LXXIII (1931), 142–146; C. E. Schorer, "The Maturing of Glenway Wescott," *College English*, XVIII (1957), 320–326; and M. D. Zabel, "The Whisper of the Hawk," in *Craft and Character in Modern Fiction*, 1957, 304–308.

ARNOLD WESKER

Born: London, England
Date: May 24, 1932

Principal Works

PLAYS: *Chicken Soup with Barley*, 1958; *Roots*, 1959; *The Kitchen*, 1959; *I'm Talking About Jerusalem*, 1960; *Chips with Everything*, 1962; *The Four Seasons*, 1965; *Their Very Own and Golden City*, 1966; *The Friends*, 1970.

Playwright Arnold Wesker burst upon the English theatrical scene in 1960 with four highly praised plays: his "trilogy" (*Chicken Soup with Barley, Roots, I'm Talking About Jerusalem*) and *The Kitchen*. The young writer—he was not yet 30—was widely hailed as a new Odets.

Much of Wesker's appeal to critics lay in his background; his early life seemed particularly appropriate to the image of a creative artist. Wesker was born in the lean years of the 1930's, and grew up in the East End slums of London. His education was minimal and, after two years in the Royal Air Force (which provided the setting for *Chips with Everything*), he held a variety of jobs. Most were menial: pastry cook, kitchen helper, plumber's mate.

Since his initial successes, Wesker has written several plays and administered Centre 42, a project created in 1962 to bring culture to the working classes. His early plays, however, remain his best. In the "trilogy" Wesker described, with a rare passion and sincerity, life in London's slums. The plays are heavily didactic: like those of Odets, Wesker implies that only Socialism could free his characters from their spirit-crushing poverty.

Unlike Odets, however, Wesker seemed to possess a deeper comprehension of the human experience and was also aware that, ultimately, no political system provided all the answers. The power of the plays came from his burning moral concern for his characters, but an added element of sympathy and forgiveness gave them a depth unusual in the didactic social drama.

Perhaps the most striking aspect of the early plays was Wesker's urgent sincerity. The plays are structurally naïve, obviously written by a very young playwright with virtually no technical knowledge of playwrighting or of the commercial theater's limitations. Although his later works are interesting, Wesker has yet to fulfill his youthful promise.

BIBLIOGRAPHICAL REFERENCES: For biography and criticism see Ronald Hayman, *Arnold Wesker*, 1970; H. Ribalow, *Arnold Wesker*, 1965; M. Page, "Whatever Happened to Arnold Wesker," *Modern Drama*, XI (1968), 317–325; Clifford Leech, "Two Romantics: Arnold Wesker and Harold Pinter," *Contemporary Theatre*, edited by John Russell Brown and Bernard Harris, 1962; and Jacqueline Latham, "*Roots*: A Reassessment," *Modern Drama*, VIII (1965), 192–197.

Also of interest are references to Wesker in John Russell Taylor, *Anger and After*, 1962, revised edition, 1969; W. A. Armstrong, editor, *Experimental Drama*, 1963; John Russell Brown, editor, *Modern British Dramatists*, 1968; C. Marowitz, *Theatre at Work*, 1967; G. Wellworth, *The Theater of Protest and Paradox*, 1964; and John Kershaw, *The Present Stage*, 1966.

NATHANAEL WEST

Born: New York, N. Y.
Date: October 17, 1903 (?)

Died: El Centro, California
Date: December 22, 1940

Principal Works

NOVELS: *The Dream Life of Balso Snell*, 1931; *Miss Lonelyhearts*, 1933; *A Cool Million*, 1934; *The Day of the Locust*, 1939.

Nathanael West's literary life has an irony which almost parodies his own novels. Completely original and a deadly serious craftsman, he achieved in his short life little fame, except among a discerning few, and no popular success. Now, seventeen years after his death, two paperback editions have sold in the hundred thousands, and his *Complete Works* (1957) won critical acclaim and a place on best-seller lists.

Born Nathan Weinstein, in New York City, October 17, 1903 (?), he used the name Nathaniel von Wallenstein-Weinstein in Brown University (Ph.B., 1924), where he was labeled eccentric and a genius, and nicknamed "Pep" for the opposite characteristics the word suggests. Literary friends included I. J. Kapstein, Quentin Reynolds, and S. J. Perelman, who later married his sister Laura; but he wrote few pieces for undergraduate publications. In Paris during 1925–1926 he came under surrealist influences and wrote his first novel, *The Dream Life of Balso Snell*, a fantasy on his hero's wanderings inside the Trojan Horse, where he meets a naked man in a derby writing about Saint Puce (a flea who lived in Christ's armpit), and a twelve-year-old boy wooing his schoolmistress with Russian journals. This work was ignored following its publication in 1931.

Back in New York, West worked as a hotel manager, as associate editor of *Contact* with William Carlos Williams in 1932, and also as associate on *Americana* with George Grosz in 1933. *Contact* and a third little magazine, *Contempo*, contained early drafts of *Miss Lonelyhearts*, the story of an agony columnist who is destroyed when he takes too seriously the problems and miseries of his correspondents. This minor classic was issued in 1933 by a publisher who shortly afterward went bankrupt. By the time copies and plates were rescued from the unpaid printer by another publishing house, demand for the book had ceased.

West's third and weakest novel, *A Cool Million*, is a broad satire on the Horatio Alger myth, in which Lemuel Pitkin loses his teeth, eye, scalp, money, and eventually his life after being victimized by capitalists, communists, and neo-fascists. It was quickly remaindered.

Unsuccessful as a short story writer and playwright, West made a living in Hollywood writing B-grade movies. Here he took five years to finish his most mature work, *The Day of the Locust*, and in 1940 he married Eileen McKenney, of *My Sister Eileen* fame. Seven months later, on December 22, they were killed together in an auto crash at El Centro, California.

Although *The Day of the Locust* has Hollywood as its locale and minor actors and hangers-on from the periphery of the studios as its characters, the novel is no more about motion pictures than *Miss Lonelyhearts* is about newspapers. Fantastic and exaggerated in theme and treatment, West's two chief novels convey, more clearly than most twentieth century fiction, a sense of horror and revulsion from the universe man lives in and the world he makes for his fellows and himself.

BIBLIOGRAPHICAL REFERENCES: There are two book-length studies: James F. Light, *Nathanael West: An Interpretive Study,* 1961; and Randall Reid, *The Fiction of Nathanael West: No Redeemer, No Promised Land,* 1967.

Useful critical material is found in Robert M. Coates, Introduction to the New Directions edition of *Miss Lonelyhearts* (1946); Edmund Wilson, "Postscript," *The Boys in the Back Room,* 1941, reprinted in *Classics and Commercials,* 1950; Daniel Aaron, "The Truly Monstrous: A Note on Nathanael West," *Partisan Review,* XIV (1947), 98–106; Alan Ross, "The Dead Centre: An Introduction to Nathanael West," *Horizon,* XVIII (1948), 284–296, reprinted, with changes, in the Grey Walls Press edition of *Miss Lonelyhearts,* 1949, and the *Complete Works,* 1957; Richard B. Gehman, "Nathanael West: A Novelist Apart," *Atlantic,* CLXXXVI (1950), 69–72, reprinted in the New Directions edition of *The Day of the Locust,* 1950; Cyril M. Schneider, "The Individuality of Nathanael West," *Western Review,* XX (1955), 7–28, 254–256; Arthur Cohen, "Nathanael West's Holy Fool," *Commonweal,* LXIV (June 15, 1956), 276–278; and James F. Light, *"Miss Lonelyhearts:* The Imagery of Nightmare," *American Quarterly,* VIII (1956), 316–327. See also William White, "Nathanael West: A Bibliography," *Studies in Bibliography,* XI (1958), 207–224.

REBECCA WEST
Cicily Isabel Fairfield

Born: County Kerry, Ireland
Date: December 25, 1892

Principal Works

NOVELS: *The Return of the Soldier*, 1918; *The Judge*, 1922; *Harriet Hume*, 1929; *The Thinking Reed*, 1936; *The Fountain Overflows*, 1956; *The Birds Fall Down*, 1966.
CRITICAL ESSAYS AND STUDIES: *Henry James*, 1916; *The Strange Necessity*, 1928; *D. H. Lawrence, An Elegy*, 1930; *Arnold Bennett Himself*, 1931; *Ending in Earnest: A Literary Log*, 1931; *The Court and the Castle*, 1957.
POLITICAL STUDIES: *The Meaning of Treason*, 1947; *A Train of Powder*, 1955.
TRAVEL SKETCHES AND IMPRESSIONS: *Black Lamb and Grey Falcon*, 1941.

Few writers in modern times have taken as much interest in the world about them as Rebecca West, and even fewer have done so much to illuminate that world by their writing. Miss West's interest in the condition of man began at an early age. She was born Cicily Isabel Fairfield in County Kerry, Ireland, on December 25, 1892, but spent her childhood in Edinburgh, where she attended George Watson's Ladies' College. By the time she was eighteen she was contributing to radical periodicals. One of her primary interests was female suffrage, a cause she defended in much of her early writing. It is significant that she took her pen name from the "emancipated" heroine of Ibsen's *Rosmersholm*. After a brief period on the London stage, she turned to journalism in 1911 and became a reviewer for *The Freewoman*. Becoming also an advocate of Socialism, she was for a time active in the Fabian Society.

Her first separate publication was *Henry James*, a closely reasoned and detailed analysis of that author's work. As a writer she has always admired James's powers of insight; he, along with Proust, is thought of as being one of her models. Her literary criticism is characterized by uncompromising attacks on the reputations of accepted writers. Rebecca West has always been willing to sacrifice convention for what she considers the truth.

The Return of the Soldier, her first novel, reflects the postwar emphasis on psychology. It is the story of a veteran, a victim of amnesia who is led, by a woman with whom he had had an early love affair, back to health and his wife and family. *The Judge* also displays Miss West's interest in applied psychology, although the subject here is the obsessive love of a mother for her son. Miss West's next novel, *Harriet Hume*, is subtitled *A London Fantasy*; it is just that, the end being capable of several interpretations. In this novel the writer shows her ability to draw full and carefully observed descriptions of the London scene, a power of description which was to enrich greatly her later travel writing. In the previous year she had published another volume of literary criticism, *The Strange Necessity*; with its appearance Miss West's reputation as a penetrating critic was secure.

She married Henry Maxwell Andrews, a British banker, in 1930, and she has often declared her debt to him for his help and encouragement in her literary efforts. Another book of criticism, *Ending in Earnest,* added further to her reputation as a fearless and skillful critic. The subject of her next novel, *The Thinking Reed,* is the excessive demands made by wealth upon the people who have it. The story concerns a rich American widow who marries a wealthy Frenchman.

The Meaning of Treason is a collection of essays about the Nuremberg war crimes trials, particularly that of William Joyce, "Lord Haw-Haw." In this book Miss West tries to arrive at a decision about the true significance of treasonous acts. One of the six essays in *A Train of Powder* deals with the same subject, but the other essays are concerned with topics as divergent as German economical growth and a lynching trial in South Carolina.

Her novel, *The Fountain Overflows,* won Miss West renewed fame in America. It tells of the dawning of awareness of an artistic gift in a member of a talented family in London. In this novel, as in her others, Miss West displays a richness of style and clarity of insight. Her last novel, *The Birds Fall Down,* a story of intrigue written in the tradition of the nineteenth century novel, was also highly praised. The most impressive literary product of her career, however, is the massive *Black Lamb and Grey Falcon.* This book, which Miss West calls a journal of a trip through Yugoslavia, is really a fully detailed exposition of her views on history, society, and art.

In this book, as in all her others, Rebecca West brings to the reader what is perhaps her most important quality, her ability and willingness to undertake any literary, historical, or social problem that interests her and to treat it with care, detail, and courage.

BIBLIOGRAPHICAL REFERENCES: There is no comprehensive biographical study and surprisingly little criticism, although several critical studies are reported in preparation. See Patrick Braybrooke, *Novelists, We Are Seven,* 1926, and *Philosophies in Modern Fiction,* 1929; Arthur St. John Adcock, *The Glory That Was Grubb Street,* 1928; Frank Swinnerton, *The Georgian Literary Scene,* 1935; Richard Church, *British Authors,* 1948 (rev. ed.); and Dachine Rainer, "Rebecca West: Disturber of the Peace," *Commonweal,* 88 (1968), 227–230.

EDWARD NOYES WESTCOTT

Born: Syracuse, New York
Date: September 27, 1846

Died: Syracuse
Date: March 31, 1898

Principal Works

NOVEL: *David Harum,* 1898.
SHORT STORIES: *The Teller,* 1901.

Edward Noyes Westcott, author of the popular *David Harum,* is something of an anomaly in the history of American literature, being a banker turned author. The son of a dentist, he was born in Syracuse, New York, on September 27, 1846. He attended the public schools in Syracuse until he was sixteen and then left school to take a job as a junior clerk in a local bank. At the age of twenty he left Syracuse to work for an insurance company in New York City. He returned to Syracuse, however, to become a teller and cashier in banks in that city. In 1874 he married Jane Dows, of Buffalo, New York, and the couple had three children, two sons and a daughter.

Anxious to get ahead in life and to provide for his children's education, Westcott formed the company of Westcott and Abbott, a banking and brokerage house, in 1880. For several years the firm was successful, but the bankruptcy of an allied company caused its failure in the late 1880's, at which time Wescott took a job with the Syracuse water commission. Having to retire because of tuberculosis in 1895, Westcott went to the Adirondack Mountains to recuperate. While there he began to write for his own amusement. In 1895–1896 he went to Naples, still searching for good health, and while there he wrote *David Harum,* his famous novel about a shrewd, but good-hearted Yankee with a penchant for horse trading. The novel, rejected by six publishing houses before it was finally accepted, appeared in 1898, just a few months after the death of the author at Syracuse on March 31 of that year. Its success was immediate, with six printings within three months. Within two years over 400,000 copies were sold, and the eventual sales ran over a million copies. In 1901 *The Teller,* a group of stories, with some letters by Westcott, was published.

The popularity of *David Harum* has continued into the media of the stage and a motion picture. The novel, among the first of a type which portrayed the Yankee character as hard on the outside but gentle and kind within, is competently written; but its literary value is slight, and scholars, unlike the public, have passed it by with but slight attention.

BIBLIOGRAPHICAL REFERENCES: *The Teller,* 1901, contains a selection of letters by Edward Noyes Westcott and an account of his life. See also the sketch by Brice Harris in the *Dictionary of National Biography.*

EDITH WHARTON

Born: New York, N. Y.
Date: January 24, 1862

Died: St. Brice sous Foret, France
Date: August 11, 1937

Principal Works

NOVELS: *The Touchstone,* 1900; *The Valley of Decision,* 1902 (2 vols.); *Sanctuary,* 1903; *The House of Mirth,* 1905; *The Fruit of the Tree,* 1907; *Madame de Treymes,* 1907; *Ethan Frome,* 1911; *The Reef,* 1912; *The Custom of the Country,* 1913; *Summer,* 1917; *The Marne,* 1918; *The Age of Innocence,* 1920; *The Glimpses of the Moon,* 1922; *A Son at the Front,* 1923; *Old New York,* 1924 (*False Dawn: The Forties, The Old Maid: The Fifties, The Spark: The Sixties,* and *New Year's Day: The Seventies*); *The Mother's Recompense,* 1925; *Twilight Sleep,* 1927; *The Children,* 1928; *Hudson River Bracketed,* 1929; *The Gods Arrive,* 1932; *The Buccaneers,* 1938.

SHORT STORIES: *The Greater Inclination,* 1899; *Crucial Instances,* 1901; *The Descent of Man,* 1904; *The Hermit and the Wild Woman,* 1908; *Tales of Men and Ghosts,* 1910; *Xingu,* 1916; *Here and Beyond,* 1926; *Certain People,* 1930; *Human Nature,* 1933; *The World Over,* 1936; *Ghosts,* 1937.

POEMS: *Artemis to Actaeon,* 1909; *Twelve Poems,* 1926.

CRITICISM: *The Writing of Fiction,* 1925.

AUTOBIOGRAPHY: *A Backward Glance,* 1934.

Edith Newbold Jones was born in New York City on January 24, 1862, into a wealthy, upper middle-class family of distinguished ancestry. She learned as a girl, according to her own account, to love good literature, good English, and good manners. Traveling extensively with her socially active parents, and reading under the encouragement of tutors, she acquired a perspective of people and an enjoyment of literature which led her into writing stories on her own. With the publication of poetry and stories in magazines her literary career began. But her own social circle disapproved of her work, and she in turn discovered that their good manners were motivated by status rather than love. In 1885 she married Edward Wharton, a Boston banker, but their marriage was clouded by the husband's mental breakdown. In 1907, following the example of her literary mentor and personal friend, Henry James, Mrs. Wharton went abroad to live and settled permanently in France. However, she did not forget her society; she contemplated it from a distance and re-created it in art with irony and nostalgia.

Though Edith Wharton must be considered a major writer because of her artistry, her themes are somewhat less important today than they were during the first quarter of the twentieth century. One theme she treated was that the very conventions of conduct in America tend to stifle creative activity; the second, that the rising *nouveaux riches* were adulterating the purity of upper-class standards. Essentially a writer of manners, she never attained the dispassionate view of her material that Jane Austen did, and her works are tragedies rather than comedies. Most of her novels tell the same story: the plight of an innocent victimized by the stultifying conventions of the group or the difficulties of the noble in heart in an ignoble society, a society whose lip service to the conventions makes its successful members hypocrites and its few honest ones victims. The antagonists are essentially evil, and their inevitable triumph is the real tragedy. However, the very defeat of the protagonists gives them a spiritual victory, for their defeat, as in *The House of Mirth,* is the result of their moral integrity.

All of her works are colored by the business of maneuvering for position, usually social. The first work to achieve critical recognition was the novel *The House of Mirth,* published in 1905. The protagonist, Lily Bart, a sensitive, ethical girl, is punished by society for following the direction of her sympathies rather than the demands of the "respectable"; she makes attractive friendships rather than socially acceptable ones, is snubbed by family and old acquaintances, and commits suicide in an agony of bewildered despair. In line with the literature of revolt of the period, this novel was unique in the restraint of its style, and perhaps all the more effective for its keyed-down qualities.

Edith Wharton rejected the "middle" class with prejudiced scorn. *The Custom of the Country* is cutting in its delineation of the character of the barbarian climber, Undine Spragg. However, she felt for the lower class, especially the rural, the same sympathy and identification with its victims of convention. *Ethan Frome* is a classic story of tragic frustration. Ethan, a farmer, marries out of loneliness. When his wife's cousin comes to live with them in poverty, and they fall in love —the first love in both their lives— they cannot see any way out to consummate their love; so they attempt suicide. Mrs. Wharton, as she does in many of her short stories, adds an ironic denouement to this plot: the suicide attempt fails, both are crippled, and the wife-in-name who refused to allow them their freedom is chained to them forever as their nurse. The novel *Summer* is similar in subject, milieu, and theme.

The Age of Innocence presents a starkly classic quality in its picture of the inevitabliity of spiritual destruction suffered by two noble people because of their moral flaw, which allows their social status to take precedence over love. The protagonists, Newland Archer and Ellen Olenska, are defeated by a code of their group, a group that willingly breaks the codes only when there is an assurance of not getting caught. "It was a dull association of material and social interests held together by ignorance on the one side and hypocrisy on the other." This novel comes closest to the polished perfection of the manners genre in that there is a comic tone that restrains the pathos of the dilemma of Newland and married Ellen who, afraid to face ostracism, must either destroy their love for each other or destroy themselves. The very restraint allows the perceptive reader to live the tragedy of their thwarted emotional lives, and the impression is deep and lasting.

After 1920 only the short stories continued as art; the novels were mechanical repetitions of the earlier works or quickly contrived propaganda pieces, like *A Son at the Front.* The world that Edith Wharton had known was gone and there was little more to say.

The success of Mrs. Wharton's work was achieved by "disengaging crucial moments from the welter of existence," keeping the plot true to the characters' motivations, and using a language that was dispassionate yet moving in its clarity and restraint. Before she died, at St. Brice sous Foret, France, on August 11, 1937, she had received more honors for her work than any other woman writer in American history.

BIBLIOGRAPHICAL REFERENCES: There is no definitive biography of Edith Wharton. Her autobiography, *A Backward Glance*, was published in 1934 and reprinted in 1964. The most recent biographical study is Percy Lubbock, *Portrait of Edith Wharton*, 1947; the most recent critical study, Nevius Blake, *Edith Wharton: A Study of Her Fiction*, 1953. For earlier biographical and critical works see Katherine F. Gerould, *Edith Wharton: A Critical Study*, 1922; Robert M. Lovett, *Edith Wharton*, 1925; and E. K. Brown, *Edith Wharton: Étude Critique*, 1935. The best criticism is to be found in Irving Howe, ed., *Edith Wharton: A Collection of Critical Essays*, 1962.

See also Percy H. Boynton, *Some Contemporary Americans*, 1924; Régis Michaud, *The American Novel To-day*, 1928; N. Elizabeth Monroe, *The Novel and Society*, 1941; Alfred Kazin, *On Native Grounds*, 1942; also Percy Lubbock, "The Novels of Edith Wharton," *Quarterly Review*, CCXXIII (1915), 182–201; Charles K. Trueblood, "Edith Wharton," *Dial*, LXVIII (1920), 80–91; Frances T. Russell, "Melodramatic Mrs. Wharton," *Sewanee Review*, XL (1932), 425–437; E. K. Brown, "Edith Wharton," *Études Anglaises*, II (1938), 12–26; Edmund Wilson, "Justice to Edith Wharton," *New Republic*, XCV (1938), 209–213; and Larry Rubin, "Aspects of Naturalism in Four Novels by Edith Wharton," *Twentieth Century Literature*, II (1957), 182–192.

PATRICK WHITE

Born: London, England
Date: May 28, 1912

Principal Works

NOVELS: *Happy Valley,* 1939; *The Living and the Dead,* 1941; *The Aunt's Story,* 1948; *The Tree of Man,* 1955; *Riders in the Chariot,* 1961; *Solid Mandala,* 1966; *The Vivisector,* 1970.
SHORT STORIES: *The Burnt Ones,* 1964.

Patrick White was born in London May 28, 1912. A fourth-generation Australian, he was taken to Sydney at the age of six and spent his childhood there. He later attended an English public school, returning afterward to Australia and living in the country where he worked at two sheep stations and practiced writing. In 1932 he moved again to England, where he studied modern languages at King's College, Cambridge, until 1935. During this period he wrote a number of plays, all unsuccessful. His first work to receive wide critical notice was *Happy Valley,* a scathing and ironically titled novel about a small town in Australia. It was awarded the Australian Literature Society's Gold Medal. White traveled extensively in the United States in 1939 and 1940, leaving in the latter year to join the Royal Air Force. He served in the Sudanese and Egyptian campaigns, returning to Australia after the war. His second novel, *The Living and the Dead,* was published in 1941; one of his plays, *Return to Abyssinia,* was produced in London shortly after the war. A third novel, *The Aunt's Story,* appeared in 1948. Four more novels were produced between that date and 1970.

White's earlier novels were written in the tradition of James Joyce's *Ulysses,* and in them the "stream-of-consciousness" device was explored to what may well be its practical limits. The characters evidenced his interest in psychological abnormality; his style has been noted as possessing a vitality peculiarly his own, together with great clarity of observation. *The Aunt's Story,* an unusual mixture of wit and pathos, was somewhat less Joycean; however, its grotesque qualities evoked a mixed critical response. *The Tree of Man,* a long and ambitious novel of an Australian homesteader, derives its scope and power from the accumulation of a vast amount of detail that gradually builds a solid and closely-woven fabric. It has been likened in some respects to the work of D. H. Lawrence, particularly in an unusually vivid understanding of nature. *Riders in the Chariot* is a still more ambitious work that interweaves four separate novels into one; an allegory dealing with fundamental aspects of love, it is structurally complex and largely symbolic. *Solid Mandala* is a story of two brothers—one the competent man of reason, the other a visionary—over a period of fifty years. Here the characters are made to live through the accumulation of great masses of revealing detail. *The Vivisector* concerns itself with a painter of enormous talent who analyzes the world about him and paints it as he sees it. Critical response has been favorable; the novel has been characterized as "haunting, obsessed, magnificent"; White's prose is seen as Faulknerian in its complexity, analytical, precise, and at the same time voluptuous. Patrick White continues to experiment, to develop, and to grow as a writer.

BIBLIOGRAPHICAL REFERENCES: Important studies include Geoffrey Dutton, *Patrick White,* 1961, revised edition, 1963; R. F. Brissenden, *Patrick White,* 1966; Barry Argyle, *Patrick White,* 1967; G. A. Wilkes, *Ten Essays on Patrick White,* 1970; and Patricia A. Morley, *The Mystery of Unity: Theme and Technique in the Novels of Patrick White,* 1972. See also Maria Antonini, "Voss di Patrick White," *Convivium,* XXXVII (1969), 218–228; Clement Semmler, *Twentieth Century Australian Literary Criticism,* 1968; and *Approaches to the Novel,* edited by John Colmer, 1967.

J. Finch compiled a *Bibliography of Patrick White,* 1966.

T. H. WHITE

Born: Bombay, India
Date: May 29, 1906

Died: Piraeus, Greece
Date: January 17, 1964

Principal Works

NOVELS: *Darkness at Pemberley*, 1932; *Farewell Victoria*, 1934; *The Sword in the Stone*, 1938; *The Witch in the Wood*, 1939; *The Ill-Made Knight*, 1940; *Mistress Masham's Repose*, 1946; *The Elephant and the Kangaroo*, 1947; *The Master*, 1957; *The Candle in the Wind*, 1958; *The Once and Future King* (a tetralogy including *The Sword in the Stone*, *The Witch in the Wood*, *The Ill-Made Knight*, and *The Candle in the Wind*), 1958.

MISCELLANEOUS: *England Have My Bones*, 1936; *The Age of Scandal: An Excursion Through a Minor Period*, 1950; *The Scandalmonger*, 1952; *The Goshawk*, 1952; *The Book of Beasts*, 1954; *Godstone and the Blackymor*, 1959; *America at Last*, 1965.

Although Terence Hanbury White was born in India, he spent most of his adult life in the British Isles. Educated at Cheltenham College and Queen's College, Cambridge, he taught school at Stowe Ridings, Buckinghamshire, until 1937, when he resigned to devote full time to writing. His first major success was *The Sword in the Stone*, published in 1938. Although White was a prolific writer, he did not attain financial security until 1960, when his Arthurian tetralogy was used as the basis for Lerner and Lowe's musical comedy *Camelot*. From 1948 until his death in 1964, he lived on the tiny island of Alderney in the English Channel.

White's greatest successes have been his modernizations of Malory's *Le Morte D'Arthur*. These four novels —*The Sword in the Stone*, *The Witch in the Wood*, *The Ill-Made Knight*, and *The Candle in the Wind* —with some revisions were collected under the title *The Once and Future King* in 1958. In these retellings of the legends of King Arthur, White shows a vast knowledge of the Middle Ages and a keen appreciation of medieval culture. More important, he is able to make the sometimes shadowy figures of the legends vital and real, often interpreting his characters with the aid of modern psychology. In particular, the character of King Arthur is sympathetically depicted; the King becomes an almost tragic figure as he struggles, in the face of mounting opposition, to build an ideal kingdom founded on law and justice instead of on naked force.

Although White's retellings of Arthurian legend have been widely praised, some critics have objected to the mixture of fantasy and social satire that is characteristic of his novels of contemporary life. Of these, the best known is *Mistress Masham's Repose*, a story of a little girl's encounter with a group of Lilliputians living on an island in a lake on the grounds of a ruined castle. *The Elephant and the Kangaroo* is a fantasy about an Irishman and an Englishman who build a modern Noah's ark, and *The Master* tells how two children and their dog foil the schemes of an eccentric old man who is planning world conquest.

White's nonfiction, however, best exemplifies the wide range of his knowledge and interest. For instance,

The Age of Scandal and *The Scandalmonger* are anthologies of gossipy and scandalous anecdotes about men and women of eighteenth century England; *The Goshawk* is an account of his attempt to train a hawk after the manner of a medieval falconer; *The Book of Beasts* is a translation of a medieval bestiary (a collection of legends about actual and legendary animals); and *England Have My Bones, Godstone and the Blackymor,* and *America at Last* are autobiographical accounts of White's life in England, Ireland, and America.

BIBLIOGRAPHICAL REFERENCES: The most complete study of White's life and works at present is Sylvia Townsend Warner's *T. H. White: A Biography,* 1967. Valuable insights into White's life may also be found in *The White-Garnett Letters,* edited by David Garnett, 1968.

For criticism of White's Arthurian novels, see Stephen P. Dunn, "Mr. White, Mr. Williams, and the Matter of Britain," *Kenyon Review,* XXIV (Spring, 1962), 363–371; J. R. Cameron, "T. H. White in Camelot: The Matter of Britain Revitalized," *Humanities Association Bulletin,* XV (Spring, 1965), 45–48; and Barbara Floy, "A Critique of T. H. White's *The Once and Future King,*" *Riverside Quarterly,* I (1965), 175–180; II (1966), 54–57, 127–133, 210–213.

WALT WHITMAN

Born: West Hills, Long Island
Date: May 31, 1819

Died: Camden, New Jersey
Date: March 26, 1892

Principal Works

POEMS: *Leaves of Grass,* 1855, 1856, 1860, 1867, 1871, 1876, 1881–1882, 1888, 1891–1892; *Drum-Taps,* 1865; *Passage to India,* 1871; *After All, Not to Create Only,* 1871; *As a Strong Bird on Pinions Free,* 1872; *Two Rivulets,* 1876; *November Boughs,* 1888; *Good-bye My Fancy,* 1891.

ESSAYS, NOTES, AND STUDIES: *Democratic Vistas,* 1871; *Memoranda During the War,* 1875–1876; *Specimen Days and Collect,* 1882–1883; *Complete Prose Works,* 1892; *An American Primer,* 1904.

LETTERS AND JOURNALS: *Calamus,* edited by Richard M. Bucke, 1897; *The Wound Dresser,* edited by Richard M. Bucke, 1898; *Letters Written by Walt Whitman to His Mother, 1866–1872,* edited by Thomas B. Harned, 1902; *Walt Whitman's Diary in Canada,* edited by William S. Kennedy, 1904; *The Letters of Anne Gilchrist and Walt Whitman,* edited by Thomas B. Harned, 1918.

NOVEL: *Franklin Evans,* 1842.

SHORT STORIES: *The Half-Breed and Other Stories,* 1927.

Walt (christened Walter) Whitman was born at West Hills, near Huntington, Long Island, May 31, 1819, the second child of Walter Whitman and Louisa Van Velsor, of English and Dutch descent. The father, a farmer and carpenter by turns, had difficulty in supporting his large family, which grew to nine children, though one died in infancy. In 1823 he moved to Brooklyn, where Walt, his only son ever to show marked ability, received a meager public school education, learned the printing trade, became a journalist, and finally a poet.

After teaching school on Long Island and starting and abandoning a newspaper, the *Long Islander,* Walt Whitman worked as a printer in New York City, and at twenty-three edited a daily paper, the New York *Aurora.* Returning to Brooklyn in 1845, he worked on the Long Island *Star* and for two years edited the Brooklyn *Eagle,* from which he was dismissed because of his editorial defense of the "free soil" faction of the Democratic Party. For three months in 1848 he was employed on the New Orleans *Crescent,* but again returned to Brooklyn and for a few months edited a "free soil" paper called the *Freeman.* Thereafter for five years he built and sold houses and dabbled in real estate. He did not edit another paper until 1857, when he took charge of the Brooklyn *Times* for approximately two years.

While employed as printer, journalist, and editor Whitman published sentimental poems and stories in newspapers and magazines, but he first became a serious poet when he printed at his own expense the first edition of *Leaves of Grass.* This book was acclaimed by Emerson and a few others, but was mostly ignored or denounced as unpoetic because the lines did not rhyme or scan, or as indecent because of the frank language. Undaunted, the poet brought out a second edition in 1856, and a third in 1860, the latter published by Thayer and Eldridge in Boston; but the outbreak of the Civil War bankrupted this firm, and Whitman did not have another commercial publisher until 1881. He himself participated in the war by ministering to the wounded, writing accounts for the New York and Brooklyn newspapers, and composing his *Drum-Taps* poems, which he printed in 1865. After the assassination of President Lincoln he wrote what were to become his two best-known poems, "O Captain! My Captain!" and "When Lilacs Last in the Dooryard Bloom'd," which he included in an annex to the second issue of *Drum-Taps*. From 1865 until 1873, when he suffered a paralytic stroke, he was employed as a government clerk in Washington. His mother having died in 1873, for several years he lived with his brother George in Camden, N. J., a "battered, wrecked old man." Although a semi-invalid for the remainder of his life, he recovered sufficiently to make some trips, several to New York, one as far west as Denver in 1879, and another to Canada the following year.

In 1881 James Osgood, a respected Boston publisher, issued another edition of *Leaves of Grass*, but stopped distribution after the poet refused to withdraw several lines (for a new printing) which had provoked the threat of criminal prosecution. Whitman secured a new publisher in Philadelphia, first Rees Welsh and Company, followed by David McKay, who thereafter remained his publisher during his lifetime. In 1882 McKay published *Specimen Days and Collect*, a volume of prose containing sketches of the poet's early life, experiences in the hospitals, and old-age diary notes. *November Boughs*, 1888, also contained some prose, and an important literary apologia, "A Backward Glance O'er Travel'd Roads." With the income from the 1881 edition Whitman was able to buy a small house for himself in Camden, on Mickle Street, which soon began to be visited by many prominent writers and artists from England, where Whitman's reputation was greater than in his own country. At the time of his death in Camden, March 26, 1892, he was one of the best known poets in the United States, partly because of the publicity resulting from the accusations made against the Boston edition of 1881 and partly because he had relentlessly publicized himself. Consequently, the metropolitan newspapers gave many columns of space to his death, and it was even mentioned in many European papers. But he was not generally accepted by the literary critics and historians of his own country for another quarter century. By mid-twentieth century, however, he was almost universally regarded as the greatest poet America had produced. *Leaves of Grass* has now been translated in whole or in part into nearly every language of the world. Successful complete translations have been published in France, Germany, Spain, Italy, and Japan. *Leaves of Grass* is today an acknowledged masterpiece in world literature.

In its growth and structure *Leaves of Grass* is very nearly unique in literary history. Between 1855 and 1892 Whitman used the same title for nine editions of his collected poems, no two alike, and several dramatically different in size, content, and arrangement. Not only did the poet constantly revise and augment his poems, but he also altered titles, divided or combined poems, dropped some, and constantly shifted their relative positions in the book until 1881, when he solidified the order, thereafter merely annexing new poems.

A posthumous tenth edition, published in 1897 contains the final annex, "Old Age Echoes," made up of poems first collected by the literary executors. On his deathbed the poet declared the 1892 edition to be definitive, but critics and biographers have often found earlier editions to be more interesting, more revealing, and even of higher literary merit—especially the first (1855) and third (1860).

Great controversy has arisen over the sexual imagery of two groups of poems first assembled in 1860 and titled "Enfans d'Adam" (later "Children of Adam") and "Calamus." Theoretically, the former group treats procreative or sexual love, the latter friendship or "manly love." Earlier critics objected to the realism of "Children of Adam"; later critics have been more concerned with the eroticism of "Calamus," but there is no universal agreement. Another critical problem is ideology vs. aesthetics. Whitman openly espoused didacticism and preferred to be known as the spokesman of democracy—and in many foreign lands he has become a symbol of American democracy—but his poems have survived as poems and not as the repository of ideas. Whitman's most characteristic poem is "Song of Myself," which celebrates *the self*, not himself primarily. Though uneven, it contains some of the finest lyrical passages in the whole range of American poetry.

BIBLIOGRAPHICAL REFERENCES: The most extensive edition of Whitman's poetry and prose is the Camden Edition, *The Complete Writings of Walt Whitman*, edited by Richard M. Bucke, Horace L. Traubel, and Thomas B. Harned, 10 vols., 1902. In addition to titles already noted, supplementary material may be found in *Notes and Fragments*, edited by Richard M. Bucke, 1899; *The Gathering of the Forces*, edited by Cleveland Rodgers and John Black, 2 vols., 1920; *The Uncollected Poetry and Prose of Walt Whitman*, edited by Emory Holloway, 2 vols., 1921; *Walt Whitman's Workshop*, edited by Clifton J. Furness, 1928; *Rivulets of Prose*, edited by Carolyn Wells and Alfred F. Goldsmith, 1928; *A Child's Reminiscence*, edited by Thomas O. Mabbott and Rollo G. Silver, 1930; *I Sit and Look Out*, edited by Emory Holloway and Vernolian Schwarz, 1932; and *Walt Whitman and the Civil War*, edited by Charles I. Glicksberg, 1933.

Available one-volume editions of selections include *Walt Whitman's Complete Poetry and Selected Prose and Letters*, edited by Emory Holloway, 1938; *The Portable Walt Whitman*, edited by Mark Van Doren, 1945; *Leaves of Grass and Selected Prose*, edited by Sculley Bradley, Rinehart Editions, 1949; and *The Complete Poetry and Prose of Walt Whitman*, edited by Malcolm Cowley, 1954. Emory Holloway also edited the inclusive *Leaves of Grass*, 1924, and *Leaves of Grass: The Collected Poems*, 1942. Other editions have been prepared by Stuart P. Sherman, 1922; John Valente, 1928; Sherwood Anderson, 1933; and Carl Sandburg, 1944.

The fullest biography is by Gay Wilson Allen, *The Solitary Singer: A Critical Biography of Walt Whitman*, 1955. A companion volume is this author's *Walt Whitman Handbook*, 1946 (reissued 1957), a work useful in all Whitman studies. Allen has also edited *Walt Whitman Abroad: Critical Essays from Germany, France, Scandinavia, Russia, Italy, Spain, Latin America, Israel, Japan, and India* [in translation], 1955, and, with Charles T. Davis, *Walt Whitman's Poems*, 1955, an anthology containing extensive critical commentary. For additional biographical and critical studies see also Bliss Perry, *Walt Whitman: His Life and Works*, 1906; Basil de Sélincourt, *Walt Whitman: A Critical Study*, 1914; Emory Holloway, *Whitman: An*

Interpretation in Narrative, 1926; Frederik Schyberg, *Walt Whitman,* 1933, translated by Evie Allison Allen, 1951; Henry S. Canby, *Walt Whitman, An American,* 1943; Joseph Beaver, *Walt Whitman: Poet of Science,* 1951; Roger Asselineau, *L'Évolution de Walt Whitman après la première édition des Feuilles d'Herbe,* 1954 (tr. *The Evolution of Walt Whitman,* 1960); and Richard Chase, *Walt Whitman Reconsidered,* 1955.

For briefer studies see also Norman Foerster, *Nature in American Literature,* 1923; *idem, American Criticism,* 1928; Henry S. Canby, *Classic Americans,* 1931; Gay Wilson Allen, *American Prosody,* 1935; F. O. Matthiessen, *American Renaissance,* 1941; *Literary History of the United States,* edited by Robert E. Spiller, Willard Thorp, Thomas H. Johnson, and Henry S. Canby, Vol. II, 1948; and William M. White, "The Dynamics of Whitman's Poetry," *Sewanee Review* (Spring, 1972), 347–360.

JOHN GREENLEAF WHITTIER

Born: Haverhill, Massachusetts
Date: December 17, 1807

Died: Hampton Falls, New Hampshire
Date: September 7, 1892

PRINCIPAL WORKS

POEMS: *Legends of New England,* 1931; *Moll Pitcher,* 1832; *Mogg Megone,* 1836; *Lays of My Home,* 1843; *Ballads and Other Poems,* 1844; *Voices of Freedom,* 1846; *Songs of Labor,* 1850; *The Chapel of the Hermits,* 1853; *The Panorama,* 1856; *The Sycamores,* 1857; *Home Ballads,* 1860; *In War-Time,* 1864; *Snow-Bound,* 1866; *The Tent on the Beach,* 1867; *Among the Hills,* 1869; *Miriam,* 1871; *The Pennsylvania Pilgrim,* 1872; *Hazel-Blossoms,* 1875; *The Bay of Seven Islands,* 1883; *St. Gregory's Guest,* 1886; *At Sundown,* 1890.

PROSE NARRATIVES: *Narrative of James Williams,* 1838; *Leaves from Margaret Smith's Journal,* 1849.

ESSAYS: *Old Portraits and Modern Sketches,* 1850; *Literary Recreations and Miscellanies,* 1854.

Time and geography link John Greenleaf Whittier with such American literary figures as Emerson, Longfellow, Lowell, and Holmes—the socalled New England Group. Whittier's New England, however, was never the same as theirs; and he stands apart from them in background, schooling, and the general direction of his writing talents. To begin with, he did not share their Puritan heritage—Whittier was a Quaker, derived from Quaker stock. Nor did he inherit a ticket of admission to the cultural benefits which nineteenth century Cambridge, Concord, and Boston were able to provide. Instead, "the American Burns" was born to the rugged labors and simple pleasures of rural life, and to such limited educational opportunities as were open to a Massachusetts farm lad.

Whittier was born near Haverhill, Massachusetts, on December 17, 1807. His birthplace was the plain colonial homestead that he later made famous in "Snow-Bound" and his boyhood environment, though not povertystricken, provided no luxury or special incentives to a literary career. His formal education was confined to winter sessions of a district school and two terms at Haverhill Academy. It was the village schoolmaster, Joshua Coffin, who introduced him to Burns's poems, a powerful source of inspiration to the imaginative boy.

Whittier's early poems appeared chiefly in local newspapers, one of which was published by William Lloyd Garrison. When he was about twenty-one, Whittier left home to embark on a career of itinerant journalism which led him to Boston, back to Haverhill, then to Hartford and Philadelphia. In 1833 he attended an anti-slavery convention in Philadelphia, thus launching abolitionist efforts so zealous as to engage his best strength for the next thirty years. The end of the Civil War, however, freed him to endeavors less didactic; and in 1866 "Snow-Bound" gave him not only important literary recognition but the beginnings of financial security. As the poet of rural New England and as a voice of calm and sincere religious faith, he became increasingly popular; and his seventieth and eightieth birthdays were widely celebrated. Whittier died at Hampton Falls, New Hampshire, on September

7, 1892, at the age of eighty-five.

Whittier's reputation today rests on poems which, at their best, express the very heart of rural New England. It cannot be disputed, however, that his literary reputation has suffered a marked decline during the twentieth century, nor are the reasons far to seek. For one thing, most of Whittier's anti-slavery poems have not survived the cause in which they were written. For another, the author's work, despite its sincerity and intensity, often suffers from limitations of range and craftsmanship. Finally, his poetry is direct, simple, and emotional, qualities to which modern criticism tends to turn its deaf ear. Interesting also is the now almost-forgotten *Leaves from Margaret Smith's Journal,* a fictitious but accurate account of Colonial life.

Nevertheless, "Snow-Bound" alone is enough to place posterity in debt to Whittier. The simplicity and dignity of family affection, the sharply-etched view of a winter-bound farmhouse, and the recaptured charm of a lost way of life: in these features no other American poem can display a greater, or perhaps even equal, degree of felicity.

BIBLIOGRAPHICAL REFERENCES: The standard biography is still Samuel T. Pickard, *The Life and Letters of John Greenleaf Whittier,* 2 vols., 1907 (rev. ed.). Less extensive biographical studies are Albert Mordell: *Quaker Militant: John Greenleaf Whittier,* 1933; Whitman Bennett, *Whittier: Bard of Freedom,* 1941; John A. Pollard, *John Greenleaf Whittier: Friend of Man,* 1949; and Edward Wagenknecht, *John Greenleaf Whittier: A Portrait in Paradox,* 1967.

For criticism see George E. Woodberry, *Makers of Literature,* 1901; George R. Carpenter, *John Greenleaf Whittier,* in the American Men of Letters Series, 1903; Iola K. Eastburn, *Whittier's Relation to German Life and Thought,* 1904; Norman Foerster, *Nature in American Literature,* 1923; Gay Wilson Allen, *American Prosody,* 1935; R. Brenner, *Twelve American Poets before 1900,* 1933; Arthur E. Christy, "Orientalism in New England: Whittier," *American Literature,* I (1930), 372–392; Winfield T. Scott, "Poetry in America: A New Consideration of Whittier's Verse," *New England Quarterly,* VII (1934), 258–275; and Desmond Powell, "Whittier," *American Literature,* IX (1937), 335–342.

GEORGE J. WHYTE-MELVILLE

Born: Near St. Andrews, Scotland
Date: June 19, 1821

Died: Berkshire, England
Date: December 5, 1878

Principal Works

Novels: *Digby Grand,* 1853; *Tilbury Nogo,* 1854; *Kate Coventry,* 1856; *The Interpreter,* 1858; *Holmby House,* 1860; *Market Harborough,* 1861; *The Queen's Maries,* 1862; *The Gladiators,* 1863; *Cerise,* 1866; *The White Rose,* 1868; *Sarchedon,* 1871; *Satanella,* 1873; *Uncle John,* 1874; *Katerfelto,* 1875.

George John Whyte-Melville was born near St. Andrews, Scotland, June 19, 1821, into society, his father being a landowner in Scotland and his mother a daughter of the Duke of Leeds. As a boy Whyte-Melville attended Eton, the famous English public school, and at the age of seventeen became a commissioned officer in the Ninety-third Highlanders Regiment. After seven years with that regiment he transferred to the Coldstream Guards and retired from the British army at the age of twenty-seven with the rank of captain. When the Crimean War broke out in 1853, Whyte-Melville volunteered his services to the government and went on active duty with the rank of major. He served with units of Turkish irregular cavalry. During his service in the Crimean War he wrote some poetry and a portion of it was published. After the war he returned to civilian life to continue writing, along with hunting, his favorite sport.

The novels of Whyte-Melville fall easily into two categories: sporting novels, for which he is best known, and historical romances. As a wealthy man of property, and a retired officer, Whyte-Melville was completely familiar with the society he depicted in his sporting novels. He wrote from first-hand knowledge of fashionable, military, and sporting people, and all of those groups furnished him with the characters, actions, and background for his fiction. His novels about fox hunting had an especial appeal for British sportsmen, for they were authentically written, with a great deal of attention to realistic detail. In addition to the realistic detail, they are also filled with action. The best-known of the sporting novels is *Market Harborough,* a picaresque account of a series of fox-hunting episodes, with plenty of realistic detail about life among people in rural England and London society who follow the hounds. Other novels in this category are *Digby Grand, Tilbury Nogo,* and *Kate Coventry.* One interesting sidelight to these novels is that horses are often important characters.

Whyte-Melville's later fiction is largely in the field of historical romance. In 1858 he published *The Interpreter,* a novel based on the Crimean War and relating the activities of a beautiful female spy. *Holmby House* is a novel about the English Civil War of the seventeenth century, with an interesting depiction of Oliver Cromwell. In *Cerise* the author moved from backgrounds he knew well to write a novel about France and the court of Louis XIV. In *The Gladiators* and *Sarchedon* appear the times and deeds of exotic countries, the former being laid in Rome and Palestine and the latter depicting Egypt and Assyria under the rule of Semiramis. Perhaps the best of Whyte-Melville's historical novels, from one standpoint, is *Katerfelto*, the story of a famous horse of eighteenth century England.

Whyte-Melville did not write to earn money, and most of his income from his books was spent in charitable activity, especially among the poor people who were hangers-on about stables. In non-fiction, as in his novels and his charity, Whyte-Melville illustrated his love of horses with *Riding Recollections* (1875). Of his personal life little is known except that it was not happy with respect to marriage. Whyte-Melville met his death in the hunting field in White Horse Vale, Berkshire, on December 5, 1878, when one of his favorite horses stumbled and fell while at a gallop, throwing his rider and killing him instantly.

BIBLIOGRAPHICAL REFERENCES: There are interesting essays on Whyte-Melville in Lewis Melville's *Victorian Novelists*, 1906, and in *The Eighteen-sixties*, edited by John Drinkwater, 1932. See also Ernest A. Baker, *History of the English Novel*, Vol. VII, 1936.

RICHARD WILBUR

Born: New York, N. Y.
Date: March 1, 1921

Principal Works

POEMS: *The Beautiful Changes and Other Poems,* 1947; *Ceremony and Other Poems,* 1950; *Things of This World,* 1956; *Advice to a Prophet and Other Poems,* 1961; *The Poems of Richard Wilbur,* 1963; *Walking to Sleep,* 1968; *Digging for China,* 1970.

TRANSLATIONS: Molière's *The Misanthrope,* 1956; *Candide: A Comic Opera* (with Lillian Hellman and Others), 1957; Molière's *Tartuffe,* 1963.

Richard Wilbur, the son of Lawrence Lazear Wilbur, an artist, and Helen Ruth Purdy Wilbur was born March 1, 1921, in New York City. He lived with his brother Lawrence for two years in New York, then moved to a rural area near North Caldwell, New Jersey. He asserts that this country experience, spent in an area now suburbanized, accounts for his earlier nature poetry. He wrote his first poem, "That's When the Nightingales Wake," at the age of eight. Graduated from Montclair High School, he attended Amherst College and received an A.B. in 1942. There he edited the college newspaper and considered a career in journalism. That same year he married Charlotte Ward; his children are Ellen, Christopher, Nathan, and Aaron.

At that time he had been writing poetry for several years, but says it was the experience of the war which turned him toward writing as a serious endeavour. He served as an enlisted man in the army in Europe from 1943 to 1945, at some of the major fronts.

After the war he returned to school, and received an M.A. in English at Harvard University in 1947. He was retained as a junior fellow at Harvard until 1950. In 1947 and 1950 his first two books of poems, *The Beautiful Changes* and *Ceremony,* were published. In 1950, committed to an academic career and thereby becoming still another of the modern academic poets, he became an assistant professor of English at Harvard—an unusual post for one without a doctorate. He took time out in 1952 to visit Mexico on a grant from the Guggenheim Foundation. During this time he won the Harriet Monroe and the Oscar Blumenthal prizes from *Poetry* magazine, and in 1954 won the three-thousand dollar Prix de Rome from the American Academy of Arts and Sciences. His scholarly work was centered on Edgar Allen Poe, whose complete poems he edited.

In 1955, Wilbur was made an associate professor of English at Wellesley College, where he taught for two years. In that same year his translation of Molière's *Le Misanthrope* was published and produced in Cambridge, Massachusetts, at the Poet's Theatre; the following year it was staged at the Theatre East off Broadway. *A Bestiary* (an anthology) was published at this time; later came *The Pelican from a Bestiary of 1120.*

In 1957, he received a Pulitzer Prize and a National Book Award for *Things of This World,* published in 1956. The same year he was appointed professor of English at Wesleyan University in Middletown, Connecticut.

He won the Boston Festival Award in 1959, and in 1960 received a Ford Fellowship and was awarded an honorary L.H.D. degree by Sarah Lawrence College. He became vice-president of the National Institute of Arts and Letters in 1959. In September of the year of his fourth book of poems, *Advice to a Prophet,* 1961, he traveled to Russia as an American literary "specialist" for the State Department. In 1963 his four volumes of poems were collected by his publisher. His second translation from Molière, *Tartuffe,* was also produced in New York. His most recent book of poems is *Digging for China.*

BIBLIOGRAPHICAL REFERENCES: Important studies of Wilbur include Donald Hill, *Richard Wilbur,* 1967, and Paul F. Cummins' pamphlet, *Richard Wilbur: A Critical Essay,* 1971. *The Hollins Critic,* VI (1969), was a special Wilbur number. See also Don Cameron Allen, editor, *The Moment of Poetry,* 1962; and M. L. Rosenthal, *The Modern Poets,* 1965. For additional critical material see John P. Field, "Richard Wilbur: A Bibliographical Checklist," *Serif,* no. 16 (1971).

OSCAR WILDE

Born: Dublin, Ireland
Date: October 15, 1856

Died: Paris, France
Date: November 30, 1900

Principal Works

PLAYS: *Vera, or the Nihilists*, 1882; *The Duchess of Padua*, 1884; *A Florentine Tragedy*, 1885; *Lady Windermere's Fan*, 1892; *Salome*, 1893; *A Woman of No Importance*, 1893; *An Ideal Husband*, 1895; *The Importance of Being Earnest*, 1895.
NOVEL: *The Picture of Dorian Gray*, 1891.
TALES AND SKETCHES: *The Happy Prince and Other Tales*, 1888; *Lord Arthur Savile's Crime*, 1891; *A House of Pomegranates*, 1891.
POEMS: *Poems*, 1881; *The Sphinx*, 1894; *The Ballad of Reading Gaol*, 1898.
ESSAYS AND STUDIES: *Intentions*, 1891; *The Soul of Man Under Socialism*, 1891; *De Profundis*, 1905.

One of the most famous of Irish expatriates, Oscar (Fingal O'Flahertie Wills) Wilde, second son of Sir William Robert Wills Wilde and Jane Francisca Elgee Wilde, best known as "Speranza" of political fame, was born in Dublin, October 15, 1856. Early noted for his brilliance and sloth, characteristics he carried with him throughout life, he won prizes at the Portora Royal School in Ennis Killen, and later in Trinity College, Dublin. But it was in London that he first distinguished himself, although he had acquired fame at Magdalen College, Oxford, for his prize-winning poem "Ravenna" (1878) and as the most famous student of a famous master, John Ruskin.

As the leader of the Art-for-Art's-Sake school of aesthetics, Wilde was associated with his famous symbols: a peacock feather, sunflowers, dados, blue china, long hair, and velveteen breeches. A slight stigma was attached to his name even before his graduation from Oxford in 1878, but Wilde preached the doctrine that he did not care what was said as long as he was talked about. He was lampooned in cartoons, in novels, and even in comic opera; but he remained for years the center of attention, the lion of the hour, the most sought after of many famous talkers. His talents were conceded to be great by Shaw, Harris, Whistler, and, of course, Wilde himself. Even his early effusions in such magazines as *Month*, *The Catholic Mirror*, and the *Irish Monthly* were considered witty, artistic, and accomplished.

In a sense, his fortune was made in America where he lectured in the early 1880's and where his first play, *Vera*, was produced with fair success. His outrageous affectations and witty sayings and paradoxes were eagerly followed by everyone. Certainly this triumphant tour prepared England better to accept his later and best works. In 1884 his marriage to Constance Lloyd allayed somewhat the scabrous gossip of his deprecators. In fact, there seems little evidence for his homosexuality at this time. Only through hearsay and the later Wilde apologia, *De Profundis*, published posthumously in 1905, is there evidence of the depths of degradation to which he later sank. In direct contrast was his delicate language; no one ever heard him utter an oath or make an off-color remark.

Wilde's picture of the successive

stages of degradation in man was openly presented in the character of Dorian Gray, who remained young outwardly while his pact with evil allowed his portrait to take on his many sins. Later Wilde's drama *Salome* aroused Philistines everywhere. Some of his poems, read at his famous trials, also caused much tongue-wagging which finally culminated in the Marquis of Queensberry's attack and Wilde's ill-advised slander suit against Lord Alfred Douglas' father. The reversal of this libel case caused Oscar Wilde to spend two years (1895–1897) in the Old Bailey and Reading Gaol, an experience which he immortalized in his famous poem. Much comment has been made on this work, regarded by many as a notable statement against man's inhumanity to man.

Many of the unsavory aspects of Wilde's personal life have been forgotten, but his witty paradoxes remain alive, especially in the plays, for his real reputation rests on his witty comedies of manners. *Lady Windermere's Fan* is a kind of moral tract with the fan used to turn public feeling from a compromising situation; in this case the mother takes on the sins of the daughter in order to prevent the daughter from making a mistake in decorum. As in all the plays, the epigrams are more noteworthy than the plot, especially in *The Importance of Being Earnest*, his last, best, and most popular drama. A *Woman of No Importance* protests the double standard, while *An Ideal Husband* suggests the old ways are best: the way to have an ideal husband is to be an ideal, old-fashioned wife. None of these plays can stand beside the work of Congreve or even Sheridan, but they keep the stream of comedy flowing from the eighteenth century into the twentieth century of Maugham and Coward.

After his release from prison, Wilde lived out a miserable few years on the Continent, estranged from his wife, cut off from his friends, always short of funds. During this time he wrote (and rewrote previously published works) under the assumed name of Sebastian Melmoth. He died at the Hôtel d'Alcace in Paris on November 30, 1900, his death still shrouding the mystery, revulsion, and untruth which colored most of his life and a great deal of his legend.

BIBLIOGRAPHICAL REFERENCES: Wilde's *Works* were published in 14 vols. in 1908. Richard Aldington edited the *Selected Works*, 1946. Vyvyan Holland edited the *Works* in 1966, and Rupert Hart-Davis the *Letters* (complete) in 1962. The standard bibliography is R. E. Cowan and William Andrews Clark, Jr., *The Library of William Andrews Clark: Wilde and Wildeiana*, 5 vols., 1922–1931. For years the standard biography was Frank Harris, *Oscar Wilde; His Life and Confessions*, 2 vols., 1916, which also contains *Memories of Oscar Wilde* by G. B. Shaw; but this work is now superseded by Hesketh Pearson, *Oscar Wilde: His Life and Wit*, 1946. V. B. Holland has made a unique contribution to biographical data in *Son of Oscar Wilde*, 1954. See also H. Montgomery Hyde, *Oscar Wilde: The Aftermath*, 1963. Critical works include Vincent O'Sullivan, *Aspects of Wilde*, 1936; Frances Winwar, *Oscar Wilde and the Yellow 'Nineties*, 1942; Edouard Roditi, *Oscar Wilde*, 1947; George Woodcock, *The Paradox of Oscar Wilde*, 1949; St. John Ervine, *Oscar Wilde: A Present Time Appraisal*, 1951; and Richard Ellman, *Oscar Wilde: A Collection of Critical Essays*, 1969. An important brief study is Eric Bentley's essay in *The Playwright as Thinker*, 1946. Other critical articles are the chapter on Wilde in Archibald Henderson, *Interpreters of Life and the Modern Spirit,* 1911; Hugh Kingsmill, "The Intelligent Man's Guide to Wilde," *Fortnightly Review,* CL (1938), 296–303; A. H. Nethercot, "Oscar Wilde and the Devil's Advocate," *Publications of the Modern Language Association,* LIX (1944), 833–850; and Edouard Roditi, "Oscar Wilde's Poetry as Art History," *Poetry,* LXVII (1945), 322–337.

THORNTON WILDER

Born: Madison, Wisconsin
Date: April 17, 1897

Principal Works

NOVELS: *The Cabala,* 1926; *The Bridge of San Luis Rey,* 1927; *The Woman of Andros,* 1930; *Heaven's My Destination,* 1934; *The Ides of March,* 1948; *The Eighth Day,* 1967.

PLAYS: *The Angel That Troubled the Waters and Other Plays,* 1928; *The Long Christmas Dinner and Other Plays,* 1931; *Our Town,* 1938; *The Merchant of Yonkers,* 1939; *The Skin of Our Teeth,* 1942; *The Matchmaker,* 1955 (revised from *The Merchant of Yonkers*).

Thornton (Niven) Wilder is a writer whose work displays individual qualities of wit, imaginaton, and careful workmanship, all combined with beauty and precision of style. As a novelist and playwright he has always followed his own course, even in decades when the literary current was flowing in quite different channels, such as naturalism, reportage, social documentation. Among the veering trends by which his contemporaries have reacted to the special concerns of our time, his work takes root in the humaneness and restraint of a classical tradition. A literary figure of some distinction in his own right, he has also been a teacher of students on both sides of the Atlantic, and in this role he has helped to create a cultural link between the Old World and the New.

Wilder was born in Madison, Wisconsin, on April 17, 1897, the son of Amos P. Wilder, who was at that time editor of the *Wisconsin State Journal.* When he was nine, he accompanied his family to China, where his father was consul general at Hong Kong and Shanghai. This was the first of a series of wanderings and international contacts which have in part shaped the outward pattern of his life and the inward habit of detached observation characteristic of his novels and plays. He finished high school in California and in 1915 entered Oberlin College, only to leave that school two years later for service in the Coast Artillery Corps during World War I. After the war he transferred to Yale, received his B.A. degree in 1920, studied for a year at the American Academy in Rome, and in 1921 became an instructor in a preparatory school at Lawrenceville, New Jersey. In 1926 he received his M.A. degree from Princeton.

In the same year he published his first novel, *The Cabala,* the gracefully written story of a young American in postwar Rome and his contacts with a group of talented and wealthy aristocrats who exert a mysterious influence on affairs of state and Church. Drawn into their secret confidences and councils, he sees them at last for what they are: the pagan gods of Europe grown old and unable, in spite of their ancient wisdom, to save themselves from the sufferings and follies of ordinary humanity. With a great leap in time and space, Wilder's imagination moved to Colonial Peru for his second novel, *The Bridge of San Luis Rey,* a brief but evocative retelling of events in five lives snuffed out in the collapse of a bridge on the road between Lima and Cuzco. The stories are beautifully told; not without irony, Wilder seeks to discover the working of a providential plan in the disaster, and only at the end does the reader perceive that his characters represent in their different persons the bitterness, innocence, sorrow, and humility of love. Some critics, noting his use of the celebrated French letter writer, Madame de Sévigné, as the model for one of his characters, suggested that there was a strong element of pastiche in Wilder's writing. It is, in fact, an open secret that Wilder's mind often finds imaginative stimulus in a forgotten nineteenth century play, in Roman histories, in work as modern as James Joyce's *Finnegan's Wake*. What his critics minimize, however, is Wilder's own note, his detached but not unkind gaze to which he subjects the materials toward which his mind and imagination have turned. Thus his third novel, *The Woman of Andros,* is more than a story based on the *Andria* of Terence; it is another probing into hidden meanings in human experience, presented through man's blundering impulses toward truth in a twilight age that waited for the birth of a great faith.

Although Wilder's sources are usually "literary," his manipulation of them is not pedantic; he displays in whatever he touches the same sure craftsmanship and the working of a mind enlivened by considerable imagination and wit. In *Heaven's My Destination* he took the pattern of the picaresque novel and imposed on it a new subject matter, evangelistic activity in the Middle West, so that the story of George Brush becomes the amusing yet touching saga of a cornfed Faithful and his travels through a modern Vanity Fair. *The Ides of March*, epistolary in form, takes for its subject events in the closing years of Julius Caesar's life; unlike the usual popular historical novel, however, this book represents full knowledge of a past period and full imaginative and artistic domination over it. *The Eighth Day,* the story of a fictitious murder, seemed to one critic to recall *The Bridge of San Luis Rey* in that it dealt with the effect of "a central and violent event on a widening circle of characters."

The same note of controlled experimentation sounds in Wilder's plays. His two most noteworthy, *Our Town* and *The Skin of Our Teeth,* are at once experimental and derivative in form; we can trace his progress toward these efforts in the one-act plays and dramatic character sketches written during his Lawrenceville years and collected in *The Angel That Troubled the Waters* and *The Long Christmas Dinner. Our Town* is the account of life in a New England village, but it is acted out on a bare stage, much in the manner of Oriental drama, and the lack of furnishings such as those which clutter the modern stage becomes an effective device in centering attention upon events which make this play a morality drama revealing the religious feeling that underlies Wilder's best work. *The Skin of Our Teeth* takes elements from Joyce and European expressionism and tells, in terms of the trials and temptations of one household, of the full course of human history on the planet. But beneath this surface diversity Wilder's own note persists, the point of view of the wise observer who is not involved in what he sees but who does not, for that reason, despise what he is observing in the failures and triumphs of mankind. The play became a subject of literary controversy when critics pointed out his debt to Joyce, but much of this curious critical flurry was negated by the fact that Joyce had in turn borrowed from the theories of Giovanni Battista Vico, eighteenth century Italian philosopher, in the writing of *Finnegan's Wake*.

Wilder's intellectual history lies open to view in his novels and plays. During World War II he served as a combat-intelligence officer with the Air Force in Italy. He has taught at the University of Chicago and at Harvard and has given special courses of lectures before various universities and learned societies throughout Europe. His most recent work is *The Matchmaker*, a revised version of *The Merchant of Yonkers*, first presented in 1939.

BIBLIOGRAPHICAL REFERENCES: For biographical and critical studies see Rex Burbank, *Thornton Wilder*, 1961; Bernard Grebanier, *Thornton Wilder*, 1964; Malcolm Goldstein, *The Art of Thornton Wilder*, 1965; and Donald Haberman, *The Plays of Thornton Wilder*, 1967. Three of his novels were reprinted in the *Thornton Wilder Trio*, 1956, for which Malcolm Cowley wrote a discerning and helpful preface. For criticism see Edmund Wilson, *Classics and Commercials*, 1950, and *Shores of Light*, 1952; Pierre Loving, "The Bridge of Casuistry," *This Quarter*, II (1929), 150–161; E. G. Twitchett, "Thornton Wilder," *London Mercury*, XXII (1930), 32–39; Robert McNamara, "Phases of American Religion in Thornton Wilder and Willa Cather," *Catholic World*, CXXXV (1932), 641–649; E. K. Brown, "A Christian Humanist, Thornton Wilder," *University of Toronto Quarterly*, IV (1935), 356–370; Dayton Kohler, "Thornton Wilder," *English Journal*, XXVIII (1939), 1–11; Martin Gardner, "Thornton Wilder and the Problem of Providence," *University of Kansas City Review*, VII (1940), 83–91; J. J. Firebaugh, "The Humanism of Thornton Wilder," *Pacific Spectator*, IV (1950), 426–438; and Arthur H. Ballet, "'In Our Living and in Our Dying,'" *English Journal*, XLV (1956), 243–249. For a Marxian view of Wilder see also Michael Gold, "Wilder: Prophet of the Genteel Christ," *New Republic*, LXIV (1930), 266, and "The Economic Interpretation of Wilder," *ibid.*, LXV (1930), 31–32.

CHARLES WILLIAMS

Born: London, England
Date: September 20, 1886

Died: Oxford, England
Date: May 15, 1945

Principal Works

NOVELS: *War in Heaven,* 1930; *Many Dimensions,* 1931; *The Place of the Lion,* 1932; *The Greater Trumps,* 1932; *Shadows of Ecstasy,* 1933; *Descent into Hell,* 1937; *All Hallows Eve,* 1945; *Flecker of Dean Close,* 1946.
PLAYS: *Three Plays,* 1931; *Thomas Cranmer of Canterbury,* 1936; *Judgment at Chelmsford,* 1939; *The House of the Octopus,* 1945; *Seed of Adam and Other Plays,* 1948.
BIOGRAPHY AND HISTORY: *Heroes and Kings,* 1930, *Bacon,* 1934; *James I,* 1934; *Rochester,* 1935.
CRITICISM: *The Myth of Shakespeare,* 1928; *Poetry at Present,* 1930; *The English Poetic Mind,* 1932; *Reason and Beauty in the Poetic Mind,* 1933; *Religion and Love in Dante,* 1941; *The Figure of Beatrice,* 1943.
PHILOSOPHY AND RELIGION: *The Rite of the Passion,* 1936; *He Came Down from Heaven,* 1938; *The Descent of the Dove,* 1939.
POEMS: *Taliessin Through Logres,* 1938; *The Region of the Summer Stars,* 1944.

Charles Williams was born in London in 1886, the son of R. W. Stansby Williams, a translator and poet. He was educated at St. Albans School and had two years at the University of London before he was forced to earn his living. During lean years in a publishing job, he continued his studies and without any formal degrees became a profound literary scholar, historian, theologian, poet, and novelist. Throughout his career as an editor with the Oxford University Press, he taught, lectured, and wrote prolifically. In 1917 he married Florence Conway, and they had one son. He lived all his life in London, except for a few years during World War II when the Press was evacuated to Oxford, where he became the moving spirit in a literary group which included C. S. Lewis and J. R. R. Tolkien. After his death in 1945 the tributes of these and other literary friends such as Auden, Eliot, and Dorothy Sayers brought him wider recognition than he had had during his lifetime.

Williams' literary career developed gradually, with four volumes of poems published between 1912 and 1924. His first critical study, *The Myth of Shakespeare,* indicated the direction of his thought toward the religious and mythic elements in literature. During the next decade he published eighteen books covering the entire range of his varied but closely related interests. The three critical works are in essence a series of variations on the theme of the religious basis of the creative imagination: *Poetry at Present, The English Poetic Mind,* and *Reason and Beauty in the Poetic Mind.* His historical studies were concerned with the relationship between the individual and the pattern of history: *Heroes and Kings, Bacon, James I,* and *Rochester.* The depth of his thought as an original but profoundly orthodox Anglican was revealed in two religious books: *The Rite of the Passion,* and *He Came Down from Heaven.* The predominantly religious emphasis was also maintained in his plays: *Three Plays* and *Thomas Cranmer of Canterbury*. His religious conviction was combined with an interest in witchcraft and the occult which formed the basis of a remarkable series of novels: *War in Heaven, Many Dimensions, The Place of the Lion, The Greater Trumps, Shadows of Ecstasy,* and *Descent into Hell.* Described by critics as "supernatural thrillers," these novels employ a realistic contemporary English setting as the background for the eternal conflict between good and evil, revealing both the mystic and the sensuous facets of Williams' personality.

In 1938 Williams published his first verse since 1924, *Taliessin Through Logres,* a series of brilliant but difficult poems based on Arthurian legends. His historical, poetic, and religious interests became focused on two of the greatest myths of European culture: the English legend of the king and the Italian poet's legend of the beloved lady. Williams' two books about Dante, *Religion and Love in Dante* and *The Figure of Beatrice,* are among the most stimulating interpretations of Dante in English. The fundamental ideas which are brought out in his treatment both of Arthur and of Beatrice were developed specifically in three religious and philosophical studies: *Descent of the Dove, Witchcraft,* and *The Forgiveness of Sins.* In 1944 he published the second volume of Arthurian poems, *The Region of the Summer Stars.* He also continued to write plays with a historical background and religious theme: *Judgment at Chelmsford, The House of the Octopus,* and *Seed of Adam and Other Plays* (published posthumously). His last novel, *All Hallows Eve,* was published shortly before his death in 1945, and *Flecker of Dean Close* in 1946.

Williams' sudden death was a shock to his friends, who felt that he was at the height of his literary power. He left behind a large body of material which he had intended to use in both poetic and critical interpretations of the Arthurian myth, which had increasingly absorbed him during the war years. C. S. Lewis edited and enlarged upon this material in a volume called *Arthurian Torso.* Williams' Arthurian studies during the war were in no sense escapist. He saw England's role in the conflict as part of a pattern in history which had been foreshadowed in the Arthurian cycle. The image of the Fisher King, as used by Eliot in the conclusion of *The Waste Land,* was to Williams not merely a poetic image but a spiritual reality, and he felt that a deeper understanding of the legendary past led to fuller understanding of the present. The fact that his last novel, written before the end of the war, was set in the autumn after the end of the war, is typical of the coherence of his imagination. The wide range of his interests and considerable scope of his literary powers were all concentrated, in Eliot's phrase, "to apprehend the point of intersection of the timeless with time."

BIBLIOGRAPHICAL REFERENCES: There is good biographical material in the preface to *Essays Presented to Charles Williams,* edited by C. S. Lewis, 1947. Biographical and critical studies include John Heath-Stubbs, *Charles Williams,* 1955; Alice M. Hadfield, *An Introduction to Charles Williams,* 1959; Mary M. Shideler, *Theology of Romantic Love: A Study in the Writings of Charles Williams,* 1962; and *idem.*

Charles Williams: A Critical Essay, 1966.

See also Charles Moorman, *Arthurian Triptych,* 1960; Kathleen E. Morgan, *Christian Themes in Contemporary Poets,* 1965; W. H. Auden, *Secondary Worlds,* 1968; R. J. Reilly, *Romantic Religion: A Study in the Work of Owen Barfield, C. S. Lewis, Charles Williams, and J. R. R. Tolkien,* 1971; and Patricia M. Spacks, "Charles Williams: The Fusions of Fiction," in *Shadows of Imagination: The Fantasies of C. S. Lewis, J. R. R. Tolkien, and Charles Williams,* edited by Mark R. Hillegas, 1969.

There are also T. S. Eliot's Introduction to *All Hallows Eve,* 1948; and W. H. Auden's Introduction to *The Descent of the Dove,* 1956.

TENNESSEE WILLIAMS

Born: Columbus, Mississippi
Date: March 26, 1914

Principal Works

PLAYS: *American Blues*, 1939, 1948; *Battle of Angels*, 1940; *The Glass Menagerie*, 1945; *You Touched Me!*, 1945 (with Donald Windham); *27 Wagons Full of Cotton*, 1946, 1953; *A Streetcar Named Desire*, 1947; *Summer and Smoke*, 1948; *The Rose Tattoo*, 1951; *I Rise in Flame, Cried the Phoenix*, 1951; *Camino Real*, 1953; *Cat on a Hot Tin Roof*, 1955; *Orpheus Descending*, 1957; *Suddenly Last Summer*, 1958; *Sweet Bird of Youth*, 1959; *The Night of the Iguana*, 1962; *The Milk Train Doesn't Stop Here Anymore*, 1964; *The Eccentricities of a Nightingale*, 1965; *Kingdom of Earth: The Seven Descents of Myrtle*, 1968; *In the Bar of a Tokyo Hotel*, 1969; *Dragon Country*, a book of plays, 1970.

NOVEL: *The Roman Spring of Mrs. Stone*, 1950.

SHORT STORIES: *One Arm and Other Stories*, 1948; *Hard Candy, a Book of Stories*, 1954; *Three Players of a Summer Game, and Other Stories*, 1960; *The Knightly Quest*, a novella and 4 short stories, 1967.

POEMS: *Five Young American Poets*, 1939; *In the Winter of Cities*, 1956.

When *The Glass Menagerie* became the hit of the 1945 Broadway season, it was evident that America had in Tennessee Williams a playwright of new sensibility. For here he suffused the naturalism of his St. Louis upbringing with a rare theater poetry. It was also evident, and has become increasingly so, that he was a writer of the South, largely symbolized in the fading beauty and neuroses of its womanhood.

Born Thomas Lanier Williams in his grandfather's rectory in Columbus, Mississippi, on March 26, 1914, Williams has led a peripatetic life after the fashion of his shoe-salesman father. His youth consisted of aborted academic stands at the universities of Iowa and Washington and odd jobs from Florida to California; today, in well-heeled security, he still moves restlessly from Key West to Rome to New Orleans, his favorite city.

Williams' first recognition came in 1939 when his collection of one-act plays, *American Blues*, received a Group Theatre award. In 1940 the Theatre Guild backed an ill-starred production of *Battle of Angels*. Although the play never got past third-act trouble and censorship in Boston, its early demise failed to check Williams' certain but uneven career as a playwright.

The success of *The Glass Menagerie* was followed immediately by a tepid merger of Shaw and D. H. Lawrence, otherwise a vital influence upon Williams, in *You Touched Me!*, done in collaboration with Donald Windham. Two years later *A Streetcar Named Desire* brought to the stage that great portrayal of female psychosis Blanche Dubois, somewhat after the image of Strindberg's *Miss Julie*, and carried Williams' name around the world. An earlier play, *Summer and Smoke*, finally found its proper medium in the arena style and revealed Williams' fine ear for the Southern idiom.

Having examined Italianate love in

The Roman Spring of Mrs. Stone, his only novel, Williams juxtaposed the fiery Sicilian temperament against a Gulf of Mexico sterility in *The Rose Tattoo*, a lurid, uncertain play compounded of sex and ashes. In *Camino Real*, Williams created a canvas of desiccation and despair, brilliantly theatrical but immature in its symbolism. In *Cat on a Hot Tin Roof* Williams returned to the Mississippi Delta to deal in sexual ambiguity and the decay of plantation power. Here, as so often before, the conjunctive talents of Williams as writer and Elia Kazan as director resulted in a swift, brilliant production, the "achievement of continual flow," as they called it. Their collaboration on the film *Baby Doll* (1956) accomplished a fine fusion of social protest and lingering affection for the South.

By revising *Battle of Angels* into the *Orpheus Descending* of 1957, Williams again displayed what is perhaps his greatest theatrical talent, the capacity for incessant revision, a revision which always advances into a new poetry of the theater. And in *The Night of the Iguana*, 1962, another study of what has been called "futile degeneration," Williams wrote a play that has become as famous as his earlier successes.

BIBLIOGRAPHICAL REFERENCES: The Williams bibliography is extensive. For full-length studies see S. L. Falk, *Tennessee Williams*, 1961; Benjamin Nelson, *Tennessee Williams: The Man and His Work*, 1961; Francis Donahue, *The Dramatic World of Tennessee Williams*, 1964; Gerald Weales, *Tennessee Williams*, 1965; and Nancy M. Tischler, *Tennessee Williams*, 1969. For further discussion see John Gassner, "Tennessee Williams: Dramatist of Frustration," *College English*, X (October 1948), 1–7; and *passim.*, *The Theatre in Our Times*, 1954; Joseph Wood Krutch, *"Modernism" in Modern Drama*, 1953; Paul Moor, "A Mississippian Named Tennessee," *Harper's*, CXCVIII (1948), 63–71; David Sievers, *Freud on Broadway*, 1955; C. N. Stavrou, "The Neurotic Heroine in Tennessee Williams," *Literature and Psychology*, V (1955), 26–34; Kenneth Tynan, "American Blues: The Plays of Arthur Miller and Tennessee Williams," *Encounter* (London), II (1954), 13–19; Richard B. Vowles, "Tennessee Williams och Strindberg," *Svenska Dagbladet* (Stockholm), April 11, 1956, 8–9; and A. B. Waters, "Tennessee Williams: Ten Years Later," *Theatre Arts Monthly*, XXXIX (1955), 72–73, 96.

WILLIAM CARLOS WILLIAMS

Born: Rutherford, New Jersey
Date: September 17, 1883

Died: Rutherford, New Jersey
Date: March 4, 1963

Principal Works

POEMS: *Poems,* 1909; *The Tempers,* 1913; *Al Que Quiere!,* 1917; *Kora in Hell: Improvisations,* 1920; *Sour Grapes,* 1921; *Spring and All,* 1922; *Collected Poems, 1921–1931,* 1934; *An Early Martyr and Other Poems,* 1935; *Adam and Eve & the City,* 1936; *The Complete Collected Poems of William Carlos Williams, 1906–1938,* 1938; *The Broken Span,* 1941; *The Wedge,* 1944; *Paterson,* Book I, 1946; *The Clouds,* 1948; *Paterson,* Book II, 1948; *Paterson,* Book III, 1949; *Collected Later Poems,* 1950; *Paterson,* Book IV, 1951; *Collected Earlier Poems,* 1951; *The Desert Music and Other Poems,* 1954; *Journey to Love,* 1956; *Collected Later Poems* (rev. ed.), 1963.

NOVELS: *A Voyage to Pagany,* 1928; *White Mule,* 1937; *In the Money,* 1940; *The Build-Up,* 1952.

SHORT STORIES: *The Knife of the Times,* 1932; *Life Along the Passaic River,* 1938; *Make Light of It: Collected Stories,* 1950.

ESSAYS AND BELLES-LETTRES: *The Great American Novel,* 1923; *In the American Grain,* 1925; *A Novelette and Other Prose,* 1932; *Selected Essays of William Carlos Williams,* 1954.

AUTOBIOGRAPHY: *The Autobiography of William Carlos Williams,* 1951.

LETTERS: *The Selected Letters of William Carlos Williams,* 1957.

William Carlos Williams, the New Jersey doctor who has become one of America's leading contemporary poets, was born on September 17, 1883, in Rutherford, New Jersey, where he practiced medicine from 1910 until his retirement in 1951. He received his preparatory education in Geneva and his M.D. from the University of Pennsylvania. He did graduate work in pediatrics at the University of Leipzig. He wrote all his adult life, and his first volume, *Poems,* was published in 1909. His long career as doctor and poet was crowned by the receipt of many honors and awards. He received the Russell Loines Memorial Award of the National Institute of Arts and Letters in 1948 and the National Book Award for Poetry in 1950. He was named a fellow of the Library of Congress in 1949 and in 1952 was appointed consultant in poetry to the Library, although objections to his politics prevented him from ever occupying the post. In 1953 he shared the Yale University Library's Bollingen Prize for 1952 with Archibald MacLeish. He held honorary degrees from the University of Buffalo, Rutgers University, Bard College, and the University of Pennsylvania.

Williams' early poems gave little indication of the kind of work which would make him famous later. The poems in *The Tempers,* an early volume, are heavily influenced by Yeats, Joyce, and the Imagists. Conventional in rhyme and verse pattern, they are filled with mythological and classical allusions. In the *Transitional* (1915) poems, however, Williams' characteristic free-verse form began to develop, with its short, sharp lines, colloquial speech, and rhythms arbitrarily molded to the accents of contemporary speech. Equally important was Williams' change in choice of subject matter; from a concentration on mythology and the past he turned to an intense concentration on the world he knew and lived in, and began his lifelong poetic search for the universals of human existence among the minutiae of everyday urban life. In *Al Que Quiere!* and in his "Pastorals" of city streets and back yards these changes became increasingly evident.

During the 1920's and 1930's Williams continued to write the numerous short poems which formed the *Complete Collected Poems,* and which show an ever-increasing concern with structural movement and with the inseparability of image and thought. Although sometimes marred by the opacity which his friend Ezra Pound encouraged, Williams' poems of this period are enhanced by their vivid and dynamic imagery, sometimes even going to extremes of onomatopoeia and visual patterns on the page.

Between 1928 and 1952 Williams wrote four novels: *A Voyage to Pagany, White Mule, In the Money,* and *The Build-Up.* He has also written short stories and essays. Perhaps his most important book of prose is *In the American Grain,* a minor masterpiece in which he re-creates a living American tradition from the historical figures of the national past. His prose, while casual and colloquial and sometimes even slangy, is warm and vital in the love of humanity it expresses. But it is in the realm of poetry that Williams excels as an artist, and his long poem *Paterson,* published in four books between 1946 and 1951, is the culmination of his artistic skill and sensitivity. In this poem, which has been called Williams' personal epic, he writes about what he knows best, seeking "in the particular to discover the universal." Writing about a city and a world he has been observing all his life, he seems to share Walt Whitman's ability to weave descriptions of ordinary people and commonplace incidents into a saga of American life itself. It is an older and sadder America than Whitman saw, but still worthy of the love which Williams, despite his occasional precise and biting social criticism, offered it in the creation of his masterpiece.

BIBLIOGRAPHICAL REFERENCES: There is no definitive edition of the poems. In addition to the volumes of collected verse listed under Williams' principal works, he has also published *Collected Later Poetry of William Carlos Williams,* 1950 (rev. ed., 1963), and *Collected Earlier Poems,* 1951. The four books of *Paterson* were printed in a single volume in 1951.

For biographical information see his *Autobiography,* 1951. The most authoritative critical study is Vivienne Koch, *William Carlos Williams,* 1950. For criticism in books and periodicals see, further, Paul Rosenfeld, *Port of New York,* 1924; Yvor Winters, *Primitivism and Decadence,* 1937; Linda Wagner, *The Poems of William Carlos Williams,* 1964; Alan B. Ostram, *The Poetic World of William Carlos Williams,* 1966; and Bram Dijkstra, *The Hieroglyphics of a New Speech,* 1966; Carl Rakosi, "William Carlos Williams," *Symposium,* IV (1933), 439–447; Ruth Lechlitner, "The Poetry of William Carlos Williams," *Poetry,* LIV (1939), 326–335; Vivienne Koch, "William Carlos Williams: The Man and the Poet," *Kenyon Review,* XIV (1952), 502–510; Sister M. Bernetta Quinn, "William Carlos Williams: A Testament of Perpetual Change," *Publications of the Modern Language Association,* LXX (1955), 292–322—the most comprehensive discussion of *Paterson* to date; and

Frank Thompson, "The Symbolic Structure of *Paterson*," *Western Review,* XIX (1955), 285–293.

HENRY WILLIAMSON

Born: Bedfordshire, England
Date: December 1, 1895

Principal Works

NOVELS: *The Flax of Dreams*, 4 vols., 1921–1928 (*The Beautiful Years*, 1921; *Dandelion Days*, 1922; *The Dream of Fair Women*, 1924; *The Pathways*, 1928); *The Old Stag*, 1926; *Tarka the Otter*, 1927; *The Star-Born*, 1933; *Salar the Salmon*, 1935; *The Phasian Bird*, 1948; *A Chronicle of Ancient Sunlight*, 15 vols., 1951–1969.

SHORT STORIES: *Tales of a Devon Village*, 1945; *Tales of Moorland and Estuary*, 1953; *The Henry Williamson Animal Saga*, 1959.

NATURE AND NATURAL HISTORY: *Anthology of Modern Nature Writing*, 1936 (editor); *Selections from Richard Jefferies*, 1937 (editor); *The Story of a Norfolk Farm*, 1940; *Life in a Devon Village*, 1945; *A Clear Water Stream*, 1958.

Henry Williamson was born in Bedfordshire, England, on December 1, 1895. His lonely childhood was spent in a house that had belonged to his family for more than four centuries. During his formative years he read and admired the writings of Richard Jefferies, who thus provided the inspiration for his later work. When World War I began Williamson enlisted; he was then nineteen. He served throughout the war in Flanders, where some of the bitterest fighting occurred and casualties were appalling. He returned to civilian life with gray hair and shattered nerves in 1920. Completely unable to cope with the hectic pettiness of the life around him, he attempted to earn a living as reporter for the *Weekly Dispatch* and was forced to give the position up. He then tried to eke out an existence on his pension, which provided the meager income of forty pounds a year; this was supplemented by small sums received for nature articles which he contributed weekly to the *Daily Express*. He slept in haystacks in the nearby countryside, or under trees on the Thames embankment. He was depressed, morbid, and contemplated suicide. He had almost reached the end of his tether when he got hold of himself and abandoned this impossible existence: he walked to Devonshire and settled down in a cottage at Exmoor to complete his first novel. As time passed he found it possible to earn a living with his pen, and he found contentment in his rural surroundings. His work was admired by such famous and successful writers as Walter De La Mare, Arnold Bennett, Thomas Hardy, and T. E. Lawrence. His nature novel *Tarka the Otter* won the Hawthornden Prize in 1927 and brought him widespread recognition. It has remained a modern nature classic. Two of his later books, *Salar the Salmon* and *The Phasian Bird*, the story of a pheasant, are considered equally significant. Although a prolific writer, the majority of his works have not appeared in the United States. He is looked upon as one of the most gifted of nature writers; his novels reveal the lives of wild creatures from their own viewpoints, as evoked by a mind of deep insight and understanding. His somber prose transmits, faithfully, the eternal struggle of living things to survive, and with it a deep awareness of the transitory fragility of life itself.

BIBLIOGRAPHICAL REFERENCES: Williamson's early work is discussed in I. W. Girvan, *A Bibliography and Critical Survey of the Works of Henry Williamson,* 1931. See also Bernard Bergonzi, *Heroes' Twilight: A Study of the Literature of the Great War,* 1965; and Denys Val Baker, editor, *Modern British Writing,* 1947.

For review of various works see Frank N. Magill, *Masterplots:* Comprehensive Library Edition, 1968.

EDMUND WILSON

Born: Red Bank, New Jersey
Date: May 8, 1895

Died: Talcottville, New York
Date: June 12, 1972

Principal Works

CRITICISM AND ESSAYS: *Axel's Castle,* 1931; *The American Jitters: A Year of the Slump,* 1932; *Travels in Two Democracies,* 1936; *The Triple Thinkers,* 1938; *To the Finland Station,* 1940; *The Wound and the Bow,* 1941; *The Boys in the Back Room,* 1941; *The Shock of Recognition,* 1943; *Europe Without Baedeker,* 1947; *Classics and Commercials,* 1950; *The Shores of Light,* 1952; *The Scrolls from the Dead Sea,* 1955; *Red, Black, Blond and Olive,* 1956; *A Piece of My Mind,* 1956; *Apologies to the Iroquois,* 1959; *Patriotic Gore,* 1962; *The Cold War and the Income Tax,* 1963; *O Canada,* 1965; *The Bit Between My Teeth,* 1965; *A Prelude,* 1967; *The Fruits of the MLA,* 1969; *Upstate: Records and Recollections of Northern New York,* 1971.

NOVEL: *I Thought of Daisy,* 1929.

SHORT STORIES: *Memoirs of Hecate County,* 1946.

PLAYS: *Five Plays,* 1954; *The Duke of Palermo and Other Plays,* 1969.

POEMS: *The Undertaker's Garland* (with J. P. Bishop), 1922; *Poets, Farewell!,* 1929; *Notebooks of Night,* 1942; *Night Thoughts,* 1961.

Edmund Wilson almost single-handedly created an American tradition of literary criticism. Productive for more than fifty years, his enormous output of criticism was consistently clear and comprehensible to the layman. Wilson was an incredibly well-read and erudite man; the breadth of knowledge which he brought to virtually any topic makes his writing, often extremely personal in its content, always illuminating and never limited by intellectual narrowness.

Wilson was, preëminently, a historical critic. His precepts of criticism included a conviction that literature must be comprehended within its social and political context. His work thus stands in direct opposition to the more rigid views of the formalists and the "New Critics." Wilson did not, however, extend his views on the nature of criticism to an extreme; art should not, he said, be judged on an ideological basis. And despite quite definitive political views, often forcibly expressed, his criticism remained detached from such concerns.

Wilson's insistence upon seeing literary works in context but not encumbering them with meaningless and misleading material led to a lifelong battle with the confusing apparatus of professional scholarship. He remained aloof from the university approach to literature, and in *The Fruits of the MLA* (originally published in the influential *New York Review of Books*), unleashed a blistering attack upon the Modern Language Association and its publications. Such scholarship, he charged, treats literature as an object rather than as art. The close textual analysis of literature and lengthy discussions of variant readings make it impossible, he averred, to retain an aesthetic enjoyment of the work of art. He further dismissed such criticism as the work of men unable to explicate clearly the text, who therefore take refuge in a meaningless scholarly structure to conceal their ignorance.

In addition to providing a powerful and constant opposition to critics whose writings are often impenetrable without knowledge of their specialized jargon, Wilson's critical stance included a passionate hatred of all commercial literary works. As a result, he searched for merit, and often found it, in obscure and little-known writers. His influential examination of the Symbolist tradition in literature, *Axel's Castle,* was among the first explorations of Yeats, Joyce, and Proust in more than sensationalist terms. His interest in Freudianism led to the searching reëvaluation of Dickens in *The Wound and the Bow* which has informed most of Dickens scholarship ever since.

Edmund Wilson's own creative writing has been called ultimately critical, and certainly it is clearly the work of a critical temperament. His plays are rarely performed, and are more important as social histories documenting American mores at the time of their composition than as dramas.

His novel, *I Thought of Daisy,* is more interesting for its critical discussion of Greenwich Village bohemian writers during the 1920's than for its fictive plot, while his short stories, *Memoirs of Hecate County,* received their principal fame when banned in the New York courts as obscene.

His major contribution to American literature, then, was as a critic. His analytical works have been attacked for their lack of humor, and Wilson himself was called snobbish in his approach to new literature. In the enormous amount of criticism which he wrote, numerous essays are undoubtedly dull, and many of his judgments suspect. But Edmund Wilson, over the length of his career, consistently wrote with elegance, erudition, and clarity. His criticism illuminated often obscure literary works, bringing fresh insight to the average reader. His attacks on self-satisfied establishments, whether governmental or academic, caused those organizations to face unpleasant realities. Edmund Wilson was, in short, that rarity on the American literary scene, the complete man of letters.

BIBLIOGRAPHICAL REFERENCES: The most detailed studies to date are Sherman Paul, *Edmund Wilson: A Study of Literary Vocation in Our Time,* 1967; Charles Frank, *Edmund Wilson,* 1970; and Leonard Kriegel, *Edmund Wilson,* 1971. See also Warner Berthoff's pamphlet, *Edmund Wilson,* 1968; Robert Penn Warren, "Edmund Wilson's Civil War," *Commentary,* XXXIV (August, 1962), 151–158; R. Gilmon, "Edmund Wilson, Then and Now," *New Republic,* CLV (July 2, 1966), 23–28; Alfred Kazin, "Edmund Wilson: His Life and Books," *Atlantic Monthly,* CCXX (July, 1967), 80–83; and Daniel Aaron, *Writers on the Left,* 1961.

For additional references see Richard D. Ramsey, *Edmund Wilson: A Bibliography,* 1971.

OWEN WISTER

Born: Philadelphia, Pennsylvania
Date: July 14, 1860

Died: North Kingstown, Rhode Island
Date: July 21, 1938

Principal Works

NOVELS: *The Dragon of Wantley*, 1892; *The Virginian*, 1902; *Lady Baltimore*, 1906.

SHORT STORIES: *Red Men and White*, 1896; *Lin McLean*, 1898; *The Jimmyjohn Boss and Other Stories*, 1900; *Philosophy 4*, 1903; *Padre Ignacio*, 1911; *When West Was West*, 1928.

BIOGRAPHY: *Ulysses S. Grant*, 1900; *The Seven Ages of Washington*, 1907; *Roosevelt: The Story of a Friendship, 1880-1919*, 1930.

Owen Wister, born in Philadelphia, Pennsylvania, on July 14, 1860, began his career with a serious interest in music and only later became interested in writing. After being educated in private schools in the United States and abroad, he attended Harvard University, where he was graduated with highest honors in music in 1882. He then spent two years abroad, studying composition in Paris before ill health forced his return to the United States. Following a period as the employee of a bank in New York City, he suffered a nervous breakdown and traveled to Wyoming to recuperate in the healthful atmosphere of a Western cattle ranch. From 1885 to 1888 he attended the Harvard Law School. After graduation he was admitted to the bar and practiced law in Philadelphia.

Having grown extremely fond of the West while recuperating from his illness, Wister made frequent trips back to his favorite country. Two short stories based on western life, "Hank's Woman" (1891) and "How Lin McLean Went West" (1891), published in *Harper's Magazine*, were his first published literary works to gain recognition. Such volumes as *Red Men and White* and *The Jimmyjohn Boss* followed. In the meantime, Wister was married to Mary Channing, of Philadelphia, in 1898.

Wister's only well-known novel, *The Virginian*, was enough to make him famous. The book was a best seller for years, and succeeding generations have discovered this pioneer "Western" to their delight. The volume was dedicated to another outdoorsman and lover of the West, Theodore Roosevelt, who was a close friend of Owen Wister. One of the men who illustrated an edition of *The Virginian* was Frederic Remington, the famous painter of life in the West. Owen Wister continued to write, and he explored other themes than the West, but his other works were never widely accepted, largely because of their subject matter. *Philosophy 4*, for example, was a story about life at Harvard University, with limited appeal to general readers. *Lady Baltimore* is his one venture into the field of historical romance.

In the years after World War I, Wister wrote little. His last book was *Roosevelt: The Story of a Friendship*. He died of a cerebral hemorrhage at North Kingstown, Rhode Island, July 21, 1938.

BIBLIOGRAPHICAL REFERENCES: The collected edition is *The Writings of Owen Wister*, 11 vols., 1928, which includes writings previously unpublished in book form. There is also Fanny Kemble Wister, ed., *Owen Wister Out West: His Journals and Letters*, 1958. There is no full-scale study of Wister, but a fair and economical estimate is Jay B. Hubbell, "Owen Wister's Work," *South Atlantic Quarterly*, XXIX (1930), 440–443. Two opposing views of Wister's career are E. C. Marsh, "Representative American Story Tellers: Owen Wister," *Bookman*, XXVII (1908), 456–548; and H. W. Boynton, "A Word on the Genteel Critic: Owen Wister's Quack Novels and Democracy," *Dial*, LIX (1915), 303–306.

GEORGE WITHER

Born: Bentworth, England
Date: June 11, 1588

Died: London, England
Date: May 2, 1667

Principal Works

POEMS: *Abuses Stript and Whipt*, 1611; *Fidelia*, 1615; *Wither's Motto; Nec habeo, nec careo, nec curo*, 1621; *Faire-Virtue, The Mistresse of Philarete*, 1622; *Britain's Remembrancer*, 1628; *Collection of Emblemes, Ancient and Moderne*, 1635; *Heleluiah: Or Britain's Second Remembrancer*, 1641.

George Wither, son of a Hampshire gentleman, was born in Bentworth, Hampshire, on June 11, 1588. He was sent to Oxford in 1603, where he apparently did not do well. Two years later, at the age of seventeen, he left the university without graduating and went to London, where he entered one of the Inns of Chancery to study law. He was eventually introduced at court. In 1612 and 1613 respectively he wrote an elegy on the death of Prince Henry and a poem celebrating the marriage of Princess Elizabeth. Also, in 1613, he published his collection of satires *Abuses Stript and Whipt*, in which, among other unwise things, he insulted the Lord Chancellor. The poet was imprisoned for a few months but was released at the intercession of Princess Elizabeth.

While in prison, Wither continued to write. After his release he was admitted to Lincoln's Inn (1615); the same year he published *Fidelia*, the book in which first appeared his best-known lyric, "Shall I, wasting in despair." By 1621, he was again writing satire; in that year appeared his *Motto*, a biting poem that is said to have quickly sold 30,000 copies, and which again landed him in jail accused of libel. He was soon released without trial, however, and in 1622 he published *Faire-Virtue, the Mistresse of Philarete*, his best single volume of poetry. This book was a watershed in Wither's career; it ended what he himself later called his juvenilia. Most of the rest of his writing is religious in character.

Wither had begun as a moderate in religion and politics, but now he became increasingly Puritan. He published a book of hymns in 1623, and in 1628, after witnessing the London plague of 1625, he published *Britain's Remembrancer* in which he described what he saw and prophesied disaster for England.

In 1639 the poet served as a captain of horse in King Charles I's expedition against the Scottish Covenanters, but at the outbreak of the Civil War he sided with Parliament and sold his estate to raise a troop of cavalry. During the war he was once captured by the Royalist forces and threatened with execution. He was saved, it is said, by the intervention of the Royalist and poet, Sir John Denham. Denham is supposed to have begged Wither's life on the ground that as long as Wither was alive, Denham could not be called the worst poet in England. In 1641, Wither's best book of religious poems, *Heleluiah: Or Britain's Second Remembrancer*, was published in Holland.

Before the end of the Civil War,

the poet was promoted to the rank of major; he was present at the siege of Gloucester (1643) and the battle of Naseby (1645), though because of legal troubles he had been deprived of command in 1643. During the years of Cromwell's administration the poet was in various financial troubles and also managed to lose the favor of the Protector by, claims Wither, "declaring unto him those truths which he was not willing to hear of." After the Restoration of Charles II in 1660, the poet was imprisoned for three years. On May 2, 1667, at the age of seventy-nine, he died in London.

BIBLIOGRAPHICAL REFERENCES: The best edition is *The Poetry of George Wither*, edited by F. Sidgwick, 2 vols., 1902. There is no full critical study, but material on Wither may be found in H. Genouy, *L'élément pastoral*, 1928; I. Tramer, *Studien zu den Anfängen der puritanischen Emblemliteratur in England: Andrew Willet—George Wither*, 1934; and W. K. Jordan, *Development of Religious Toleration*, II, 1936. Of special interest is Charles Lamb's essay, "On the Poetical Works of George Wither," *Works*, 1918. For a summary of Wither's accomplishments and a brief bibliography see Douglas Bush, *English Literature in the Earlier Seventeenth Century*, 1945.

THOMAS WOLFE

Born: Asheville, North Carolina
Date: October 3, 1900

Died: Baltimore, Maryland
Date: September 15, 1938

Principal Works

NOVELS: *Look Homeward, Angel*, 1929; *Of Time and the River*, 1935; *The Web and the Rock*, 1939; *You Can't Go Home Again*, 1940.

SHORT STORIES: *From Death to Morning*, 1935; *The Hills Beyond*, 1941.

PLAYS: *The Return of Buck Gavin*, 1924 (in *Carolina Folk-Plays: Second Series*, edited by Frederick H. Koch); *Mannerhouse*, 1948.

BELLES-LETTRES: *The Story of a Novel*, 1936.

LETTERS: *Thomas Wolfe's Letters to His Mother*, edited by J. S. Terry, 1943; *The Letters of Thomas Wolfe*, edited by Elizabeth Nowell, 1956.

MISCELLANEOUS: *A Note on Experts*, 1939; *Gentlemen of the Press*, 1942; *A Western Journal*, 1951; *Notebooks*, edited by Richard S. Kennedy and Paschal Reeves, 1970.

Thomas (Clayton) Wolfe was born October 3, 1900, in Asheville, North Carolina. He was the youngest child in the family, with older brothers and sisters. His father, W. O. Wolfe, was a stonecutter who had been born in central Pennsylvania and who went south to live soon after the Civil War. His mother was Julia Westall, of Asheville. Wolfe was educated in public schools until he was twelve, when he was entered at the North State School under the direction of Mr. and Mrs. J. M. Roberts. Attending school here until graduation (1912–1916), he entered the University of North Carolina (1916–1920). His stay at Chapel Hill was maturing and exciting; he stood well in his classes, became interested in the Carolina Playmakers and wrote plays of his own in which he acted, and became one of the most popular and outstanding figures on the campus of his time. Encouraged by Professor Frederick H. Koch of the Playmakers, Wolfe decided to do graduate work at Harvard in George Pierce Baker's 47 Dramatic Workshop, and to make playwriting his career.

He remained three years at Harvard, two of them as student, taking his A.M. degree in 1922, and hoping to place at least one of his plays for Broadway production. During his years at Harvard, his father died, and Wolfe accepted a teaching appointment as instructor in English at New York University. He began teaching in February, 1924.

Soon afterward he was diverted from playwriting to fiction. *Look Homeward, Angel* was started in England in 1924, when Wolfe made his first visit abroad; it was finished in 1928, placed by Madeleine Boyd with Maxwell Perkins, managing editor of Scribner's, and published in October, 1929. The book was generally well received; only at home in North Carolina were the reactions antagonistic. The turmoil occasioned by *Look Homeward, Angel* in his home town hurt Wolfe; he was naïvely surprised that his novel should be so patently recognized for what it was, a very thinly disguised autobiography, and he avoided a return to Asheville until the year before his death.

Recognition came slowly for Wolfe, but surely. In 1930, in his address of acceptance of the Nobel Prize for literature, Sinclair Lewis paid Wolfe tribute on the basis of his only book, *Look Homeward, Angel,* and prophesied a great future for the younger novelist. In the meantime Wolfe was working on a second novel, a continuation of the story of Eugene Gant, which was published in 1935 as *Of Time and the River.* Although equally autobiographical, *Of Time and the River* stirred no local animosities in Asheville, perhaps because the scenes of the book were removed to Boston, New York, and Europe. In the summer of 1935 Wolfe was invited to speak at a writers' conference at Boulder, Colorado, where he delivered a series of lectures which became an account of the writer's craft and which was published the following year as *The Story of a Novel.* Also published in 1935 were the sketches and short stories called *From Death to Morning.*

By 1937 Wolfe had come to a momentous decision with himself: he had smarted from criticism and gossip which suggested too much dependence upon the guiding editorship of Maxwell Perkins, and so Wolfe decided to change publishers and become "far more objective in his approach to fiction." He signed a new contract with Harper and Brothers, and delivered to his new editor the continuing development of "the book," a work in progress incorporating some changes which Wolfe mistakenly believed to be much greater than they actually were. "The book"—Wolfe's name for the constantly accumulating manuscript of his writings—was still the story of Eugene Gant-Thomas Wolfe. Now, however, the chief protagonist was renamed George Webber, and he varied somewhat in physical appearance and family background from Eugene Gant, but the other circumstances were much the same. In 1937 Wolfe returned to Asheville to find himself recognized as famous and forgiven for the shock of *Look Homeward, Angel;* but other things had also changed, and Wolfe, the man, like Gant-Webber, the character, discovered that "You can't go home again."

In the Spring of 1938 Wolfe was invited to lecture at Purdue University. From there he started on a trip to the Far West, stopping at Denver and making a great sweep through the National Park country. In Seattle he was ill with a cold, locally diagnosed as pneumonia; he was removed to a hospital and his brother Fred was called West to attend him. When his condition grew worse, Fred Wolfe was joined by his sister, Mrs. Mabel Wheaton. Consulting physicians suspected a brain tumor; certainly an operation was indicated. The family conference determined that any operation should be done at Johns Hopkins, in Baltimore, and there Wolfe was brought in August. The operation revealed multiple tuberculosis of the brain. Wolfe never came out of the coma which followed the operation, and he died in Baltimore on September 15, 1938, less than a month before his thirty-eighth birthday. His body was taken to Asheville for burial; only in death could the wanderer "go home again."

Wolfe's third and fourth novels, *The Web and the Rock* and *You Can't Go Home Again,* were readied for posthumous publication by Edward C. Aswell, Wolfe's editor and personal friend at Harper. The novels added stature to Wolfe's increasing position as a major writer, and brought his fictional work to a reasonable conclusion. In 1941 appeared *The Hills Beyond*, another series of short stories and sketches, and "The Hills Beyond," a fragmentary and incomplete novel introducing some of the Gant-Webber family members of an earlier time in the Carolina mountains. *Mannerhouse,* a play first written by Wolfe during his stay at Harvard, appeared in published form in 1948. His *Letters to His Mother* came out in 1943. *The Letters of Thomas Wolfe,* collected and edited by his literary agent, Elizabeth Nowell, appeared in 1956; these letters constitute what amounts to an autobiography.

Before his death Thomas Wolfe was already becoming a legend. Everything about him was greater than lifesize. He was six feet five inches tall; his capacities for vividly rendering sense impressions and physical appetites and energies were widely known and praised; his books confirmed the statement of the American Dream better than it had been expressed since Walt Whitman, and characters of his fiction had already entered general allusive consciousness. He is still a controversial figure, but his popularity seems to continue growing and to encourage new studies and new converts.

BIBLIOGRAPHICAL REFERENCE: : The definitive biography is Elizabeth Nowell, *Thomas Wolfe,* 1960. Herbert J. Muller, *Thomas Wolfe,* 1947, is the pioneer critical study. Other biographical and critical studies include Pamela Hansford Johnson, *Thomas Wolfe: A Critical Study,* 1947 [*Hungry Gulliver: An English Critical Appraisal*]; Agatha B. Adams, *Thomas Wolfe: Carolina Student,* 1950; Daniel L. Delakas, *Thomas Wolfe: La France et les romanciers français,* 1950; T. C. Pollock and Oscar Cargill, *Thomas Wolfe at Washington Square,* 1954; Louis D. Rubin, Jr., *Thomas Wolfe: The Weather of His Youth,* 1955; C. Hugh Holman, *Thomas Wolfe,* 1960; Richard S. Kennedy, *The Window of Memory: The Literary Career of Thomas Wolfe,* 1962; and Bruce R. McElderry, *Thomas Wolfe,* 1964. Related materials are found in Hayden Norwood, *The Marble Man's Wife,* 1947; and Maxwell Perkins, *Editor to Author: The Letters of Maxwell E. Perkins,* edited by John Hall Wheelock, 1950; and T. C. Pollock and Oscar Cargill, eds., *The Correspondence of Thomas Wolfe and Homer Andrew Watts,* 1954.

For articles on Wolfe in books see Herbert J. Muller, *Modern Fiction: A Study of Values,* 1937; Joseph Warren Beach, *American Fiction, 1920–1940,* 1941; Maxwell Geismar, *Writers in Crisis,* 1942; Alfred Kazin, *On Native Grounds,* 1942; George Snell, *Shapers of American Fiction, 1798–1947,* 1947; E. B. Burgum, *The Novel and the World's Dilemma,* 1947; F. J. Hoffman, *The Modern Novel in America, 1900–1950,* 1951; Gerald S. Sloyan, "Thomas Wolfe: A Legend of a Man's Youth in His Hunger," in *Fifty Years of the American Novel,* edited by Harold C. Gardiner, 1952; and Louis D. Rubin, Jr., "Thomas Wolfe in Time and Place," in *Southern Renascence,* edited by Rubin and Robert D. Jacobs, 1953.

See also Hamilton Basso, "Thomas Wolfe: A Portrait," *New Republic,* LXXXVII (1936), 199–202; Dayton Kohler, "Thomas Wolfe: Prodigal and Lost," *College English,* I (1939), 1–10; William Braswell, "Thomas Wolfe Lectures and Takes a Holiday," *ibid.,* 11–22; John Peale Bishop, "The Sorrows of Thomas Wolfe," *Kenyon Review,* I (1939), 7–17; Henry T. Volkening, "Thomas Wolfe: Penance No More," *Virginia Quarterly Review,* XV (1939), 196–215; E. K. Brown: "Thomas Wolfe: Realist and Symbolist," *University of Toronto Quarterly,* X (1941), 153–166; John M. Maclachan, "Folk Concepts in the Novels of Thomas Wolfe," *Southern Folklore*

Quarterly, IX (1945), 28–36; Margaret Church, "Thomas Wolfe: Dark Time," *Publications of the Modern Language Association,* LXIV (1949), 629–638; and Betty Thompson, "Thomas Wolfe: Two Decades of Criticism," *South Atlantic Quarterly,* LXIX (1950), 378–392.

The Portable Thomas Wolfe, 1946, contains an excellent introduction by Maxwell Geismar.

WOLFRAM VON ESCHENBACH

Born: Eschenbach, Germany
Date: c. 1170

Died: Eschenbach
Date: c. 1220

Principal Works

CHIVALRIC ROMANCES: *Parzival*, c. 1200; *Willehalm*, c. 1212.

Few facts are known about Wolfram von Eschenbach, the strongest personality of the thirteenth century epic poets writing in Middle High German. Born in Eschenbach, Germany, about 1170, he was a member of a noble Bavarian family, apparently impoverished, as he says jestingly in his poetry. Many scholars claim that he was a younger son. He served powerful overlords, like the counts of Wertheim and the Landgrave Hermann of Thüringia. His feats of sword and spear are subjects for his boasting, rather than his poetry. He mentions being unlettered, yet the French *chanson de geste La Bataille d'Aliscans* was his source for *Willehalm* and French originals inspired much of his other poetry. His own contributions were the acute observation, deep psychology, broad toleration, and sense of humor found in his work.

Greatest of his poems is *Parzival*, a romance of 25,000 lines believed to have been composed between 1200 and 1212. Its popularity is proved by the fifteen complete manuscripts of the work still in existence. Wolfram accredited it to the troubadour Kyot le Provençal, who has never been identified. Its praise of noble marriage and its high moral tone may derive from the personality of the author. Wolfram was admired by all as a deeply religious man; in fact, one contemporary wrote a poem selecting him as the champion of Christianity against an evil enchanter. *Willehalm* deals also with a noble knight remarkable for his chivalrous treatment of the Saracens. This work, unfinished at Wolfram's death, was continued by Ulrich von Türkheim (fl. 1235–1250) and Ulrich von dem Türlin (fl. 1261–1270). *Titurel*, a third romance left only in fragments, was completed by one Albrecht about 1260.

When the landgrave died in 1216, Wolfram apparently left Wartburg Castle and returned to his native town, where he died about 1220. He was reported buried in the Church of Our Lady in Eschenbach, but the location of his grave has never been determined.

BIBLIOGRAPHICAL REFERENCES: For commentary and criticism in English see Margaret F. Richey, *Gahmuret Anschevin: A Contribution to the Study of Wolfram von Eschenbach*, 1923; *The Story of Parzifal*, 1935; *Essays on the Mediaeval Love Lyric*, 1943; Hugh Sacker, *An Introduction to Wolfram's Parzival*, 1963; and David Blamires, *Characterization and Individuality in Wolfram's 'Parzival'*, 1966. See also A. Schulz, *Parzifal Studien*, 3 vols. 1861–1862; Ernst E. Martin, *Zur Gralsage*, 1880; Samuel Singer, *Wolframs Willehalm*, 1918, and *Wolfram und der Graal*, 1939; and Kate Laserstein, *Wolfram von Eschenbach, germanische Sendung*, 1928.

VIRGINIA WOOLF

Born: London, England
Date: January 25, 1882

Died: Lewes, Sussex, England
Date: March 28, 1941

PRINCIPAL WORKS

NOVELS: *The Voyage Out,* 1915; *Night and Day,* 1919; *Jacob's Room,* 1922; *Mrs. Dalloway,* 1925; *To the Lighthouse,* 1927; *Orlando: A Biography,* 1928; *The Waves,* 1931; *The Years,* 1937; *Between the Acts,* 1941.

SHORT STORIES: *Kew Gardens,* 1919; *The Mark on the Wall,* 1919; *Monday or Tuesday,* 1921; *The Haunted House,* 1943.

LITERARY CRITICISM: *Mr. Bennett and Mrs. Brown,* 1924; *The Common Reader,* 1925; *The Common Reader: Second Series,* 1932 [*The Second Common Reader*].

ESSAYS AND STUDIES: *A Room of One's Own,* 1929; *Three Guineas,* 1938; *The Death of the Moth,* 1942; *The Moment and Other Essays,* 1947; *The Captain's Deathbed and Other Essays,* 1950; *Granite and Rainbow,* 1958.

BIOGRAPHY: *Flush: A Biography,* 1933; *Roger Fry: A Biography,* 1940.

JOURNALS: *A Writer's Diary,* 1953.

The greatest woman novelist of this century was born Adeline Virginia Stephen in London on January 25, 1882, the daughter of Sir Leslie Stephen, eminent editor, biographer, and critic. The youngest of eight children (four were half-brothers and sisters), Virginia was frail and found her education at home in her father's superb library. Reflections of these early years were to appear in her fiction: the close-knit family group, the brilliant and domineering father, the lovely and conciliating mother, all seen in London or at seasides resembling that of their Cornish summer home. Her mother's death in 1895 was a traumatic shock, but Virginia Stephen continued reading voluminously, studying Greek, and imitating the Elizabethan prose masters. Then, following Sir Leslie's death in 1904, Vanessa, Thoby, Virginia, and Adrian Stephen took a house in the Bloomsbury district. In 1905, however, Virginia suffered the first onslaught of the mental illness which was to recur during World War I. Two years later, after Vanessa's marriage and Thoby's tragic death, Virginia and Adrian took another house among a congenial set which included economist John Maynard Keynes, artist Roger Fry, biographer Lytton Strachey, and others who became associated with the Bloomsbury Group. Reviewing books and publishing essays and criticism, Virginia Stephen worked at her art. In 1912 she married Leonard Woolf, a journalist and political essayist. Sympathetic and protective, he encouraged her in her work.

Three years later, *The Voyage Out* appeared. This story of young Rachel Vinrace's South American voyage was conventional in technique and desultory in plot, but its sensitive treatment of Rachel's maturation, abruptly stopped by death, foreshadowed a rejection of conventional plot and realistic description. *Night and Day,* longer, more sure and solid, dealt specifically with Katherine Hilbery's finding of the right fiancé and generally with a young woman's intellectual and emotional growth in an environment such as Virginia Woolf's own as a girl.

Her new goals and experimental methods were indicated in *Monday or Tuesday* in 1921. Its eight sketches ranged from impressionistic creation of moods in short pieces to the use of symbolic imagery in longer ones. Still others attempted to convey through highly suggestive lyrical prose the sound of music and the quality of color. (This arresting book was published by the Hogarth Press. Founded by the Woolfs in 1917, it was to publish all her books as well as work by T. S. Eliot, E. M. Forster, and Sigmund Freud.) *Jacob's Room* used some of the devices of *Monday or Tuesday* in a novel built around the magnetic Jacob Flanders, modeled on Thoby Stephen. Here the author's interest in her characters lies principally in their relationship with Jacob as he grows into manhood and even after his death in World War I. Despite uncertain health, Virginia Woolf continued to produce literary criticism and essays. A number were collected in *The Common Reader: First Series* which appeared in 1925. She ranged from the Greeks to her contemporaries, writing as a sensitive critic who was also a creative artist.

In *Mrs. Dalloway* she explored her characters' streams-of-consciousness as she depicted twelve hours in the inner and outer life of a sensitive woman. Unlike Dorothy Richardson, she revealed the interior monologues of other characters besides the central one; unlike James Joyce, she presented these thoughts so as to avoid any seemingly chaotic effect. In 1927 came her finest achievement, *To The Lighthouse*. Plotless in the ordinary sense, like *Mrs. Dalloway*, this story of the Ramsays was based on her childhood. Rich in image and symbol, it treated her favorite themes of love, marriage, time, and death. She combined experiment and lyricism in "Time Passes," an interlude describing the decay of the summer home in the seven years following Mrs. Ramsay's death. In *Orlando*, a dashing Elizabethan nobleman unaccountably changes into a woman during the Restoration and continues thus into the present. This pleasant fantasy, based on Vita Sackville-West's family, re-emphasized Mrs. Woolf's interest in the merging flow of time and experience. *A Room of One's Own* discussed fiction and women, protesting against the widespread discrimination women faced. Two years later Virginia Woolf published a novel that some said signalized the end of that form. *The Waves* comprised the impressionistic interior monologues of six characters from early childhood to old age. Separated by italicized lyrical descriptions of a seaside from dawn to dark, the book's sections traced the characters' developing natures, interaction, and relationship to a dominating character named Percival who resembled Jacob Flanders. Here again Virginia Woolf intended recurrent, interrelated images and symbols to impose the unity and coherence which Bennett and Galsworthy sought through conventional plotting, narration, and description.

The Common Reader: Second Series was followed a year later by *Flush*, a pleasant little biography of a spaniel whose mistress, Elizabeth Barrett Browning, dominates the story. *The Years* was not stylized like *The Waves*. This overlong novel emphasized the flow of time by tracing the Pargiters' fortunes from 1880 to the present. *Three Guineas* returned sharply to Virginia Woolf's feminist concerns. *Roger Fry: A Biography*, although a sympathetic memoir, lacked the characteristic incandescence of her prose. Fry's death had deepened the shadows which, cast by ill health and the specter of war, were gathering around her. On March 28, 1941, she left her work table and walked across the fields of her Sussex home into the river Ouse to her death. A note revealed her fear of oncoming incurable madness. *Between the Acts*, a poetically evocative and symbolic book built around a country pageant spanning Britain's history, showed both her weariness and continued intent to expand, here through symbol, the novel's scope. *The Death of the Moth, The Moment and Other Essays*, and *The Captain's Deathbed and Other Essays* included new and old essays displaying her characteristic perception. *A Writer's Diary*, published in 1953, is an invaluable record of the inner feelings and creative processes of this modern master. *Virginia Woolf and Lytton Strachey: Letters* (1956) reveals personal aspects of these two gifted Bloomsburyites.

BIBLIOGRAPHICAL REFERENCES: The *Collected Essays* were edited in 4 vols. by Leonard Woolf, 1966–1967. The definitive biography is Quentin Bell, Vol. I, *Virginia Stephen, 1882–1912*, and Vol. II, *Mrs. Woolf, 1912–1941*, 1972. See also Aileen Pippett, *The Moth and the Star: A Biography of Virginia Woolf*, 1955; and Leonard Woolf, *Growing*, 1962, and *Beginning Again*, 1964. The following contain authoritative critical commentary: Winifred Holtby, *Virginia Woolf*, 1932; Ruth Gruber, *Virginia Woolf: A Study*, 1935; David Daiches, *Virginia Woolf*, 1942; E. M. Forster, *Virginia Woolf*, 1942; Joan Bennett, *Virginia Woolf: Her Art as a Novelist*, 1945; R. L. Chambers, *The Novels of Virginia Woolf*, 1947; Bernard Blackstone, *Virginia Woolf: A Commentary*, 1949; James Hafley, *The Glass Roof: Virginia Woolf as Novelist*, University of California English Studies, No. 9, 1954; and David Daiches, *Virginia Woolf*, 1963.

See also Elizabeth N. Monroe, *The Novel and Society*, 1941; Edward Wagenknecht, *Cavalcade of the English Novel*, 1943; E. B. Burgum, *The Novel and the World's Dilemma*, 1947; Lord David Cecil, *Poets and Story-Tellers*, 1949; Elizabeth Bowen, *Collected Impressions*, 1950; D. S. Savage, *The Withered Branch*, 1950; Robert Humphrey, *The Stream of Consciousness in the Modern Novel*, 1954; and J. K. Johnstone, *The Bloomsbury Group*, 1954.

For criticism in magazines see Edwin Muir, "Virginia Woolf," *Bookman*, LXXIV (1931), 362–367; William Troy, "Virginia Woolf: The Poetic Method," *Symposium*, III (1932), 53–63, and "Virginia Woolf: The Poetic Style," *ibid.*, 153–166; J. H. Roberts, "Towards Virginia Woolf," *Virginia Quarterly Review*, X (1934), 587–612; Joseph Warren Beach, "Virginia Woolf," *English Journal*, XXVI (1937), 603–612; T. S. Eliot, "Virginia Woolf," *Horizon*, III (1941), 313–316; W. H. Mellers, "Virginia Woolf: The Last Phase," *Kenyon Review*, IV (1942), 381–387; Martin Turnell, "Virginia Woolf," *Horizon*, IV (1942), 44–56; James Southall Wilson, "Time and Virginia Woolf," *Virginia Quarterly Review*, XVIII (1942), 267–276; J. H. Roberts, "'Vision and Design' in Virginia Woolf," *Publications of the Modern Language Association*, LXI (1946), 835–847; Dayton Kohler, "Time in the Modern Novel," *College English*, X (1948), 15–24; W. Y. Tindall, "Many Leveled Fiction: Virginia Woolf to Ross Lockridge," *College English*, X (1948), 65–71; John Graham, "Time in the Novels of Virginia Woolf," *University of Toronto Quarterly*, XVIII (1949), 186–201; Margaret Church, "Concepts of Time in the Novels of Virginia Woolf and Aldous Huxley," *Modern Fiction Studies*, I (May, 1955), 19–24; and Dean Doner, "Virginia Woolf: The Service of Style," *Modern*

Fiction Studies, II (February, 1956), 1–12.

The Virginia Woolf Number of *Modern Fiction Studies,* II (February, 1956) contains a selected checklist of criticisms of Virginia Woolf with an index to studies of her separate works, 36–45.

DOROTHY WORDSWORTH

Born: Cockermouth, England
Date: December 25, 1771

Died: Rydal Mount, England
Date: January 25, 1855

Principal Works

JOURNALS: *The Alfoxden Journal,* 1798 et seq; *Journal of a Visit to Hamburg and of a Journey from Hamburg to Goslar,* 1798; *The Grasmere Journal,* 1800–1803; *Recollections of a Tour Made in Scotland,* 1803; *Excursion of the Banks of Ullswater,* 1805; *Excursion up Scawfell Pike,* 1818; *Journal of a Tour on the Continent,* 1820; *Journal of My Second Tour in Scotland,* 1822; *Journal of a Tour in the Isle of Man,* 1828.

Dorothy Wordsworth was the only sister of William Wordsworth, the great English Romantic poet. She was separated from her brothers at the age of six, upon the death of her mother. While living at Halifax with her mother's cousin, Elizabeth Threlkeld, she attended a day school, except for one six-month stay at a boarding school. In 1787 young Dorothy went to live with her maternal grandparents, her education at an end. Life with her grandparents was unhappy, especially as they made her four brothers unwelcome as visitors. The following year, 1788, her maternal uncle, the Rev. William Cookson, married and took his niece into his household until 1794. In 1795, through a legacy and the loan of a house, Dorothy Wordsworth finally achieved a childhood dream, living with her older brother, William. From that time to his death in 1850 she was seldom separated from him, living amicably in his household even after he was married.

In 1798, while Dorothy and William were living at Alfoxden to be near Samuel Taylor Coleridge, Dorothy began the first of her journals, from which both Coleridge and her brother drew descriptions for some of their poems in *Lyrical Ballads.* This practice continued for Wordsworth; often in later years he depended upon his sister's descriptions of people and places to furnish him with poetic material. She wrote her journals for her own pleasure and her brother William's, none of the journals being published until after her death, although she did allow some of the manuscripts to circulate among their friends. Living in his home, acting as a second mother to his children, Dorothy Wordsworth was a constant companion to her brother, except for her brief periods of travel and visiting with friends.

But this happy existence was shattered when she was stricken by illness in April, 1829. Although she recovered physically, after she had not been expected to live, she no longer had sufficient vitality for the activities she loved: walking, mountain climbing, traveling, and writing her journals. Her mind began to fail, and she became like an excitable young child. She died five years after her brother, passing away at Rydal Mount, where she and her William had lived for more than half a century.

1937

BIBLIOGRAPHICAL REFERENCES: The *Poetry of Dorothy Wordsworth* was edited by H. Eigerman, 1940. Important biographical materials are the *Journals of Dorothy Wordsworth*, edited by Helen Darbishire, 1958, and the *Letters of William and Dorothy Wordsworth*, edited by E. de Selincourt, 6 vols., 1935–1938.

Helpful biographical and critical studies include E. de Selincourt, *Dorothy Wordsworth: A Biography*, 1933; C. M. Maclean, *Dorothy and William Wordsworth*, 1927; *idem.*, *Dorothy Wordsworth: The Early Years*, 1932; Amanda M. Ellis, *Rebels and Conservatives: Dorothy and William Wordsworth and Their Circle*, 1967; and Margaret Willy, *Three Women Diarists: Celia Fiennes, Dorothy Wordsworth, Katherine Mansfield*, 1964.

WILLIAM WORDSWORTH

Born: Cockermouth, England
Date: April 7, 1770

Died: Rydal Mount, England
Date: April 23, 1850

PRINCIPAL WORKS

POEMS: *Lyrical Ballads,* 1798 (with Coleridge); *Lyrical Ballads,* enlarged, with Preface, 1800; *Poems in Two Volumes,* 1807; *The Excursion,* 1814; *The White Doe of Rylstone,* 1815; *Peter Bell and the Waggoner,* 1819; *The River Duddon,* 1820; *Ecclesiastical Sketches,* 1822; *Memorials of a Tour on the Continent,* 1822; *Yarrow Revisited and Other Poems,* 1835; *Sonnets,* 1838; *Poems, Chiefly of Early and Late Years,* 1842; *Collected Poems,* 1849–1850; *The Prelude,* 1850.

To compare Wordsworth with other great English poets has long been a parlor game for critics. Matthew Arnold places him below only Shakespeare and Milton; others, ranging less widely, are content to call him the greatest of the Romantics. Incontestably, however, he stands supreme among English nature poets; and the stamp of his influence so strongly marks the short, glorious period of nineteenth century Romanticism that perhaps those can be forgiven who have gone so far as to call it the Age of Wordsworth.

The second son of a lower middle-class family, William Wordsworth was born April 7, 1770, at Cockermouth in the Lake District of Cumberland. When he was eight, his mother died; the loss of his father, five years later, made him dependent upon his uncles for an education. School at Hawkshead was followed by matriculation at Cambridge, where he entered St. John's College in 1787. His career there was interrupted in 1790 by a summer tour of Switzerland, France, and Italy; and in 1791, after receiving his degree, he returned to France, ostensibly to learn the language.

Much besides language, however, quickly absorbed Wordsworth's attention. The years 1791–1792 found Wordsworth developing two passions, one for Annette Vallon and the other for the French Revolution. Both were probably sincere, while they lasted; but both were soon to suffer from a change of heart. His daughter Anne Caroline was born to Annette Vallon while Wordsworth was still in France; for reasons which have never become clear, he acknowledged the child without marrying the mother. Wordsworth's other passion, the Revolution, stirred him deeply and left an indelible impression. His enthusiasm waned chiefly because of its growing excesses and because of the accession of Napoleon. Even so, the philosophy he acquired from Michel Beaupuy and his fellow revolutionists was an important factor in making Wordsworth the great poetic spokesman for that element as yet relatively voiceless—the common man.

Back in England, Wordsworth briefly found congeniality in the circle of young freethinkers surrounding William Godwin. Godwin, future father-in-law of Percy Shelley, was a radical philosopher and the author of *Political Justice.* Like Wordsworth himself, he was an ardent disciple of Rousseau, a fact which helps to explain his temporary hold on the young man's attention. In 1795, however, a fortunate legacy enabled Wordsworth to settle at Racedown with his devoted and talented sister Dorothy. Here occurred a brush with fate which was to change the lives of two men. In meeting Samuel Taylor Coleridge, Wordsworth formed the most significant connection of his career. Mutual intellectual stimulation and constant companionship were its immediate dividends; and when, in 1797, Coleridge moved into Somersetshire, the Wordsworths followed. The next year the two men published jointly that little volume which would eventually come into its own as one of the most magnificent milestones of English literature.

Nevertheless, the initial reception of the 1798 edition of *Lyrical Ballads* gave no clue to the status it would achieve in the future. Most of its contents came from the industrious Wordsworth, including the sublime nature poem, "Tintern Abbey," and a group of shorter, ballad-like compositions in which the author undertook to preach the kindness of Nature and exalt familiar reality. Coleridge, on the other hand, attempted the project of making supernatural subjects seem real, a project carried to superb completion in his single contribution, *The Ancient Mariner*.

Laughed at by some critics and ignored by others, *Lyrical Ballads* survived its reception sufficiently well to justify a second printing in 1800. Though this edition contained some interesting new poems, its most significant feature was Wordsworth's long Preface, which amounted to a literary declaration of independence and broke completely with neo-classical theory. The main points of this credo reflected strongly the continuing influence of Rousseau and stated formally the ideals of sincerity, democracy, nature worship, and simple, natural diction to which Wordsworth and Coleridge had vowed allegiance.

With *Lyrical Ballads* as its starting point, most of Wordsworth's great poetry was compressed into the quarter century between 1798 and 1823. Many of his celebrated short poems, such as "I Wandered Lonely as a Cloud" and "The Solitary Reaper," illustrate beautiful effects and essential truths achieved through the Wordsworthian simplicity of vocabulary advocated in his famous Preface. Still, he could successfully depart from his principles when he felt the need. That he could employ more elevated diction with telling effect finds ample illustration in his excellent sonnets, as well as in such longer poems as "Tintern Abbey" and "The Prelude." The content of his work conveys feelings of humanitarianism, liberalism, and—finally and most distinctively—a thoroughly pantheistic worship of nature. Biographical interest combined with distinguished poetry are found in "The Prelude" and, to a lesser extent, in "The Excursion"; both of these were written as parts of a longer autobiographical work, *The Recluse*, which was never completed.

If Wordsworth's work could scale the heights, it could also make inexplicable plunges into utter sterility; hardly another major poet can be named who is capable of such extremes in his published poetry. Completely devoid of a sense of humor, his tendency to complacency led him into such demonstrations of bathos and infelicity as "Andrew Jones" and "The Idiot Boy." His detractors, Byron notable among them, seized on these lapses with unholy glee; and the failure of Wordsworth's critical faculty in such instances is difficult to explain.

His failures in human relationships were sometimes equally conspicuous. The friendship with Coleridge, which had had such an auspicious beginning, tapered off during the years which followed *Lyrical Ballads*. In 1803, a misunderstanding arose during a tour of Scotland, leading to a breach between the two men which was never fully mended.

In 1802 Wordsworth married his childhood friend, Mary Hutchinson, the inspiration for "She Was a Phantom of Delight." As he grew older, Wordsworth became more and more conservative in matters of religion and politics. From the government which had once been the object of his youthful censure he now received employment, being appointed, in 1813, Distributor of Stamps in Westmorland County. In 1843, long after the passing of his really creative period, he was appointed Poet Laureate, succeeding Robert Southey. He died at Rydal Mount on April 23, 1850, and was buried in Grasmere churchyard. A monument to him was erected in Westminster Abbey.

BIBLIOGRAPHICAL REFERENCES: The definitive edition, excluding *The Prelude*, is *The Poetical Works of William Wordsworth*, edited by Ernest de Selincourt and Helen Darbishire, 5 vols., 1940–1949. The variorum edition of *The Prelude* was edited by Ernest de Selincourt, 1926, 1932. Editions of the letters include *Letters of the Wordsworth Family*, edited by William Knight, 3 vols., 1907; H. C. Robinson, *Correspondence with the Wordsworth Circle, 1808–1866*, 1927; and Ernest de Selincourt, *The Early Letters of William and Dorothy Wordsworth, 1780–1805*, 1937, and *Letters of William and Dorothy Wordsworth: The Middle Years*, 2 vols., 1937. This editor also prepared the *Journals of Dorothy Wordsworth*, 2 vols., 1941.

The standard biography is George McLean Harper, *William Wordsworth, His Life, Works, and Influence*, 2 vols., 1916. See also Émile Legouis, *The Early Years of William Wordsworth, 1770–1798*, 1897; Edith Batho, *The Later Wordsworth*, 1933; G. W. Meyer, *Wordsworth's Formative Years*, University Publications in Language and Literature, XX (1943); and Mary Moorman, *William Wordsworth: A Biography*, Vol. I, *The Early Years*, 1957, Vol. II, *The Later Years*, 1965. For criticism see Samuel Taylor Coleridge, *Biographia Literaria*, 1817; Matthew Arnold, *Essays in Criticism: Second Series*, 1888; Alfred North Whitehead, *Science and the Modern World*, 1925; Earl Leslie Griggs, ed., *Wordsworth and Coleridge: Studies in Honor of George McLean Harper*, 1939; R. D. Havens, *The Mind of a Poet*, 1941; Helen Darbishire, *The Poet Wordsworth*, 1950; Gilbert T. Dunklin, ed., *Wordsworth: Centenary Studies Presented at Cornell and Princeton Universities*, 1951; David Ferry, *The Limits of Mortality: An Essay on Wordsworth's Major Poems*, 1959; and G. H. Hartman, *Wordsworth's Poetry, 1787–1814*, 1965.

RICHARD WRIGHT

Born: Near Natchez, Mississippi
Date: September 4, 1908

Died: Paris, France
Date: November 28, 1960

PRINCIPAL WORKS

NOVELS: *Native Son*, 1940; *Black Boy*, 1945; *The Outsider*, 1953.
SOCIAL STUDIES: *Twelve Million Black Voices*, 1941; *Black Power*, 1954.

Richard Wright's childhood was an unpleasant one. Born near Natchez, Mississippi, on September 4, 1908, he grew up, according to his own account, as an unruly and unwanted Negro child in the American South. His father, a laborer, deserted the family when Wright was five years old, and Wright's mother became totally paralyzed when the boy was ten. Leaving the home of relatives at the age of fifteen, Wright went to Memphis, Tennessee, where he worked at various unskilled jobs. During the depression years of the 1930's he traveled north, arriving in Chicago in 1934. There, becoming interested in the labor movement and communism, he joined the Communist Party in 1936. He worked on WPA Writers' Projects in Chicago and New York, later became a contributing editor of the *New Masses*.

Wright's "Uncle Tom's Children" won the prize offered by *Story* in 1938. Awarded a Guggenheim Fellowship the following year, he wrote *Native Son*, a fictional study of a Negro murderer. In 1940 he received the Spingarn Medal for achievement in the field of Negro interests. *Twelve Million Black Voices* is a history of the American Negro and his problems. In 1944 Wright broke with the Communists; an essay describing his career as a Party member was published in *The God That Failed* (1950). *Black Boy* is an autobiographical novel based on Wright's childhood. *The Outsider* is a novel about a Negro's experience as a Communist. *Black Power* is a nonfictional personal study of conditions in Africa, on the Gold Coast, as Wright saw them on a visit to the region in 1953. *Native Son* has been Wright's most popular novel. As a stage play produced in the United States and as a motion picture filmed in Argentina, *Native Son* was fairly successful. The author played the lead role in the motion picture version.

After World War II Wright and his family moved to France because he found life there less difficult. In Paris he associated himself with the existentialist group. He died in a Paris clinic in 1960.

BIBLIOGRAPHICAL REFERENCES: For biographical and critical discussion see H. M. Gloster, *Negro Voices in American Fiction*, 1948; William A. Owens, Introduction to *Native Son*, Harper Modern Classics edition, 1957; James Baldwin, "Many Thousands Gone," *Partisan Review*, XVIII (1951), 665–680; and Nathan A. Scott, "Search for Beliefs: Fiction of Richard Wright," *University of Kansas City Review*, XXIII (1956), 19–24.

SIR THOMAS WYATT

Born: Kent, England
Date: 1503(?)

Died: Sherborne, England
Date: October, 1542

Principal Works

POEMS: *Poems,* c. 1525–1542, first published in Richard Tottel's *Songes and Sonettes,* 1557, and in the *Courte of Venus,* 1558.

Throughout the Renaissance the European nobleman was expected to be a creditable poet as well as a capable soldier and diplomat, and much of the best poetry of sixteenth century England was written by members of high-ranking families, men who contributed much to their country's development. Sir Thomas Wyatt and Henry Howard, Earl of Surrey, who inaugurated the golden age of English poetry with their adoption of the verse forms and subject matter of French and Italian works, fall into the long line of courtier poets who wrote sonnets, songs, and satires for their own satisfaction and that of their friends.

Wyatt's poems were composed at intervals in a busy, if chequered, career as a public official. The son of Sir Henry Wyatt, a minor nobleman, he was born about 1503 at Allington Castle in Kent. He went to St. John's College, Cambridge, when he was thirteen, and was made Master of Arts in 1520. In that year he married Elizabeth, daughter of Lord Cobham, and began to serve as a court official.

In 1526 he was sent to France as a courier for the English ambassador. However, his mission to Italy in the following year was probably more significant for his poetic development; it gave him an opportunity to become familiar with the works of the Italian poets who greatly influenced his own writing, among them Petrarch and Pietro Aretino.

During the course of his Italian mission Wyatt was captured by Spanish troops, but he escaped before his ransom was paid. For the next four years he served as Marshal of Calais, returning to England in 1532 as Commissioner of the Peace in Essex.

Wyatt was imprisoned in May, 1536, probably because of a quarrel with the powerful Duke of Suffolk, although there has been considerable speculation about his involvement with Queen Anne Boleyn, who was executed that same year. There is a strong tradition, supported by some evidence, that Anne was Wyatt's mistress before her marriage to Henry VIII, and several of his poems have been interpreted as references to his love for her. These lines, translated from a sonnet by Petrarch, are often quoted:

Noli me tangere, for Caesar's I am;
And wild for to hold, though I seem tame.

Wyatt remained in prison only briefly; after a few months at his father's home he was appointed ambassador to Spain, faced with the unenviable task of placating the Emperor Charles V, nephew of Henry VIII's divorced Queen, Catherine of Aragon. The last years of Wyatt's life were turbulent ones, marked by the execution of his friend, Thomas Cromwell, Henry's capable minister, who fell from royal favor and was convicted of treason in 1540, and by the enmity of Thomas Bonner, Bishop of London, who had Wyatt himself brought to trial on charges of treason in 1541.

Wyatt spoke brilliantly in his own defense and received full pardon. He was made both a member of Parliament and a Vice-Admiral, but before he could begin to enjoy his new positions he died of a fever contracted as he was traveling to the coast to greet the Spanish ambassador.

A fine poem by Wyatt's young friend and disciple, the Earl of Surrey, pays tribute to his intelligence, his integrity, and his faith:

> Wyatt resteth here, that quick could never rest;
> Whose heavenly gifts increaséd by disdain,
> And virtue sank the deeper in his breast;
> Such profit he by envy could obtain.

BIBLIOGRAPHICAL REFERENCES: The standard edition is *Poems*, edited by Kenneth Muir, 1949, revised edition, 1963. Muir's *The Life and Letters of Sir Thomas Wyatt*, 1963, is the definitive biographical study.

Other significant studies include E. M. W. Tillyard, *Sir Thomas Wyatt: A Selection and a Study*, 1929; E. K. Chambers, *Sir Thomas Wyatt and Some Collected Studies*, 1933; Sergio Baldi, *La poesia di Sir Thomas Wyatt*, 1953, translated by F. T. Prince, 1961; Patricia Thomson, *Sir Thomas Wyatt and His Background*, 1964; and Raymond Southall, *The Courtly Maker: An Essay on the Poetry of Wyatt and His Contemporaries*, 1964.

Wyatt's poems are also discussed in C. S. Lewis, *English Literature in the Sixteenth Century*, 1954; J. B. Broadbent, *Poetic Love*, 1964; J. W. Lever, *The Elizabethan Love Sonnet*, 1966; John Buxton, *A Tradition of Poetry*, 1967; and Douglas L. Peterson, *The English Lyric from Wyatt to Donne*, 1967.

WILLIAM WYCHERLEY

Born: Clive, Shropshire, England
Date: 1640

Died: London, England
Date: January 1, 1716

Principal Works

PLAYS: *Love in a Wood,* 1671; *The Gentleman Dancing Master,* 1672; *The Country Wife,* 1673; *The Plain Dealer,* 1677.

William Wycherley was born of an old family at Clive, near Shrewsbury, Shropshire, in 1640. When he was about fifteen years of age, he was sent to France, where he frequented refined circles, notably the salon of the Duchess de Montausier, the atmosphere of which was impregnated with the spirit of the Hôtel de Rambouillet. Also, while in France, Wycherley became a Catholic. In 1660 he spent a short time at Oxford, from where he went to the Inner Temple in London. In London he soon found a place in the pleasure-loving society of the town, rejoicing after eighteen years of enforced Puritan virtue; and he gravitated toward the theater, the most notable social entertainment of the day.

In 1671 his first play, *Love in a Wood,* gained him the intimacy of a royal mistress, the Duchess of Cleveland, through whose influence he secured in 1672 a commission in a foot regiment. This acquaintance with the duchess also brought him into favor with the king, which favor, however, he lost when about 1680 he married the Countess of Drogheda. This rich marriage, which led to his temporary retirement from the theater, proved disappointing, and Wycherley shortly found himself in debt and, consequently, in Fleet Prison. He was released in 1685 by the proceeds of a benefit performance of his last play, *The Plain Dealer.*

After 1704 he formed a friendship with young Alexander Pope, who "somewhat too zealously" revised many of his later verses. On his deathbed Wycherley put into posterity's quiver many barbed shafts against himself by his second marriage, ostensibly contracted to prevent the passing of his property to his nephew. He died in London on January 1, 1716.

Wycherley, with four plays, stands next after Etherege, with three plays, as the innovator of modern English comedy. Wycherley probably learned little from Etherege's cynical avoidance of genuine emotion, or from his flexible empty dialogue. Etherege transcribed life, but he lacked philosophy; life was to him a frivolous game, and to become emotionally engrossed in it was perhaps slightly vulgar. Wycherley, on the other hand, while he partook of Etherege's cynicism, felt not aloof amusement, but more than a little resentment. There is bitterness, even malice, in Wycherley's satire; he himself is not immune to his own poison.

In typical Restoration fashion, to Wycherley the greatest sin is foolishness. For instance, in *Love in a Wood,* his first play, Alderman Gripe, a hypocritical Puritan, ultimately marries a wench; Dapperwit, a fop, gets Gripe's daughter for his wife, but does not get her fortune, which he was really after. Wycherley's third play, *The Country Wife,* is an extremely realistic picture of cuckold-gulling, the great aristocratic pastime of the day. Horner, recently returned from France, pretends impotence in order better to practice his formidable art of despoiling chastity. His chief success is to win the favor of Margery, the country wife of the superannuated sensualist, Pinchwife. Without subtlety, but certainly with power, Wycherley makes his spectators partisans in condemning selfishness, pretentiousness, and hypocrisy.

The Country Wife is nowadays considered Wycherley's best play, but in his own day The Plain Dealer was considered his finest achievement; it is still more commonly included in anthologies. The same theme of exposing pretension and hypocrisy is present in this play as in *The Country Wife*. Manly, the Plain Dealer, has been robbed and wronged by his mistress Olivia, and his closest friend, Vernish. Wycherley's attack on selfishness and treachery in the persons of Vernish and Olivia is open and savage. Indeed, the play is not at all typical of the Restoration. It is hardly funny, hardly even amusing. Since it has more than a little of the near-repellent naturalistic abandon so noticeable in today's most esteemed playwrights, it is certain to make a strong impression on the modern reader.

BIBLIOGRAPHICAL REFERENCES: The standard edition is *The Complete Works of William Wycherley*, edited by Montague Summers, 4 vols., 1924. The *Complete Plays* were edited by Gerald Weales in 1967. An early biographical study, but an interesting one, is Lord Lansdowne's *Memoirs of the Life of William Wycherley*, 1718. See also A. W. Ward, *The History of English Dramatic Literature*, 1899; Bonamy Dobrée, *Restoration Comedy, 1600–1720*, 1924; Allardyce Nicoll, *A History of English Drama, 1660–1900*, Vol. I, 1952 (rev. ed.); Rose A. Zimbardo, *Wycherley's Drama: A Link in the Development of English Satire*, 1965; and Anne Righter, "William Wycherley," in *Restoration Theatre*, edited by John Russell Brown and Bernard Harris, 1965, 71–91.

ELINOR WYLIE

Born: Somerville, New Jersey
Date: September 7, 1885

Died: New York, N. Y.
Date: December 16, 1928

Principal Works

POEMS: *Nets to Catch the Wind*, 1921; *Black Armour*, 1923; *Trivial Breath*, 1928; *Angels and Earthly Creatures*, 1928; *Last Poems*, 1943.
NOVELS: *Jennifer Lorn: A Sedate Extravaganza*, 1923; *The Venetian Glass Nephew*, 1925; *The Orphan Angel*, 1926; *Mr. Hodge and Mr. Hazard*, 1928.

A woman of mercurial temperament and a dedicated artist in both poetry and prose, Elinor Wylie had one of the briefest and most integrated careers in the history of American literature. In a space of eight years she wrote four books of poems and four novels in which her tragic vision of life is grained with fantasy and satire. Within these her message is complete. Dying at forty-three, she had already made her demand on posterity for recognition of her brilliant craftsmanship and the revelation of the stoic in woman contained in her work.

Her life was a turbulent seedbed for the development of her singular talent. She was born Elinor Morton Hoyt in Somerville, New Jersey, on September 7, 1885, the oldest child of Henry Martyn and Anne (McMichael) Hoyt, both descended from old Pennsylvania families distinguished in society and public affairs. Her education was as fashionably correct as her family background. She attended private schools in Bryn Mawr and Washington, where her father, appointed to the post of assistant attorney-general of the United States in 1897, became Solicitor-General in 1903. During her schooldays her interests were divided between art and poetry, the latter chiefly through her discovery of Shelley. Following her debut and a brief, unhappy love affair, she married Philip Hichborn in 1905. For the next five years she lived the life of a fashionable young matron according to the standards of Philadelphia society and official Washington. In 1910, to the surprise of family and friends, she abandoned her husband and small son and eloped with Horace Wylie, a cultivated scholarly man fifteen years her senior. Two years later her husband committed suicide. Because of the prominent names involved, this elopement created a scandal kept alive by gossip and the press for more than a decade.

When Horace Wylie found it impossible to obtain a divorce, the couple went to England and lived there under an assumed name. *Incidental Numbers*, her first book of poems, was privately printed in London in 1912. Published anonymously, for presentation only, it holds only occasional promise of her mature powers as a poet. Unable to remain in England under wartime conditions, she and Wylie returned to Boston in 1916. His divorce having been granted, they were married the next year. After several years of restless travel from Maine to Georgia, Horace Wylie secured a minor government post and they returned to Washington in 1919. Cut off from most of her former friends, Elinor Wylie became one of a literary group that included William Rose Benét and Sinclair Lewis, and with their encouragement she continued to write poetry. In 1921 she left Washington to make her home in New York.

She came late upon the literary scene, but with the manner of one whom no disastrous circumstance could subdue. When one possesses charm and talent, as Elinor Wylie did, and to these adds a deep knowledge of life and the craftsmanship of crystal-cool words, the result is likely to be poetry which rises phoenix-like from the ashes of disillusionment. *Nets to Catch the Wind*, published in 1921, was awarded the Julia Ellsworth Ford Prize by the Poetry Society of America. To those who knew her best she remained a person of contradictions. She could be high-handed and remote and proud (the iced chalk to which one critic compared her), but she was also comradely and mirthful and gracious, and her speech, like her writing, crackled with the wit and vigor of her mind. She had become a figure of literary legend when, having divorced Horace Wylie, she married William Rose Benét in 1923, and in the same year published her second book of poems and a successful first novel.

Although Shelley was her lifelong passion, to the extent that she often identified herself with him, he was not the only influence on her work. Her loans of power, as reflected in *Nets to Catch the Wind* and *Black Armour*, were also in the tradition of Donne and Blake, poets who found an approach to spiritual truth in a disembodied ecstasy of thought and emotion. Her erudition and wit are plain in her use of the sharpened epithet, the aristocratic scorn, the language framing stark abstractions, a delight in subtleties of thought, an imagery of symbolic birds and beasts. On the whole, the poems in these books are songs of experience, with much bitterness in the singing. *Trivial Breath* is a more uneven collection, divided as it is between lyrics of personal experience and payment of her literary debts. But there is little of the "overfine" in the elegiac moods which pervade *Angels and Earthly Creatures*. Most of these poems were written in England during the summer of 1928, when some presentiment of death seemed to have given Elinor Wylie a final certainty of vision and language. The desire for escape is less persistent, the note of resignation less profound. Instead, there is exultant affirmation of love and faith transcending all fears of death in the magnificent sonnet sequence, "One Person." These poems, her most passionate revelation of the woman and the poet, are in the great tradition.

Her novels are like much of her poetry, exquisite and erudite. *Jennifer Lorn*, set against a droll background blending sophisticated elegance with simple manners, is a satire on the twin themes of magnificence and folly, reflected in the ambitions of an eighteenth century empire builder and the attitude of a heroine unmoved by the bustle of all practical affairs until death frees her at last from a husband who bores her and a world that intrudes upon her romantic dreaming. The artifice of *The Venetian Glass Nephew* seems on the suface as brittle as its spun-glass hero, but under its bright surface are deeper meanings in the story of a heroine willing to be transformed into a porcelain figure to decorate the sharp angles and cold corners of the world. *The Orphan Angel* is apocryphal legend, a picaresque romance in which Shelley is miraculously rescued off Viareggio and brought to America aboard a Yankee ship. *Mr. Hodge and Mr. Hazard* is a more personal fable, in many ways her best. The disillusioned poet who returns to England in the twilight of the Romantic Period is not Shelley, as many readers have supposed, but any artist who survives into a later period than his own. The summer idyl of the old poet ends in a fiasco of stale cream buns and an epigram; his fate is the crack of doom in a teacup, and the whole is an ironic allegory of the poet's tragedy and the world's indifference.

Elinor Wylie was not to share her hero's fate. In England, where she spent the summer of 1928, she fell while visiting a country house and suffered a painful but temporary back injury. In October a light stroke left one side of her face partly paralyzed. She returned to New York early in December of that year. On December 16 she had arranged the poems in *Angels and Earthly Creatures* for the printer and was sitting reading in the Benét apartment when she had a second stroke and died before her husband could summon assistance.

BIBLIOGRAPHICAL REFERENCES: *Collected Poems of Elinor Wylie* was edited by her husband, William Rose Benét, 1932. *Collected Prose of Elinor Wylie*, 1933, contains biographical and critical prefaces by Stephen Vincent Benét, William Rose Benét, Isabel Patterson, Carl Van Doren, and Carl Van Vechten. There is no authorized biography. *Elinor Wylie: The Portrait of an Unknown Lady*, 1935, is an informal biographical study by her sister, Nancy Hoyt. For brief studies in books and periodicals see Elizabeth S. Sergeant, *Fire Under the Andes*, 1927; James Branch Cabell, *Some of Us*, 1930; Emily Clark, *Innocence Abroad*, 1931; Rebecca West, *Ending in Earnest*, 1931; William Rose Benét, *The Prose and Poetry of Elinor Wylie*, 1934; Carl Van Doren, *Three Worlds*, 1936; Henry S. Canby, *American Memoir*, 1947; Mary M. Colum, *Life and the Dream*, 1947; Mary M. McClain, "Elinor Wylie's Poetry and Prose: Her Artistic Evolution," in *Writers and Their Critics*, 1956; Archibald MacLeish, "Black Armour," *New Republic*, XXXVII (December 5, 1923), Suppl., 16–18; Herbert S. Gorman, "Daughter of Donne," *North American Review*, CCXIX (1924), 679–686; Harriet Monroe, "Elinor Wylie," *Poetry*, XXXIII (1929), 266–272; Morton Dauwen Zabel, "The Pattern of the Atmosphere," *Poetry*, XL (1932), 273–282; Osbert Burdett, "The Novels of Elinor Wylie," *English Review*, LIX (1934), 488–490, 492; Dayton Kohler, "Elinor Wylie: Heroic Mask," *South Atlantic Quarterly*, XXXVI (1937), 218–228; Henry Lüdeke, "Venetian Glass: The Poetry and Prose of Elinor Wylie," *English Studies*, XX (1938), 241–250; Julia Cluck, "Elinor Wylie's Shelley Obsession," *Publications of the Modern Language Association*, LVI (1941), 841–860; Babette Deutsch, "The Ghostly Member," *Poetry in Our Time*, 1963, 243–268; Thomas J. Wertenbaker, Jr., "Into the Poet's Shoes," *English Journal*, LIII (1964), 370–372; and Evelyn Helmick, "Elinor Wylie's Novels, Allegories of Love," *Carrell*, 9 (1968), 17–28.

JOHANN RUDOLF WYSS

Born: Bern, Switzerland
Date: March 13, 1781

Died: Bern
Date: March 31, 1830

Principal Work

NOVEL: *Der Schweizerische Robinson*, 1812–1813 (*The Swiss Family Robinson*).

Johann Rudolf Wyss, who is usually credited with being the author of *The Swiss Family Robinson*, was born in Bern, Switzerland, on March 13, 1781. He studied at several German universities and in 1806 became a professor of philosophy at the University of Bern, where he also served as the chief librarian. In his native land of Switzerland he became known as a collector and editor of Swiss folklore, publishing such volumes as *Idyllen und Erzählungen aus der Schweiz* (*Idyls and Tales from the Swiss*, 1815–1822), *Reise im Berner Oberland* (*Travels in the Bernese Uplands*, 1808), and the fifteen-volume *Die Alpenrose* (1811–1830). He was also the author of the Swiss national anthem.

Johann Rudolf Wyss, although given credit often as the author, apparently did not compose *The Swiss Family Robinson*, but only wrote it down in revised form and had it published. The story, obviously in partial imitation of Daniel Defoe's *Robinson Crusoe* (1719), was concocted by Wyss's father, named Rudolf David, for the enjoyment of his sons. Of the father, who was a chaplain in the Swiss army, little is known, except that he was born in 1749, became a chaplain, served in Italy, and died in 1818.

The history of *The Swiss Family Robinson* is an interesting one. Apparently Pastor Wyss committed his story to writing before his son revised the manuscript and had it published at Zurich, Switzerland, under the title *Der Schweizerische Robinson, Oder der Schiffbruchige Schweizerpredige und Seine Familie. Ein Lehrreiches Buch für Kinder und Kinderfreunde zu Stadt und Land*. All that long German title can be translated as *The Swiss Family Robinson, or the Shipwrecked Swiss Preacher and His Family: An Instructional Book for Children and Their Friends in City or Country*. The first known English translation was by William Godwin, British philosopher, reformer, and novelist, a short time after the Zurich edition appeared. But a Frenchwoman, Baroness de Montolieu, with Johann Rudolf Wyss's approval, enlarged the story, translated it into French, and published it in 1824. Two years later the original publisher in Zurich brought out a new German edition which incorporated the baroness's additions. The first English translation of the enlarged story was made in 1868, by Mrs. H. B. Paull, who also translated Grimm's fairy tales. Most later editions have followed Baroness Montolieu's edition. The book has been immensely popular in America and Europe with generations of children.

Wyss died in Bern on March 31, 1830.

BIBLIOGRAPHICAL REFERENCES: For brief studies of Wyss in English see William Dean Howells, Introduction to *The Swiss Family Robinson*, 1909; and R. B. Glaenzer, "The Swiss Family Robinson," *Bookman,* XXXIV (1911), 139–142. See also P. Dottin "Le Robinson suisse," *Mercure de France,* CLXIX (January 1, 1924), 114–126.

XENOPHON

Born: Athens, Greece
Date: c. 430 B.C.

Died: Corinth, Greece
Date: c. 354 B.C.

PRINCIPAL WORKS
(Dates uncertain)

HISTORY AND BIOGRAPHY: The *Hellenica*, the *Anabasis*, *Agesilaus*.
ROMANCE: The *Cyropaedia, or Education of Cyrus*.
SOCRATIC DIALOGUES: The *Memorabilia of Socrates*, the *Oeconomicus* (*Household Management*), the *Apology of Socrates*, the *Symposium*.
TREATISES: *Hippike* (*On Horsemanship*), *Hipparchicus* (*On the Cavalry General*), *Cynegeticus* (*On Hunting*), *De Vectigalibus* (*On Ways and Means*), *Polity of the Lacedaemonians*, *Hiero*.

Born at Athens about 430 B.C., Xenophon, son of Gryllus of the Attic deme Erchia, belonged to a well-to-do family and was a disciple of Socrates, though not a member of his intimate circle. After an adventurous participation in an expedition to overthrow the King of Persia in 401 B.C., he then spent a few years in Asia Minor with mercenary troops under Spartan command. Exiled from Athens around 394, he settled in the Peloponnese, where he lived as a country gentleman on an estate granted him by the Spartans at Scillus near Olympia. He lost this estate around 371 when the Eleans recovered Scillus from the Spartans. In 369 the decree of exile was rescinded, after Athens entered into an alliance with Sparta. Thereafter he occasionally visited Athens and sent his sons to serve in the Athenian cavalry. He died at Corinth about 354 B.C.

It is as a writer that Xenophon is best known. He wrote history, romance, and essays of practical and moral import. His most famous work is the *Anabasis*, an account of the expedition of ten thousand mercenaries hired by Cyrus, the younger brother of King Artaxerxes, to win for himself the throne of Persia. Though Cyrus' army defeated the king's, Cyrus was killed. The Greek generals having been treacherously captured and slain, Xenophon found himself in command of the hazardous retreat of the mercenaries to Trebizond on the Black Sea. After making contact with the Spartan general Thibron, Xenophon turned the mercenaries over to him; Xenophon himself remained in Asia with the Spartans for some years. The *Anabasis* is a thrilling adventure story, written in good, if somewhat uninspired, Greek.

In the *Hellenica* Xenophon completed the unfinished *History of the Peloponnesian War* of Thucydides and continued the history of Greek war and politics down to the battle of Mantinea in 362 B.C. The work is inferior to that of Thucydides both in style and in historical understanding, but it is a primary source for the history of the period it covers.

Association with Socrates supplied the material and motive for several works: The *Memorabilia of Socrates* is a defense of Socrates, with illustrative anecdotes and many short dialogues between Socrates and his friends, usually on moral questions. Xenophon lacked Plato's interest in speculative philosophy. The *Apology* of *Socrates* purports to explain why Socrates did not defend himself any better than he did. The *Symposium* consists of an imagined dinner party conversation at the house of Callias, with some serious philosophizing by Socrates. In general these works portray a more matter-of-fact Socrates than the protagonist of Plato's dialogues, but one probably no nearer the historical truth. Another dialogue, the *Oeconomicus*, between Socrates and Critoboulos sets forth Xenophon's views on the management of an estate. It reflects the life at Scillus and is a valuable document for the economy of the period.

A work of a different sort, the *Cyropaedia* is a romantic account of the youth and education of Cyrus the Great of Persia. It is intended to lay down the ideals of education for political leadership. It is unfavorably remarked on by Plato in the *Republic*. Xenophon's political interests were also expressed in the laudatory *Polity of the Lacedaemonians* and in the *Hiero*. The latter is a dialogue between the King of Syracuse and the poet Simonides, dealing with the relative happiness of the despot and the private citizen and with the question of how a despot should rule in order to win the affection of his people.

Four technical treatises were also written by Xenophon: The *Hipparchicus*, on the duties of a cavalry commander; *On Horsemanship*, an authoritative manual, the first of its kind to come down to us from antiquity; *Ways and Means*, suggestions for improving the finances of Athens; and the *Cynegeticus*, a treatise on hunting, including, oddly enough, an attack on the Sophists.

Xenophon was a man of affairs, with intelligence and wide interests, who wrote plainly and with a taste for platitude. He reflects the attitudes of a Greek gentleman and for this reason alone is worth much to us for the insights his writings provide.

BIBLIOGRAPHICAL REFERENCES: E. C. Marchant edited the *Opera Omnia*, 5 vols., 1900–1919. Among available translations are the following: H. A. Holden, *Cyropaedia*, 4 vols., 1887–1890; C. L. Brownson and O. J. Todd, *Hellenica, Anabasis, Apology*, and *Symposium*, 3 vols., 1914–1923; and E. C. Marchant, *Memorabilia* and *Oeconomicus*, 1923, and *Scripta Minora*, 1925. For criticism and comment see H. Richards, *Xenophon and Others*, 1907; J. B. Bury, *Ancient Greek Historians*, 1909; Edith Hamilton, *The Greek Way*, 1930; Kathleen Atkinson, *The Republica Lacedaemoniorum Ascribed to Xenophon: Its Manuscript Tradition and General Significance*, 1948; and Leo Strauss, *Xenophon's Socratic Discourse: An Interpretation of the Oeconomicus*, 1970; also A. Croiset, *Xenophon, son caractère et son talent*, 1873; and Jean Luccioni, *Xenophon et le socratisme*, 1953.

AGUSTÍN YÁÑEZ

Born: Guadalajara, Mexico
Date: May 4, 1904

Principal Works

NOVELS: *Pasión y convalecencia,* 1943; *Al filo del agua,* 1947; *La tierra prótiga,* 1960; *Las tierras flacas,* 1962.
NOVELLAS: *Archipiélago de mujeres,* 1943.
SHORT STORIES AND SKETCHES: *Espejismo de Juchitán,* 1940; *Flor de juegos antiguos,* 1942; *Esta es mala suerte,* 1945.
BIOGRAPHY: *Fray Bartolomé de las Casas, el conquistador conquistado,* 1942; *Alfonso Gutiérrez Hermosillo y algunos amigos,* 1945; *Don Justo Sierra, su vida, sus ideas y su obra,* 1950.
MISCELLANEOUS: *Genio y figuras de Guadalajara,* 1940; *El contenido social de la literatura iberoamericana,* 1944; *Yahualica,* 1946.

Agustín Yáñez has given us, in two of his books, some glimpses into his literary life. "Very early," he writes of himself in the third person, "there awoke in him a rigorous critical sense that inhibited the expansiveness of the child and the adolescent; but his sentimental temperament was so intense and overflowing that it could not but manifest itself, even exaggeratedly, and ended in coloring his life absolutely. Intelligence imposed on him an essential severity; . . . art was his star, his great ambition, the window through which he looked at existence." These characteristics of seriousness, austerity, and preoccupation with artistic form have shaped all his literary work.

He associated himself with other young writers of Guadalajara and founded the literary journal, *Bandera de Provincias,* the establishment of which was a national event. He received his law degree in Guadalajara and later moved to Mexico City where he devoted himself to university teaching and literary production, and held several important public offices.

According to the aesthetic creed of Yáñez, the ideal of art is form: "Not art dehumanized, nor purely aesthetical as mere pleasure in form, nor, even less, verbalism." For him, the idea of literary form is inward, a theory of composition initiated by means of living the reality, and then reliving it in the literary work until one completes it in the appropriate verbal form. "I never write—least of all when writing novels—with the intention of sustaining a premeditated thesis, committed to predetermined conclusions." After intuiting a form, he develops it until it takes on consistency; it is then necessary to follow it, striving not to falsify characters, situations, and atmosphere.

Yáñez as a writer is very conscious and cognizant of his function. His style is elaborate, reflective, grave, and refined. "Here extend the supreme ambition and limit of my style: When I succeed in making the words sparkle like the colors in crystal and in combining them magnificently and solemnly." His knowledge of contemporary philosophy, of the Spanish classics, and of the resources of the modern novel has given to his work robustness, rigor, and an abundant vocabulary.

Almost all of Yáñez' works have reminiscence as a common ingredient. On the occasion of the commemoration of the Fourth Centennial of the founding of Guadalajara, he wrote two books: *Flor de juegos antiguos*, lyrical memories of his childhood and of the games of his province, and *Genio y figuras de Guadalajara*, in which he presents a brief description of this city in 1930 and character studies of its principal citizens throughout its history. In 1943 he published, *Archipiélago de mujeres*, a collection of seven stories, each one called by the name of a woman who represents a step on the author's "ladder of adolescence": music, revelation, desire, beauty, folly, death, and love.

In *Al filo del agua*, published in 1947, Yáñez produced his best novel and, according to many critics, one of the finest Mexican novels of the last twenty-five years. In a prose that is dense, unhackneyed, and subtle, he presents the life of a typical pueblo of Jalisco. In the routine and monotony of everyday life, passion and religion are the two stimuli of these townspeople. The dramas of conscience brought about by the conflicts of flesh and spirit are here analyzed with subtle introspection.

Two other books compose his trilogy of novels about Jalisco, his native State—*La tierra pródiga* and *Las tierras flacas*. During the time he held the office of governor of that state, he had the opportunity of obtaining first-hand knowledge of the inhabitants of its coastal region. From this contact, *La tierra pródiga* was born as a portrait of the struggle between barbarism and civilization which results in man's finally overcoming nature. In *Las tierras flacas* he recreates the atmosphere of *Al filo del agua*, namely, the secluded, traditional life of small towns, with arid lands, menaced by the appearance of technology.

Yáñez' studies on Mexican literature have attained a high eminence. Particularly outstanding are those devoted to the chronicles of the Spanish Conquest of Mexico, the novel of Lizardi, and the native myths of the pre-Hispanic epoch. After holding the Ministry of Public Education of his country, Yáñez now leads a private life, filled with the prestige of being one of the foremost representatives of the new Spanish-American fiction.

BIBLIOGRAPHICAL REFERENCES: There is no helpful criticism of Yáñez in English. For biographical and critical studies in Spanish see Manuel de Ezcurdia, *Trayectoria novelística de Agustín Yáñez*, 1954 (Mexico); F. Morton Rand, *Los Novelistas de la Revolución mexicana*, 1949 (Mexico); José Luis Martínez, *Literatura mexicana, siglo XX*, I, 1949 (Mexico); Manuel Pedro González, *Trayectoria de la novela en Mexico*, 1951 (Mexico); and Raúl Cardiel Reyes, "El ser de America en Agustín Yáñez," *Filosofía y Letras*, No. 38 (April–June, 1950), 301–321. Two collections of critical and appreciative essays by various hands have been printed in Mexican periodicals: "Homenaje a Agustín Yáñez," in *Tiras de Colores*, II, No. 27 (July, 1944), and "Homenaje a Agustín Yáñez," in *Novedades*, 1952. For studies of individual works see also the following journals printed in Mexico City: Julio Jiménez Rueda on *Archipiélago de mujeres*, *Filosofía y Letras*, No. 16 (Oct.–Dec., 1944), 232–233; Francisco Monterde on *Al filo del agua*, *ibid.*, No. 25 (Jan.–Mar., 1947), 136–140; Gabriel Méndez Plancarte on *Fray Bartolome de las Casas* in "Yáñez, el silencioso," *Abside*, VI, No. 2, 212–217; and Elena Orozco on *Don Justo Sierra* in *Filosofía y*

Letras, No. 40 (Oct.–Dec., 1950). A good introduction to Yáñez is Antonio Castro Leal, Introduction to *Al filo del agua,* 1955 (2nd ed., Mexico).

WILLIAM BUTLER YEATS

Born: Sandymount, Ireland
Date: June 13, 1865

Died: Roquebrune, France
Date: January 28, 1939

Principal Works

POEMS: *Mosada: A Dramatic Poem*, 1886; *The Wanderings of Oisin*, 1889; *Poems*, 1895; *The Wind Among the Reeds*, 1899; *In the Seven Woods*, 1903; *The Green Helmet and Other Poems*, 1910; *Responsibilities*, 1914; *The Wild Swans at Coole*, 1917; *Michael Robartes and the Dancer*, 1920; *Later Poems*, 1922; *The Cat and the Moon and Certain Poems*, 1924; *The Tower*, 1928; *The Winding Stair*, 1933; *Collected Poems*, 1933; *The King of the Great Clock Tower*, 1934; *A Full Moon in March*, 1935; *New Poems*, 1938; *Last Poems and Plays*, 1940; *Collected Poems*, 1949.

PLAYS: *The Countess Kathleen*, 1892; *The Land of Heart's Desire*, 1894; *The Shadowy Waters*, 1900; *Cathleen ni Houlihan*, 1902; *Where There Is Nothing*, 1902; *The Hour Glass*, 1903; *The Pot of Broth*, 1904; *The King's Threshold*, 1904; *Deirdre*, 1907; *The Unicorn from the Stars and Other Plays*, 1908 (with Lady Gregory); *Plays for an Irish Theatre*, 1911; *Four Plays for Dancers*, 1921; *Wheels and Butterflies*, 1934; *Collected Plays*, 1934; *The Herne's Egg*, 1938; *Collected Plays*, 1952.

SHORT STORIES AND TALES: *The Celtic Twilight*, 1893; *Stories of Red Hanrahan*, 1904.

MEMOIRS: *Reveries Over Childhood and Youth*, 1915; *Four Years*, 1921; *The Trembling of the Veil*, 1922; *Autobiographies*, 1926; *Estrangement*, 1926; *Reflections from a Diary Kept in 1909*, 1926; *The Death of Synge and Other Passages from an Old Diary*, 1928; *Dramatis Personae*, 1936.

ESSAYS: *Ideas of Good and Evil*, 1903; *Discoveries*, 1907; *Poetry and Ireland*, 1908 (with Lionel Johnson); *Synge and the Ireland of His Time*, 1911; *The Cutting of an Agate*, 1912; *Essays*, 1924; *A Vision*, 1925.

LETTERS: *Letters on Poetry to Dorothy Wellesley*, 1940; *Letters to Katharine Tynan*, 1953.

TRANSLATIONS: Sophocles' *King Oedipus*, 1928; *Oedipus at Colonus*, 1934.

William Butler Yeats was born at Sandymount, near Dublin, on June 13, 1865. His father, John Butler Yeats, was an artist of considerable merit who had given up a moderately lucrative law practice in order to devote himself to painting; his mother was a frail, beautiful woman who nurtured in her son a deep love for the "west country" of Ireland that was to last all his life. His early childhood and later vacations were spent there, among the green hills and lakes of Sligo which were to become, in such poems as "The Lake Isle of Innisfree," a symbol of his imaginative escape from the disappointments and unpleasant realities of life.

Much of Yeats's early life was spent in London, but between 1880 and 1887 the family was in Dublin, years which had a lasting effect on the impressionable young poet. Stimulated by his father, who loved to read aloud, Yeats discovered Shakespeare, the Romantic poets, and the Pre-Raphaelites, explored popular works on Eastern mysticism, became interested in Irish myths and folklore, and, perhaps most important, met the poets and intellectuals of the Irish Literary Revival, many of whom were to remain lifelong friends. During the period he made several attempts at poetic drama, but the plays were highly imitative and hopelessly cluttered with magic islands and timid shepherds. Back in London, Yeats embarked on a serious study of Irish folk tales in the British Museum and published his first major poem, *The Wanderings of Oisin,* in 1889. Although the poem is superficially reminiscent of Spenser, Shelley, and his friend William Morris, the Gaelic theme and unorthodox rhythms are characteristic of Yeats's quest for a fresh tradition and an individual style.

There is, however, little that is imitative in poetic plays such as *The Countess Kathleen* and *The Land of Heart's Desire,* or in the lyrics that accompanied the former. The continued use of Irish themes evident in these volumes is indicative of an important and complex aspect of Yeats's early development. In common with the other writers of the nationalistic Irish Literary Revival, he wished to create a literature that was purely Irish in tone and subject matter. As part of the same general movement, he strove to reawaken in his people a sense of the glory and significance of Ireland's historical and legendary past. Furthermore, the remoteness of these Celtic themes was consistent with Yeats's aesthetic theory, later repudiated in part, of the separation of art from life. Finally, Irish folklore offered an answer to his search for a personal and individual mythology, for he found there a treasury of symbols hitherto unused in English poetry. Yeats's tendency to make mythical figures into private symbols was encouraged by his contacts with such Symbolist poets as Arthur Symons and Mallarmé, and by his undisciplined but enthusiastic dabbling in such esoteric subjects as "hermetic" philosophy, astrology, and spiritualism. *The Secret Rose* (1897) and *The Wind Among the Reeds* are representative of Yeats's work at this time, and while the clues to the meaning of the poems in these volumes is not always readily accessible to the uninitiated reader, they reveal a major step forward in terms of artistic skill and emotional maturity.

In spite of Yeats's theoretic dissociation from contemporary Irish life and politics, he could not escape his environment, the less so because he was in love, and was to be for two decades, with the beautiful and fiery actress and nationalist, Maud Gonne. In 1899 he and Isabella Augusta, Lady Gregory, founded the Irish National Theatre Society, which presently became the famous Abbey Theatre of Dublin. During the first decade of the twentieth century, working alongside Lady Gregory and J. M. Synge, Yeats wrote several plays for the Abbey, the best of which is a patriotic propaganda piece, *Cathleen ni Houlihan,* and the tragedy *Deirdre.* In the poetry of this period, too, Yeats reacted against what he considered the sentimentality and divorce from reality of his earlier work. As the legendary past became less important, in order to rescue his imagination from abstractions and bring it closer to actuality, he pressed everything into his poetry: the theater, patriotism, contemporary controversies.

The Green Helmet characteristically shows a tremendous advance in precision of imagery and syntax, as well as an increased use of personal and contemporary themes. Yet along with the substitution of a hard, dry manner and lively, homely detail for the dreamy vagueness of the early poetry, the symbolism which he was evolving becomes more and more esoteric and obscure. In 1917, having had proposals of marriage rejected by both Maud Gonne and her daughter Iseult, Yeats precipitously married Miss Georgie Hyde-Lees. The marriage was on the whole a success; one of its curious by-products was their joint experiment in spiritualism and "automatic writing," begun by his wife as a game to distract Yeats from personal worries. From the renewed interest in the occult and the mystical which arose out of these investigations Yeats developed a system of symbols by means of which he hoped to express his philosophy of life and art. This symbolism, which Yeats discusses in detail in *A Vision,* privately printed in 1925, is extremely complex, but while it provided the poet with a device which gave unity to his ideas on history, art, and human experience, its difficulties need not be a barrier to an understanding of his poems. It is probably enough for the average reader to recognize in the gyre, or ascending spiral, and the phases of the moon, Yeats's theories regarding the cyclical natures of both human nature and history.

For the aging Yeats this concept of the cyclical character of history was in a sense his defense against time. The poems of his later years are dominated by the figure of the poet, withdrawn from the "blood and mire" of life into the eternal realm of art, smiling with "tragic joy" at the cycles of life and death, creation and destruction, which mark human existence. But Yeats could not, either in his life or in his art, consistently maintain this withdrawal. In 1923 he was made a senator of the new Irish Free State, a post he entered into with enthusiasm, if not always tact.

Some of Yeats's last poems, such as the "Crazy Jane" group, are a harsh, almost bitter glorification of the physical and even the sensual. As he says in "The Circus Animal's Desertion" from *Last Poems,* he "must lie down where all the ladders start, / In the foul rag-and-bone shop of the heart." The period after 1923, when Yeats was awarded the Nobel Prize in Literature, saw the production of some of his best and most exciting poetry. On January 28, 1939, his mind still alert and active, Yeats died at Roquebrune, on the French Riviera.

No sparse biographical outline can adequately characterize the complex personality of William Butler Yeats. He was fascinated by strange and supernatural phenomena but scorned the wonders of modern science; he was by nature inclined towards mysticism, but found little that attracted him in Christianity; he was an ardent patriot who dissociated himself as far as possible from the revolutionary course his country was following; he was a disciple of the doctrine of the separation of life from art. He was all these, yet his poetry had its basis in his own quick response to life, and was indeed a criticism *of* life. Yeats himself was aware of the contradictions in his nature and in life, and throughout his career he sought for a philosophical and artistic system that would resolve the conflict between his vision of what art should be and the recognition of what life is. Perhaps he found it, but it was in many ways too private, too personal a vision to be communicated. Yeats is not always an easy poet to read, but his compact, intellectually intense, but supremely lyrical poetry deserves the careful attention it demands.

BIBLIOGRAPHICAL REFERENCES: There is no collected edition of Yeats. The definitive edition of the poems is *The Collected Poems of William Butler Yeats*, 2 vols., 1949, incorporating revisions made by the poet before his death. For those interested in a reading of the texts an indispensable work is *The Variorum Edition of the Poems of William Butler Yeats*, edited by George Daniel Peter Allt and Russell K. Alspach, 1957. A revised edition of the *Collected Plays* was published in 1952. There is also *Collected Prose* edited by John P. Frayne, Vol. I, *First Reviews and Articles, 1880–1896*, 1970. There are two bibliographies: A. J. H. Symons, *A Bibliography of William Butler Yeats*, 1924, and Allan Wade, *A Bibliography of the Writings of William Butler Yeats*, 1953.

The Yeats bibliography is extensive. The best and most recent study is Harold Bloom, *William Butler Yeats*, 1970. Also valuable is Joseph Hone, *The Life of William Butler Yeats*, 1942. For biography and criticism see also Forrest Reid, *W. B. Yeats: A Critical Study*, 1915; C. L. Wrenn, *William Butler Yeats: A Literary Study*, 1920; J. H. Pollock, *William Butler Yeats*, 1935; J. P. O'Donnell, *Sailing to Byzantium: A Study of the Later Style and Symbolism of William Butler Yeats*, 1939; Lennox Robinson, *William Butler Yeats: A Study*, 1939; Louis MacNeice, *The Poetry of William Butler Yeats*, 1941 (rev. ed. 1967); V. K. N. Menon, *The Development of W. B. Yeats*, 1942; Peter Ure, *Towards a New Mythology*, 1946; Richard Ellman, *Yeats: The Man and the Masks*, 1948; and *The Identity of Yeats*, 1950; A. N. Jeffares, *W. B. Yeats: Man and Poet*, 1949; Donald Stauffer, *Golden Nightingale*, 1949; T. R. Henn, *Lonely Tower*, 1950; Vivienne Koch: *William Butler Yeats: The Tragic Phase*, 1951; Virginia Moore, *The Unicorn: William Butler Yeats' Search for Reality*, 1954; Frank Kermode, *Romantic Images*, 1957; and John R. Moor, *Masks of Love and Death* (plays), 1971.

For briefer studies in books and periodicals see, further, Cornelius Weygandt, *The Time of Yeats*, 1937; Arland Ussher, *Three Great Irishmen*, 1952; R. P. Blackmur, "The Later Poetry of W. B. Yeats," *Southern Review*, II (1936), 339–362; Morton Dauwen Zabel, "Yeats at Thirty and Seventy," *Poetry*, XLVII (1936), 268–277; Cleanth Brooks, "The Vision of W. B. Yeats," *Southern Review*, IV (1938), 116–142; W. K. Tindall, "The Symbolism of W. B. Yeats," *Accent*, V (1945), 203–212; D. S. Savage, "The Aestheticism of W. B. Yeats," *Kenyon Review*, VII (1945), 118–134; Harold H. Watts, "Yeats and Lapsed Mythology," *Renascence*, III (1951), 107–112; Peter Allt, "Yeats, Religion, and History," *Sewanee Review*, LX (1952), 624–658; Robert M. Adams, "Now That My Ladder's Gone—Yeats Without Myth," *Accent*, XIII (1953), 140–152; Richard Ellman, "The Art of Yeats: Affirmative Capability," *Kenyon Review*, XV (1953), 357–385; T. R. Henn, "W. B. Yeats and the Irish Background," *Yale Review*, XLII (1953), 351–364; Hugh Kenner, "The Sacred Book of the Arts," *Sewanee Review*, LXIV (1956), 574–590; and Peter Ure, "Yeats' Supernatural Songs," *Review of English Studies*, VII (1956), 38–51.

The Permanence of Yeats, edited by James Hall and Martin Steinmann, 1950, is a collection of essays by various hands. The special Yeats Issue of the *Southern Review*, VII (Winter, 1942), was devoted entirely to studies of Yeats as poet and mystic.

EDWARD YOUNG

Born: Upham, near Winchester, England
Date: July, 1683

Died: Welwyn, England
Date: April 5, 1765

Principal Works

POEMS: *The Universal Passion,* "first satire," 1725, 2nd, 3rd, and 4th satires, 1725, "last satire," 1726, 5th, 1727; collected under the title *The Love of Fame,* in Seven Characteristic Satires, 1728; *The Complaint, or Night Thoughts on Immortality* (anonymous), 1742–1745; "Conjectures on Original Composition," 1759; *Works* 1741 (2 vols.); *Works,* 1757, (4 vols.) and a fifth in 1767 and a seventh in 1778.

Edward Young, poet, critic and dramatist, was born at Upham, near Winchester, probably in early July, 1683, the son of Edward Young, rector of Upham and fellow of Winchester. Young as a youth probably deserved the comment of Alexander Pope, that he had had "a foolish youth, the sport of peers and poets." He very likely was not then the pious man of religion and morality that he later became.

Young was graduated from Oxford on April 23, 1714, as B.C.L., and as D.C.L. on June 10, 1719. Thereafter he capitalized on his friendships and acquaintances, trying to push ahead in the world and gain admittance to literary circles. He wrote many and various "literary" works on many and various subjects, from literature to politics, some of which he was later to regret.

He wrote two plays, among other things, that met with varying degrees of success; *Busirus,* for example, ran nine nights at Drury Lane, in March, 1718, and was ridiculed by Fielding. In April, 1721, *Revenge,* a variation of Shakespeare's *Othello,* ran at the same theater for six nights but later enjoyed great popularity. Young's most memorable work is his *Night Thoughts,* which was immediately popular.

By the early 1740's Young had become wealthy, and though he continued to write, his power—such as it had been—had weakened, and he sank into melancholy and irritability.

BIBLIOGRAPHICAL REFERENCES: The standard edition is still the *Complete Works,* edited by J. Doran, 2 vols., 1854, reprinted in 1968. The *Conjectures on Original Composition* was edited by Edith J. Morley in 1918. The best biographies are Walter Thomas, *La Poète Edward Young,* 1901; and H. C. Shelley, *The Life and Letters of Edward Young,* 1914. The *Correspondence* was edited by Henry Petit, 1971.

For critical comment see J. W. Mackail, *Studies of English Poets,* 1926; M. Bailey, "Edward Young," *The Age of Johnson: Essays Presented to C. B. Tinker,* 1949; C. V. Wicker, *Edward Young and the Fear of Death: A Study in Romantic Melancholy,* 1952; Martin Price, *To the Palace of Wisdom: Studies in Order and Energy from Dryden to Blake,* 1964; and Isabel St. John Bliss, *Edward Young,* 1969.

STARK YOUNG

Born: Como, Mississippi
Date: October 11, 1881

Died: New York, N. Y.
Date: January 6, 1963

Principal Works

NOVELS: *Heaven Trees*, 1926; *The Torches Flare*, 1928; *River House*, 1929; *So Red the Rose*, 1934.

SHORT STORIES: *The Street of the Islands*, 1930; *Feliciana*, 1935.

PLAYS: *Guenevere*, 1906; *Addio, Madretta, and Other Plays*, 1912; *The Queen of Sheba*, 1922; *The Colonnade*, 1924; *The Saint*, 1925.

POEMS: *The Blind Man at the Window*, 1906.

ESSAYS AND SKETCHES: *Encaustics*, 1926.

THEATRICAL CRITICISM: *The Flower in Drama*, 1923; *Glamour*, 1925; *Theatre Practice*, 1926; *The Theatre*, 1927; *Immortal Shadows*, 1948.

TRAVEL SKETCHES AND IMPRESSIONS: *The Three Fountains*, 1924.

REMINISCENCES: *The Pavilion*, 1951.

Stark Young, known chiefly as the author of *So Red the Rose* and often ranked as a minor figure among the Southern Agrarians, was born in Como, Mississippi, on October 11, 1881. When a typhoid epidemic closed the preparatory school he was attending, he was allowed to enter the University of Mississippi at the age of fourteen. Graduated in 1901, he continued his studies at Columbia University, from which he received his master's degree in English in 1902.

His first career was in the classroom. After a short period of teaching in a military school for boys he became an instructor in English at the University of Mississippi in 1904. Three years later he joined the faculty of the University of Texas, where he taught until 1915, when he became professor of English at Amherst College. In 1921 he resigned to become a member of the editorial staff of the *New Republic*, a position he held until 1947, except for one year (1924–1925) when he served as drama critic of the *New York Times*. Concurrently he was an associate editor of *Theatre Arts Monthly* from 1921 to 1940. His close association with the theater resulted in five books of drama criticism, the plays he himself wrote in both prose and verse, translations, and the direction of several plays, including Lenormand's *The Failures* and Eugene O'Neill's *Welded*, on Broadway.

Stark Young's most sustained work was in the novel. *So Red the Rose*, one of the earliest and most popular of the Civil War novels, achieves scope and depth because the writer has dramatized against a factual historical background the symbolic conflict between opposing forces of tradition and disintegration implicit in Southern life and character. This novel and its predecessors—*Heaven Trees*, a nostalgic re-creation of plantation life in antebellum days, and *The Torches Flare* and *River House*, which deal with later periods of the regional experience—make up, in effect, four panels of a dramatic and somberly realized social and moral history of the South. Young also declared his local loyalties in the essay written for *I'll Take My Stand: The South and the Agrarian Tradi-*

tion, a symposium by "Twelve South- erners" published in 1930.

BIBLIOGRAPHICAL REFERENCES: There is no full-length biographical or critical study of Stark Young, but an excellent picture of his background and personality may be gathered from his book of reminiscences, *The Pavilion,* 1951. For brief critical sketches see Donald Davidson, Introduction to *So Red the Rose,* Modern Standard Authors Series, 1953; Abbott Martin, "Stark Young and the Ransomists," Sewanee Review, XXXVIII (1930), 114–115; John Donald Wade, "Two Souths," *Virginia Quarterly Review,* X (1934), 616–619; Emily Clark, "Stark Young's South," *ibid.,* XI (1935), 626–628; J. W. Miller, "Stark Young, Chekhov, and the Method of Indirect Action," *Georgia Review,* XVIII (1964), 98–115; John Pilkington, "Stark Young at the Southern Literary Festival," *University of Mississippi Studies in English,* V (1964), 35–42; and John J. Sommers, "The Critic as Playwright: A Study of Stark Young's *The Saint,*" Modern Drama, VII (1965), 446–453.

MARGUERITE YOURCENAR
Marguerite de Crayencour

Born: Brussels, Belgium
Date: June 8, 1903

Principal Works

NOVELS AND SHORT STORIES: *Alexis ou le Traité du Vain Combat,* 1929; *La Nouvelle Eurydice,* 1931; *La Mort conduit l'Attelage,* 1934; *Denier du Rêve,* 1934, revised version, 1971; *Nouvelles Orientales,* 1938; *Le Coup de Grâce,* 1939 (*Coup de Grace*); *Mémoires d'Hadrien,* 1951 (*Hadrian's Memoirs*); *L'Oeuvre au Noir,* 1968.

ESSAYS: *Pindare,* 1932; *Les Songes et les Sorts,* 1938; *Sous Bénéfice d'Inventaire,* 1962.

PLAYS: *Electre ou la Chute des Masques,* 1954; *Le Mystère d'Alceste et Qui n'a pas son Minotaure?,* 1963.

POEMS: *Feux,* 1936; *Les Charités d'Alcippe,* 1956.

Marguerite Yourcenar was born in Brussels, Belgium, on June 8, 1903. Her parents were French citizens. She was the daughter of Michel de Crayencour, a distinguished Latinist and bibliophile; Yourcenar, the pseudonym under which she writes, is an anagram of the family name. Her mother, Fernande de Cartier de Marchienne, died a few days after Marguerite was born, and she was brought up by her father. From him she acquired a love of scholarship and an interest in the ancient world. Privately educated, she began learning Latin and Greek by the time she was eight; these studies were continued in conjunction with French and English, and she became an accomplished classicist. She has written a number of novels, plays, essays, poems, and scholarly articles; she has also translated a number of works from English to French. A lecturer at various American and European universities since 1940, she has become a naturalized American citizen and now lives on a small island off the New England coast. She received a Litt. D. from Smith College in 1961.

Her principal work, and that for which she is best known, is *Hadrian's Memoirs,* a brilliant and entirely credible reconstruction of a man and his time. She has imagined Hadrian's thought processes so skillfully, viewed a civilization and a time so sharply through his eyes, and tied her creation so carefully to all the extant historical evidence concerning both, that it becomes extremely difficult for the reader to remember that this is a novel and a work of the imagination. Hadrian's mind and character are developed fully in a noble and austere prose that is entirely in keeping with him. The book contains no false notes; it is a remarkable tour-de-force, and has been highly acclaimed. It won its author the Prix Femina Vacaresco in 1952.

The high quality of Miss Yourcenar's writing has brought other awards. She received the Page One Award of the Newspaper Guild, New York, in 1955; her essay *Sous Bénéfice d'Inventaire* and her other work brought her the Prix Combat in

1963. Her novel, *L'Oeuvre au Noir,* was awarded the Prix Femina in 1968. The latter work is a powerful and unusually vivid evocation of sixteenth century Flanders and of the Renaissance, as they are seen through the eyes of one of that period's "universal men." He is an adventurer, a poet, a man of the arts and sciences: philosopher, alchemist and physician. The high intellectual content thus infused into the novel gives it added dimension.

Miss Yourcenar has been more fortunate in the translations of her work than has been the case with many authors; she and her translator have collaborated and the result is an unimpaired transmission conforming entirely to the author's wishes.

BIBLIOGRAPHICAL REFERENCES: For criticism see Jean Blot, *Marguerite Yourcenar,* 1971; P. de Boisdeffre, *Une Histoire vivante de la litterature d'aujourd'hui,* 1968; and Jean Blot, "Marguerite Yourcenar, *L'oeuvre au noir,*" *Nouvelle Revue Française,* XVI (November, 1968), 659–663.

For a review of *Hadrian's Memoirs* see Frank N. Magill, *Masterplots:* Comprehensive Library Edition, 1968, 1900–1902.

ISRAEL ZANGWILL

Born: London, England
Date: February 14, 1864

Died: Midhurst, Sussex, England
Date: August 1, 1926

Principal Works

NOVELS: *Children of the Ghetto*, 1892; *Merely Mary Ann*, 1893; *The King of the Schnorrers*, 1894; *The Master*, 1895; *The Mantle of Elijah*, 1900.

SHORT STORIES: *Ghetto Tragedies*, 1893.

PLAYS: *Children of the Ghetto*, 1899; *Merely Mary Ann*, 1903; *The Melting Pot*, 1908.

ESSAYS: *Dreamers of the Ghetto*, 1898.

Israel Zangwill, born in London on February 14, 1864, was one of the outstanding Jewish authors and leaders of his time. His family, Russian Jews, had fled Russia and settled in England before his birth. A graduate of the Jews' Free School in London, he remained at the school as a teacher in order to finance his studies at London University, which he attended at the same time he was teaching. Despite the disadvantage of this dual program, Zangwill was graduated from the university with highest honors. After graduation he left teaching for a career in journalism. He founded and edited *Ariel, The London Puck*, and also wrote for various other London periodicals. His critical fame began with the publication of *Children of the Ghetto: A Study of a Peculiar People*, the first of his novels of Jewish life. At the time the novel attracted considerable attention largely because of its subject matter, and Zangwill has been credited with the prevention of anti-Jewish legislation by Parliament through its publication. Other novels about Jewish people followed, including *The Last of the Schnorrers, The Master*, and *The Mantle*. Another work, *Dreamers of the Ghetto*, was a series of essays on such notable Jewish thinkers and leaders as Spinoza, Heine, and Disraeli.

Although he won fame and will probably be remembered as a novelist interpreting Jews and Jewish life, Zangwill wished to excel as a dramatist rather than as a writer of fiction; some of his most popular plays were dramatizations of novels which had been published earlier, such as *Merely Mary Ann*, his most popular comedy, and *Children of the Ghetto*. Zangwill's plays were produced in Jewish communities everywhere, in both Yiddish and English, and he tried for more than a decade to be the great dramatist of the Yiddish theater. Later critics have not been kind to his plays, and even the dramatist admitted that they were less successful artistically than they were popular.

In addition to being a writer, Zangwill was an influential Jewish leader and a popular lecturer whose work in the cause of modern Zionism was of considerable historical importance. He died in Sussex on August 1, 1926.

BIBLIOGRAPHICAL REFERENCES: The pioneer critical biography is Joseph Leftwich, *Israel Zangwill*, 1957. A briefer study appeared in Arthur St. John Adcock, *Gods of Modern Grub Street*, 1928. See also Maurice Wohlgelernter, *Israel Zangwill: A Study*, 1964.

STEFAN ŻEROMSKI

Born: Near Kielce, Poland
Date: November 14, 1864

Died: Warsaw, Poland
Date: November 20, 1925

Principal Works

NOVELS: *Ludzie Bezdomni*, 1900 (*The Homeless*); *Popioly*, 1904 (*Ashes*); *Wierna rzeka*, 1912 (*The Faithful River*); *Wiatr od morza*, 1922 (*The Wind from the Sea*); *Puszcza jodlowa*, 1925 (*The Fir Forest*).
PLAYS: *Róża*, 1909; *Uciekla mi przepióreczka*, 1924 (*My Little Quail Has Fled*).

Stefan Żeromski was born near Kielce in Russian Poland, November 14, 1864, of an impoverished noble family. Throughout his life he chafed under this Tsarist domination, and frequently his short stories take as their subject the resistance of Polish secret organizations. Żeromski himself was even more directly involved. In 1905, during the revolt against Russia, he was imprisoned; later he went into semi-voluntary exile in France and Austrian Galicia, where he remained until the end of World War I.

Żeromski wrote plays and poetry, but his claim to greatness comes out of his novels. Most famous of these is *Ashes*, which has been called the *War and Peace* of Poland. Although his great lyrical descriptive vein is not so evident in this work as it is in *The Wind from the Sea*, the novel possesses scope and richness of characterization to make it an authentic masterpiece.

There is a dark pessimism to Żeromski's writing which is characteristic of the Polish positivist school. Perhaps it was this quality as well as his extreme nationalism that kept him from winning the Nobel Prize. During his career he contributed many characters to the Polish national consciousness, and for that he was honored by his countrymen. He died in Warsaw on November 20, 1925.

BIBLIOGRAPHICAL REFERENCES: A good introduction to the work of Żeromski is W. Borowy, "Żeromski," *Slavonic Review*, XIV (1936), 403–416. See also Z. L. Zaleski, "Etienne Żeromski," in *Attitudes et destinées*, 1932; and Jan Lechoń, "Stefan Żeromski," *Harvard Slavic Studies*, II (1954), 323–342.

ÉMILE ZOLA

Born: Paris, France
Date: April 2, 1840

Died: Paris
Date: September 29, 1902

PRINCIPAL WORKS

NOVELS: *Thérèse Raquin,* 1867; *Madeleine Férat,* 1868; *La Fortune des Rougons,* 1871 (*The Rougon Family*); *La Curée,* 1872; *La Ventre de Paris,* 1873; *La Conquête de Plassans,* 1874; *La Faute de l'abbé Mouret,* 1875 (*The Abbe Mouret's Transgression*); *Son excellence Eugène Rougon,* 1876; *L'Assommoir,* 1877 (*Drink*); *Une Page d'amour,* 1878; *Nana,* 1880; *Pot-Bouille,* 1882; *Au bonheur des dames,* 1883; *La Joie de vivre,* 1884; *Germinal,* 1885; *L'Œuvre,* 1886 (*Labor*); *La Terre,* 1887 (*Earth*); *Le Rêve,* 1888; *La Bête humaine,* 1890; *L'Argent,* 1891; *La Débâcle,* 1892; *Le Docteur Pascal,* 1893; *Lourdes,* 1894; *Rome,* 1896; *Paris,* 1898.

CRITICAL STUDIES: *Le Roman expérimental,* 1880 (*The Experimental Novel*); *Les Romanciers naturalistes,* 1881.

TRACT: *J'accuse,* 1898 (*I Accuse*).

Probably the most important and certainly the most controversial of the French novelists of the second half of the nineteenth century was Émile Zola. Born in Paris, April 2, 1840, the son of an engineer of mixed Greek and Italian ancestry who died when his son was only seven, Zola was educated at Aix and returned to Paris in 1858 to start his career as a writer. He began as a critic, then changed, in 1867, to the writing of novels. In 1871 he published *The Rougon Family,* the first volume of twenty in a series, called the "Rougon-Macquart Novels," which was to deal with the history of a family under the Second Empire. The first of these novels attracted little attention; it was *Drink,* a merciless study of the effects of alcohol that placed Zola among the foremost French writers of a brilliant literary period.

In the Rougon-Macquart series it was Zola's intention to study, with scientific precision and detachment, the fortunes of the various branches of a typical French family of his time, showing, in the vast and complicated web of relationships thus created, how the members of the family were affected by their combined heredity and environment. This approach was a reaction against the romanticism of the generation of Hugo and the elder Dumas and meant an advance beyond anything that realism had as yet accomplished in fiction. The explanation of his method was set forth in his essay *The Experimental Novel.* To the literary school he thus established has been given the name of naturalism.

The naturalists claimed that they descended from Stendhal, through Balzac and Flaubert, all of whom minutely dissected the personality of the individual and the society in which he found himself, thus giving a realistic picture of the contemporary world as it actually is. The naturalists, however, went considerably further. Literature, according to them, must be scientific in its approach, not imaginative; and in this attitude they were echoing the mechanistic statements of mid-nineteenth century science. Man, according to this point of view, is merely an animal among other animals, the product of his heredity and environment which can be studied almost as in a laboratory and his behavior then predicted. When transferred to literature, this theory means, as the naturalists contended, that the novelist should invent nothing; he should observe facts and collect data as the scientist does. If the observations have been complete, if the facts are all gathered, then the behavior and even the final end of the individual can be predicted with scientific accuracy. The plot of the novel will be as inevitable as the solution to a problem in mathematics.

The scientific spirit in which Zola approached his gigantic task is shown by his submitting to his publisher a detailed outline of ten of the projected novels. Further, the sub-title of the series, "The natural and social history of a family under the Second Empire," gives the impression that he was studying his characters as an entomologist might study a colony of ants. He was astonishingly painstaking in preparing his material; if he wished to introduce some minor characters engaged in a particular trade, he was capable of spending weeks at the task of mastering the technical jargon peculiar to that trade. He was endlessly taking notes so that his details might be correct. It is not surprising that it took him twenty-five years to complete the series.

Although Zola tried to include all strata of society, the volumes by which he is best known deal with the lower— at times the lowest—classes. It is in this picture of the brutalized, almost animalistic existence of the poor that his uncompromising realism was strongest. The details aroused protest even in France; in England there was a cry of outrage from the few readers who became familiar with his work. Tennyson's lines will be remembered: "Feed the budding rose of boyhood with the drainage of your sewer." The dose was too strong for the general Anglo-Saxon reader of that day.

In the course of studying, under the microscope, the fortunes of a particular family, Zola also gave an analysis of the whole world of the Second Empire, a glittering, ornate façade with very little back of it. The hollowness of this society is best shown in *Nana,* where we are given a picture of the corruption of Paris even among the rich. Nana, risen from the position of a simple prostitute to that of a *grande cocotte,* literally devours men; there is no amount of money too great to be spent on her. She is the epitome of the vast luxury and vice of Paris where men ruin themselves for a worthless harlot. The novel ends with the terrible irony of the dead Nana, a loathsome mass of disease, abandoned by everyone, while outside in the streets the crowds are shouting "To Berlin!"; the scene is a prelude to the downfall that is to follow.

Near the end of his life Zola became involved in a cause which brought him an international recognition far beyond his fame as an author: the Dreyfus case that split France at that time. In 1898, having become convinced that Dreyfus was the innocent victim of a plot, Zola published his famous article *I Accuse,* in which he attacked the General Staff and French officialdom for seeking to persecute Dreyfus. He was tried twice for libel and had to flee to England, returning to Paris only after a general amnesty had been proclaimed.

Although Zola's scientific conception of literature is outmoded, his influence on the modern novel cannot be overemphasized. It was his work, along with that of his French imitators, that helped to shatter Victorian reticence in English literature; and, while some lamentable lapses of taste resulted, novelists were free to deal truthfully with their subjects. Dreiser's *An American Tragedy* is an example of Zola's influence on American fiction.

He died of accidental asphyxiation at his home in Paris on September 29, 1902.

BIBLIOGRAPHICAL REFERENCES: The fullest study of Zola in English is E. A. Vizetelly's rather eulogistic *Émile Zola, Novelist and Reformer*, 1904. More balanced estimates are given in R. H. Sherard, *Émile Zola: A Biographical and Critical Study*, 1903; Matthew Josephson, *Zola and His Time*, 1929; Martin Kanes, *Zola's La Bête machine: A Study in Literary Creation*, 1962; Angus Wilson, *Emile Zola: An Introductory Study of His Novels*, 1965. See also F. Brunetière, *Le Roman Naturaliste*, 1883; and Henri Barbusse, *Zola*, 1932 (English translation, 1933). An account of Zola's activities in connection with the Dreyfus case is given in *Le Procès Zola*, 2 vols., 1898.

JOSÉ ZORRILLA Y MORAL

Born: Valladolid, Spain
Date: February 21, 1817

Died: Madrid, Spain
Date: January 23, 1893

Principal Work

play: *Don Juan Tenorio*, 1844.

José Zorrilla y Moral, called the "spoiled darling of Spanish Romanticism," is its representative not only in his writing, but in his life. Born in Valladolid, February 21, 1817, he was lured, in spite of parental opposition, from the study of law by his love for poetry. Marriage to a woman somewhat older than he, against the wishes of his stern father, widened the breach, and as a bohemian, he lived in frequent poverty. Yet he was able to visit France in 1846 to meet the leading poets of Paris and later to travel to Mexico at the request of Emperor Maximilian to direct the National Theater. He lived in Mexico from 1855 until 1866.

He sprang into fame in 1837, when as a gaunt youth he leaped into the grave of the suicide Larra and read his emotional verses about the loneliness of a poet and the sacredness of his mission. This act initiated fifteen years of literary production. He became a member of the Royal Academy in 1848. Lyrical and dramatic poetry with themes of mystery, melancholy, and religion, against a background of wild nature, characterized him. Old legends provided him with themes, and he wrapped himself in the splendor of his country's past.

As a playwright, Zorrilla was author of about twenty original dramas, all written with speed and facility and many patterned on the cape-and-sword dramas of the Golden Age. His mastery of many verse forms established him as one of Spain's leading poets. *Don Juan Tenorio* brought him his highest fame, though he called it "the greatest nonsense ever written." In spite of its exaggerations, melodramatic improbability, and technical flaws, the drama expresses the spirit of Spain's Golden Age and is usually performed throughout the Spanish-speaking world on November 1. A good performance of it is an artistic delight. Audiences like to believe that the play, outwardly a melodramatic representation of amorous intrigues, dramatizes fundamental eternal truths, with the characters personifying the inner duality of earthy and spiritual elements inherent in human nature. Zorrilla died in Madrid, January 23, 1893.

BIBLIOGRAPHICAL REFERENCES: For criticism of Zorrilla in English see F. C. Tarr, *Romanticism in Spain*, 1939; E. A. Peers, *History of the Romantic Movement in Spain*, 1940; William Mills, *Don Juan Tenorio, Introduction, Notes, Appendixes*, 1966; in Spanish, José Zorrilla's *Recuerdos del tiempo viejo*, 1880–1882, an interesting but unreliable account; N. Alonso Cortés, *Zorrilla, su vida y sus obras*; 3 vols., 1916-1920; and G. Díaz Plaja, *Introducción al estudio del romanticism español*, 1942 (2nd ed.).

ARNOLD ZWEIG

Born: Gross-Glogau, Prussia
Date: November 10, 1887

Died: East Berlin, Germany
Date: November 26, 1968

Principal Works

NOVELS: *Novellen um Claudia*, 1912 (*Claudia*); *Der Streit um den Sergeanten Grischa*, 1927 (*The Case of Sergeant Grischa*); *Junge Frau von 1914*, 1931; (*Young Woman of 1914*); *De Vriendt kehrt heim*, 1932 (*De Vriendt Goes Home*); *Erziehung vor Verdun*, 1935 (*Education before Verdun*); *Einsetzung eines Königs*, 1937 (*The Crowning of a King*); *Das Beil von Wandsbek*, 1946 (*The Axe of Wandsbek*); *Die Zeit ist reif*, 1957 (*The Time is Ripe*).

SHORT STORIES: *Geschichtenbuch*, 1916; *Spielzeug der Zeit*, 1933 (*Playthings of Time*); *Stufen*, 1949.

PLAYS: *Abigail und Nebel*, 1913; *Ritualmord in Ungarn*, 1914; *Die Lucilla*, 1919; *Papiergeld Brennt*, 1920; *Das Spiel vom Segeanten Grischa*, 1921; *Die Umkehr*, 1927.

ESSAYS: *Juden auf der deutschen Bühne*, 1928; *Bilanz der deutschen Judenheit*, 1934 (*Insulted and Exiled*); *Literatur und Theater*, 1959.

The author of *The Case of Sergeant Grischa*, one of the greatest war novels ever written, was born into a Jewish middle-class family at Gross-Glogau, Prussia, on November 10, 1887. His father was Adolf Zweig, a saddler and remover, and his mother was Bianca von Spandow. He was educated at the technical school in Kattowitz, Upper Silesia, and then at several German universities, including schools at Breslau, Munich, Berlin, Göttingen, Rostock, and Tubingen, where he studied philosophy and languages and developed an interest in psychology, history, and the arts.

Arnold Zweig had planned to be a teacher, but during the course of his education he began to devote a considerable amount of time to writing; his earliest short stories date from 1909. His first novel, actually a series of episodes unified by a central character, Claudia, appeared in 1912. Traces of his careful, ironic style showed in that early work, an experimental book in which he portrayed the sufferings and growth of a sensitive, upper-class girl as she strives, while married to a shy professor, to free herself from her inhibitions and release her natural forces. Zweig's interest in the psychology of the individual continued to govern most of his work in the novel and drama.

During World War I he served as a private in a labor battalion in France and Serbia, and from 1917 to the armistice worked in the press section of Ober-Ost. He had already attracted some attention with his short stories and plays. *Abigail and Nebel* was presented in 1913, and *Ritualmord in Ungarn*, written in 1914, was produced seven years later as *Die Sendung Semaels* by Max Reinhardt in Berlin. After a successful tour in Germany and Austria, the play received the Kleist Prize in 1915.

After the war Zweig lived in Bavaria to recover his strength. A play, *Das Spiel vom Sergeanten Grischa*, prepared the way for his war novel, *The Case of Sergeant Grischa*, which appeared after the Hitler *Putsch* of 1923 compelled him to leave his home in

Starnberg. The novel is a powerful story about a Russian sergeant who fell victim to the power of the Prussian war machine. As a study of war and the individual, the book ranks as Zweig's best and has won a place as one of the outstanding war novels in modern literature. It demonstrated Zweig's progress from a concern with the problems of young intellectuals to an absorption in the inner lives of persons confronting situations in which their entire systems of values are upset.

Zweig lived in Berlin until he was forced to leave by the Nazis in 1933. He traveled across Europe and settled in Palestine, where he became closely identified with the Zionist movement. At the time he was suffering from a serious eye disease which forced him to dictate his books, including *Education before Verdun*, the manuscript of which was destroyed when he left Berlin. Many of Zweig's essays and some of his novels and plays show his concern for the Zionist cause; *De Vriendt Goes Home* has its setting in Palestine and centers about the Jewish problem.

After 1948, Zweig lived in East Berlin, where he won prizes and other honors from the Communist government. He served as president of the East German Academy of Letters.

BIBLIOGRAPHICAL REFERENCES: *The Letters of Sigmund Freud and Arnold Zweig* were edited by Ernst Freud, 1970. The work of Arnold Zweig is discussed in W. K. Pfeiler, *War and the German Mind*, 1941. See also Werner Mahrholz, *Deutsche Literatur der Gergenwart,* 1930. A brief, specialized study is Solomon Fishman, "The War Novels of Arnold Zweig," *Sewanee Review*, XLIX (1941), 433–451. See further Lothar Kahn, "Arnold Zweig: From Zionism to Marxism," *Mirrors of the Jewish Mind*, 1968, 194–209; and *ibid.*, "The Two Worlds of Arnold Zweig," *Chicago Jewish Forum*, XIX (1960), 144–151.

AUTHOR INDEX

AUTHOR INDEX

Abélard, Pierre, 1
About, Edmond François, 2
Adamov, Arthur, 3
Adams, Henry, 5
Adams, John, 7
Addison, Joseph, 11
AE, 14
Aeschylus, 16
Aesop, 19
Agee, James (Rufus), 20
Aiken, Conrad Potter, 22
Ainsworth, William Harrison, 24
Alain-Fournier, 26
Alarcón, Juan Ruiz de
 see Ruiz de Alarcón, Juan
Alarcón, Pedro Antonio de, 27
Albee, Edward, 29
Alcayaga, Lucila Godoy
 see Mistral, Gabriela
Alcott, Louisa May, 32
Aldington, Richard, 34
Aldrich, Thomas Bailey, 36
Alegría, Ciro, 38
Alemán, Mateo, 39
Alighieri, Dante
 see Dante Alighieri
Allen, Hervey, 41
Altamirano, Ignacio Manuel, 43
Amado, Jorge, 45
Ambrogini, Angelo
 see Politian
Amicis, Edmondo de, 46
Amis, Kingsley, 48
Ammers-Küller, Johanna van, 50
Andersen, Hans Christian, 52
Andersen, Nexö, Martin
 see Nexö, Martin Andersen
Anderson, Maxwell, 55
Anderson, Sherwood, 57
Andreyev, Leonid, 60
Andrić, Ivo, 62
Annunzio, Gabriele D'
 see D'Annunzio, Gabriele
Anouilh, Jean, 65
Apollinaire, Guillaume, 67
Apuleius, Lucius, 69
Aquinas, Thomas, 71
Aretino, Pietro, 73
Arihara no Narihira, 75
Aristo, Ludovico, 76
Aristophanes, 78
Aristotle, 81
Arnold, Matthew, 83

Artsybashev, Mikhail, 86
Asch, Sholem, 87
Assís, Joaquim Maria Machado de
 see Machado de Assís, Joaquim Maria
Asturias, Miguel Angel, 89
Aubrey, John, 91
Auden, W. H., 93
Aue, Hartmann von
 see Hartmann, von Aue
Augustine, St., 95
Augustinus, Aurelius
 see Augustine, St.
Aurelius, Marcus
 see Marcus Aurelius
Austen, Jane, 97
Azuela, Mariano, 100

Bacchelli, Riccardo, 101
Bacon, Sir Francis, 103
Baldwin, James, 106
Bale, John, 108
Balzac, Honoré de, 109
Barbusse, Henri, 113
Barclay, John, 115
Barham, Richard Harris
 see Ingoldsby, Thomas
Barker, George, 116
Baroja y Nessi, Pío, 118
Barrie, Sir James Matthew, 120
Barrios, Eduardo, 123
Barth, John, 125
Bashô, Matsuo, 127
Basoalto, Neftalí Ricardo Reyes y
 see Neruda, Pablo
Baudelaire, Charles, 129
Baum, Vicki, 131
Beach, Rex, 132
Beard, Charles and Mary, 133
Beauchamp, Kathleen Mansfield
 see Mansfield, Katherine
Beaumarchais, Pierre Augustin Caron de, 135
Beaumont, Francis and John Fletcher, 137
Beckett, Samuel, 141
Beckford, William, 143
Beddoes, Thomas Lovell, 145
Beerbohm, Sir Max, 147
Behn, Aphra, 149
Bellamann, Henry, 151
Bellamy, Edward, 152
Bellay, Joachim Du, 154
Belloc, Hilaire, 156
Bellow, Saul, 158
Benavente y Martínez, Jacinto, 160

I

AUTHOR INDEX

Benét, Stephen Vincent, 162
Bennett, Arnold, 164
Berdyaev, Nicholas, 167
Bergson, Henri, 169
Berkeley, George, 171
Bernanos, Georges, 173
Berryman, John, 175
Beyle, Marie Henri
 see Stendhal
Bierce, Ambrose, 177
Bird, Robert Montgomery, 179
Björnson, Björnstjerne, 180
Blackmore, R. D., 183
Blair, Eric Hugh
 see Orwell, George
Blake, William, 185
Blasco Ibáñez, Vicente, 188
Blixen-Finecke, Baroness Karen
 see Dinesen, Isak
Blok, Aleksandr, 190
Blunden, Edmund Charles, 192
Boas, Franz, 193
Boccaccio, Giovanni, 195
Boethius, Anicius Manlius Severinus, 197
Boiardo, Matteo Maria, 198
Boileau-Despréaux, Nicolas, 199
Bojer, Johan, 201
Booth, Philip, 203
Borges, Jorge Luis, 204
Borrow, George Henry, 209
Boswell, James, 211
Bourget, Paul, 214
Bowen, Elizabeth, 216
Bowers, Claude G., 218
Boyd, James, 219
Brackenridge, Hugh Henry, 220
Bradford, Gamaliel, 221
Bradford, William, 223
Braine, John, 225
Brecht, Bertolt, 227
Breton, André, 229
Breton, Nicholas, 231
Broch, Hermann, 232
Brome, Richard, 234
Bromfield, Louis, 235
Brontë, Anne
 see Brontës, The
Brontë, Charlotte
 see Brontës, The
Brontë, Emily (Jane)
 see Brontës, The
Brontës, The 237
Brooke, Henry, 241
Brooke, Rupert, 242
Brooks, Gwendolyn, 244
Brooks, Van Wyck, 246
Brown, Charles Brockden, 248
Brown, George Douglas
 see Douglas, George
Browne, Sir Thomas, 250
Browning, Elizabeth Barrett, 252
Browning, Robert, 254
Bryant, William Cullen, 257
Bryce, James Viscount, 260

Buchan, John, 261
Büchner, Georg, 263
Buck, Pearl S., 265
Bullen, Frank Thomas, 268
Bulwer-Lytton, Edward George Earle, 269
Bunin, Ivan Alexeyevich, 272
Bunyan, John, 274
Buonarroti, Michelangelo, 277
Burke, Edmund, 279
Burney, Fanny, 281
Burns, Robert, 283
Burton, Robert, 286
Butler, Samuel, 288
Butler, Samuel, 289
Byrne, Donn, 291
Byron, Lord, George Gordon, 293

Cabell, James Branch, 296
Cable, George Washington, 299
Caesar, 301
Caesar, Gaius Julius
 see Caesar
Cain, James M., 303
Calderón, de la Barca, Pedro, 305
Caldwell, Erskine, 308
Camoëns, Luis de, 310
Campion, Thomas, 312
Camus, Albert, 314
Čapek, Karel, 316
Carducci, Giosuè, 317
Carew, Thomas, 319
Carleton, William, 321
Carlyle, Thomas, 322
Carroll, Lewis, 325
Cary, Joyce, 328
Casanova, 330
Casanova de Seingalt, Giovanni Jacopo
 see Casanova
Castiglione, Baldassare, 332
Cather, Willa, 334
Catullus, 338
Catullus, Gaius Valerius
 see Catullus
Cavafy, Constantine P., 339
Cavendish, George, 340
Cela, Camilo José, 341
Céline, Louis-Ferdinand, 343
Cellini, Benvenuto, 345
Cervantes, 347
Cervantes, Saavedra, Miguel de
 see Cervantes
Challans, Mary
 see Renault, Mary
Chapman, George, 351
Chateaubriand, François René de, 353
Chatterton, Thomas, 355
Chaucer, Geoffrey, 357
Cheever, John, 360
Chekhov, Anton, 361
Chesnutt, Charles Waddell, 364
Chesterfield, Lord, Philip Dormer Stanhope, 365
Chesterton, G. K., 366
Chikamatsu Monzaemon, 368

AUTHOR INDEX

Choderlos de Laclos, Pierre
  see Laclos, Pierre Choderlos de
Chrétien de Troyes, 370
Churchill, Winston, 371
Churchill, Sir Winston, 373
Cibber, Colley, 376
Cicero, 378
Cicero, Marcus Tullius
  see Cicero
Clare, John, 380
Clarendon, Earl of
  see Hyde, Edward
Clark, Walter Van Tilburg, 382
Clark, William
  see Lewis, Meriwether and William Clark
Claudel, Paul, 384
Clemens, Samuel Langhorne
  see Twain, Mark
Cocteau, Jean, 386
Coleridge, Samuel Taylor, 388
Colette, 391
Collins, Wilkie, 393
Collins, William, 396
Compton-Burnett, Ivy, 398
Congreve, William, 400
Connell, Evan S., Jr., 403
Conrad, Joseph, 405
Conscience, Hendrik, 411
Constant, Benjamin, 412
Cooke, John Esten, 413
Cooper, James Fenimore, 415
Coppard, A(lfred) E(dgar), 418
Corbière, Édouard Joachim
  see Corbière, Tristan
Corbière, Tristan, 420
Corneille, Pierre, 422
Corvo, Baron, 424
Coster, Charles De, 426
Couperus, Louis, 427
Coward, Sir Noel, 429
Cowley, Abraham, 431
Cowper, William, 432
Cozzens, James Gould, 434
Crabbe, George, 436
Craik, Dinah Maria Mulock
  see Mulock, Dinah Maria
Crane, Hart, 437
Crane, Stephen, 439
Crashaw, Richard, 442
Crayencour, Marguerite de
  see Yourcenar, Marguerite
Crébillon, Prosper Jolyot de, 444
Crèvecoeur, Michel-Guillaume Jean de, 445
Croce, Benedetto, 446
Crockett, David, 448
Cruz, Sor Juana Inés de La, 449
Cummings, E. E., 451

Dana, Richard Henry, 453
Daniel, Samuel, 454
D'Annunzio, Gabriele, 456
Dante, Alighieri, 458
Darío, Rubén, 462
Darwin, Charles, 464

Daudet, Alphonse, 466
Davenant, Sir William, 468
da Vinci, Leonardo
  see Leonardo da Vinci
Davis, H. L., 469
Day, Clarence, 471
Day, Thomas, 473
de Amicis, Edmondo
  see Amicis, Edmondo de
De Coster, Charles
  see Coster, Charles De
Defoe, Daniel, 475
De Forest, John William, 478
Dekker, Eduard Douwes
  see Multatuli
Dekker, Thomas, 480
de la Mare, Walter, 482
de la Roche, Mazo, 484
Deledda, Grazia, 485
Deloney, Thomas, 487
De Morgan, William, 488
Demosthenes, 490
De Quincey, Thomas, 492
Descartes, René, 494
Destouches, Louis Fuch
  see Céline, Louis-Ferdinand
Dickens, Charles, 496
Dickey, James, 499
Dickinson, Emily, 501
Diderot, Denis, 504
Dinesen, Isak, 506
Disraeli, Benjamin, 508
Dodgson, Charles Lutwidge
  see Carroll, Lewis
Donn-Byrne, Brian Oswald
  see Byrne, Donn
Donne, John, 510
Dos Passos, John, 514
Dostoevski, Fyodor Mikhailovich, 516
Doughty, Charles M., 520
Douglas, George, 522
Douglas, Lloyd C., 523
Douglas, Norman, 524
Dowson, Ernest (Christopher), 526
Doyle, Sir Arthur Conan, 528
Drayton, Michael, 530
Dreiser, Theodore, 531
Dryden, John, 534
Dudevant, Amandine Lucile Aurore Dupin
  see Sand, George
du Gard, Roger Martin
  see Martin du Gard, Roger
Duggan, Alfred, 537
Dumas, Alexandre, *père*, 539
Dumas, Alexandre, *fils*, 542
du Maurier, Daphne, 543
du Maurier, George, 544
Dumitriu, Petru, 546
Dupin, Amandine Lucile Aurore
  see Sand, George
Durrell, Lawrence, 548
Duun Olav, 551

Eberhart, Richard, 552

III

AUTHOR INDEX

Echegaray y Eizaguirre, José, 554
Eckermann, Johann Peter, 556
Edgeworth, Maria, 558
Edmonds, Walter D., 560
Edwards, Jonathan, 562
Egan, Pierce, 564
Eggleston, Edward, 566
Eichendorff, Joseph von, 568
Eliot, George, 570
Eliot, T. S., 573
Ellison, Ralph (Waldo), 576
Emerson, Ralph Waldo, 578
Erasmus, Desiderius, 582
Eschenbach, Wolfram von
 see Wolfram von Eschenbach
Esenin, Sergei, 584
Etherege, Sir George, 586
Euripides, 588
Evans, Marian or Mary Ann
 see Eliot, George
Evelyn, John, 591

Fairfield, Cicily Isabel
 see West, Rebecca
Fanu, Joseph Sheridan Le
 see Le Fanu, Joseph Sheridan
Farquhar, George, 593
Farrell, James T., 595
Faulkner, William, 597
Ferber, Edna, 601
Fernández de Lizardi, José Joaquín, 603
Ferreira, António, 604
Feuchtwanger, Lion, 605
Fielding, Henry, 607
Fisher, Vardis, 610
Fitzgerald, Edward, 612
Fitzgerald, F. Scott, 613
Flaccus, Quintus Horatius
 see Horace
Flaubert, Gustave, 615
Flecker, James Elroy, 618
Fletcher, John
 see Beaumont, Francis and John Fletcher
Fogazzaro, Antonio, 620
Fontaine, Jean de La
 see La Fontaine, Jean de
Fontane, Theodor, 622
Forbes, Esther, 623
Ford, Ford Madox, 624
Ford, John, 626
Forester, C. S., 627
Forster, E. M., 628
Foqué, Friedrich de La Motte-
 see La Motte-Fouqué, Friedrich de
Fournier, Henri Alain
 see Alain-Fournier
France, Anatole, 630
Franklin, Benjamin, 633
Frazer, Sir James George, 638
Frederic, Harold, 640
Freeman, Douglas Southall, 642
Freneau, Philip, 643
Freud, Sigmund, 645
Freytag, Gustav, 648

Froissart, Jean, 649
Fromentin, Eugène, 650
Frost, Robert, 651
Fry, Christopher, 656
Fuentes, Carlos, 658
Fuller, Thomas, 662

Gaboriau, Émile, 664
Galdós, Benito Pérez
 see Pérez Galdós, Benito
Gallegos, Rómulo, 665
Galsworthy, John, 666
Galt, John, 669
García Lorca, Federico, 671
Garland, Hamlin, 673
Garnett, David, 675
Garrett, George, 677
Gascoigne, George, 679
Gaskell, Mrs. Elizabeth, 682
Gass, William H., 684
Gautier, Théophile, 685
Gay, John, 687
George, Stefan, 689
Gibbon, Edward, 691
Gibbons, Stella, 693
Gide, André, 695
Gilbert, Sir William Schwenck, 698
Giono, Jean, 700
Giraudoux, Jean, 702
Gironella, José María, 704
Gissing, George, 706
Glasgow, Ellen, 708
Godwin, William, 712
Goethe, Johann Wolfgang von, 714
Gogol, Nikolai Vasilyevich, 718
Golding, William, 721
Goldoni, Carlo, 724
Goldsmith, Oliver, 725
Goncharov, Ivan Alexandrovich, 729
Goncourt, Edmond Louis Antoine Huot de
 see Goncourts, The
Goncourt, Jules Alfred Huot de
 see Goncourts, The
Goncourts, The, 731
Gordon, Caroline, 733
Gorky, Maxim, 734
Gottfried von Strassburg, 737
Gourmont, Remy de, 738
Grahame, Kenneth, 740
Granville-Barker, Harley, 742
Grass, Günter, 743
Graves, Robert, 745
Gray, Thomas, 747
Green, Henry, 749
Green, Julian, 751
Greene, Graham, 753
Greene, Robert, 756
Gregory, Lady Augusta, 758
Griffin, Gerald, 760
Grillparzer, Franz, 761
Grimmelshausen, J. J. C. von, 763
Grotius, Hugo, 765
Guillaume de Lorris, 767
Güiraldes, Ricardo, 768

AUTHOR INDEX

Gunnarsson, Gunnar, 769
Guthrie, A. B., Jr., 771
Guzmán, Martin Luis, 772

Hāfiz, 775
Haggard, H. Rider, 776
Hakluyt, Richard, 778
Hale, Edward Everett, 779
Halévy, Ludovic, 780
Hall, Donald, 781
Hall, James Norman
   see Nordoff, Charles and
   James Norman Hall
Hamilton, Alexander, 782
Hammett, Dashiell, 787
Hamsun, Knut, 788
Hardy, Thomas, 791
Harris, Joel Chandler, 794
Harte, Bret, 796
Hartmann von Aue, 798
Hasek, Jaroslav, 799
Hauptmann, Gerhart, 801
Hawkes, John, 803
Hawkins, Sir Anthony Hope
   see Hope, Anthony
Hawthorne, Nathaniel, 806
Haydon, Benjamin Robert, 810
Hazlitt, William, 812
H. D., 814
Hearn, Lafcadio, 815
Hebbel, Friedrich, 817
Heggen, Thomas O., 819
Heidenstam, Verner von, 820
Heine, Heinrich, 821
Heller, Joseph, 824
Hellman, Lillian, 826
Hemingway, Ernest, 827
Hémon, Louis, 830
Henley, William Ernest, 831
Henry, O., 833
Herbert, George, 836
Heredia, José María de, 837
Hergesheimer, Joseph, 839
Herlihy, James Leo, 840
Hernández, José, 841
Herodotus, 842
Herrick, Robert, 844
Hersey, John, 846
Hesiod, 848
Hesse, Hermann, 849
Heyward, DuBose, 851
Heywood, Thomas, 853
Hilda Doolittle
   see H. D.
Hilton, James, 855
Hiraoka, Kimitake
   see Mishima, Yukio
Hobbes, Thomas, 857
Hodgson, Ralph, 858
Hoffmann, Ernst Theodor Amadeus, 860
Hofmannsthal, Hugo von, 861
Hölderlin, Johann Christian Friedrich, 863
Holmes, Oliver Wendell, 865
Homer, 868

Hope, Anthony, 870
Hopkins, Gerard Manley, 872
Horace, 874
Horatius Flaccus, Quintus
   see Horace
Housman, A. E., 876
Howard, Henry, Earl of Surrey, 878
Howe, E. W., 880
Howells, William Dean, 881
Hudson, W. H., 884
Hueffer, Ford Madox
   see Ford, Ford Madox
Hughes, Langston, 886
Hughes, Richard, 888
Hughes, Thomas, 889
Hugo, Victor, 890
Huizinga, Johan, 893
Hume, David, 894
Hunt, Leigh, 896
Hutchinson, A. S. M., 898
Huxley, Aldous, 899
Huxley, Sir Julian, 902
Huxley, Thomas Henry, 904
Huysmans, Charles Marie Georges
   see Huysmans, J(oris)-K(arl)
Huysmans, J(oris)-K(arl), 906
Hyde, Edward, Earl of Clarendon, 908

Ibáñez, Vicente Blasco
   see Blasco Ibáñez, Vicente
Ibara, Saikaku, 910
Ibsen, Henrik, 912
Icaza, Jorge, 916
Ikku, Jippensha
   see Jippensha Ikku
Ingoldsby, Thomas, 917
Ionesco, Eugène, 919
Irving, Washington, 921

Jackson, Charles, 925
Jacobsen, Jens Peter, 926
James, Henry, 927
James, William, 931
Jarrell, Randall, 933
Jay, John, 935
Jean de Meung
   see Guillaume de Lorris and
   Jean de Meung
Jeffers, Robinson, 937
Jefferson, Thomas, 939
Jensen, Johannes V., 943
Jerome, Jerome K., 945
Jewett, Sarah Orne, 946
Jiménez, Juan Ramón, 949
Jippensha, Ikku, 951
Johnson, Samuel, 953
Johnson, Uwe, 957
Johnston, Mary, 959
Jókai, Maurus, 961
Jolyot, Prosper
   see Crébillon, Prosper Jolyot de
Jones, Henry Arthur, 962
Jones, James, 963
Jonson, Ben, 965

AUTHOR INDEX

Joyce, James, 968
Jung, Carl Gustaf, 972
Juvenal, 974
Juvenalis, Decimus Junius
  see Juvenal

Kabaphes, Konstantinos P.
  see Cavafy, Constantine P.
Kafka, Franz, 975
Kalidasa, 977
Kant, Immanuel, 978
Kao Ming
  see Kao Tse-ch'eng
Kao Tse-ch'eng, 980
Kawabata, Yasunari, 981
Kaye-Smith, Sheila, 982
Kazantzakis, Nikos, 984
Keats, John, 986
Keller, Gottfried, 989
Kempis, Thomas à
  see Thomas à Kempis
Kennedy, John Pendleton, 990
Kierkegaard, Sören, 992
Kingsley, Charles, 994
Kingsley, Henry, 996
Kipling, Rudyard, 998
Kleist, Heinrich von, 1001
Knight, Eric, 1003
Koestler, Arthur, 1004
Korzeniowski, Teodor Jósef Konrad Nalecz
  see Conrad, Joseph
Kostrowitsky, Wilhelm Apollinaris de
  see Apollinaire, Guillaume
Kyd, Thomas, 1006
Kyôden, Santô
  see Santô Kyôden

Labrunie, Gérard
  see Nerval, Gérard de
Laclos, Pierre Choderlos de, 1008
La Fayette, Madame Marie de, 1009
La Fontaine, Jean de, 1010
Laforgue, Jules, 1012
Lagerkvist, Pär, 1014
Lagerlöf, Selma, 1016
Lamartine, Alphonse de, 1018
Lamb, Charles, 1020
La Motte-Fouqué, Friedrich de, 1023
Lampedusa, Giuseppe Tomasi di, 1024
Landor, Walter Savage, 1025
Langland, William, 1027
Lanier, Sidney, 1028
Lardner, Ring, 1030
Larkin, Philip, 1032
La Rochefoucauld, François, 1033
Lawrence, D. H., 1035
Lawrence, T. E., 1039
Laxness, Halldór Kiljan, 1041
Layamon, 1043
Le Fanu, Joseph Sheridan, 1045
Léger, Alexis St.-Léger
  see Perse, St.-John
Leonardo da Vinci, 1046
Leopardi, Giacomo, 1049

Lermontov, Mikhail Yurievich, 1051
Le Sage, Alain René, 1053
Lessing, Gotthold Ephraim, 1055
Lever, Charles James, 1057
Lewis, Cecil Day, 1059
Lewis, C. S., 1061
Lewis, Matthew Gregory, 1064
Lewis, Meriwether and William Clark, 1065
Lewis, Sinclair, 1067
Lewis, Wyndham, 1070
Lie, Jonas, 1072
Lincoln, Abraham, 1074
Lindsay, Vachel, 1078
Lins do Rêgo, José, 1080
Livius, Titus
  see Livy
Livy, 1082
Lizardi, José Joaquín Fernández de
  see Fernández de Lizardi, José Joaquín
Llewellyn, Richard, 1083
Lloyd, Richard David Vivian Llewellyn
  see Llewellyn, Richard
Lo Kuan-chung, 1085
Lobeira, Vasco de, 1086
Locke, John, 1087
Lockridge, Ross, Jr., 1089
London, Jack, 1090
Longfellow, Henry Wadsworth, 1092
Longinus, Cassius, 1094
Longstreet, Augustus Baldwin, 1095
Longus, 1096
Lönnrot, Elias, 1097
Lope de Vega
  see Vega, Lope de
Lorca, Federico García
  see García Lorca, Federico
Lorris, Guillaume de
  see Guillaume de Lorris and
    Jean de Meung
Loti, Pierre, 1098
Lovelace, Richard, 1099
Lover, Samuel, 1100
Lowell, James Russell, 1101
Lowell, Robert, 1104
Lowry, Malcolm, 1105
Lucian, 1106
Lucretius, 1107
Lucretius Carus, Titus
  see Lucretius
Lyly, John, 1108
Lytle, Andrew, 1110
Lytton, Edward Lytton Bulwer-
  see Bulwer-Lytton, Edward George Earle

Macaulay, Thomas Babington, 1111
McCoy, Horace, 1113
McCullers, Carson, 1115
McFee, William, 1118
Machado, Antonio, 1120
Machado de Assís, Joaquim Maria, 1122
Machen, Arthur, 1124
Machiavelli, Niccolò, 1126
Mackenzie, Henry, 1128
MacLeish, Archibald, 1129

AUTHOR INDEX

MacNeice, Louis, 1131
Madison, James, 1133
Maeterlinck, Maurice, 1137
Mailer, Norman, 1139
Malamud, Bernard, 1141
Mallarmé, Stéphane, 1143
Mallea, Eduardo, 1145
Malory, Sir Thomas, 1147
Malraux, André, 1149
Mann, Thomas, 1151
Mansfield, Katherine, 1154
Manzoni, Alessandro, 1157
Maran, René, 1159
Marcus Aurelius, 1160
Marie de France, 1161
Marivaux, Pierre de, 1162
Marlowe, Christopher, 1163
Marot, Clément, 1166
Marquand, John Phillips, 1168
Marryat, Frederick, 1171
Marston, John, 1173
Martial, 1175
Martialis, Marcus Valerius,
  see Martial
Martin du Gard, Roger, 1176
Martínez Sierra, Gregorio, 1178
Marvell, Andrew, 1180
Marx, Karl, 1182
Masefield, John, 1185
Massinger, Philip, 1187
Masters, Edgar Lee, 1189
Mather, Cotton, 1191
Matthiessen, Peter, 1193
Maturin, Charles Robert, 1195
Maugham, W. Somerset, 1196
Maupassant, Guy de, 1199
Mauriac, François, 1202
Maurier, Daphne du
  see du Maurier, Daphne
Maurier, George du
  see du Maurier, George
Mayakovsky, Vladimir, 1204
Meleager, 1206
Melville, Herman, 1208
Menander, 1211
Mencken, H. L., 1212
Meredith, George, 1215
Merejkowski, Dmitri, 1218
Mérimée, Prosper, 1220
Meung, Jean de
  see Guillaume de Lorris and
  Jean de Meung
Middleton, Thomas, 1222
Mikszáth, Kálmán, 1224
Mill, John Stuart, 1225
Millay, Edna St. Vincent, 1227
Miller, Arthur, 1229
Miller, Henry, 1231
Milton, John, 1233
Ming, Kao
  see Kao Tse-ch'eng
Mirandola, Pico Della, 1236
Mishima, Yukio, 1238
Mistral, Gabriela, 1240

Mitchell, Margaret, 1242
Mitchell, S. Weir, 1243
Mitford, Mary Russell, 1245
Molière, 1247
Molnar, Ferenc, 1250
Montaigne, Michel Eyquem de, 1252
Montesquieu, Charles de, 1255
Moore, George, 1257
Moore, Marianne, 1259
Moore, Thomas, 1261
Moravia, Alberto, 1263
More, Paul Elmer, 1265
More, Sir Thomas, 1267
Morgan, William De
  see De Morgan, William
Morier, James Justinian, 1269
Mörike, Eduard, 1270
Morris, William, 1272
Morris, Wright, 1274
Motte-Fouqué, Friedrich de la
  see La Motte-Fouqué, Friedrich de
Muir, John, 1276
Mulock, Dinah Maria, 1278
Multatuli, 1280
Mumford, Lewis, 1281
Munro, Hector Hugh
  see Saki
Murasaki Shikibu, Lady, 1283
Murdoch, Iris, 1284
Murger, Henri, 1286
Musset, Alfred de, 1287

Nabokov, Vladimir Vladimirovich, 1289
Narayan, Rasipuram Krishnaswami, 1291
Narihira, Arihara no
  see Arihara no Narihira
Nash, Thomas, 1293
Nekrasov, Nikolai, 1294
Neruda, Pablo, 1296
Nerval, Gérard de, 1298
Newman, John Henry, 1300
Newton, Sir Isaac, 1303
Nexö, Martin Andersen, 1305
Nicolson, Sir Harold George, 1307
Nietzsche, Friedrich Wilhelm, 1309
Nievo, Ippolito, 1312
Nordhoff, Charles and
  James Norman Hall, 1314
Norris, Frank, 1316
Norton, Thomas and Thomas Sackville, 1319

Oates, Joyce Carol, 1321
O'Brien, Kate, 1323
O'Casey, Sean, 1324
O'Connor, Flannery, 1326
Odets, Clifford, 1327
O'Faoláin, Seán, 1328
O'Flaherty, Liam, 1330
O'Hara, John, 1332
Oldenbourg, Zoé, 1334
O'Neill, Eugene, 1336
Ortega y Gasset, José, 1339
Orwell, George, 1341
Osborne, John, 1344

AUTHOR INDEX

Otway, Thomas, 1346
Ouida, 1347
Ovid, 1349
Ovidius Naso, Publius
    see Ovid
Owen, Wilfred, 1351

Page, Thomas Nelson, 1353
Paine, Thomas, 1355
Parkman, Francis, 1357
Parrington, Vernon Louis, 1359
Pascal, Blaise, 1361
Passos, John Dos
    see Dos Passos, John
Pasternak, Boris Leonidovich, 1362
Pater, Walter, 1364
Paton, Alan, 1365
Paz, Octavio, 1366
Peacock, Thomas Love, 1369
Peattie, Donald Culross, 1371
Peele, George, 1373
Péguy, Charles-Pierre, 1375
Pepys, Samuel, 1377
Pereda, José María de, 1380
Pérez Galdós, Benito, 1382
Perse, St.-John, 1384
Peshkov, Aleksei Maksimovich
    see Gorky, Maxim
Petrarch, Francesco, 1386
Petronius, 1388
Petronius Arbiter, Gaius
    see Petronius
Pilnyak, Boris, 1390
Pincherle, Alberto
    see Moravia, Alberto
Pindar, 1392
Pinero, Sir Arthur Wing, 1393
Pinter, Harold, 1395
Pirandello, Luigi, 1397
Plato, 1400
Plautus, 1403
Plautus, Titus Maccius
    see Plautus
Pliny the Younger, 1405
Plutarch, 1407
Poe, Edgar Allen, 1409
Politian, 1412
Polo, Marco, 1413
Pontoppidan, Henrik, 1415
Pope, Alexander, 1417
Poquelin, Jean Baptiste
    see Molière
Porter, Jane, 1419
Porter, Katherine Anne, 1420
Porter, William Sydney
    see Henry, O.
Pound, Ezra, 1423
Powell, Anthony (Dymoke), 1426
Powys, John Cowper, 1428
Powys, Llewelyn, 1430
Powys, T. F., 1432
Prescott, William Hickling, 1434
Prévost, The Abbé, 1435
Price, Reynolds, 1437

Priestley, J. B., 1438
Prior, Matthew, 1440
Prokosch, Frederic, 1442
Propertius, Sextus, 1444
Proust, Marcel, 1446
Purdy, James, 1449
P'u Sung-ling, 1451
Pushkin, Alexander, 1453

Rabelais, François, 1455
Racine, Jean Baptiste, 1458
Radcliffe, Mrs. Ann, 1460
Raleigh, Sir Walter, 1462
Ramée, Marie Louise de la
    see Ouida
Ramuz, Charles-Ferdinand, 1464
Ransom, John Crowe, 1465
Raspe, Rudolph Erich, 1467
Rawlings, Marjorie Kinnan, 1469
Reade, Charles, 1470
Reid, Forrest, 1472
Remark, Erich Paul
    see Remarque, Erich Maria
Remarque, Erich Maria, 1474
Renault, Mary, 1476
Reyes, Alfonso, 1477
Reymont, Ladislas, 1480
Rice, Elmer, 1482
Richards, I. A., 1484
Richardson, Dorothy M., 1486
Richardson, Henry Handel, 1487
Richardson, Samuel, 1488
Richter, Conrad, 1491
Riggs, Lynn, 1494
Rilke, Rainer Maria, 1495
Rimbaud, Arthur, 1498
Roberts, Elizabeth Madox, 1500
Roberts, Kenneth, 1503
Robertson, Ethel Florence Richardson
    see Richardson, Henry Handel
Robertson, Thomas William, 1505
Robinson, Edwin Arlington, 1506
Robinson, Henry Crabb, 1509
Rochefoucauld, François La
    see La Rochefoucauld, François
Roethke, Theodore, 1511
Rojas, Fernando de, 1512
Rolfe, Frederick William
    see Corvo, Baron
Rolland, Romain, 1513
Rölvaag, O. E., 1516
Ronsard, Pierre de, 1518
Rossetti, Christina, 1519
Rossetti, Dante Gabriel, 1521
Rostand, Edmond, 1523
Roth, Henry, 1525
Rousseau, Jean Jacques, 1527
Ruiz de Alarcón, Juan, 1530
Rulfo, Juan, 1531
Ruskin, John, 1533
Russell, George William
    see AE
Russell, W. Clark, 1535
Rydberg, Viktor, 1536

AUTHOR INDEX

Sachs, Hans, 1537
Sackville, Thomas
  see Norton, Thomas and
  Thomas Sackville
Sade, The Marquis de, 1538
Sage, Alain René Le
  see Le Sage, Alain René
St. Augustine
  see Augustine, St.
Sainte-Beauve, Charles Augustin, 1540
Saint-Exupéry, Antoine de, 1542
Saki, 1544
Salinger, J. D., 1546
Salten, Felix, 1548
Salzmann, Siegmund
  see Salten, Felix
Sánchez, Florencio, 1549
Sand, George, 1551
Sandburg, Carl, 1553
Santayana, George, 1556
Santô, Kyôden, 1559
Sappho, 1561
Saroyan, William, 1562
Sartre, Jean-Paul, 1564
Sassoon, Siegfried, 1566
Schiller, Friedrich, 1568
Schopenhauer, Arthur, 1571
Schreiner, Olive, 1573
Scott, Michael, 1574
Scott, Robert F., 1575
Scott, Sir Walter, 1577
Scudéry, Madeleine de, 1580
Seneca, Lucius Annaeus, 1581
Sévigné, Madame de, 1583
Shakespeare, William, 1585
Shams ud-din Mohammed
  see Hâfiz
Shapiro, Karl, 1589
Shaw, Bernard, 1591
Shelley, Mary Wollstonecraft Godwin, 1596
Shelley, Percy Bysshe, 1598
Sheridan, Richard Brinsley, 1601
Sherriff, Robert C., 1604
Sherwood, Robert E., 1605
Shih Nai-an, 1607
Shirley, James, 1608
Sholokhov, Mikhail, 1609
Shorthouse, Joseph Henry, 1611
Shudraka, 1612
Sidney, Sir Philip, 1613
Sienkiewicz, Henryk, 1615
Sierra, Gregorio Martínez
  see Martinez Sierra, Gregorio
Sillanpää, Frans Eemil, 1617
Silone, Ignazio, 1618
Simms, William Gilmore, 1620
Sinclair, May, 1622
Sinclair, Upton, 1624
Singer, Israel Joshua, 1627
Singmaster, Elsie, 1628
Sitwell, Edith, 1631
Skelton, John, 1633
Smart, Christopher, 1635

Smith, Adam, 1637
Smith, Betty, 1639
Smith, Homer W., 1640
Smollett, Tobias, 1642
Snorri Sturluson, 1644
Snow, C. P., 1646
Socrates, 1648
Solzhenitsyn, Aleksandr, 1651
Sophocles, 1653
Southey, Robert, 1656
Spark, Muriel, 1658
Spender, Stephen, 1660
Spenser, Edmund, 1662
Spinoza, Benedictus de, 1665
Staël, Madame de, 1667
Stanhope, Philip Dormer
  see Chesterfield, Lord, Philip Dormer
  Stanhope
Statius, 1668
Statius, Publius Papinius
  see Statius
Steele, Sir Richard, 1669
Steinbeck, John, 1672
Stendhal, 1675
Stephens, James, 1677
Sterne, Laurence, 1679
Stevens, James, 1683
Stevens, Wallace, 1684
Stevenson, Robert Louis, 1687
Still, James, 1690
Stoker, Bram, 1692
Stong, Phil, 1693
Stowe, Harriet Beecher, 1695
Strachey, Lytton, 1697
Strassburg, Gottfried von
  see Gottfried von Strassburg
Strindberg, August, 1699
Strong, L. A. G., 1702
Stuart, Jesse, 1704
Sturluson, Snorri
  see Snorri Sturluson
Styron, William, 1707
Suckling, Sir John, 1709
Suckow, Ruth, 1711
Sudermann, Hermann, 1713
Sue, Eugène, 1715
Suetonius, 1717
Suetonius Tranquillus, Gaius
  see Suetonius
Sumner, William Graham, 1718
Surrey, Earl of
  see Howard, Henry
Surtees, Robert Smith, 1720
Swedenborg, Emanuel, 1723
Swift, Jonathan, 1725
Swinburne, Algernon Charles, 1729
Swinnerton, Frank, 1732
Synge, John Millington, 1734

Tacitus, 1736
Tacitus, Cornelius
  see Tacitus
Taine, Hippolyte, 1737

AUTHOR INDEX

Tarkington, Booth, 1739
Tasso, Torquato, 1741
Tate, Allen, 1743
Taylor, Edward, 1745
Tegnér, Esaias, 1747
Tennyson, Lord Alfred, 1748
Terence, 1751
Thackeray, William Makepeace, 1753
Theocritus, 1756
Thibault, Jacques Anatole
  see France, Anatole
Thomas, Dylan, 1757
Thomas à Kempis, 1760
Thomas Aquinas
  see Aquinas, Thomas
Thompson, Daniel Pierce, 1761
Thompson, Francis, 1762
Thomson, James, 1763
Thoreau, Henry David, 1765
Thucydides, 1768
Thurber, James, 1769
Tocqueville, Alexis de, 1771
Tolkien, John Ronald Reuel, 1773
Tolstoy, Count Leo, 1775
Tomlinson, H. M., 1778
Toomer, Jean, 1780
Torsvan, Traven
  see Traven, B.
Tourgée, Albion Winegar, 1782
Tourneur, Cyril, 1784
Toynbee, Arnold, 1786
Traherne, Thomas, 1788
Traven, B., 1790
Trevelyan, George Macaulay, 1793
Trollope, Anthony, 1795
Trowbridge, John Townsend, 1798
Troyes, Chrétien de
  see Chrétien de Troyes
Turgenev, Ivan, 1799
Turner, Frederick Jackson, 1803
Tutuola, Amos, 1805
Twain, Mark, 1807
Tweedsmuir, Baron
  see Buchan, John

Udall (Woodall), Nicholas, 1811
Unamuno y Jugo, Miguel de, 1813
Undset, Sigrid, 1814
Updike, John, 1816

Valera y Alcalá Galiano, Juan, 1818
Valéry, Paul, 1820
Valmiki, 1822
Vanbrugh, Sir John, 1823
Van Vechten, Carl, 1825
Vaughan, Henry, 1826
Vazov, Ivan, 1828
Veblen, Thorstein, 1829
Vega, Lope de, 1831
Verga, Giovanni, 1834
Vergil, 1836
Vergilius Maro, Publius
  see Vergil

Verlaine, Paul, 1838
Verne, Jules, 1840
Viaud, Louis Marie Julien
  see Loti, Pierre
Vigny, Alfred de, 1842
Villon, François, 1844
Vogau, Boris Andreyevich
  see Pilnyak, Boris
Voltaire, François Marie Arouet de, 1846

Wallace, Lewis, 1849
Wallant, Edward Lewis, 1850
Waller, Edmund, 1851
Walpole, Horace, 1853
Walpole, Sir Hugh, 1855
Walton, Izaak, 1857
Warren, Robert Penn, 1859
Wassermann, Jakob, 1861
Wast, Hugo, 1863
Waugh, Evelyn, 1865
Webb, Mary, 1867
Webb, Walter Prescott, 1869
Webster, John, 1871
Wedekind, Frank, 1872
Wells, H. G., 1873
Welty, Eudora, 1877
Werfel, Franz, 1879
Wescott, Glenway, 1881
Wesker, Arnold, 1883
West, Nathanael, 1884
West, Rebecca, 1886
Westcott, Edward Noyes, 1888
Wharton, Edith, 1889
White, Patrick, 1892
White, T. H., 1894
Whitman, Walt, 1896
Whittier, John Greenleaf, 1900
Whyte-Melville, George J., 1902
Wilbur, Richard, 1904
Wilde, Oscar, 1906
Wilder, Thornton, 1909
Williams, Charles, 1912
Williams, Tennessee, 1915
Williams, William Carlos, 1917
Williamson, Henry, 1920
Wilson, Edmund, 1922
Wister, Owen, 1924
Wither, George, 1926
Wolfe, Thomas, 1928
Wolfram von Eschenbach, 1932
Woolf, Virginia, 1933
Wordsworth, Dorothy, 1937
Wordsworth, William, 1939
Wright, Richard, 1942
Wyatt, Sir Thomas, 1943
Wycherley, William, 1945
Wylie, Elinor, 1947
Wyss, Johann Rudolf, 1950

Xenophon, 1952

Yáñez, Augustín, 1954
Yeats, William Butler, 1957

CYCLOPEDIA OF WORLD AUTHORS: CRITICAL BIOGRAPHIES OF 975 AUTHORS

Biographical Update

Andric, Ivo
Died: Belgrade, Yugosalvia
Date: March 13, 1975

Asturias, Miguel Angel
Died: Madrid, Spain
Date: June 9, 1974

Blunden, Edmund Charles
Died: Sudbury, England
Date: January 20, 1974

Cain, James M.
Died: Hyattsville, Maryland
Date: October 27, 1977

Cheever, John
Died: Ossining, New York
Date: June 18, 1982

Cozzens, James Gould
Died: Stuart, Florida
Date: August 9, 1978

Farrell, James T.
Died: Chicago, Illinois
Date: August 22, 1979

Gordon, Caroline
Died: Cristobal de las Cas, Mexico
Date: April 11, 1981

Green, Henry
Died: London, England
Date: December 13, 1973

Gunnarsson, Gunnar
Died: Reykjavik, Iceland
Date: November 21, 1975

Hughes, Richard
Died: Near Harlech, Wales
Date: April 28, 1976

Huxley, Julian
Died: London, England
Date: February 14, 1975

Icaza, Jorge
Died: Quito, Ecuador
Date: May 26, 1978

Jones, James
Died: Southampton, New York
Date: May 9, 1977

Koestler, Arthur
Died: London, England
Date: March 3, 1983

Lagerkvist, Pär
Died: Stockholm, Sweden
Date: July 11, 1974

Lowell, Robert
Died: New York, New York
Date: September 12, 1977

MacLeish, Archibald
Died: Boston, Massachusetts
Date: April 20, 1982

Malraux, André
Died: Paris, France
Date: November 23, 1976

Miller, Henry
Died: Pacific Palisades, California
Date: June 7, 1980

Nabokov, Vladimir
Died: Montreux, Switzerland
Date: July 2, 1977

O'Brien, Kate
Died: Faversham, England
Date: August 13, 1974

Perse, St.-John
Died: Giens, France
Date: September 20, 1975

Porter, Katherine Anne
Died: College Park, Maryland
Date: September 18, 1980

Ransom, John Crowe
Died: Gambier, Ohio
Date: July 3, 1974

Renault, Mary
Died: Capetown, South Africa
Date: December 13, 1983

Richards, I.A.
Died: Cambridge, England
Date: September 7, 1979

Saroyan, William
Died: Fresno, California
Date: May 18, 1981

Sarte, Jean-Paul
Died: Paris, France
Date: April 15, 1980

Sherriff, Robert C.
Died: London, England
Date: November 13, 1975

Sholokhov, Mikhail
Died: Kruzhlino, U.S.S.R.
Date: February 21, 1984

Silone, Ignazio
Died: Geneva, Switzerland
Date: August 21, 1978

Snow, C.P.
Died: London, England
Date: July 1, 1980

Stuart, Jesse
Died: W-Hollow, Kentucky
Date: February 17, 1984

Swinnerton, Frank
Died: Cranleigh, England
Date: November 6, 1982

Tate, Allen
Died: Nashville, Tennessee
Date: February 9, 1979

Tolkien, J.R.R.
Died: Bournemouth, England
Date: September 2, 1973

Toynbee, Arnold
Died: York, England
Date: October 22, 1975

West, Rebecca
Died: London, England
Date: March 15, 1983

Wilder, Thornton
Died: Hamden, Connecticut
Date: December 7, 1975

Williams, Tennessee
Died: New York, New York
Date: February 25, 1983

Williamson, Henry
Died: England
Date: August 13, 1977

AUTHOR INDEX

Yorke, Henry Vincent
   see Green, Henry
Young, Edward, 1961
Young, Stark, 1962
Yourcenar, Marguerite, 1964

Zangwill, Israel, 1966

Żeromski, Stefan, 1967
Zola, Émile, 1968
Zorrilla y Moral, José, 1971
Zuviría, Gustavo Martínez
   see Wast, Hugo
Zweig, Arnold, 1972